SOLARO

STUDY GUIDE

Geometry

SOLARO Study Guide is designed to help students achieve success in school. The content in each study guide is 100% curriculum aligned and serves as an excellent source of material for review and practice. To create this book, teachers, curriculum specialists, and assessment experts have worked closely to develop the instructional pieces that explain each of the key concepts for the course. The practice questions and sample tests have detailed solutions that show problem-solving methods, highlight concepts that are likely to be tested, and point out potential sources of errors. **SOLARO Study Guide** is a complete guide to be used by students throughout the school year for reviewing and understanding course content, and to prepare for assessments.

Copyright © 2013 Castle Rock Research Corporation

All rights reserved. No part of this book covered by the copyright hereon may be reproduced or used in any form or by any means graphic, electronic, or mechanical, including photocopying, recording, taping, or information storage and retrieval systems without the express permission of the publisher.

Rao, Gautam, 1961 –
SOLARO STUDY GUIDE – Geometry (Traditional) (2013 Edition)

1. Mathematics – Juvenile Literature. I. Title

Castle Rock Research Corporation
2410 Manulife Place
10180 – 101 Street
Edmonton, AB T5J 3S4

    1 2 3 MP 15 14 13

Printed in Canada

Publisher
Gautam Rao

Dedicated to the memory of Dr. V. S. Rao

THE *SOLARO STUDY GUIDE*

The *SOLARO Study Guide* is designed to help students achieve success in school and to provide teachers with a road map to understanding the concepts of the Common Core State Standards. The content in each study guide is 100% curriculum aligned and serves as an excellent source of material for review and practice. The *SOLARO Study Guide* introduces students to a process that incorporates the building blocks upon which strong academic performance is based. To create this resource, teachers, curriculum specialists, and assessment experts have worked closely to develop instructional pieces that explain key concepts. Every exercise question comes with a detailed solution that offers problem-solving methods, highlights concepts that are likely to be tested, and points out potential sources of errors.

The *SOLARO Study Guide* is intended to be used for reviewing and understanding course content, to prepare for assessments, and to assist each student in achieving their best performance in school.

The *SOLARO Study Guide* consists of the following sections:

TABLE OF CORRELATIONS

The Table of Correlations is a critical component of the *SOLARO Study Guide*.

Castle Rock Research has designed the *SOLARO Study Guide* by correlating each question and its solution to Common Core State Standards. Each unit begins with a Table of Correlations, which lists the standards and questions that correspond to those standards.

For students, the Table of Correlations provides information about how each question fits into a particular course and the standards to which each question is tied. Students can quickly access all relevant content associated with a particular standard.

For teachers, the Table of Correlations provides a road map for each standard, outlining the most granular and measurable concepts that are included in each standard. It assists teachers in understanding all the components involved in each standard and where students are excelling or require improvement. The Table of Correlations indicates the instructional focus for each content strand, serves as a standards checklist, and focuses on the standards and concepts that are most important in the unit and the particular course of study.

Some concepts may have a complete lesson aligned to them but cannot be assessed using a paper-and-pencil format. These concepts typically require ongoing classroom assessment through various other methods.

LESSONS

Following the Table of Correlations for each unit are lessons aligned to each concept within a standard. The lessons explain key concepts that students are expected to learn according to Common Core State Standards.

As each lesson is tied to state standards, students and teachers are assured that the information will be relevant to what is being covered in class.

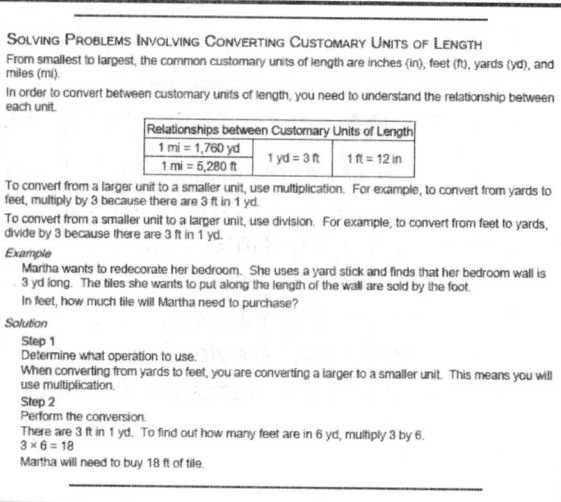

EXERCISE QUESTIONS

Each set of lessons is followed by two sets of exercise questions that assess students on their understanding of the content. These exercise questions can be used by students to give them an idea of the type of questions they are likely to face in the future in terms of format, difficulty, and content coverage.

DETAILED SOLUTIONS

Some study guides only provide an answer key, which will identify the correct response but may not be helpful in determining what led to the incorrect answer. Every exercise question in the *SOLARO Study Guide* is accompanied by a detailed solution. Access to complete solutions greatly enhances a student's ability to work independently, and these solutions also serve as useful instructional tools for teachers. The level of information in each detailed solution is intended to help students better prepare for the future by learning from their mistakes and to help teachers discern individual areas of strengths and weaknesses.

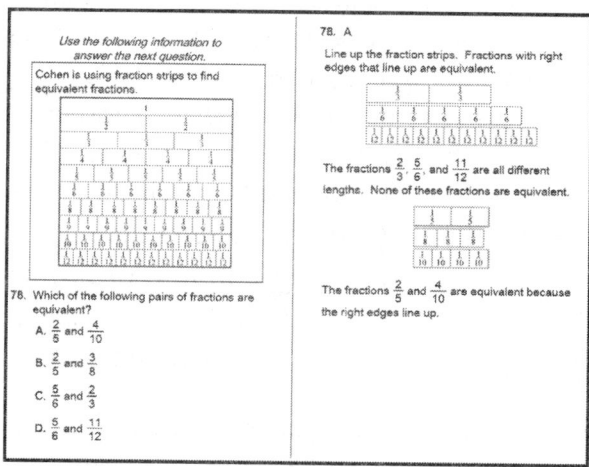

For the complete curriculum document, visit www.corestandards.org/the-standards.

SOLARO Study Guides are available for many courses. Check www.solaro.com/orders for a complete listing of books available for your area.

For more enhanced online resources, please visit www.SOLARO.com.

Student-Oriented Learning, Assessment, and Reporting Online

SOLARO is an online resource that provides students with regionally and age-appropriate lessons and practice questions. Students can be confident that SOLARO has the right materials to help them when they are having difficulties in class. SOLARO is 100% compliant with each region's core standards. Teachers can use SOLARO in the classroom as a supplemental resource to provide remediation and enrichment. Student performance is reported to the teacher through various reports, which provide insight into strengths and weaknesses.

TABLE OF CONTENTS

KEY TIPS FOR BEING SUCCESSFUL AT SCHOOL 1
    Key Factors Contributing to School Success 2
    How to Find Your Learning Style 3
    Scheduling Study Time 4
    Creating Study Notes 5
    Memorization Techniques 7
    Key Strategies for Reviewing 7
    Key Strategies for Success: A Checklist 8

CLASS FOCUS

TRANSFORMATIONS 9
    Table of Correlations 10
    Concepts 12
        Defining Angles, Circles, Arcs and Lines
        Transformations in the Plane
        Rotations and Reflections in Different Shapes
        Defining Rotations, Reflections, and Translations
        Drawing 2D Images after Multiple Transformations
    Exercise #1—Transformations 47
    Exercise #1—Transformations Answers and Solutions 51
    Exercise #2—Transformations 56
    Exercise #2—Transformations Answers and Solutions 60

RIGID MOTION 67
    Table of Correlations 68
    Concepts 69
        Properties of Congruence
        Properties of Congruent Triangles
        Problem Solving with Congruent Triangles
    Exercise #1—Rigid Motion 77
    Exercise #1—Rigid Motion Answers and Solutions 79
    Exercise #2—Rigid Motion 81
    Exercise #2—Rigid Motion Answers and Solutions 83

GEOMETRIC THEOREMS 87
Table of Correlations 88
Concepts 89
Proving Theorems about Lines and Angles
Proving Theorems about Triangles
Proving Theorems about Parallelograms
Exercise #1—Geometric Theorems 113
Exercise #1—Geometric Theorems Answers and Solutions 118
Exercise #2—Geometric Theorems 123
Exercise #2—Geometric Theorems Answers and Solutions 128

GEOMETRIC CONSTRUCTIONS 133
Table of Correlations 134
Concepts 135
Making Geometric Constructions
Constructing Equilateral Triangles
Exercise #1—Geometric Constructions 146
Exercise #1—Geometric Constructions Answers and Solutions 148
Exercise #2—Geometric Constructions 151
Exercise #2—Geometric Constructions Answers and Solutions 154

SIMILARITY TRANSFORMATIONS 157
Table of Correlations 158
Concepts 159
Verifying Dilations
Determining the Scale Factor of a Diagram
Determining the Similarity of Polygons
Proving the Similarities of Triangles
Exercise #1—Similarity Transformations 171
Exercise #1—Similarity Transformations Answers and Solutions 174
Exercise #2—Similarity Transformations 178
Exercise #2—Similarity Transformations Answers and Solutions 181

THEOREMS INVOLVING SIMILARITY 185
Table of Correlations 186
Concepts 187
Pythagorean Theorem
Proving Relationships in Geometric Figures
Exercise #1—Theorems Involving Similarity 198
Exercise #1—Theorems Involving Similarity Answers and Solutions 199
Exercise #2—Theorems Involving Similarity 201
Exercise #2—Theorems Involving Similarity Answers and Solutions 203

RIGHT ANGLE TRIANGLES IN TRIGONOMETRY ... 205
Table of Correlations ... 206
Concepts ... 207
Tangent, Sine, and Cosine Ratios
Verifying Equivalent Trigonometric Expressions
Solving Problems Using Trigonometric Ratios and the Pythagorean Theorem
Exercise #1—Right Angle Triangles in Trigonometry ... 228
Exercise #1—Right Angle Triangles in Trigonometry Answers and Solutions ... 233
Exercise #2—Right Angle Triangles in Trigonometry ... 239
Exercise #2—Right Angle Triangles in Trigonometry Answers and Solutions ... 242

APPLYING GEOMETRIC CONCEPTS ... 249
Table of Correlations ... 250
Concepts ... 251
Solving Problems Involving the Volume of Geometric Shapes
Geometric Methods to Solve Design Problems
Exercise #1—Applying Geometric Concepts ... 273
Exercise #1—Applying Geometric Concepts Answers and Solutions ... 276
Exercise #2—Applying Geometric Concepts ... 280
Exercise #2—Applying Geometric Concepts Answers and Solutions ... 283

GENERAL TRIANGLES IN TRIGONOMETRY ... 287
Table of Correlations ... 288
Concepts ... 289
Calculating the Area of a Triangle Given One Angle and Two Adjacent Sides
Applying the Sine and Cosine Laws
Solving Problems Using the Sine and Cosine Laws
Exercise #1—General Triangles in Trigonometry ... 301
Exercise #1—General Triangles in Trigonometry Answers and Solutions ... 304
Exercise #2—General Triangles in Trigonometry ... 307
Exercise #2—General Triangles in Trigonometry Answers and Solutions ... 309

VOLUME FORMULAS ... 313
Table of Correlations ... 314
Concepts ... 315
Using Volume Formulas to Solve Problems
Exercise #1—Volume Formulas ... 320
Exercise #1—Volume Formulas Answers and Solutions ... 321
Exercise #2—Volume Formulas ... 322
Exercise #2—Volume Formulas Answers and Solutions ... 323

TWO AND THREE-DIMENSIONAL OBJECTS ... 325
Table of Correlations ... 326
Concepts ... 327
Identifying and Sketching 3-D Objects and Cross Sections
Exercise #1—Two and Three-Dimensional Objects ... 335
Exercise #1—Two and Three-Dimensional Objects Answers and Solutions ... 337
Exercise #2—Two and Three-Dimensional Objects ... 339
Exercise #2—Two and Three-Dimensional Objects Answers and Solutions ... 340

USING COORDINATES ... 343
Table of Correlations ... 344
Concepts ... 346
Proving Simple Geometric Theorems Using Coordinates
Proving Slope for Parallel and Perpendicular Lines
Applying the Distance Formula
Using Coordinates to Perimeters and Areas
Exercise #1—Using Coordinates ... 366
Exercise #1—Using Coordinates Answers and Solutions ... 369
Exercise #2—Using Coordinates ... 376
Exercise #2—Using Coordinates Answers and Solutions ... 380

EQUATIONS FOR CONIC SECTIONS ... 387
Table of Correlations ... 388
Concepts ... 389
Defining Foci and Eccentricity of Conic Sections
Exercise #1—Equations for Conic Sections ... 394
Exercise #1—Equations for Conic Sections Answers and Solutions ... 395
Exercise #2—Equations for Conic Sections ... 396
Exercise #2—Equations for Conic Sections Answers and Solutions ... 397

CIRCLE THEOREMS ... 399
Table of Correlations ... 400
Concepts ... 401
Relationships among Inscribed Angles, Radii, and Chords
Cyclic Quadrilaterals
Exercise #1—Circle Theorems ... 413
Exercise #1—Circle Theorems Answers and Solutions ... 414
Exercise #2—Circle Theorems ... 415
Exercise #2—Circle Theorems Answers and Solutions ... 416

ARC LENGTHS AND SECTOR AREAS OF CIRCLES ... 419
Table of Correlations ... 420
Concepts ... 421
Arc Lengths and Sectors of Circles
Exercise #1—Arc Lengths and Sector Areas of Circles ... 424
Exercise #1—Arc Lengths and Sector Areas of Circles Answers and Solutions ... 425
Exercise #2—Arc Lengths and Sector Areas of Circles ... 426
Exercise #2—Arc Lengths and Sector Areas of Circles Answers and Solutions ... 427

RELATING CONIC SECTIONS TO THEIR EQUATIONS ... 429
Table of Correlations ... 430
Concepts ... 431
Equation of a Circle
Exercise #1—Relating Conic Sections to Their Equations ... 437
Exercise #1—Relating Conic Sections to Their Equations Answers and Solutions ... 439
Exercise #2—Relating Conic Sections to Their Equations ... 441
Exercise #2—Relating Conic Sections to Their Equations Answers and Solutions ... 442

INDEPENDENCE AND CONDITIONAL PROBABILITY ... 445
Table of Correlations ... 446
Concepts ... 447
Sample Space
Identifying Sample Space for Two Independent Events
Identifying Conditional Probability
Finding Conditional Probability Given a Frequency Table
Identifying Conditional Probability
Exercise #1—Independence and Conditional Probability ... 460
Exercise #1—Independence and Conditional Probability Answers and Solutions ... 462
Exercise #2—Independence and Conditional Probability ... 465
Exercise #2—Independence and Conditional Probability Answers and Solutions ... 468

PROBABILITIES OF COMPOUND EVENTS 471
Table of Correlations 472
Concepts 474
- Calculating Probability of Independent Events
- Calculating Probability of Mutually and Non-Mutually Exclusive Events
- Calculating the Probability of Dependent Events
- Using Permutations and Combinations to Compute Probabilities

Exercise #1—Probabilities of Compound Events 510
Exercise #1—Probabilities of Compound Events Answers and Solutions 513
Exercise #2—Probabilities of Compound Events 518
Exercise #2—Probabilities of Compound Events Answers and Solutions 521

EVALUATING OUTCOMES USING PROBABILITY 527
Table of Correlations 528
Concepts 529
- Making Decisions Based on Probability
- Analyzing Decisions Based on Probability

Exercise #1—Evaluating Outcomes Using Probability 532
Exercise #1—Evaluating Outcomes Using Probability Answers and Solutions 533
Exercise #2—Evaluating Outcomes Using Probability 534
Exercise #2—Evaluating Outcomes Using Probability Answers and Solutions 536

CREDITS

Every effort has been made to provide proper acknowledgement of the original source and to comply with copyright law. However, some attempts to establish original copyright ownership may have been unsuccessful. If copyright ownership can be identified, please notify Castle Rock Research Corp so that appropriate corrective action can be taken.

Some images in this document may be from www.clipart.com, copyright (c) 2013 Jupiter images Corporation.

Some images in this document may be from www.nasa.com.

Some images may be from National Atmospheric and Oceanic Administration http://www.noaa.gov/.

Some images may be from www.usgs.gov/.

Key Tips for Being Successful at School

KEY TIPS FOR BEING SUCCESSFUL AT SCHOOL

KEY FACTORS CONTRIBUTING TO SCHOOL SUCCESS

In addition to learning the content of your courses, there are some other things that you can do to help you do your best at school. You can try some of the following strategies:

- **Keep a positive attitude:** Always reflect on what you can already do and what you already know.
- **Be prepared to learn:** Have the necessary pencils, pens, notebooks, and other required materials for participating in class ready.
- **Complete all of your assignments:** Do your best to finish all of your assignments. Even if you know the material well, practice will reinforce your knowledge. If an assignment or question is difficult for you, work through it as far as you can so that your teacher can see exactly where you are having difficulty.

- **Set small goals for yourself when you are learning new material:** For example, when learning the parts of speech, do not try to learn everything in one night. Work on only one part or section each study session. When you have memorized one particular part of speech and understand it, move on to another one. Continue this process until you have memorized and learned all the parts of speech.
- **Review your classroom work regularly at home:** Review to make sure you understand the material you learned in class.
- **Ask your teacher for help:** Your teacher will help you if you do not understand something or if you are having a difficult time completing your assignments.

- **Get plenty of rest and exercise:** Concentrating in class is hard work. It is important to be well-rested and have time to relax and socialize with your friends. This helps you keep a positive attitude about your schoolwork.
- **Eat healthy meals:** A balanced diet keeps you healthy and gives you the energy you need for studying at school and at home.

HOW TO FIND YOUR LEARNING STYLE

Every student learns differently. The manner in which you learn best is called your learning style. By knowing your learning style, you can increase your success at school. Most students use a combination of learning styles. Do you know what type of learner you are? Read the following descriptions. Which of these common learning styles do you use most often?

- **Linguistic Learner:** You may learn best by saying, hearing, and seeing words. You are probably really good at memorizing things such as dates, places, names, and facts. You may need to write down the steps in a process, a formula, or the actions that lead up to a significant event, and then say them out loud.

- **Spatial Learner:** You may learn best by looking at and working with pictures. You are probably really good at puzzles, imagining things, and reading maps and charts. You may need to use strategies like mind mapping and webbing to organize your information and study notes.

- **Kinesthetic Learner:** You may learn best by touching, moving, and figuring things out using manipulatives. You are probably really good at physical activities and learning through movement. You may need to draw your finger over a diagram to remember it, tap out the steps needed to solve a problem, or feel yourself writing or typing a formula.

SCHEDULING STUDY TIME

You should review your class notes regularly to ensure that you have a clear understanding of all the new material you learned. Reviewing your lessons on a regular basis helps you to learn and remember ideas and concepts. It also reduces the quantity of material that you need to study prior to a test. Establishing a study schedule will help you to make the best use of your time.

Regardless of the type of study schedule you use, you may want to consider the following suggestions to maximize your study time and effort:

- Organize your work so that you begin with the most challenging material first.
- Divide the subject's content into small, manageable chunks.
- Alternate regularly between your different subjects and types of study activities in order to maintain your interest and motivation.
- Make a daily list with headings like "Must Do," "Should Do," and "Could Do."
- Begin each study session by quickly reviewing what you studied the day before.
- Maintain your usual routine of eating, sleeping, and exercising to help you concentrate better for extended periods of time.

CREATING STUDY NOTES

MIND-MAPPING OR WEBBING

Use the key words, ideas, or concepts from your reading or class notes to create a mind map or web (a diagram or visual representation of the given information). A mind map or web is sometimes referred to as a knowledge map. Use the following steps to create a mind map or web:

1. Write the key word, concept, theory, or formula in the centre of your page.
2. Write down related facts, ideas, events, and information, and link them to the central concept with lines.
3. Use coloured markers, underlining, or symbols to emphasize things such as relationships, timelines, and important information.

The following examples of a Frayer Model illustrate how this technique can be used to study vocabulary.

Definition	Notes
• Perimeter is the distance around the outside of a polygon.	• Perimeter is measured in linear units (e.g., metres, centimetres, and so on).

Perimeter

Examples	Non-Examples
• The length of a fence around a yard	• The area of grass covering a lawn
• The distance around a circle (circumference)	• The size of a rug lying on a floor

Definition	Notes
• A cube is a solid 3-D object with six faces.	• A cube is different from other shapes because it has six equally-sized square faces, eight vertices, and twelve equal edges.

Cube

Examples	Non-Examples
 (dice, block with B, cube)	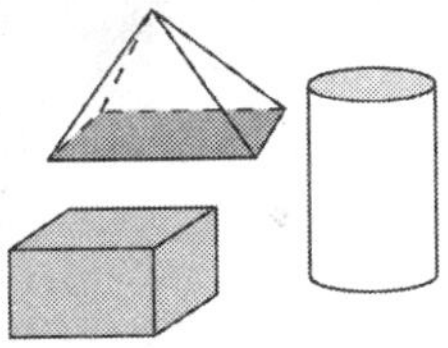 (pyramid, cylinder, rectangular prism)

INDEX CARDS

To use index cards while studying, follow these steps:

1. Write a key word or question on one side of an index card.
2. On the reverse side, write the definition of the word, answer to the question, or any other important information that you want to remember.

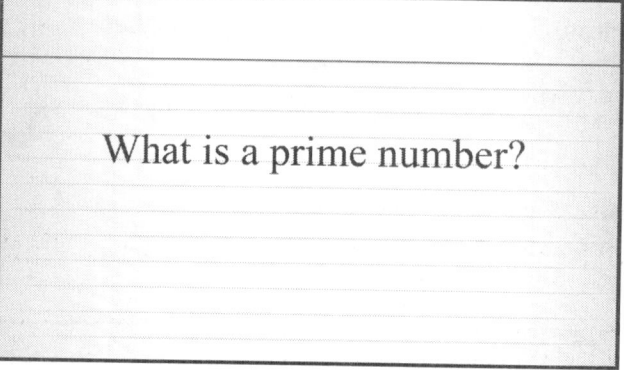

> What is a prime number?

> What is a prime number?
> A prime number is any number that has exactly 2 factors.
> A prime number can be divided evenly only by itself and one.
> For example, 2, 3, 5, 7, 19.
> The number 1 is not a prime number.

SYMBOLS AND STICKY NOTES—IDENTIFYING IMPORTANT INFORMATION

Use symbols to mark your class notes. The following are some examples:

- An exclamation mark (!) might be used to point out something that must be learned well because it is a very important idea.
- A question mark (?) may highlight something you are not certain about
- A diamond (◊) or asterisk (*) could highlight interesting information that you want to remember.

Sticky notes are useful in the following situations:

- Use sticky notes when you are not allowed to put marks in books.
- Use sticky notes to mark a page in a book that contains an important diagram, formula, explanation, or other information.
- Use sticky notes to mark important facts in research books.

MEMORIZATION TECHNIQUES

- **Association** relates new learning to something you already know. For example, to remember the spelling difference between dessert and desert, recall that the word *sand* has only one *s*. So, because there is sand in a desert, the word *desert* has only one *s*.

- **Mnemonic** devices are sentences that you create to remember a list or group of items. For example, the first letter of each word in the phrase "Every Good Boy Deserves Fudge" helps you to remember the names of the lines on the treble-clef staff (E, G, B, D, and F) in music.

- **Acronyms** are words that are formed from the first letters or parts of the words in a group. For example, RADAR is actually an acronym for Radio Detecting and Ranging, and MASH is an acronym for Mobile Army Surgical Hospital. HOMES helps you to remember the names of the five Great Lakes (Huron, Ontario, Michigan, Erie, and Superior).

- **Visualizing** requires you to use your mind's eye to "see" a chart, list, map, diagram, or sentence as it is in your textbook or notes, on the chalkboard or computer screen, or in a display.

- **Initialisms** are abbreviations that are formed from the first letters or parts of the words in a group. Unlike acronyms, an initialism cannot be pronounced as a word itself. For example, GCF is an initialism for **G**reatest **C**ommon **F**actor.

KEY STRATEGIES FOR REVIEWING

Reviewing textbook material, class notes, and handouts should be an ongoing activity. Spending time reviewing becomes more critical when you are preparing for a test. You may find some of the following review strategies useful when studying during your scheduled study time:

- Before reading a selection, preview it by noting the headings, charts, graphs, and chapter questions.

- Before reviewing a unit, note the headings, charts, graphs, and chapter questions.

- Highlight key concepts, vocabulary, definitions, and formulas.

- Skim the paragraph, and note the key words, phrases, and information.

- Carefully read over each step in a procedure.

- Draw a picture or diagram to help make the concept clearer.

KEY STRATEGIES FOR SUCCESS: A CHECKLIST

Reviewing is a huge part of doing well at school and preparing for tests. Here is a checklist for you to keep track of how many suggested strategies for success you are using. Read each question, and put a check mark (✓) in the correct column. Look at the questions where you have checked the "No" column. Think about how you might try using some of these strategies to help you do your best at school.

Key Strategies for Success	Yes	No
Do you attend school regularly?		
Do you know your personal learning style—how you learn best?		
Do you spend 15 to 30 minutes a day reviewing your notes?		
Do you study in a quiet place at home?		
Do you clearly mark the most important ideas in your study notes?		
Do you use sticky notes to mark texts and research books?		
Do you practise answering multiple-choice and written-response questions?		
Do you ask your teacher for help when you need it?		
Are you maintaining a healthy diet and sleep routine?		
Are you participating in regular physical activity?		

Transformations

Copyright Protected

TRANSFORMATIONS

Table of Correlations

Standard		Concepts	Exercise #1	Exercise #2
Unit 1.1	Experiment with transformations in the plane.			
G-CO.1	*Know precise definitions of angle, circle, perpendicular line, parallel line, and line segment, based on the undefined notions of point, line, distance along a line, and distance around a circular arc.*	Understanding and Identifying Five Classical Axioms		
		Identifying Undefined Terms: Point, Line, Segment, and Ray		
		Calculating Arc Lengths	1	15
		Identifying Undefined Terms: Plane, Intersection, Collinear, and Non-Collinear		
		Understanding and Identifying Postulates on Angles	2	16
G-CO.2	*Represent transformations in the plane using, e.g., transparencies and geometry software; describe transformations as functions that take points in the plane as inputs and give other points as outputs. Compare transformations that preserve distance and angle to those that do not.*	Translations	3	17
		Rotations	4	18
		Reflections	5	19
		Dilations	6	20
		Drawing 2D Images after Multiple Transformations	7	21
		Identifying Single Transformations	8	22
		Applying Glide Reflections on a Two-Dimensional Shape	9	23
		Using Proper Function Notation for Isometries	10	24
		Investigating and Applying Invariant Isometric Properties	11	25
G-CO.3	*Given a rectangle, parallelogram, trapezoid, or regular polygon, describe the rotations and reflections that carry it onto itself.*	Identifying Lines of Symmetry in a Tessellation	12	26
		Identifying Rotational Symmetry in a Tessellation	13	27
		Calculating the Rotational Symmetry of Two-Dimensional Shapes	14	28
G-CO.4	*Develop definitions of rotations, reflections, and translations in terms of angles, circles, perpendicular lines, parallel lines, and line segments.*	Translations	3	17
		Rotations	4	18
		Reflections	5	19
		Applying Glide Reflections on a Two-Dimensional Shape	9	23
		Investigating and Applying Invariant Isometric Properties	11	25
G-CO.5	*Given a geometric figure and a rotation, reflection, or translation, draw the transformed figure using, e.g., graph paper, tracing paper, or geometry software. Specify a sequence of transformations that will carry a given figure onto another.*	Translations	3	17
		Rotations	4	18
		Reflections	5	19
		Drawing 2D Images after Multiple Transformations	7	21

| | | Applying Glide Reflections on a Two-Dimensional Shape | 9 | 23 |

G-CO.1 Know precise definitions of angle, circle, perpendicular line, parallel line, and line segment, based on the undefined notions of point, line, distance along a line, and distance around a circular arc.

UNDERSTANDING AND IDENTIFYING FIVE CLASSICAL AXIOMS

An **axiom** (or **postulate**) is a statement or proposition that is accepted as being true. An axiom is often a self-evident proposition. The following axioms are some of the cornerstone propositions that are used in geometry to construct objects and to prove a given **theorem**.

It is important to remember and understand that axioms are meant to be self-evident or obvious statements. They are basic ideas that provide a common starting point for a discussion of geometry. The application of axioms usually involves naming them when appropriate.

LINE SEGMENT POSTULATE

Along a straight line, there exists a line segment of any **finite** length.

This axiom states that along an existing line, and from an existing point, a line segment of any given length can be constructed. For example, consider the following diagram.

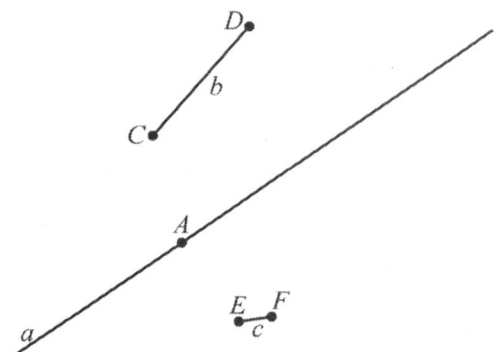

This postulate states that there exists a line segment, *AG* (when the position of *G* is not given), on the line through point *A*, such that *AG* is the same length as *CD*, *EF*, or any other finite length. These possible line segments are shown in the following diagrams.

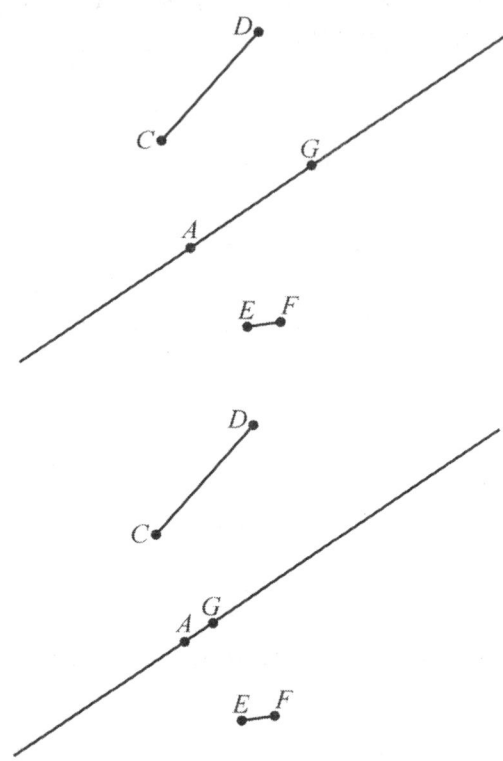

This postulate only suggests that such line segments exist or are possible. The postulate does not, however, explain how these line segments are constructed.

Transformations — Castle Rock Research

STRAIGHT LINE POSTULATE

A straight line may be drawn between any two given points.

The following two images represent an illustration of this postulate. The first image shows two points on a plane. The second image shows a line through the two points.

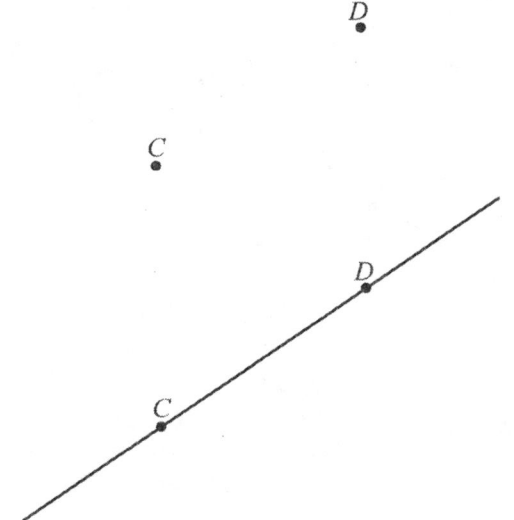

This postulate simply states that it is possible to draw such a line.

CIRCLE POSTULATE

A circle may be described with any given point as its center and any distance as its radius.

Imagine a point on a plane labeled O. This postulate states that there can be a circle around point O made with any given radius, as illustrated in the following diagrams.

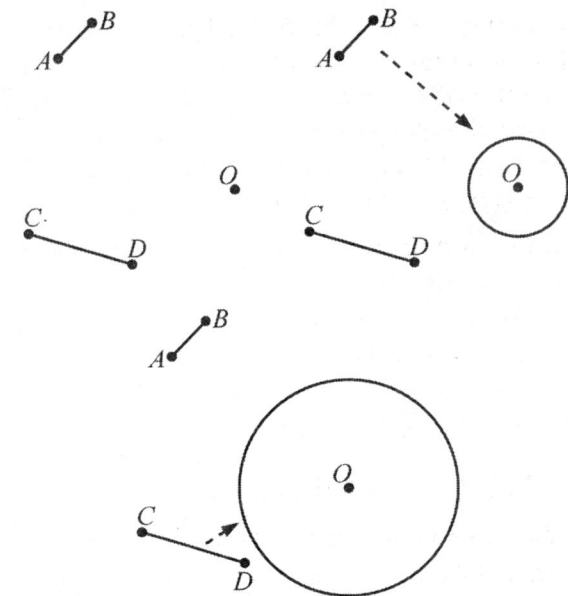

In the second diagram, the circle has the same radius as the length of line segment AB. In the third diagram, the circle has the same radius as the length of line segment CD.

Right Angle Postulate

All right angles are equal.

This is Euclid's first postulate and the first mention of angles. An **angle** is formed between two intersecting lines or two rays that originate at the same point. One interpretation of this postulate is that if two or more right angles are constructed anywhere, they will be equal. Another interpretation of this postulate is that if two right angles are constructed from lines that intersect a point on another line, the two lines forming the right angles will coincide, as illustrated in the following diagram.

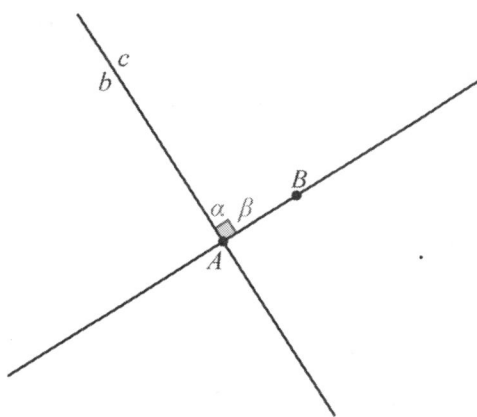

In the given diagram, two separate right angles are constructed by drawing lines *b* and *c* through point *A* of line *AB*. The two perpendicular lines (lines forming right angles) coincide, and angles α and β are equal.

Parallel Line Postulate

Imagine two straight lines in a plane. A third straight line intersects the two straight lines. If the two interior angles on one side of the third line are less than two right angles, then the first two straight lines will meet at a point if extended far enough on the side on which the angles are less than two right angles.

The postulate can be illustrated as follows: Start with two lines, *a* and *b*.

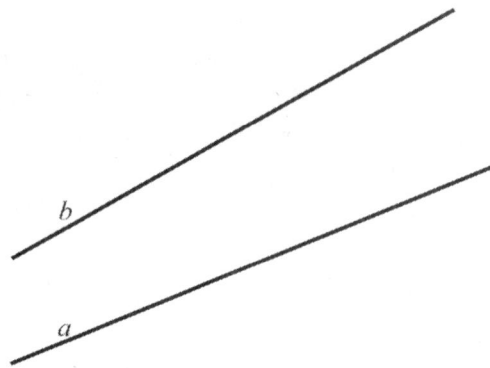

Draw the third line, *c*.

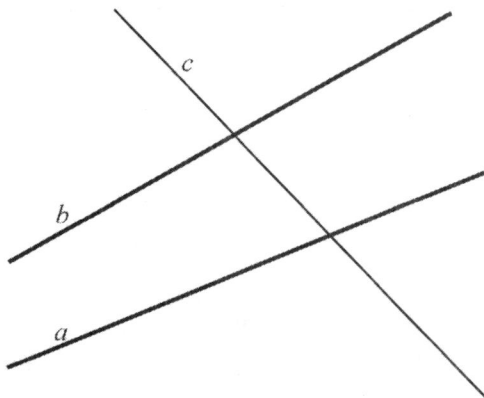

Lines *a* and *c* form an angle, α, while lines *b* and *c* form angle β. If angles α and β are put together, the result is less than two right angles.

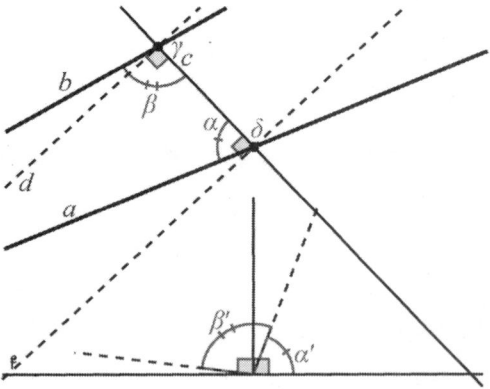

When extended, lines *a* and *b* intersect on the same side as angles *α* and *β*.

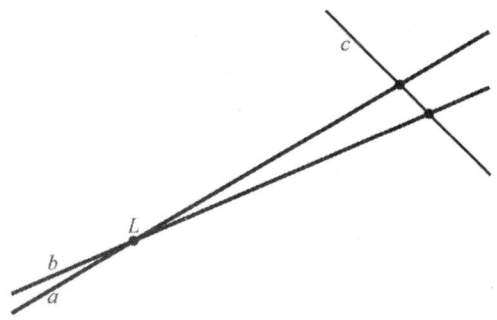

The parallel line postulate describes how two lines cannot be parallel. For two lines to be parallel, the sum of the interior angles must be equal to two right angles (the two interior angles must be **supplementary**).

IDENTIFYING UNDEFINED TERMS: POINT, LINE, SEGMENT, AND RAY

The terms point, line, segment, and ray are geometric concepts that do not have clear definitions.

A **point** is best understood as a particular location. A point can be described using coordinates on a Cartesian plane; for example, the coordinates (2, −5) refer to a point in a two-dimensional space that is 2 units to the right and 5 units down from an origin. A point can also be described as a specific location where an intersection takes place. A point has no size or sign.

A **line** is best thought of as a geometric tool with the following properties:

- A line has no beginning or end, which signifies that it can be extended indefinitely.
- A line is straight with no turns or bends, which signifies a particular direction.
- A line has no determinate length or width.
- A line contains all the points along it.

Since each point can be thought of as having coordinates, a line can be represented as a set of all points that follow a certain rule; for example, all points 2 units to the right of an origin represent a vertical line.

A **segment** or **line segment** is best thought of as a section of a line between two points. A line segment has no width. However, since it represents a portion of a line between two points, a line segment can be thought of as representing the specific distance between two points; i.e., a line segment has length. The points at either end of a line segment are called the endpoints.

A **ray** is best thought of as the direction in which a line is extended from a particular point. A ray shares the following properties with a line: a ray is straight, has no width, has no length, and follows a particular rule. However, a ray has a starting point and can only be extended in a particular direction.

This image show some representations of points, lines, line segments, and rays. Note that each line and ray may be extended beyond the edges of a computer screen or a page.

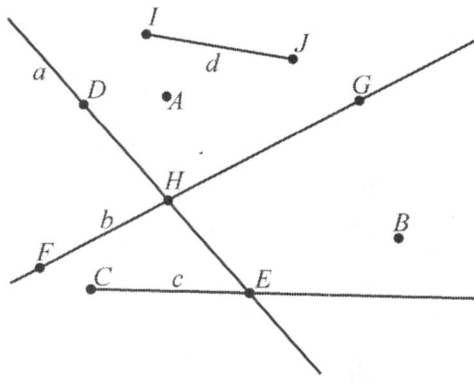

In the given image, points are generally represented by capital letters. *A*, *B*, *C*, *D*, *E*, *F*, *G*, *H*, *I*, and *J* are all examples of points. Although each point is represented by a small circle, in reality, each point has no size.

The image contains three lines labeled with lowercase letters *a* and *b*. Each line extends beyond the edges of the computer screen or page. Line *a* contains points *D*, *H*, and *E*, as well as an uncountable number of other points. Line *b* contains points *F*, *H*, and *G*, as well as infinitely many other points.

There are many line segments in the image. The segment between points *I* and *J* (labeled *d*) is the clearest example of a segment.
Other examples include segments between any pair of points, such as *C* and *E*, *H* and *G*, and *D* and *E*. There is no line segment between *B* and *G* because there is no line connecting the two points.

There are many rays shown in the image. One ray begins at point *C* and extends past point *E*. The ray is labeled with the lowercase letter *c*. Other rays include a ray from point *E* and away from point *D*, a ray from point *H* and past point *E*, and a ray starting at point *G* and beyond point *F*.

CALCULATING ARC LENGTHS

One of the advantages of measuring angles in radians becomes evident when calculating arc lengths.

Recall that there is a close relationship between the arc length on a circle and the size of the angle subtended by that arc.

For an angle measuring 2 rad, the corresponding arc length is 2 radii.

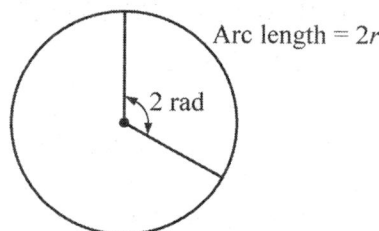

For an angle measuring 3 rad, the corresponding arc length is 3 radii.

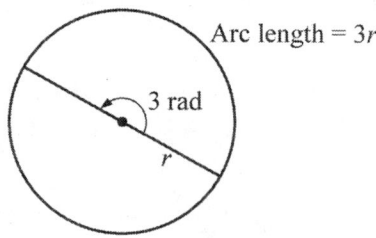

In general, given an angle of θ radians and a radius, r, the arc length, a, can be calculated using the equation $a = r\theta$, where θ is measured in radians, a is the arc length, and r is the radius.

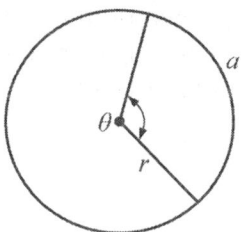

Example
An arc subtends an angle of 1.8 rad. If the radius of the circle is 6 cm, what is the arc length?

Solution
$\theta = 1.8$ rad and $r = 6$ cm
$a = r\theta$
$ = (6)(1.8)$
$ = 10.8$

The arc length is 10.8 cm.

When the measure of an angle is given in degrees, convert it to radians first, and then apply the formula.

Example
An arc subtends an angle of 150°. The radius of the circle is 11 mm. Find the arc length. Round your answer to the nearest tenth of a millimeter.

Solution
Step 1
Determine the radian measure of the angle.
$150° = 150 \times \dfrac{\pi}{180} = \dfrac{150\pi}{180} = \dfrac{5\pi}{6}$ rad

Step 2
Apply the formula to determine the length of the arc.
$a = r\theta$
$ = (11)\left(\dfrac{5\pi}{6}\right)$
$ \doteq 28.8$

The arc length is approximately 28.8 mm.

When asked to calculate the unknown measures of the radius or the angle, rearrange the given formula, substitute in the known values, and solve.

Example

An arc subtends the angle θ. If the radius of the circle is 18.5 cm and the arc length is 88.8 cm, what is the measure of angle θ to the nearest tenth of a radian?

Solution

Step 1
Use the formula $a = r\theta$ to solve for θ.
$$\theta = \frac{a}{r}$$

Step 2
Substitute given values and solve for θ.
It is given that $r = 18.5$ and $a = 88.8$.
$$\theta = \frac{a}{r}$$
$$= \frac{88.8}{18.5}$$
$$\approx 4.8$$

Therefore, $\theta \approx 4.8$ rad.

IDENTIFYING UNDEFINED TERMS: PLANE, INTERSECTION, COLLINEAR, AND NON-COLLINEAR

Like the terms *point* and *line*, **plane** refers to a concept rather than a physical object. A plane is a flat surface that is similar to the surface of a desk or a sheet of paper. However, unlike a desk or a sheet of paper, a plane has no thickness, has only one side (a top), and can be extended indefinitely. A plane contains points, lines, rays, and line segments.

A plane is very much like a canvas upon which lines and geometric shapes are drawn. This drawing of lines and shapes on a plane is called **geometric construction** because it requires special tools such as a straight edge and a compass.

A geometric construction is often based on the idea of **intersection**. For example, two lines in the same plane that do not run side by side (parallel) or coincide (one on top of the other) will always intersect at one point. Drawing two lines in a plane allows the construction of the point of intersection.

Two lines drawn in two different planes, however, may never intersect. To illustrate the concept, hold up a book and imagine that the front cover of the book represents one plane and the back cover represents another plane. If one line is drawn on the front cover and another line is drawn on the back cover and both lines are extended, the two lines will never intersect.

Accordingly, two intersecting lines will always exist in a single plane. In fact, two intersecting lines are often used to describe the plane. Points along a single line in a plane are called **collinear** points because they all belong to the same line. However, points on both intersecting lines are called **non-collinear points** because they belong to more than one line.

If you use the surface of a desk to represent a plane, it is possible to imagine the plane being extended to the left and right as well as forward and backward. In other words, a plane can be extended in two dimensions, which is often written as 2-D. A Cartesian representation of the plane in two dimensions assigns pairs of numbers, called coordinates (x, y), to every point on the plane.

UNDERSTANDING AND IDENTIFYING POSTULATES ON ANGLES

The angle measure, angle addition, and angle bisector postulates all deal with angles. An **angle** is formed when two rays share a common endpoint. The endpoint is called the **vertex**.

The postulates dealing with angles are similar to the postulates about line segments.

ANGLE MEASURE POSTULATE

The angle measure postulate states that every angle has a unique measure between 0 and 360. A common unit for angle measure is degrees represented by the symbol °.

This postulate is sometimes called the protractor postulate as the common **protractor** tool for drawing and measuring angles is based on this postulate.

Let O be a point on a plane. Consider an infinite number of non-overlapping rays originating at point O. For every ray, there exists a real number from 0 to 360, and for any pair of rays forming an angle at point O, the angle measure is equal to the difference of the corresponding numbers.

The given diagrams illustrate the angle measure postulate. This image shows some of the possible rays originating at point O. This image shows several angles formed by pairs of rays.

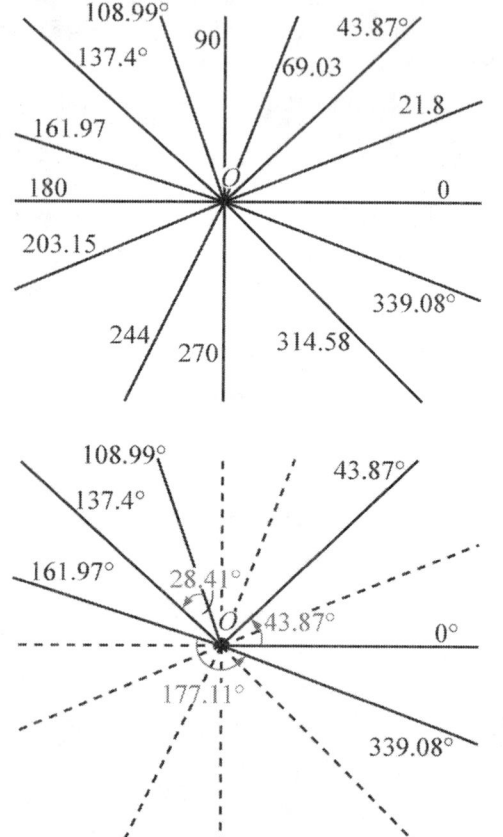

The angle formed between the ray at 0° and the ray at 43.87° is 43.87° − 0° = 43.87°.

The angle formed between the ray at 108.99° and the ray at 137.4° is 137.4° − 108.99° = 28.41°.

The angle formed between the ray at 161.97° and the ray at 339.08° is 339.08° − 161.97° = 177.11°.

ANGLE ADDITION POSTULATE

The angle addition postulate states that $\alpha = \beta + \lambda$. For example, rays r, p, and t originate from point O and extend in different directions so that ray p lies between ray r and ray t. Angle α is formed by rays r and t, and angle β is formed between rays r and p. Angle λ is formed by rays p and t. This postulate is illustrated in the given example.

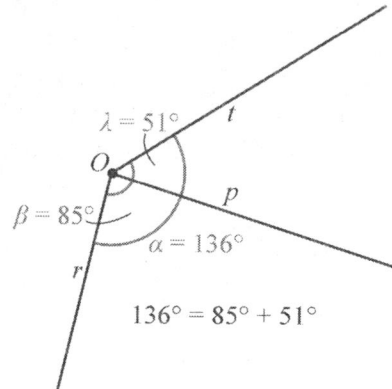

$$136° = 85° + 51°$$

ANGLE BISECTOR POSTULATE

The angle bisector postulate states that for any angle θ, there exists a ray, a, from the vertex of the angle that cuts θ in half. Ray a is called an **angle bisector**.

The given diagram illustrates the postulate.

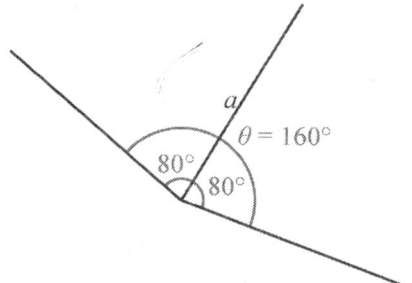

G-CO.2 Represent transformations in the plane using, e.g., transparencies and geometry software; describe transformations as functions that take points in the plane as inputs and give other points as outputs. Compare transformations that preserve distance and angle to those that do not.

TRANSLATIONS

A translation is one type of transformation performed in geometry. In a **translation**, sometimes referred to as a slide, a shape is moved up or down, right or left, or a combination of these. To move the shape, values are added or subtracted from the *x*- or *y*-coordinate of each original ordered pair.

- Movements to the left require a subtraction from the original *x*-coordinate.
- Movements to the right require an addition to the original *x*-coordinate.
- Movements up require an addition to the original *y*-coordinate.
- Movements down require a subtraction from the original *y*-coordinate.

A translated shape is called an **image**. It is identical, or congruent, to the original shape except for its location.

Shapes can be translated horizontally (to the left or right).

Example

Draw △*ABC* with vertices *A*(2, 3), *B*(4, 6), and *C*(6, 1). Translate the triangle 2 units to the right. Label the translated image *A'*, *B'* and *C'*.

Solution

Step 1

Draw the original shape on the Cartesian plane. Plot and label each point as given in the question, then connect the points with line segments.

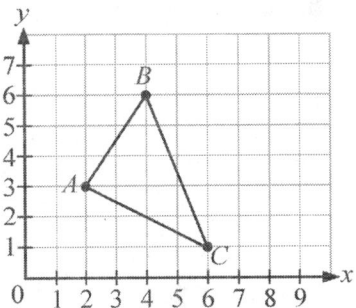

Step 2

Add or subtract, from the original coordinates of the vertices, the number of units the image will move horizontally or vertically.

The image is moving to the right. Motion to the right affects the *x*-coordinate. Add 2 to each of the given *x*-coordinates. There is no up or down movement, so the *y*-coordinates stay the same.

A'(2 + 2 = 4, 3),
B'(4 + 2 = 6, 6), *C'*(6 + 2 = 8, 1)

Step 3

Draw the translated image on the Cartesian plane.

Plot and label each new point, then connect the new points with line segments to form the translated triangle, $\triangle A'B'C'$.

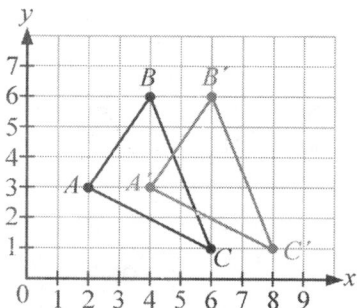

Shapes can be translated vertically (up or down).

Example

Draw $\triangle ABC$ with vertices $A(2, 3)$, $B(4, 6)$, and $C(6, 1)$. Translate the triangle 2 units down. Label the translated image A', B' and C'.

Solution

Step 1

Draw the original shape on the Cartesian plane. Plot and label each point as given in the question, then connect the points with line segments.

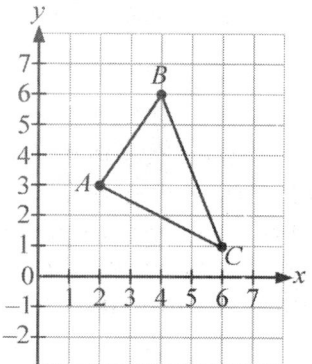

Step 2

Add or subtract, from the original coordinates of the vertices, the number of units the image will move horizontally or vertically.

The image is moving down. Downward motion affects the *y*-coordinate. Subtract 2 from each of the given *y*-coordinates. There is no right or left movement, so the *x*-coordinates stay the same.

$A'(2, 3 - 2 = 1)$,
$B'(4, 6 - 2 = 4)$, $C'(6, 1 - 2 = -1)$

Step 3

Draw the translated image on the Cartesian plane.

Plot and label each new point, then connect new the points with line segments to form the translated triangle, $\triangle A'B'C'$.

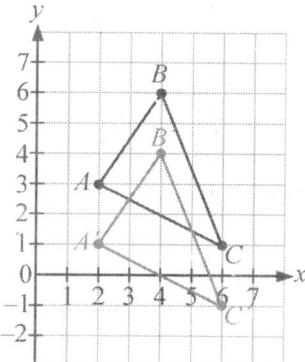

Shapes can be translated both horizontally and vertically.

Example

Draw △ABC with vertices A(2, 3), B(4, 6), and C(6, 1). Translate the triangle 4 units left and 3 units down. Label the translated image A', B' and C'.

Solution

Step 1

Draw the original shape on the Cartesian plane. Plot and label each point as given in the question, then connect the points with line segments.

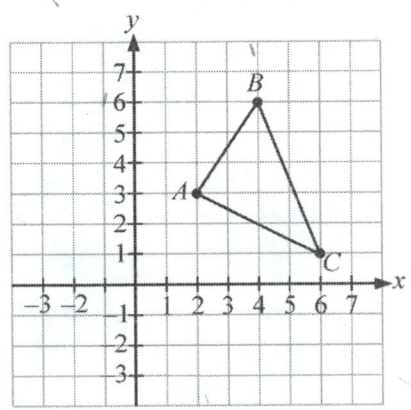

Step 2

Add or subtract, from the original coordinates of the vertices, the number of units the image will move horizontally or vertically.

For each point, subtract 4 from the x-coordinate and 3 from the y-coordinate.

A'(2 − 4, 3 − 3) = (−2, 0)
B'(4 − 4, 6 − 3) = (0, 3)
C'(6 − 4, 1 − 3) = (2, −2)

Step 3

Draw the translated image on the Cartesian plane.

Plot and label each new point, then connect the new points with line segments to form the translated triangle, △A'B'C'.

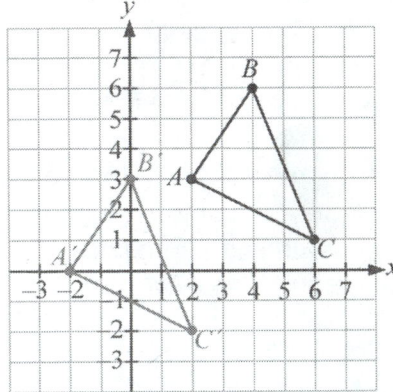

When given the translated image and asked to find the original shape, do the opposite of what was done to the original shape.

Example

The quadrilateral M'N'P'Q' was formed by connecting the vertices M'(−4, 3), N'(−5, 0), P'(1, −2), and Q'(1, 1) after translating the original shape 3 units to the left.

Draw the original shape MNPQ.

Solution

Step 1

Draw the translated image on the Cartesian plane.

Plot and label each translated point, as given in the question, then connect these points with line segments to form a quadrilateral.

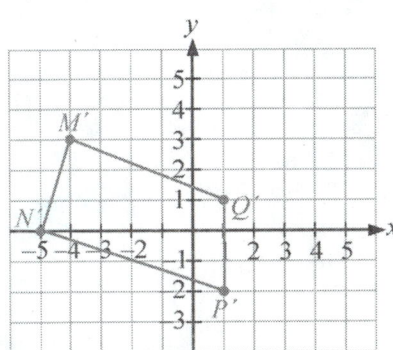

Step 2

Perform the inverse transformation.
The image moved to the left. Motion to the left affects the *x*-coordinate. Three units were subtracted from the *x*-coordinates. Perform the inverse operation to determine the original *x*-coordinates. For each point, add 3 to the *x*-coordinate.
$M(-4 + 3 = -1, 3)$, $N(-5 + 3 = -2, 0)$,
$P(1 + 3 = 4, -2)$, $Q(1 + 3 = 4, 1)$

Step 3

Draw the original shape on the Cartesian plane. Plot and label each new point, then connect the new points with line segments to form the original quadrilateral *MNPQ*.

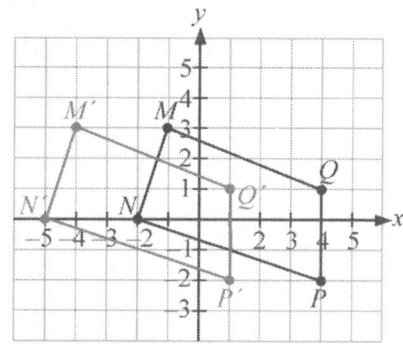

ROTATIONS

A **rotation** is one type of transformation performed in geometry. In a **rotation**, sometimes referred to as a turn, a shape is pivoted about a point. Rotations can be clockwise (cw) or counterclockwise (ccw). Some common rotation angles are shown in the following list. In each case the pivot point is point *B*.

- 90° clockwise $\left(\dfrac{1}{4} \text{ turn right}\right)$ or 270° counterclockwise $\left(\dfrac{3}{4} \text{ turn left}\right)$

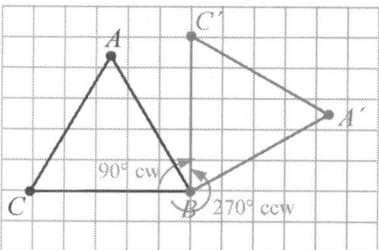

- 180° clockwise or counterclockwise $\left(\dfrac{1}{2} \text{ turn right or left}\right)$

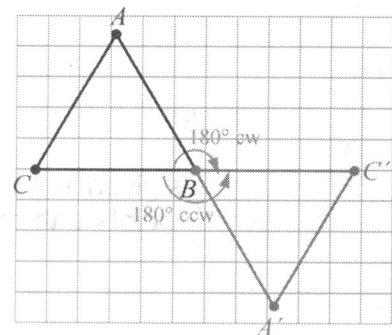

- 270° clockwise $\left(\dfrac{3}{4} \text{ turn right}\right)$ or 90° counterclockwise $\left(\dfrac{1}{4} \text{ turn left}\right)$

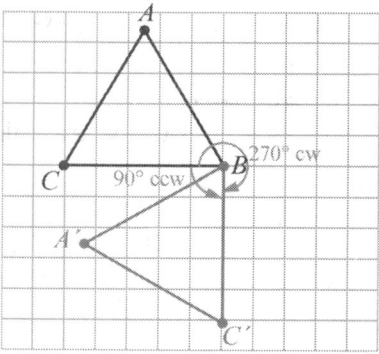

The easiest way to rotate a shape is to trace the original shape. Then, rotate the traced shape about the pivot point as directed in the question. After the rotation is completed lift up the traced image and draw the rotated image on the Cartesian plane.

Example

Draw △*DEF* with vertices *D*(3, 4), *E*(3, 1), and *F*(1, 1). Rotate △*DEF* 90° counterclockwise about the point *P*(0, 0). Use *D'*, *E'* and *F'* to label the rotated triangle. Then rotate △*D'E'F'* clockwise about the point (1, 1). Use *D''*, *E''* and *F''* to label this triangle.

Solution

Rotate the original triangle 90° counterclockwise.

Step 1
Draw the original triangle on the Cartesian plane.
Plot and label each point as given in the question, then connect the points with line segments.

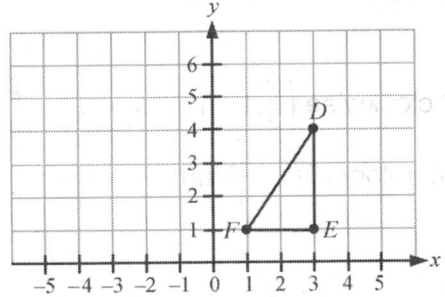

Step 2
Trace the original triangle and rotate as directed in the question.
When you turn something counterclockwise, you turn it to the left. Make sure the traced triangle is directly on top of the original triangle. Place your pencil on (0, 0) and turn the tracing paper 90° counterclockwise or a $\frac{1}{4}$ turn to the left.

Step 3
Draw the rotated triangle on the Cartesian plane.
Plot and label each new point, then connect these new points with line segments to form the rotated triangle, △*D'E'F'*.

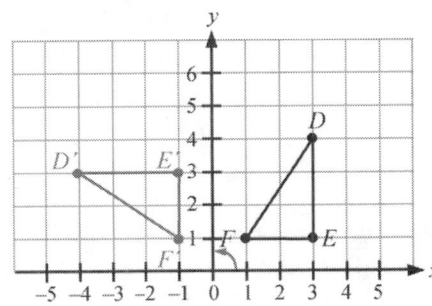

Step 4
Rotate the new △*D'E'F'*, 90° clockwise.
Use the traced original triangle from the previous rotation. Rotate as directed in the question.
When you turn something clockwise, you turn it to the right (the direction the arms on a clock move). Make sure the traced triangle is directly on top of the new triangle, △*D'E'F'*. Place your pencil on (1, 1) and turn the tracing paper 90° clockwise or a $\frac{1}{4}$ turn to the right.

Step 5
Draw the rotated triangle on the Cartesian plane.
Plot and label each new point, then connect these new points with line segments to form the rotated triangle, △*D''E''F''*.

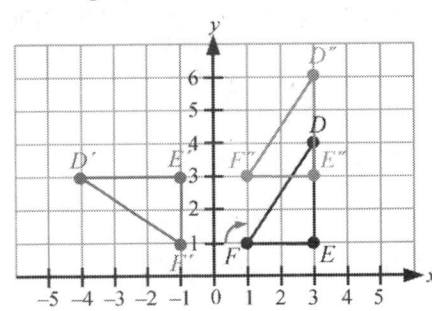

A rotation point can be on the shape or outside the shape. It can also be within the shape.

Example

Draw a quadrilateral with vertices $H(0, 3)$, $I(0, 10)$, $J(-4, 8)$, and $K(-4, 3)$. Rotate it 180° counterclockwise about the point $(1, 8)$. Use H', I', J', and K' to label the rotated image.

Solution

Step 1

Draw the original quadrilateral on the Cartesian plane.

Plot and label each point as given in the question, then connect the points with line segments.

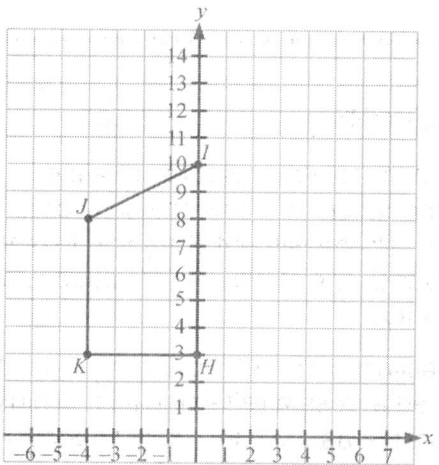

Step 2

Trace the original quadrilateral and rotate it as directed in the question.

When rotating an image 180°, direction does not matter, as a turn clockwise or counterclockwise will result in the image being in the same place. Make sure the traced quadrilateral is directly on top of the original quadrilateral. Place your pencil on $(1, 8)$ and turn the tracing paper 180° or a $\frac{1}{2}$ turn to the right or left.

Step 3

Draw the rotated image on the Cartesian plane. Plot and label each new point then connect the new points with line segments to form the rotated quadrilateral, quadrilateral $H'I'J'K'$.

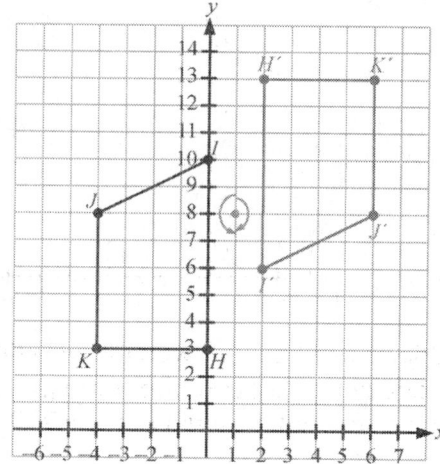

Transformations

Castle Rock Research

When given the translated image and asked to draw the original shape, do the opposite of what was done to the original shape.

Example

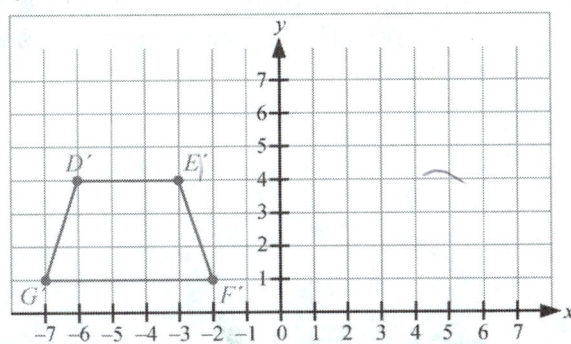

Quadrilateral $D'E'F'G'$ was drawn after a 270° clockwise rotation about the point (0, 0). Draw the original quadrilateral $DEFG$.

Solution

Step 1
Perform the inverse transformation.
Trace the rotated image, quadrilateral $D'E'F'G'$, and rotate it in the opposite direction stated in the question.
The question said the original quadrilateral was rotated clockwise. Rotate the traced image in the opposite direction: counterclockwise. Make sure the traced quadrilateral is directly on top of quadrilateral $D'E'F'G'$. Place your pencil on (0, 0). Turn the tracing paper 270° counterclockwise or a $\frac{3}{4}$ turn to the left. You could also use an equivalent shortcut and turn the page 90° clockwise or a $\frac{1}{4}$ turn to the right.

Step 2
Draw the rotated image on the Cartesian plane. Plot and label each new point, then connect these new points with line segments to form the original quadrilateral, $DEFG$.

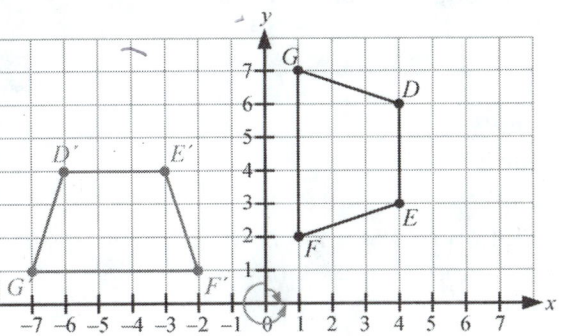

REFLECTIONS

The word *transform* means to change.
A **transformation** changes the position of a geometric shape without changing its shape.
A reflection is one of the transformations performed in geometry.

In a **reflection**, often referred to as a flip, the shape is mirrored across a reflection line. Think of the reflection line as the line that is folded to create a mirror image on the other side of the line.
The coordinates of a reflected image are the same distance away from the mirror, or reflecting line, as in the original shape. The reflection image is on the opposite side of the reflection line from the original shape.

For instance, if the reflection line is the *x*-axis and the original point is at $A(2, 3)$, then the reflected image would be at $(2, -3)$. Point A is 3 units above the *x*-axis, and A' is 3 units below the *x*-axis.
The shape and the reflected image are an equal distance from the line of reflection.

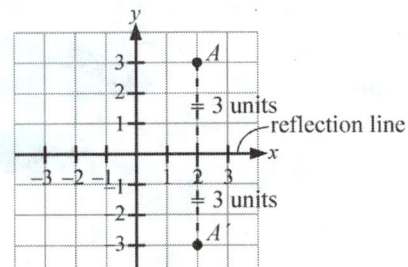

Example

Draw △ABC with vertices A(−5, −2), B(−3, −1), and C(−3, −3). Then, draw the reflection image using a line of symmetry (reflection line) one unit above the x-axis. The equation of the reflection line is $y = 1$. Label the image with single primes on the letters.

Solution

Step 1
Draw the original shape on the Cartesian plane. Plot and label each point as given in the question. Then, connect the points with line segments.
Add the reflection line.

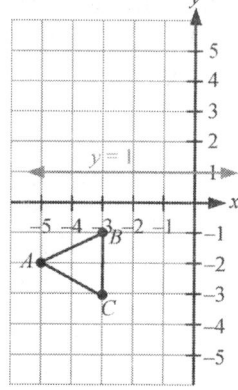

Step 2
Determine the coordinates of the reflected image.
The image is reflected about the x-axis. This means the x-coordinates will remain the same while the y-coordinates change.
Calculate the distance each vertex is from the reflection line.
Since A is 3 units below the reflection line, A′ will be 3 units above the reflection line.
A′(−5, 4)
Since B is 2 units below the reflection line, B′ will be 2 units above the reflection line.
B′(−3, 3)
Since C is 4 units below the reflection line, C′ will be 4 units above the reflection line.
C′(−3, 5)

Step 3
Draw the reflected image on the Cartesian plane.
Plot and label each new point with a prime on the letter to indicate that it is the image of the original shape. Then, connect the points with line segments.

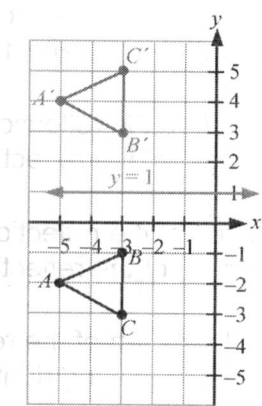

When you are given the reflected image and want to find the original shape, work backwards from the instructions given for the reflection.

Example

The image of shape A′B′C′D′ was formed by connecting the vertices A′(−6, 1), B′(−3, 1), C′(−3, −3), and D′(−8, −3) after reflecting the original shape using a line of symmetry (reflection line) one unit left of the y-axis. The equation of the reflection line is $x = −1$.

Draw the original shape ABCD.

Solution

Step 1
Draw the reflected image on the Cartesian plane.
Plot and label each point as given in the question. Then, connect the points with line segments. Add the reflection line.

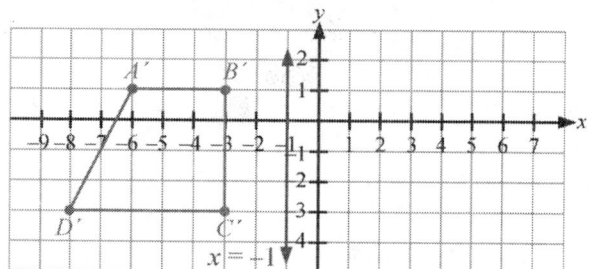

Transformations • Castle Rock Research

Step 2

Perform the inverse transformation.
The image is reflected about the *y*-axis.
This means the *y*-coordinates will remain the same while the *x*-coordinates change.
Calculate the distance each vertex is from the reflection line.
If A′ is 5 units left of the reflection line, then A will be 5 units right of the reflection line.
A(4, 1)
If B′ is 2 units left of the reflection line, then B will be 2 units right of the reflection line.
B(1, 1)
If C′ is 2 units left of the reflection line, then C will be 2 units right of the reflection line.
C(1, −3)
If D′ is 7 units to the left of the reflection line, then D will be 7 units to the right of the reflection line.
D(6, −3)

Step 3

Draw the original shape on the Cartesian plane. Plot and label each new point. Then, connect the points with line segments.

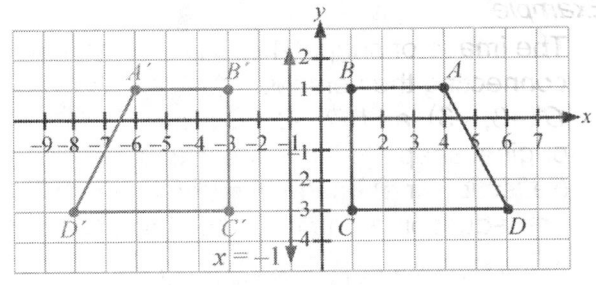

DILATIONS

The word *transform* means to change.
A **transformation** changes the position of a geometric shape without changing its shape.
A dilation is one of the transformations performed in geometry.

In a **dilation**, sometimes referred to as resizing, a shape is proportionally increased or decreased in size. When you order school pictures, your package will contain examples of dilations. It contains both large and small pictures of you. However, while the picture size may differ, it remains the same shape. Also, think of the pupil of the eye dilating. It gets larger or smaller depending on the amount of light striking it while remaining the same shape.

To create a dilation image, use a scale factor. A **scale factor** is the ratio of any two corresponding lengths in two similar geometric shapes. If the scale factor is greater than 1, the image is enlarged. For example, if an image has a scale factor of 2, the distance from the center of the dilation to a point on the image is twice as long as the distance from the center of the dilation to the same point on the original shape.

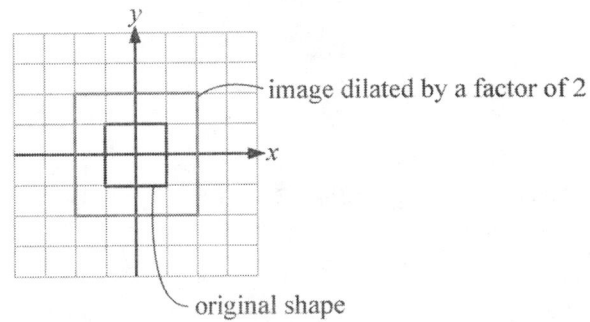

Most dilations in geometry use the origin (0, 0) as the center of the dilation. Because of this, it is easy to dilate a shape by multiplying the *x*- and *y*-coordinates by the scale factor.

Example

△ABC has vertices A(1, 2), B(2, 3), and C(3, 1).

Draw the dilation image after a scale factor of 2 is applied to the dilation center at (0, 0). Label the image appropriately with primes.

Solution

Step 1

Draw the original shape on the Cartesian plane.

Plot and label each point as given in the question. Then, connect the points with line segments.

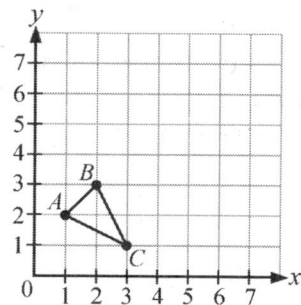

Step 2

Multiply the coordinates of the points by the scale factor.

The scale factor is 2.
A'(1 × 2 = 2, 2 × 2 = 4)
B'(2 × 2 = 4, 3 × 2 = 6)
C'(3 × 2 = 6, 1 × 2 = 2)

Step 3

Draw the dilated image on the Cartesian plane.

Plot and label each new point with a prime on the letter to indicate that it is the image of the original shape. Then, connect the points with line segments.

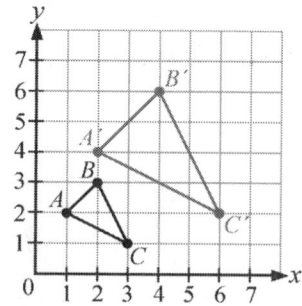

If the scale factor is less than one, the image is reduced. For example, if an image has a scale factor of $\frac{1}{2}$, the distance from the center of the dilation to a point on the image is half as long as the distance from the center of the dilation to the same point on the original shape.

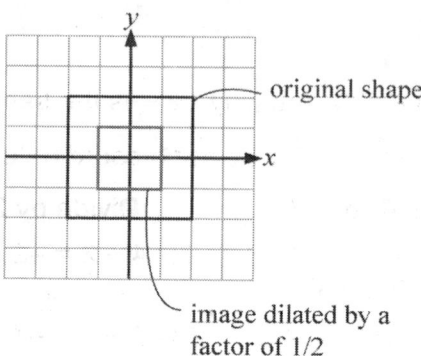

Example

Draw a triangle with vertices A(−4, 6), B(−2, 2), and C(0, 4). Locate the dilation image of the triangle with the dilation center at (0, 0) and a scale factor of $\frac{1}{2}$.

Solution

Step 1

Draw the original shape on the Cartesian plane. Plot and label each point as given in the question. Then, connect the points with line segments.

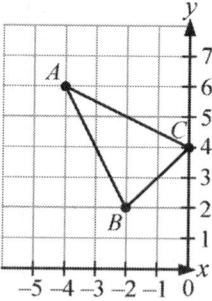

Transformations

Step 2
Multiply the coordinates of the points by the scale factor.

The scale factor is $\frac{1}{2}$.

There are two ways to do this calculation.
- Method 1: Multiply each coordinate by 0.5 $\left(\frac{1}{2} = 0.5\right)$.
- Method 2: Multiplying by $\frac{1}{2}$ is the same as dividing by 2. Divide each coordinate by 2.

Multiply by 0.5	Divide by 2
$A'(-4 \times 0.5 = -2, 6 \times 0.5 = 3)$	$A'(-4 \div 2 = -2, 6 \div 2 = 3)$
$B'(-2 \times 0.5 = -1, 2 \times 0.5 = 1)$	$B'(-2 \div 2 = -1, 2 \div 2 = 1)$
$C'(0 \times 0.5 = 0, 4 \times 0.5 = 2)$	$C'(0 \div 2 = 0, 4 \div 2 = 2)$

Step 3
Draw the dilated image on the Cartesian plane. Plot and label each new point with a prime on the letter to indicate that it is the image of the original shape. Then, connect the points with line segments.

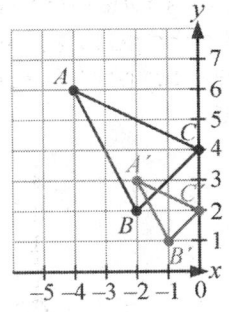

When you are given the transformed image and want to find the original shape, do the opposite of what was done to the original shape.

Example
The image of figure $M'N'O'P'$ was formed by connecting the vertices $M'(-3, 3)$, $N'(6, 3)$, $O'(3, -3)$, and $P'(-6, -3)$ after applying a scale factor of 3 to the original shape with the dilation center $(0, 0)$.

Draw the original shape $MNOP$.

Solution
Step 1
Draw the transformed image on the Cartesian plane.

Plot and label each point with a prime on the letter as given in the question. Then, connect the points with line segments.

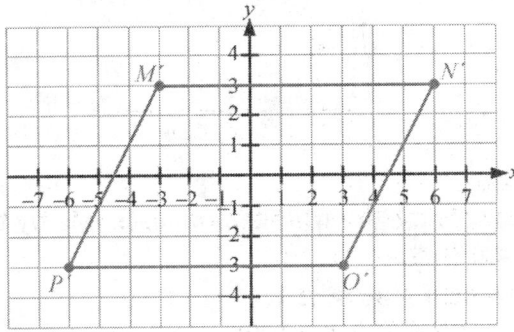

Step 2
Perform the inverse transformation.

Multiply the coordinates of the points by the inverse of the scale factor.

The coordinates were multiplied by a scale factor of 3. The inverse of multiplication is division; divide each of the coordinates by 3.
$M(-3 \div 3 = -1, 3 \div 3 = 1)$
$N(6 \div 3 = 2, 3 \div 3 = 1)$
$O(3 \div 3 = 1, -3 \div 3 = -1)$
$P(-6 \div 3 = -2, -3 \div 3 = -1)$

Step 3

Draw the original shape on the Cartesian plane. Plot and label each new point without a prime on the letter to indicate that it is the original shape. Then, connect the points with line segments.

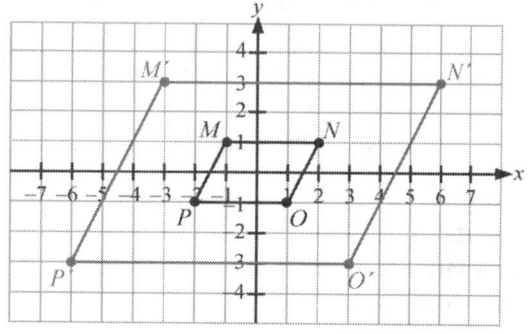

DRAWING 2D IMAGES AFTER MULTIPLE TRANSFORMATIONS

When completing **multiple transformations**, complete them in the order they are given in the question.

- Perform the first transformation using the original shape.
- Perform the second transformation using the transformed image.

Example

Quadrilateral *DEFG* has vertices of *D*(2, −1), *E*(1, 2), *F*(4, 3), and *G*(4, −1).

Draw quadrilateral *DEFG* and its images after it is reflected in the *y*-axis and then translated 4 right and 4 up. Label the reflected image as *D′E′F′G′* and the translated image as *D″E″F″G″*.

Solution

Step 1

Draw the original shape on the Cartesian plane.

Plot and label each point as given in the question. Then, connect the points with line segments.

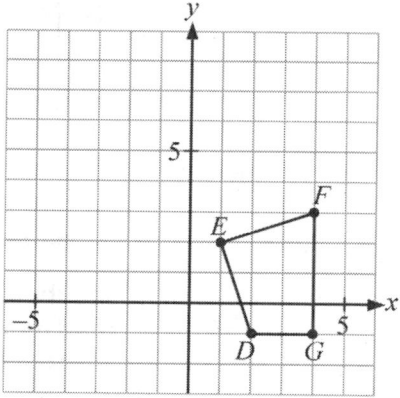

Step 2

Perform the first transformation using the original shape.

The first transformation is a reflection about the *y*-axis.

Draw the reflected image on the Cartesian plane.

Plot and label each new point, then connect these points with line segments to form the reflected quadrilateral *D′E′F′G′*.

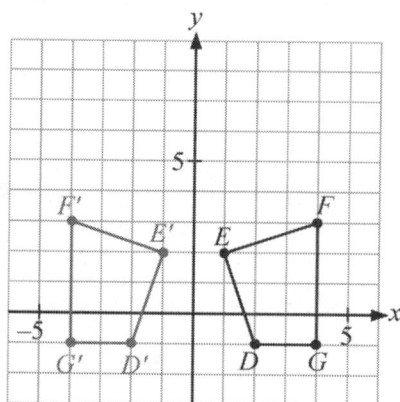

Transformations · 30 · Castle Rock Research

Step 3

Perform the second transformation using the transformed image.

The second transformation is a translation 4 units right and 4 units up.

Draw the translated image on the Cartesian plane.

Plot and label each new point, then connect these points with line segments to form the translated quadrilateral $D''E''F''G''$.

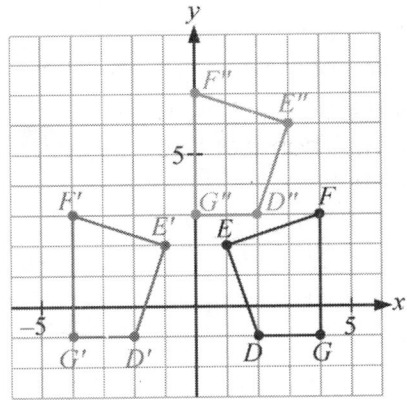

Sometimes, you are asked to find the original shape after it has been transformed multiple times. In order to do this, you must complete the transformations in the opposite order.

Example

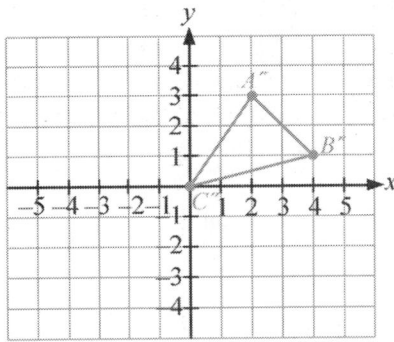

The given triangle was moved from its original position by adding 1 to its *x*-coordinates and 3 to its *y*-coordinates. It was then reflected about the *y*-axis.

Draw the original shape and first image, $\triangle A'B'C'$, and the original triangle, $\triangle ABC$.

Solution

Step 1

Identify the last transformation, and perform the inverse transformation.

The last transformation was a reflection about the *y*-axis.

Reflect the triangle back across the *y*-axis.

Plot and label each new point, then connect these new points with line segments to from the reflected triangle $\triangle A'B'C'$.

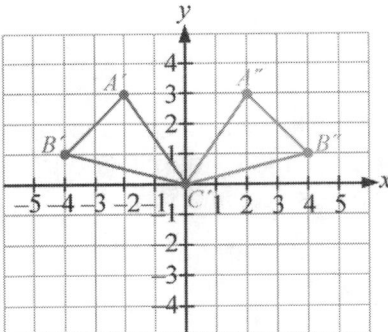

Step 2

Identify the first transformation, and perform the inverse transformation.

The first transformation was a translation, adding 1 to the *x*-axis coordinate and 3 to the *y*-axis coordinate.

Translate the triangle by inversing the movement: subtract 1 from the *x*-coordinate and 3 from the *y*-coordinate.

$A(-2 - 1 = -3, 3 - 3 = 0)$
$B(-4 - 1 = -5, 1 - 3 = -2)$
$C(0 - 1 = -1, 0 - 3 = -3)$

Draw the translated image on the Cartesian plane.

Plot and label each new point, then connect these new points with line segments to from the reflected triangle $\triangle ABC$.

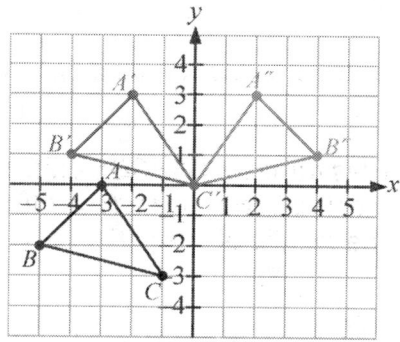

IDENTIFYING SINGLE TRANSFORMATIONS

When given the original shape and the transformed image, it is possible to identify the transformation performed by using elimination.

The easiest transformation to identify is a dilation because it is the only transformation where the size of the shape changes.

The next transformation to look for is a reflection. In a reflection, the transformation takes on a mirror image of the original shape.

In a translation, the sides of the original shape and the image are parallel to each other.

In a rotation, the vertices of the original shape move the same distance from the rotation point as the vertices of the rotated image.

Example

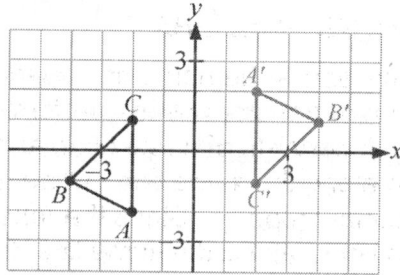

Identify the transformation of triangle *ABC* to triangle *A'B'C'*.

Solution

Compare the shape and image to each of the transformation movements.

Dilation: The image is not a dilation because the size of the triangle is the same.

Reflection: The image is not a reflection because the image is not a mirror image of the original.

Translation: The image is not a translation because the sides are not parallel. Points *A* and *C* have switched places.

Rotation: The image is a rotation of 180° about the point (0, 0). This rotation could have been either clockwise or counter-clockwise and resulted in the same final image.

APPLYING GLIDE REFLECTIONS ON A TWO-DIMENSIONAL SHAPE

A glide reflection is the name of a specific combination of transformations performed in geometry. It consists of a reflection and a translation along the same line. Glide reflections have a special property. Since the reflection and translation occur along the same line, the order in which they are applied does not affect the resulting image.

Example
Image $A''B''C''D''$ is an image of the figure $ABCD$, which has undergone a glide reflection. In this case, the figure $ABCD$ was reflected to become figure $A'B'C'D'$ and then translated down to become the image $A''B''C''D''$.

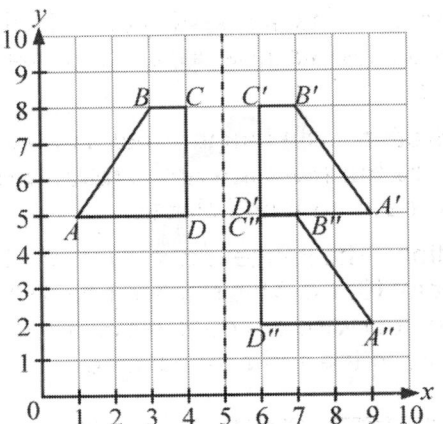

In the next example, image $A''B''C''D''$ is still an image of the figure $ABCD$, which has undergone a glide reflection. In this case, however, the figure $ABCD$ was translated down to become the image $A'B'C'D'$ and then reflected to become figure $A''B''C''D''$.

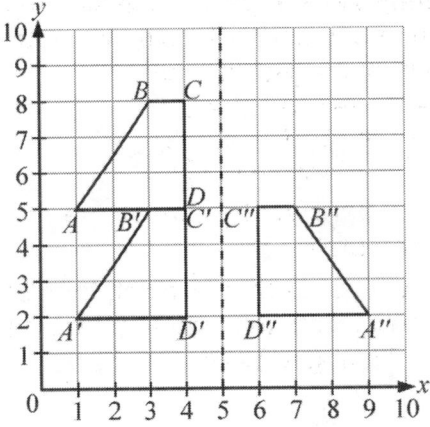

Example
Kate slides trapezoid $ABCD$ 5 units to the right. Next, she flips the trapezoid over the horizontal line in the middle of the grid.

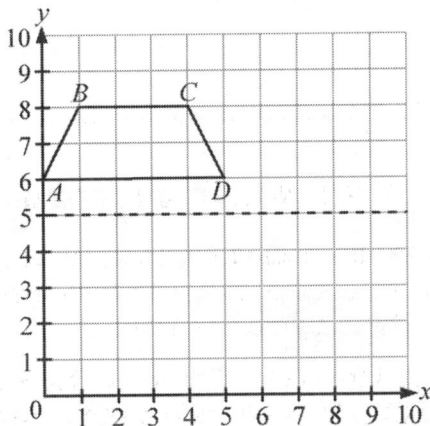

What are the coordinates of trapezoid ABCD after the two transformations?

Solution

Step 1
Move the trapezoid 5 units to the right.

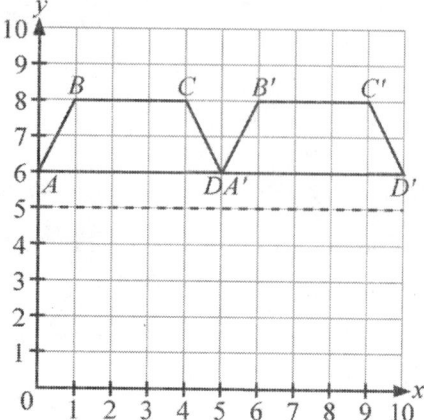

The new coordinates of the trapezoid are A'(5, 6), B'(6, 8), C'(9, 8), and D'(10, 6).

Step 2
Flip the trapezoid so it is reflected across the line in the middle of the grid.

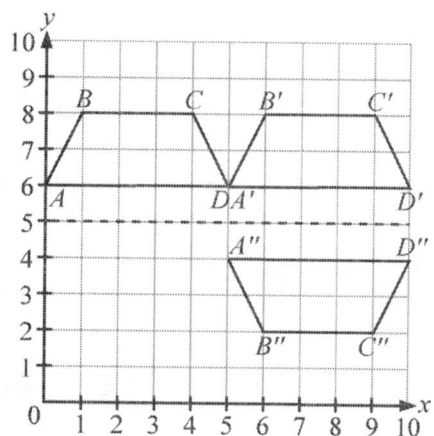

When reflected, the coordinates of the new trapezoid A" B" C" D" are
A"(5, 4), B"(6, 2), C"(9, 2), and D"(10, 4).

USING PROPER FUNCTION NOTATION FOR ISOMETRIES

Isometries are geometric transformations that maintain the shape and size of a figure but change its location. Translations, reflections, and rotations are all transformations that are classified as isometries.

Recall that a function describes a relationship between input and output values. Function notation for an isometry is a concise method of representing a transformation of points and figures on the coordinate plane.

TRANSLATIONS

The notation for a translation is of the form $T_{a,b}$, where T indicates a translation and a and b indicate that a coordinate (x, y) becomes $(x + a, y + b)$. The function that represents a translation is $T_{a,b}(x, y) = (x + a, y + b)$.

Example
A translation of △ABC is given.

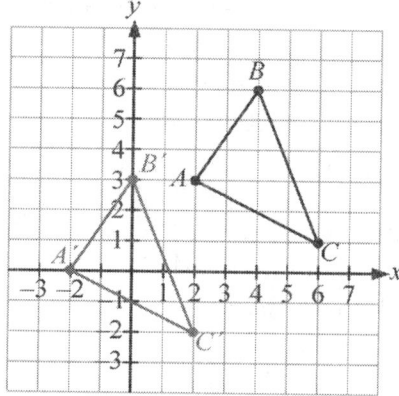

When △ABC is under $T_{-4,-3}$, it becomes △A'B'C'.

The function $T_{-4,-3}(x, y) = (x - 4, y - 3)$ can be used to verify the coordinates of △A'B'C'.
$T_{-4,-3}(2, 3) = (2 - 4, 3 - 3)$
$T_{-4,-3}(2, 3) = (-2, 0)$
$T_{-4,-3}(4, 6) = (4 - 4, 6 - 3)$
$T_{-4,-3}(4, 6) = (0, 3)$
$T_{-4,-3}(6, 1) = (6 - 4, 1 - 3)$
$T_{-4,-3}(6, 1) = (2, -2)$

The coordinates of △A'B'C' are (−2, 0), (0, 3), and (2, −2).

REFLECTIONS

An example of notation for a reflection is $r_{x\text{-axis}}$, where r indicates a reflection and the x-axis indicates that a coordinate (x, y) is reflected in the x-axis to become $(x, -y)$.

The following function notations are used for reflections:

- $r_{x\text{-axis}}(x, y) = (x, -y)$
- $r_{y\text{-axis}}(x, y) = (-x, y)$
- $r_{x=y}(x, y) = (y, x)$
- $r_{x=-y}(x, y) = (-y, -x)$

Example
A reflection of △ABC is given.

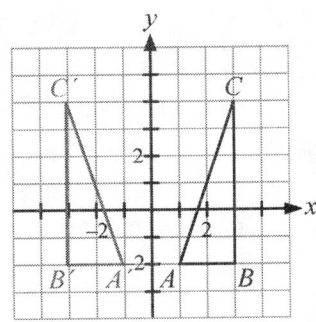

When △ABC is under $r_{y\text{-axis}}$, it becomes △A'B'C'.

The function $r_{y\text{-axis}}(x, y) = (-x, y)$ can be used to verify the coordinates of △A'B'C'.

$r_{y\text{-axis}}(1, -2) = (-1, -2)$
$r_{y\text{-axis}}(3, -2) = (-3, -2)$
$r_{y\text{-axis}}(3, 4) = (-3, 4)$

The coordinates of △A'B'C' are (−1, −2), (−3, −2), and (−3, 4).

ROTATIONS

An example of notation for a rotation is $R_{O,90°}$, which means that an image is rotated about point O with an angle of rotation of 90°.
The notation $R_{O,90°}$ indicates that each coordinate (x, y) becomes $(-y, x)$. If the location of the center of rotation is not listed, it is assumed to be the origin.

The following function notations are used for rotations about the origin:

- $R_{90°}(x, y) = (-y, x)$
- $R_{180°}(x, y) = (-x, -y)$
- $R_{270°}(x, y) = (y, -x)$
- $R_{360°}(x, y) = (x, y)$

Example
A rotation of △ABC about the origin is given.

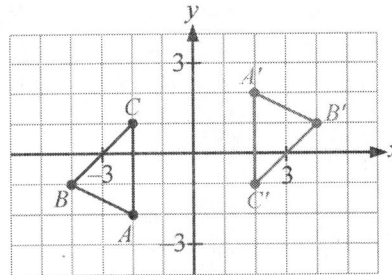

When △ABC is under $R_{180°}$, it becomes △A'B'C'.

The function $R_{180°}(x, y) = (-x, -y)$ can be used to determine the coordinates of △A'B'C'.
$R_{180°}(-2, -2) = (-(-2), -(-2))$
$R_{180°}(-2, -2) = (2, 2)$
$R_{180°}(-4, -1) = (-(-4), -(-1))$
$R_{180°}(-4, -1) = (4, 1)$
$R_{180°}(-2, 1) = (2, -1)$

The coordinates of △A'B'C' are (2, 2), (4, 1), and (2, −1).

Note that rotations of a measure that is not a multiple of 90° are possible, but they require trigonometry.

COMPOSITIONS OF ISOMETRIES

A composition of the form $F(G(x)) = y$, or $F \circ G(x) = y$, means that the function G is computed first and then used as the input for the function F. Compositions of isometries follow the same standard rules of function notation. The innermost transformations are carried out first.

Example

A glide reflection of $\triangle ABC$ is given. A glide reflection consists of a reflection and a translation along the same line.

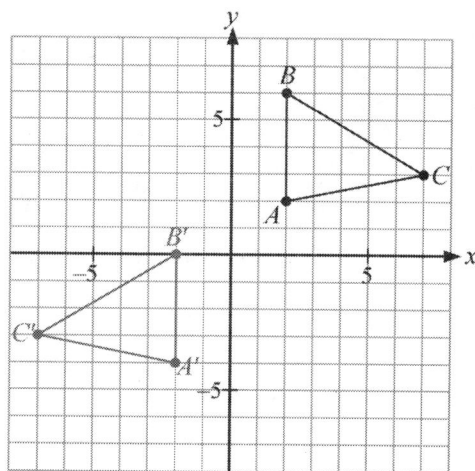

When $\triangle ABC$ is under $T_{0,-6} \circ r_{y\text{-axis}}$, it becomes $\triangle A'B'C'$.

$T_{0,-6} \circ r_{y\text{-axis}}(x, y) = T_{0,-6}(-x, y)$
$T_{0,-6} \circ r_{y\text{-axis}}(x, y) = (-x, y - 6)$

The function $T_{0,-6} \circ r_{y\text{-axis}}(x, y) = (-x, y - 6)$ can be used to verify the coordinates of $\triangle A'B'C'$.

$T_{0,-6} \circ r_{y\text{-axis}}(2, 2) = (-2, 2 - 6)$
$T_{0,-6} \circ r_{y\text{-axis}}(2, 2) = (-2, -4)$
$T_{0,-6} \circ r_{y\text{-axis}}(2, 6) = (-2, 6 - 6)$
$T_{0,-6} \circ r_{y\text{-axis}}(2, 6) = (-2, 0)$
$T_{0,-6} \circ r_{y\text{-axis}}(7, 3) = (-7, 3 - 6)$
$T_{0,-6} \circ r_{y\text{-axis}}(7, 3) = (-7, -3)$

The coordinates of $\triangle A'B'C'$ are $(-2, -4)$, $(-2, 0)$, and $(-7, -3)$.

With glide reflections, the order can be reversed and the outcome will remain the same. Therefore, the previous example could have also been written as $r_{y\text{-axis}} \circ T_{0,-6}$. However, for some compositions, the order in which the transformations are written must be taken into consideration.

For a rotation centered somewhere other than the origin, the resulting function is a composition of three transformations performed in the following order:

1. Translate the center of the rotation to the origin.
2. Rotate the image about the origin.
3. Translate the center back to its initial location.

For a reflection about a line that does not pass through the origin, the resulting function is a composition of three transformations performed in the following order:

1. Translate the image so that the reflection line passes through the origin.
2. Reflect the image.
3. Translate the image back the same amount as before.

Example

Triangle ABC is given.

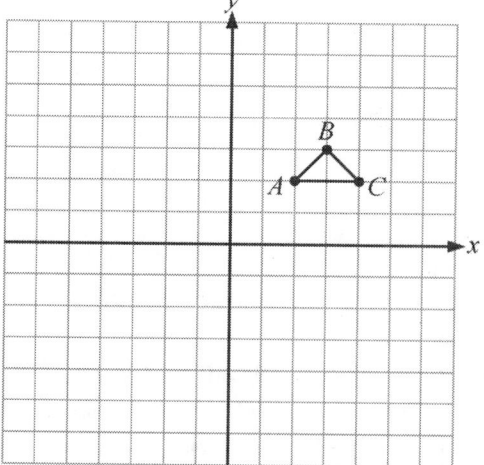

Determine a function to describe the coordinates of the image if it is rotated 90° about point A.

Solution

The rotation of the image about point A can be represented by $R_{A,90°}$. To find the function $R_{A,90°}$, translate the image to the origin, rotate the image 90°, and translate the image back to the initial location.

1. Translate the image so the center of rotation is located at the origin. Since the center of rotation is located at (2, 2), it will need to be translated left 2 units and down 2 units to become (0, 0). The function notation for this translation is $T_{-2,-2}$. The translation is as shown.

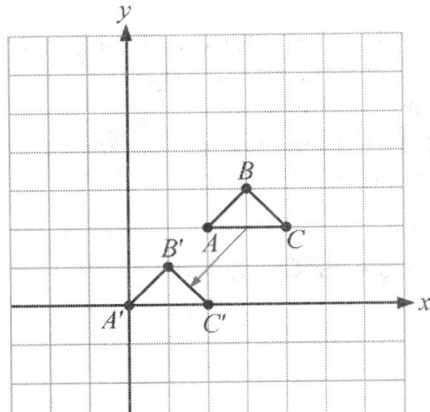

2. Rotate the image about the origin. To apply the rotation $R_{90°}$, the center of rotation must first be translated to the origin. Therefore, the function notation for the rotation about the origin is $R_{90°} \circ T_{-2,-2}$. The rotation about the origin of the translated image is shown here.

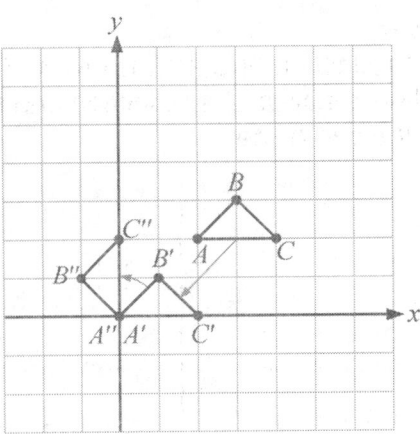

3. Translate the image so the center of location is located at its initial location. Since the center of rotation is located at (0, 0), it will need to be translated right 2 units and up 2 units to become the initial center of rotation, (2, 2). The function for this translation is $T_{2,2}$. Therefore, the function notation for the composition of isometries is $T_{2,2} \circ R_{90°} \circ T_{-2,-2}$. Each part of the composition is manageable and can be used to determine the function.

$T_{2,2} \circ R_{90°} \circ T_{-2,-2}(x, y)$
$= T_{2,2} \circ R_{90°}(x - 2, y - 2)$
$= T_{2,2}(-y + 2, x - 2)$
$= (-y + 4, x)$

A function that can be used to determine the coordinates of the transformation is $R_{A,90°}(x, y) = (-y + 4, x)$. The translation of the rotated image to its initial location is shown here.

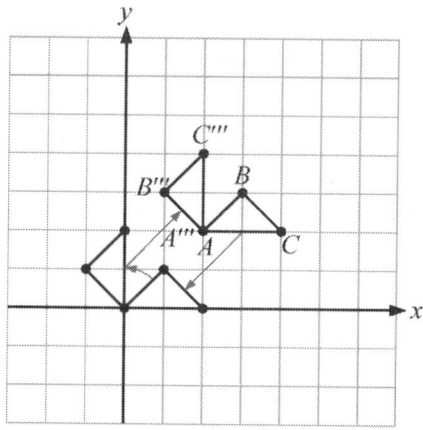

Therefore, the transformation of $\triangle ABC$ under $R_{A,90°}$ creates $\triangle A'''B'''C'''$.

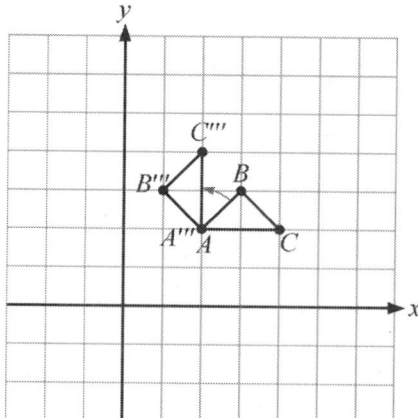

4. Compare the calculated coordinates from the function with the coordinates on the image using $R_{A,90°}(x, y) = (-y + 4, x)$.

$R_{A,90°}(2, 2) = (-2 + 4, 2)$
$R_{A,90°}(2, 2) = (2, 2)$
$R_{A,90°}(3, 3) = (-3 + 4, 3)$
$R_{A,90°}(3, 3) = (1, 3)$
$R_{A,90°}(x, y) = (-2 + 4, 4)$
$R_{A,90°}(x, y) = (2, 4)$

Each calculated coordinate matches the coordinate from the image.

INVESTIGATING AND APPLYING INVARIANT ISOMETRIC PROPERTIES

Isometries are geometric transformations that maintain the shape and size of a figure but change its location. Sometimes they are referred to as distance-preserving transformations because the distances between all the points on the figure remain constant. Translations, reflections, and rotations are transformations that are classified as isometries.

A figure that experiences an isometry always becomes an image that is congruent to the original figure. Since the image is congruent to the original figure, the following properties of both the figure and the image are invariant:

- Distance—the distance between a set of transformed points does not change.
- Collinearity—transformed lines contain the same set of corresponding points.
- Betweenness—a point will be surrounded by the same corresponding points on a transformed line.
- Midpoint—the midpoint between corresponding points does not change.
- Angle Measure—the angle formed between corresponding lines does not change.

Orientation is a property that remains constant under translations and rotations but not under reflections.

Example
The given triangle, ABC, has been rotated to become triangle A'B'C'.

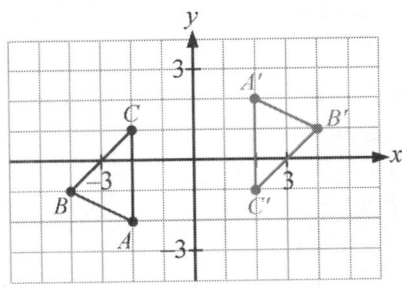

The labels of the vertices of both triangle ABC and triangle A'B'C' can be read in the clockwise direction. The orientation of triangle ABC is the same as the orientation of triangle A'B'C'.

Example
The given triangle, ABC, has been reflected to become triangle A'B'C'.

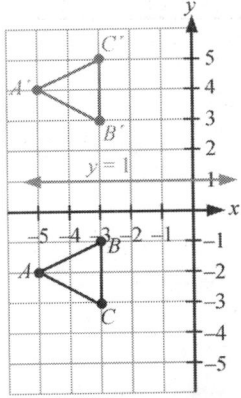

The labels of the vertices of triangle ABC can be read in the clockwise direction. The labels of the vertices of triangle A'B'C' can be read in the counterclockwise direction. As a result of the reflection of triangle ABC, the orientation of the image, triangle A'B'C', is reversed.

Since any one isometry produces a congruent image, it follows that any combination of isometries will also produce a congruent image.

Example
Image A"B"C"D" is an image of the figure ABCD that has undergone a glide reflection. A glide reflection is a combination of isometries. First a reflection and then a translation occur along the same line. In this case, the figure ABCD was reflected to become figure A'B'C'D', and then translated down to become the image A"B"C"D".

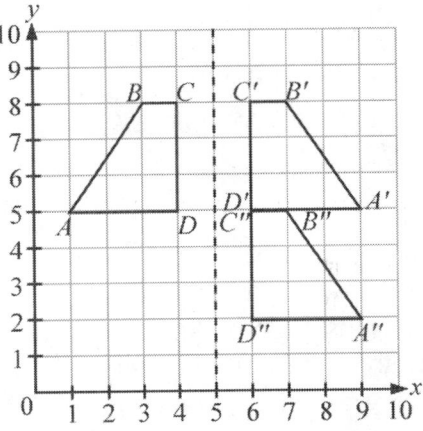

After two isometries, the image is still congruent to the original figure. With the exception of the orientation of the image, all of the given properties of the original figure are invariant in the image.

Example

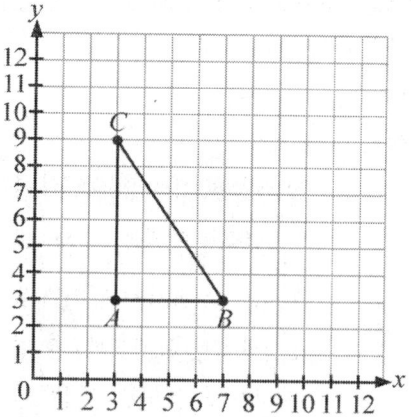

Triangle *ABC* is given.

If △*ABC* is translated into △*A'B'C'*, what is the length of *A'B'* and the measure of ∠*C'A'B'*?

Solution

Step 1
Determine the length of *A'B'*.
Since a translation makes a congruent image, the length of *AB* and *A'B'* is invariant.
In the given triangle, the length of *AB* = 4, so *A'B'* = 4.

Step 2
Determine the measure of ∠*C'A'B'*.
In the given triangle, *CA* and *AB* are perpendicular, so ∠*CAB* = 90°.
Since the angle formed between corresponding lines is an invariant, both ∠*CAB* and ∠*C'A'B'* are 90°.

G-CO.3 Given a rectangle, parallelogram, trapezoid, or regular polygon, describe the rotations and reflections that carry it onto itself.

IDENTIFYING LINES OF SYMMETRY IN A TESSELLATION

A **tessellation** is a collection of figures that fit together without any gaps. For example, a tile mosaic is a tessellation.

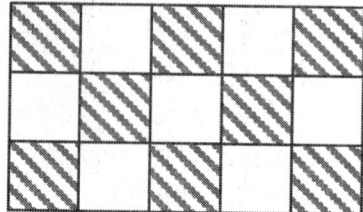

Tessellations may also have lines of symmetry. If a tessellation can be folded in half in such a way that both sides are exactly the same, it is said to be symmetrical.

Example

Four tessellations are shown.

Determine the number of lines of symmetry each tessellation has, and draw in the lines of symmetry.

Solution

The first tessellation has no lines of symmetry.

The second tessellation has one line of symmetry.

The third tessellation has two lines of symmetry.

The fourth tessellation has four lines of symmetry.

Identifying Rotational Symmetry in a Tessellation

A **tessellation** is a collection of figures that fit together without any gaps. For example, a tile mosaic is a tessellation.

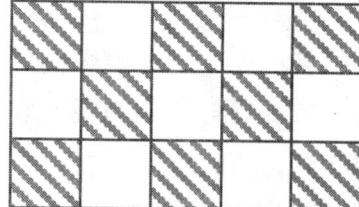

Tessellations may have **rotational symmetry**. A tessellation has rotational symmetry if it can be rotated about its center and come to rest in a different position in which it looks exactly like the original. The number of times that the rotated tessellation looks exactly like the original is called the **order of rotational symmetry** for that tessellation.

The relationship between the **angle of rotation** and the order of rotation is given in the formula

angle of rotation = $\dfrac{360°}{\text{order of rotation}}$.

Example

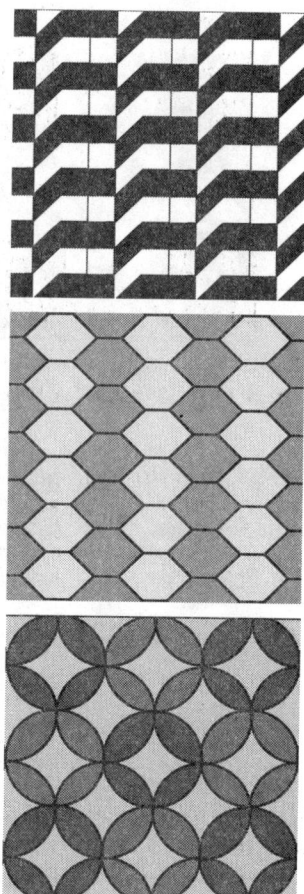

Three tessellations are given.

Determine the order of rotational symmetry and the angle of rotation of each of the given tessellations.

Solution

Each of the given images must be rotated in order to determine the angle of rotation and any rotational symmetry. A small dot is placed in a corner of the original image to track the changes made by each rotation. Since each tessellation is in the shape of a square, they will be rotated 90° at a time.

Step 1
Rotate the first image.

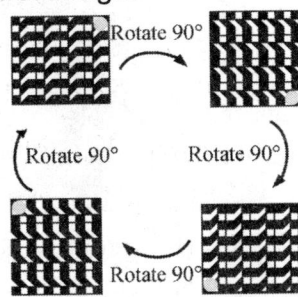

Since none of the rotations look alike, this tessellation does not have rotational symmetry.

Step 2
Rotate the second image.

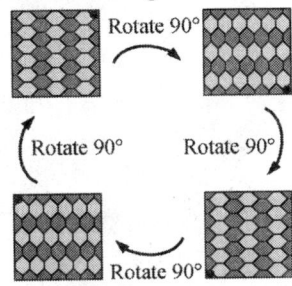

Positions 1 and 3 look exactly alike, as do positions 2 and 4. Therefore, the second tessellation has rotational symmetry of order two and an angle of rotation of 180°.

angle of rotation = $\dfrac{360°}{\text{order of rotation}}$
= $\dfrac{360°}{2}$
= 180°

Step 3
Rotate the third image.

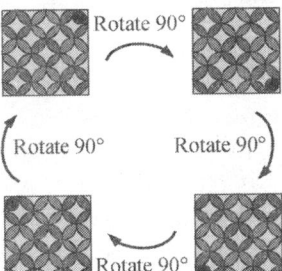

Each position looks exactly alike. Therefore, the third tessellation has rotational symmetry of order 4 and an angle of rotation of 90°.

angle of rotation = $\dfrac{360°}{\text{order of rotation}}$
= $\dfrac{360°}{4}$
= 90°

Determine the order of rotational symmetry and the angle of rotation for the given tessellation.

Solution

Rotate the image to determine if it has any rotational symmetry.

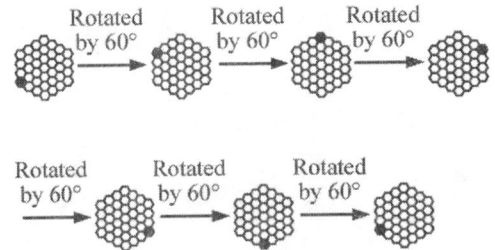

The tessellation looks exactly like the first position each time it is rotated 60°; therefore, it has rotational symmetry of order six and an angle of rotation of 60°.

angle of rotation = $\dfrac{360°}{\text{order of rotation}}$
= $\dfrac{360°}{6}$
= 60°

Calculating the Rotational Symmetry of Two-Dimensional Shapes

Rotational symmetry is seen in shapes that can be turned about a point of rotation in such a way that the rotated shape coincides exactly with its original position at least once in a complete rotation (360°). If a shape that is rotated about its center comes to rest in a different position and still looks exactly like the original, then the shape has rotational symmetry.

The **order of rotational symmetry** for two-dimensional (2-D) shapes varies. To determine the order of rotational symmetry for any 2-D shape, follow these steps:

1. Join the center of the shape to a point on the perimeter of the shape. This will help track the rotation.
2. Trace the shape, and rotate it around the center.
3. Determine how many times the rotated shape looks exactly like the original. The number of times the shape looks exactly like the original is the order of rotational symmetry.

Once you have determined the order of rotational symmetry, you can calculate the **angle of rotation**. The relationship between the angle of rotation and the order of rotation is given in the formula

$$\text{angle of rotation} = \frac{360°}{\text{order of rotation}}.$$

Example
An image of a hexagon is given.

Determine the order of rotational symmetry and the angle of rotation of the given shape.

Solution

Step 1
Determine the order of rotational symmetry.
Join the center of the shape to the perimeter of the shape.
Trace the shape, and rotate it around the center.

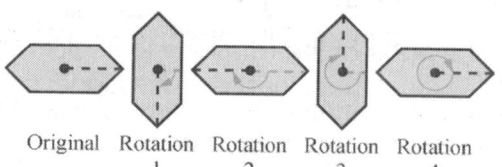

Original   Rotation   Rotation   Rotation   Rotation
               1   2   3   4

The rotated shape looks exactly like the original in two positions throughout the entire 360° rotation, which means the order of rotational symmetry is 2.

Step 2
Calculate the angle of rotation.
Apply the formula for angle of rotation.

$$\text{angle of rotation} = \frac{360°}{\text{order of rotation}}$$

$$\text{angle of rotation} = \frac{360°}{2}$$

$$\text{angle of rotation} = 180°$$

The order of rotational symmetry of the given hexagon is 2, and the angle of rotation is 180°.

Regular Polygons

The order of rotational symmetry for all regular polygons can be determined by rotating the two-dimensional shape through one complete rotation and keeping track of the number of times the shape looks exactly like the original.

Example
Three regular polygons (a triangle, a square, and a hexagon) are given.

Determine the order of rotational symmetry for the given regular polygons.

Solution

The order of rotational symmetry can be determined for all regular polygons by rotating the shape through one complete rotation.

Step 1
Determine the order of rotational symmetry for an equilateral triangle.
Join the center of the triangle to a point on the perimeter.
Trace the triangle onto a new piece of paper, and cut out the shape.
Rotate the shape around the center in a 360° rotation, and count the number of times the shape looks exactly like the original triangle.

Original   Rotation 1   Rotation 2   Rotation 3

The shape looks exactly like the original triangle three times in a 360° rotation. Therefore, the order of rotational symmetry for an equilateral triangle is 3.

Step 2
Determine the order of rotational symmetry for a square.
Join the center of the square to a point on the perimeter.
Trace the square onto a new piece of paper, and cut out the shape.
Rotate the shape around the center in a 360° rotation, and count the number of times the shape looks exactly like the original square.

 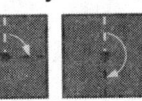  

Original   Rotation 1   Rotation 2   Rotation 3   Rotation 4

The shape looks exactly like the original square four times in a 360° rotation. Therefore, the order of rotational symmetry for a square is 4.

Step 3
Determine the order of rotational symmetry for a hexagon.
Join the center of the hexagon to a point on the perimeter.
Trace the hexagon onto a new piece of paper, and cut out the shape.
Rotate the shape around the center in a 360° rotation, and count the number of times the shape looks exactly like the original hexagon.

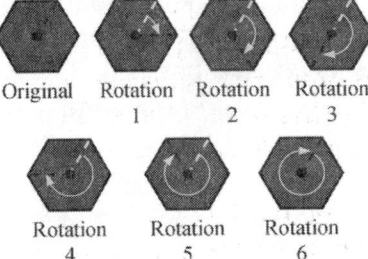

The shape looks exactly like the original hexagon six times in a 360° rotation. Therefore, the order of rotational symmetry of a hexagon is 6.

For regular polygons, the order of rotational symmetry is equal to the number of sides the polygon has. This can be summarized by the following statements:

- The order of rotational symmetry for an equilateral triangle is equal to the number of sides the triangle has.
- The order of rotational symmetry for a square is equal to the number of sides the square has.
- The order of rotational symmetry for a regular hexagon is equal to the number of sides the hexagon has.

Example

Determine the order of rotational symmetry and the angle of rotation of a regular pentagon.

Solution

Step 1

Determine the order of rotational symmetry. Since a regular pentagon has 5 equal sides and 5 lines of symmetry, its order of rotational symmetry will also be 5.

The rotational symmetry means that the pentagon can be rotated 5 times before it reaches its original position. It will look exactly like the first position each time it is rotated.

Step 2

Calculate the angle of rotation.
Apply the following formula:

$$\text{angle of rotation} = \frac{360°}{\text{order of rotation}}$$
$$= \frac{360°}{5}$$
$$= 72°$$

This set of diagrams shows how a pentagon can be rotated until it reaches its first position. The dot on the pentagon shows how the pentagon rotates 72° each time.

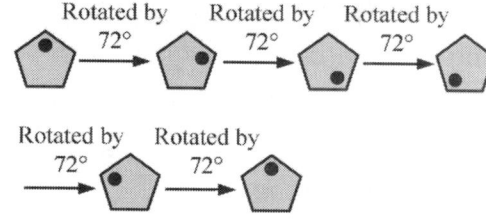

EXERCISE #1—TRANSFORMATIONS

Use the following information to answer the next question.

A circle has a radius of 10 cm. A sector within the circle is subtended by an arc with a length of 45 cm.

1. To the nearest degree, what is the measure of the angle subtended by the arc? _____°

Use the following information to answer the next question.

A diagram is given.

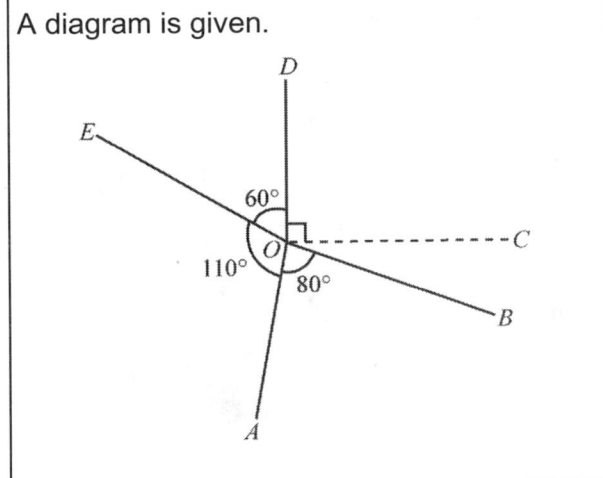

2. In the given diagram, what is the measure of ∠COB?
   A. 10°
   B. 20°
   C. 30°
   D. 40°

Use the following information to answer the next question.

△ABC has vertices A(2, 3), B(4, 6), and C(6, 1).

3. If △ABC is translated L4 and D3, the new vertices for the translated image will be
   A. A'(6, 6), B'(8, 9), and C'(10, 4)
   B. A'(5, 7), B'(7, 10), and C'(9, 5)
   C. A'(2, −2), B'(−2, 0), and C'(0, 3)
   D. A'(−2, 0), B'(0, 3), and C'(2, −2)

Use the following information to answer the next question.

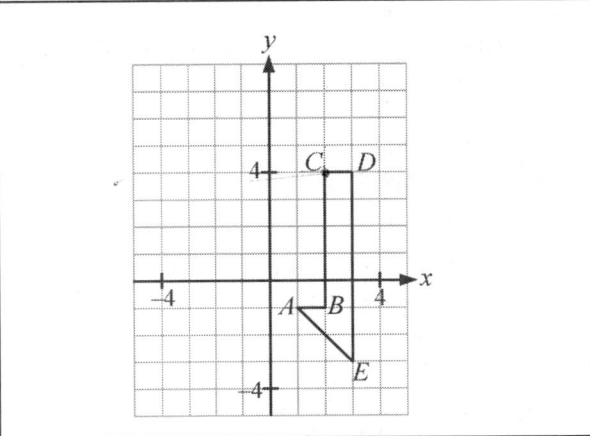

4. If figure ABCDE is rotated 270° counterclockwise about point C, then the coordinates of A' will be
   A. (−1, −1)   B. (−3, 5)
   C. (−4, 4)   D. (8, 3)

Use the following information to answer the next question.

Triangle PQR is reflected across the y-axis to form triangle P'Q'R'.

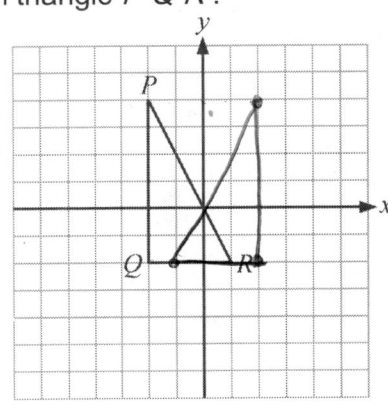

5. What are the coordinates of triangle P'Q'R' after the reflection?
   A. P'(2, −4), Q'(2, 2), R'(−1, 2)
   B. P'(2, 4), Q'(2, −2), R'(4, −2)
   C. P'(4, 2), Q'(−2, 2), R'(−2, −1)
   D. P'(2, 4), Q'(2, −2), R'(−1, −2)

Use the following information to answer the next question.

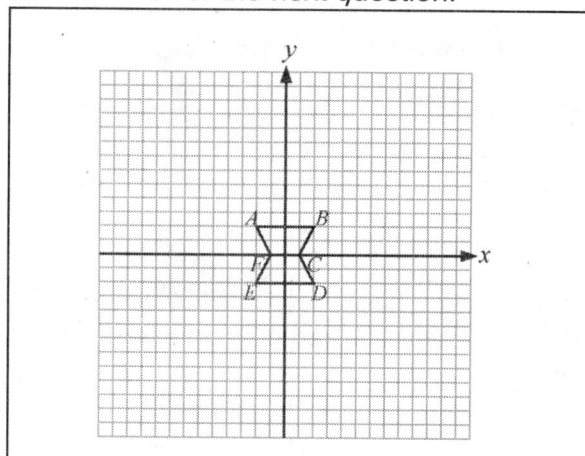

6. Figure ABCDEF is dilated by a scale factor of 3, with the center of dilation at (0, 0), to form figure A'B'C'D'E'F'. What are the coordinates of A'B'C'D'E'F'?

 A. A'(−3, 9), B'(9, 9), C'(6, 3), D'(9, 3), E'(−3, −3), F'(0, −3)

 B. A'(−6, 6), B'(6, 6), C'(3, 0), D'(6, −6), E'(−6, −6), F'(−3, 0)

 C. A'(−9, 3), B'(3, 3), C'(0, −3), D'(3, −9), E'(−9, −9), F'(−6, −3)

 D. A'(−3, 3), B'(3, 3), C'(1.5, 0), D'(3, −3), E'(−3, −3), F'(−1.5, 0)

Use the following information to answer the next question.

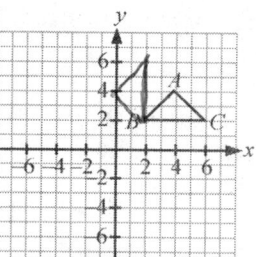

Triangle ABC is plotted on a coordinate plane. The image undergoes two transformations: a counterclockwise rotation of 90° about point B and a translation of $(x + 2, y - 1)$.

7. Which of the following diagrams represents the results of the two transformations performed on the image?

A. 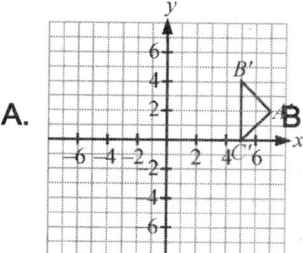   B.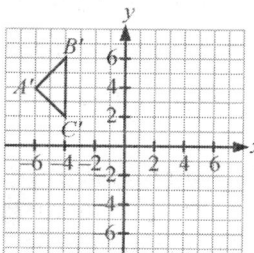

C. 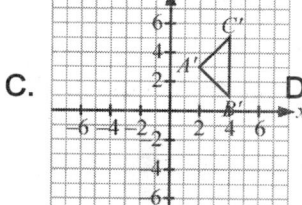   D.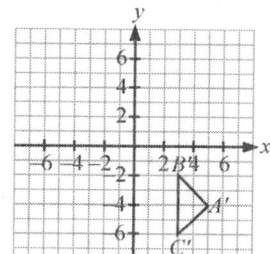

Use the following information to answer the next question.

Triangle ABC is transformed into triangle AB'C'.

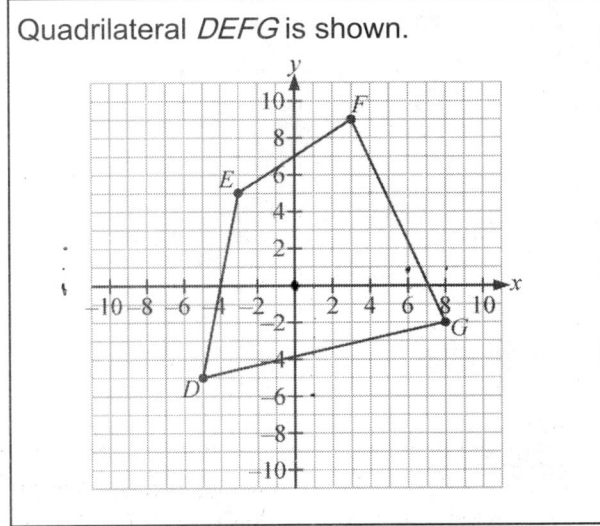

8. This transformation is an example of a
   A. dilatation
   B. translation
   C. rotation about point A
   D. reflection across line l

9. If figure ABC is translated 4 units down and reflected in the line $x = -1$, which of the following transformations would return ABC to its original location?
   A. A reflection in the line $x = -1$ and a translation 4 units down
   B. A translation 4 units to the right and a reflection in the y-axis
   C. A reflection in the x-axis and a translation 4 units to the left
   D. A translation 4 units up and a reflection in the line $x = -1$

Use the following information to answer the next question.

Quadrilateral DEFG is shown.

10. If quadrilateral DEFG has integral vertices and is transformed under $T_{3,-2} \circ R_{270°}$ to the image quadrilateral D'E'F'G', what are the coordinates of vertex G' in quadrilateral D'E'F'G'?
    A. (−5, −4)　　B. (−5, 0)
    C. (1, −6)　　 D. (1, −10)

Use the following information to answer the next question.

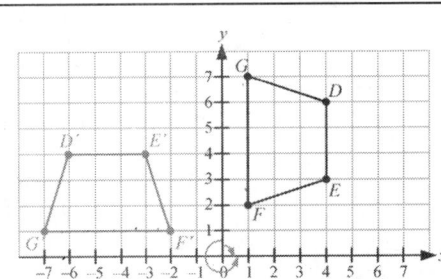

Image DEFG is transformed to image D'E'F'G'.

11. Which of the following statements about the transformation is **true**?
    A. The angles between corresponding sides increased.
    B. The orientation of the image remained constant.
    C. The distances between the points increased.
    D. The size of the image decreased.

Use the following information to answer the next question.

A tessellation is given.

12. How many lines of symmetry does the given tessellation have? _____

13. Which of the following tessellations has a rotational symmetry of order 2?

A. 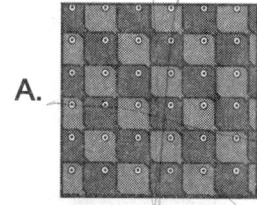 B.

C.  D.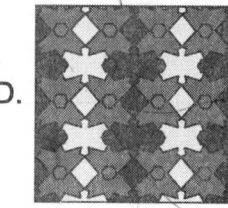

Use the following information to answer the next question.

A given two-dimensional shape has an order of rotational symmetry of 12.

14. For the given shape, the angle of rotation is _____°.

EXERCISE #1—TRANSFORMATIONS ANSWERS AND SOLUTIONS

1. 258	5. D	9. D	13. D
2. B	6. B	10. D	14. 30
3. D	7. C	11. B	
4. B	8. C	12. 1	

1. 258

The arc length formula, $a = r\theta$, can be used to determine the measure of the central angle θ in radians, where r is the radius of the circle and a is the arc length.

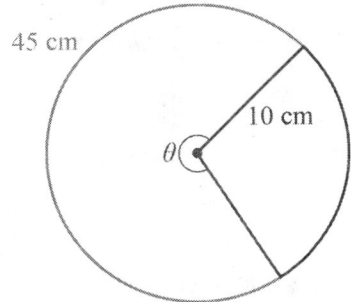

Step 1
Rearrange the formula $a = r\theta$ for θ.
$$\theta = \frac{a}{r}$$

Step 2
Substitute the known values, and solve.
The known values are $a = 45$ and $r = 10$.
$$\theta = \frac{a}{r}$$
$$\theta = \frac{45}{10}$$
$$\theta = 4.5$$
The angle is 4.5 rad.

Step 3
Convert the angle from radians to degrees.
An angle in radians can be converted to degrees by multiplying it by $\frac{180}{\pi}$.
$$4.5 \times \frac{180}{\pi} \approx 257.83°$$
The central angle to the nearest degree is 258°.

2. B

According to the angle measure postulate, every angle has a unique measure between 0° and 360°. Therefore, one rotation from line OC to line OC again is 360°.

Therefore, $\angle COB$ can be determined using the angle addition postulate by subtracting the sum of all the known angles in the diagram from 360°.

$$\angle COB = 360° - \begin{pmatrix} \angle COD + \angle DOE \\ + \angle EOA + \angle AOB \end{pmatrix}$$
$$= 360° - \begin{pmatrix} 90° + 60° \\ +110° + 80° \end{pmatrix}$$
$$= 360° - 340°$$
$$= 20°$$

The measure of $\angle COB$ is 20°.

3. D

Step 1
Draw the original shape on the Cartesian plane. Plot and label each point as given in the question, and then connect the points with line segments.

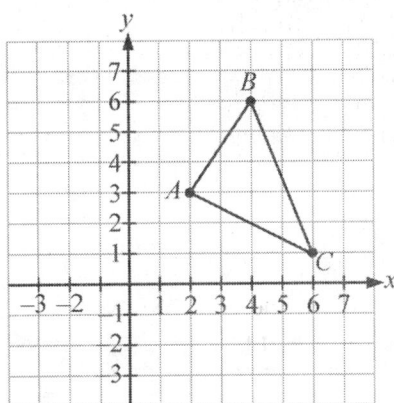

Step 2
Calculate the coordinates of the translated image. For each point, subtract 4 from the x-coordinate and 3 from the y-coordinate.
$A'(2 - 4, 3 - 3) = (-2, 0)$
$B'(4 - 4, 6 - 3) = (0, 3)$
$C'(6 - 4, 1 - 3) = (2, -2)$

Step 3
Draw the translated image on the Cartesian plane. Plot and label each new point. Then, connect the new points with line segments to form the translated triangle △A'B'C'.

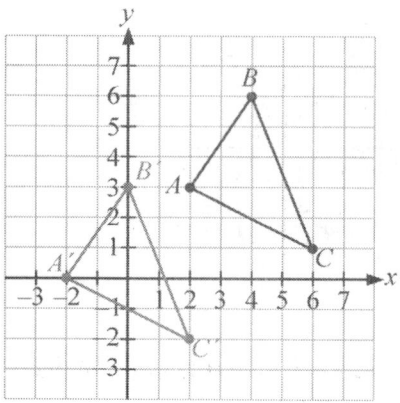

The corresponding ordered pairs are A'(−2, 0), B'(0, 3), and C'(2, −2).

4. B
Step 1
Rotate the figure.
Start with the original shape on the coordinate plane.

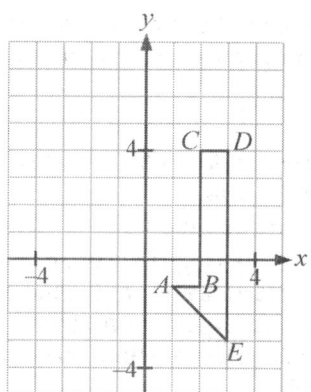

Trace the original shape on a piece of tracing paper. Place your pencil on point C, and turn the tracing paper 270° counterclockwise, or a $\frac{3}{4}$ turn to the right.

Step 2
Draw the rotated image on the coordinate plane. Plot and label each new point, adding a prime symbol to each point to indicate the shape is an image of the original shape.

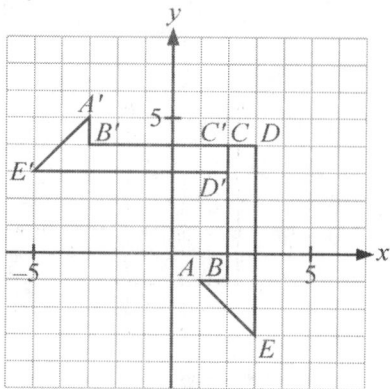

Step 3
Determine the coordinates of A'.
The coordinates of A' are (−3, 5).

5. D
Step 1
Start with the original shape on a coordinate plane.

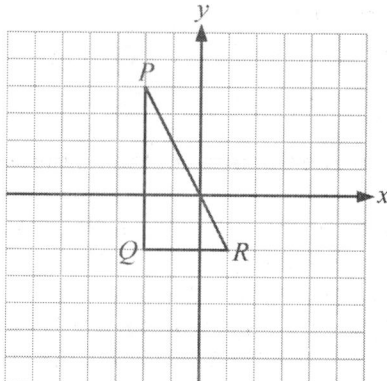

Step 2
Determine the coordinates of the reflected image. The image is reflected about the y-axis which means that the y-coordinates will remain the same and the x-coordinates will change to their opposites. Calculate the distance each vertex is away from the reflection line.
P is 2 units to the left of the y-axis. P' will be 2 units to the right of the y-axis.
Q is 2 units to the left of the y-axis. Q' will be 2 units to the right of the y-axis.
R is 1 unit to the right of the y-axis. R' will be 1 unit to the left of the y-axis.

Step 3
Draw the reflected image on the coordinate plane.

Plot and label each new point with a prime to indicate that it is an image of the shape. Connect the points with line segments.

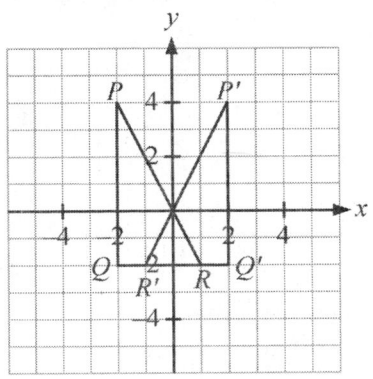

Step 4
Identify the coordinates for $P'Q'R'$.
$P'(2, 4)$, $Q'(2, -2)$, $R'(-1, -2)$

6. B
Step 1
Identify the coordinates of each point in figure $ABCDEF$.
$A(-2, 2)$, $B(2, 2)$, $C(1, 0)$, $D(2, -2)$, $E(-2, -2)$, $F(-1, 0)$

Step 2
Multiply the coordinates of the points by a scale factor of 3.

$A(-2, 2) \rightarrow A(-2 \times 3, 2 \times 3) = A'(-6, 6)$
$B(2, 2) \rightarrow B(2 \times 3, 2 \times 3) = B'(6, 6)$
$C(1, 0) \rightarrow C(1 \times 3, 0 \times 3) = C'(3, 0)$
$D(2, -2) \rightarrow D(2 \times 3, -2 \times 3) = D'(6, -6)$
$E(-2, -2) \rightarrow E(-2 \times 3, -2 \times 3) = E'(-6, -6)$
$F(-1, 0) \rightarrow F(-1 \times 3, 0 \times 3) = F'(-3, 0)$

The coordinates of the dilated figure are $A'(-6, 6)$, $B'(6, 6)$, $C'(3, 0)$, $D'(6, -6)$, $E'(-6, -6)$, $F'(-3, 0)$.

7. C
Step 1
First, apply the counter-clockwise rotation about point B.

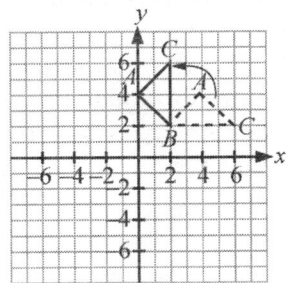

Step 2
Next, apply the translation.

Every x-coordinate moves 2 units to the right and every y-coordinate moves 1 unit down. This image illustrates the transformations.

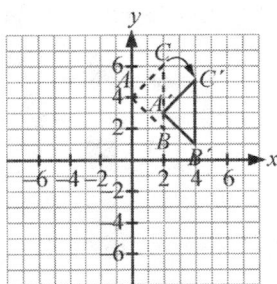

8. C
Compare the shape and image to each of the transformation movements.

Step 1
In a dilatation, the size of the image changes.
Since the size of the triangle remains the same, the transformation is not a dilatation.

Step 2
In a translation, the sides of the transformed shape are parallel to the original.
Since the sides of the transformed triangle are not parallel to the original triangle, the transformation is not a translation.

Step 3
In a reflection, the transformed image is a mirror image of the original.
The image appears to be a reflection, but the points of the triangles are not directly across from each other. Point B is across from C, and point C is across from B. Since B would be across from B and C across from C in a reflection, the transformation is not a reflection.

Step 4
In a rotation, the shape rotates around a fixed point.
The given transformation is a rotation of 180° about point A. After the rotation is applied, the points B and C correspond to B and C, respectively.

9. **D**

A transformation that would return *ABC* to its original location would have to undo the original transformation. In this case, the image would need to be reflected in the line $x = -1$ and then translated 4 units up. This transformation is a reflection and a translation along the same line, which makes it a glide reflection. The order in which the transformations are applied in a glide reflection does not affect the resulting image. Therefore, applying a translation 4 units up and then a reflection in the line $x = -1$ would be equivalent to applying them in the opposite order and would return *ABC* to its original location.

10. **D**

Step 1
Identify the coordinates of vertex *G* in quadrilateral *DEFG*.
The coordinates of vertex *G* are (8, –2).

Step 2
Determine a function to describe the coordinates of the given transformation.
$R_{270°}$ indicates a rotation of 270° about the origin, where the coordinates (*x*, *y*) become (*y*, –*x*), and $T_{3,-2}$ indicates a translation 3 units right and 2 units down.
$T_{3,-2} \circ R_{270°}(x, y)$
$= T_{3,-2}(y, -x)$
$= (y + 3, -x - 2)$

Step 3
Apply the function $T_{3,-2} \circ R_{270°}(x, y)$
$= (y + 3, -x - 2)$ to determine the coordinates of vertex *G′*.
Since the coordinates of vertex *G* are (8, –2), it is possible to determine the coordinates of vertex *G′*.
$T_{3,-2} \circ R_{270°}(x, y) = (y + 3, -x - 2)$
$T_{3,-2} \circ R_{270°}(8, -2) = ((-2) + 3, -(8) - 2)$
$T_{3,-2} \circ R_{270°}(8, -2) = (1, -10)$
The coordinates of vertex *G′* in quadrilateral *D′E′F′G′* are (1, –10).

11. **B**

Image *DEFG* has been transformed to image *D′E′F′G′*. The size and shape of the transformed image, the distances between the points, the angles between corresponding sides, and the orientation of the transformed image remain the same.

12. **1**

Only one line of symmetry can be drawn. That line runs vertically through the center of the tessellation.

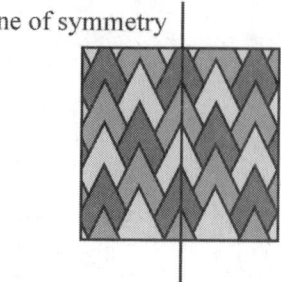

13. **D**

Determine the angle of rotation needed to have a rotational symmetry of order 2.

$$\text{angle of rotation} = \frac{360°}{\text{order of rotation}}$$
$$= \frac{360°}{2}$$
$$= 180°$$

Determine the tessellation that has an angle of rotation of 180°.

- These tessellations only appear the same when they are rotated a full 360°. Therefore, they have rotational symmetries of order 1.

 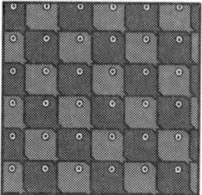

Exercise #1 Answers and Solutions

- This tessellation appears the same at every 90° rotation. Therefore, it has a rotational symmetry of order 4.

- If this tessellation is rotated 180°, it appears identical to its original position. Therefore, it has a rotational symmetry of order 2.

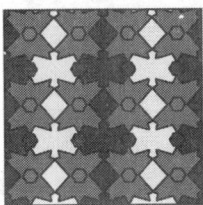

14. 30

To calculate the angle of rotation, apply the formula
angle of rotation = $\dfrac{360°}{\text{order of rotation}}$.

angle of rotation = $\dfrac{360°}{12}$

angle of rotation = 30°

The angle of rotation is 30°.

EXERCISE #2—TRANSFORMATIONS

15. An arc subtends an angle of 320°, and the radius of the circle is 12 mm. Determine the arc length.

Use the following information to answer the next question.

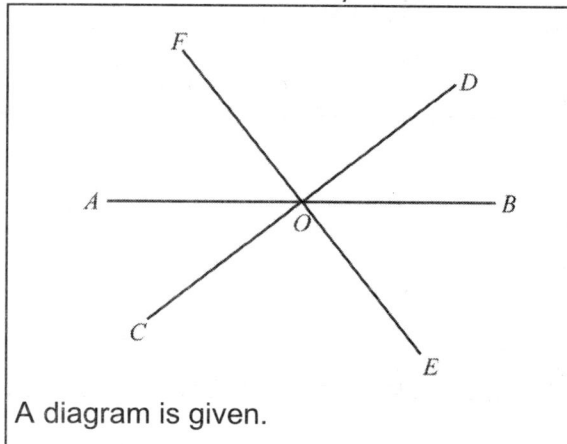

A diagram is given.

16. If ∠AOC = 38° and ∠COE = 90°, what is the measure of ∠BOE?
    A. 46°
    B. 52°
    C. 59°
    D. 63°

Use the following information to answer the next question.

Figure ABCDE is plotted on a coordinate plane.

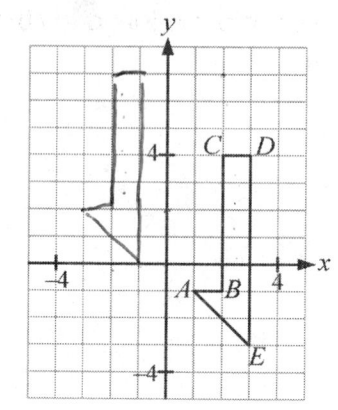

17. When the given figure is translated U3 and L4, the coordinates of B' will be
    A. (−3, 2)
    B. (−2, 2)
    C. (2, −1)
    D. (−1, 0)

Use the following information to answer the next question.

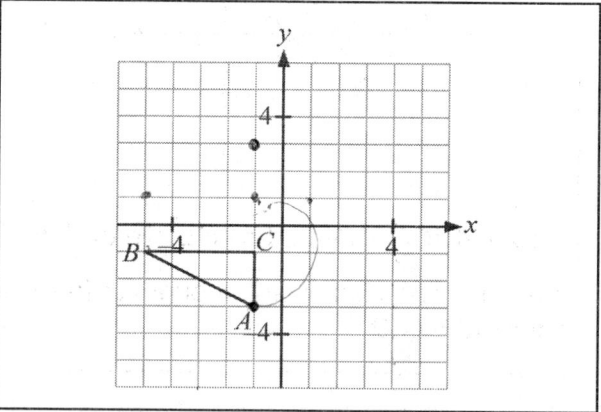

18. If triangle ABC is rotated 270° counterclockwise about point A, what are the coordinates of B'?
    A. (1, 1)
    B. (4, −5)
    C. (−3, −7)
    D. (−5, −1)

Use the following information to answer the next question.

Shape $A'B'C'D'$ is formed by connecting the vertices $A'(-4, 5)$, $B'(0, 5)$, $C'(1, 3)$, and $D'(-3, 3)$ after reflecting the original shape $ABCD$ about $x = 2$.

19. From the given information, draw the original shape $ABCD$.

Use the following information to answer the next question.

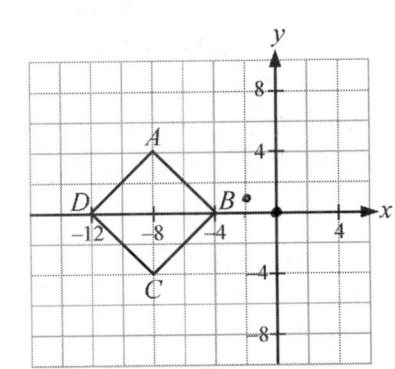

Figure $ABCD$ is dilated by a scale of $\dfrac{1}{4}$ with the center of dilation at the origin to form figure $A'B'C'D'$.

20. What are the coordinates of figure $A'B'C'D'$?
    A. $A'(-4, 8)$, $B'(0, 4)$, $C'(-4, 0)$, $D'(-8, 0)$
    B. $A'(-2, 1)$, $B'(-1, 0)$, $C'(-2, -1)$, $D'(-3, 0)$
    C. $A'(-12, 0)$, $B'(-8, -4)$, $C'(-12, -8)$, $D'(-16, -4)$
    D. $A'(-32, 16)$, $B'(-16, 0)$, $C'(-32, -16)$, $D'(-24, 0)$

Use the following information to answer the next question.

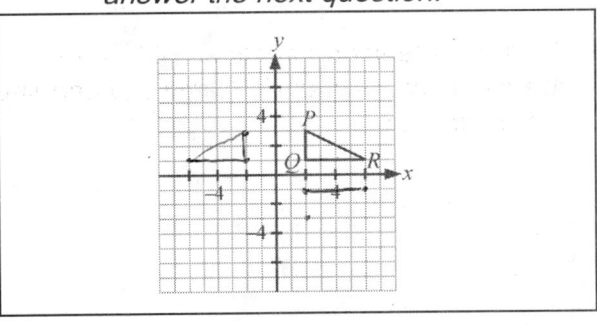

21. If $\triangle PQR$ is reflected about the y-axis and translated 4 units down and 1 unit to the right, what will the transformed image look like?

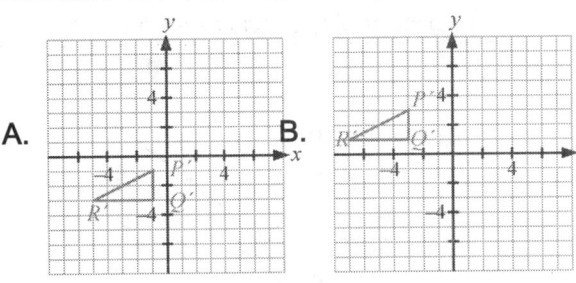

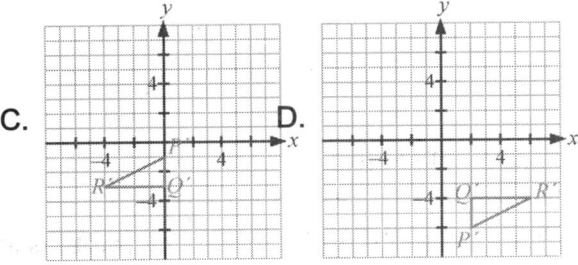

Use the following information to answer the next question.

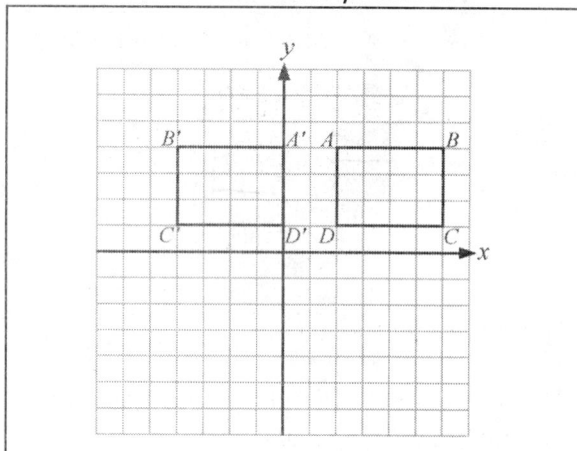

22. On the grid shown, rectangle ABCD was transformed into rectangle A'B'C'D' following a
    A. reflection about $x = 1$
    B. reflection about $x = 2$
    C. rotation 270° cw
    D. rotation 90° cw

Use the following information to answer the next question.

A graph of the circle C is given.

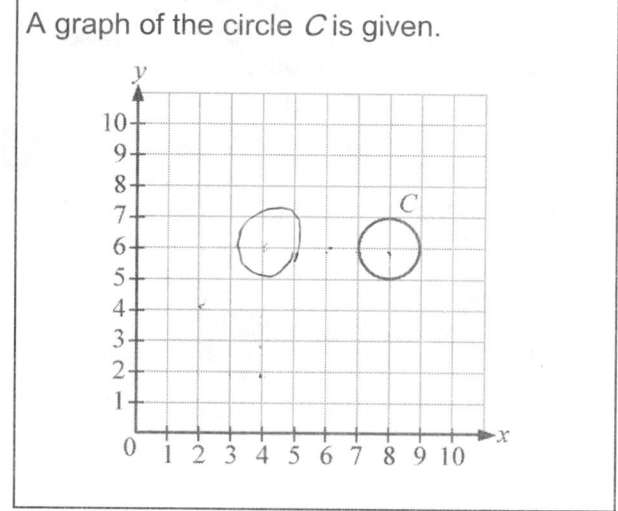

23. If the given circle, C, is reflected in the line $y = x$ and then translated 4 units down and 4 units left, what are the coordinates of the center of the transformed circle?
    A. (2, 4)
    B. (4, 2)
    C. (−10, −12)
    D. (−12, −10)

Use the following information to answer the next question.

Triangle MNP has vertices M(−3, 2), N(1, −1), and P(−5, −4). Under a particular transformation, triangle MNP produces the image triangle M'N'P'. The coordinates of the vertices of triangle M'N'P' are M'(3, −2), N'(−1, 1), and P'(5, 4).

24. Which of the following transformations could have been used to arrive at the coordinates of the image triangle M'N'P'?
    A. $R_{180°}$
    B. $R_{270°}$
    C. $r_{x\text{-axis}}$
    D. $r_{y\text{-axis}}$

Use the following information to answer the next question.

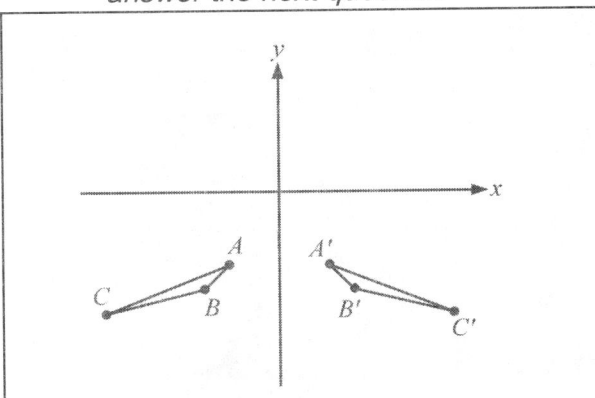

The triangle ABC is transformed to the triangle A'B'C'.

25. Which property does **not** remain the same under the given transformation?
    A. The shape and size of the triangle
    B. The orientation of the reflected triangle
    C. The distance between the points of the transformed triangle
    D. The angle between the corresponding sides of the transformed triangle

26. Which of the following tessellations does **not** have any lines of symmetry?

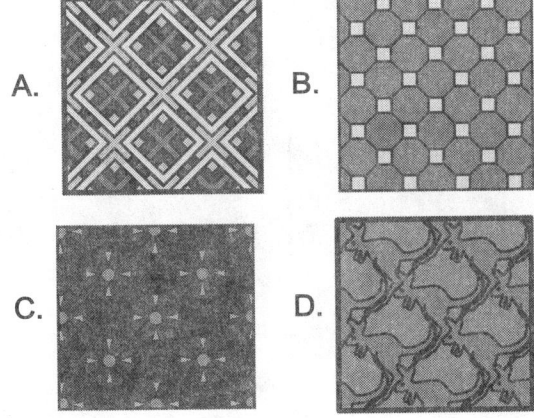

Use the following information to answer the next question.

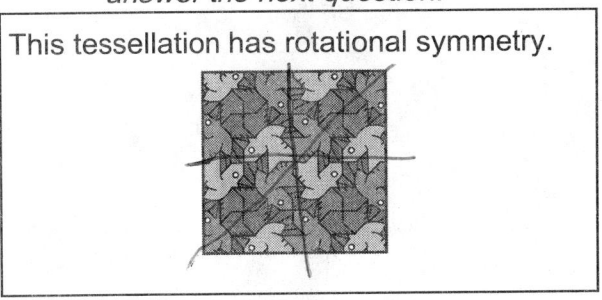

This tessellation has rotational symmetry.

27. The angle of rotation is _____°.

28. Which of the letters in the word *vest* has rotational symmetry of order 2?

A. 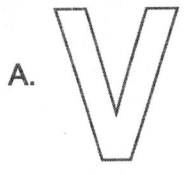 B.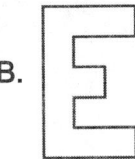

C.  D.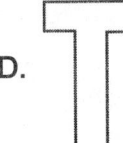

EXERCISE #2—TRANSFORMATIONS ANSWERS AND SOLUTIONS

15. See solution	19. See solution	23. A	27. 180
16. B	20. B	24. A	28. C
17. B	21. A	25. B	
18. A	22. A	26. D	

15.

Step 1
Convert from degrees to radians.
Multiply the angle degree measure by $\frac{\pi}{180}$.

$320° = 320 \times \frac{\pi}{180}$

$320° = \frac{320\pi}{180}$

$320° = \frac{16\pi}{9}$

Step 2
Calculate the arc length using the arc length formula.
$a = r\theta$
$a = (12)\left(\frac{16\pi}{9}\right)$
$a \approx 67.02$

The arc length is about 67.02 mm.

16. B

According to the angle addition postulate, the measure of ∠AOB is the sum of ∠AOC, ∠COE, and ∠BOE.

∠AOB = ∠AOC + ∠COE + ∠BOE
180° = 38° + 90° + ∠BOE
180° = 128° + ∠BOE
52° = ∠BOE

Therefore, the measure of ∠BOE is 52°.

17. B

Step 1
Apply the vertical translation.
Translate the figure ABCDE 3 units up.

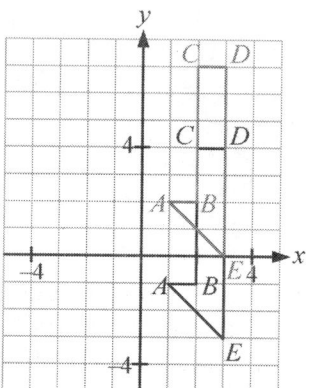

Step 2
Apply the horizontal translation.
Translate the figure 4 units to the left.

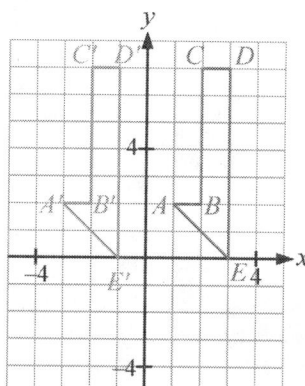

Step 3
Determine the coordinates of B'.
The coordinates of B' are (−2, 2).

18. A

Step 1
Start with the original shape on the coordinate plane.

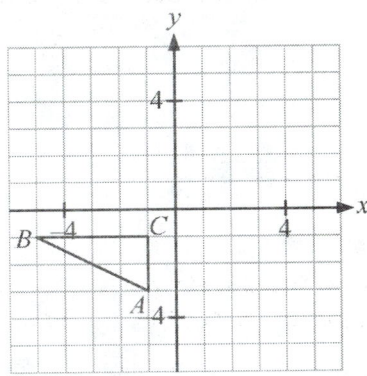

Step 2
Trace the original shape, and rotate it 270° counterclockwise about point A.
Place your pencil on point A, and turn the tracing paper 270° or a $\frac{3}{4}$ turn to the left.

Step 3
Draw the rotated image on the coordinate plane. Plot and label each new point with a prime on the point to indicate it is the image of the shape.

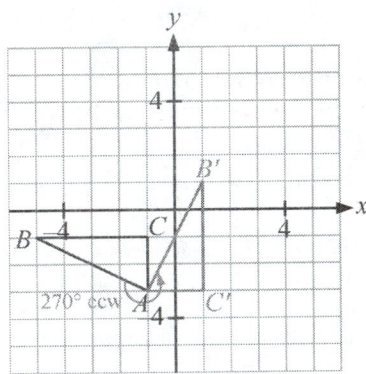

Step 4
Determine the coordinates of B'.
The coordinates of B' are (1, 1).

19.

Step 1
Draw the reflected image on a Cartesian plane. Plot and label each point as given. Then, connect the points with line segments.
Add the reflection line.

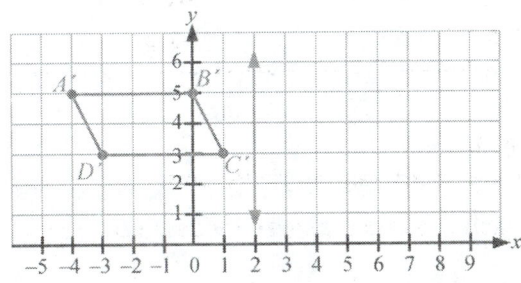

Step 2
Perform the inverse transformation.
The image is reflected about the y-axis. This means the y-coordinates will remain the same while the x-coordinates change.
Calculate the distance that each vertex is from the reflection line.
If A' is 6 units left of the reflection line, then A will be 6 units right of the reflection line: A(8, 5)
If B' is 2 units left of the reflection line, then B will be 2 units right of the reflection line: B(4, 5)
If C' is 1 unit left of the reflection line, then C will be 1 unit right of the reflection line: C(3, 3)
If D' is 5 units left of the reflection line, then D will be 5 units right of the reflection line: D(7, 3)

Step 3
Draw the original shape on the Cartesian plane. Plot and label each new point. Then, connect the points with line segments.

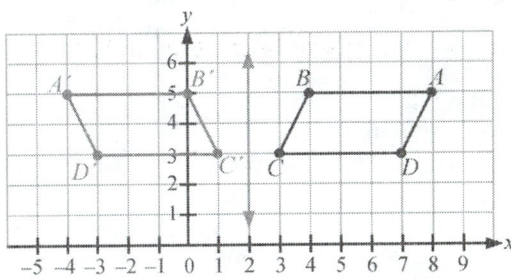

20. B

Step 1
Identify the coordinates of each point in figure ABCD.
A(−8, 4), B(−4, 0), C(−8, −4), D(−12, 0)

Step 2
Multiply the coordinates of the points by a scale factor of $\frac{1}{4}$.

$A(-8, 4) \to A\left(-8 \times \frac{1}{4}, 4 \times \frac{1}{4}\right) = A'(-2, 1)$

$B(-4, 0) \to B\left(-4 \times \frac{1}{4}, 0 \times \frac{1}{4}\right) = B'(-1, 0)$

$C(-8, -4) \to C\left(-8 \times \frac{1}{4}, -4 \times \frac{1}{4}\right) = C'(-2, -1)$

$D(-12, 0) \to D\left(-12 \times \frac{1}{4}, 0 \times \frac{1}{4}\right) = D'(-3, 0)$

The coordinates of the dilated figure are $A'(-2, 1)$, $B'(-1, 0)$, $C'(-2, -1)$, and $D'(-3, 0)$.

21. A

Step 1
Determine the coordinates of $\triangle PQR$:
$P(2, 3)$, $Q(2, 1)$, $R(6, 1)$

Step 2
Apply the reflection.
When a figure is reflected over the y-axis, all the x-coordinates change to their opposite values.
$P(2, 3) = (-2, 3)$
$Q(2, 1) = (-2, 1)$
$R(6, 1) = (-6, 1)$
After the reflection the image is at $P(-2, 3)$, $Q(-2, 1)$, $R(-6, 1)$

Step 3
Apply the translation.
When a figure is translated 4 units down, subtract 4 from each y-coordinate.
$P'(-2, 3 - 4) = (-2, -1)$
$Q'(-2, 1 - 4) = (-2, -3)$
$R'(-6, 1 - 4) = (-6, -3)$
After translating the image 4 units down it is at $P(-2, -1)$, $Q(-2, -3)$, $R(-6, -3)$

Step 4
When a figure is translated 1 unit to the right, add 1 to each x-coordinate.
$P'(-2 + 1, -1) = P'(-1, -1)$
$Q'(-2 + 1, -3) = Q'(-1, -3)$
$R'(-6 + 1, -3) = R'(-5, -3)$
Plot the points on the graph.

Step 5
Identify the image with these coordinates.

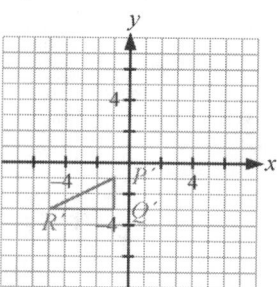

22. A

Step 1
Determine if the transformation is a rotation.
The image has not changed its orientation, therefore, its not a rotation.

Step 2
Determine the reflection line.
The images are 2 units apart. The midpoint is 1 unit from either image. Subtract 1 unit from the x-coordinate of A.
$A(2, 4) \to 2 - 1 = 1$
The x-coordinate that this location is 1. Therefore, the reflection line is at $x = 1$.

Step 3
Verify by adding 1 to the x-coordinate of A'.
$A'(0, 4) \to 0 + 1 = 1$

Step 4
Verify for a second point on the figure. Lets use points C and C'.
The coordinates of point C are $(6, 1)$.
The coordinates of point C' are $(-4, 1)$.
To find the distance between points C and C', consider the x coordinates. The distance from -4 to 6 is 10 units. This means both points C and C' are $\frac{10}{2} = 5$ units from reflection line.

For point C subtract 5 from the x coordinate because the original is to the right of the reflection line.
$6 - 5 = 1$

For point C' add 5 to the x coordinate because the image is to the left of the reflection line. $-4 + 5 = 1$
Since the x coordinate in both cases is 1, the line of reflection is $x = 1$.

23. A

The given transformation is as shown.

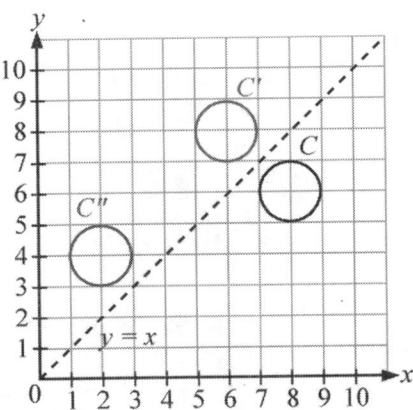

The center of the original circle, C, is found at (8, 6). A reflection in the line $y = x$ will create a circle, C', centered at (6, 8). A translation 4 units down and 4 units to the left will create a circle, C", centered at (2, 4).

24. A

Step 1
Determine if the transformation $R_{180°}$ could have been used to arrive at the coordinates of the image triangle M'N'P'.

The transformation $R_{180°}$ indicates a rotation of 180° about the origin. The coordinates (x, y) therefore become $(-x, -y)$; that is, $R_{180°}(x, y) = (-x, -y)$.

The coordinates of the vertices of this transformed image are as follows:
$R_{180°}(-3, 2) = (-(-3), -2) = (3, -2)$
$R_{180°}(1, -1) = (-1, -(-1)) = (-1, 1)$
$R_{180°}(-5, -4) = (-(-5), -(-4)) = (5, 4)$

The ordered pairs (3, -2), (-1, 1), and (5, 4) match the given coordinates of the vertices of triangle M'N'P'.

Step 2
Determine if the transformation $R_{270°}$ could have been used to arrive at the coordinates of the image triangle M'N'P'.

The transformation $R_{270°}$ indicates a rotation of 270° about the origin. The coordinates (x, y) therefore become $(y, -x)$; that is, $R_{270°}(x, y) = (y, -x)$.

The coordinates of the vertices of this transformed image are as follows:
$R_{270°}(-3, 2) = (2, -(-3)) = (2, 3)$
$R_{270°}(1, -1) = (-1, -1)$
$R_{270°}(-5, -4) = (-4, -(-5)) = (-4, 5)$

The ordered pairs (2, 3), (-1, -1), and (-4, 5) do not match the given coordinates of the vertices of triangle M'N'P'. Thus, the transformation $R_{270°}$ could not have been used to arrive at the coordinates of the image triangle M'N'P'.

Step 3
Determine if the transformation $r_{x\text{-axis}}$ could have been used to arrive at the coordinates of the image triangle M'N'P'.

The transformation $r_{x\text{-axis}}$ indicates a reflection about the x-axis. The coordinates (x, y) therefore become $(x, -y)$; that is, $r_{x\text{-axis}}(x, y) = (x, -y)$.

The coordinates of the vertices of this transformed image are as follows:
$r_{x\text{-axis}}(-3, 2) = (-3, -2)$
$r_{x\text{-axis}}(1, -1) = (1, -(-1)) = (1, 1)$
$r_{x\text{-axis}}(-5, -4) = (-5, -(-4)) = (-5, 4)$

The ordered pairs (-3, -2), (1, 1), and (-5, 4) do not match the given coordinates of the vertices of triangle M'N'P'. Thus, the transformation $r_{x\text{-axis}}$ could not have been used to arrive at the coordinates of the image triangle M'N'P'.

Step 4

Determine if the transformation $r_{y\text{-axis}}$ could have been used to arrive at the coordinates of the image triangle $M'N'P'$.

The transformation $r_{y\text{-axis}}$ indicates a reflection about the y-axis. The coordinates (x, y) therefore become $(-x, y)$; that is, $r_{y\text{-axis}}(x, y) = (-x, y)$.

The coordinates of the vertices of this transformed image are as follows:

$r_{y\text{-axis}}(-3, 2) = (-(-3), 2) = (3, 2)$
$r_{y\text{-axis}}(1, -1) = (-1, -1)$
$r_{y\text{-axis}}(-5, -4) = (-(-5), -4) = (5, -4)$

The ordered pairs $(3, 2)$, $(-1, -1)$, and $(5, -4)$ do not match the given coordinates of the vertices of triangle $M'N'P'$. Thus, the transformation $r_{y\text{-axis}}$ could not have been used to arrive at the coordinates of the image triangle $M'N'P'$.

Of the given alternatives, $R_{180°}$ is the only transformation that could have been used to arrive at the coordinates of the image triangle $M'N'P'$.

25. B

Triangle ABC undergoes a reflection in the y-axis to form triangle $A'B'C'$. After a reflection, the distance between the points, the measure of the angles, and the shape and size of the triangle all remain the same.

Notice that points A, B, and C occur in a clockwise direction, while points A', B', and C' occur in a counterclockwise direction. The orientation of the reflected triangle changed from that of the original triangle.

26. D

Tessellation A has four lines of symmetry. Those lines run vertically, horizontally, and diagonally through the center of the tessellation.

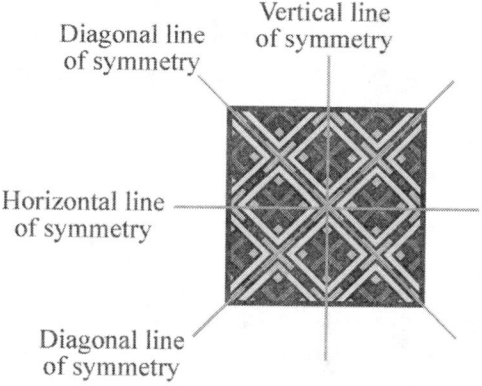

Tessellation B has one line of symmetry. That line runs vertically through the center of the tessellation.

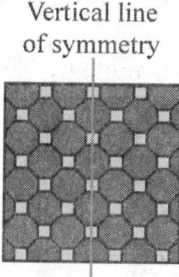

Tessellation C has four lines of symmetry. Those lines run vertically, horizontally, and diagonally through the center of the tessellation.

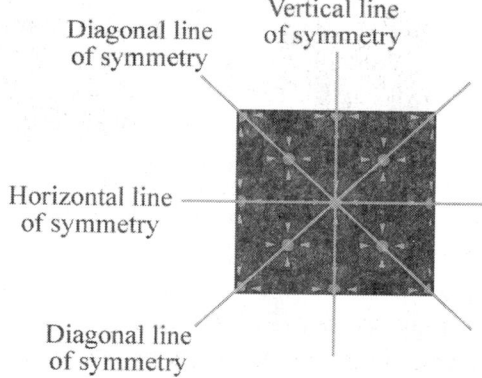

It is impossible to draw a line through tessellation D in such a way that both sides are identical; therefore, it does not have a line of symmetry.

27. 180

Step 1

Determine the order of rotational symmetry.

Place a small dot in a corner of the original image to track the changes made by each rotation. Since the tessellation is in the shape of a square, it will be rotated 90° at a time.

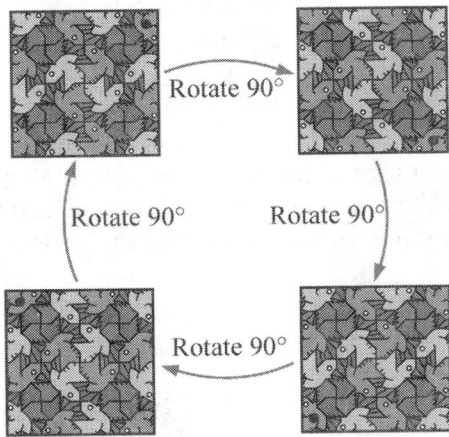

Positions 1 and 3 look exactly alike, as do positions 2 and 4. Therefore, this tessellation has rotational symmetry of order 2.

Step 2

Determine the angle of rotation.

You can determine the angle of rotation using the formula angle of rotation = $\frac{360°}{\text{order of rotation}}$.

angle of rotation = $\frac{360°}{2}$

angle of rotation = 180°

28. C

Step 1

Join the center of the V to the perimeter of the shape. Trace the V, and rotate it about the center.

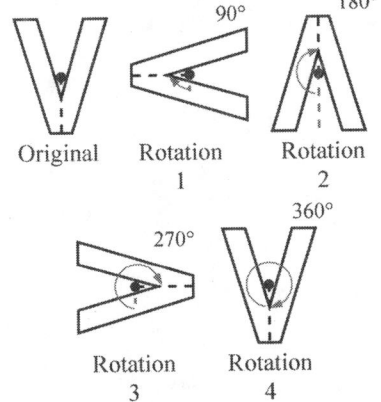

The rotated shape does not look like the original throughout the entire 360° rotation. Therefore, the letter V does not have rotational symmetry.

Step 2

Join the center of the E to the perimeter of the shape. Trace the E, and rotate it about the center.

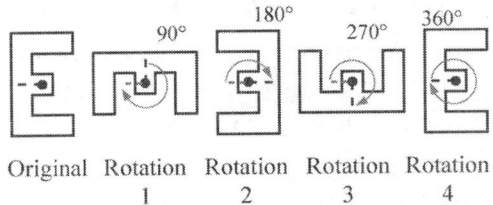

The rotated shape does not look like the original throughout the entire 360° rotation. Therefore, the letter E does not have rotational symmetry.

Step 3

Join the center of the S to the perimeter of the shape. Trace the S, and rotate it about the center.

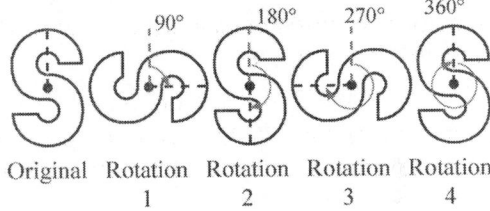

The rotated shape looks exactly like the original in two positions throughout the entire 360° rotation. Therefore, the order of rotational symmetry is 2.

Step 4

Join the center of the T to the perimeter of the shape. Trace the T, and rotate it about the center.

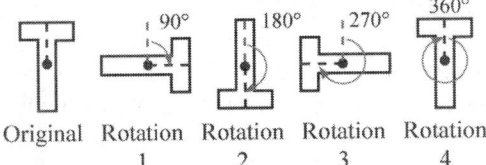

The rotated shape does not look like the original throughout the entire 360° rotation. Therefore, the letter T does not have rotational symmetry.

NOTES

Rigid Motion

RIGID MOTION

Table of Correlations

Standard		Concepts	Exercise #1	Exercise #2
Unit1.2	Understand congruence in terms of rigid motions.			
G-CO.6	Use geometric descriptions of rigid motions to transform figures and to predict the effect of a given rigid motion on a given figure; given two figures, use the definition of congruence in terms of rigid motions to decide if they are congruent.	Investigating and Applying Invariant Isometric Properties	11	25
		Properties of Congruent Triangles	32	34
		Understanding and Identifying the Properties of Congruence	30	35
		Using Coordinate Geometry to Prove Two Quadrilaterals Are Congruent	31	36
		Properties of Congruent Solids	29	37
G-CO.7	Use the definition of congruence in terms of rigid motions to show that two triangles are congruent if and only if corresponding pairs of sides and corresponding pairs of angles are congruent.	Properties of Congruent Triangles	32	34
G-CO.8	Explain how the criteria for triangle congruence (ASA, SAS, and SSS) follow from the definition of congruence in terms of rigid motions.	Problem Solving with Congruent Triangles	33	38

G-CO.6 Use geometric descriptions of rigid motions to transform figures and to predict the effect of a given rigid motion on a given figure; given two figures, use the definition of congruence in terms of rigid motions to decide if they are congruent.

PROPERTIES OF CONGRUENT TRIANGLES

A **property** is an attribute, quality, or characteristic of something. Triangles that are congruent are shown with the symbol ≅.

There are two properties of congruent triangles.

1. All corresponding angles are equal.
2. All corresponding sides are equal.

In other words, congruent triangles have the same shape and are the same size.

In triangles, corresponding angles refer to the matching pairs of angles that are found in the same place in both triangles. The corresponding sides are the matching pairs of sides found in the same place in both triangles.

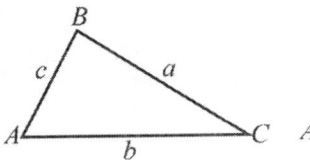

- Angles A and A' are corresponding angles.
- Angles B and B' are corresponding angles.
- Angles C and C' are corresponding angles.

- Sides a and a' are corresponding sides.
- Sides b and b' are corresponding sides
- Sides c and c' are corresponding sides.

For these two triangles to be congruent, it is necessary to prove the following:

- The corresponding angles are equal, meaning $\angle A = \angle A'$, $\angle B = \angle B'$, and $\angle C = \angle C'$.
- The corresponding sides are equal, meaning $a = a'$, $b = b'$, and $c = c'$.

Example

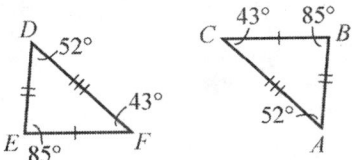

Determine whether the triangles are congruent.

Solution

For triangles to be congruent, the lengths of the corresponding sides and the corresponding angle measures must be equal.

Step 1
Identify the corresponding angles.
Corresponding angles have the same place in the triangle.

- $\angle A$ corresponds to $\angle D$.
- $\angle B$ corresponds to $\angle E$.
- $\angle C$ corresponds to $\angle F$.

Step 2
Verify whether the corresponding angles are equal.
$\angle A = 52°$ corresponds to $\angle D = 52°$.
$\angle B = 85°$ corresponds to $\angle E = 85°$.
$\angle C = 43°$ corresponds to $\angle F = 43°$.
Therefore,
$\angle A = \angle D$
$\angle B = \angle E$
$\angle C = \angle F$

Step 3
Identify the corresponding sides.
Corresponding sides have the same place in the triangle.

- AB corresponds to DE.
- BC corresponds to EF.
- AC corresponds to DF

Step 4
Verify whether the corresponding side lengths are equal.
$AB = DE$
$BC = EF$
$AC = DF$

Since the corresponding angle measures are equal and the corresponding side lengths are equal, $\triangle ABC \cong \triangle DEF$.

Understanding and Identifying the Properties of Congruence

In geometry, the term **congruent** has a very specific meaning. Two congruent objects have exactly the same shape and size. For any two congruent objects or shapes, all the following statements are true.

- Corresponding sides are equal.
- Corresponding angles are equal.
- The area of one is equal to the area of the other.
- The shape of one is the same as the shape of the other.
- For three-dimensional objects, the volume of one is equal to the volume of the other.

In other words, if two triangles are congruent, each side of the first triangle has the same length as the corresponding side of the second triangle, each angle of the first triangle is equal to the corresponding angle of the second triangle, and the area of the first triangle is equal to the area of the second triangle.

The term *congruent* is different from the term *equal*. The term *equal* only describes having the same particular value, such as the same length, the same angle, or the same area, while the term *congruent* means having the same size and shape exactly.

To identify two shapes that are not congruent, you need to point to only one item that is not the same. The item may be an angle measure, a side length, or a shape. To identify two shapes that are congruent, you must confirm one of the following conditions:

- Show that when the shapes are superimposed, they are identical.
- Make a convincing argument that the shapes are identical using common properties, postulates, and reasoning.

Example

Two polygons with their measurements are given.

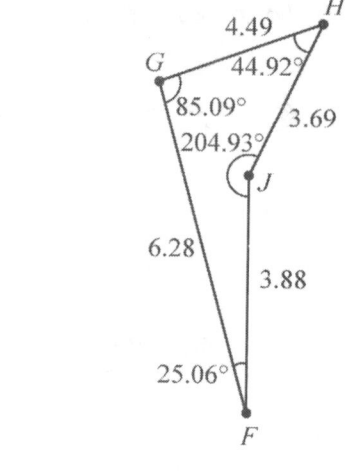

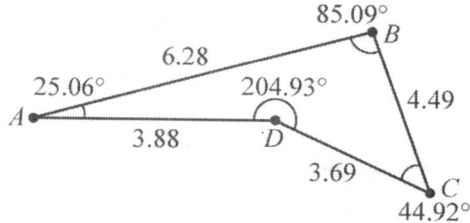

Determine whether the given polygons are congruent.

Solution

The easiest way to determine if two shapes are congruent is to place one shape on top of the other.

If you rotate polygon *FGHJ* and place it on top of polygon *ABCD*, it will match exactly.

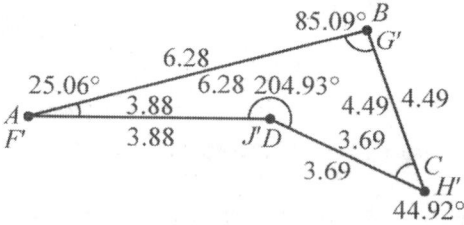

Since the two polygons have exactly the same shape and size, they are congruent.

Example

Two quadrilaterals with their measurements are shown.

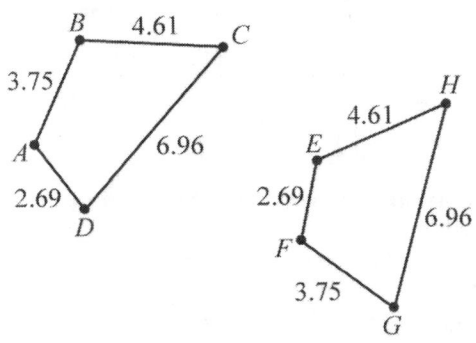

Determine whether the given quadrilaterals are congruent.

Solution

Although the two quadrilaterals do have sides with the same length measurements, the corresponding sides are not equal. Consequently, it would be impossible to superimpose one quadrilateral on the other.

Therefore, the given quadrilaterals are not congruent.

USING COORDINATE GEOMETRY TO PROVE TWO QUADRILATERALS ARE CONGRUENT

Quadrilaterals are congruent if they have the same shape and are the same size. In other words, quadrilaterals are congruent when all corresponding sides are the same length and all corresponding interior angles are of equal measure. The given diagram shows two congruent quadrilaterals.

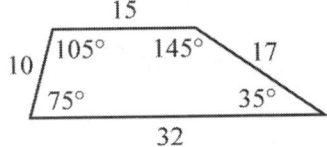

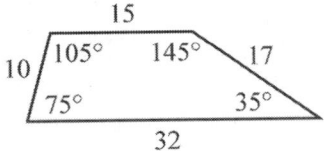

To prove whether or not two quadrilaterals are congruent using coordinate geometry, follow these steps:

1. Determine the length of every side of each quadrilateral using the distance formula $d = \sqrt{(x_2 - x_1)^2 + (y_2 - y_1)^2}$.
   - If corresponding side lengths are the same length, then the quadrilaterals may be congruent.
   - If any corresponding side lengths are not the same length, then the quadrilaterals are **not** congruent.
2. Draw corresponding diagonals within each quadrilateral.
3. Determine the length of the corresponding diagonals within each quadrilateral.
4. Use the SSS triangle congruency theorem to determine whether or not corresponding angles are of equal measure.
   - If corresponding triangles are congruent, then corresponding angles are of equal measure. Thus, the quadrilaterals are congruent.
   - If corresponding triangles are not congruent, then the quadrilaterals are not congruent.

Example

A pair of quadrilaterals are given.

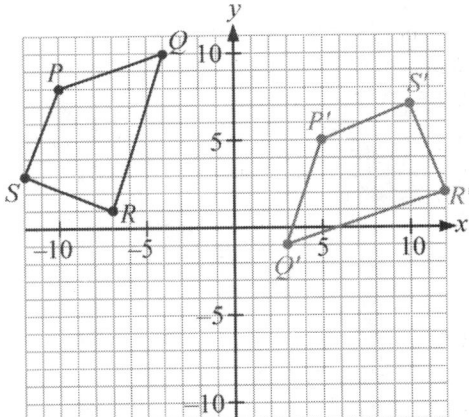

Determine if quadrilateral *PQRS* is congruent to quadrilateral *P'Q'R'S'*.

Solution

Determine the length of every side of each quadrilateral using the distance formula $d = \sqrt{(x_2 - x_1)^2 + (y_2 - y_1)^2}$.

Determine the side lengths of quadrilateral *PQRS*.

- Calculate the length of side *PQ*.
$d_{PQ} = \sqrt{(x_2 - x_1)^2 + (y_2 - y_1)^2}$
$d_{PQ} = \sqrt{(-4 - (-10))^2 + (10 - 8)^2}$
$d_{PQ} = \sqrt{6^2 + 2^2}$
$d_{PQ} = \sqrt{36 + 4}$
$d_{PQ} = \sqrt{40}$

- Calculate the length of side *QR*.
$d_{QR} = \sqrt{(x_2 - x_1)^2 + (y_2 - y_1)^2}$
$d_{QR} = \sqrt{(-7 - (-4))^2 + (1 - 10)^2}$
$d_{QR} = \sqrt{(-3)^2 + (-9)^2}$
$d_{QR} = \sqrt{9 + 81}$
$d_{QR} = \sqrt{90}$

- Calculate the length of side *RS*.
$d_{RS} = \sqrt{(x_2 - x_1)^2 + (y_2 - y_1)^2}$
$d_{RS} = \sqrt{(-12 - (-7))^2 + (3 - 1)^2}$
$d_{RS} = \sqrt{(-5)^2 + 2^2}$
$d_{RS} = \sqrt{25 + 4}$
$d_{RS} = \sqrt{29}$

- Calculate the length of side *SP*.
$d_{SP} = \sqrt{(x_2 - x_1)^2 + (y_2 - y_1)^2}$
$d_{SP} = \sqrt{(-12 - (-10))^2 + (3 - 8)^2}$
$d_{SP} = \sqrt{(-2)^2 + (-5)^2}$
$d_{SP} = \sqrt{4 + 25}$
$d_{SP} = \sqrt{29}$

Calculate the corresponding side length of *PQ*, *P'Q'*.
$d_{P'Q'} = \sqrt{(x_2 - x_1)^2 + (y_2 - y_1)^2}$
$d_{P'Q'} = \sqrt{(3 - (5))^2 + (-1 - 5)^2}$
$d_{P'Q'} = \sqrt{(-2)^2 + (-6)^2}$
$d_{P'Q'} = \sqrt{4 + 36}$
$d_{P'Q'} = \sqrt{40}$

Calculate the corresponding side length of *QR*, *Q'R'*.
$d_{Q'R'} = \sqrt{(x_2 - x_1)^2 + (y_2 - y_1)^2}$
$d_{Q'R'} = \sqrt{(12 - 3)^2 + (2 - (-1))^2}$
$d_{Q'R'} = \sqrt{9^2 + 3^2}$
$d_{Q'R'} = \sqrt{81 + 9}$
$d_{Q'R'} = \sqrt{90}$

Calculate the corresponding side length of *RS*, *R'S'*.
$d_{R'S'} = \sqrt{(x_2 - x_1)^2 + (y_2 - y_1)^2}$
$d_{R'S'} = \sqrt{(10 - 12)^2 + (7 - 2)^2}$
$d_{R'S'} = \sqrt{(-2)^2 + 5^2}$
$d_{R'S'} = \sqrt{4 + 25}$
$d_{R'S'} = \sqrt{29}$

Calculate the corresponding side length of *SP*, *S'P'*.
$d_{S'P'} = \sqrt{(x_2 - x_1)^2 + (y_2 - y_1)^2}$
$d_{S'P'} = \sqrt{(10 - 5)^2 + (7 - 5)^2}$
$d_{S'P'} = \sqrt{5^2 + 2^2}$
$d_{S'P'} = \sqrt{25 + 4}$
$d_{S'P'} = \sqrt{29}$

Draw corresponding diagonals within each quadrilateral.

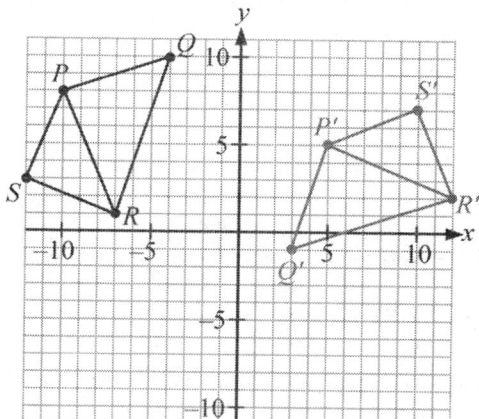

Determine the length of the corresponding diagonals within each quadrilateral.

- Calculate the length of the diagonal PR.

$d_{PR} = \sqrt{(x_2 - x_1)^2 + (y_2 - y_1)^2}$
$d_{PR} = \sqrt{(-7 - (-10))^2 + (1 - 8)^2}$
$d_{PR} = \sqrt{3^2 + (-7)^2}$
$d_{PR} = \sqrt{9 + 49}$
$d_{PR} = \sqrt{58}$

- Calculate the corresponding length of the diagonal PR, P'R'.

$d_{P'R'} = \sqrt{(x_2 - x_1)^2 + (y_2 - y_1)^2}$
$d_{P'R'} = \sqrt{(12 - 5)^2 + (2 - 5)^2}$
$d_{P'R'} = \sqrt{7^2 + (-3)^2}$
$d_{P'R'} = \sqrt{49 + 9}$
$d_{P'R'} = \sqrt{58}$

Use the SSS triangle congruency theorem to determine whether or not corresponding angles are of equal measure.

- According to the SSS congruency theorem, triangle PRS is congruent to triangle P'R'S', and triangle PQR is congruent to triangle P'Q'R'. Thus, all corresponding angles are of equal measure.
- Therefore, quadrilaterals PQRS and P'Q'R'S' are congruent; that is, all corresponding sides have the same length and all interior angles are of equal measure.

PROPERTIES OF CONGRUENT SOLIDS

When two figures are described as congruent, it means they are identical. Just like two-dimensional shapes, solids must meet certain criteria in order to be considered congruent.

Congruent solids have the following properties:

- Corresponding angles are equal
- Corresponding edges are equal
- Corresponding faces are equal
- Volume is equal
- Surface area is equal

In other words, congruent solids have the same shape and size.

In the given diagram, the congruent pyramids are the same size and shape, but they have been rotated differently. Edge a corresponds to edge a', and edge b corresponds to edge b'.

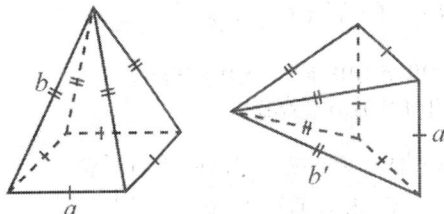

For solids, corresponding angles are the matching pairs of angles that are found in the same place in both solids. Corresponding edges are the matching pairs of edges found in the same place in both solids. Corresponding faces are the faces that appear in the same place in each object. Corresponding faces, volume, and surface area are equal because the corresponding angles and edges are equal.

Solids with the same surface area or volume are not necessarily congruent. You must still determine whether corresponding edges or angles are equal.

Example

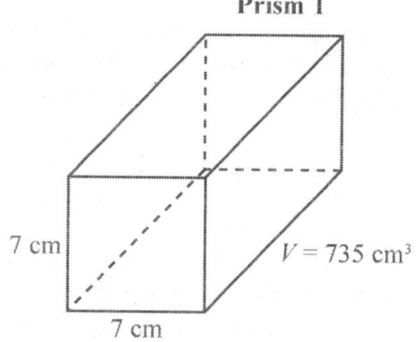

Prism 1

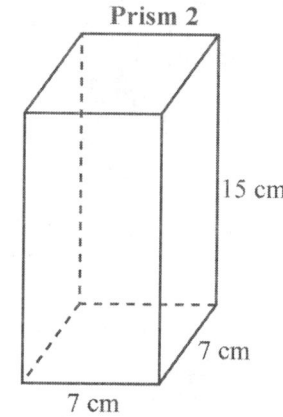

Prism 2

You can use the properties of these rectangular prisms to determine whether they are congruent.

Volume and edge lengths are given. The volume formula for a rectangular prism will help you find the missing edge length of the first prism.

$V_{Prism\ 1} = l \times w \times h$
$735 = l \times 7 \times 7$
$735 = 49 \times l$
$l = 15$

The corresponding edges of both prisms are equal; therefore, the two prisms are congruent.

When determining whether two solids are congruent, first, determine as many of the solids' dimensions as you can. Then, compare the two solids based on the information you have determined.

Example

Two cylinders and their dimensions are shown.

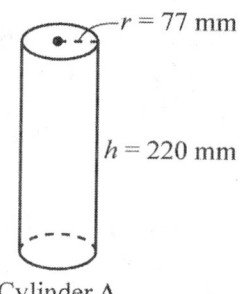

Cylinder A

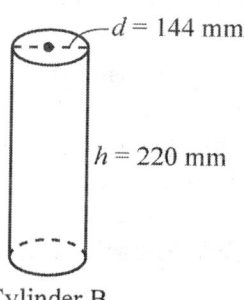

Cylinder B

Determine whether the given cylinders are congruent.

Solution

Step 1
State the properties (dimensions) that can to be used to determine if the two cylinders are congruent to each other.

In order for the cylinders to be congruent, they must have the properties of congruent solids. Since the dimensions are given for each cylinder, you can apply the property that corresponding edges must be equal.

The height and circumference of the cylinders are corresponding edges to each other, so they can be used to determine if the two cylinders are congruent.

Step 2
Compare the cylinders' heights.

The heights of both cylinders are given.
$h_{Cylinder\ A} = h_{Cylinder\ B} = 220$ mm

Step 3

Compare the cylinders' circumferences.

Use the given radius to determine the circumference of cylinder A.

$C_A = 2\pi r$
$C_A = 2\pi(77)$
$C_A = 154\pi$
$C_A \approx 483.81$ mm

Use the given diameter to determine the circumference of cylinder B.

$C_B = \pi d$
$C_B = 144\pi$
$C_B \approx 452.39$ mm

The circumferences are not equal; therefore, the cylinders are not congruent.

G-CO.8 Explain how the criteria for triangle congruence (ASA, SAS, and SSS) follow from the definition of congruence in terms of rigid motions.

Problem Solving with Congruent Triangles

One way to identify congruence is to trace one triangle and then slide the tracing over the other triangle to show that it fits exactly over the other.

Another way to identify congruence is to use one of the five triangle relationships:

1. If three sides of one triangle are equal to three sides of another triangle, the triangles are congruent. This is called the side-side-side condition, or **SSS**.

2. If two sides of one triangle and the included angle are equal to two sides of another triangle and the included angle, the triangles are congruent. This is called the side-angle-side condition, or **SAS**.

 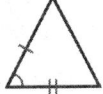

3. If two angles of one triangle and the side included by them are equal to two angles of another triangle and the side included by them, the triangles are congruent. This is called the angle-side-angle condition, or **ASA**.

 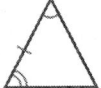

4. If two angles of one triangle and a non-included side of one triangle are congruent to two angles and the corresponding non-included side of another triangle, the triangles are congruent. This is called the angle-angle-side condition, or **AAS**.

5. If the hypotenuse and leg of one right triangle are equal to the hypotenuse and leg of the other right triangle, the triangles are congruent. This is called the right angle-hypotenuse-leg condition, or **RHL**.

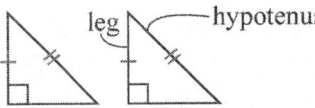

Example

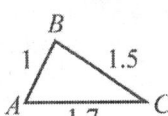 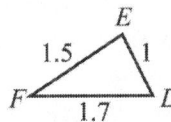

State why $\triangle ABC \cong \triangle DEF$.

Solution

Step 1
Identify which sides or angles are given.
All the sides are given.

Step 2
Identify the condition that will prove congruency.
Side-side-side (SSS) is the condition that proves congruency, since three sides of one triangle are equal to three sides of another triangle.

Step 3
Apply the condition.
Verify that the corresponding sides are equal.
AB = DE
BC = EF
AC = DF
△ABC ≅ △DEF satisfies the condition SSS.

Example

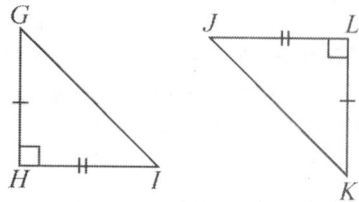

State why △GHI ≅ △KLJ.

Solution

Step 1
Identify which sides or angles are given.
Two sides and an angle are given.

Step 2
Identify the condition that will prove congruency.
Side-angle-side (SAS) is the condition that proves congruency, since two sides and one included angle are equal to the two sides and one included angle of the other triangle.

Step 3
Apply the condition.
Verify that the corresponding sides and angles are equal.
GH = KL
∠H = ∠L
HI = LJ
△GHI ≅ △KLJ satisfies the condition of SAS.

Example

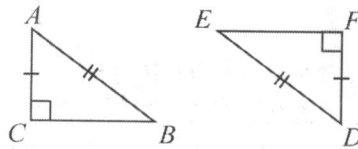

Explain why the triangles are or are not congruent.

Solution

Step 1
Identify which sides or angles are given.
The hypotenuse and leg are given.

Step 2
Identify the condition that will prove congruency.
Right angle-hypotenuse-leg (RHL) is the condition that proves congruency, since the hypotenuse and leg of one triangle are equal to the hypotenuse and leg of the other triangle.

Step 3
Apply the condition.
Verify that the corresponding hypotenuse, leg, and angle measures are equal.
AB = DE
AC = DF
∠C = ∠F
△ABC ≅ △DEF satisfies the condition of RHL.

All pairs of corresponding sides and angles in congruent triangles are equal.

EXERCISE #1—RIGID MOTION

Use the following information to answer the next question.

Two square-based pyramids with volumes of 32,928 cm³ are shown.

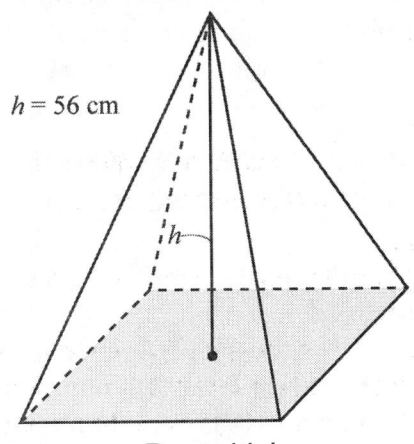

Pyramid J

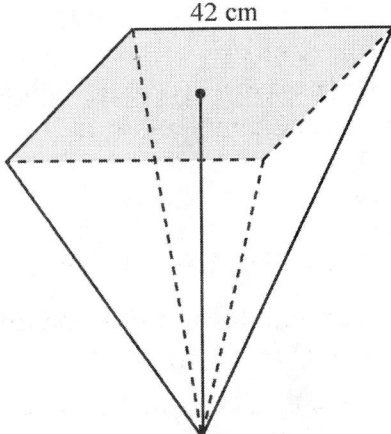

Pyramid K

The volume, V, of a square-based pyramid can be determined by applying the formula $V = \frac{1}{3}b^2h$, where b represents the side length of the base and h represents the height of the pyramid.

29. Which of the following statements about the two given pyramids is **true**?
    A. Pyramid J is not congruent to pyramid K because the two pyramids do not have the same height.
    B. Pyramid J is not congruent to pyramid K because the side length of the base is not the same for the two pyramids.
    C. Pyramid J is congruent to pyramid K because they have the same shape and each pyramid has a height of 56 cm and a base length of 42 cm.
    D. Pyramid J is congruent to pyramid K because they have the same shape and the height of pyramid J is more than the side length of the base of pyramid K.

Use the following information to answer the next question.

Two congruent rectangles are shown in the given diagram. For rectangle KNML, the length is 4 cm and the width is 2 cm.

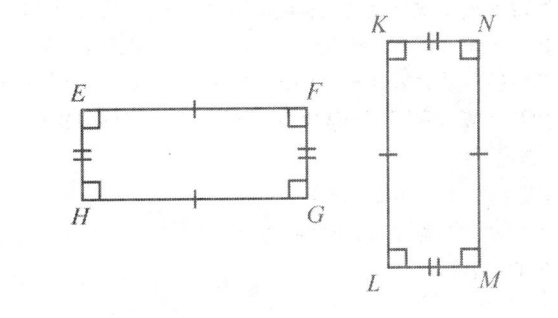

30. What is the area of rectangle EFGH?
    A. 4 cm² B. 6 cm²
    C. 8 cm² D. 12 cm²

Use the following information to answer the next question.

Josh is asked to prove whether or not quadrilaterals *ABCD* and *EFGH* are congruent.

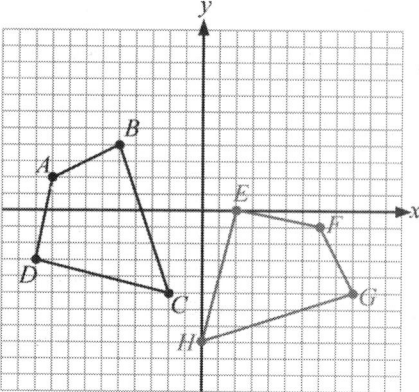

The steps in Josh's solution are as follows:

1. Calculate the length of every side of each quadrilateral using the distance formula.
2. Draw corresponding diagonals *DB* and *HF*.
3. Determine the length of corresponding diagonals within each quadrilateral using the distance formula.
4. Apply the SSS triangle congruency theorem to determine whether or not corresponding angles are of equal measure.

31. In which step did Josh make his first mistake?
    A. Step 1   B. Step 2
    C. Step 3   D. Step 4

Use the following information to answer the next question.

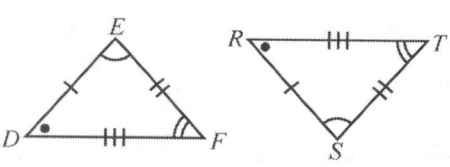

Triangle *DEF* and triangle *RST* are considered congruent triangles.

32. The reason the triangles in the diagram are congruent is that their
    A. angles are equal
    B. sides are equal and their angles are not equal
    C. sides are equal and their angles are equal
    D. angles are equal and their sides are not equal

Use the following information to answer the next question.

Triangles *ABC* and *DEF* are given.

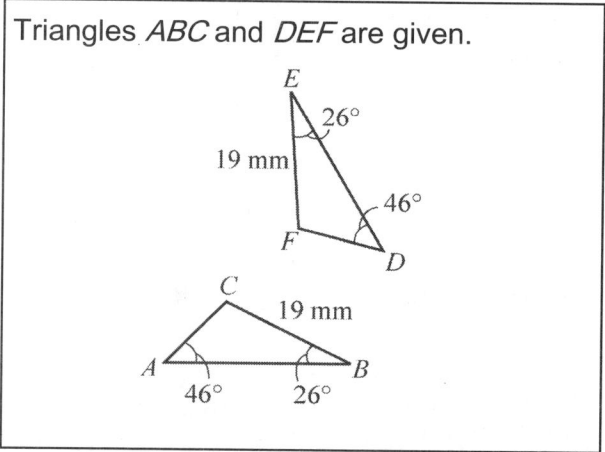

33. Determine whether triangle *ABC* is congruent to triangle *DEF*, and explain your answer.

EXERCISE #1—RIGID MOTION ANSWERS AND SOLUTIONS

| 29. C | 31. B | 33. See solution |
| 30. C | 32. C | |

29. C

Since dimensions are given for each pyramid, determine if the corresponding edges are equal.

Step 1
Determine the base length, b, of pyramid J by applying the formula $V = \frac{1}{3}b^2h$.

Substitute 32,928 for V, 56 for h, and then solve for b.

$$32{,}928 = \frac{1}{3}b^2(56)$$
$$3 \times 32{,}928 = 3 \times \frac{1}{3}b^2(56)$$
$$98{,}784 = 56b^2$$
$$\frac{98{,}784}{56} = \frac{56b^2}{56}$$
$$1{,}764 = b^2$$
$$\sqrt{1{,}764} = b$$
$$42 = b$$

Step 2
Determine the height, h, of pyramid K by applying the formula $V = \frac{1}{3}b^2h$.

Substitute 32,928 for V, 42 for b, and then solve for h.

$$32{,}928 = \frac{1}{3}(42)^2 h$$
$$32{,}928 = \frac{1}{3}(1{,}764)h$$
$$32{,}928 = 588h$$
$$\frac{32{,}928}{588} = \frac{588h}{588}$$
$$56 = h$$

Step 3
Determine if the two given pyramids are congruent to each other.

Pyramid J and pyramid K have the same base length, 42 cm, and the same height, 56 cm. Therefore, it follows that the corresponding edges of the two pyramids must be equal.

Since the corresponding edges of the two pyramids are equal, pyramid J must be congruent to pyramid K.

30. C

Step 1
Calculate the area of rectangle $KNML$.

$$A_{KNML} = l \times w$$
$$= 4 \times 2$$
$$= 8 \text{ cm}^2$$

Step 2
Determine the area of rectangle $EFGH$.

It is given that the two rectangles are congruent. According to the properties of congruency, the area of the first rectangle is equal to the area of the second rectangle.

$$A_{EFGH} = A_{KNML}$$
$$A_{EFGH} = 8 \text{ cm}^2$$

31. B

The diagonals Josh drew in step 2 were not corresponding diagonals.

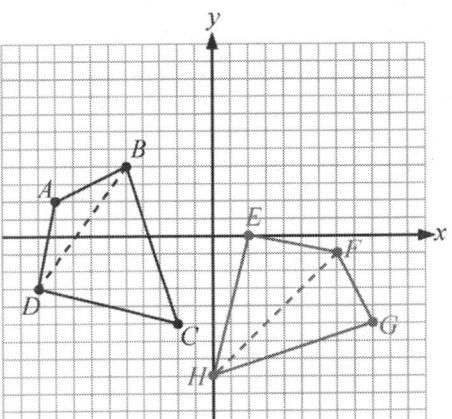

SOLARO Study Guide – Geometry

Diagonal *BD* corresponds to diagonal *GE*.
The correct diagram is as shown.

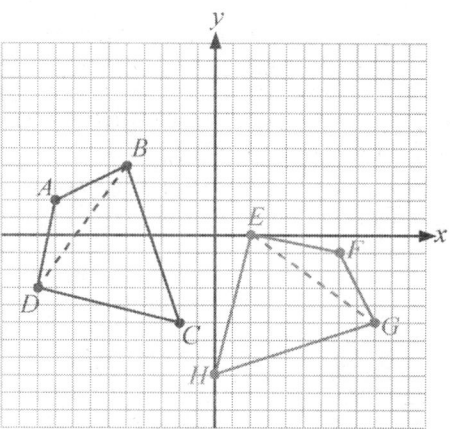

32. C

There are two properties of congruent triangles.

- Property 1: All corresponding angles are equal.
- Property 2: All corresponding sides are equal.

Triangle *ABC* and triangle *RST* are congruent because both their sides and their angles are equal.

33.

Step 1
Locate the sides or angles that are identified.
Two angles and a side are given.

Step 2
Identify the condition that will prove congruency.
The angle-angle-side condition, or AAS, will prove congruency.

Step 3
Apply the condition.
Verify the corresponding sides and angles are equal.
∠A = ∠D
∠B = ∠E
BC = EF

The given triangles satisfiy the condition AAS: two angles of one triangle and a non-included side are equal to the two angles and a non-included side of the other triangle.
Therefore, △ABC ≅ △DEF.

EXERCISE #2—RIGID MOTION

Use the following information to answer the next question.

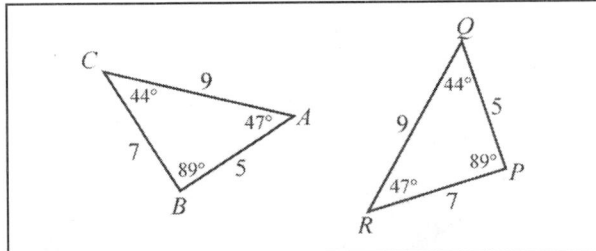

34. Which of the following statements is **true** about the given triangles?
    A. They are congruent because the sides are all equal.
    B. They are congruent because the angles are all equal.
    C. They are not congruent because the corresponding sides are not equal in length.
    D. They are not congruent because the corresponding angles are not equal in measure.

Use the following information to answer the next question.

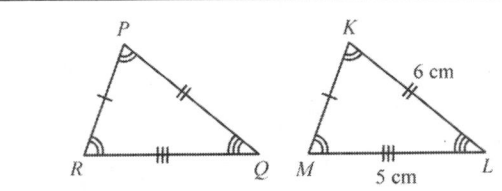

Two congruent triangles are shown in the given diagram.

35. What is the measure of *PQ*?
    A. 4 cm
    B. 5 cm
    C. 6 cm
    D. 7 cm

Use the following information to answer the next question.

Mrs. Dawson asked four students to determine whether or not quadrilaterals *ABCD* and *FGHI* are congruent.

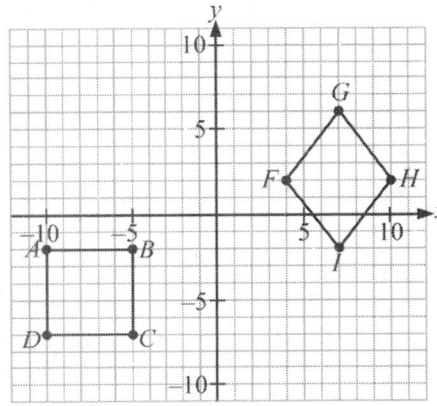

The given table displays the students' results.

Student	Thomas	Crystal	Jack	Tanis
Corresponding Side Lengths	Not Equal	Not Equal	Equal	Equal
Corresponding Angles	Not Equal	Equal	Not Equal	Equal
Congruency	No	No	No	Yes

36. Which student correctly identified the relationship between quadrilateral *ABCD* and quadrilateral *FGHI*?
    A. Thomas
    B. Crystal
    C. Tanis
    D. Jack

Use the following information to answer the next question.

The surface area, SA, of a sphere can be found by applying the formula $SA = 4\pi r^2$. The volume, V, of a sphere can be found by applying the formula $V = \frac{4}{3}\pi r^3$.

The surface area of sphere M is $2,916\pi \text{ cm}^2$, and the volume of sphere N is $26,244\pi \text{ cm}^3$.

37. Which of the following statements about spheres M and N is **true**?
    A. Spheres M and N are congruent, because they have the same shape and each has a radius of 24 cm.
    B. Spheres M and N are congruent, because they have the same shape and each has a radius of 27 cm.
    C. The radii of spheres M and N are unequal in length, so the spheres are not congruent.
    D. The surface areas of spheres M and N are unequal, so the spheres are not congruent.

Use the following information to answer the next question.

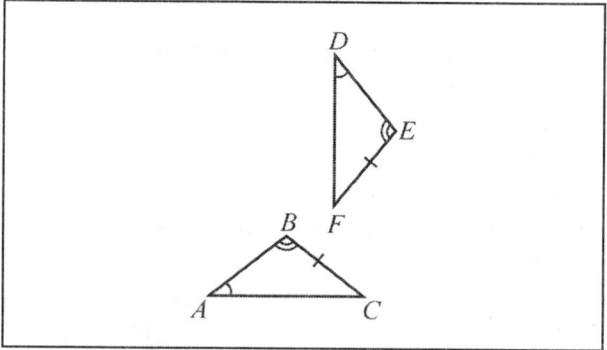

38. Determine if the two given triangles are congruent.

Exercise #2   82   Castle Rock Research

EXERCISE #2—RIGID MOTION ANSWERS AND SOLUTIONS

34. D	36. D	38. See solution
35. C	37. B	

34. D

Step 1
Identify the corresponding sides.
Corresponding sides have the same place in the triangle and are equal in measure.
$AB = QP$
$BC = PR$
$CA = RQ$

Step 2
Identify the corresponding angles.
Corresponding angles have the same place in the triangle, so using the side lengths as a guide, determine which angles correspond.
$\angle A \sim \angle Q$
$\angle B \sim \angle P$
$\angle C \sim \angle R$

Step 3
Identify the measure of each corresponding angle.
$\angle A = \angle Q = 47° \neq 44°$
$\angle B = \angle P = 89°$
$\angle C = \angle R = 44° \neq 47°$
Since the sides of the triangles do not have the same angle measures, they are not congruent.

35. C

According to the property of congruency, each side of the first triangle has the same length as the corresponding side of the second triangle.

Step 1
Match the corresponding sides of the triangles.
$PQ = KL$
$PR = KM$
$RQ = ML$

Step 2
Determine the measure of PQ.
$PQ = KL$
$PQ = 6$ cm

36. D

Step 1
Determine the length of each side of both quadrilaterals using the distance formula
$d = \sqrt{(y_2 - y_1)^2 + (x_2 - x_1)^2}$.

Determine the length of AB.
$d_{AB} = \sqrt{(x_2 - x_1)^2 + (y_2 - y_1)^2}$
$d_{AB} = \sqrt{(-5 - (-10))^2 + (-2 - (-2))^2}$
$d_{AB} = \sqrt{5^2 + 0^2}$
$d_{AB} = \sqrt{25 + 0}$
$d_{AB} = \sqrt{25}$
$d_{AB} = 5$

Determine the length of FG.
$d_{FG} = \sqrt{(x_2 - x_1)^2 + (y_2 - y_1)^2}$
$d_{FG} = \sqrt{(7 - 4)^2 + (6 - 2)^2}$
$d_{FG} = \sqrt{3^2 + 4^2}$
$d_{FG} = \sqrt{9 + 16}$
$d_{FG} = \sqrt{25}$
$d_{FG} = 5$

Determine the length of BC.
$d_{BC} = \sqrt{(x_2 - x_1)^2 + (y_2 - y_1)^2}$
$d_{BC} = \sqrt{(-5 - (-5))^2 + (-7 - (-2))^2}$
$d_{BC} = \sqrt{0^2 + (-5)^2}$
$d_{BC} = \sqrt{0 + 25}$
$d_{BC} = \sqrt{25}$
$d_{BC} = 5$

Determine the length of GH.
$d_{GH} = \sqrt{(x_2 - x_1)^2 + (y_2 - y_1)^2}$
$d_{GH} = \sqrt{(10 - 7)^2 + (2 - 6)^2}$
$d_{GH} = \sqrt{3^2 + (-4)^2}$
$d_{GH} = \sqrt{9 + 16}$
$d_{GH} = \sqrt{25}$
$d_{GH} = 5$

Determine the length of CD.
$d_{CD} = \sqrt{(x_2 - x_1)^2 + (y_2 - y_1)^2}$
$d_{CD} = \sqrt{(-10 - (-5))^2 + (-7 - (-7))^2}$
$d_{CD} = \sqrt{(-5)^2 + 0^2}$
$d_{CD} = \sqrt{25 + 0}$
$d_{CD} = \sqrt{25}$
$d_{CD} = 5$

Determine the length of HI.
$d_{HI} = \sqrt{(x_2 - x_1)^2 + (y_2 - y_1)^2}$
$d_{HI} = \sqrt{(7 - 10)^2 + (-2 - 2)^2}$
$d_{HI} = \sqrt{(-3)^2 + (-4)^2}$
$d_{HI} = \sqrt{9 + 16}$
$d_{HI} = \sqrt{25}$
$d_{HI} = 5$

Determine the length of AD.
$d_{AD} = \sqrt{(x_2 - x_1)^2 + (y_2 - y_1)^2}$
$d_{AD} = \sqrt{(-10 - (-10))^2 + (-7 - (-2))^2}$
$d_{AD} = \sqrt{0^2 + (-5)^2}$
$d_{AD} = \sqrt{0 + 25}$
$d_{AD} = \sqrt{25}$
$d_{AD} = 5$

Determine the length of FI.
$d_{FI} = \sqrt{(x_2 - x_1)^2 + (y_2 - y_1)^2}$
$d_{FI} = \sqrt{(7 - 4)^2 + (-2 - 2)^2}$
$d_{FI} = \sqrt{3^2 + (-4)^2}$
$d_{FI} = \sqrt{9 + 16}$
$d_{FI} = \sqrt{25}$
$d_{FI} = 5$

The sides are all the same length.

Step 2
Draw corresponding diagonals within each quadrilateral.

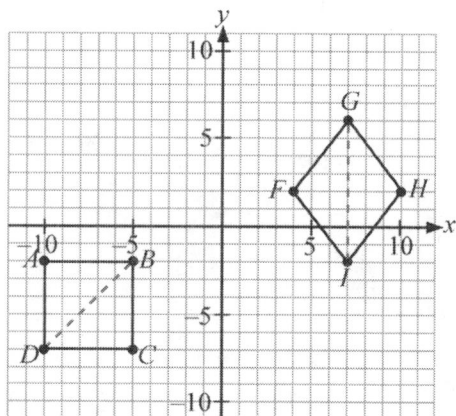

Step 3
Determine the length of the corresponding diagonals within each quadrilateral.
$d_{BD} = \sqrt{(x_2 - x_1)^2 + (y_2 - y_1)^2}$
$d_{BD} = \sqrt{((-10) - (-5))^2 + (-7 - (-2))^2}$
$d_{BD} = \sqrt{(-5)^2 + (-5)^2}$
$d_{BD} = \sqrt{25 + 25}$
$d_{BD} = \sqrt{50}$

$d_{GI} = \sqrt{(x_2 - x_1)^2 + (y_2 - y_1)^2}$
$d_{GI} = \sqrt{(7 - 7)^2 + (-2 - 6)^2}$
$d_{GI} = \sqrt{0^2 + (-8)^2}$
$d_{GI} = \sqrt{0 + 64}$
$d_{GI} = \sqrt{64}$
$d_{GI} = 8$

The corresponding diagonals are not the same length.

Step 4
Use the *SSS* triangle congruency theorem to determine whether or not corresponding angles are of equal measure.

Even though the corresponding sides are equal in length, since diagonals BD and GI are not equal in length, triangles ABD and FGI and triangles BCD and GHI are not congruent. Therefore, the corresponding angles in quadrilaterals ABCD and FGHI are not equal in measure.

Thus, quadrilaterals ABCD and FGHI are not congruent. Jack is correct.

37. B

Step 1
Determine the radius of sphere M by applying the formula $SA = 4\pi r^2$.
Substitute $2{,}916\pi$ for SA, and solve for r.
$2{,}916\pi = 4\pi r^2$
$\dfrac{2{,}916\pi}{4\pi} = \dfrac{4\pi r^2}{4\pi}$
$729 = r^2$
$\sqrt{729} = r$
$27 = r$

The radius of sphere M is 27 cm.

Step 2
Determine the radius of sphere N by applying the formula $V = \frac{4}{3}\pi r^3$.

Substitute $26,244\pi$ for V, and solve for r.

$$26,244\pi = \frac{4}{3}\pi r^3$$
$$3 \times 26,244\pi = 3 \times \frac{4}{3}\pi r^3$$
$$78,732\pi = 4\pi r^3$$
$$\frac{78,732\pi}{4\pi} = \frac{4\pi r^3}{4\pi}$$
$$19,683 = r^3$$
$$\sqrt[3]{19,683} = r$$
$$27 = r$$

The radius of sphere N is 27 cm.

Step 3
Determine whether the spheres are congruent.
The spheres have the same shape and size (each has a radius of 27 cm), so they are congruent.

38.

Step 1
Identify the given sides or angles.
Two angles and a side are given.

Step 2
Identify the condition that will prove congruency.
The condition that will prove congruency is angle-angle-side (AAS). Two angles and a non-included side of one triangle are equal to two angles and the non-included side of the other triangle.

Step 3
Apply the condition.
Verify that the corresponding angles and sides are equal.
$\angle A = \angle D$
$\angle B = \angle E$
$BC = EF$
Since $\triangle ABC = \triangle DEF$, the condition of AAS is satisfied.
Therefore, the given triangles are proven to be congruent.

NOTES

Geometric Theorems

GEOMETRIC THEOREMS

Table of Correlations

Standard		Concepts	Exercise #1	Exercise #2
Unit1.3	Prove geometric theorems.			
G-CO.9	Prove theorems about lines and angles. Theorems include: vertical angles are congruent; when a transversal crosses parallel lines, alternate interior angles are congruent and corresponding angles are congruent; points on a perpendicular bisector of a line segment are exactly those equidistant from the segment's endpoints.	Problem Solving with Parallel Lines and a Transversal	39	57
		Proving Parallel-Line Theorems	40	
		Determining the Measure of Vertically Opposite Angles	41	58
		Calculating Interior Angles in Transversals	39, 42	59
		Calculating Exterior Angles in Transversals	43	60
		Calculating Corresponding Angles in Transversals	44	61
		Identifying and Labeling Angles in a Transversal	45	62
G-CO.10	Prove theorems about triangles. Theorems include: measures of interior angles of a triangle sum to 180°; base angles of isosceles triangles are congruent; the segment joining midpoints of two sides of a triangle is parallel to the third side and half the length; the medians of a triangle meet at a point.	Understanding the Triangle Inequality Theorem		
		Applying the Triangle Inequality Theorem	46	63
		Concurrency of Medians, Altitudes, Angle Bisectors, and Perpendicular Bisectors of Triangles	47	64
		Applying the Angle Sum Theorem for Triangles	48	65
		Applying Isosceles Triangle Theorems	49	66
		Applying the Exterior Angle Theorem	50	67
		Identifying the Longest Side or Largest Angle of a Triangle	51	68
		Applying the Triangle Midsegment Theorem	52	69
		Applying Theorems about the Mean Proportional	53	70
		Understanding and Applying the Hinge Theorem for Triangles	54	71
G-CO.11	Prove theorems about parallelograms. Theorems include: opposite sides are congruent, opposite angles are congruent, the diagonals of a parallelogram bisect each other, and conversely, rectangles are parallelograms with congruent diagonals.	Applying Theorems about Parallelograms	55	72
		Applying Theorems about Special Parallelograms	56	73

G-CO.9 Prove theorems about lines and angles. Theorems include: vertical angles are congruent; when a transversal crosses parallel lines, alternate interior angles are congruent and corresponding angles are congruent; points on a perpendicular bisector of a line segment are exactly those equidistant from the segment's endpoints.

PROBLEM SOLVING WITH PARALLEL LINES AND A TRANSVERSAL

Many problems involve situations in which parallel lines are crossed by transversal lines. Landscaping, carpentry, and fashion design, as well as many other activities, often require working with parallel lines and transversal lines. The parallel lines can represent the edges of the material or the borders of the lot, and the transversal lines can represent the cut of the fabric or the path of a walkway. Solving problems concerning angles that are formed when a transversal cuts two parallel lines requires a certain approach.

Follow these steps to determine the measure of unknown angles in a problem:

1. Determine the relationship between the given angle and the unknown angles.
2. Determine the measure of the unknown angles using the appropriate relationships.

Example

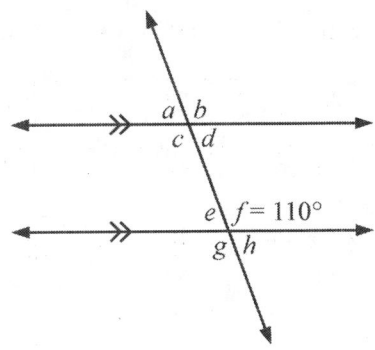

What is the measure of ∠a and ∠c?

Solution

Step 1
Determine the relationship between the given angle and the unknown angles.
Determine the relationship between ∠f, which has a measure of 110°, and ∠a and ∠c.
Angle c and angle f are alternate interior angles, and angle a and angle c are supplementary angles.

Step 2
Determine the measure of the unknown angles using the appropriate relationships.
Alternate interior angles have the same measure.
If ∠f = 110°, then ∠c = 110°.
Since ∠a and ∠c are supplementary angles, their sum is 180°. If ∠c = 110°, then ∠a = 70°.
Thus, the measure of ∠a = 70°, and the measure of ∠c = 110°.

Example

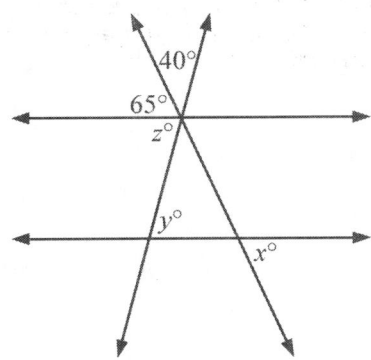

What are the measures of ∠x and ∠y?

Solution

Step 1
Determine the relationship between the given angle and the unknown angles.
Angle x and the 65° angle are alternate exterior angles.
Angle y and angle z are alternate interior angles.

Step 2

Determine the measures of the unknown angles using the appropriate relationships.

Alternate exterior angles have the same measure, which means ∠x = 65°.

Alternate interior angles also have the same measure, which means ∠y = ∠z.

To determine the measure of ∠z, identify its relationship to the other given angles.

Angle z forms a supplementary angle with the 65° angle and the 40° angle. Therefore, its measure is 180° − 65° − 40° = 75°.

If ∠z = 75°, then ∠y = 75°.

Knowing how parallel and transversal lines create angles can help solve real-world problems.

Example

In a certain city, Platinum Lane intersects Bronze Lane at an angle of 90°. Gold Lane intersects Bronze Lane, creating angles of 110° and 70°.

Silver Lane is a road that is going to be built parallel to Bronze Lane. It will intersect Platinum Lane at a 90° angle.

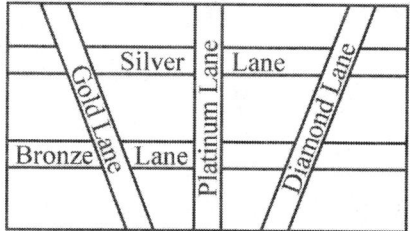

What can be assumed about the angles where Silver Lane will intersect Gold Lane?

Solution

When Silver Lane is built, it will be parallel to Bronze Lane. Gold Lane forms a transversal line that will intersect both Bronze Lane and Silver Lane. Since Gold Lane is intersecting two roads that are parallel, the angles the road makes with Silver Lane will be the same as the angles made where the road intersects Bronze Lane.

Gold Lane will create angles of 110° and 70° when it intersects Silver Lane.

PROVING PARALLEL-LINE THEOREMS

When two parallel lines are cut by a transversal (another line that is not parallel to the given lines), eight angles are produced. These eight angles have specific names and relationships.

The theorems that apply to these angles are called parallel-line theorems. These theorems can be used to solve problems involving parallel lines and transversals.

The given diagram shows the angles that are formed when two parallel lines are cut by a transversal. Refer to this diagram for an illustration of the various angles that are described in this lesson (alternate interior angles, corresponding angles, and interior angles).

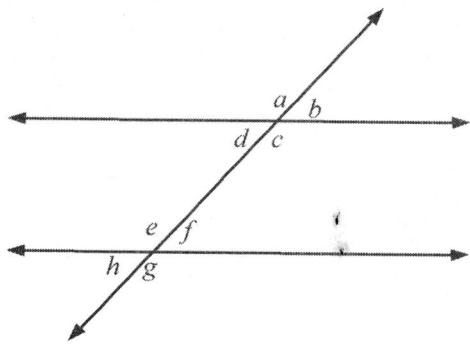

CONGRUENT ALTERNATE INTERIOR ANGLES

Two lines that are intersected by a transversal are parallel if the alternate interior angles are congruent. In the above diagram, ∠c, ∠e and ∠d, ∠f are the pairs of alternate interior angles.

Example

Two parallel lines, N and M, have a transversal intersecting line N at point D and line M at point B.

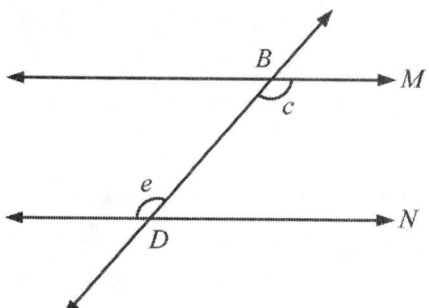

Geometric Theorems   90   Castle Rock Research

Prove that ∠c = ∠e.

Solution

Draw a perpendicular line to line N that goes through the midpoint of DB.

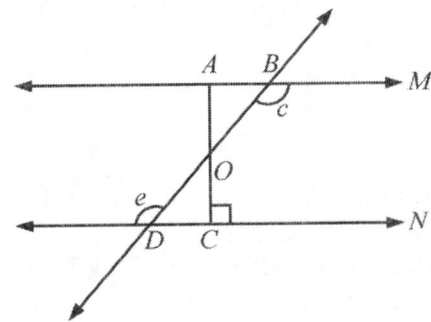

Statement	Reason
∠BAO = ∠DCO	Lines M and N are parallel, so a line perpendicular to one is perpendicular to the other.
DO = BO	Point O is the midpoint of DB.
∠DOC = ∠AOB	Opposite angle theorem
△AOB ≅ △COD	Angle-angle-side congruency
∠CDO = ∠ABO	Since △AOB ≅ △COD
∠e + ∠CDO = 180°	Angles adjacent to each other on a line are supplementary.
∠c + ∠ABO = 180°	Angles adjacent to each other on a line are supplementary.
∠c + ∠ABO = ∠e + ∠CDO ∠c + ∠CDO = ∠e + ∠CDO ∠c = ∠e	By substitution

Therefore, it is proven that ∠c is congruent to ∠e.

Congruent Corresponding Angles

Two lines that are intersected by a transversal are parallel if the corresponding angles are congruent. In the given diagram, ∠a and ∠e, ∠b and ∠f, ∠c and ∠g, and ∠d and ∠h are the pairs of corresponding angles.

Example

Two parallel lines that are cut by a transversal produce eight angles, as shown.

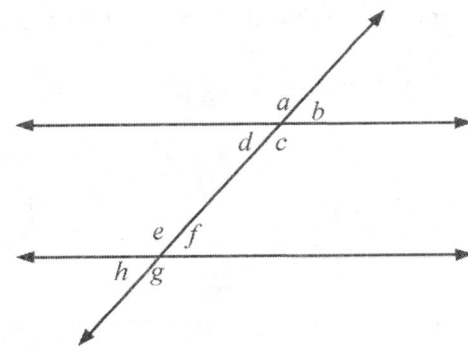

Prove that ∠a = ∠e.

Solution

Create a statement-reason table.

Statement	Reason
∠c = ∠e	Alternate angle theorem
∠c = ∠a	Opposite angle theorem
∠e = ∠a	By substitution

Therefore, it is proven that ∠a is congruent to ∠e.

The proofs that ∠b = ∠f, ∠g = ∠c, and ∠d = ∠h follow the same procedure.

Supplementary Interior Angles

Two lines that are intersected by a transversal are parallel if the interior angles on the same side of the transversal are supplementary (add up to 180°). In the given diagram, angles d and e and angles c and f are the interior angles on the same side of the transversal.

Example

Two parallel lines cut by a transversal produce eight angles, as shown.

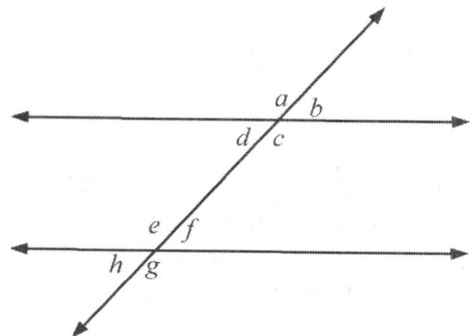

Prove that $\angle e + \angle d = 180°$.

Solution

Create a statement-reason table.

Statement	Reason
$\angle d = \angle f$	Alternate angle theorem
$\angle e + \angle f = 180°$	Angles adjacent to each other on a line are supplementary.
$\angle e + \angle d = 180°$	By substitution

Therefore, it is proven that $\angle e + \angle d = 180°$.

The proof that $\angle c + \angle f = 180°$ follows the same procedure.

Determining the Measure of Vertically Opposite Angles

A **transversal** is a line that cuts across two **parallel lines**.

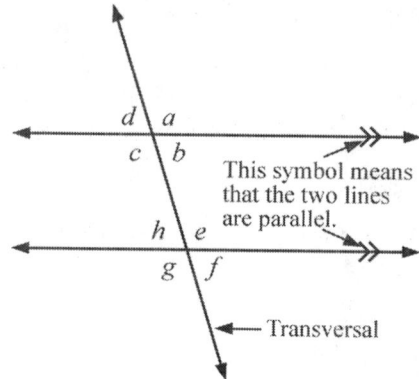

When the transversal intersects two parallel lines, four opposite angles are formed. Opposite angles have the same measure. In the given diagram, $\angle d = \angle b$, $\angle a = \angle c$, $\angle h = \angle f$, and $\angle g = \angle e$ are opposite angles.

If the measure of one opposite angle is known, the measure of its opposite angle must be the same.

Example

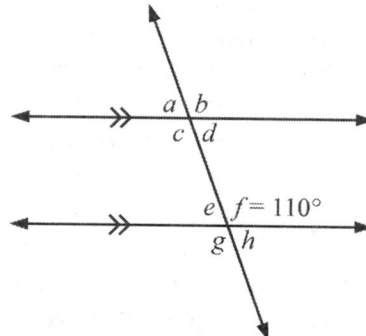

A transversal cuts across two parallel lines, as shown. The measure of $\angle f$ is given.

What is the measure of $\angle g$?

Solution

Step 1

Determine the relationship between the given angle ($\angle f$) and $\angle g$.

Angle g and angle f are opposite angles.

Step 2
Determine the measure of the unknown angle using the relationship of opposite angles. Opposite angles have the same measure.
If $\angle f = 110°$, then $\angle g = 110°$.
The measure of $\angle g$ is 110°.

CALCULATING INTERIOR ANGLES IN TRANSVERSALS

A transversal is a line that crosses two parallel lines.

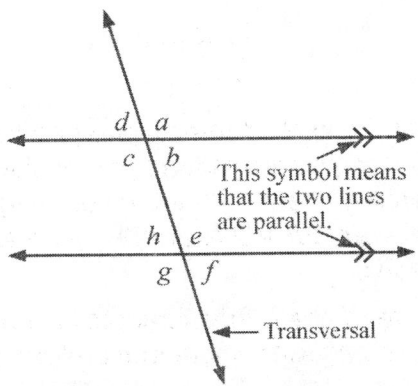

Interior angles are located between the two parallel lines. In the given diagram, $\angle b$, $\angle c$, $\angle e$, and $\angle h$ are all interior angles. These angles are also classified as **alternate angles** when they are on different sides of the transversal or **same-side angles** when they are on the same side of the transversal. Alternate interior angles are equal. In the given diagram, $\angle b$ and $\angle h$ are equal and $\angle c$ and $\angle e$ are also equal. Same-side interior angles are supplementary. In the given diagram, $\angle b$ and $\angle e$ have a sum of 180° and $\angle c$ and $\angle h$ also have a sum of 180°.

When determining the measure of an unknown angle in a transversal, follow these steps:

1. Determine the relationship between the given angle and the unknown angle.
2. Determine the measure of the unknown angle by using the appropriate relationship.

Example
A diagram is given.

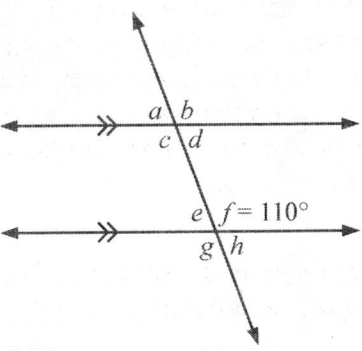

Determine the measure of $\angle c$.

Solution
Step 1
Determine the relationship between the given angle and the unknown angle.
Since $\angle f$ and $\angle c$ are on opposite sides of the transversal, they are alternate interior angles.

Step 2
Calculate the value of $\angle c$ by using the appropriate relationship.
Alternate interior angles are equal.
$\angle f = \angle c$
$110° = \angle c$

Determine the measure of $\angle d$.

Solution
Step 1
Determine the relationship between the given angle and the unknown angle.
Since $\angle d$ and $\angle f$ are on the same side of the transversal, they are same-side interior angles.

Step 2
Calculate the value of $\angle d$ by using the appropriate relationship.
Same-side interior angles are supplementary.
$\angle d + \angle f = 180°$
$\angle d + 110° = 180°$
$\angle d = 70°$

CALCULATING EXTERIOR ANGLES IN TRANSVERSALS

A transversal is a line that crosses two parallel lines. When two parallel lines are cut by a transversal, four exteriors angles are formed.

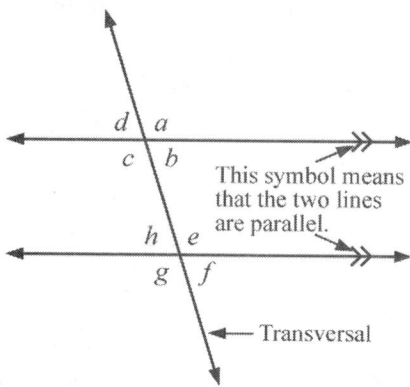

Exterior angles are located outside the two parallel lines. In the given diagram, $\angle a$, $\angle d$, $\angle f$, and $\angle g$ are exterior angles. These angles are also classified as either **alternate angles** when they are on different sides of the transversal or **same-side angles** when they are on the same side of the transversal.

Alternate exterior angles are equal. In the given diagram, $\angle a = \angle g$ and $\angle d = \angle f$. Same-side exterior angles are supplementary. In the given diagram, $\angle d + \angle g = 180°$ and $\angle a + \angle f = 180°$.

When determining the measure of an unknown angle in a transversal, follow these steps:

1. Determine the relationship between the given angle and the unknown angle.
2. Determine the measure of the unknown angle by using the appropriate relationship.

Example
In the given diagram, $\angle w = 70°$.

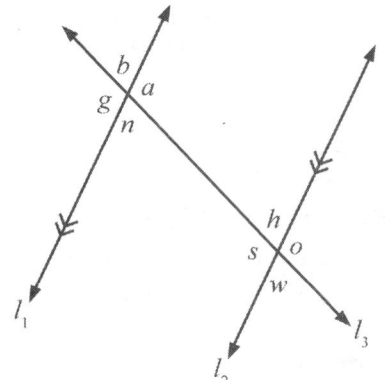

Determine the measure of $\angle b$.

Solution
Step 1
Determine the relationship between the given angle and the unknown angle.
Angles b and w are alternate exterior angles.
Step 2
Determine the measure of $\angle b$ by using the appropriate relationship.
Alternate exterior angles are equal.
$\angle w = \angle b$
$70° = \angle b$

Determine the measure of $\angle g$.

Solution
Step 1
Determine the relationship between the given angle and the unknown angle.
Angles g and w are same-side exterior angles.
Step 2
Determine the measure of $\angle g$ by using the appropriate relationship.
Same-side exterior angles are supplementary.
$\angle g + \angle w = 180°$
$\angle g + 70° = 180°$
$\angle g = 110°$

CALCULATING CORRESPONDING ANGLES IN TRANSVERSALS

A transversal is a line that crosses two parallel lines.

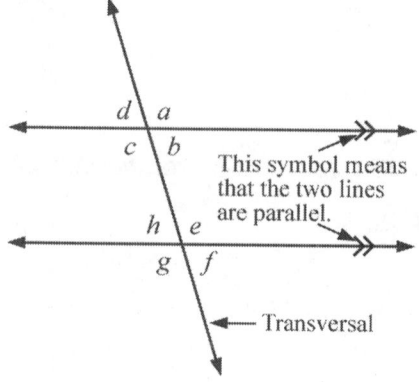

Geometric Theorems

Corresponding angles are pairs of angles that are in the same position relative to each of the parallel lines and the transversal. For example, one pair of corresponding angles in the given diagram is ∠a and ∠e. The property of corresponding angles states that corresponding angles are equal. Therefore, ∠a = ∠e.

When determining the measure of an unknown angle in a transversal, follow these steps:

1. Determine the relationship between the given angle and the unknown angle.
2. Determine the measure of the unknown angle by using the appropriate relationship.

Example
A diagram is given. What is the measure of ∠b?

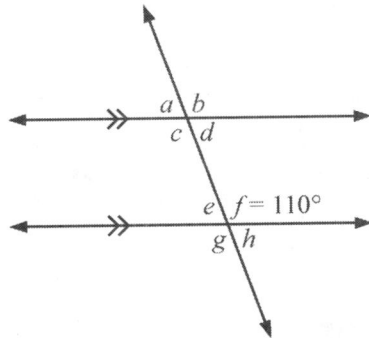

Solution

Step 1
Determine the relationship between the given angle and the unknown angle.

The given angle, f, and the unknown angle, b, are corresponding angles.

Step 2
Determine the measure of ∠b by using the appropriate relationship.

Since corresponding angles are equal, ∠f = ∠b. Therefore, ∠b = 110°.

IDENTIFYING AND LABELING ANGLES IN A TRANSVERSAL

Parallel lines are lines that always stay the same distance apart and never intersect. Parallel lines usually have matching arrow markings on them to indicate that they are parallel.

A **transversal** is a line that crosses two parallel lines.

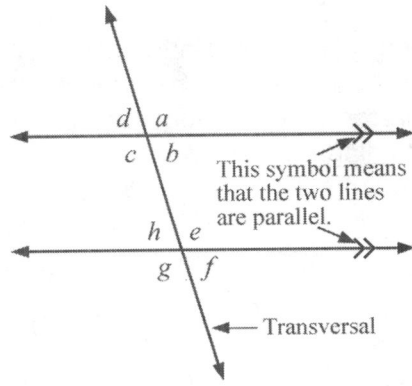

The angles that are formed between the transversal and the two parallel lines are described and named according to their positions in the diagram and their positions relative to one another.

Opposite angles are angles that are across the intersection point. Opposite angles are also called **vertical angles**. They are not across a straight line. In the given diagram, ∠d is across the intersection point from ∠b and across a line from ∠c. The pairs of opposite angles are ∠a and ∠c, ∠b and ∠d, ∠e and ∠g, and ∠f and ∠h.

Interior angles are located between the two parallel lines. In the given diagram, ∠c, ∠b, ∠h, and ∠e are interior angles. **Exterior angles** are located outside the two parallel lines. In the given diagram, ∠d, ∠a, ∠g, and ∠f are exterior angles. Interior and exterior angles are also classified as either **alternate angles** when they are on different sides of the transversal or **same-side angles** when they are on the same side of the transversal.

These types of angles have the following properties:

- Alternate interior angles are equal. In the given diagram, ∠h = ∠b and ∠c = ∠e.
- Same-side interior angles are supplementary. In the given diagram, ∠c + ∠h = 180° and ∠b + ∠e = 180°.
- Alternate exterior angles are equal. In the given diagram, ∠a = ∠g and ∠d = ∠f.
- Same-side exterior angles are supplementary. In the given diagram, ∠d + ∠g = 180° and ∠a + ∠f = 180°.

Corresponding angles are pairs of angles that are in the same position compared to each of the parallel lines and the transversal. If one of the parallel lines was placed on top of the other, their angles would match (or correspond with) each other. Therefore, corresponding angles are equal. In the given diagram, one pair of corresponding angles is ∠a and ∠e. These angles are equal.

Example

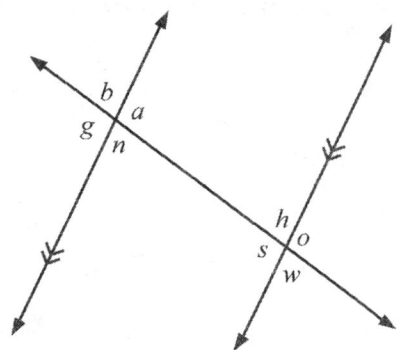

The transversal cuts across two parallel lines.
Name four pairs of opposite angles in the given diagram.

Solution

Step 1
Identify which two lines are parallel and which line is the transversal.
The two parallel lines are the lines angling up to the right. The transversal is the single line angling down to the right.

Step 2
Identify the pairs of opposite angles.
The opposite angles are angles ∠b and ∠n, ∠a and ∠g, ∠s and ∠o, and ∠h and ∠w.

Example
A diagram is given.

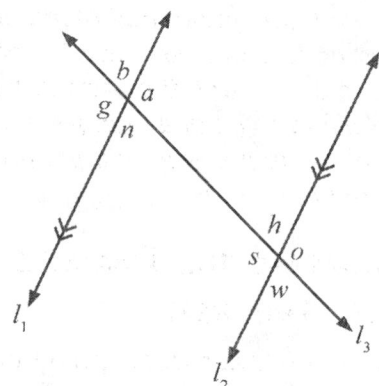

Identify and properly name all the pairs of interior angles in the given diagram.

Solution

Step 1
First, identify which two lines are parallel and which line is the transversal.
Lines l_1 and l_2 are parallel since they contain parallel marker signs and they do not intersect. Line l_3 intersects two parallel lines, so it is the transversal line.

Step 2
Identify all angles in the interior of the diagram.
Angles *a*, *n*, *h*, and *s* are located in the space between two parallel lines. These angles are the interior angles.

Step 3
Name the pairs of interior angles.
There are six pairs of interior angles:

1. Angles *a* and *n* are supplementary interior angles.
2. Angles *a* and *h* are same-side interior angles.
3. Angles *a* and *s* are alternate interior angles.
4. Angles *h* and *n* are alternate interior angles.
5. Angles *s* and *n* are same-side interior angles.
6. Angles *s* and *h* are supplementary interior angles.

Geometric Theorems

G-CO.10 Prove theorems about triangles. Theorems include: measures of interior angles of a triangle sum to 180°; base angles of isosceles triangles are congruent; the segment joining midpoints of two sides of a triangle is parallel to the third side and half the length; the medians of a triangle meet at a point.

UNDERSTANDING THE TRIANGLE INEQUALITY THEOREM

Intuition tells you that a direct path from one location to another is the shortest distance between those two locations. For example, in an open field, walking directly toward an object is always the shortest path to that object. The **triangle inequality theorem** states that one side of any triangle is less than the sum of the other two sides.

Example
In the given triangle ABC, select points A and B as the origin and destination, respectively. The path AB is less than the path $AC + CB$.
Using mathematical notation, $AB < AC + CB$.

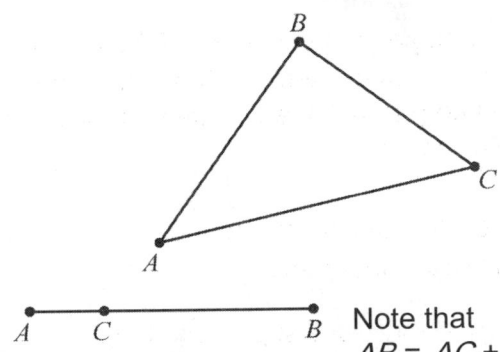

Note that $AB = AC + CB$ is true if points A, B, and C are **collinear** and point C is located between points A and B (the addition of line segments postulate).

Example
Prove that the length of a **diagonal** of any **quadrilateral** is less than the sum of the two sides connecting the vertices of the diagonal.

Solution

Step 1
Draw a diagram.
Let $ABCD$ be a quadrilateral. Draw a diagonal, e, between vertex A and vertex C.

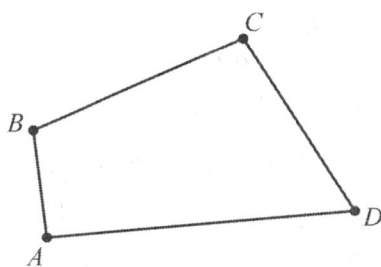

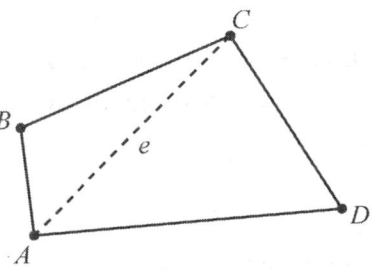

Step 2
Prove that diagonal e is less than the sum of two sides of the quadrilateral connecting point A and point C.
There are two pairs of sides: AB and BC, and AD and DC.
Prove that $e < AB + BC$.
Together with the diagonal, there is a triangle, $\triangle ABC$, formed. Diagonal e is side AC of the triangle. By the triangle inequality theorem, side $AC < AB + BC$. Therefore, $e < AB + BC$. Similarly, $e < AD + DC$.

Applying the Triangle Inequality Theorem

The **triangle inequality theorem** states that the length of one side of any triangle is less than the sum of the other two sides. This can be applied in solving for a range of unknown side lengths of triangles.

Example

If a triangle has side lengths of $7 + x$, $7 - x$, and 7, what are the possible values of x?

Solution

The triangle inequality theorem states that the length of one side of any triangle is less than the sum of the other two sides. Solve for possible values of x for each of the three sides as follows:

Step 1
Use the first side:
$7 + x < (7 - x) + 7$
$x + x < 14 - 7$
$\quad 2x < 7$
$\quad\quad x < \dfrac{7}{2}$

Step 2
Use the second side:
$7 - x < 7 + (7 + x)$
$7 - 14 < x + x$
$\quad -7 < 2x$
$\quad -\dfrac{7}{2} < x$

Step 3
Use the third side:
$7 < (7 + x) + (7 - x)$
$7 < 14$

This inequality results in $7 < 14$. This means that, for this particular side, any value of x would be valid to produce a triangle.

Step 4
Identify all possible values for x.

By combining the first two inequalities, the values of x that can form the triangle are $-\dfrac{7}{2} < x < \dfrac{7}{2}$.

Example

Triangle ABC has side lengths of $AB = 4$, $BC = 8$, and $AC = x$. What are the possible values of x that would allow $\triangle ABC$ to exist as a triangle?

Solution

The triangle inequality theorem states that the length of one side of any triangle is less than the sum of the other two sides. Solve for possible values of x for each of the three sides as follows:

Step 1
Use the first side:
$BC + AC > AB$
$\quad 8 + x > 4$
$\quad\quad\quad x > -4$

This inequality results in $x > -4$. Since negative values of measurement are not possible, the value of x will always be greater than -4. This means that, for this particular side, any positive value of x would be valid to produce a triangle. Therefore, this inequality must be disregarded.

Step 2
Use the second side:
$AB + AC > BC$
$\quad 4 + x > 8$
$\quad\quad\quad x > 4$

Step 3
Use the third side:
$AB + BC > AC$
$\quad 4 + 8 > x$
$\quad\quad 12 > x$

Step 4
Identify all possible values for x.
By combining the last two inequalities, the values of x that can form the triangle are $4 < x < 12$.

Concurrency of Medians, Altitudes, Angle Bisectors, and Perpendicular Bisectors of Triangles

Two or more lines are **concurrent** if the lines intersect each other at one single point.

There are four points of concurrency in a triangle:

1. Incentre
2. Circumcentre
3. Orthocentre
4. Centroid

Incentre

The angle bisectors of a triangle are concurrent at a point called the **incentre**. The incentre is of equal perpendicular distance from each side of the triangle. An inscribed circle with its center at the incentre touches each side of the triangle only once. This circle is called the **incircle**.

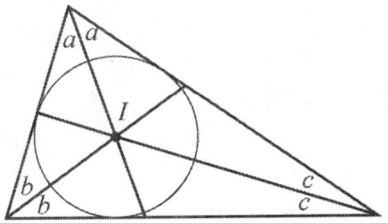

Circumcentre

The perpendicular bisectors of a triangle are concurrent at a point called the **circumcentre**. The circumcentre is most commonly marked with the letter *O*. The circumcentre is of equal distance from each vertex of the triangle. The circumcentre is located inside an acute triangle, outside an obtuse triangle, and midway on the hypotenuse of a right triangle. A circle that is centered on the circumcentre and passes through each vertex of the triangle is called the **circumcircle**.

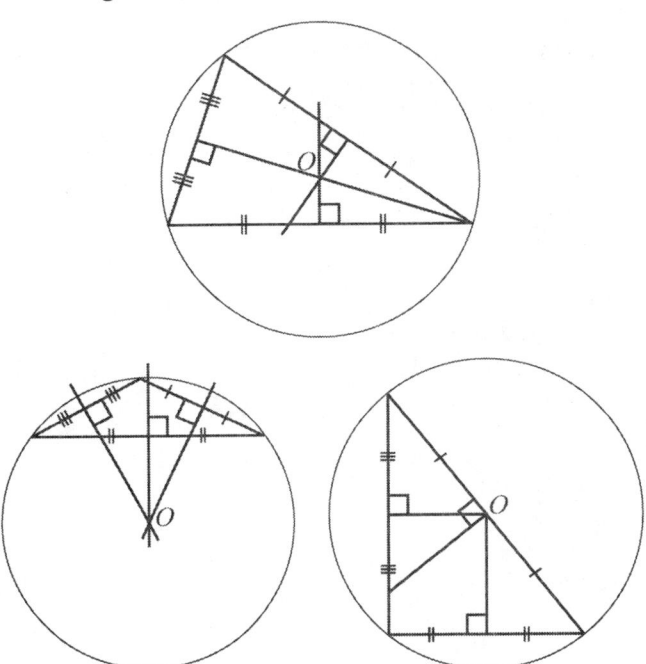

ORTHOCENTRE

The altitudes of a triangle are concurrent at a point called the **orthocentre**. The orthocentre is most commonly marked with the letter *H*.

The orthocentre is found inside an acute triangle, outside an obtuse triangle, and on the right angle of a right triangle.

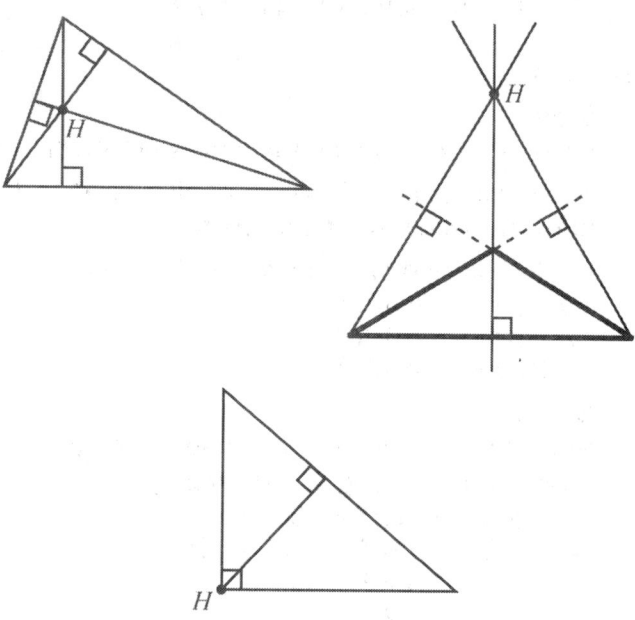

CENTROID

In a triangle, the medians are concurrent at a point called the **centroid**. The centroid divides each median two-thirds of the way from a vertex to the opposite side. The centroid is most commonly marked with the letter *G*.

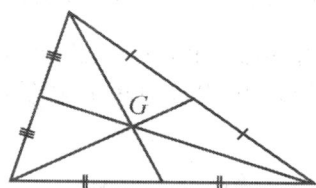

Example

Triangle *ABC* is given. Lines extending for each vertex are concurrent at point *D*.

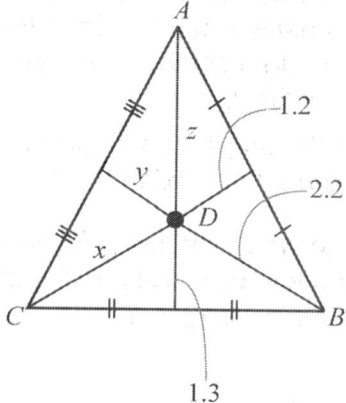

Determine the lengths of *x*, *y*, and *z*.

Solution

Step 1

Determine the point of concurrency.

Since the line from each vertex divides the opposite side into two equal lengths, each line is a median. The medians of a triangle are concurrent at the centroid, so *D* is the centroid of the triangle.

Step 2

Determine the unknown lengths.

The centroid divides each median $\frac{2}{3}$ of the way from a vertex to the opposite side. Since the short section is $\frac{1}{3}$ of the total length and the long section is $\frac{2}{3}$ of the total length, there is a 1:2 ratio between the two sections. This ratio can be used to set up proportions.

$$\frac{1}{2} = \frac{1.2}{x}$$
$$x = 2.4$$
$$\frac{1}{2} = \frac{y}{2.2}$$
$$1.1 = y$$
$$\frac{1}{2} = \frac{1.3}{z}$$
$$z = 2.6$$

The lengths of *x*, *y*, and *z* are 2.4, 1.1, and 2.6 units, respectively.

APPLYING THE ANGLE SUM THEOREM FOR TRIANGLES

The sum of the interior angles of any triangle is 180°. This means that the sum of the interior angles of a triangle can be represented as ∠a + ∠b + ∠c = 180°.

You can use the angle sum theorem to find missing angles in a triangle by following these steps:

1. Determine which angles are given.
2. Substitute the given values into the angle property for a triangle, and simplify.

Example

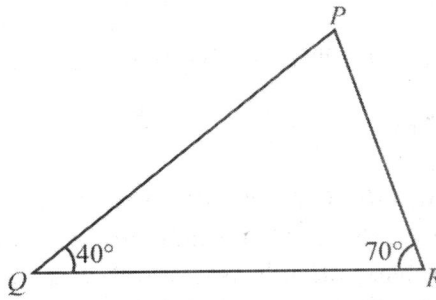

Find the measure of ∠P.

Solution

Step 1
Determine which angle measures are given.
∠Q = 40°
∠R = 70°

Step 2
Substitute the given values into the formula for the angle property for a triangle, and simplify.
∠P + ∠Q + ∠R = 180°
∠P + 70° + 40° = 180°
∠P + 110° = 180°
∠P = 70°

The measure of ∠P is 70°.

Example

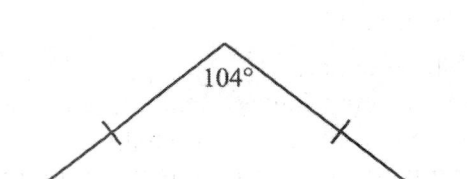

Find the measures of ∠a and ∠b.

Solution

Step 1
Determine what angle measures are given.

Since this is an isosceles triangle, ∠a and ∠b have the same measure: ∠a = ∠b.

So, the property is modified and becomes
∠a + ∠b + ∠c = 180°
∠a + ∠a + ∠c = 180°.
2∠a + ∠c = 180°

Step 2
Substitute the given values into the angle property for a triangle and simplify.
$$2\angle a + (104°) = 180°$$
$$2\angle a + 104° - 104° = 180° - 104°$$
$$\frac{2\angle a}{2} = \frac{76°}{2}$$
$$\angle a = 38°$$

Therefore, ∠a and ∠b each have a measure of 38°.

APPLYING ISOSCELES TRIANGLE THEOREMS

An isosceles triangle is a triangle with two congruent sides and two equal angles.

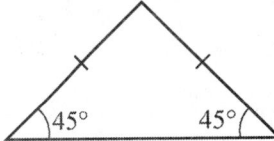

The isosceles triangle theorem states that if two sides of a triangle are congruent, then the angles opposite them are congruent. Conversely, if two angles are congruent, then the sides opposite them are congruent.

The isosceles triangle theorem and its converse are useful when solving problems involving isosceles triangles.

Example

The triangle angle sum theorem states that the sum of the interior angles of any triangle is 180°. In $\triangle DEF$, $\angle D$ measures 130°.

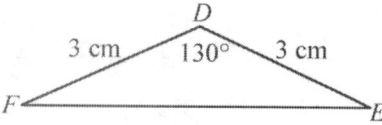

What is the measure of $\angle E$?

Solution

Since $DE = DF = 3$ cm, $\triangle DEF$ is an isosceles triangle. Thus, the angles' opposite sides, DE and DF, are equal in measure. $\angle F = \angle E$

Step 1
Label the measure of $\angle F$ and $\angle E$ as θ.

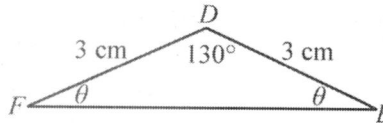

Step 2
Write an equation for the sum of the interior angles of a triangle.
$$\begin{pmatrix}\text{sum of the interior}\\ \text{angles of } \triangle DEF\end{pmatrix} = \angle D + \angle E + \angle F$$

Step 3
Substitute all known values into the interior angle equation.
$$\begin{pmatrix}\text{sum of the interior}\\ \text{angles of } \triangle DEF\end{pmatrix} = \angle D + \angle E + \angle F$$
$$180° = 130° + \theta + \theta$$

Step 4
Solve for θ.
$180° = 130° + \theta + \theta$
$180° = 130° + 2\theta$
$50° = 2\theta$
$25° = \theta$

The measure of $\angle E$ is equal to θ. Therefore, $\angle E$ measures 25°.

Example

The perimeter of $\triangle ABC$ is 14.5 cm.

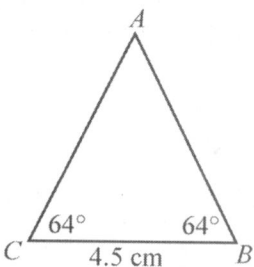

What is the length of side AB?

Solution

Since $\angle B = \angle C = 64°$, $\triangle ABC$ is an isosceles triangle. Thus, the sides opposite $\angle B$ and $\angle C$ are equal in length. $AB = AC$

Step 1
Label sides AB and AC as x.

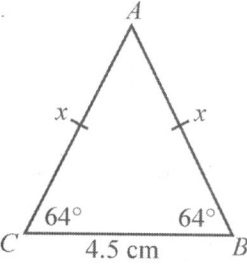

Step 2
Write an equation for the perimeter of $\triangle ABC$.
$P = AB + AC + BC$

Step 3
Substitute all known values into the perimeter equation.
$P = AB + AC + BC$
$14.5 = x + x + 4.5$

Step 4
Solve for x.
$14.5 = x + x + 4.5$
$14.5 = 2x + 4.5$
$10 = 2x$
$5 = x$

The length of side AB is equal to x. Therefore, side AB is 5 cm long.

Applying the Exterior Angle Theorem

The exterior angle theorem states that an exterior angle of a triangle is equal to the sum of the remote (opposite) interior angles.

Example

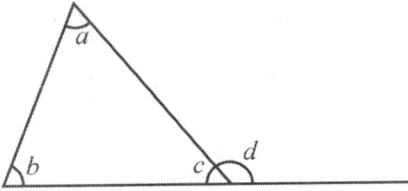

According to the exterior angle theorem, in the given triangle, $\angle d = \angle a + \angle b$.

You can apply the exterior angle theorem to find unknown measures in triangles.

Example
Triangle *STU* is given.

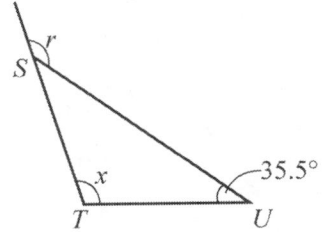

If $\angle r = 143.5°$, determine the measure of $\angle x$.

Solution

The exterior angle theorem states that an exterior angle of a triangle is equal to the sum of the remote (opposite) interior angles. Therefore, $\angle r = \angle x + \angle U$.

Substitute the known measures and solve for $\angle x$.

$\angle r = \angle x + \angle U$
$143.5° = \angle x + 35.5°$
$108° = \angle x$

The measure of $\angle x$ is 108°.

Example
Triangle *MNO* is given with an exterior angle at *M*.

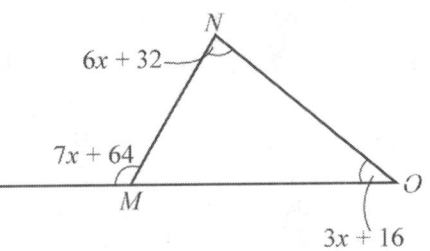

Determine the value of *x* in the given triangle.

Solution

The exterior angle theorem states that an exterior angle of a triangle is equal to the sum of the remote (opposite) interior angles.

Determine the value of *x*.
$7x + 64 = (6x + 32) + (3x + 16)$
$7x + 64 = 9x + 48$
$-2x = -16$
$x = 8$

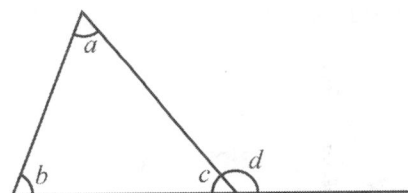

It follows from the equality $\angle d = \angle a + \angle b$ that the exterior angle is greater than both opposite interior angles. Therefore, in the given diagram, $\angle d > \angle a$ and $\angle d > \angle b$.

Example
The triangle *ABC* is given.

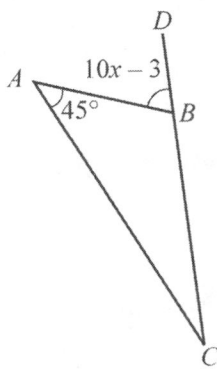

What are the possible values of x if $0° < x < 180°$?

Solution

Step 1

Determine the value that x must be less than. Since $\angle ABD$ and $\angle ABC$ produce a straight line, $\angle ABD < 180°$ and $\angle ABC < 180°$. Substitute $10x - 3$ for $\angle ABD$, and solve for x.

$\angle ABD < 180°$
$10x - 3 < 180°$
$10x < 183°$
$x < 18.3°$

Step 2

Determine the angle that x must be greater than.

The exterior angle theorem states that an exterior angle of a triangle is equal to the sum of the remote (opposite) interior angles, so $\angle ABD = \angle A + \angle C$. From this it is possible to conclude that the exterior angle is greater than both opposite interior angles, so $\angle ABD > \angle A$ and $\angle ABD > \angle C$. In the diagram, $\angle C$ is not given, so use the value of $\angle A$.

$\angle ABD > \angle A$
$10x - 3 > 45°$
$10x > 48°$
$x > \dfrac{48°}{10}$
$x > 4.8°$

Therefore, the possible values of x are $4.8° < x < 18.3°$.

IDENTIFYING THE LONGEST SIDE OR LARGEST ANGLE OF A TRIANGLE

In a triangle, the longest side is opposite the largest angle. Similarly, the largest angle is opposite the longest side.

Example

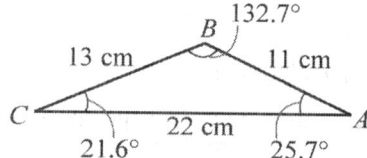

From the given measurements of this triangle, you can see that the longest side, AC, is opposite the largest angle, $\angle B$.

Example

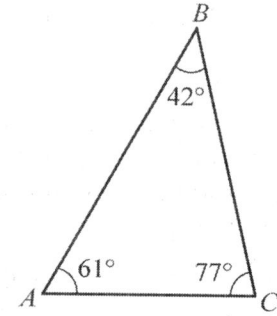

Triangle ABC is shown.

What is the longest side of this triangle?

Solution

The longest side of a triangle is the side opposite the largest angle. The diagram shows that the largest angle is $\angle C$. Therefore, the longest side of the given triangle is side AB.

Example

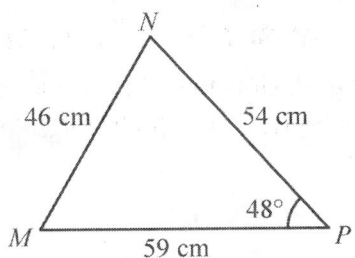

Triangle *MNP* is shown.

Determine the largest angle in △*MNP*.

Solution

The largest side of a triangle is opposite the largest angle. The diagram shows that the longest side is *MP*. Therefore, the largest angle is ∠*N*.

APPLYING THE TRIANGLE MIDSEGMENT THEOREM

The triangle midsegment theorem states that the line segment joining the midpoints of two sides of a triangle is parallel to and half the length of the third side of the triangle.

In triangle *ABC*, $\overline{DE}$ joins the midpoints of $\overline{AB}$ and $\overline{AC}$. By the triangle midsegment theorem, $\overline{DE} \parallel \overline{BC}$ and $\overline{DE} = \frac{1}{2}(\overline{BC})$.

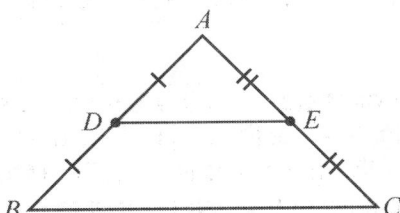

Example

In triangle *ACT*, $\overline{DG}$ joins the midpoints of $\overline{AC}$ and $\overline{CT}$.

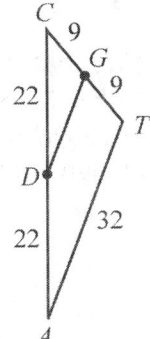

The length of $\overline{DG}$ can be found by applying the triangle midsegment theorem. From the diagram, it is clear that $\overline{DG}$ joins the midpoints of $\overline{AC}$ and $\overline{CT}$, so $\overline{DG} = \frac{1}{2}(\overline{AT})$.

$\overline{DG} = \frac{1}{2}(\overline{AT})$

$\overline{DG} = \frac{1}{2}(32)$

$\overline{DG} = 16$

The length of $\overline{DG}$ is 16 units.

Example

Triangle *XYZ* and line segment *UV* are given.

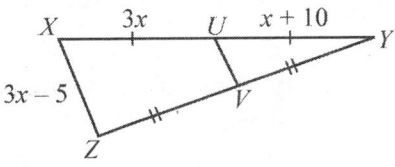

Find the length of $\overline{UV}$.

Solution

Step 1
Find the value of *x*.
From the diagram, $\overline{XU} = \overline{UY}$.
$\overline{XU} = \overline{UY}$
$3x = x + 10$
$2x = 10$
$x = 5$

Step 2
Determine the value of $\overline{UV}$.

Since $\overline{UV}$ joins the midpoints of $\overline{XY}$ and $\overline{YZ}$, the triangle midsegment theorem can be applied.

From the theorem, $\overline{UV} = \frac{1}{2}(\overline{XZ})$. Substitute the know values into the theorem, and solve.

$\overline{UV} = \frac{1}{2}(\overline{XZ})$
$\overline{UV} = \frac{1}{2}(3x - 5)$
$\overline{UV} = \frac{1}{2}(3(5) - 5)$
$\overline{UV} = \frac{1}{2}(15 - 5)$
$\overline{UV} = \frac{1}{2}(10)$
$\overline{UV} = 5$

The length of $\overline{UV}$ is 5 units.

APPLYING THEOREMS ABOUT THE MEAN PROPORTIONAL

The mean proportional is a number, X, that satisfies the proportional relationship $\frac{A}{X} = \frac{X}{B}$, where A and B are positive numbers. In geometry, the mean proportional is also called the **geometric mean**. Such a relationship exists within the sides of a right angle triangle divided by an altitude.

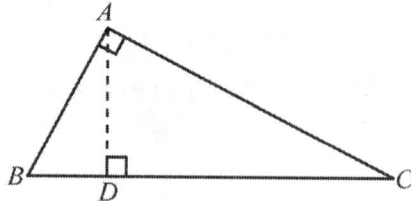

All three triangles in this figure are similar through the angle-angle-angle (AAA) condition.
$\triangle ABC \sim \triangle DAC \sim \triangle BDA$

Since the triangles are similar and they share several side lengths, proportions can be set up to determine unknown side lengths.

The two following rules can be applied to save time in setting up proportions:

1. The altitude rule is applied when the altitude and the two sections of the hypotenuse are used. The altitude is the mean proportional.

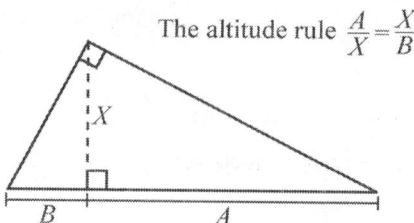

The altitude rule $\frac{A}{X} = \frac{X}{B}$

2. The leg rule is applied when part of the hypotenuse, the whole hypotenuse, and a leg of the triangle are used. The section of the hypotenuse used is adjacent to the leg. The leg is the mean proportional.

The leg rule $\frac{A}{X} = \frac{X}{B}$

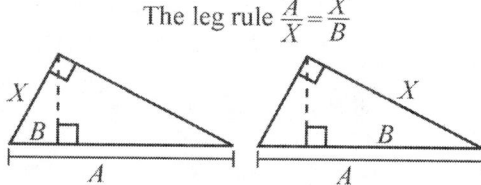

As long as the mean proportional is the correct value, the remaining two values can be used in either variable. To find unknown values, recognize which relationship is present and substitute the appropriate values into the proportion.

Example
Triangle XYZ is given.

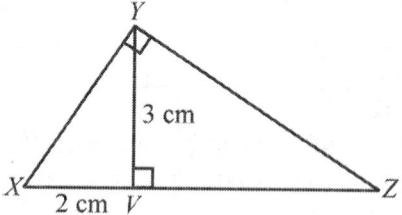

Determine the length of $\overline{VZ}$.

Solution
Step 1
Determine which proportional rule to use. Since the altitude and two sections of the hypotenuse are involved, the altitude rule can be used.

Step 2
Substitute the appropriate values into the proportion.
Since the altitude rule is being used, the length of the altitude is the mean proportional.

$$\frac{A}{X} = \frac{X}{B}$$
$$\frac{2}{3} = \frac{3}{VZ}$$
$$2\overline{VZ} = 9$$
$$\overline{VZ} = 4.5$$

The length of $\overline{VZ}$ is 4.5 cm.

Triangle *IJK* is given.

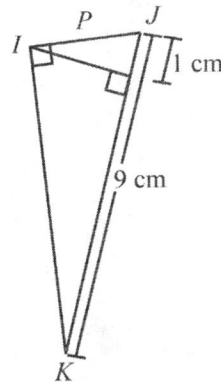

Determine the length of *P*.

Solution

Step 1
Determine which proportional rule to use.
Since the hypotenuse, a section of the hypotenuse, and the leg from the same side of the triangle as the section are involved, the leg rule can be used.

Step 2
Substitute the appropriate values into the proportion.
Since the leg rule is being used, the length of the leg is the mean proportional.

$$\frac{A}{X} = \frac{X}{B}$$
$$\frac{1}{P} = \frac{P}{9}$$
$$9 = P^2$$
$$\sqrt{9} = P$$
$$3 = P$$

The length of *P* is 3 cm.

UNDERSTANDING AND APPLYING THE HINGE THEOREM FOR TRIANGLES

The **hinge theorem** states that if two sides of a triangle are each equal to two corresponding sides of a second triangle and the included angle of the first triangle is larger than the second, then the third side of the first triangle is longer than the third side of the second.

In the given triangles, since $AB = A'B'$, $AC = A'C'$, and $\angle A > \angle A'$, then according to the hinge theorem, $CB > C'B'$.

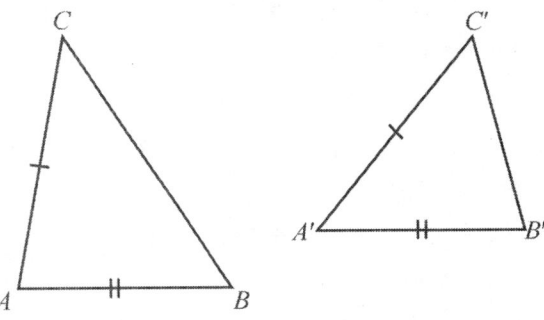

Example
In the given triangles, $PR = SW$ and $PQ = ST$. Also, $\angle P > \angle S$.

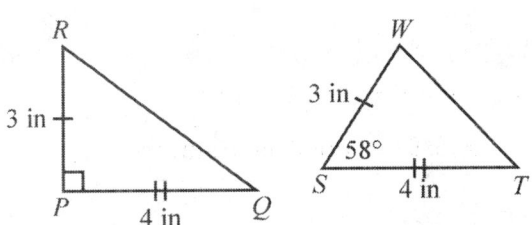

You can see that $RQ > WT$. The length of RQ is 5 in, while the length of WT is about 3.5 in.

You can apply the hinge theorem to solve problems involving triangles.

Example
In the given triangle, $\theta_1 > \theta_2$.

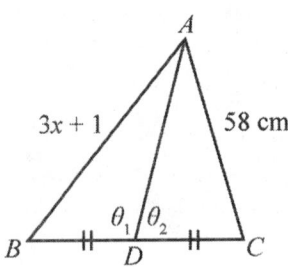

In order for triangle ABC to exist, what value must x be greater than?

Solution

The median from A to side BC forms two triangles, ABD and ADC. In the two triangles, AD is a shared side, BD = DC, and the relationship between the included angles is $\theta_1 > \theta_2$. Therefore, using the hinge theorem, AB > AC.

Use the relationship AB > AC to determine what value x is greater than.
$$AB > AC$$
$$3x + 1 > 58$$
$$3x > 57$$
$$x > 19$$

In order for triangle ABC to exist, x must be greater than 19 cm.

Example

Darrin and Irene are both driving home from the same restaurant. Darrin has to drive 7 km west and then 6 km north to get to his house. Irene needs to drive 7 km east and then 6 km 30° south of west to get to her house.

Who lives closer to the restaurant?

Solution

Step 1
Draw a diagram using the given information.
Let D represent Darrin's house, I represent Irene's house, and R represent the restaurant.

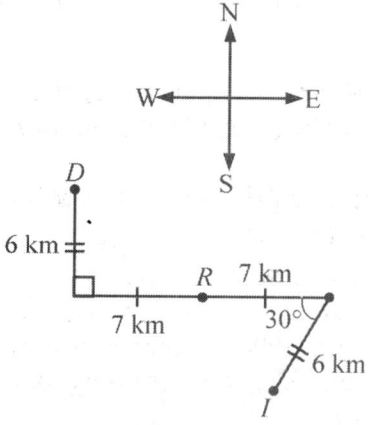

Step 2
Using the diagram, determine who lives closer to the restaurant.
Draw a line from point D to point R and a line from point I to point R. Label turning points X and Y to form triangles DRX and RIY.

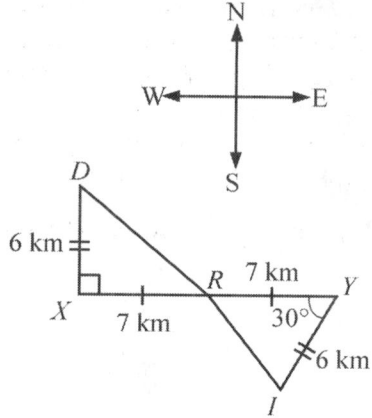

In the two triangles, DX = IY, XR = RY, and ∠X > ∠Y. According to the hinge theorem, DR > RI. Therefore, Irene lives closer to the restaurant.

G-CO.11 Prove theorems about parallelograms. Theorems include: opposite sides are congruent, opposite angles are congruent, the diagonals of a parallelogram bisect each other, and conversely, rectangles are parallelograms with congruent diagonals.

APPLYING THEOREMS ABOUT PARALLELOGRAMS

A parallelogram is a quadrilateral that has two pairs of parallel lines. The opposite sides of a parallelogram are equal in length and parallel.

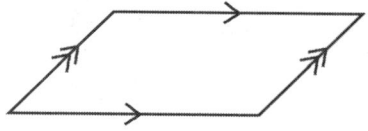

There are several specific properties of parallelograms that can be used to solve problems involving parallelograms. These properties make up the following theorems:

1. Opposite angles in parallelograms are equal.
2. Consecutive (same side interior) angles within a parallelogram are supplementary.
3. A diagonal of a parallelogram divides it into two congruent triangles.
4. The diagonals of a parallelogram bisect each other.

This parallelogram illustrates theorems 1 and 2.

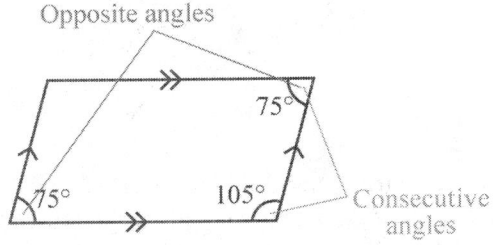

This parallelogram illustrates theorems 3 and 4.

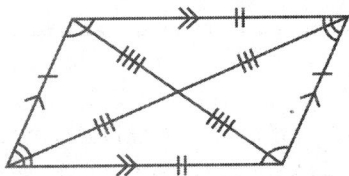

Example

The given quadrilateral *ABCD* is a parallelogram with diagonals *AC* and *BD* intersecting at *E*, where $AE = 9x$, $EC = 10x - 2$, and $\angle BCD = 125°$.

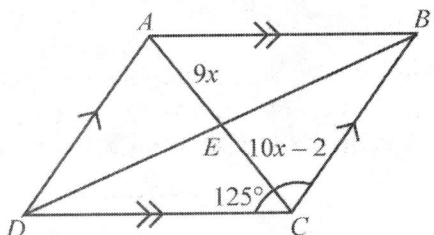

Find the measure of $\angle ADC$.

Solution

If consecutive angles within parallelograms are supplementary, then $\angle ADC + \angle BCD = 180°$.
$\angle ADC + \angle BCD = 180°$
$\angle ADC + 125° = 180°$
$\angle ADC = 55°$

The measure of $\angle ADC$ is 55°.

Find the length of *EC*.

Solution

Step 1
Find the value of *x*.
Since the diagonals of a parallelogram bisect each other, $AE = EC$.
$AE = EC$
$9x = 10x - 2$
$-x = -2$
$x = 2$

Step 2
Substitute the value of *x* into the equation given for the length of *EC*.
$EC = 10x - 2$
$EC = 10(2) - 2$
$EC = 20 - 2$
$EC = 18$
The length of *EC* is 18 units.

APPLYING THEOREMS ABOUT SPECIAL PARALLELOGRAMS

The specific properties of parallelograms can be used to solve problems involving parallelograms. These properties are summarized in the following list:

1. A parallelogram has two pairs of parallel lines. The opposite sides of a parallelogram are parallel.
2. The area of a parallelogram can be calculated using the formula $A_{parallelogram} = b \times h$.
3. Opposite angles in parallelograms are equal.
4. Consecutive (same-side interior) angles within a parallelogram are supplementary.
5. A diagonal divides a parallelogram into two congruent triangles.
6. The diagonals of a parallelogram bisect each other.

This parallelogram illustrates property 1.

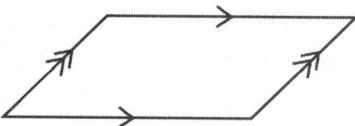

This parallelogram illustrates how area is calculated in property 2.

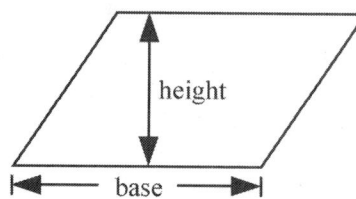

This parallelogram illustrates properties 3 and 4.

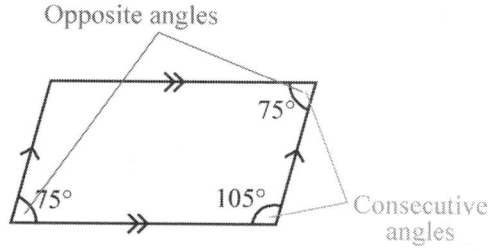

This parallelogram illustrates properties 5 and 6.

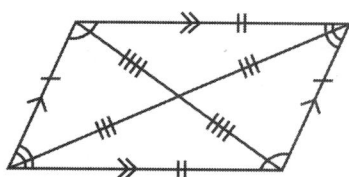

Special parallelograms include rhombuses, rectangles, and squares. These shapes have all the standard properties of parallelograms as well as their own specific properties. You can apply these properties to solve problems involving special parallelograms.

RHOMBUS

A rhombus is a parallelogram with four sides of equal length.

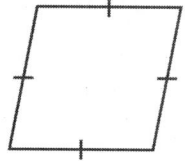

The following theorems result from this information and the definition of a parallelogram:

- The diagonals are perpendicular to each other.
- The diagonals will produce four congruent triangles.
- The diagonals will bisect each angle in the rhombus.

Example

In the given diagram, rhombus *KLMN* has angle *LKN* with a measure of 50°.

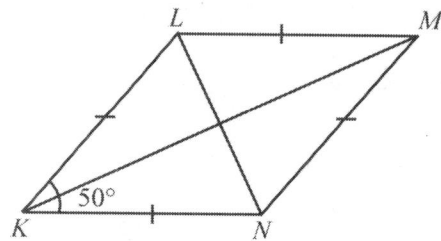

What is the measure of ∠*MLN*?

Solution

Apply the appropriate theorems about special parallelograms to the given diagram.

Step 1
Adjacent angles in a parallelogram are supplementary, so ∠*KLM* + ∠*LKN* = 180°.

The diagonals of a rhombus bisect each angle in the rhombus, so ∠*MLN* = ∠*KLN*. Therefore, ∠*KLM* = 2∠*MLN*.

Step 2
Solve for the measure of ∠*MLN*.
2∠*MLN* + ∠*LKN* = 180°
2∠*MLN* + 50° = 180°
2∠*MLN* = 130°
∠*MLN* = 65°

The measure of ∠*MLN* is 65°.

RECTANGLE

A rectangle is a parallelogram with four equal angles.

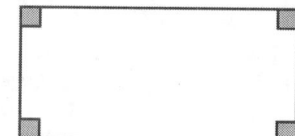

The following theorems result from this information and the definition of a parallelogram:

- The diagonals are congruent.
- Each diagonal produces two congruent triangles.
- The four triangles produced by the diagonals are congruent.

Example

The given rectangle has diagonals AD and BC that intersect at E, where $AE = 12x - 2$ and $ED = 2x + 3$.

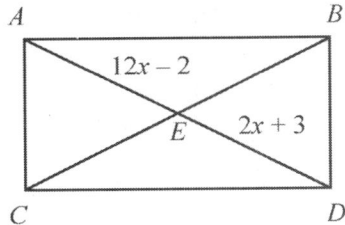

Determine the length of diagonal BC.

Solution

Apply the appropriate theorems about special parallelograms to the given diagram.

Step 1
Find the value of x.
A rectangle is a special parallelogram.
The diagonals of a parallelogram bisect each other, so $AE = ED$.
$$AE = ED$$
$$12x - 2 = 2x + 3$$
$$10x = 5$$
$$x = \frac{1}{2}$$

Step 2
Determine the length of BC.
The diagonals in a rectangle are congruent, so $BC = AD$.
From the diagram, $AD = AE + ED$. Therefore, $BC = AE + ED$.
$BC = AE + ED$
$BC = \left(12\left(\frac{1}{2}\right) - 2\right) + \left(2\left(\frac{1}{2}\right) + 3\right)$
$BC = (6 - 2) + (1 + 3)$
$BC = 4 + 4$
$BC = 8$
The length of diagonal BC is 8 units.

SQUARE

A square is a special example of a parallelogram that is both a rhombus and a rectangle. It has four equal sides and four equal angles. Since it can be classified as all of these shapes, every property that applies to one of these shapes applies to the square also. The following theorems result from this information:

- The diagonals are perpendicular to each other.
- The diagonals are congruent.
- The diagonals bisect each angle in the square.
- The diagonals produce four congruent triangles.

These images illustrate the theorems that apply to the rhombus, the rectangle, and the square.

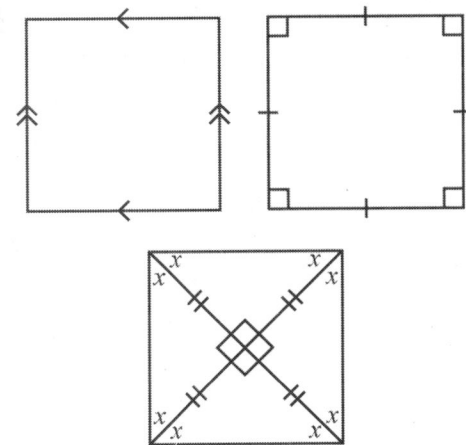

Example

In the given diagram, quadrilateral $HARE$ is a square with $HA = 2x - 1$, $AR = \frac{x}{2} + 5$, and $RE = 4x - 9$.

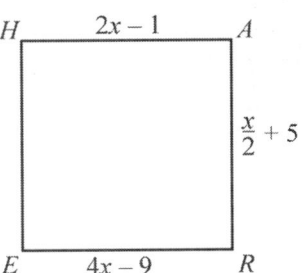

What is the length of *HE*?

Solution

Apply the appropriate theorems about special parallelograms to the given diagram.

Step 1

Find the value of *x*.

Since all sides of a square are equal, $HA = AR = RE$.

You can use any two of these sides to solve for *x*.

$HA = RE$
$2x - 1 = 4x - 9$
$-2x = -8$
$x = 4$

Step 2

Determine the length of *HE*.

The length of *HE* is equal to the length of any side of the square.

$HE = HA = AR = RE$

Substitute the value of *x* into the equation for any side of the square to find *HE*.

$HE = HA$
$HE = 2x - 1$
$HE = 2(4) - 1$
$HE = 8 - 1$
$HE = 7$

Therefore, the length of *HE* is 7 units.

EXERCISE #1—GEOMETRIC THEOREMS

Use the following information to answer the next question.

In the given figure, $AB \parallel CD \parallel EF$.

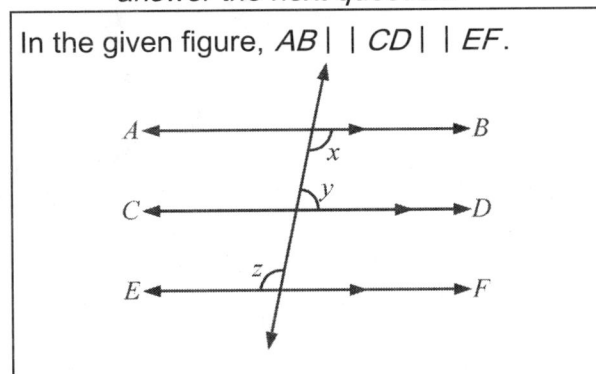

39. If $y = 63°$, what are the values of x and z?
    A. $x = 117°$, $z = 117°$
    B. $x = 120°$, $z = 118°$
    C. $x = 125°$, $z = 120°$
    D. $x = 130°$, $z = 117°$

40. Prove that same-side exterior angles on a transversal are supplementary.

Use the following information to answer the next question.

A transversal cuts through two parallel lines as shown. The measure of $\angle a$ is 30°.

41. What is the measure of $\angle d$?
    A. 30°   B. 40°
    C. 140°   D. 150°

Use the following information to answer the next question.

In the given figure, lines AB, CD, and EF are parallel.

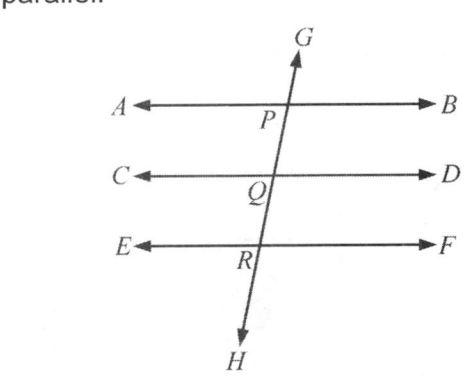

42. If $\angle QRF = 78°$, then the measure of $\angle QPB$ is _____°.

Use the following information to answer the next question.

A transversal line cuts through two parallel lines as shown. The measure of ∠a is 30°.

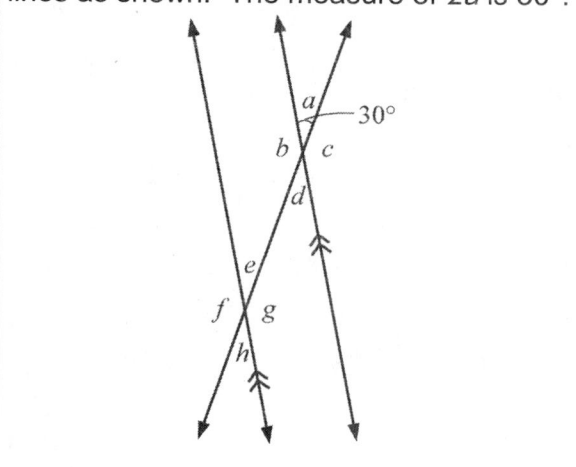

43. What is the measure of ∠f?
    A. 30° B. 50°
    C. 130° D. 150°

Use the following information to answer the next question.

A transversal line intersects two parallel lines. The measure of ∠u is 50°.

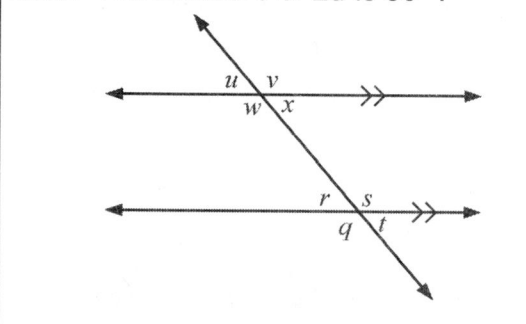

44. What is the measure of ∠r?
    A. 25° B. 50°
    C. 80° D. 130°

Use the following information to answer the next question.

The given figure shows two parallel lines, p and q, and two transversal lines, l and m.

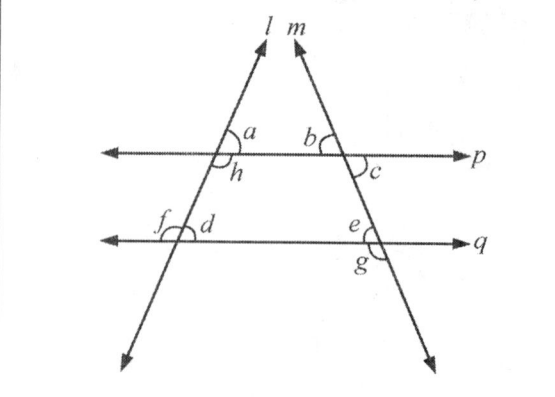

45. Which of the following pairs of angles are alternate interior angles?
    A. ∠a and ∠h
    B. ∠b and ∠c
    C. ∠d and ∠f
    D. ∠f and ∠h

Use the following information to answer the next question.

Triangle RST has the side lengths RS = 6, ST = 8, and RT = x. The possible values for x that make △RST true are given in the form $a < x < b$.

46. The value of $a + b$ is _____.

Use the following information to answer the next question.

The orthocentre of △DEF is determined and marked with the letter H, as illustrated in the given diagram.

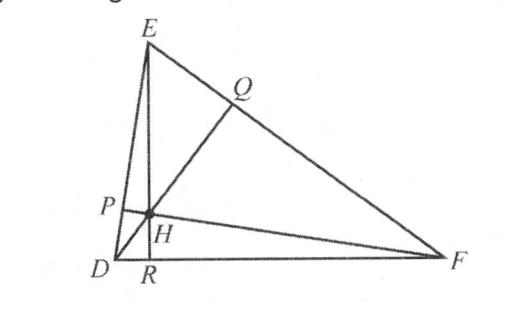

47. If ∠QEH = 53° and ∠RFH = 9°, then the measure of ∠QHF is
    A. 44°   B. 59°
    C. 62°   D. 71°

Use the following information to answer the next question.

Triangle ABC is an isosceles triangle, where ∠A = ∠B.

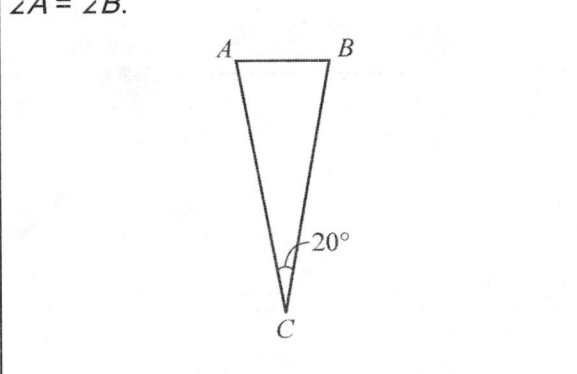

48. What is the measure of ∠A?
    A. 60°   B. 70°
    C. 80°   D. 90°

Use the following information to answer the next question.

Quadrilateral ABCD is shown.

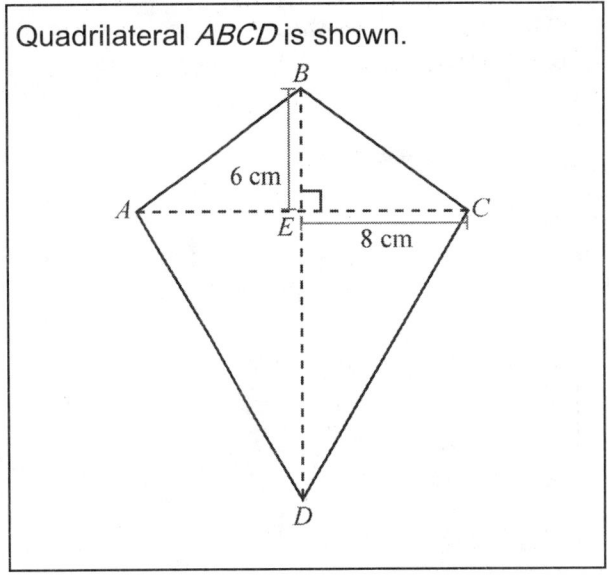

49. If ∠CAB = ∠ACB, ∠DAC = ∠DCA, and the perimeter of quadrilateral ABCD is 54 cm, then the length of side AD is _____ cm.

Use the following information to answer the next question.

Two triangles are shown.

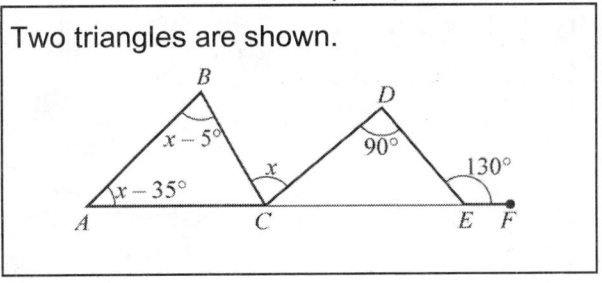

50. The value of x is _____ °.

Use the following information to answer the next question.

In triangle XYZ, the angle measurements are ∠X = 40°, ∠Y = 28°, and ∠Z = 112°.

51. If the longest side of triangle XYZ is 16 cm, what is the measure of the angle opposite this side? _____ °

Use the following information to answer the next question.

In the given triangle, $\overline{QS} \parallel \overline{TU}$, $\overline{RU} = \overline{US}$, $\overline{QS} = 7x + 6$, $\overline{TU} = 4x$, and $\overline{QR} = 8x - 4$.

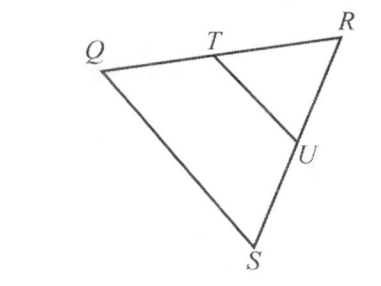

52. What is the length of $\overline{QT}$?
    A. 22 units
    B. 24 units
    C. 44 units
    D. 48 units

Use the following information to answer the next question.

Right triangle DEF with altitude EG is shown.

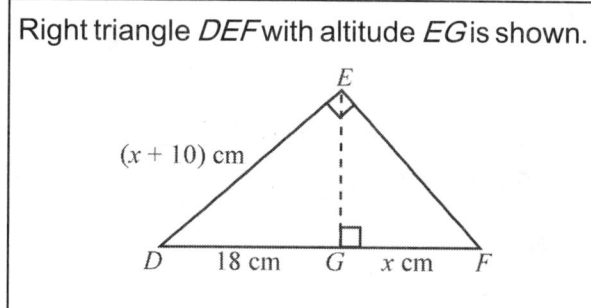

53. The length of side DE in right triangle DEF is
    A. 15.9 cm
    B. 19.8 cm
    C. 22 cm
    D. 24 cm

Use the following information to answer the next question.

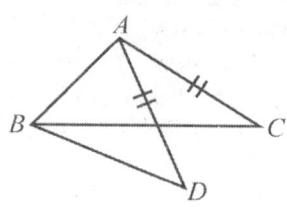

Triangles ABD and ABC are given.

54. According to the hinge theorem, BC must be longer than BD in the given diagram because
    A. $AB = AB$, $AC = AD$, and $\angle BAC > \angle BAD$
    B. $AB = BA$, $BC = DC$, and $\angle BAC > \angle BAD$
    C. $AB = CA$, $AC = CA$, and $\angle BAC < \angle BAD$
    D. $AB = BA$, $AC = AC$, and $\angle BAC < \angle BAD$

Use the following information to answer the next question.

The given diagram shows parallelogram GOAT with diagonals intersecting at S.

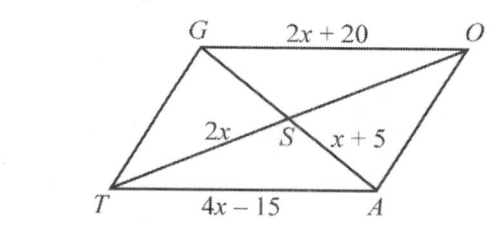

55. What is the length of ST?
    A. 22 units
    B. 35 units
    C. 42 units
    D. 55 units

Use the following information to answer the next question.

In the given parallelogram, *STAR* is a rectangle with diagonals *SA* and *TR* intersecting at *E*. It is also known that *SA* = 2x + 27 and *TR* = 11x + 45.

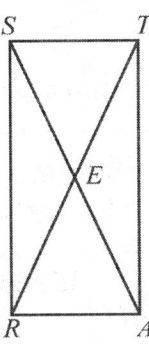

56. What is the length of *TE*?
  A. 2 units
  B. 7.5 units
  C. 11.5 units
  D. 23 units

EXERCISE #1—GEOMETRIC THEOREMS ANSWERS AND SOLUTIONS

39. A	44. B	49. 17	54. A
40. See solution	45. D	50. 80	55. B
41. A	46. 16	51. 112	56. C
42. 102	47. C	52. A	
43. D	48. C	53. D	

39. A

It is given that $y = 63°$.

Since x and y are supplementary angles (equal 180°), you can find the values of x and z.

$x + y = 180°$
$x + 63° = 180°$
$\quad x = 180° - 63°$
$\quad x = 117°$
$\quad z = 117°$

The values of x and z are both 117° because x and z are alternate angles.

40.

Step 1
Draw a diagram.

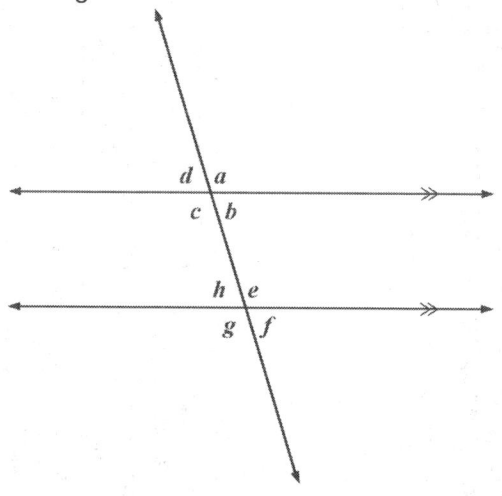

Angles d and g are same-side exterior angles. Angles a and f are also same-side exterior angles. Proving the result for one pair is enough because a similar proof can be reconstructed for the second pair of angles.

To prove that angles a and f are supplementary, prove that $\angle a + \angle f = 180°$.

Step 2
Prove the given statement.

Statement	Reason
$\angle b + \angle e = 180°$ Angles b and e are supplementary.	Supplementary interior angles. This is defined by the parallel-line postulate.
$\angle b + \angle a = 180°$ Angles b and a are supplementary.	Angles adjacent to each other on a line are supplementary.
$\angle a = \angle e$	$\angle b + \angle e = 180°$ $= \angle b + \angle a$
$\angle e + \angle f = 180°$ Angles e and f are supplementary.	Angles adjacent to each other on a line are supplementary.
$\angle a + \angle f = 180°$ Angles a and f are supplementary.	By substitution

41. A

Step 1
Determine the relationship between $\angle a$ and $\angle d$.
In the diagram shown, $\angle a$ and $\angle d$ are vertically opposite angles.

Step 2
Determine the measure of $\angle d$.
Vertically opposite angles have the same measure. Because $\angle a$ and $\angle d$ are opposite angles, $\angle a = \angle d$. If $\angle a = 30°$, then $\angle d = 30°$.
The measure of $\angle d$ is 30°.

42. 102

Step 1
Determine the relationship between the given angle and the unknown angle.
Both $\angle QRF$ and $\angle QPB$ are same-side interior angles.

Step 2
Calculate the value of ∠QPB by using the appropriate relationship.
Same-side interior angles are supplementary.
∠QRF + ∠QPB = 180°
78° + ∠QPB = 180°
∠QPB = 102°

43. D

Step 1
Determine the relationship between the given angle and the unknown angle.
Angles a and f are same-side exterior angles.

Step 2
Determine the measure of ∠f using the appropriate relationship.
Same-side exterior angles are supplementary.
∠a + ∠f = 180°
30° + ∠f = 180°
∠f = 150°

44. B

Step 1
Determine the relationship between the given angle and the unknown angle.
Angles u and r are corresponding angles.

Step 2
Determine the measure of ∠r using the appropriate relationship.
Since the angles are corresponding angles, ∠u = ∠r. Therefore, ∠r = 50°.

45. D

Alternate interior angles are angles located between two parallel lines and on opposite sides of the transversal.

Of the choices given, only ∠f and ∠h are alternate interior angles.

46. 16

The triangle inequality theorem states that the length of one side of any triangle is less than the sum of the other two sides. Solve for possible values of x for each of the three sides.

Step 1
Use the first side.
Substitute 6 for RS, 8 for ST, and x for RT in the formula RS + ST > RT.
RS + ST > RT
6 + 8 > x
14 > x

Step 2
Use the second side.
Substitute 6 for RS, 8 for ST, and x for RT in the formula ST + RT > RS.
ST + RT > RS
8 + x > 6
x > −2
This inequality results in x > −2. Since negative values of measurement are not possible, the value of x will always be greater than −2. This means that for this particular side, any positive value of x would be valid to produce a triangle. Therefore, this inequality must be disregarded.

Step 3
Use the third side.
Substitute 6 for RS, 8 for ST, and x for RT in the formula RS + RT > ST.
RS + RT > ST
6 + x > 8
x > 2

Step 4
Identify all possible values for x.
The values of x that satisfy all three inequalities are 2 < x < 14.
Therefore, the possible values of x are 2 < x < 14.

Step 5
Determine the value of $a + b$.
The possible values of x are 2 < x < 14. Therefore, a = 2 and b = 14.
$a + b$
= 2 + 14
= 16

47. C

The altitudes of a triangle are concurrent at a point called the orthocentre. Therefore, RE, PF, and QD are the altitudes of △DEF.

Step 1
Determine the measure of ∠RHF.
Since RE is an altitude of △DEF, the measure of ∠FRH is 90°.
The sum of the measures of the interior angles of a triangle is equal to 180°. Therefore,
∠RHF + ∠RFH + ∠FRH = 180°.
The measure of ∠RHF can be determined as follows:
∠RHF + ∠RFH + ∠FRH = 180°
Substitute 9° for ∠RFH and 90° for ∠FRH.
∠RHF + 9° + 90° = 180°
∠RHF + 99° = 180°
∠RHF = 81°

Step 2

Determine the measure of ∠QHE.

Since QD is an altitude of △DEF, the measure of ∠EQH is 90°. The sum of the measures of the interior angles of a triangle is 180°.

The measure of ∠QHE can therefore be determined as follows:

∠QHE + ∠EQH + ∠QEH = 180°

Substitute 90° for ∠EQH and 53° for ∠QEH.

∠QHE + 90° + 53° = 180°
∠QHE + 143° = 180°
∠QHE = 37°

Step 3

Determine the measure of ∠QHF.

Recall that a straight line has a measure of 180°. Therefore, ∠QHE + ∠QHF + ∠RHF = 180°.

The measure of ∠QHF can be determined as follows:

∠QHE + ∠QHF + ∠RHF = 180°

Substitute 37° for ∠QHE and 81° for ∠RHF.

37° + ∠QHF + 81° = 180°
∠QHF + 118° = 180°
∠QHF = 62°

The measure of ∠QHF is 62°.

48. C

Step 1

Determine which angle measures are given.
∠C = 20°

Step 2

Substitute the given values into the angle property for a triangle, and simplify.

Since this is an isosceles triangle, ∠A and ∠B have the same measure.

Modify the property.

∠A + ∠B + ∠C = 180°
∠A + ∠A + ∠C = 180°
2∠A + ∠C = 180°
2∠A + 20° = 180°
2∠A + 20° − 20° = 180° − 20°
$\frac{2∠A}{2} = \frac{160°}{2}$
∠A = 80°

Therefore, ∠A and ∠B each have a measure of 80°.

49. 17

Step 1

Determine the length of side BC in triangle BEC by applying the Pythagorean theorem.

$(BE)^2 + (CE)^2 = (BC)^2$

Substitute 6 for BE and 8 for CE, and then solve for BC.

$6^2 + 8^2 = (BC)^2$
$36 + 64 = (BC)^2$
$100 = (BC)^2$
$\sqrt{100} = BC$
$10 = BC$

The length of side BC is 10 cm.

Step 2

Determine the length of side AD.

Since ∠CAB = ∠ACB, triangle ABC is an isosceles triangle. It then follows, by the corollary of the isosceles triangle theorem, that AB = BC.

Similarly, since ∠DAC = ∠DCA, triangle ADC is an isosceles triangle. It then follows, by the corollary of the isosceles triangle theorem, that AD = CD.

In order to determine the length of side AD, let AD = CD = x. Then, using the fact that the perimeter of quadrilateral ABCD is 54 cm, solve for x.

AB + BC + CD + AD = 54

Substitute 10 for both AB and BC, and x for both CD and for AD.

10 + 10 + x + x = 54
20 + 2x = 54
2x = 34
x = 17

The length of side AD is 17 cm.

50. 80

The exterior angle theorem states that the measure of an exterior angle of a triangle is equal to the sum of the measures of the two remote interior angles of the triangle.

Step 1

Determine the measure of ∠ECD by applying the exterior angle theorem.

When the exterior angle theorem is applied to triangle ECD, the resulting equation is
∠FED = ∠ECD + ∠CDE.

The measure of ∠ECD can be determined as follows:
∠FED = ∠ECD + ∠CDE

Substitute 130° for ∠FED and 90° for ∠CDE.

130° = ∠ECD + 90°
130° − 90° = ∠ECD
40° = ∠ECD

The measure of ∠ECD is 40°.

Step 2
Determine an expression for the measure of ∠BCD.
Since ∠BCE = ∠BCD + ∠ECD, it follows that, by substitution, the measure of ∠BCE can be expressed as ∠BCE = $x + 40°$.

Step 3
Apply the exterior angle theorem to triangle ABC.
When the exterior angle theorem is applied to triangle ABC, the resulting equation is ∠BCE = ∠CAB + ∠ABC. Substituting $x + 40°$ for ∠BCE, $x - 35°$ for ∠CAB, and $x - 5°$ for ∠ABC, the equation ∠BCE = ∠CAB + ∠ABC becomes $x + 40° = x - 35° + x - 5°$.

Step 4
Solve for x in the equation
$x + 40° = x - 35° + x - 5°$.
$x + 40° = x - 35° + x - 5°$
$x + 40 = 2x - 40°$
$40° + 40° = 2x - x$
$80° = x$

The value of x is $80°$.

51. 112
In a triangle, the largest angle is opposite the longest side.

In the given triangle, the largest angle is ∠Z = 112°.

Therefore, the measure of the angle opposite the side with a length of 16 cm is 112°.

52. A
Step 1
Find the value of x.
Given that $\overline{QS} \parallel \overline{TU}$ and $\overline{RU} = \overline{US}$, you can conclude that $\overline{TU}$ joins the midpoints of $\overline{QR}$ and $\overline{RS}$.

Therefore, $\overline{TU} = \frac{1}{2}(\overline{QS})$.

$\overline{TU} = \frac{1}{2}(\overline{QS})$
$4x = \frac{1}{2}(7x + 6)$
$8x = 7x + 6$
$x = 6$

Step 2
Determine the length of $\overline{QT}$.
Since $\overline{TU}$ joins the midpoints of $\overline{QR}$ and $\overline{RS}$,
$\overline{QT} = \frac{1}{2}\overline{QR}$.

$\overline{QT} = \frac{1}{2}\overline{QR}$
$\overline{QT} = \frac{1}{2}(8x - 4)$
$\overline{QT} = \frac{1}{2}(8(6) - 4)$
$\overline{QT} = \frac{1}{2}(44)$
$\overline{QT} = 22$

The length of $\overline{QT}$ is 22 units.

53. D
Step 1
Determine which proportional rule to use.
Notice that the length of the hypotenuse of right triangle DEF, DF, is represented by $(x + 18)$ cm. The leg rule can be used to determine the length of side DE since the length of the whole hypotenuse, a leg of the triangle, and a section of the hypotenuse adjacent to the leg are represented (the leg, DE, is the mean proportional). Thus, $\frac{DF}{DE} = \frac{DE}{DG}$.

Step 2
Substitute the appropriate values into the proportion.
Substitute $18 + x$ for DF, $x + 10$ for DE, and 18 for DG.

$\frac{18 + x}{x + 10} = \frac{x + 10}{18}$

Cross-multiply.
$(18 + x)(18) = (x + 10)(x + 10)$
$324 + 18x = x^2 + 10x + 10x + 100$
$324 + 18x = x^2 + 20x + 100$
$0 = x^2 + 2x - 224$

Step 3
Solve for x.

Factor the trinomial $x^2 + 2x - 224$.
$0 = (x + 16)(x - 14)$
Set each factor equal to zero.
$x + 16 = 0$ or $x - 14 = 0$
$x = -16$ $x = 14$

If $x = -16$, the length of side DE, $(x + 10)$ cm, would be $-16 + 10 = -6$ cm, which is not possible. Thus, the value of x must be 14. It follows that the length of side DE in right triangle DEF is $14 + 10 = 24$ cm.

54. A

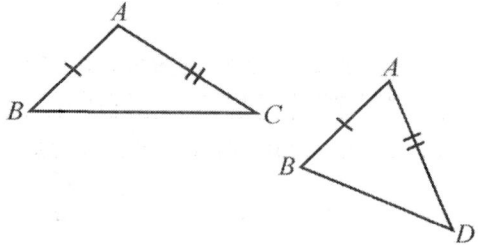

In triangles ABD and ABC it is clear that AB = AB and that AC = AD. According to the hinge theorem, if ∠BAC is larger than ∠BAD, then BC > BD.

55. B

Step 1
Find the value of x.
Since the given quadrilateral is a parallelogram, opposite sides are equal in length. Therefore, GO = TA.
$$GO = TA$$
$$2x + 20 = 4x - 15$$
$$-2x = -35$$
$$x = \frac{35}{2}$$

Step 2
Substitute the value of x into the equation given for the length of ST.
$$ST = 2x$$
$$ST = 2\left(\frac{35}{2}\right)$$
$$ST = 35$$
The length of ST is 35 units.

56. C

Step 1
Find the value of x.
The diagonals in a rectangle are congruent, so SA = TR.
$$SA = TR$$
$$2x + 27 = 11x + 45$$
$$-9x = 18$$
$$x = -2$$

Step 2
Determine the length of TE.
Since the diagonals of a parallelogram bisect each other, $TE = \frac{1}{2}TR$.
$$TE = \frac{1}{2}TR$$
$$TE = \frac{1}{2}(11x + 45)$$
$$TE = \frac{1}{2}(11(-2) + 45)$$
$$TE = \frac{1}{2}(-22 + 45)$$
$$TE = \frac{1}{2}(23)$$
$$TE = 11.5$$
The length of TE is 11.5 units.

EXERCISE #2—GEOMETRIC THEOREMS

Use the following information to answer the next question.

The given figure shows a pair of parallel lines L and M that are intersected by a transversal P. The measure of angle x is 78°.

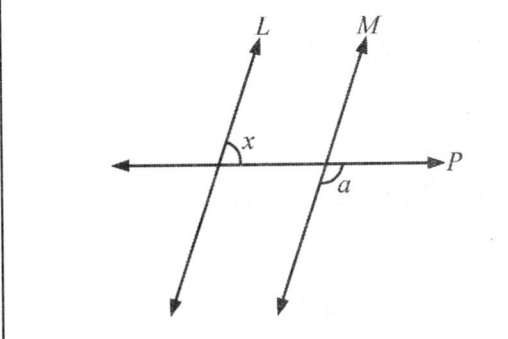

57. What is the measure of angle a in the given figure?
    A. 78° B. 90°
    C. 102° D. 114°

Use the following information to answer the next question.

A transversal cuts through two parallel lines, as shown.

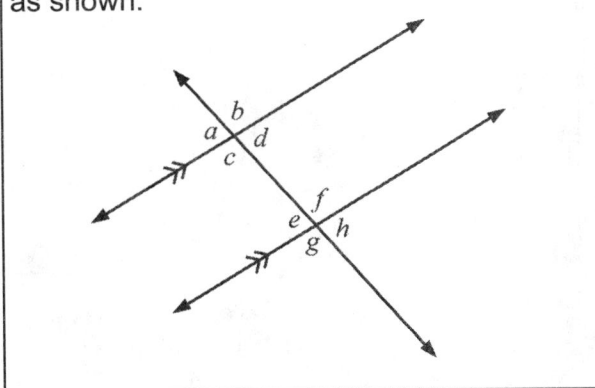

58. If ∠b = 100° and ∠h = 80°, what is the measure of ∠c?
    A. 80° B. 90°
    C. 100° D. 110°

Use the following information to answer the next question.

The given diagram shows four lines.

59. What is the measure of ∠e?
    A. 60° B. 80°
    C. 120° D. 180°

Use the following information to answer the next question.

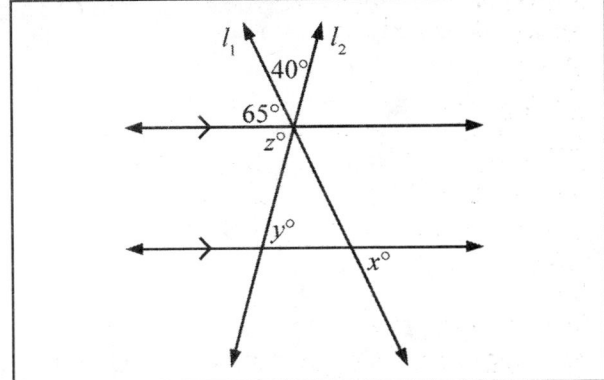

60. What is the value of x?
    A. 35 B. 40
    C. 50 D. 65

Use the following information to answer the next question.

In the given figure, lines *AB* and *CD* are parallel. Lines *EG* and *FH* are also parallel and intersect lines *AB* and *CD* at points *P*, *Q*, *R*, and *S*.

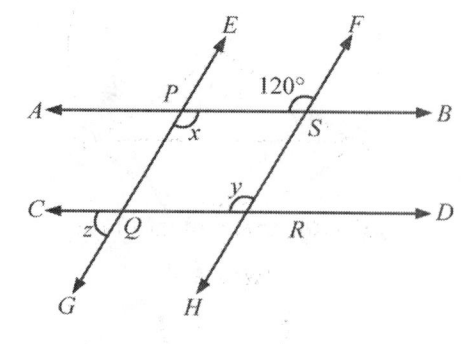

61. What is the measure of ∠*y*?
   A. 60°   B. 75°
   C. 110° D. 120°

Use the following information to answer the next question.

Two parallel horizontal lines are intersected by three lines to create angles.

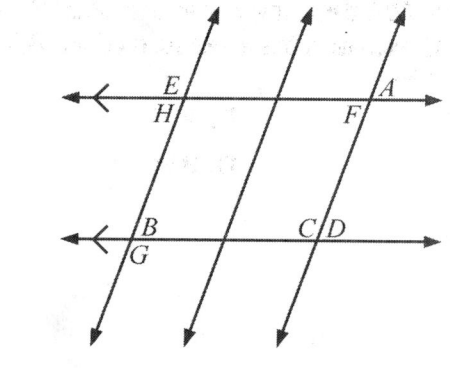

62. Which of the following pairs of angles are vertically opposite to each other?
   A. ∠*A* and ∠*F*
   B. ∠*C* and ∠*D*
   C. ∠*B* and ∠*G*
   D. ∠*H* and ∠*E*

63. Which of the following side-length measurements will be able to form a triangle?

   A. KL = 3
      LM = 9
      MK = 5

   B. NO = 14
      OP = 7
      PN = 6

   C. RS = 5
      ST = 9
      TR = 7

   D. XY = 2
      YZ = 15
      ZX = 21

Use the following information to answer the next question.

The given diagram shows the perpendicular bisector of each side of △*MNP*. The circumcircle for △*MNP*, with center *O*, is also shown.

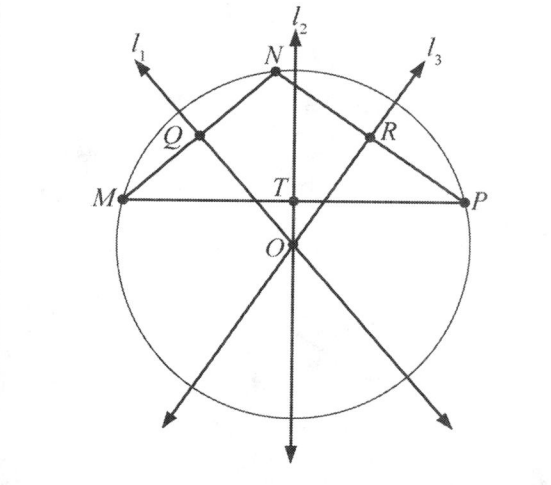

64. If the length of $\overline{MP}$ is 126 cm and the length of $\overline{TO}$ is 16 cm, then the radius of the circumcircle is _____ cm.

Use the following information to answer the next question.

A triangle is given.

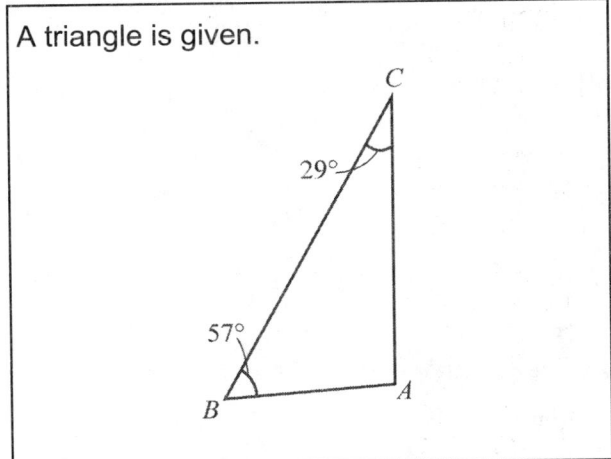

65. What is the measure of ∠A?
 A. 84°
 B. 94°
 C. 104°
 D. 114°

Use the following information to answer the next question.

Two different geometrical figures are given.

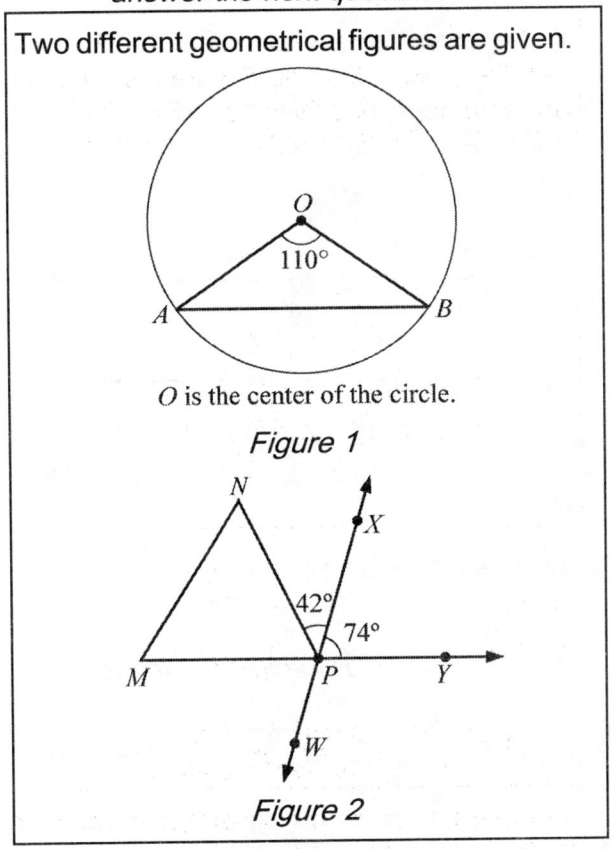

O is the center of the circle.
Figure 1

Figure 2

66. If MP = NP, then the measure of ∠PNM in figure 2 exceeds the measure of ∠OAB in figure 1 by
 A. 23°
 B. 29°
 C. 32°
 D. 36°

Use the following information to answer the next question.

Triangle RST is given.

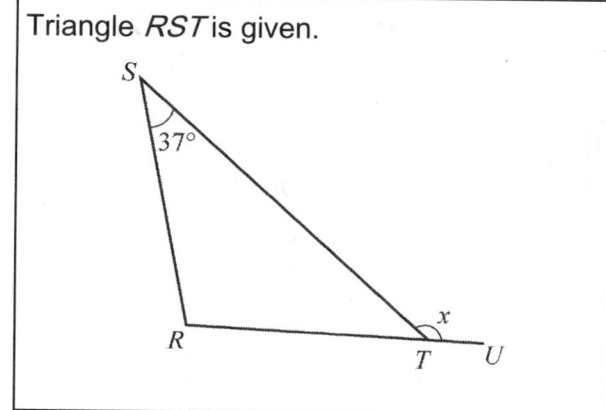

67. Which of the following measures is **not** a possible measure for ∠x?
    A. 28°
    B. 76°
    C. 134°
    D. 171°

Use the following information to answer the next question.

In △ABC the side lengths are AC = 1.9 cm, CB = 2.1 cm, and AB = 2.8 cm.

68. If the largest angle in this triangle is 90°, what is the measure of the side opposite to this angle? _____ cm

Use the following information to answer the next question.

In triangle ACE, $\overline{BD} = x + 2$, $\overline{CD} = \frac{x}{2} + 1$, and $\overline{DE} = 3x - 4$.

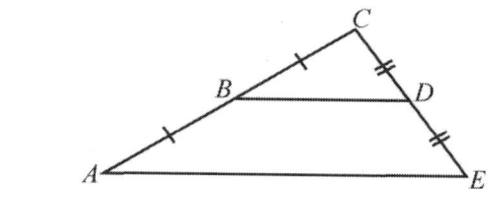

69. What is the length of $\overline{AE}$?
    A. 2 units
    B. 4 units
    C. 6 units
    D. 8 units

Use the following information to answer the next question.

Right triangle RST with altitude SU is shown.

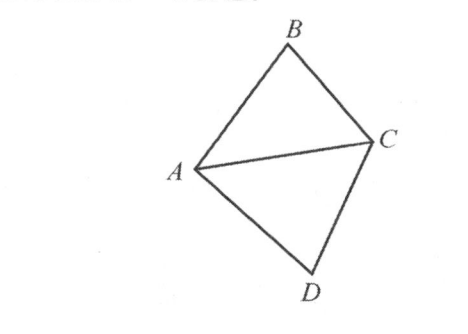

70. The length of side ST in right triangle RST is _____ cm.

Use the following information to answer the next question.

In the given diagram, AB = AC, AB = AD, and ∠CAD > ∠CAB.

71. According to the hinge theorem, which of the following inequalities is true with respect to the given triangles?
    A. CD < CB
    B. CD > CB
    C. AC < CD
    D. AC < CB

Use the following information to answer the next question.

Quadrilateral WXYZ is a parallelogram with diagonals WY and XZ intersecting at V. The lengths of WY and XZ respectively are 44 cm and 32 cm.

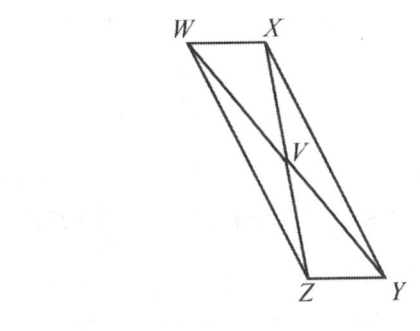

72. What is the value of ZV + YV?
    A. 32 cm
    B. 38 cm
    C. 44 cm
    D. 48 cm

Use the following information to answer the next question.

The area of the shaded part of this square is 5 cm².

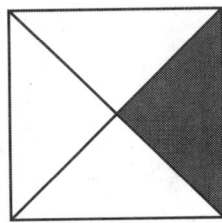

73. What is the area of the entire square?
    A. 15 cm²
    B. 20 cm²
    C. 25 cm²
    D. 30 cm²

Copyright Protected

EXERCISE #2—GEOMETRIC THEOREMS ANSWERS AND SOLUTIONS

57. C	62. A	67. A	72. B
58. C	63. C	68. 2.8	73. B
59. C	64. 65	69. D	
60. D	65. B	70. 15	
61. D	66. A	71. B	

57. C

Insert y as shown. This will help determine the value of a.

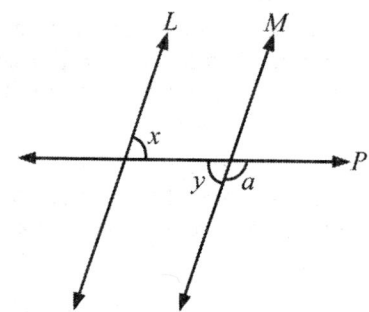

x and y are alternate interior angles, so $x = y$.
$x = 78°$
$y = 78°$

Also, y and a form a straight line which means they are supplementary angles. Supplementary angles have a sum of 180°.
$y + a = 180°$
$78° + a = 180°$
$a = 180° - 78°$
$a = 102°$

The measure of a is 102°.

58. C

Step 1
Determine the relationship between $\angle b$ and $\angle c$.
In the diagram shown, $\angle b$ and $\angle c$ are vertically opposite angles.

Step 2
Determine the measure of $\angle c$.
Vertically opposite angles have the same measure. Because $\angle b$ and $\angle c$ are opposite angles, $\angle b = \angle c$. If $\angle b = 100°$, then $\angle c = 100°$.
The measure of $\angle c$ is 100°.

59. C

Alternate interior angles are angles located between two parallel lines and on opposite sides of the transversal.

Step 1
Identify the parallel lines and the transversal.
Lines l_1 and l_2 are parallel, since they contain parallel marker signs and never intersect. Line l_3 intersects the two parallel lines, so it is a transversal line.
Lines l_3 and l_4 are also parallel, since they contain parallel marker signs and never intersect. Line l_1 intersects the two parallel lines, so it is a transversal line.

Step 2
Identify the alternate interior angles.
Angles a and c are alternate interior angles.
Angles c and e are also alternate interior angles.

Step 3
Determine the measure of $\angle e$.
Alternate interior angles are congruent.
$\angle a = 120°$
$\angle a = \angle c$
$\angle c = \angle e$
$\angle a = \angle e$
$\angle e = 120°$
The measure of $\angle e$ is 120°.

60. D

Step 1
Determine the relationship between a given angle and the unknown angle.
In the diagram, there are two transversals and two given angles. For l_1, $x°$ and 65° are alternate exterior angles.

Step 2
Calculate the value of x using the appropriate relationship.
Alternate exterior angles are equal.
$x° = 65°$
$x = 65$

61. D

Step 1
Determine the relationship between the given angle and the unknown angle.
Angle FSP and angle y are corresponding angles.

Exercise #2 Answers and Solutions 128 Castle Rock Research

Step 2
Determine the measure of ∠y by using the appropriate relationship.
Since the angles are corresponding angles, ∠FSP = ∠y.
Since ∠FSP equals 120°, ∠y = 120°.

62. A

Vertically opposite angles are formed when two intersecting lines form angles that are opposite to each other.

The only pair of angles that are vertically opposite in the given diagram are ∠A and ∠F.

63. C

The triangle inequality theorem states that the length of one side of any triangle is less than the sum of the other two sides.

Step 1
Apply the triangle inequality theorem to determine if the measurements in alternative A can form a triangle.
KL = 3
LM = 9
MK = 5
LM < KL + MK
 9 < 3 + 5
 9 ≮ 8
Since 9 ≮ 8, these measurements will not be able to form a triangle.

Step 2
Apply the triangle inequality theorem to determine if the measurements in alternative B can form a triangle.
NO = 14
OP = 7
PN = 6
NO < OP + PN
 14 < 7 + 6
 14 ≮ 13
Since 14 ≮ 13, these measurements will not be able to form a triangle.

Step 3
Apply the triangle inequality theorem to determine if the measurements in alternative C can form a triangle.
RS = 5
ST = 9
TR = 7
RS < ST + TR
 5 < 9 + 7
 5 < 16
ST < RS + TR
 9 < 5 + 7
 9 < 12
TR < RS + ST
 7 < 5 + 9
 7 < 14
Since the triangle inequality theorem is true for all possible combinations of side lengths, the measurements in alternative C will be able to form a triangle.

Step 4
Apply the triangle inequality theorem to determine if the measurements in alternative D can form a triangle.
XY = 2
YZ = 15
ZX = 21
ZX < YZ + XY
 21 < 15 + 2
 21 ≮ 17
Since 21 ≮ 17, these measurements will not be able to form a triangle.

64. 65

Step 1
Determine the measure of ∠PTO.
Since l_2 is the perpendicular bisector of $\overline{MP}$, it follows that the measure of ∠PTO is 90°.

Step 2
Determine the length of $\overline{PT}$.
Since l_2 is the perpendicular bisector of $\overline{MP}$ and the length of $\overline{MP}$ is 126 cm, it follows that the length of $\overline{PT}$ is 126 ÷ 2 = 63 cm.

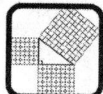

Step 3
Determine the radius of the circumcircle.
Since $\overline{OP}$ is one of the radii of the circumcircle, the radius of the circumcircle can be determined by calculating the length of $\overline{OP}$. This can be done by applying the Pythagorean theorem with respect to $\triangle PTO$.
$(\overline{PT})^2 + (\overline{TO})^2 = (\overline{OP})^2$
Substitute 63 for $\overline{PT}$ and 16 for $\overline{TO}$, and then solve for $\overline{OP}$.
$(63)^2 + (16)^2 = (\overline{OP})^2$
$3{,}969 + 256 = (\overline{OP})^2$
$4{,}225 = (\overline{OP})^2$
$\sqrt{4{,}225} = \overline{OP}$
$65 = \overline{OP}$
The radius of the circumcircle is 65 cm.

65. B
Step 1
Determine what angle measures are given.
In the given triangle, $\angle B = 57°$ and $\angle C = 29°$.

Step 2
Substitute the given values into the formula for the angle property for a triangle, and simplify.
$\angle A + \angle B + \angle C = 180°$
$\angle A + 57° + 29° = 180°$
$\angle A + 86° = 180°$
$\angle A + 86° - 86° = 180° - 86°$
$\angle A = 94°$
The measure of $\angle A = 94°$.

66. A
Recall that the isosceles triangle theorem states that if two sides of a triangle are congruent, then the angles opposite to them are congruent.

Step 1
Determine the measure of $\angle OAB$ in figure 1.
Since OA and OB are each a radius of the given circle, their respective lengths must be equal. Therefore, $\triangle AOB$ is an isosceles triangle. It follows, by the isosceles triangle theorem, that $\angle OAB = \angle OBA$.
In order to determine the measure of $\angle OAB$, let $\angle OAB = \angle OBA = x$ and then apply the triangle angle sum theorem.
$\angle OAB + \angle AOB + \angle OBA = 180°$
Substitute 110° for $\angle AOB$ and x for both $\angle OAB$ and for $\angle OBA$.
$x + 110° + x = 180°$
$2x + 110° = 180°$
$2x = 70°$
$x = 35°$
The measure of $\angle OAB$ is 35°.

Step 2
Determine the measure of $\angle NPY$.
$\angle NPY = \angle NPX + \angle YPX$
Substitute 42° for $\angle NPX$ and 74° for $\angle YPX$.
$\angle NPY = 42° + 74°$
$\angle NPY = 116°$
The measure of $\angle NPY$ is 116°.

Step 3
Determine the measure of $\angle PNM$.
Since $MP = NP$, $\triangle MNP$ is an isosceles triangle. It follows, by the isosceles triangle theorem, that $\angle PNM = \angle PMN$. Also, by the exterior angle theorem, $\angle YPN = \angle PNM + \angle PMN$.
In order to determine the measure of $\angle PNM$, let $\angle PNM = \angle PMN = x$ and then solve for x.
$\angle YPN = \angle PNM + \angle PMN$
Substitute 116° for $\angle YPN$ and x for both $\angle PNM$ and for $\angle PMN$.
$116° = x + x$
$116° = 2x$
$58° = x$
The measure of $\angle PNM$ is 58°.

Step 4
Determine the angle measurement difference between $\angle PNM$ and $\angle OAB$.
$58° - 35° = 23°$
The measure of $\angle PNM$ exceeds the measure of $\angle OAB$ by 23°.

67. A
The exterior angle theorem states that an exterior angle of a triangle is equal to the sum of the remote (opposite) interior angles, so $\angle x = \angle R + \angle S$. From this, you can conclude that the exterior angle is greater than both opposite interior angles, so $\angle x > \angle R$ and $\angle x > \angle S$. In the diagram, $\angle R$ is not given, so you can use the value of $\angle S$.
$\angle x > \angle S$
$\angle x > 37°$
Of the given alternatives, the only value that is not possible for $\angle x$ is 28° since it is the only value that is less than 37°.

68. 2.8
In a triangle, the longest side is opposite the largest angle. According to the information given about this triangle, the longest side is 2.8 cm. Therefore, the measure of the side opposite the 90° angle in $\triangle ABC$ is 2.8 cm.

69. D

Step 1
Find the value of x.
From the diagram, $\overline{CD} = \overline{DE}$.
$$\overline{CD} = \overline{DE}$$
$$\frac{x}{2} + 1 = 3x - 4$$
$$-\frac{5x}{2} = -5$$
$$5x = 10$$
$$x = 2$$

Step 2
Determine the length of $\overline{AE}$.
Since $\overline{BD}$ joins the midpoints of $\overline{AC}$ and $\overline{CE}$, the triangle mid-segment theorem can be applied.
The triangle mid-segment theorem states that $\overline{BD} = \frac{1}{2}(\overline{AE})$. This equation can be modified to solve for $\overline{AE}$.
$$\frac{1}{2}(\overline{AE}) = \overline{BD}$$
$$\overline{AE} = 2(\overline{BD})$$
$$\overline{AE} = 2(x + 2)$$
$$\overline{AE} = 2(2 + 2)$$
$$\overline{AE} = 2(4)$$
$$\overline{AE} = 8$$
The length of $\overline{AE}$ is 8 units.

70. 15

Step 1
Determine which proportional rule to use.
Two sections of the hypotenuse and the leg from the same side of the triangle as one of the sections are involved.
Since the two sections added together give the measure of the hypotenuse, the leg rule can be used.

Step 2
Determine the length of the hypotenuse.
$RT = RU + UT$
$RT = 16 + 9$
$RT = 25$

Step 3
Substitute the appropriate values into the proportion.
Since the leg rule is being used, the length of the leg is the mean proportional.
$$\frac{RT}{ST} = \frac{ST}{UT}$$
$$\frac{25}{ST} = \frac{ST}{9}$$
$$225 = ST^2$$
$$\sqrt{225} = ST$$
$$15 = ST$$

The length of ST is 15 cm.

71. B

To apply the hinge theorem, look for two triangles, each of which has two sides congruent to two sides in the other triangle. In this case, the two triangles are $\triangle CAD$ and $\triangle CAB$.

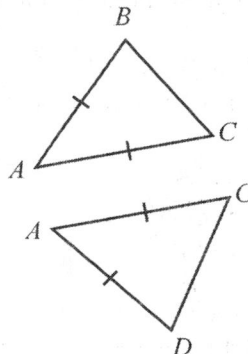

Applying the hinge theorem to the sides opposite the angles, since $AB = AC$, $AB = AD$, and $\angle CAD > \angle CAB$, it follows that $CD > CB$.

72. B

Step 1
Determine the value of ZV.
Since the diagonals of a parallelogram bisect each other, $ZV = \frac{1}{2}XZ$. Substitute 32 for XZ, and solve.
$$ZV = \frac{1}{2}(32)$$
$$ZV = \frac{32}{2}$$
$$ZV = 16 \text{ cm}$$

Step 2
Determine the value of YV.
Since the diagonals of a parallelogram bisect each other, $YV = \frac{1}{2}WY$. Substitute 44 for WY, and solve.
$$YV = \frac{1}{2}(44)$$
$$YV = \frac{44}{2}$$
$$YV = 22 \text{ cm}$$

Step 3
Determine the value of $ZV + YV$. Substitute 16 for ZV and 22 for YV.
$ZV + YV$
$= 16 + 22$
$= 38$
The value of $ZV + YV$ is 38 cm.

73. B

Use the fact that the diagonals of a square produce four congruent triangles.

Congruent triangles have equal sides and thus have equal areas.

Since there are four congruent triangles covering the square, its area is four times the area of the shaded triangle.

$A_{square} = 4 \times 5$

$A_{square} = 20 \text{ cm}^2$

The area of the entire square is 20 cm².

Geometric Constructions

GEOMETRIC CONSTRUCTIONS

Table of Correlations

Standard		Concepts	Exercise #1	Exercise #2
Unit 1.4	Make geometric constructions.			
G-CO.12	Make formal geometric constructions with a variety of tools and methods (compass and straightedge, string, reflective devices, paper folding, dynamic geometric software, etc.). Copying a segment; copying an angle; bisecting a segment; bisecting an angle; constructing perpendicular lines, including the perpendicular bisector of a line segment; and constructing a line parallel to a given line through a point not on the line.	Constructing Angle Bisectors	74	81
		Constructing Perpendicular Bisectors	75	82
		Drawing a Parallel Line Using a Straightedge and Compass	76	83
		Constructing a Perpendicular Line Through a Point Using a Straightedge and Compass	77	86
		Constructing Congruent Line Segments with a Compass and a Straightedge	79	84
		Constructing Congruent Angles with a Compass and a Straightedge	78	85
G-CO.13	Construct an equilateral triangle, a square, and a regular hexagon inscribed in a circle.	Constructing Equilateral Triangles with a Straightedge and Compass	80	87

G-CO.12 Make formal geometric constructions with a variety of tools and methods (compass and straightedge, string, reflective devices, paper folding, dynamic geometric software, etc.). Copying a segment; copying an angle; bisecting a segment; bisecting an angle; constructing perpendicular lines, including the perpendicular bisector of a line segment; and constructing a line parallel to a given line through a point not on the line.

CONSTRUCTING ANGLE BISECTORS

When an angle is divided into two equal parts by a line, the angle has been **bisected**. *Bi* means two, and *sect* means cut. The line that cuts an angle into two equal parts is called the **angle bisector**. The angles are marked with the same symbol to indicate that they are equal in measure.

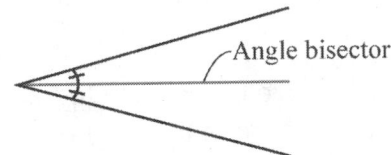

To bisect the angle using a compass and ruler, follow these steps:

1. Draw and label the angle if it is not already provided.
2. Draw an arc to intersect the two line segments of the angle.
3. From both points of intersection between the arc and the arms of the angle, draw two more intersecting arcs.
4. Using a ruler, draw a line from the angle to this intersection point.

Example
Angle *NOP* is 128°.

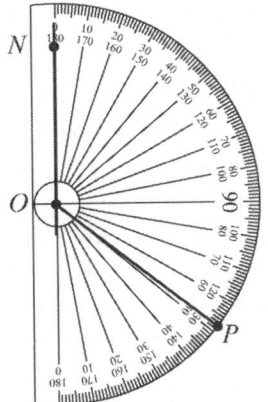

Using a compass and a straightedge, draw the angle bisector of angle *NOP*.

Solution

Step 1
Draw an arc to intersect the two line segments of the angle.

Place the point of the compass on point *O*. Draw an arc intersecting line segment *NO* and line segment *OP*. Label the points of intersection as *R* and *S*.

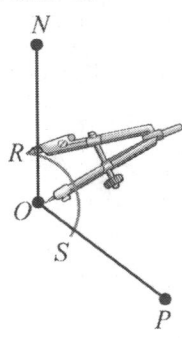

Step 3
Draw two more intersecting arcs from points *R* and *S*.

Place the point of the compass on point *R*. Draw an arc toward the middle of the angle. Repeat the process at point *S*, keeping the size of the compass opening the same. Label the point of intersection as *T*.

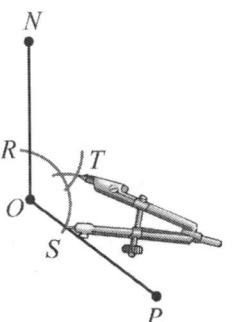

Step 4

Draw a line from the angle to the intersection point.

Use a straight edge to connect point *O* to point *T*.

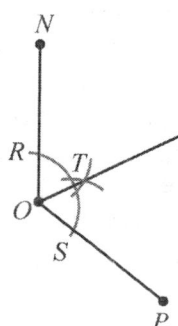

To verify that the angles are equal, use a protractor to measure the two new angles.

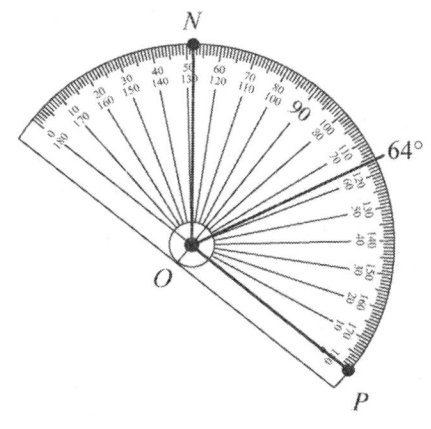

To draw an angle bisector using a protractor, follow these steps:

1. Draw and label the angle if it is not already provided.
2. Calculate the size of the bisected angle.
3. Use a protractor to mark this angle.
4. Draw the angle bisector.

Example

Angle *ABC* is 100°.

Using a protractor, draw angle *ABC* and the angle bisector.

Solution

Step 1

Draw and label the angle.

Draw line segment *AB*. Use a protractor to add line segment *BC* at 100°.

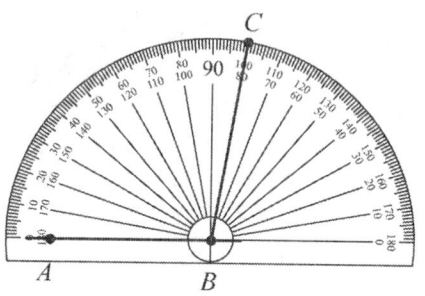

Step 2

Calculate the size of the bisected angle.

Divide the measure of the angle by 2.

100 ÷ 2 = 50

Step 3

Use a protractor to mark this angle.

Place the zero line on one of the line segments. Follow the outside numbers to 50. Plot point *U* at 50°.

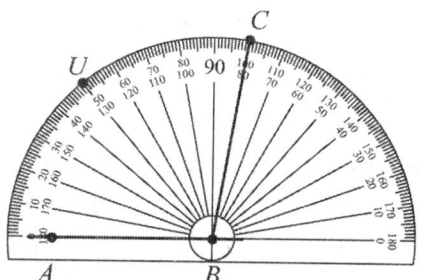

Geometric Constructions

Step 4
Draw the angle bisector.
Use a straight edge to connect point *B* to point *U*.

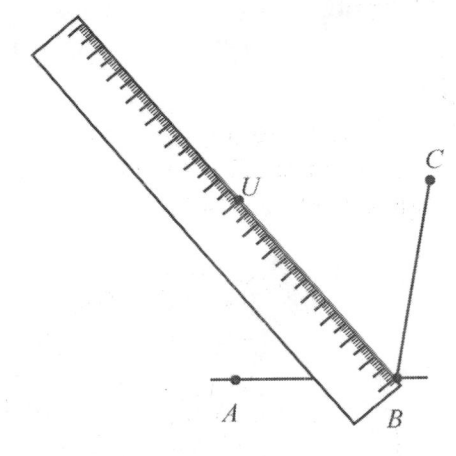

CONSTRUCTING PERPENDICULAR BISECTORS

When a line segment is divided into two equal parts by another line, the segment is bisected. *Bi* means two, and *sect* means cut. The line that divides the line segment is called the **bisector**. The line segment is marked with the same number of ticks on each side to indicate that both sides are the same length.

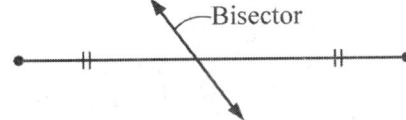

When the bisector is at a right angle to the line segment, it is called a **perpendicular bisector**.

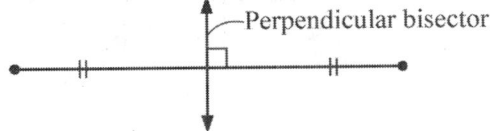

To draw the perpendicular bisector using a compass, follow these steps:

1. Place the pointed end of a compass on one endpoint of the line segment. Draw a large arc that crosses the line segment more than halfway between the two points.
2. Keep the compass exactly the same. Draw another arc from the other endpoint.
3. Draw a line that connects the points where the two arcs cross each other. This is the perpendicular bisector.

Example

Draw the perpendicular bisector of line segment *AB*.

Solution

Step 1
Draw the first arc.
Place the pointed end of the compass on point *A* of the line segment. Draw an arc that crosses the line segment at a distance greater than halfway between the two points.

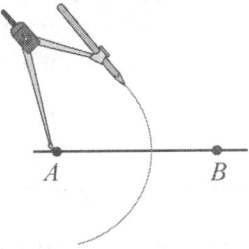

Step 2
Draw the second arc.
Repeat the same process with the pointed end of the compass on point *B* of the line segment. Label the points where the arcs intersect *C* and *D*.

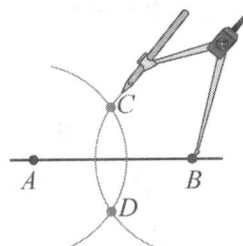

Step 3
Draw the perpendicular bisector.
Use a straightedge to connect points C and D.

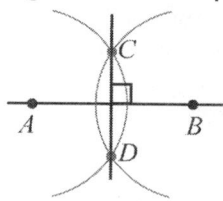

DRAWING A PARALLEL LINE USING A STRAIGHTEDGE AND COMPASS

Parallel lines are straight lines that do not intersect; they remain the same distance apart. You can draw a line parallel to a given line by using a straightedge and compass. To draw a line parallel to a given line AB through a given point P, use the following steps:

1. Use a straightedge to draw a line at an angle through point P and line AB. Label the point of intersection R.
2. Place the compass needle on point R, and set the width to approximately half the length between point R and point P.
3. Draw an arc between both lines. Label the points of intersection C and D. With the compass set to the same width, place the compass needle on point P, and draw a similar arc. Label the point of intersection E.
4. Set the width of the compass by placing the compass needle on point C and the other end at point D. With the compass set to the same width, place the compass needle on point E. Draw an arc and label the point of intersection F.
5. Using a straightedge, draw a line through points P and F.

Example
A line, AB, and a point, P, are given.

Draw a line parallel to AB.

Solution
Step 1
Use a straightedge to draw a line at an angle through point P and line AB. Label the point of intersection R.

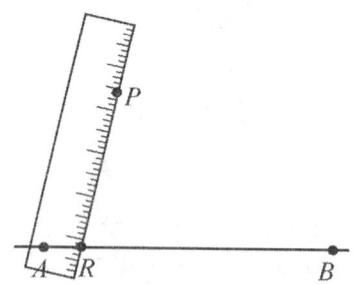

Step 2
Place the compass needle on point R, and set the width to approximately half the length between point R and point P.

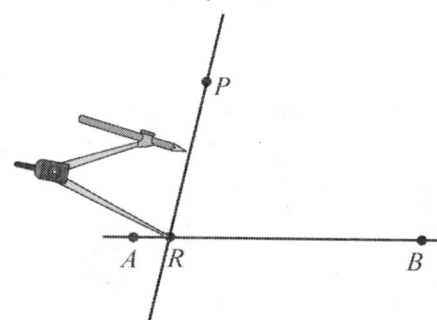

Step 3
Draw an arc between both lines. Label the points of intersection C and D.

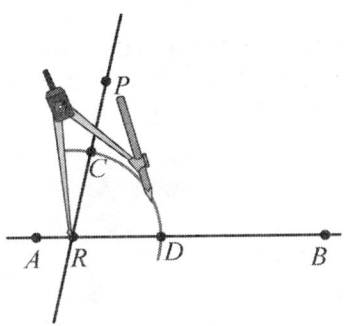

With the compass set to the same width, place the compass needle on point P, and draw a similar arc. Label the point of intersection E.

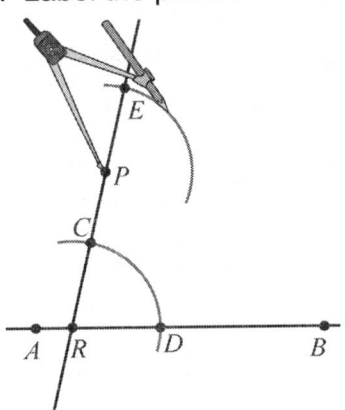

Step 4
Set the width of the compass by placing the compass needle on point C and the other end at point D.

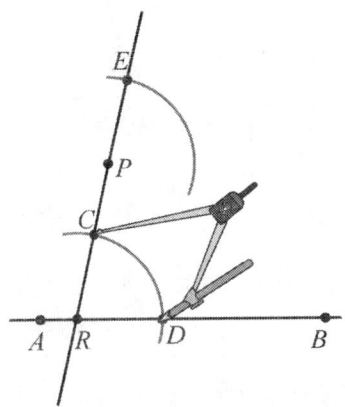

With the compass set to the same width, place the compass needle on point E. Draw an arc, and label the point of intersection F.

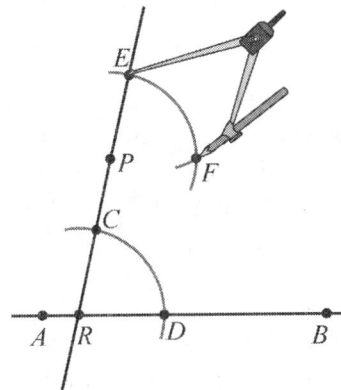

Step 5
Using a straightedge, draw a line through points P and F.

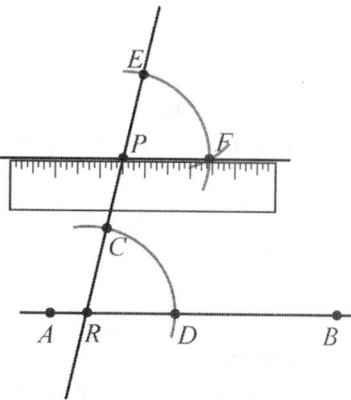

Line PF is parallel to line AB.

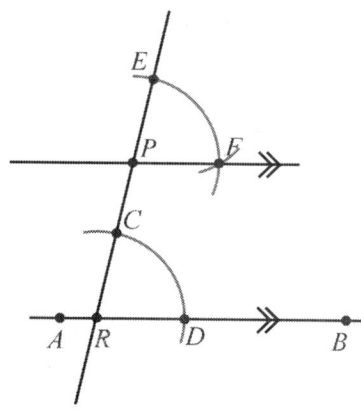

CONSTRUCTING A PERPENDICULAR LINE THROUGH A POINT USING A STRAIGHTEDGE AND COMPASS

Perpendicular lines are two lines in the same plane that intersect at 90° to form a right angle. It is possible to construct a perpendicular line through a point using only a straightedge and a compass.

To construct a perpendicular line using a straightedge and a compass, follow these steps:

1. Use a straightedge to draw a line segment. Draw a point, P, above the line segment but not touching it.
2. Place the compass needle on point P, and open the compass to a width greater than the distance between point P and the line segment.
3. Draw an arc that intersects the line segment to the left of point P. Keeping the width of the compass the same, draw an arc that intersects the line segment to the right of point P.
4. Place the compass needle on the point of intersection on the left, and draw an arc below the line segment.
5. Without adjusting the width of the compass, place the compass needle on the point of intersection on the right, and draw an arc below the line segment that intersects the arc drawn in step 4.
6. Use a straightedge to connect point P to the point of intersection drawn in step 5.

The construction of a perpendicular line through a point is shown here.

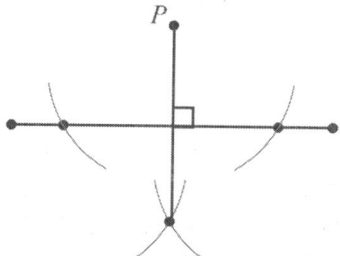

Geometric Constructions

Example

Construct a line segment perpendicular to $\overline{AB}$ through point P.

Solution

Step 1

Use a straightedge to draw $\overline{AB}$. Draw a point, P, above the line segment but not touching it.

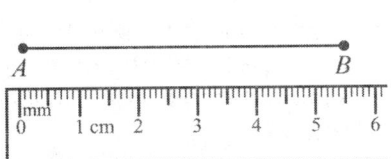

Step 2

Place the compass needle on point P, and open the compass to a width greater than the distance between point P and $\overline{AB}$. The exact width is not important.

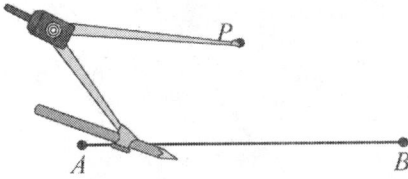

Step 3

Draw an arc that intersects $\overline{AB}$ to the left of point P. Label the point of intersection Q. Keeping the width of the compass the same, draw an arc that intersects $\overline{AB}$ to the right of point P. Label the point of intersection R.

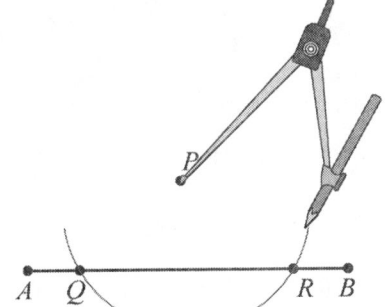

Step 4

Place the compass needle on point Q, and draw an arc below $\overline{AB}$.

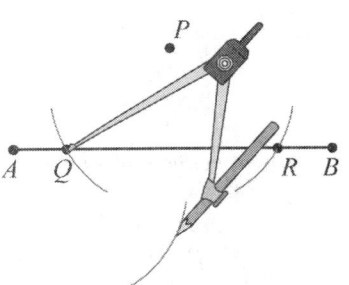

Step 5

Without adjusting the width of the compass, place the compass needle on point R and draw an arc below $\overline{AB}$ that intersects the arc drawn in step 4. Label the point of intersection S.

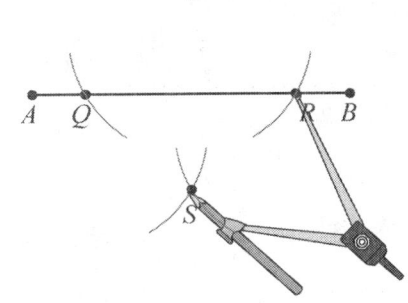

Step 6
Use a straightedge to connect point S to point P.

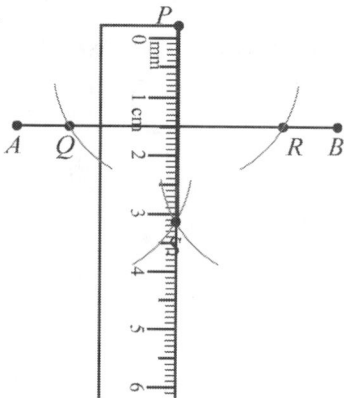

The line segment perpendicular to $\overline{AB}$ through point P is $\overline{PS}$.

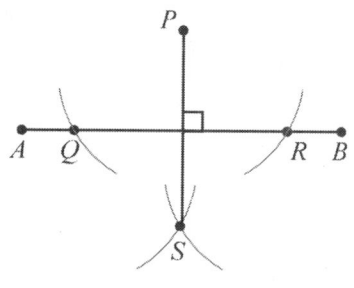

CONSTRUCTING CONGRUENT LINE SEGMENTS WITH A COMPASS AND A STRAIGHTEDGE

Congruent line segments can be drawn using a compass and a straightedge.

Use the following steps to draw a congruent line segment when given a line segment:

1. Draw a point to represent the endpoint of the new line segment.
2. Measure the length of the given line using a compass.
3. Position the compass with the set measurement on the endpoint of the new line segment, and draw a point where the new endpoint will be.
4. Use a straightedge to draw a line connecting the two endpoints.

Example
Kim draws the given line segment.

Draw a line that is congruent to line segment AB.

Solution

Step 1
Draw a point to represent the endpoint of the new line segment.

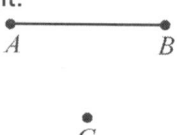

Step 2
Measure the length of line AB using a compass. Place one end on point A, and extend the other end of the compass until it reaches point B.

Step 3
Position the compass with the set measurement on the endpoint of the new line segment. Draw a point where the new endpoint will be.

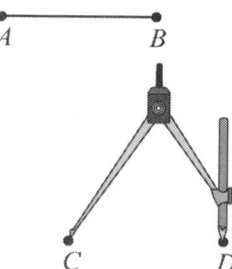

Geometric Constructions

Step 4
Use a straightedge to draw a line connecting the two endpoints.

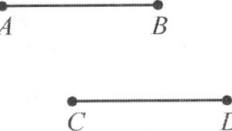

Line segment CD is congruent to line segment AB.

CONSTRUCTING CONGRUENT ANGLES WITH A COMPASS AND A STRAIGHTEDGE

You can draw congruent angles using a compass and a straightedge.

Use the following steps to draw a congruent angle when given an angle:

1. Draw the vertex and one side of the congruent angle.
2. Draw an arc that intersects both sides of the given angle to create two new points
3. With the compass set to the same width, draw a similar arc on the side of the congruent angle to create a new point.
4. Readjust the compass on the points that were created on the sides of the given angle.
5. Without changing the width of the compass, set it on the point that was created on the side of the congruent angle, and draw a new point.
6. Use a straightedge to draw a ray through this new point.

Example
Tommy draws the given angle.

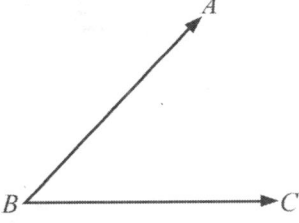

Draw an angle that is congruent to ∠ABC.

Solution
Step 1
Draw the vertex and one side of the congruent angle.

Step 2
Position the steel tip of the compass at point A of ∠ABC, and select a width.

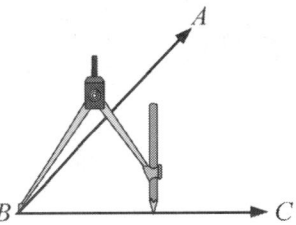

Draw an arc that intersects both sides of ∠ABC, and label each side with two new points, M and N.

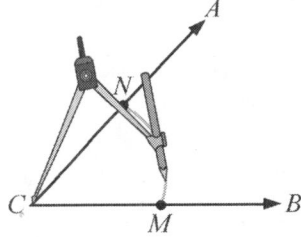

Step 3
With the compass set to the same width, draw a similar arc on side EF. Create a new point, H.

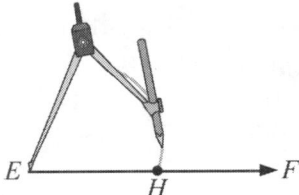

Step 4
Readjust the compass on points M and N of ∠ABC..

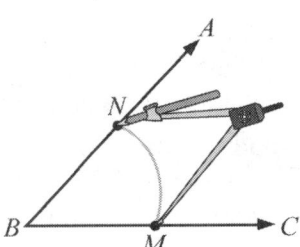

Step 5
Without changing the width of the compass, set it on point *H* of side *EF*, and draw a new point labeled *I*, where the new arc intersects the arc drawn in Step 3.

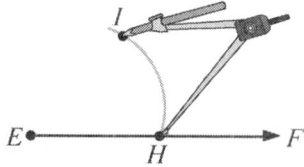

Step 5
Use a straightedge to draw a ray through point *I*, and label the endpoint *J*.

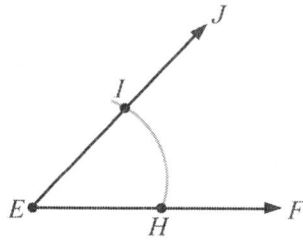

Angle *JEF* is congruent to ∠*ABC*.

G-CO.13 Construct an equilateral triangle, a square, and a regular hexagon inscribed in a circle.

CONSTRUCTING EQUILATERAL TRIANGLES WITH A STRAIGHTEDGE AND COMPASS

An equilateral triangle has three congruent sides and three congruent angles. It is possible to construct an equilateral triangle using only a straightedge and a compass. To do that, follow these steps:

1. Use a straightedge to draw line segment $\overline{AB}$.
2. Extend your compass so that it is the same length as $\overline{AB}$.
3. Put the end of the compass on point *A*, and draw an arc.
4. Put the end of the compass on point *B*, and draw an arc that intersects the first arc.
5. Label the place where the two arcs cross as point *C*.
6. Use the straightedge to draw line segments $\overline{AC}$ and $\overline{BC}$.

Example
Construct equilateral triangle *ABC*.

Solution
Step 1
Use a straightedge to draw line segment $\overline{AB}$.

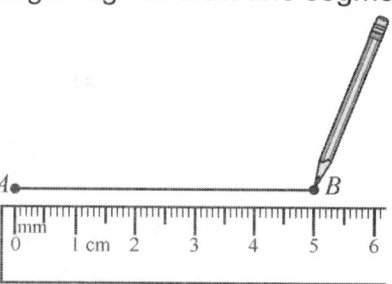

Step 2
Extend your compass so that it is the same length as $\overline{AB}$.

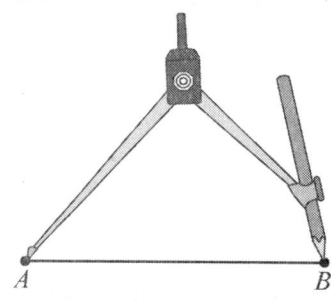

Step 3
Put the end of the compass on point *A*, and draw an arc.

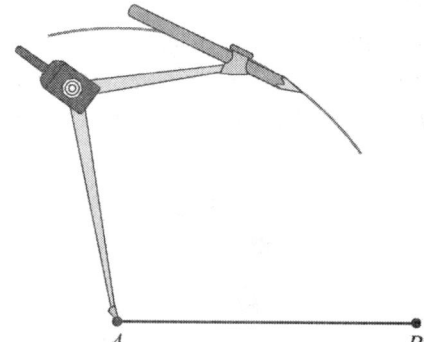

Geometric Constructions

Step 4
Make sure that your compass is still the same length as $\overline{AB}$. Put the end of the compass on point B, and draw an arc that intersects the first arc.

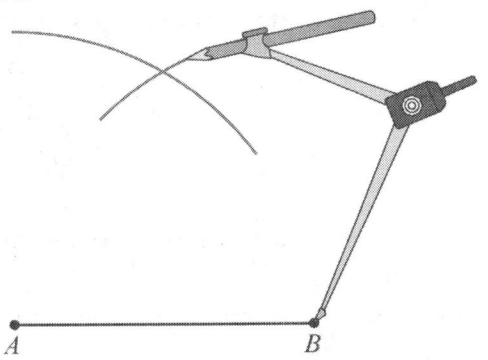

Step 5
Label the place where the two arcs cross as point C.

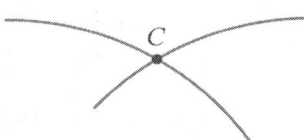

Step 6
Use the straightedge to draw line segments $\overline{AC}$ and $\overline{BC}$.

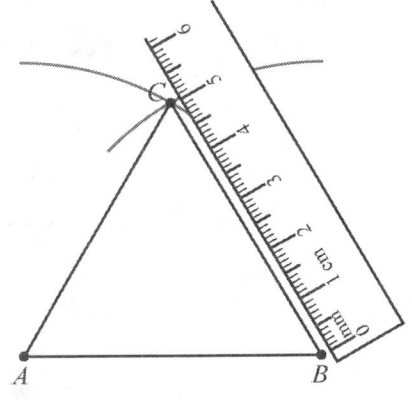

EXERCISE #1—GEOMETRIC CONSTRUCTIONS

Use the following information to answer the next question.

Angle MNO is 140°.

74. Draw ∠MNO and the angle bisector using a protractor.

Use the following information to answer the next question.

Line segment AB is 36 mm long.

75. Draw the line segment and its perpendicular bisector.

76. What are the slopes of lines that are parallel and perpendicular to a line with a slope of $m = -\dfrac{1}{5}$?

77. To the nearest hundredth, determine the shortest distance from the point (2, 1) to the line defined by the equation $y = -x + 7$.

Use the following information to answer the next question.

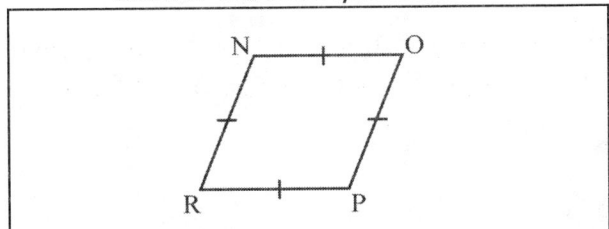

78. Using geometric properties of quadrilaterals, classify the given four-sided shape.

Use the following information to answer the next question.

Two triangles each have an area of 200 cm².

79. Prove that the two triangles do not have to be congruent.

80. Using a ruler and a protractor, draw an equilateral triangle, *ABC*, with sides measuring 6 cm.

What are the measures of each angle?

Show your work. Explain your answer

EXERCISE #1—GEOMETRIC CONSTRUCTIONS ANSWERS AND SOLUTIONS

| 74. See solution | 76. See solution | 78. See solution | 80. See solution |
| 75. See solution | 77. See solution | 79. See solution | |

74.

Step 1
Draw and label the angle.
Draw line segment NO. Use a protractor to add line segment MN at 140°.

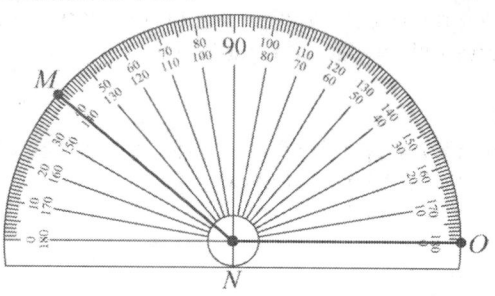

Step 2
Calculate the size of the bisected angle.
Divide the measure of the angle by 2.
140° ÷ 2 = 70°

Step 3
Use a protractor to mark this angle.
Place the zero line on one of the line segments.
Follow the inside numbers to 70. Plot point P at 70°.

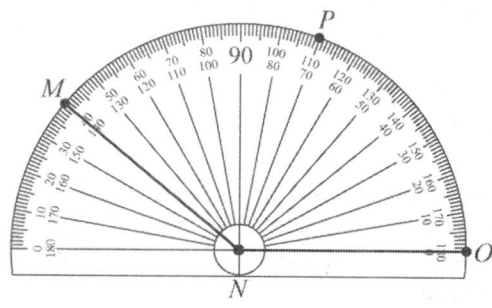

Step 4
Draw the angle bisector.
Use a straight edge to connect point N to point P.

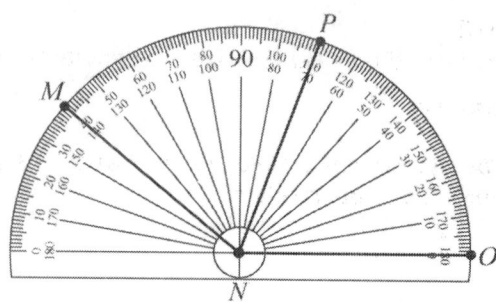

75.

Step 1
Draw the line segment.
Plot point A. Measure 36 mm, and plot point B.
Connect the two points.

Step 2
Calculate the length of the bisected line segment.
Divide the length by 2.
36 ÷ 2 = 18

Step 3
Draw the perpendicular bisector.
Plot point C 18 mm from either side. Place the corner of the right triangle at point C. Draw a line segment, making sure to extend the line above and below line segment AB.

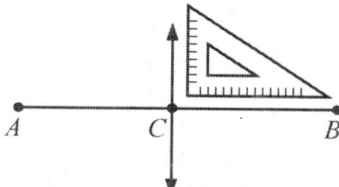

76.

Step 1
Determine the slope of a line parallel to the slope $m = -\frac{1}{5}$.

Parallel lines have the same slope. Therefore, $m_\parallel = -\frac{1}{5}$ is the slope of a line parallel to the slope $m = -\frac{1}{5}$.

Step 2
Determine the slope of a line perpendicular to the slope $m = -\frac{1}{5}$.

Perpendicular lines have slopes that are negative reciprocals of each other.

$m_\perp = -1 \times \frac{1}{m}$

$m_\perp = -1 \times \left(\frac{1}{-\frac{1}{5}}\right)$

$m_\perp = -1 \times (-5)$

$m_\perp = 5$

Therefore, $m_\perp = 5$ is the slope of a line perpendicular to the slope $m = -\frac{1}{5}$.

77.

The shortest distance from a point to a line is the perpendicular distance from that point to the line.

Line segment AD passes through the point (2, 1) and is perpendicular to $y = -x + 7$.

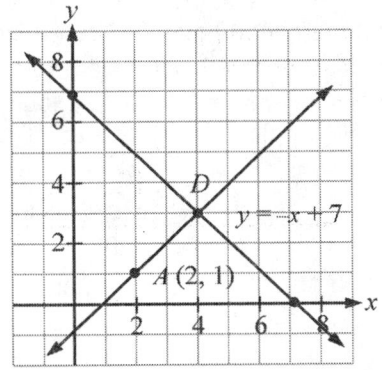

Step 1
Determine the slope of the perpendicular line segment AD.

The slope of the line $y = -x + 7$ is -1.

Thus, the slope of AD is 1 (the negative reciprocal of -1).

Step 2
Determine the equation that defines line segment AD.

Apply the point slope formula of a line using the point (2, 1) and the slope of 1.

$y = m(x - x_1) + y_1$
$y = 1(x - 2) + 1$
$y = x - 2 + 1$
$y = x - 1$

The equation of line segment AD is $y = x - 1$.

Step 3
Determine the point of intersection.

The intersection point D can be found by solving this system of two linear equations.
(1) $y = -x + 7$
(2) $y = x - 1$

Solve for x by substituting the expression for y in equation (2) into equation (1).

$x - 1 = -x + 7$
$2x - 1 = 7$
$\quad 2x = 8$
$\quad\quad x = 4$

Substitute 4 into equation (2) to find the y-coordinate of point D.

$y = x - 1$
$y = (4) - 1$
$y = 3$

The intersection point D is (4, 3).

Step 4
Determine the distance from (2, 1) to (4, 3) by applying the distance formula.

$d = \sqrt{(x_2 - x_1)^2 + (y_2 - y_1)^2}$
$d = \sqrt{(4 - 2)^2 + (3 - 1)^2}$
$d = \sqrt{(2)^2 + (2)^2}$
$d = \sqrt{4 + 4}$
$d = \sqrt{8}$

To the nearest hundredth, $d \approx 2.83$.

The shortest distance from the point (2, 1) to the line defined by the equation $y = -x + 7$ is approximately 2.83 units.

78.

Step 1
Identify the number of parallel sides.
There are two pairs of parallel sides

Step 2
Identify the number of congruent sides.
All four sides are congruent.

Step 3
Identify the number of congruent angles.
Since there are two pairs of parallel sides and there are no right angles (90°), opposite angles are equal. There are two pairs of congruent angles.

Step 4
Identify the quadrilateral.
All four sides are congruent, there are two pairs of congruent angles, and two pairs of parallel sides. The four-sided shape is a rhombus.

79.

Step 1
Calculate the area of a rectangle from the area of the triangle.
Substitute the area of the triangle into the formula for area of a triangle. Then, isolate the variables by multiplying both sides of the equation by 2.

$$A_{triangle} = \frac{bh}{2}$$
$$200 = \frac{bh}{2}$$
$$2(200) = \left(\frac{bh}{2}\right)2$$
$$400 = bh$$
$$A_{rectangle} = lw$$
$$bh = lw$$
$$lw = 400$$

Step 2
Use the product of the length and width measures to determine possible base and height measures of the triangle.
Think of two factors that equal 400 when multiplied together.
10 × 40 = 400
20 × 20 = 400

Step 3
Draw the triangles using the factors as side length measures.

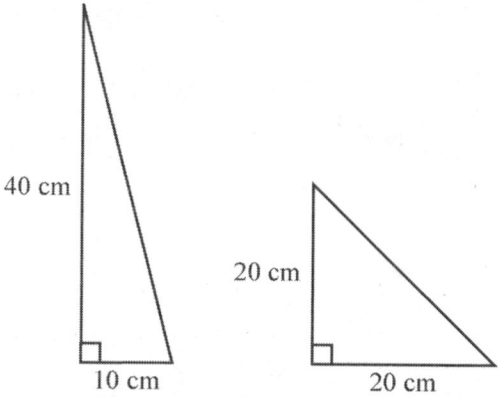

Triangles with the dimensions 20 cm × 20 cm and 40 cm × 10 cm both have an area of 200 cm² but are not congruent.

80.

Points	Rationale
4	Thorough ability in drawing an equilateral triangle using a protractor. **Sample Answer:** In an equilateral triangle, all sides are equal and all angles are equal. The inside angles of all triangles add up to 180°. Therefore, in an equilateral triangle where all the sides are equal, each angle must equal 60° (180 ÷ 3). Using a ruler, draw a line that is 6 cm. At one end of the line, use your protractor to draw an angle of 60°. Make this line 6 cm also. Draw a connecting line that is also 6 cm. The equilateral triangle should have three 60° angles and three sides that each measure 6 cm.
3	Considerable ability in drawing an equilateral triangle using a protractor.
2	Some ability in drawing an equilateral triangle using a protractor.
1	Limited ability in drawing an equilateral triangle using a protractor.

EXERCISE #2—GEOMETRIC CONSTRUCTIONS

Use the following information to answer the next question.

Angle MKL is 66°.

81. Draw ∠MKL and the angle bisector using a protractor.

Use the following information to answer the next question.

Line segment GH is 1.4 dm long.

82. Draw the line segment and its perpendicular bisector using a right triangle.

Use the following information to answer the next question.

$l_1: 2x + 3y - 18 = 0$

$l_2: 5x + \dfrac{15}{2}y - 210 = 0$

83. Use algebra to explain whether the two given lines are coincident, parallel, or intersecting.

Use the following information to answer the next question.

Five triangles are given.

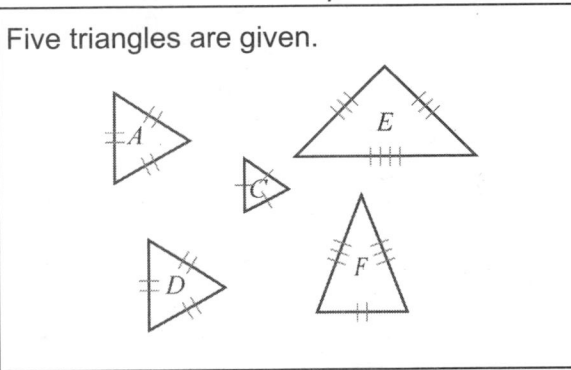

84. Which triangle is congruent to triangle A?

Use the following information to answer the next question.

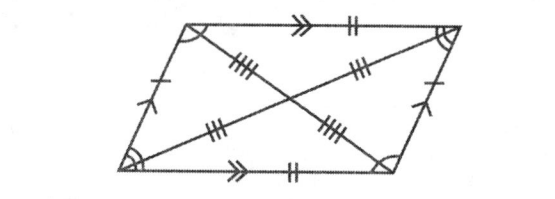

85. Using geometric properties of quadrilaterals, including diagonals, classify the given quadrilateral.

Use the following information to answer the next question.

A plane travels at a constant speed of 240 km/h for 5 h.

This table shows the total distance the plane traveled at the end of each hour of its trip.

Time (h)	Distance (km)
0	0
1	240
2	480
3	720
4	960
5	1,200

86. Plot the values from the table on a graph, and draw a line through the points.

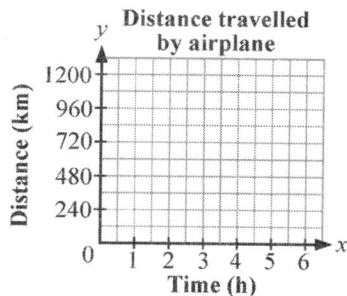

87. Design an equilateral triangle with a perimeter of 18 cm.

EXERCISE #2—GEOMETRIC CONSTRUCTIONS ANSWERS AND SOLUTIONS

| 81. See solution | 83. See solution | 85. See solution | 87. See solution |
| 82. See solution | 84. See solution | 86. See solution | |

81.

Step 1
Draw and label the angle.
Draw line segment KL. Use a protractor to add line segment MK at 66°.

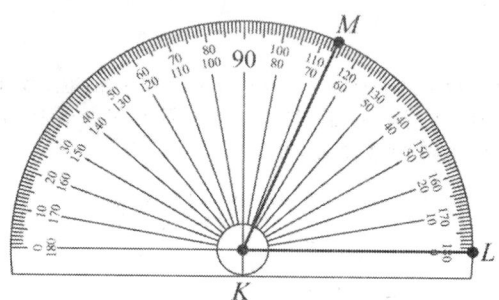

Step 2
Calculate the size of the bisected angle.
Divide the measure of the angle by 2.
66° ÷ 2 = 33°

Step 3
Use a protractor to mark this angle.
Place the zero line on one of the line segments.
Follow the inside numbers to 33. Plot point J at 33°.

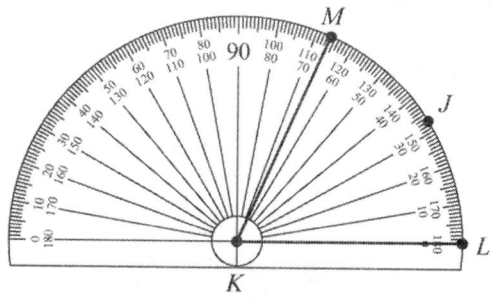

Step 4
Draw the angle bisector.
Use a straight edge to connect point K to point J.

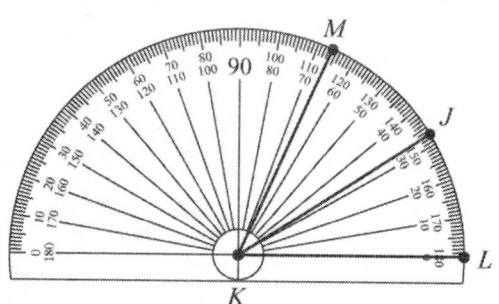

82.

Step 1
Draw a line segment.
Plot point G. Measure 1.4 dm, which is equal to 14 cm, and plot point H.
Connect the two points.

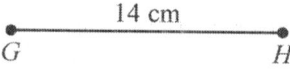

Step 2
Calculate the length of the bisected line segment.
Divide the length by 2.
14 ÷ 2 = 7

Step 3
Draw the perpendicular bisector.
Plot point I at a distance of 7 cm from either side.
Place the corner of the right triangle at point I. Draw a line segment, making sure to extend the line above and below line segment GH.

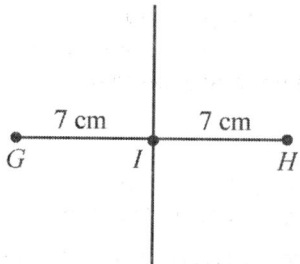

83.
Method 1

Step 1
Rewrite the equation of each line in the slope-intercept form $y = mx + b$.

$l_1: 2x + 3y - 18 = 0$
$$3y = -2x + 18$$
$$y = -\frac{2}{3}x + 6$$

$l_2: 5x + \frac{15}{2}y - 210 = 0$
$$\frac{15}{2}y = -5x + 210$$
$$y = \frac{-10}{15}x + \frac{420}{15}$$
$$y = \frac{-2}{3}x + 28$$

Step 2
Compare the slopes (*m*) and *y*-intercepts (*b*) of each line to determine the nature of the lines.

$l_1: m = -\frac{2}{3}$
$ b = 6$

$l_2: m = -\frac{2}{3}$
$ b = 28$

Since the slopes of the two lines are the same but their *y*-intercepts are different, these two lines are parallel.

Method 2
Step 1
Create a system of equations in the form $ax + by = c$.

$l_1: 2x + 3y - 18 = 0$
① $2x + 3y = 18$

$l_2: 5x + \frac{15}{2}y - 210 = 0$
② $5x + \frac{15}{2}y = 210$

Step 2
Multiply equation (1) by 5 and equation (2) by 2. Then, subtract equation (1) from equation (2).
② × 2 $(10x + 15y = 420)$
① × 5 $\underline{-(10x + 15y = 90)}$
$ 0x + 0y = 330$

Since there are no solutions (*x*, *y*) that satisfy the system, the lines are parallel.

84.

When one shape is congruent to another, the size and shape are exactly the same.

Trace triangle *A* onto a piece of paper and cut it out. Then, place it over the other triangles to see which one matches up with it exactly. Upon completing this procedure, you will notice that triangle *D* is congruent to triangle *A* because it is the same size and shape as triangle *A*.

85.

Step 1
Identify the number of sets of parallel sides.
There are two pairs of parallel sides.

Step 2
Identify the number of congruent sides.
There are two pairs of congruent sides.

Step 3
Identify the number of congruent angles.
Since the opposite sides are congruent, the opposite angles are also congruent. There are two pairs of congruent angles.

Step 4
Identify properties of the intersecting diagonals.
The diagonals bisect each other. They are not perpendicular.

Step 5
Identify the quadrilateral.
The quadrilateral is a parallelogram.

86.

Complete the graph by plotting the ordered pairs (0, 0), (1, 240), (2, 480), (3, 720), (4, 960), and (5, 1,200) on the graph.

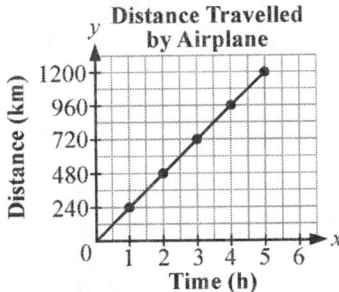

87.

An equilateral triangle has 3 equal sides, so you can divide the perimeter by 3.
$18 \div 3 = 6$
Each side will be 6 cm long.

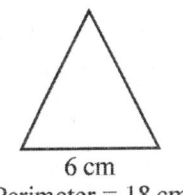

6 cm
Perimeter = 18 cm

NOTES

Similarity Transformations

SIMILARITY TRANSFORMATIONS

Table of Correlations

Standard		Concepts	Exercise #1	Exercise #2
Unit2.1	Understand similarity in terms of similarity transformations.			
G-SRT. 1a	Verify experimentally the properties of dilations given by a center and a scale factor. A dilation takes a line not passing through the center of the dilation to a parallel line, and leaves a line passing through the center unchanged.	Dilations	6	20
		Determining the Center and Magnitude of a Dilation	88	96
G-SRT. 1b	Verify experimentally the properties of dilations given by a center and a scale factor. The dilation of a line segment is longer or shorter in the ratio given by the scale factor.	Determining the Scale Factor of a Diagram	89	97
G-SRT.2	Given two figures, use the definition of similarity in terms of similarity transformations to decide if they are similar; explain using similarity transformations the meaning of similarity for triangles as the equality of all corresponding pairs of angles and the proportionality of all corresponding pairs of sides.	Identifying Similar Polygons	90	98
		Solving for Missing Angles in Similar Polygons	91	99
		Solving for Missing Side Lengths in Similar Polygons	92	100
		Using Coordinate Geometry to Prove Two Quadrilaterals Are Similar	93	101
G-SRT.3	Use the properties of similarity transformations to establish the AA criterion for two triangles to be similar.	Properties of Similar Triangles	94	102
		Proving the Similarity of Triangles	95	103

G-SRT.1a Verify experimentally the properties of dilations given by a center and a scale factor. A dilation takes a line not passing through the center of the dilation to a parallel line, and leaves a line passing through the center unchanged.

DETERMINING THE CENTER AND MAGNITUDE OF A DILATION

A dilation is a transformation that produces the same shape as the original figure, but a different size. A dilation either expands or compresses the original figure. The description of a dilation includes the center of dilation and the magnitude of dilation.

The center of dilation is a fixed point in the plane about which all points are expanded or compressed. The center of dilation is the only invariant point under a dilation. In the given diagram, point O is the center of dilation.

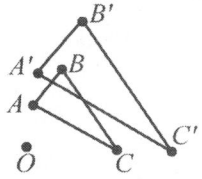

The center of dilation can be found by drawing lines through all corresponding points. The point where the lines intersect is the center of dilation.

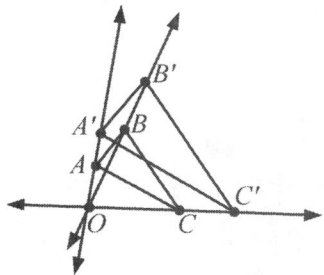

Follow these steps to determine the center of dilation:

1. Draw a line passing through each pair of corresponding points.
2. Determine the point of intersection. This is the center of dilation.

The magnitude, or scale factor, of a dilation determines how many times larger or smaller the image is than the original. The formula for the magnitude of dilation is

magnitude = $\dfrac{\text{image length}}{\text{original length}}$. When substituting into the magnitude formula, you need to use corresponding side lengths.

Follow these steps to determine the magnitude of dilation:

1. Substitute corresponding side lengths into the magnitude formula.
2. Calculate the magnitude.

Example

Rectangle *ABCD* has been dilated to produce the transformed image of *A'B'C'D'*.

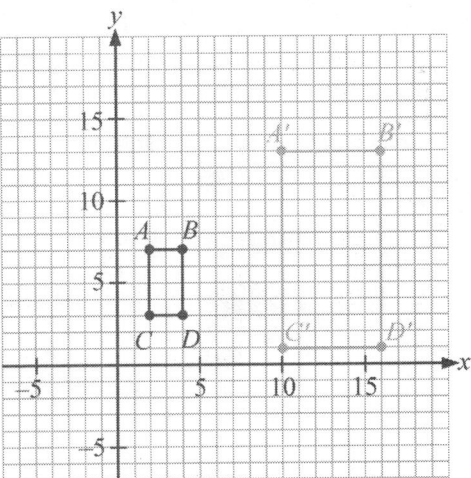

Determine the center of dilation.

Solution

Step 1
Draw a line passing through each pair of corresponding points.

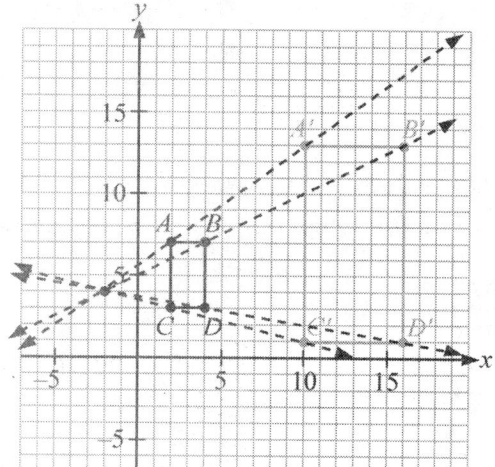

Step 2
Determine the point of intersection. This is the center of dilation.

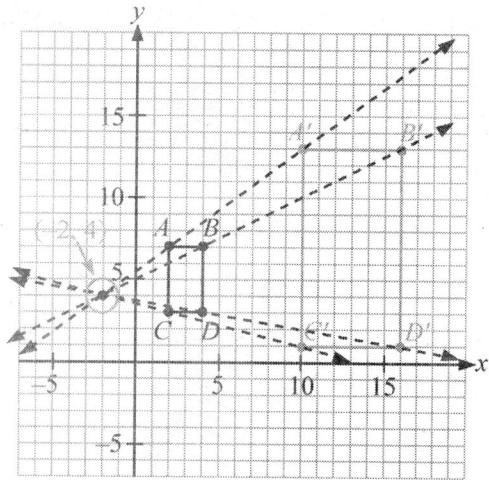

The center of dilation is located at (−2, 4).

Determine the magnitude of dilation.

Solution

Step 1
Substitute corresponding side lengths into the magnitude formula.

magnitude = $\dfrac{\text{image length}}{\text{original length}}$

magnitude = $\dfrac{A'B'}{AB}$

Step 2
Calculate the magnitude.

magnitude = $\dfrac{A'B'}{AB}$

magnitude = $\dfrac{6}{2}$

magnitude = 3

The magnitude of dilation is 3.

G-SRT.1b Verify experimentally the properties of dilations given by a center and a scale factor. The dilation of a line segment is longer or shorter in the ratio given by the scale factor.

DETERMINING THE SCALE FACTOR OF A DIAGRAM

Scale drawings are used when objects are either too large or too small to be drawn on a piece of paper.

The **scale factor** between the original shape and the new image is a number that indicates how much larger or smaller the shape was made. The scale factor can be calculated using the formula scale factor = $\dfrac{\text{image length}}{\text{original length}}$.

If the scale factor is less than 1, the image is a **reduction** of the original shape. If the scale factor is greater than 1, the image is an **enlargement** of the original shape.

When given a diagram and its image, determine the scale factor by following these steps:

1. Pick one known length in the image diagram.
2. Find the corresponding length in the original diagram.
3. Use the scale factor formula to determine the scale factor.

Example

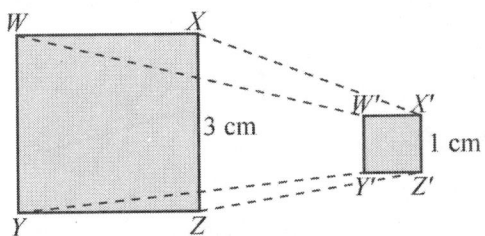

A scale drawing is given.

What is the scale factor of the given diagram?

Solution

Step 1
Pick one known length in the image diagram.
$X'Z' = 1$ cm

Step 2
Find the corresponding length in the original diagram.
$XZ = 3$ cm

Step 3
Use the scale factor formula to determine the scale factor.

$$\text{scale factor} = \frac{\text{image length}}{\text{original length}}$$
$$= \frac{X'Z'}{XZ}$$
$$= \frac{1 \text{ cm}}{3 \text{ cm}}$$
$$= \frac{1}{3}$$

The diagram shows a reduction with a scale factor of $\frac{1}{3}$.

Example

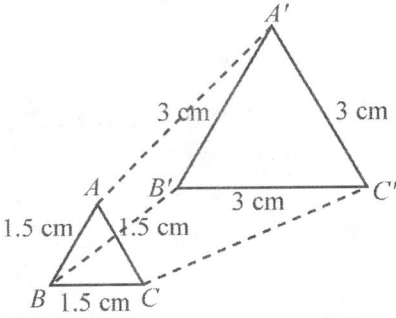

A scale drawing is given.

What is the scale factor of the given diagram?

Solution

Step 1
Pick one known length in the image diagram.
$A'C' = 3$ cm

Step 2
Find the corresponding length in the original diagram.
$AC = 1.5$ cm

Step 3
Use the scale factor formula to determine the scale factor.

$$\text{scale factor} = \frac{\text{image length}}{\text{original length}}$$
$$= \frac{A'C'}{AC}$$
$$= \frac{3 \text{ cm}}{1.5 \text{ cm}}$$
$$= 2$$

The diagram shows an enlargement with a scale factor of 2.

G-SRT.2 Given two figures, use the definition of similarity in terms of similarity transformations to decide if they are similar; explain using similarity transformations the meaning of similarity for triangles as the equality of all corresponding pairs of angles and the proportionality of all corresponding pairs of sides.

IDENTIFYING SIMILAR POLYGONS

A **polygon** is any closed plane figure constructed by three or more line segments. Similar polygons have the same shape but do not necessarily have the same size.

If you are given a set of polygons, you can identify similar polygons by following these steps:

1. Identify polygons that have equal corresponding angles.
2. Identify polygons that have corresponding sides that are proportional.

Example

Mrs. Andrews drew quadrilateral *ABCD* on the board.

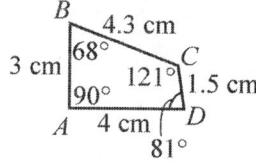

Then, she drew three quadrilaterals, as shown.

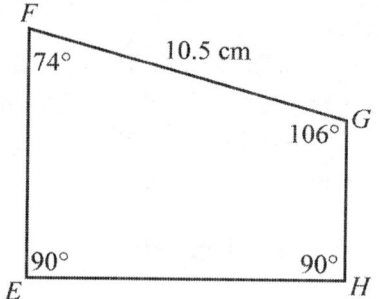

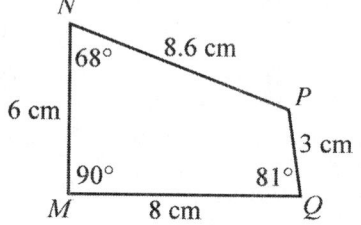

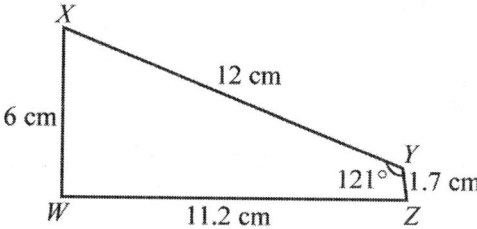

Determine which of the given quadrilaterals is similar to quadrilateral *ABCD*.

Solution

Step 1

Look for equal corresponding angles. Quadrilateral *EFGH* is not similar to quadrilateral *ABCD* because the corresponding angles are not equal.

Similarity Transformations   162   Castle Rock Research

Step 2
Look for corresponding sides that are proportional.

Quadrilateral *WXYZ* is not similar to quadrilateral *ABCD* because the corresponding sides are not proportional.

$\frac{WX}{AB} = \frac{6}{3}$

$\frac{WX}{AB} = 2$

$\frac{XY}{BC} = \frac{12}{4.3}$

$\frac{XY}{BC} \approx 2.8$

Quadrilateral *MNPQ* has corresponding sides that are proportional to quadrilateral *ABCD*.

$\frac{NP}{BC} = \frac{8.6}{4.3}$

$\frac{NP}{BC} = 2$

$\frac{MN}{AB} = \frac{6}{3}$

$\frac{MN}{AB} = 2$

$\frac{QM}{DA} = \frac{8}{4}$

$\frac{QM}{DA} = 2$

$\frac{PQ}{CD} = \frac{3}{1.5}$

$\frac{PQ}{CD} = 2$

Therefore, quadrilateral *MNPQ* is similar to quadrilateral *ABCD*, since the corresponding angles are equal and the corresponding sides are proportional.

Solving for Missing Angles in Similar Polygons

A **polygon** is any closed-plane figure constructed by three or more line segments. Similar polygons have the same shape, but they are not necessarily the same size.

One property of similar polygons is that the corresponding angles of similar polygons are equal. You can apply this property to find missing angles in similar polygons.

Example
Two similar quadrilaterals, *GHIJ* and *KLMN*, are shown.

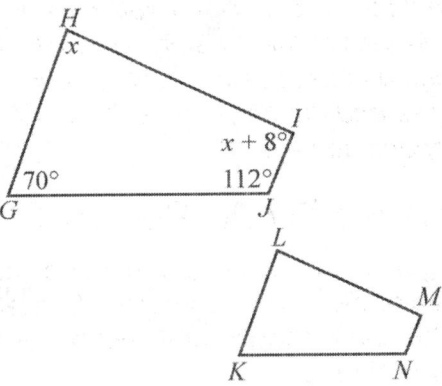

Given that the sum of the measure of the angles in a quadrilateral is 360°, what is the measure of ∠*M*?

Solution

Step 1
Determine the value of *x* in quadrilateral *GHIJ*.
The sum of the angles in the quadrilateral is 360°.

$x + (x + 8°) + 70° + 112° = 360°$

Simplify by collecting like terms.

$2x + 190° = 360°$

Apply inverse operations to isolate the variable.

$2x + 190° = 360°$
$2x + 190° - 190° = 360° - 190°$
$2x = 170°$
$\frac{2x}{2} = \frac{170°}{2}$
$x = 85°$

Step 2
Solve for ∠*I*.
∠*I* = *x* + 8°
∠*I* = 85° + 8°
∠*I* = 93°

Step 3
The properties of similar polygons state that corresponding angles are equal. Therefore, ∠*I* = ∠*M*, and ∠*M* = 93°.

Solving for Missing Side Lengths in Similar Polygons

A **polygon** is any closed-plane figure constructed by three or more line segments. Similar polygons have the same shape, but they are not necessarily the same size. One property of similar polygons is that corresponding side lengths are proportional. As a result, when given the side lengths of a polygon, you can solve for missing side lengths in a similar polygon.

To solve for missing side lengths in similar polygons, follow these steps:

1. Identify the corresponding sides.
2. Set up a ratio, and solve by applying cross multiplication.

Example
Two similar quadrilaterals, QRST and WXYZ, are given.

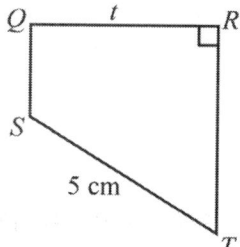 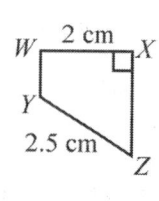

What is the length of side QR?

Solution

Step 1
Identify the corresponding sides.
Side QR in quadrilateral QRST corresponds to side WX in quadrilateral WXYZ, and side ST in quadrilateral QRST corresponds to side YZ in quadrilateral WXYZ.

Step 2
Set up a ratio, and solve by applying cross multiplication.

$$\frac{QR}{WX} = \frac{ST}{YZ}$$

$$\frac{t}{2} = \frac{5}{2.5}$$

$$t \times 2.5 = 2 \times 5$$

$$2.5t = 10$$

$$t = \frac{10}{2.5}$$

$$t = 4$$

The length of side QR is 4 cm.

Example
Similar polygons ABCD and EFGH are shown.

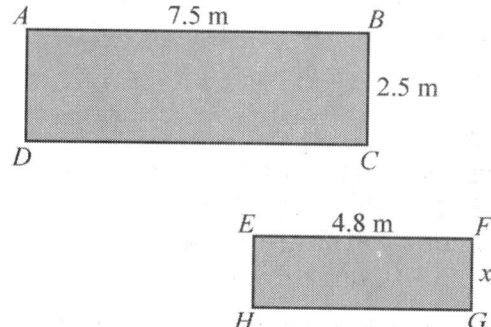

Determine the length of side FG.

Solution

Step 1
Identify the corresponding sides.
Side AB corresponds to side EF, and side BC corresponds to side FG.

Step 2
Set up a ratio, and solve by applying cross multiplication.

$$\frac{AB}{EF} = \frac{BC}{FG}$$

$$\frac{7.5}{4.8} = \frac{2.5}{FG}$$

$$7.5 \times FG = 2.5 \times 4.8$$

$$7.5(FG) = 12$$

$$\frac{7.5(FG)}{7.5} = \frac{12}{7.5}$$

$$FG = 1.6$$

The missing side FG is 1.6 m long.

Using Coordinate Geometry to Prove Two Quadrilaterals Are Similar

Coordinate geometry can be used to check if two quadrilaterals are similar. To prove two quadrilaterals are similar, verify the following three properties:

1. The corresponding sides of similar quadrilaterals are proportional.
2. The corresponding diagonals of similar quadrilaterals are proportional.
3. The ratio of the corresponding diagonals is equal to the ratio of the corresponding sides.

You can use the distance formula to prove that two quadrilaterals are similar. The distance formula states that the distance between two points, (x_A, y_A) and (x_B, y_B), is calculated using the formula $d_{AB} = \sqrt{(x_A - x_B)^2 + (y_A - y_B)^2}$.

Example
The vertices of rhombus *ABCD* are *A*(−3, 5), *B*(3, 8), *C*(9, 5) and *D*(3, 2). The vertices of rhombus *EFGH* are *E*(−4, 0), *F*(−3, −2), *G*(−4, −4), and *H*(−5, −2)
Prove these rhombuses are similar.

Solution
In a rhombus, all sides are equal in length. When comparing two rhombuses, the ratios between all corresponding sides are equal.
Thus, $\frac{AB}{EF} = \frac{BC}{FG} = \frac{CD}{GH} = \frac{DA}{HE}$. To prove that the rhombuses are similar, determine if the ratio of one set of corresponding sides and the ratio between the diagonals are equal.

Step 1
Determine the ratio between the side lengths of *AB* and *EF*.
$d_{AB} = \sqrt{(x_A - x_B)^2 + (y_A - y_B)^2}$
$d_{AB} = \sqrt{(-3 - 3)^2 + (5 - 8)^2}$
$d_{AB} = \sqrt{(-6)^2 + (-3)^2}$
$d_{AB} = \sqrt{36 + 9}$
$d_{AB} = \sqrt{45}$
$d_{EF} = \sqrt{(x_E - x_F)^2 + (y_E - y_F)^2}$
$d_{EF} = \sqrt{(-4 - (-3))^2 + (0 - (-2))^2}$
$d_{EF} = \sqrt{(-1)^2 + (2)^2}$
$d_{EF} = \sqrt{1 + 4}$
$d_{EF} = \sqrt{5}$

Determine the value of $\frac{AB}{EF}$.

$\frac{AB}{EF} = \frac{\sqrt{45}}{\sqrt{5}}$
$\frac{AB}{EF} = \sqrt{\frac{45}{5}}$
$\frac{AB}{EF} = \sqrt{9}$
$\frac{AB}{EF} = 3$

Step 2
Determine the ratio between the lengths of the diagonals *AC* and *EG*.
$d_{AC} = \sqrt{(x_A - x_C)^2 + (y_A - y_C)^2}$
$d_{AC} = \sqrt{(-3 - 9)^2 + (5 - 5)^2}$
$d_{AC} = \sqrt{(-12)^2 + (0)^2}$
$d_{AC} = \sqrt{144}$
$d_{AC} = 12$
$d_{EG} = \sqrt{(x_E - x_G)^2 + (y_E - y_G)^2}$
$d_{EG} = \sqrt{(-4 - (-4))^2 + (0 - (-4))^2}$
$d_{EG} = \sqrt{(0)^2 + (4)^2}$
$d_{EG} = \sqrt{16}$
$d_{EG} = 4$

Determine the value of $\frac{AC}{EG}$.

$\frac{AC}{EG} = \frac{12}{4}$
$\frac{AC}{EG} = 3$

Step 3
Determine the ratio between the lengths of the diagonals BD and FH.
$d_{BD} = \sqrt{(x_B - x_D)^2 + (y_B - y_D)^2}$
$d_{BD} = \sqrt{(3-3)^2 + (8-2)^2}$
$d_{BD} = \sqrt{(0)^2 + (6)^2}$
$d_{BD} = \sqrt{36}$
$d_{BD} = 6$
$d_{FH} = \sqrt{(x_F - x_H)^2 + (y_F - y_H)^2}$
$d_{FH} = \sqrt{(-3-(-5))^2 + (-2-(-2))^2}$
$d_{FH} = \sqrt{(2)^2 + (0)^2}$
$d_{FH} = \sqrt{4}$
$d_{FH} = 2$

Determine the value of $\dfrac{BD}{FH}$.

$\dfrac{BD}{FH} = \dfrac{6}{2}$
$\dfrac{BD}{FH} = 3$

Step 4
Determine if the rhombuses are similar.
Since the ratio between the diagonals and side lengths are equal, $\dfrac{AB}{EF} = \dfrac{AC}{EG} = \dfrac{BD}{FH} = 3$, the rhombuses ABCD and EFGH are similar.

Example
Parallelograms ABCD and EFGH are given.

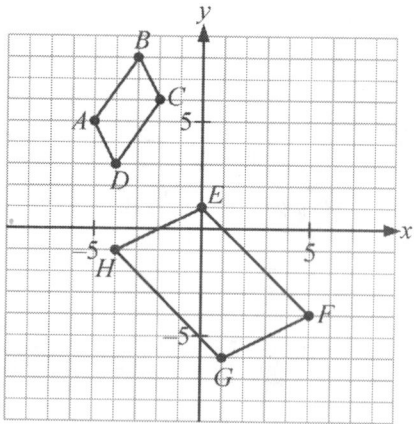

Are these parallelograms similar?

Solution
In a parallelogram, opposite sides are equal in length. The ratio between the corresponding sides of the parallelograms must be the same as the opposite corresponding sides. Thus, $\dfrac{AB}{EF} = \dfrac{CD}{GH}$, and $\dfrac{BC}{FG} = \dfrac{DA}{HE}$. To determine if the two parallelograms are similar, determine if the ratio between sides AB and EF is equal to the ratio between sides BC and FG.

Step 1
Determine the length of AB.
$d_{AB} = \sqrt{(x_A - x_B)^2 + (y_A - y_B)^2}$
$d_{AB} = \sqrt{(-5-(-3))^2 + (5-8)^2}$
$d_{AB} = \sqrt{(-2)^2 + (-3)^2}$
$d_{AB} = \sqrt{4+9}$
$d_{AB} = \sqrt{13}$

Step 2
Determine the length of BC.
$d_{BC} = \sqrt{(x_B - x_C)^2 + (y_B - y_C)^2}$
$d_{BC} = \sqrt{(-3-(-2))^2 + (8-6)^2}$
$d_{BC} = \sqrt{(-1)^2 + (2)^2}$
$d_{BC} = \sqrt{1+4}$
$d_{BC} = \sqrt{5}$

Step 3
Determine the length of EF.
$d_{EF} = \sqrt{(x_E - x_F)^2 + (y_E - y_F)^2}$
$d_{EF} = \sqrt{(0-5)^2 + (1-(-4))^2}$
$d_{EF} = \sqrt{(-5)^2 + (5)^2}$
$d_{EF} = \sqrt{25+25}$
$d_{EF} = \sqrt{50}$

Step 4
Determine the length of FG.
$d_{FG} = \sqrt{(x_F - x_G)^2 + (y_F - y_G)^2}$
$d_{FG} = \sqrt{(5-1)^2 + (-4-(-6))^2}$
$d_{FG} = \sqrt{(4)^2 + (2)^2}$
$d_{FG} = \sqrt{16+4}$
$d_{FG} = \sqrt{20}$

Step 5

Determine if $\dfrac{AB}{EF} = \dfrac{BC}{FG}$.

$$\dfrac{AB}{EF} = \dfrac{BC}{FG}$$
$$\dfrac{\sqrt{13}}{\sqrt{50}} = \dfrac{\sqrt{5}}{\sqrt{20}}$$
$$\left(\dfrac{\sqrt{13}}{\sqrt{50}}\right)^2 = \left(\dfrac{\sqrt{5}}{\sqrt{20}}\right)^2$$
$$\dfrac{13}{50} = \dfrac{5}{20}$$
$$0.26 \ne 0.25$$

Since $\dfrac{AB}{EF} \ne \dfrac{BC}{FG}$, parallelograms *ABCD* and *EFGH* are not similar.

G-SRT.3 Use the properties of similarity transformations to establish the AA criterion for two triangles to be similar.

PROPERTIES OF SIMILAR TRIANGLES

A **property** is an attribute, quality, or characteristic of something. Triangles with similar properties are shown with the symbol ~ . There are two properties of similar triangles.

1. All the corresponding angles of the triangles are equal.
2. All the corresponding sides of the triangles are proportionately equal in length.

Similar triangles have the same shape, but are not necessarily the same size.

In triangles, corresponding angles refer to matching pairs of angles found in the same place in both triangles. Corresponding sides are matching pairs of sides found in the same place in both triangles.

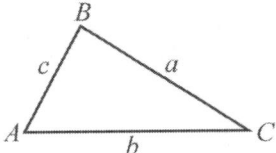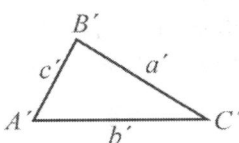

For example, the given triangles have the following properties:

- Angles *A* and *A'* are corresponding angles.
- Angles *B* and *B'* are corresponding angles.
- Angles *C* and *C'* are corresponding angles.

- Sides *a* and *a'* are corresponding sides.
- Sides *b* and *b'* are corresponding sides.
- Sides *c* and *c'* are corresponding sides.

For the given two triangles to be similar, it is necessary to prove the following:

- The corresponding angles are equal, meaning $\angle A = \angle A'$, $\angle B = \angle B'$, and $\angle C = \angle C'$.

  OR

- The corresponding sides are proportional, meaning $\dfrac{a}{a'} = \dfrac{b}{b'} = \dfrac{c}{c'}$ or $\dfrac{a'}{a} = \dfrac{b'}{b} = \dfrac{c'}{c}$.

Example

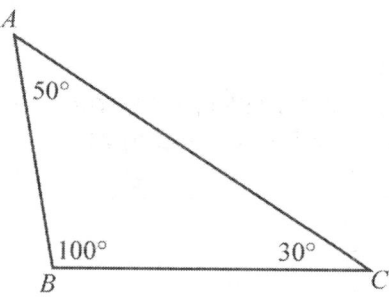

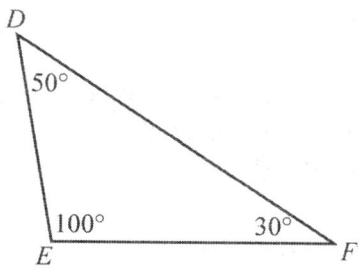

Determine whether triangles △ABC and △DEF are similar, using the property of corresponding angles.

Solution

Step 1
Identify the corresponding angles.
Corresponding angles have the same place in the triangles.

- ∠A corresponds to ∠D since ∠A = ∠D
- ∠B corresponds to ∠E since ∠B = ∠E
- ∠C corresponds to ∠F since ∠C = ∠F

All three corresponding angles are equal. Therefore, △ABC ~ △DEF.

Example

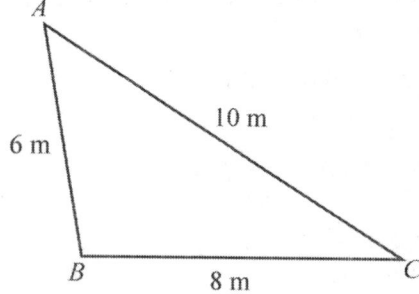

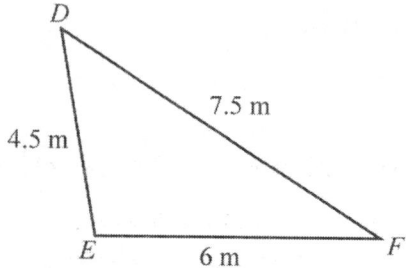

Determine whether △ABC and △DEF are similar, using the property of corresponding sides. Write the ratio of the corresponding sides in lowest terms.

Solution

Step 1
Identify the numerator and denominator of the ratios.
Place one triangle's corresponding sides in the numerator and the other triangle's corresponding sides in the denominator.

The ratio is $\frac{\triangle ABC}{\triangle DEF}$.

Step 2
Identify the corresponding sides.
Corresponding sides have the same place in the triangles.

- AB corresponds to DE
- BC corresponds to EF
- AC corresponds to DF

Similarity Transformations

Step 3
Write the ratio of the corresponding sides in lowest terms.

- $\dfrac{AB}{DE} = \dfrac{6\text{ m}}{4.5\text{ m}} = 1.3$
- $\dfrac{BC}{EF} = \dfrac{8\text{ m}}{6\text{ m}} = 1.3$
- $\dfrac{AC}{DF} = \dfrac{10\text{ m}}{7.5\text{ m}} = 1.3$

The triangles have proportional sides: $\triangle ABC \sim \triangle DEF$.

PROVING THE SIMILARITY OF TRIANGLES

When proving similarity in triangles, the following relationships should be considered:

1. The angle-angle (AA) or angle-angle-angle (AAA) relationship states that when two or three angles of one triangle are equal to two or three corresponding angles of another triangle, the two triangles must be similar.
2. The side-side-side (SSS) relationship states that when three pairs of corresponding sides are in the same ratio for two triangles, the triangles must be similar. This relationship is different from the SSS relationship of congruent triangles.
3. The side-angle-side (SAS) relationship states that when two sides and the included angle of one triangle are in the same ratio as the corresponding two sides and included angle of another triangle, the two triangles must be similar. This relationship is different from the SAS relationship of congruent triangles.

Example
Two triangles are given.

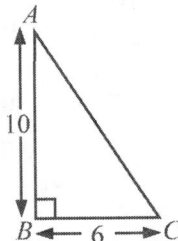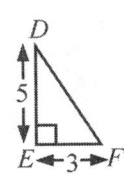

Prove that $\triangle ABC \sim \triangle DEF$.

Solution

Step 1
Determine if there is a common ratio between the sides of the two triangles.
$$\dfrac{AB}{DE} = \dfrac{10}{5} = 2$$
$$\dfrac{BC}{EF} = \dfrac{6}{3} = 2$$

Step 2
Determine if there are any congruent angles between the two triangles.
$\angle B = 90° = \angle E$

Step 3
State if the two triangles are similar.
According to the SAS (side-angle-side) relationship of similar triangles, $\triangle ABC \sim \triangle DEF$.

Example
Two triangles are given.

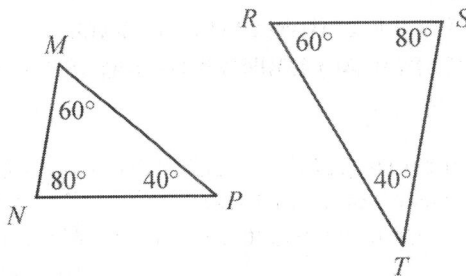

Prove that $\triangle MNP \sim \triangle RST$.

Solution
Only the angles are given in the two triangles.

Step 1
Determine if there are any congruent angles between the two triangles.
$\angle M = 60° = \angle R$
$\angle N = 80° = \angle S$
$\angle P = 40° = \angle T$

Step 2
State if the triangles are similar.
According to the AAA (angle-angle-angle) relationship of similar triangles, $\triangle MNP \sim \triangle RST$.

Example

Two triangles are given.

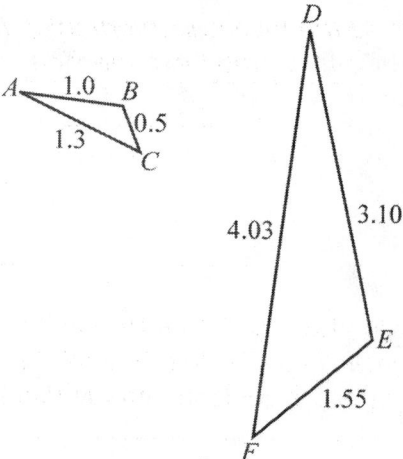

Prove that △ABC~△DEF.

Solution

Only the sides are given in the two triangles.

Step 1

Determine if there is a common ratio between the sides of the two triangles.

$$\frac{DE}{AB} = \frac{3.10}{1.0}$$
$$= 3.1$$
$$\frac{EF}{BC} = \frac{1.55}{0.5}$$
$$= 3.1$$
$$\frac{DF}{AC} = \frac{4.03}{1.3}$$
$$= 3.1$$

Step 2

State if the triangles are similar.
There is a common ratio of 3.1 between the sides of the two triangles.
By the SSS (side-side-side) relationship of similar triangles, △ABC~△DEF.

EXERCISE #1—SIMILARITY TRANSFORMATIONS

Use the following information to answer the next question.

Parallelogram *DEFG* has been transformed to produce the transformed image *D'E'F'G'*.

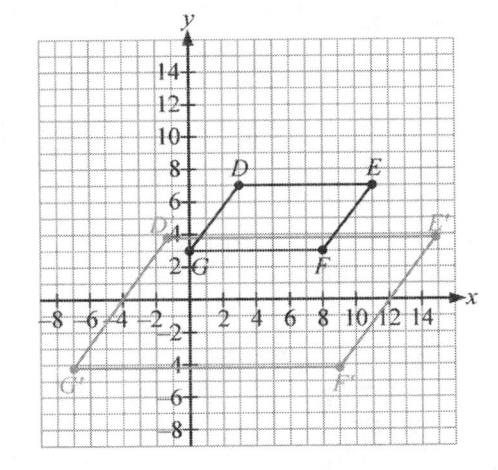

88. Which of the following statements correctly defines the dilation?
    A. The center of dilation is located at (−10, 7), and the magnitude of dilation is 2.
    B. The center of dilation is located at (−10, 7), and the magnitude of dilation is $\frac{1}{2}$.
    C. The center of dilation is located at (7, 10), and the magnitude of dilation is $\frac{1}{2}$.
    D. The center of dilation is located at (7, 10), and the magnitude of dilation is 2.

Use the following information to answer the next question.

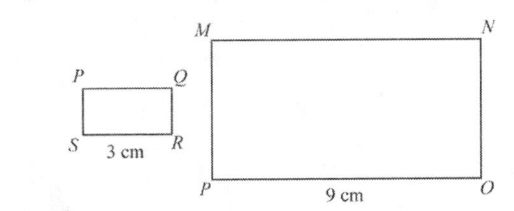

A scale drawing is given where rectangle *PQRS* is the original diagram and rectangle *MNOP* is the image diagram.

89. What is the scale factor of the given diagram? _____

Use the following information to answer the next question.

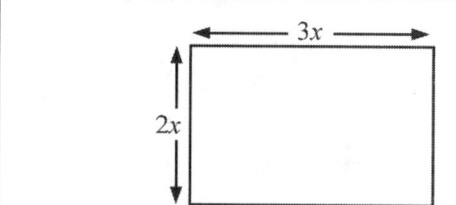

The rectangle shown has a length of $3x$ and a height of $2x$.

90. Which of the following rectangles is similar to the given rectangle?

A.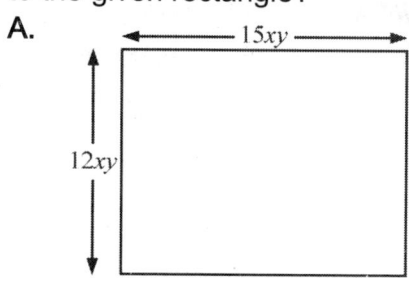

B.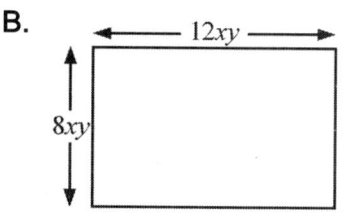

C.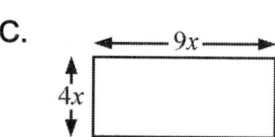

D.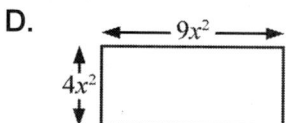

Use the following information to answer the next question.

A company that designs and manufactures crests designed the crest for the winners in a bantam hockey tournament.

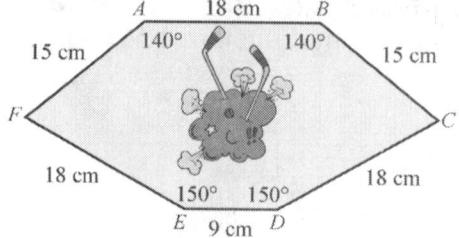

The organizers of the hockey tournament liked the design. However, they requested that the manufactured crests be 20% smaller than the original design.

91. If $\angle C = \angle F$, what is the measure of the angle that corresponds to $\angle C$ in the manufactured crests, given that the sum of the angles in a hexagon is $720°$?

A. 70° B. 65°
C. 56° D. 50°

Use the following information to answer the next question.

Polygon *ABCDEF* is similar to polygon *MNPQRS*. *AB* is 24 cm, *BC* is 28 cm, and *MN* is 36 cm.

92. If *AB* corresponds to *MN* and *BC* corresponds to *NP*, the length of side *NP* is _____ cm.

Exercise #1   Castle Rock Research

Use the following information to answer the next question.

Marie is asked to prove that the two quadrilaterals shown are similar, given that each vertex has integral x- and y-coordinates.

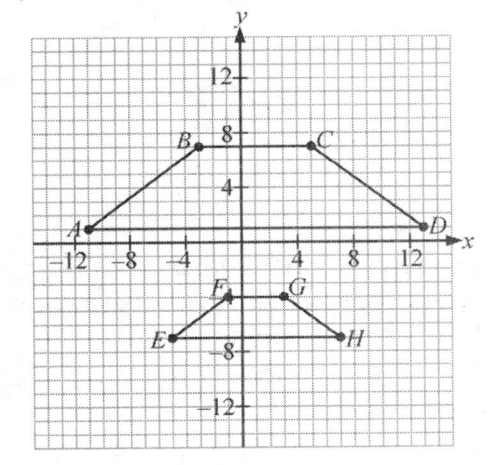

93. Assuming Marie's proof is correct, which of the following pairs of equations could be part of her proof?

   A. $\dfrac{BC}{FG} = 2$ and $\dfrac{BD}{FH} = \dfrac{1}{2}$

   B. $\dfrac{AD}{FG} = \dfrac{1}{2}$ and $\dfrac{AC}{EG} = \dfrac{1}{2}$

   C. $\dfrac{CD}{GH} = \dfrac{1}{2}$ and $\dfrac{BD}{FH} = 2$

   D. $\dfrac{AB}{EF} = 2$ and $\dfrac{AC}{EG} = 2$

Use the following information to answer the next question.

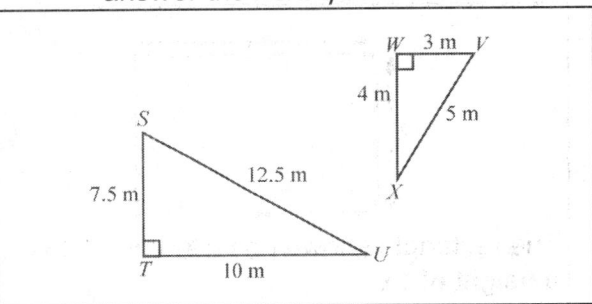

94. Prove triangle STU is similar to triangle VWX using the property of proportional corresponding sides.

    Note that ∠STU is a right angle, and is equal to ∠VWX.

Use the following information to answer the next question.

Two triangles are shown.

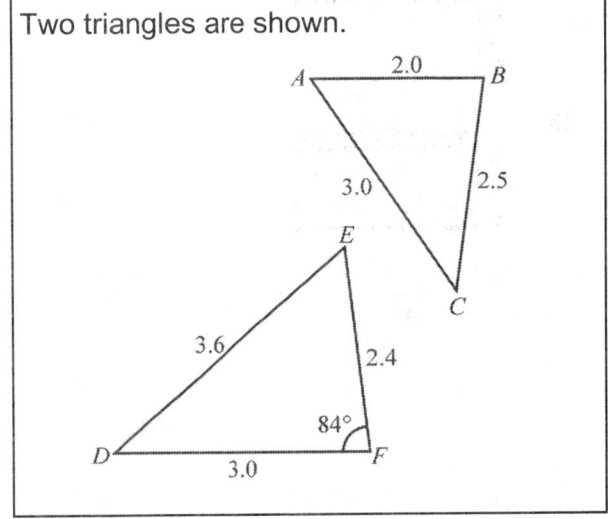

95. The measure of ∠B is _____°.

EXERCISE #1—SIMILARITY TRANSFORMATIONS ANSWERS AND SOLUTIONS

| 88. D | 90. B | 92. 42 | 94. See solution |
| 89. 3 | 91. A | 93. D | 95. 84 |

88. D

Step 1
Draw a line passing through each corresponding pair of points.

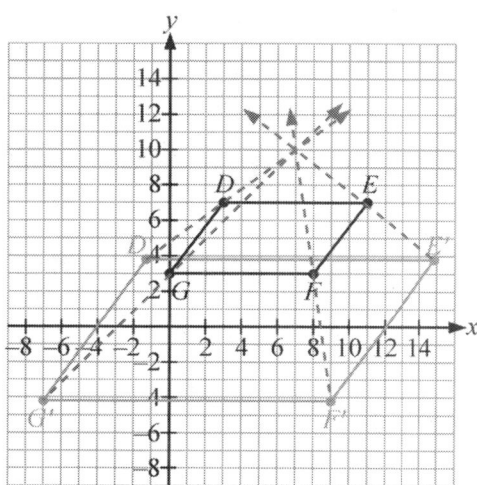

Step 2
Determine the point of intersection (center of dilation).
The center of dilation is located at (7, 10).

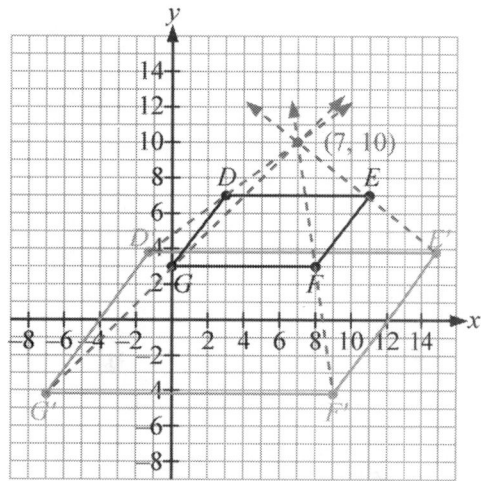

Step 3
Substitute corresponding side lengths into the magnitude formula.

magnitude = $\dfrac{\text{image length}}{\text{original length}}$

magnitude = $\dfrac{F'G'}{FG}$

Step 4
Calculate the magnitude.

magnitude = $\dfrac{F'G'}{FG}$

magnitude = $\dfrac{16}{8}$

magnitude = 2

The magnitude of dilation is 2.

Therefore, the center of dilation is located at (7, 10), and the magnitude of dilation is 2.

89. 3

Step 1
Pick one known length in the image diagram.
$PO = 9$ cm

Step 2
Find the corresponding length in the original diagram.
$SR = 3$ cm

Step 3
Use the scale factor formula to determine the scale factor.

scale factor = $\dfrac{\text{image length}}{\text{original length}}$

= $\dfrac{PO}{SR}$

= $\dfrac{9 \text{ cm}}{3 \text{ cm}}$

= 3

The diagram shows a reduction with a scale factor of 3.

90. B

Compare the lengths and widths of the possible rectangle to the given rectangle to determine similarity.

To compare the length, set up a ratio that compares the length of the possible similar rectangle to the length of the given rectangle.

$\dfrac{12xy}{3x} = 4y$

To compare the width, set up a ratio that compares the width of the possible similar rectangle to the width of the given rectangle.

$\dfrac{8xy}{2x} = 4y$

Since $\frac{12xy}{3x} = 4y$ and $\frac{8xy}{2x} = 4y$, the corresponding sides of the rectangle are proportional to the original rectangle.

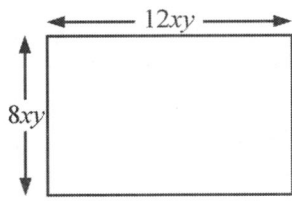

91. A

When the size of the crest is reduced by 20%, the length of each side of hexagon *ABCDEF* will be affected, but the measures of angles ∠A, ∠B, ∠C, ∠D, ∠E, and ∠F will not change. For similar polygons, corresponding sides are proportional in length, and corresponding angles are equal in measure.

Step 1
Determine the measure of ∠C.
The sum of the angles in a hexagon is 720°. Thus, ∠A + ∠B + ∠C + ∠D + ∠E + ∠F = 720°. If the measure of ∠C is represented by *x*, then the measure of ∠F will also be represented by *x*, since ∠C = ∠F.
Substitute 140° for ∠A, 140° for ∠B, *x* for ∠C, 150° for ∠D, 150° for ∠E, and *x* for ∠F in the equation ∠A + ∠B + ∠C + ∠D + ∠E + ∠F = 720°, and then solve for *x*.
140° + 140° + *x* + 150° + 150° + *x* = 720°
Simplify by collecting like terms.
$$2x + 580° = 720°$$
$$2x + 580° - 580° = 720° - 580°$$
$$2x = 140°$$
$$\frac{2x}{2} = \frac{140°}{2}$$
$$x = 70°$$

Since *x* = 70° and the measure of ∠C is represented by *x*, the measure of ∠C is 70°.

Step 2
Determine the measure of the angle that corresponds to ∠C in the manufactured crest.
Corresponding angles in similar polygons are equal in measure. Thus, the measure of the angle that corresponds to ∠C in the manufactured crest is also 70°.

92. 42

Since the figures are similar, use cross multiplication to find the missing side length.
$$\frac{AB}{MN} = \frac{BC}{NP}$$
$$\frac{24}{36} = \frac{28}{NP}$$
$$24(NP) = (28)(36)$$
$$\frac{24(NP)}{24} = \frac{1{,}008}{24}$$
$$x = 42$$
NP = 42 cm

93. D

Recall that the distance formula, $d = \sqrt{(x_2 - x_1)^2 + (y_2 - y_1)^2}$, can be used to find the length of a line segment.

Step 1
Determine the value of the ratio between the side lengths *BC* and *FG*.
$$d_{BC} = \sqrt{(x_C - x_B)^2 + (y_C - y_B)^2}$$
$$d_{BC} = \sqrt{(5 - (-3))^2 + (7 - 7)^2}$$
$$d_{BC} = \sqrt{(8)^2 + (0)^2}$$
$$d_{BC} = \sqrt{64}$$
$$d_{BC} = 8$$
$$d_{FG} = \sqrt{(x_G - x_F)^2 + (y_G - y_F)^2}$$
$$d_{FG} = \sqrt{(3 - (-1))^2 + (-4 - (-4))^2}$$
$$d_{FG} = \sqrt{(4)^2 + (0)^2}$$
$$d_{FG} = \sqrt{16}$$
$$d_{FG} = 4$$

The value of $\frac{BC}{FG}$ is $\frac{8}{4} = 2$.

Step 2
Determine the value of the ratio between the side lengths CD and GH.

$d_{CD} = \sqrt{(x_D - x_C)^2 + (y_D - y_C)^2}$
$d_{CD} = \sqrt{(13 - 5)^2 + (1 - 7)^2}$
$d_{CD} = \sqrt{(8)^2 + (-6)^2}$
$d_{CD} = \sqrt{64 + 36}$
$d_{CD} = \sqrt{100}$
$d_{CD} = 10$
$d_{GH} = \sqrt{(x_H - x_G)^2 + (y_H - y_G)^2}$
$d_{GH} = \sqrt{(7 - 3)^2 + (-7 - (-4))^2}$
$d_{GH} = \sqrt{(4)^2 + (-3)^2}$
$d_{GH} = \sqrt{16 + 9}$
$d_{GH} = \sqrt{25}$
$d_{GH} = 5$

The value of $\dfrac{CD}{GH}$ is $\dfrac{10}{5} = 2$.

Step 3
Determine the value of the ratio between the side lengths AB and EF.

$d_{AB} = \sqrt{(x_B - x_A)^2 + (y_B - y_A)^2}$
$d_{AB} = \sqrt{(-3 - (-11))^2 + (7 - 1)^2}$
$d_{AB} = \sqrt{(8)^2 + (6)^2}$
$d_{AB} = \sqrt{64 + 36}$
$d_{AB} = \sqrt{100}$
$d_{AB} = 10$
$d_{EF} = \sqrt{(x_F - x_E)^2 + (y_F - y_E)^2}$
$d_{EF} = \sqrt{(-1 - (-5))^2 + (-4 - (-7))^2}$
$d_{EF} = \sqrt{(4)^2 + (3)^2}$
$d_{EF} = \sqrt{16 + 9}$
$d_{EF} = \sqrt{25}$
$d_{EF} = 5$

The value of $\dfrac{AB}{EF}$ is $\dfrac{10}{5} = 2$.

Step 4
Determine the value of the ratio between the diagonals BD and FH.

$d_{BD} = \sqrt{(x_D - x_B)^2 + (y_D - y_B)^2}$
$d_{BD} = \sqrt{(13 - (-3))^2 + (1 - 7)^2}$
$d_{BD} = \sqrt{(16)^2 + (-6)^2}$
$d_{BD} = \sqrt{256 + 36}$
$d_{BD} = \sqrt{292}$
$d_{FH} = \sqrt{(x_H - x_F)^2 + (y_H - y_F)^2}$
$d_{FH} = \sqrt{(7 - (-1))^2 + (-7 - (-4))^2}$
$d_{FH} = \sqrt{(8)^2 + (-3)^2}$
$d_{FH} = \sqrt{64 + 9}$
$d_{FH} = \sqrt{73}$

The value of $\dfrac{BD}{FH}$ is $\dfrac{\sqrt{292}}{\sqrt{73}} = \sqrt{292 \div 73} = \sqrt{4} = 2$.

Step 5
Determine the value of the ratio between the diagonals AC and EG.

$d_{AC} = \sqrt{(x_C - x_A)^2 + (y_C - y_A)^2}$
$d_{AC} = \sqrt{(5 - (-11))^2 + (7 - 1)^2}$
$d_{AC} = \sqrt{(16)^2 + (6)^2}$
$d_{AC} = \sqrt{256 + 36}$
$d_{AC} = \sqrt{292}$
$d_{EG} = \sqrt{(x_G - x_E)^2 + (y_G - y_E)^2}$
$d_{EG} = \sqrt{(3 - (-5))^2 + (-4 - (-7))^2}$
$d_{EG} = \sqrt{(8)^2 + (3)^2}$
$d_{EG} = \sqrt{64 + 9}$
$d_{EG} = \sqrt{73}$

The value of $\dfrac{AC}{EG}$ is $\dfrac{\sqrt{292}}{\sqrt{73}} = \sqrt{292 \div 73} = \sqrt{4} = 2$.

Step 6
Identify the pair of equations that could be part of Marie's proof.

Since $\dfrac{AB}{EF} = 2$ and $\dfrac{AC}{EG} = 2$, these equations could be part of Marie's proof.

Since side AD does not correspond to side FG, it is not necessary to determine the value of the ratio $\dfrac{AD}{FG}$.

94.
Step 1
Identify the numerator and denominator of the ratio. Place the corresponding sides of triangle *STU* in the numerator and the corresponding sides of triangle *VWX* in the denominator.

The ratio is $\frac{\triangle STU}{\triangle VWX}$.

Step 2
Write the ratio of the corresponding sides in lowest terms.

The ratio is $\frac{ST}{VW} = \frac{7.5 \text{ m}}{3 \text{ m}} = 2.5$.

The ratio is $\frac{TU}{WX} = \frac{10 \text{ m}}{4 \text{ m}} = 2.5$.

The ratio is $\frac{SU}{VX} = \frac{12.5 \text{ m}}{5 \text{ m}} = 2.5$.

Since the given triangles have proportional sides, $\triangle STU \sim \triangle VWX$.

95. 84

Step 1
Determine if the triangles are similar.
Find a common ratio between the sides of the two triangles.

$\frac{EF}{AB} = \frac{2.4}{2.0}$
$= 1.2$

$\frac{DF}{BC} = \frac{3.0}{2.5}$
$= 1.2$

$\frac{DE}{AC} = \frac{3.6}{3.0}$
$= 1.2$

Since there is a common ratio of 1.2 between the sides of the two triangles, by the SSS (side-side-side) relationship of similar triangles, $\triangle ABC \sim \triangle DEF$.

Step 2
Determine the measure of $\angle B$.
By the definition of similar triangles, all the corresponding angles of the triangles are equal. Therefore, if $\angle B = \angle F$, then $\angle B = 84°$.

EXERCISE #2—SIMILARITY TRANSFORMATIONS

Use the following information to answer the next question.

Triangle ABC has been dilated to produce the transformed image A'B'C', as illustrated in the given diagram.

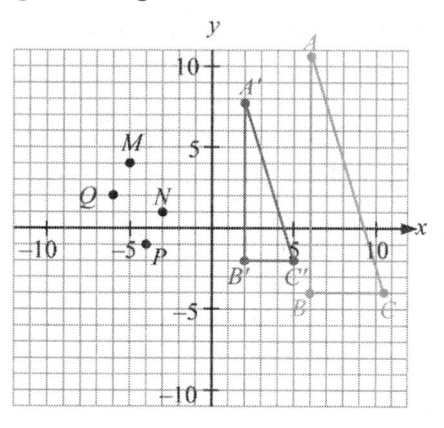

96. The center of dilation is at point
    A. M
    B. N
    C. P
    D. Q

Use the following information to answer the next question.

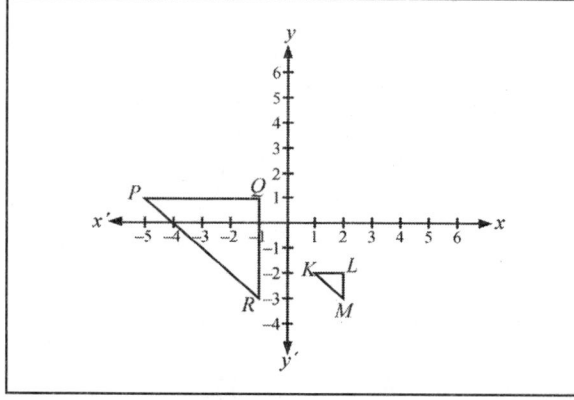

97. By what scale factor is triangle PQR larger than triangle KLM?
    A. 2
    B. 3
    C. 4
    D. 5

Use the following information to answer the next question.

A regular pentagon has sides measuring 2 cm and interior angles measuring 108°.

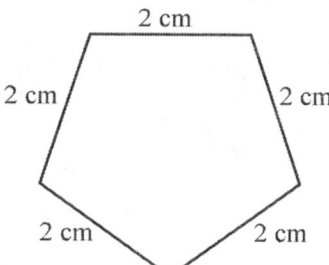

Anabel drew a pentagon that is similar to the one shown.

98. Which of the following statements about the pentagon Anabel drew is **false**?
    A. Corresponding side lengths are proportional.
    B. Corresponding side lengths are not proportional.
    C. The exterior angles of the polygon measure 72°.
    D. The interior angles of the polygon measure 108°.

Use the following information to answer the next question.

Octagons ABCDEFGH and MNOPQRST are similar.

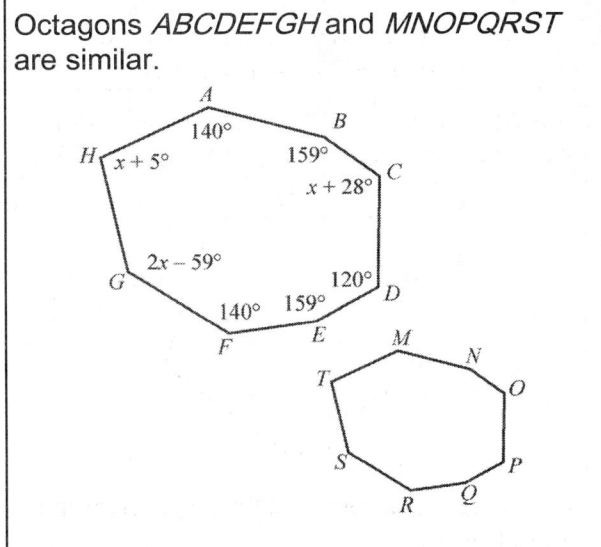

99. Given that the sum of the angles in an octagon is 1,080°, what is the measure of angle T?
   A. 95°
   B. 97°
   C. 100°
   D. 102°

Use the following information to answer the next question.

LMNO and PQRS are similar polygons.

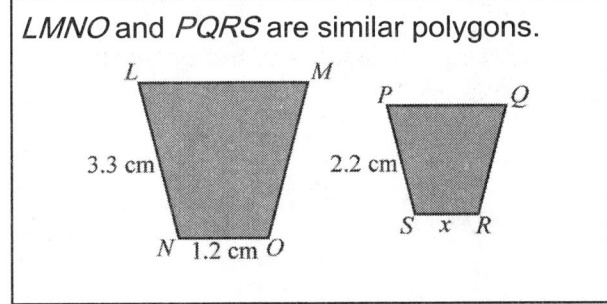

100. Expressed to the nearest tenth, the length of side SR is _____ cm.

Use the following information to answer the next question.

Miguel is asked to prove that quadrilateral EFGH, which has vertices E(3, 8), F(9, 13), G(12, 11), and H(12, −1), is similar to quadrilateral RSTU, which has vertices R(x, −3), S(9, −1), T(10, −2), and U(10, −6), where x represents a whole number less than 12. As part of his proof, Miguel correctly determines that the length of side GH is 12 units, the length of side TU is 4 units, and the length of diagonal EG is $3\sqrt{10}$ units.

101. What is the value of x? _____ units

Use the following information to answer the next question.

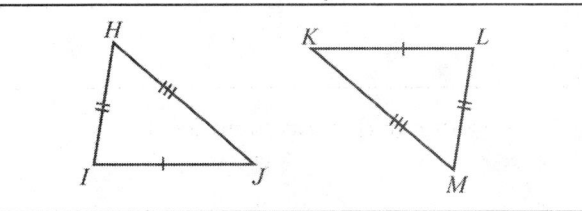

102. Using corresponding angles and sides, determine whether triangles △HIJ and △KLM are similar.

Use the following information to answer the next question.

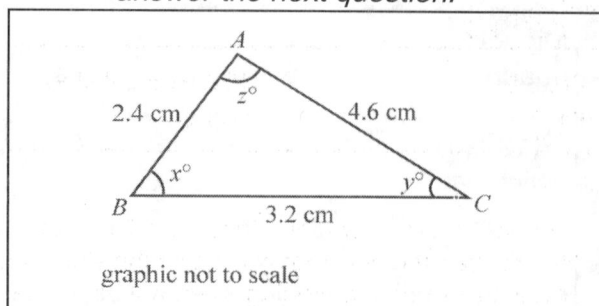

graphic not to scale

103. Which of the following triangles is **not** similar to the triangle shown?

A.
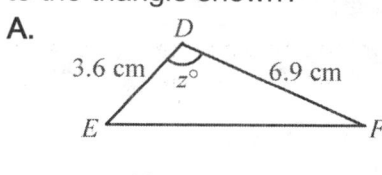

graphic not to scale

B.
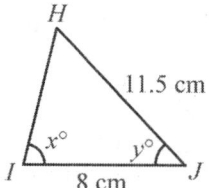

graphic not to scale

C.
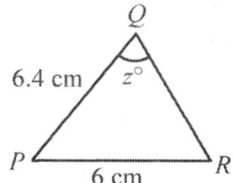

graphic not to scale

D.
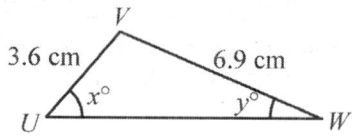

graphic not to scale

EXERCISE #2—SIMILARITY TRANSFORMATIONS ANSWERS AND SOLUTIONS

96. D	98. B	100. 0.8	102. See solution
97. C	99. D	101. 7	103. C

96. D

Step 1
Draw a line passing through each pair of corresponding vertices (A and A', B and B', and C and C') in the given diagram.

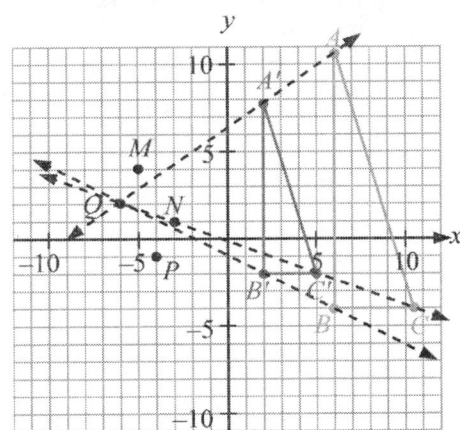

Step 2
Determine the point of intersection of the three lines. The center of dilation is the point where the three lines intersect. The three lines intersect at point Q. Therefore, point Q is the center of dilation.

97. C

Step 1
Find the lengths of the legs of the triangles.
Find the lengths of PQ, QR, KL, and LM.
The length of PQ = 4 units.
The length of QR = 4 units.
The length of KL = 1 unit.
The length of LM = 1 unit.

Step 2
Find the ratio of corresponding legs of the triangle to find the scale factor.

$$\frac{PQ}{KL} = \frac{QR}{LM}$$
$$\frac{4}{1} = \frac{4}{1}$$
$$4 = 4$$

The scale factor is 4.

98. B

If Anabel drew a pentagon that is similar to the one shown, then the ratio that compares the side lengths of any pair of corresponding sides will be the same.

This means that corresponding side lengths in similar polygons, no matter how many sides, are always proportional.

In any two proportional figures, the interior and exterior angles will remain the same.

99. D

Step 1
Determine the value of x in octagon ABCDEFGH. Given that the sum of the angles in an octagon is 1,080°, it follows that

$$\begin{pmatrix} \angle A + \angle B + \angle C + \angle D \\ + \angle E + \angle F + \angle G + \angle H \end{pmatrix} = 1,080°.$$

Substitute the provided values of angles A, B, C, D, E, F, G, and H in the equation, and solve for x.

$$\begin{pmatrix} 140° + 159° + (x + 28°) \\ + 120° + 159° + 140° \\ + (2x - 59°) + (x + 5°) \end{pmatrix} = 1,080°$$

Simplify by collecting like terms.
$$4x + 692° = 1,080°$$
$$4x = 388°$$
$$\frac{4x}{4} = \frac{388°}{4}$$
$$x = 97°$$

Step 2
Identify the angle in octagon ABCDEFGH that corresponds to ∠T in octagon MNOPQRST.
By examining the two given octagons, it can be observed that ∠T corresponds to ∠H.

Step 3
Determine the measure of ∠H.
∠H = x + 5°
Substitute 97° for x.
∠H = 97° + 5°
    = 102°

Step 4
Determine the measure of ∠T.
Corresponding angles in similar polygons are equal in measure. Since ∠T corresponds to ∠H and the measure of ∠H is 102°, it follows that the measure of ∠T is 102°.

100. 0.8

Since the polygons are similar, you can use cross multiplication to find the missing side length.

$$\frac{3.3}{2.2} = \frac{1.2}{x}$$
$$3.3x = (2.2)(1.2)$$
$$\frac{3.3x}{3.3} = \frac{2.64}{3.3}$$
$$x = 0.8$$
$$SR = 0.8 \text{ cm}$$

101. 7

The ratio between the lengths of corresponding sides in similar quadrilaterals is equal to the ratio between the lengths of corresponding diagonals in the respective quadrilaterals.

Step 1
Determine the value of the ratio between the side lengths of GH and TU.
Sides GH and TU are corresponding sides with respect to the two given quadrilaterals. Since the length of side GH is 12 units and the length of side TU is 4 units, the value of $\frac{GH}{TU} = \frac{12}{4} = 3$.

Step 2
Determine an expression for the length of diagonal RT by applying the distance formula,
$d_{AB} = \sqrt{(x_A - x_B)^2 + (y_A - y_B)^2}$.
$d_{RT} = \sqrt{(x - 10)^2 + (-3 - (-2))^2}$
$d_{RT} = \sqrt{(x - 10)^2 + (-1)^2}$
$d_{RT} = \sqrt{(x - 10)^2 + 1}$

Step 3
Determine an expression for the ratio between the lengths of the corresponding diagonals EG and RT. The expression for the length of diagonal RT is $\sqrt{(x - 10)^2 + 1}$ units, and the length of diagonal EG is given as $3\sqrt{10}$ units. Therefore, an expression for the ratio between the lengths of the diagonals EG and RT, $\frac{EG}{RT}$, is $\frac{3\sqrt{10}}{\sqrt{(x - 10)^2 + 1}}$.

Step 4
Determine the value of x.
Since the ratio between the lengths of corresponding sides in similar quadrilaterals is equal to the ratio between the lengths of corresponding diagonals in the respective quadrilaterals, it follows that
$$\frac{3\sqrt{10}}{\sqrt{(x - 10)^2 + 1}} = \frac{3}{1}.$$
Cross-multiply.
$3\sqrt{10} \times 1 = 3 \times \sqrt{(x - 10)^2 + 1}$
$3\sqrt{10} = 3\sqrt{(x - 10)^2 + 1}$
Divide each side of the equation by 3.
$\sqrt{10} = \sqrt{(x - 10)^2 + 1}$
Square each side of the equation, simplify, and set the resulting equation equal to 0.
$\sqrt{10}^2 = \sqrt{(x - 10)^2 + 1}^2$
$10 = (x - 10)^2 + 1$
$10 = x^2 - 10x - 10x + 100 + 1$
$10 = x^2 - 20x + 101$
$0 = x^2 - 20x + 91$
Factor the trinomial.
$0 = x^2 - 20x + 91$
$0 = (x - 13)(x - 7)$
Set each factor equal to 0, and solve for x.
$x - 13 = 0$ or $x - 7 = 0$
$x = 13$ or $x = 7$
The value of x must be 7 because x represents a whole number less than 12.

102.

Step 1
Identify the corresponding sides.
Corresponding sides have the same place in the triangles.
HJ is equal and corresponds to KM.
HI is equal and corresponds to LM.
IJ is equal and corresponds to KL.
△HIJ and △KLM are similar as all sides are equal and corresponding in length.

Step 2
Corresponding angles have the same place in the triangles and are equal, when the sides of the triangles are corresponding and proportional in length.
∠H corresponds to ∠M.
∠L corresponds to ∠I.
∠J corresponds to ∠K.
△HIJ is similar to △KLM as corresponding angles are equal.

103. C

In each alternative, some of the sides and angles are known. Apply the appropriate similarity relationships to the known side lengths and angles to determine which triangle is not similar.

Step 1
Compare $\triangle ABC$ with $\triangle DEF$.
$$\frac{AB}{DE} = \frac{2.4 \text{cm}}{3.6 \text{cm}} = \frac{2}{3}$$
$$\frac{AC}{DF} = \frac{4.6 \text{cm}}{6.9 \text{cm}} = \frac{2}{3}$$
$$\frac{AB}{DE} = \frac{AC}{DF}$$
Since two sides and the included angle of $\triangle ABC$ are proportional to the corresponding two sides and included angle of $\triangle DEF$, the two triangles are similar through side-angle-side similarity.

Step 2
Compare $\triangle ABC$ with $\triangle HIJ$.
Since two angles of $\triangle ABC$ are equal to two angles of $\triangle HIJ$, they are similar through angle-angle similarity.

Step 3
Compare $\triangle ABC$ with $\triangle UVW$.
Since two angles of $\triangle ABC$ are equal to two angles of $\triangle UVW$, they are similar through angle-angle similarity.

Step 4
Compare $\triangle ABC$ with $\triangle PQR$.
The $z°$ angle can be found in both triangles. To be similar triangles, BC would have to correspond to PR since they are both opposite from $z°$.
The side PQ would have to correspond to AC since AC is longer than BC in $\triangle ABC$, while PQ is longer than PR in $\triangle PQR$.
$$\frac{AC}{PQ} = \frac{4.6 \text{cm}}{6.4 \text{cm}} = \frac{5.75}{8}$$
$$\frac{BC}{PR} = \frac{3.2 \text{cm}}{6 \text{cm}} \approx \frac{4.27}{8}$$
$$\frac{AC}{PQ} \neq \frac{BC}{PR}$$
Similar triangles have proportional side lengths through the side-side-side relationship of similarity. Since the known sides of $\triangle ABC$ and $\triangle PQR$ are not proportional, it can be proven that the triangles are not similar.

NOTES

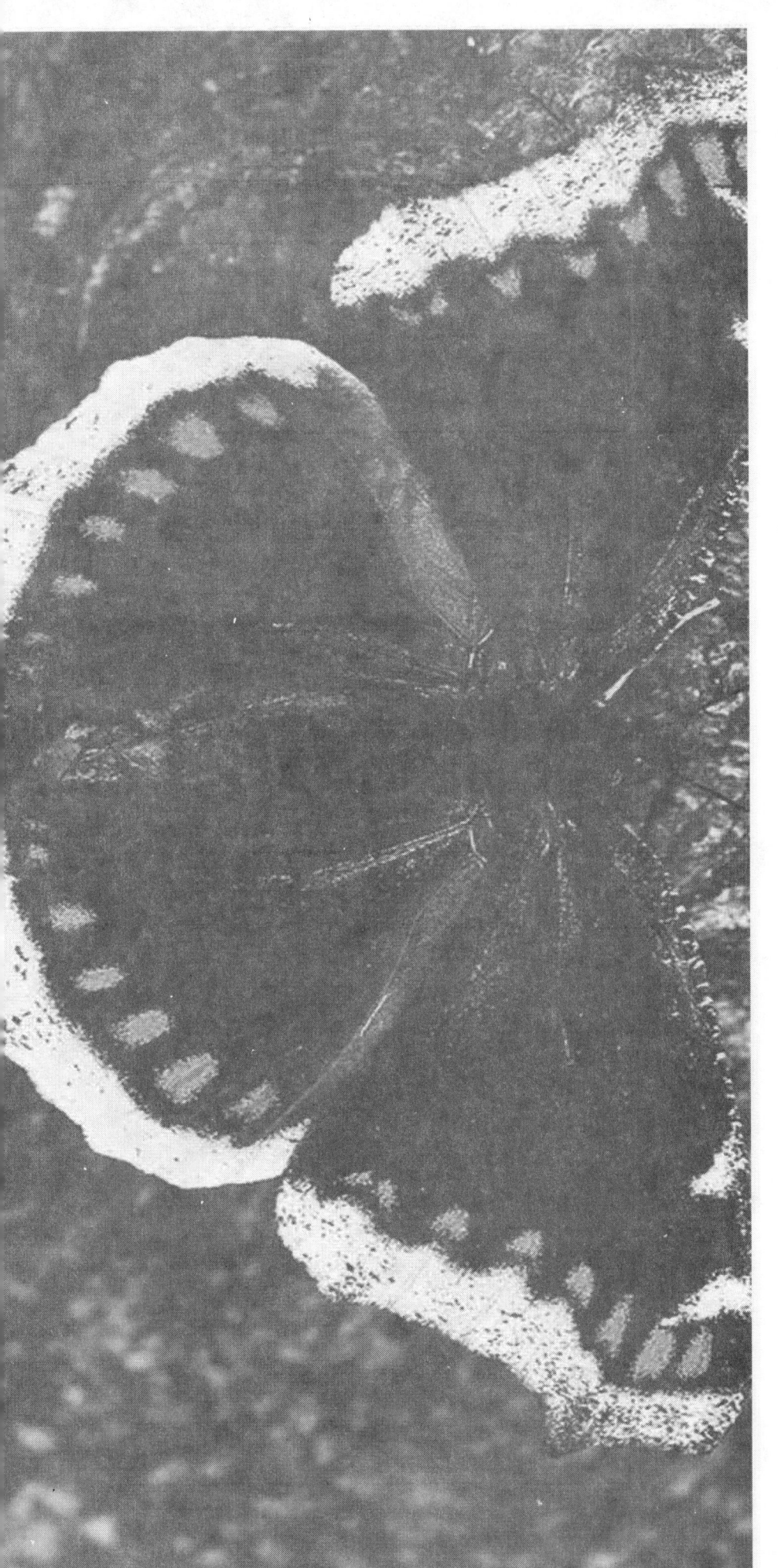

Theorems Involving Similarity

THEOREMS INVOLVING SIMILARITY

Table of Correlations

Standard		Concepts	Exercise #1	Exercise #2
Unit2.2	Prove theorems involving similarity.			
G-SRT.4	Prove theorems about triangles. Theorems include: a line parallel to one side of a triangle divides the other two proportionally, and conversely; the Pythagorean Theorem proved using triangle similarity.	Applying Theorems about the Mean Proportional	53	70
		Developing the Pythagorean Theorem Using Diagrams	104	109
		Problem Solving Using the Pythagorean Theorem	105	110
		Applying Theorems about Proportionality Among Segments of Triangles	106	111
G-SRT.5	Use congruence and similarity criteria for triangles to solve problems and to prove relationships in geometric figures.	Properties of Congruent Triangles	32	34
		Problem Solving with Congruent Triangles	33	38
		Applying Theorems about Parallelograms	55	72
		Applying Theorems about Special Parallelograms	56	73
		Properties of Similar Triangles	94	102
		Proving the Similarity of Triangles	95	103
		Problem Solving with Similar Triangles	107	112
		Applying Theorems about Trapezoids	108	113

G-SRT.4 Prove theorems about triangles. Theorems include: a line parallel to one side of a triangle divides the other two proportionally, and conversely; the Pythagorean Theorem proved using triangle similarity.

DEVELOPING THE PYTHAGOREAN THEOREM USING DIAGRAMS

The Pythagorean theorem describes the relationship between three sides of a right triangle. The theorem may be used to find the length of one side of any right triangle when the other two sides are given. This theorem is called the Pythagorean theorem because it was developed by Pythagoras, a Greek mathematician, in the 6th century BC.

Pythagoras drew the following triangle:

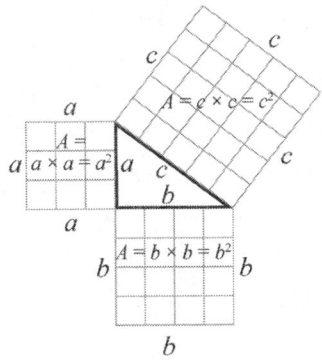

He used each side length of a triangle to make squares along each edge. He discovered that when the area of the square with the same side lengths as one leg of the triangle is added to the area of the square of the other leg of the triangle, they add up to the area of the square located along the hypotenuse.

He came up with what is now known as the Pythagorean theorem: $a^2 + b^2 = c^2$. Although the Pythagorean theorem equation is readily available on many formula sheets, it is so frequently used that it is a good idea to remember it. Therefore, most people memorize it as:

The square **on** the hypotenuse is equal to the sum of squares **on** the other two sides.

Notice that we say "on" as the squares are literally drawn on top of the sides.

Although the sides adjacent the right angle, called **legs**, are frequently labeled with letters a and b, and the *hypotenuse* is frequently labeled as c, any lower-case letters representing the hypotenuse and the legs may be used to write the Pythagorean theorem equation.

Here are some examples of right triangles with the sides properly labeled.

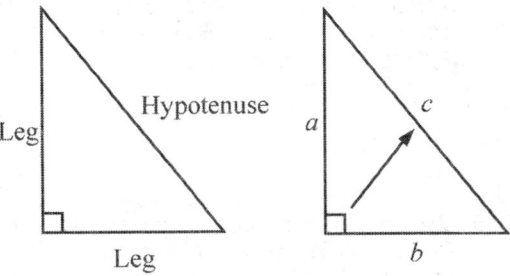

The sides a and b are interchangeable. As long as the two sides are the legs that make up the right angle, it does not matter which side is labeled a and which is labeled b.

Here are two more examples of right triangles.

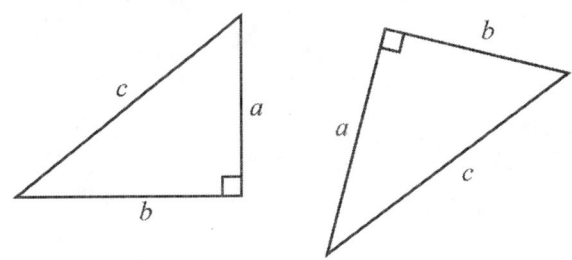

The **Pythagorean theorem** states that the area of the square on the hypotenuse is equal to the area of the squares on the legs added together.

To model the Pythagorean theorem, follow these steps:

1. Make a square using the length of one leg of the triangle (for example, a).
2. Make a square using the length of one leg of the triangle (for example, b).
3. Make a square using the length of the hypotenuse c.

Example

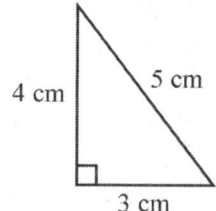

Show that the sum of the areas of the squares on the legs is equal to the area of the square on the hypotenuse.

Solution

Step 1

Make a square using the length of side a. Choose either of the two shorter sides to be side a.

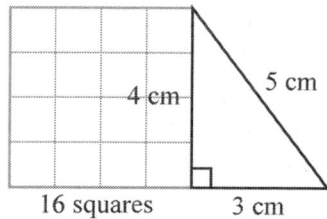

This square will have an area of 16 square centimeters.

Step 2

Make a square using the length of side b.

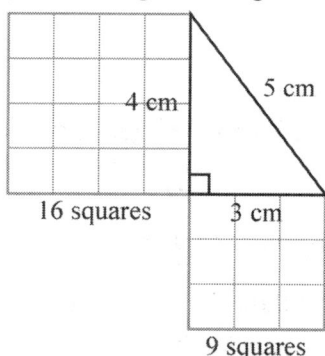

This square will have an area of 9 square centimeters.

Step 3

Make a square using the length of side c.

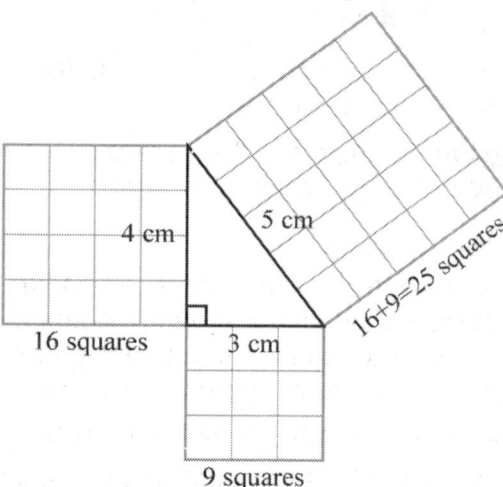

This square will have an area of 25 cm². 25 squares is equal to 16 squares and 9 squares added together. So, the area of the square on the hypotenuse is equal to the sum of the squares on the two legs of the right triangle.

The Pythagorean theorem may be used to determine whether a triangle is a right triangle.

Example

A triangle has sides lengths of 5 units, 11 units and 13 units.

Use the Pythagorean theorem to determine whether the triangle is a right triangle.

Solution

If the triangle is a right triangle, then by the Pythagorean theorem, the area of the square on the hypotenuse will equal to the sum of areas of squares on the other two sides.

The square on the side with 5 units length will have area of $5^2 = 25$ units^2 and the square on the side with 11 units will have area of $11^2 = 121$ units^2. The square on the hypotenuse has area of $13^2 = 169$ units^2. Check if the Pythagorean theorem holds:

$5^2 + 11^2 = 13^2$
$25 + 121 = 169$
$146 \ne 169$

The two sides of the equation are not equal, so the triangle is not a right triangle.

Example

Use the Pythagorean theorem to determine whether a right triangle can have sides of 5, 12, and 13 units.

Solution

If it is a right triangle, $5^2 + 12^2$ should equal 13^2. Check:

$5^2 + 12^2 = 13^2$
$25 + 144 = 169$
$169 = 169$

The two sides of the equation are equal, so this makes a right triangle.

Example

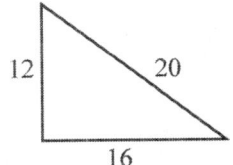

Use the Pythagorean theorem to determine whether the triangle is a right triangle.

Solution

Step 1
Label the sides.

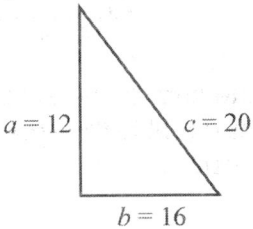

Step 2
Substitute the given values into the Pythagorean theorem, and simplify.
$a^2 + b^2 = c^2$
$12^2 + 16^2 = 20^2$
$144 + 256 = 400$
$400 = 400$

Since the two sides of the equation are equal, this is a right triangle.

Example

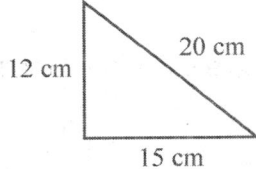

Use the Pythagorean theorem to determine whether the triangle is a right triangle.

Solution

Step 1
Label the sides.

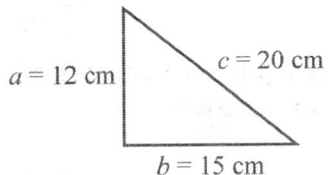

Step 2

Substitute the given values into the Pythagorean theorem, and simplify.

$a^2 + b^2 = c^2$
$12^2 + 15^2 = 20^2$
$144 + 225 = 400$
$369 \neq 400$

Since the two sides of the equation are not equal, this is not a right triangle.

Example

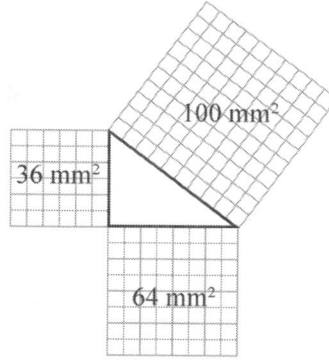

Use the Pythagorean theorem to determine whether the triangle is a right triangle.

Solution

Add the areas of the legs to see if their sum is equal to the area of the hypotenuse.

The largest value is always the hypotenuse.
$36 + 64 = 100$
$100 = 100$

The triangle is a right triangle because the sum of the area of the two legs is equal to the area of the hypotenuse.

PROBLEM SOLVING USING THE PYTHAGOREAN THEOREM

When solving problems using the Pythagorean theorem, it is important to label all the sides of a right-angled triangle correctly. The legs of the triangle are the two sides that join to form the right angle. These are often labeled a and b. The hypotenuse is the longest side of the triangle and is always opposite the right angle. The hypotenuse is often labeled c.

To find the missing side of a right triangle, follow these steps:

1. Substitute the known values into the Pythagorean Theorem equation.
2. Solve for the missing side.

Example

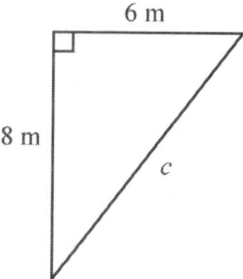

Use the Pythagorean theorem to solve for the missing side of the triangle.

Solution

Step 1

Substitute the known values into the Pythagorean theorem.

Label one side a and the other side b. Substitute the values into the equation.

$a^2 + b^2 = c^2$
$6^2 + 8^2 = c^2$

Step 2

Solve for the missing side.

Follow the order of operations.

Calculate the exponents.

$36 + 64 = c^2$
$100 = c^2$

Take the square root of both sides to solve for c.

$\sqrt{100} = \sqrt{c^2}$
$10 = c$
$c = 10$ m

Example

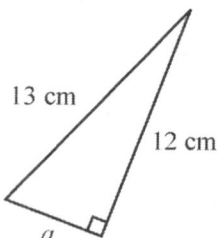

Use the Pythagorean theorem to solve for the missing side of the right triangle.

Solution

Step 1
Substitute the known values into the Pythagorean Theorem equation.
Substitute the values in for b and c.
$a^2 + b^2 = c^2$
$a^2 + 12^2 = 13^2$
$a^2 + 144 = 169$

Step 2
Solve for the missing side.
Subtract 144 from both sides of the equation to isolate a^2.
$a^2 + 144 - 144 = 169 - 144$
$a^2 = 25$
Take the square root of both sides to solve for a.
$\sqrt{a^2} = \sqrt{25}$
$a = 5$
Side a is 5 cm.

Example
A ladder is leaning against the side of a wall. The top of the ladder is 1.5 m from the ground. The base of the ladder is 2 m from the wall. The wall is **perpendicular** to the ground.

Use the Pythagorean theorem to determine the length of the ladder.

Solution

Step 1
Draw and label a figure that illustrates the problem.
Label the wall a and the ground b (or vice versa). The ladder will be side c because it is opposite the right angle.

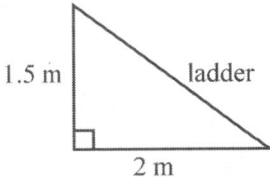

Note: Although we will use the common representation of the Pythagorean Theorem using variables a, b, and c, you may also label the triangle as w for the wall, g for the ground, and l for the ladder. In this case, the Pythagorean Theorem will lead to an expression: $w^2 + g^2 = l^2$.

Step 2
Substitute the known values into the Pythagorean theorem, and solve for the unknown.
Simplify by following the order of operations.
$a^2 + b^2 = c^2$
$1.5^2 + 2^2 = c^2$
$2.25 + 4 = c^2$
$6.25 = c^2$
$\sqrt{6.25} = \sqrt{c^2}$
$2.5 = c$
$c = 2.5$ m
The ladder is 2.5 m long.

Example

A square field has a path running diagonally across it. The sides of the field measure 4.2 m long.

Rounded to the tenth of a meter, how long is the path?

Solution

Step 1

Draw and label a figure that illustrates the problem.

Label the sides *a* and *b*; label the diagonal path *c*.

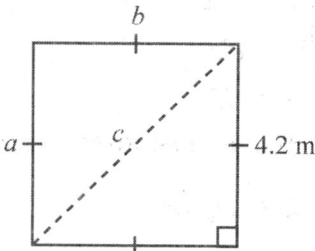

Note: In this diagram, one may choose to label sides of the square field using letter *s* representing "side", and the diagonal path using letter *p* for "path" or *d* for diagonal. Using letters *s* and *p*, the Pythagorean Theorem equation will be $s^2 + s^2 = p^2$ since both sides of the square are equal in length and represented by the same variable.

Step 2

Substitute the known values into the Pythagorean theorem, and solve for the unknown.

$$a^2 + b^2 = c^2$$
$$4.2^2 + 4.2^2 = c^2$$
$$17.64 + 17.64 = c^2$$
$$35.28 = c^2$$
$$\sqrt{35.28} = \sqrt{c^2}$$
$$5.93969692 = c$$
$$c = 5.9 \text{ m}$$

The path across the field is 5.9 m long.

APPLYING THEOREMS ABOUT PROPORTIONALITY AMONG SEGMENTS OF TRIANGLES

When a line is parallel to one side of a triangle, it intersects the other two sides of a triangle and divides them into proportional segments.

Example

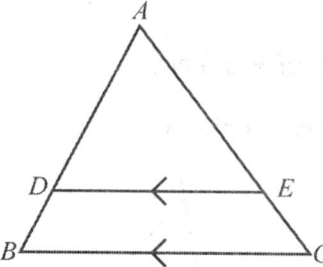

In the given triangle, $\frac{AE}{CE} = \frac{AD}{BD}$. This theorem can also be represented by $\frac{AC}{CE} = \frac{AB}{BD}$ or $\frac{AE}{AC} = \frac{AD}{AB}$.

The lengths of parallel segments are also proportional to the sides they divide.

$$\frac{AD}{AB} = \frac{DE}{BC}$$

You can use these relationships to solve for missing lengths of segments of triangles.

Example

In the given triangle *MNO*, *PQ* and *NO* are parallel line segments.

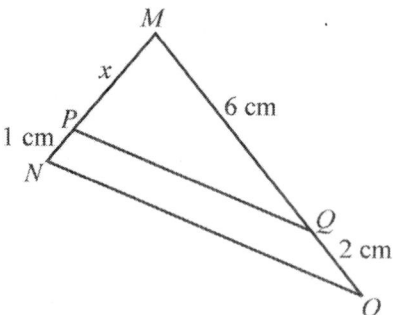

Determine the length of x.

Solution

Since PQ and NO are parallel line segments, PQ divides the sides of triangle MNO into proportional segments.

$$\frac{MP}{NP} = \frac{MQ}{OQ}$$
$$\frac{x}{1} = \frac{6}{2}$$
$$x = 3$$

The length of x is 3 cm.

Triangle ABC is given.

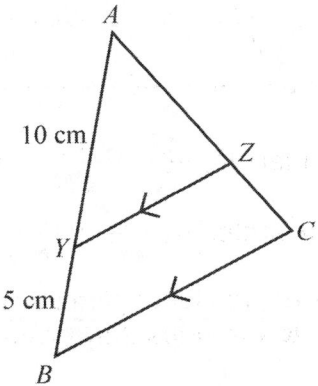

If side AC has a length of 12 cm, what is the length of line segment CZ?

Solution

Since YZ and BC are parallel line segments, YZ divides the sides of triangle ABC into proportional lengths.

$$\frac{BY}{AB} = \frac{CZ}{AC}$$
$$\frac{BY}{AY + BY} = \frac{CZ}{AC}$$
$$\frac{5}{10 + 5} = \frac{CZ}{12}$$
$$\frac{5}{15} = \frac{CZ}{12}$$
$$\frac{5 \times 12}{15} = CZ$$
$$4 = CZ$$

The length of line segment CZ is 4 cm.

Triangle IJK is given.

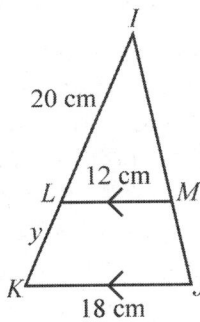

Determine the value of length *y*.

Solution

Since *LM* and *KJ* are parallel line segments, *LM* divides the sides of triangle *IJK* into proportional lengths. Line segments *LM* and *KJ* are also proportional to the lengths of the sides of the triangle that are divided.

$$\frac{IL}{LM} = \frac{IK}{JK}$$
$$\frac{IL}{LM} = \frac{IL + y}{JK}$$
$$\frac{20}{12} = \frac{20 + y}{18}$$
$$\frac{20 \times 18}{12} = 20 + y$$
$$\frac{20 \times 18}{12} - 20 = y$$
$$30 - 20 = y$$
$$10 = y$$

The length of *y* is 10 cm.

G-SRT.5 Use congruence and similarity criteria for triangles to solve problems and to prove relationships in geometric figures.

Problem Solving with Similar Triangles

When you are problem solving with similar triangles, determine missing side measures by forming and then solving an equation with respect to the ratios of the corresponding sides.

Example

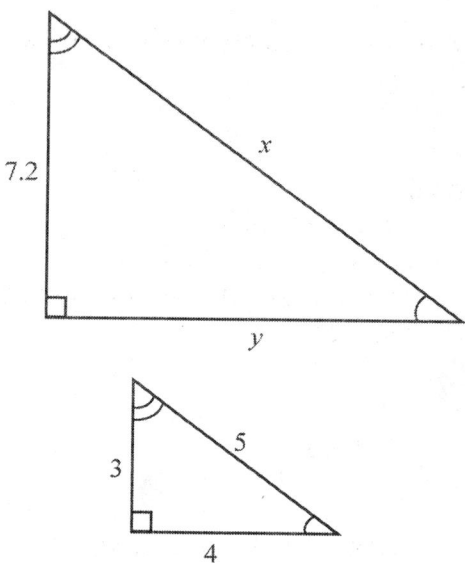

In these similar triangles, solve for the missing sides *x* and *y* by using the ratios of corresponding sides.

Solution

Step 1

Identify the numerator and denominator of the ratio.

The ratio is $\frac{\text{large } \Delta}{\text{small } \Delta}$.

Step 2

Identify the corresponding sides.

Corresponding sides have the same place in the triangle.

7.2 corresponds to 3.
x corresponds to 5.
y corresponds to 4.

Theorems Involving Similarity

Step 3
Write the ratios of the corresponding sides.
$$\frac{7.2}{3} = \frac{x}{5} = \frac{y}{4}$$

Step 4
Solve for the variable x.
Set up an equation with one ratio containing the variable x and the other ratio containing the known values.
$$\frac{7.2}{3} = \frac{x}{5}$$
Cross multiply.
$(7.2)(5) = (3)(x)$
$36 = 3x$
Divide both sides by 3 to isolate the variable.
$$\frac{36}{3} = \frac{3x}{3}$$
$12 = x$

Step 5
Solve for the variable y.
Set up an equation with one ratio containing the variable y and the other ratio containing the known values.
$$\frac{7.2}{3} = \frac{y}{4}$$
Cross multiply.
$(7.2)(4) = (3)(y)$
$28.8 = 3y$
Divide each side by 3 to isolate the variable.
$$\frac{28.8}{3} = \frac{3y}{3}$$
$9.6 = y$
The missing side lengths are $x = 12$ and $y = 9.6$.

Example
A person who stands 180 cm tall casts a shadow 45 cm long. A nearby telephone pole casts a shadow 300 cm long at the same time of day.
What is the height of the pole in meters?

Solution

Step 1
Draw a diagram to visualize the problem.
Use a variable to identify the side you are trying to find.

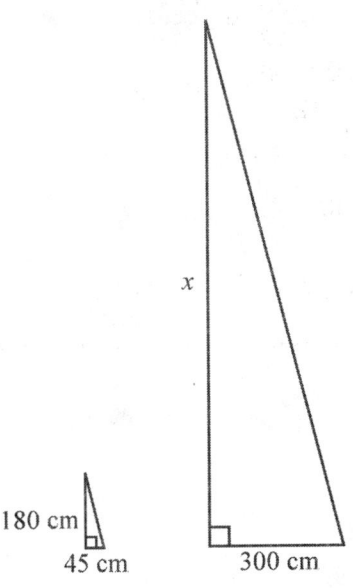

Step 2
Identify the numerator and denominator of the ratios.
The ratio is $\frac{\text{small } \Delta}{\text{large } \Delta}$.

Step 3
Identify the corresponding sides.
Corresponding sides have the same place in the triangle.
180 corresponds to x.
45 corresponds to 300.

Step 4
Set up an equation with one ratio containing the variable x and the other ratio containing the know values.
$$\frac{180}{x} = \frac{45}{300}$$

Step 5

Solve for the variable x.
Cross multiply.
$(180)(300) = (x)(45)$
$54{,}000 = 45x$

Divide each side by 45 to isolate the variable.
$$\frac{54{,}000}{45} = \frac{45x}{45}$$
$1{,}200 = x$

Convert centimeters to meters.
$$\frac{1{,}200 \text{ cm}}{100} = 12 \text{ m}$$

The height of the pole is 12 m.

APPLYING THEOREMS ABOUT TRAPEZOIDS

Specific theorems of trapezoids can be used to solve problems involving trapezoids. The following three theorems pertain to trapezoids:

1. The median of a trapezoid is parallel to the parallel sides, and its length is half the sum of the two parallel sides.
2. The side connected to both parallel sides forms supplementary angles
3. The diagonals of a trapezoid form two similar triangles.

Example

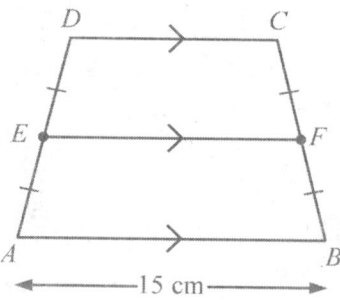

Trapezoid *ABCD* is given.

If *EF* = 12.5 cm, determine the length of *DC*.

Solution

In the given trapezoid, *EF* connects the two midpoints of the non-parallel sides and is parallel to the parallel sides. Therefore, *EF* is the median of trapezoid *ABCD*.

In a trapezoid, the length of the median is half the sum of the two parallel sides. Therefore, in trapezoid *ABCD*, $EF = \frac{1}{2}(AB + DC)$.

Using the property $EF = \frac{1}{2}(AB + DC)$, let $EF = 12.5$ cm and $AB = 15$ cm, and solve for *DC*.

$$EF = \frac{1}{2}(AB + DC)$$
$$12.5 = \frac{1}{2}(15 + DC)$$
$$25 = 15 + DC$$
$$DC = 10$$

Therefore, the length of *DC* is 10 cm.

Example

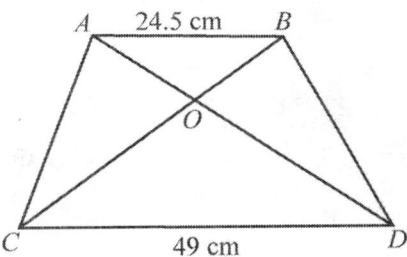

Trapezoid *ABCD* is given.

If *OB* = 14 cm, then what is the length of *CO*?

Solution

The diagonals of a trapezoid form two similar triangles. In the given trapezoid, *AD* and *BC* are diagonals that form two similar triangles, △*ABO* and △*COD*.

In a similar triangle, the ratio of corresponding sides is equal; therefore, in the given trapezoid, $\frac{AB}{CD} = \frac{OB}{CO}$.

Substitute known values into the ratio $\frac{AB}{CD} = \frac{OB}{CO}$, and solve by applying cross multiplication.

$$\frac{AB}{CD} = \frac{OB}{CO}$$
$$\frac{24.5}{49} = \frac{14}{CO}$$
$$(CO)(24.5) = (14)(49)$$
$$CO = \frac{(14)(49)}{24.5}$$
$$CO = 28$$

Therefore, the length of *CO* is 28 cm.

ISOSCELES TRAPEZOIDS

Isosceles trapezoids have the following properties:

- The non-parallel sides are equal in length.
- The adjacent base angles are in equal measure.
- The diagonals are congruent.

If one of these properties is found, then the others are also true.

Example

The diagram shows the quadrilateral *ABCD*.

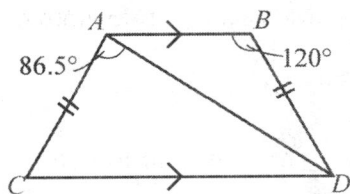

What is the measure of ∠*BDA*?

Solution

Since sides *AB* and *CD* are parallel and the non-parallel sides are equal in length, *ABCD* is an isosceles trapezoid.

In an isosceles trapezoid, adjacent base angles are equal in measure. Therefore, ∠*DBA* = ∠*CAB*.

Step 1

Using the property ∠*DBA* = ∠*CAB*, where ∠*CAB* = ∠*DAB* + ∠*CAD*, find the measure of ∠*DAB*.

∠*DBA* = ∠*CAB*
∠*DBA* = ∠*DAB* + ∠*CAD*
 120° = ∠*DAB* + 86.5°
 33.5° = ∠*DAB*

Step 2

Determine the measure of ∠*BDA*.

Since the sum of all the interior angles of a triangle is 180°, find the measure of ∠*BDA* using known angle measures in triangle *ABD*.

180° = ∠*BDA* + ∠*DAB* + ∠*DBA*
180° = ∠*BDA* + 33.5° + 120°
180° = ∠*BDA* + 153.5°
26.5° = ∠*BDA*

Therefore, the measure of ∠*BDA* is 26.5°.

EXERCISE #1—THEOREMS INVOLVING SIMILARITY

104. Which of the following sets of numbers could be the sides of a right triangle?
 A. 12, 48, 52
 B. 16, 63, 65
 C. 23, 72, 74
 D. 26, 81, 85

Use the following information to answer the next question.

The hypotenuse of a right triangle is 23 mm, and the length of one side is 15 mm.

105. To the nearest tenth, the length of the missing side is _____ mm.

Use the following information to answer the next question.

In the given diagram, *DE*, *FG*, and *BC* are parallel line segments.

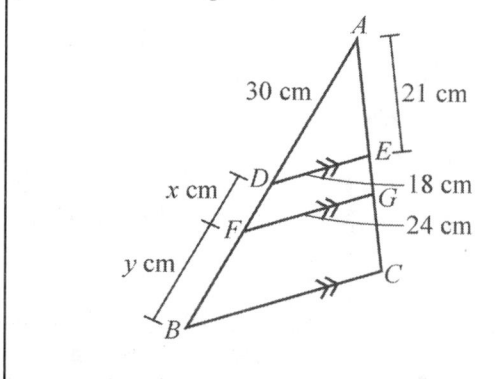

106. If the length of side *AC* in the given diagram can be represented by (*x* + 32) cm, the value of *y* is _____ cm.

Use the following information to answer the next question.

The sails of two sailboards are similar triangles, as illustrated in the given diagram.

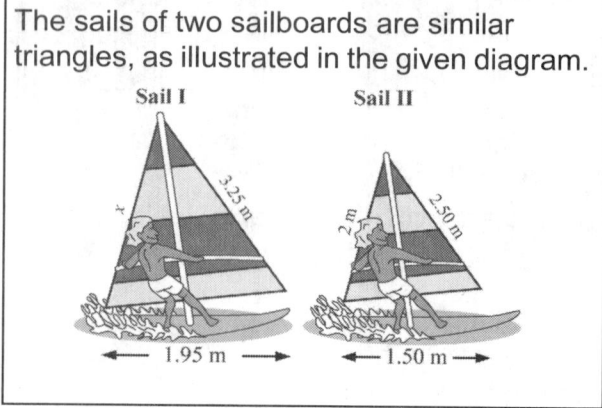

107. Rounded to the nearest hundredth of a meter, the length of side *x* is
 A. 2.45 m
 B. 2.60 m
 C. 2.75 m
 D. 3.80 m

Use the following information to answer the next question.

The given diagram illustrates an isosceles trapezoid and its respective diagonals.

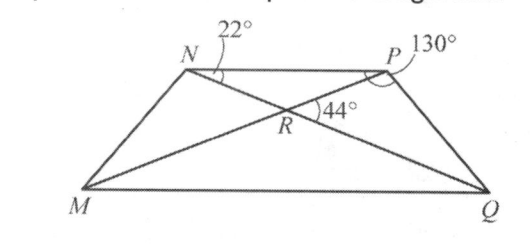

108. If the measure of ∠*NPQ* is 130°, the measure of ∠*PNQ* is 22°, and the measure of ∠*PRQ* is 44°, then the measure of ∠*NMR* is
 A. 24°
 B. 26°
 C. 28°
 D. 30°

EXERCISE #1—THEOREMS INVOLVING SIMILARITY
ANSWERS AND SOLUTIONS

104. B	106. 20	108. C
105. 17.4	107. B	

104. B

Evaluate each set of numbers using the Pythagorean theorem.

Step 1
Evaluate the set of numbers 12, 48, and 52.
$$a^2 + b^2 = c^2$$
$$12^2 + 48^2 = 52^2$$
$$144 + 2{,}304 = 2{,}704$$
$$2{,}448 \neq 2{,}704$$

Step 2
Evaluate the set of numbers 16, 63, and 65.
$$a^2 + b^2 = c^2$$
$$16^2 + 63^2 = 65^2$$
$$256 + 3{,}969 = 4{,}225$$
$$4{,}225 = 4{,}225$$

Step 3
Evaluate the set of numbers 23, 72, and 74.
$$a^2 + b^2 = c^2$$
$$23^2 + 72^2 = 74^2$$
$$529 + 5{,}184 = 5{,}476$$
$$5{,}713 \neq 5{,}476$$

Step 4
Evaluate the set of numbers 26, 81, and 85.
$$a^2 + b^2 = c^2$$
$$26^2 + 81^2 = 85^2$$
$$676 + 6{,}561 = 7{,}225$$
$$7{,}237 \neq 7{,}225$$

The set of numbers 16, 63, and 65 could be the sides of a right triangle.

105. 17.4

Step 1
Substitute the known values into the Pythagorean theorem.
$$a^2 + b^2 = c^2$$
$$a^2 + 15^2 = 23^2$$
$$a^2 + 225 = 529$$

Step 2
Solve for the missing side.
Subtract 225 from both sides of the equation to isolate a^2.
$$a^2 + 225 = 529$$
$$a^2 + 225 - 225 = 529 - 225$$
$$a^2 = 304$$

Take the square root of both sides to solve for a.
$$\sqrt{a^2} = \sqrt{304}$$
$$a \approx 17.4356$$

The length of the missing side to the nearest tenth is 17.4 mm.

106. 20

When a line is parallel to one side of a triangle, it intersects the other two sides of the triangle and divides them into proportional segments. This relationship can be used to solve for both x and y in the given diagram.

Step 1
Solve for x in $\triangle AFG$ by applying the proportion $\dfrac{AD}{AF} = \dfrac{DE}{FG}$.

Substitute 30 for AD, $30 + x$ for AF, 18 for DE, and 24 for FG.
$$\frac{30}{30 + x} = \frac{18}{24}$$
$$30(24) = 18(30 + x)$$
$$720 = 540 + 18x$$
$$180 = 18x$$
$$10 = x$$

Step 2
Solve for y in $\triangle ABC$ by applying the proportion $\dfrac{AD}{AB} = \dfrac{AE}{AC}$.

Substitute 30 for AD and 21 for AE. Next, substitute $30 + x + y$ for AB and $x + 32$ for AC. Since $x = 10$, AB will equal $40 + y$ and AC will equal 42.
$$\frac{30}{40 + y} = \frac{21}{42}$$
$$30(42) = 21(40 + y)$$
$$1{,}260 = 840 + 21y$$
$$420 = 21y$$
$$20 = y$$

The value of y is 20.

107. B

Step 1
Identify the corresponding sides.
1.95 ~ 1.5
x ~ 2

Step 2
Write the ratio of the corresponding sides.
$$\frac{1.95}{1.5} = \frac{x}{2}$$

Step 3
Solve for the variable using cross products.
$$\frac{1.95}{1.5} = \frac{x}{2}$$
$$1.95(2) = x(1.5)$$
$$3.9 = 1.5x$$
$$\frac{3.9}{1.5} = \frac{1.5x}{1.5}$$
$$2.6 = x$$

The length of x is 2.60 m.

108. C

Step 1
Determine the measure of $\angle MNP$.
In an isosceles quadrilateral, adjacent base angles are equal in measure. Therefore, $\angle MNP = \angle NPQ$. Since the measure of $\angle NPQ$ is 130°, it follows that the measure of $\angle MNP$ is 130°.

Step 2
Determine the measure of $\angle MNR$.
Since $\angle MNP = \angle MNR + \angle PNQ$, the measure of $\angle MNR$ can be determined as follows:
$\angle MNP = \angle MNR + \angle PNQ$
Substitute 130° for $\angle MNP$ and 22° for $\angle PNQ$.
$130° = \angle MNR + 22°$
$130° - 22° = \angle MNR$
$108° = \angle MNR$

Step 3
Determine the measure of $\angle NRM$.
Vertically opposite angles have the same measure. Since $\angle PRQ$ and $\angle NRM$ are vertically opposite angles and the measure of $\angle PRQ$ is 44°, it follows that the measure of $\angle NRM$ is 44°.

Step 4
Determine the measure of $\angle NMR$.
The sum of the interior angles of a triangle is 180°. Therefore, the sum of the interior angles of triangle NRM is 180°. The measure of $\angle NMR$ can be determined as follows:
$\angle MNR + \angle NRM + \angle NMR = 180°$
Substitute 108° for $\angle MNR$ and 44° for $\angle NRM$.
$108° + 44° + \angle NMR = 180°$
$152° + \angle NMR = 180°$
$\angle NMR = 180° - 152°$
$\angle NMR = 28°$

The measure of $\angle NMR$ is 28°.

EXERCISE #2—THEOREMS INVOLVING SIMILARITY

109. If △ABC has a right angle at B, the measures of sides AB, BC, and CA respectively could be
A. 12 cm, 13 cm, and 17 cm
B. 9 cm, 11 cm, and 15 cm
C. 8 cm, 15 cm, and 17 cm
D. 17 cm, 19 cm, and 24 cm

Use the following information to answer the next question.

The rope that attaches to the top of a tent pole is 170 cm long, and it is fastened to the ground 80 cm away from the foot of the pole.

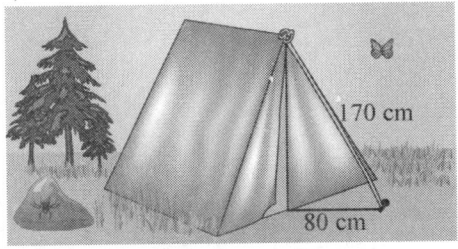

110. How tall is the tent pole? _____ cm

Use the following information to answer the next question.

In the diagram shown, DE and FG are parallel. Roberto and Ariel are each asked to determine the value of x in centimeters.

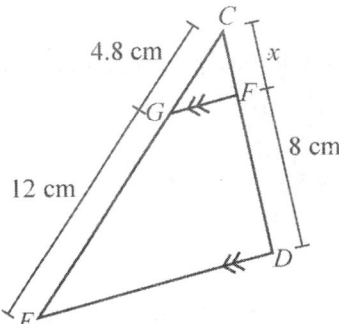

Roberto's partial solution is as follows:

1. $\dfrac{EG}{GC} = \dfrac{DF}{FC}$
2. $\dfrac{12}{4.8} = \dfrac{8}{x}$
3. $12 \times x = 8 \times 4.8$

Ariel's partial solution is as follows:

1. $\dfrac{EC}{GC} = \dfrac{DC}{FC}$
2. $\dfrac{16.8}{4.8} = \dfrac{8+x}{x}$
3. $16.8(x) = 4.8(8 + x)$

111. Which of the following statements about the partial solutions of the two students is **true**?
A. Roberto's partial solution is correct, and Ariel's is incorrect.
B. Roberto's partial solution is incorrect, and Ariel's is correct.
C. Both Roberto and Ariel have incorrect partial solutions.
D. Both Roberto and Ariel have correct partial solutions.

Use the following information to answer the next question.

During an afternoon soccer game, Samira casts a 62 cm shadow and Leah casts a 77 cm shadow.

112. If Leah is 158 cm tall, then what is Samira's height rounded to the nearest hundredth of a meter?

    A. 124.52 cm
    B. 127.22 cm
    C. 143.37 cm
    D. 173.84 cm

Use the following information to answer the next question.

In the diagram shown, point E is the midpoint of line segment BG, point F is the midpoint of line segment CH, point G is the midpoint of line segment AE, and point H is the midpoint of line segment DF.

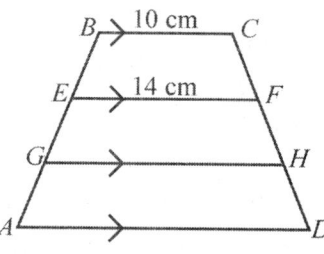

113. The length of side AD in the given diagram is
    A. 20 cm
    B. 22 cm
    C. 26 cm
    D. 28 cm

Exercise #2

EXERCISE #2—THEOREMS INVOLVING SIMILARITY
ANSWERS AND SOLUTIONS

109. C	111. D	113. B
110. 150	112. B	

109. C

Use the Pythagorean theorem of $a^2 + b^2 = c^2$ to evaluate each option.

Step 1
Substitute the values of the measures 12 cm, 13 cm, and 17 cm into the formula.
$$a^2 + b^2 = c^2$$
$$12^2 + 13^2 = 17^2$$
$$144 + 169 = 289$$
$$313 \neq 289$$
Since the two sides of the equation are not equal, this could not be the answer.

Step 2
Substitute the values of the measures 9 cm, 11 cm, and 15 cm into the formula.
$$a^2 + b^2 = c^2$$
$$9^2 + 11^2 = 15^2$$
$$81 + 121 = 225$$
$$202 \neq 225$$
Since the two sides of the equation are not equal, this could not be the answer.

Step 3
Substitute the values of the measures 8 cm, 15 cm, and 17 cm into the formula.
$$a^2 + b^2 = c^2$$
$$8^2 + 15^2 = 17^2$$
$$64 + 225 = 289$$
$$289 = 289$$
Since the two sides of the equation are equal, this is the answer.

Step 4
Substitute the values of the measures 17 cm, 19 cm, and 24 cm into the formula.
$$a^2 + b^2 = c^2$$
$$17^2 + 19^2 = 24^2$$
$$289 + 361 = 576$$
$$650 \neq 576$$
Since the two sides of the equation are not equal, this could not be the answer.

110. 150

The rope attached to the tent represents the hypotenuse of a right triangle. The height of the tent and the distance the rope is from the foot of the pole represent the legs of a right triangle.

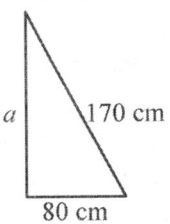

Step 1
Substitute the known values into the Pythagorean theorem.
$$a^2 + b^2 = c^2$$
$$a^2 + 80^2 = 170^2$$
$$a^2 + 6{,}400 = 28{,}900$$

Step 2
Rearrange the formula to solve for the missing side.
$$a^2 + 6{,}400 = 28{,}900$$
$$a^2 + 6{,}400 - 6{,}400 = 28{,}900 - 6{,}400$$
$$a^2 = 22{,}500$$

Take the square root of both sides to solve for a.
$$\sqrt{a^2} = \sqrt{22{,}500}$$
$$a = 150$$

The height of the tent pole is 150 cm.

111. D

When a line is parallel to one side of a triangle, it intersects the other two sides of the triangle and divides them into proportional segments.

Roberto correctly applied the proportion $\dfrac{EG}{GC} = \dfrac{DF}{FC}$ in his partial solution, and Ariel correctly applied the proportion $\dfrac{EC}{GC} = \dfrac{DC}{FC}$ in her partial solution.

The remaining steps in Roberto's partial solution could be as follows:

4. $12x = 38.4$
5. $x = 3.2$ cm

The remaining steps in Ariel's partial solution could be as follows:

4. $16.8x = 38.4 + 4.8x$
5. $12x = 38.4$
6. $x = 3.2$ cm

Thus, both Roberto and Ariel have correct partial solutions.

112. B

Step 1
Draw a diagram that represents the given situation.

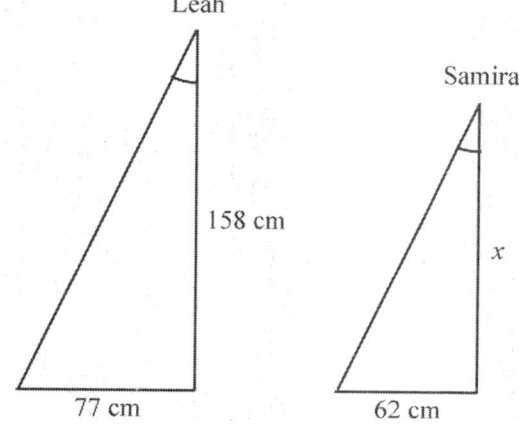

Step 2
The triangles are similar since they are created from the shadows made by the same angle of the sun at the same point in time. The remaining corresponding angles are equal. Corresponding sides have equal ratios.
Identify the corresponding sides.
77 ~ 62
158 ~ x

Step 3
Write the ratio of the corresponding sides.
$\dfrac{77}{62} = \dfrac{158}{x}$

Step 4
Solve for the variable using cross products.
$\dfrac{77}{62} = \dfrac{158}{x}$
$77(x) = 158(62)$
$77x = 9{,}796$
$\dfrac{77x}{77} = \dfrac{9{,}796}{77}$
$x = 127.2207792$

Step 5
Round to the nearest hundredth of a centimeter.
$127.2207792 \rightarrow 127.22$
Samira is 127.22 m tall.

113. B

Step 1
Determine the length of side *GH* in trapezoid *BCHG*. In trapezoid *BCHG*, *EF* connects the two midpoints of the non-parallel sides *BG* and *CH*. It is also parallel to sides *BC* and *GH*. Therefore, *EF* is the median of trapezoid *BCHG*. Since the length of a median in a trapezoid is half the sum of the lengths of the two parallel sides, it follows that the length of side *GH* can be determined using the equation $EF = \dfrac{1}{2}(BC + GH)$.

Substitute 14 for *EF* and 10 for *BC*.
$14 = \dfrac{1}{2}(10 + GH)$
$14 \times 2 = 1(10 + GH)$
$28 = 10 + GH$
$18 = GH$

The length of side *GH* is 18 cm.

Step 2
Determine the length of side *AD* in trapezoid *AEFD*. In trapezoid *AEFD*, *GH* connects the two midpoints of the non-parallel sides *AE* and *DF*. It is also parallel to sides *EF* and *AD*. Therefore, *GH* is the median of trapezoid *AEFD*. The length of side *AD* can now be determined using the equation $GH = \dfrac{1}{2}(EF + AD)$.

Substitute 18 for *GH* and 14 for *EF*.
$18 = \dfrac{1}{2}(14 + AD)$
$18 \times 2 = 1(14 + AD)$
$36 = 14 + AD$
$22 = AD$

The length of side *AD* is 22 cm.

Right Angle Triangles in Trigonometry

RIGHT ANGLE TRIANGLES IN TRIGONOMETRY

Table of Correlations

Standard		Concepts	Exercise #1	Exercise #2
Unit2.3	Define trigonometric ratios and solve problems involving right triangles.			
G-SRT.6	Understand that by similarity, side ratios in right triangles are properties of the angles in the triangle, leading to definitions of trigonometric ratios for acute angles.	The Tangent Ratio	114	131
		The Sine Ratio	115	132
		The Cosine Ratio	116	133
G-SRT.7	Explain and use the relationship between the sine and cosine of complementary angles.	Verifying Equivalent Trigonometric Expressions	117	134
		Solving Problems Using Primary Cofunctions in Degrees	118	135
G-SRT.8	Use trigonometric ratios and the Pythagorean Theorem to solve right triangles in applied problems.	Solving Problems by Applying the Primary Trigonometric Ratios and the Pythagorean Theorem	119	136
		Solving a Triangle Using Trigonometric Ratios and the Pythagorean Theorem	120	137
		Calculating Unknown Values using Two Right Triangles	121	138
		Solving Problems Using the Tangent Ratio	122	139
		Solving Problems Using the Sine Ratio	123	140
		Solving Problems Using the Cosine Ratio	124	141
		Applying the Cosine Ratio to Solve for a Missing Angle of a Right Triangle	125	142
		Applying the Tangent Ratio to Solve for a Missing Angle of a Right Triangle	126	143
		Applying the Sine Ratio to Solve for the Missing Angle of a Right Triangle	127	144
		Applying the Sine Ratio to Solve for a Missing Side of a Right Triangle	128	145
		Applying the Cosine Ratio to Solve for the Missing Side of a Right Triangle	129	146
		Applying the Tangent Ratio to Solve for a Missing Side of a Right Triangle	130	147

G-SRT.6 Understand that by similarity, side ratios in right triangles are properties of the angles in the triangle, leading to definitions of trigonometric ratios for acute angles.

THE TANGENT RATIO

One area of Trigonometry deals with the study of the relationships between the angles and sides of right triangles. A right angle triangle is a triangle that has one interior angle that measures 90°. This 90° angle is usually identified with a small square.

Each of the three sides in a right angle triangle is given a particular name. These names are:

1. **hypotenuse**—the longest side in the triangle, it is the side across from the right angle.
2. **opposite side**—the side across the angle you are observing.
3. **adjacent side**—the side, other than the hypotenuse, which is next to the angle you are observing.

Hint: When solving right triangle problems, it is helpful to first determine which side is the hypotenuse.

Example

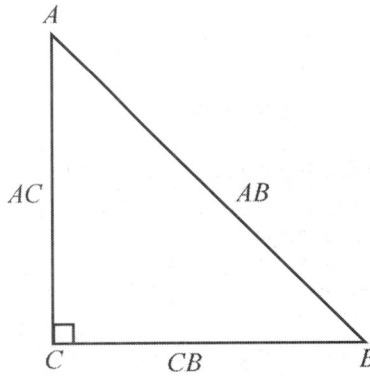

For △ABC, identify the hypotenuse and then identify the opposite and adjacent side to each acute angle.

Solution

The side across from ∠C, (the right angle), is side AB. Therefore, side AB is the hypotenuse of △ABC.

If ∠B is the angle being observed, then side AC is the opposite side and side BC is the adjacent side in △ABC.

If ∠A is the angle being observed, then side BC is the opposite side and side AC is the adjacent side in △ABC.

Be very careful in naming the opposite and adjacent sides in a right angle triangle. Always ask yourself the question "Which acute angle am I working with?"

A ratio is a comparison of two quantities. The tangent ratio in a right triangle, where ∠A is one of the acute angles, compares the length of the side opposite to ∠A to the length of the side adjacent to ∠A.

As an equation, the tangent ratio is written as follows:

tangent A
$= \dfrac{\text{length of the side opposite to } \angle A}{\text{length of the side adjacent to } \angle A}$ or

$\tan A = \dfrac{\text{opposite}}{\text{adjacent}}$

Example

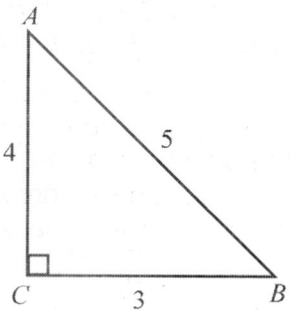

Write the ratio for tan A.

Solution

Step 1
Identify the hypotenuse for △ABC (this will help with determining the location of the side opposite to ∠A and the side adjacent to ∠A). Side AB is across from the right angle, ∠C, so side AB is the hypotenuse for △ABC.

Step 2
Identify the side opposite to angle A.
The side opposite to angle A is side BC.

Step 3
Identify the side adjacent to angle A.
The side adjacent to angle A is side AC.

Step 4
Substitute the length of side BC, 3 units, and the length of side AC, 4 units, into the tangent ratio equation.

$$\tan A = \frac{\text{opposite}}{\text{adjacent}} = \frac{3}{4}$$

When given an exact acute angle, you can use your calculator to determine the tangent ratio.

Example
Illustrate the tangent ratio to three decimal places for tan 35° with a diagram.

Solution
Make sure your calculator is in degree mode.

Step 1
Determine the length of the side opposite to the 35° angle.
Type in $\boxed{3}\boxed{5}$, and then press $\boxed{\tan}$ or type in $\boxed{\tan}\boxed{3}\boxed{5}\boxed{\text{ENTER}}$, depending on your calculator.
The screen will show 0.7002075382. Therefore, the length of the opposite side, to three decimal places is 0.700 units.

Step 2
Determine the length of the adjacent side.
When using your calculator to determine the tangent ratio for a given angle measurement, the length of the adjacent side is always 1 unit.

Step 3
Write the ratio for tan A.
The tangent ratio is the ratio of the length of the side opposite the angle measuring 35° to the length of the side adjacent to the angle measuring of a right triangle is a ratio of the side opposite the angle measuring 35°.

$$\tan \theta = \frac{\text{opposite}}{\text{adjacent}}$$

$$\tan 35° = \frac{0.700}{1}$$

You can also say that the opposite side is 0.700 times as long as the adjacent side.

Step 4
Illustrate the tangent ratio for tan 35° with a diagram.

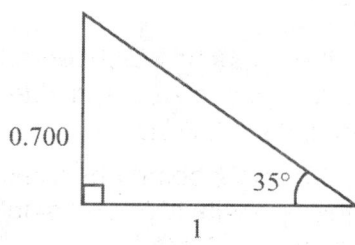

Right Angle Triangles in Trigonometry

THE SINE RATIO

One area of Trigonometry deals with the study of the relationships between the angles and sides of right triangles. A right angle triangle is a triangle that has one interior angle that measures 90°. This 90° angle is usually identified with a small square.

Each of the three sides in a right angle triangle is given a particular name. These names are:

1. **hypotenuse**—the longest side in the triangle, it is the side across from the right angle.
2. **opposite side**—the side across the angle you are observing.
3. **adjacent side**—the side, other than the hypotenuse, which is next to the angle you are observing.

Hint: When solving right triangle problems, it is helpful to first determine which side is the hypotenuse.

Example

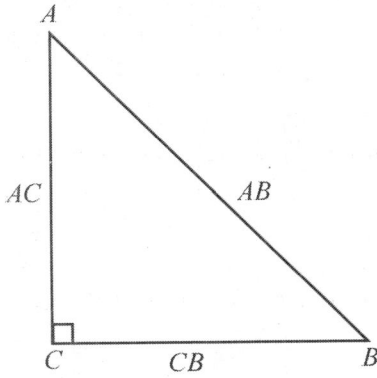

For △ABC, identify the hypotenuse and then identify the opposite and adjacent side to each acute angle.

Solution

The side across from ∠C, (the right angle), is side AB. Therefore, side AB is the hypotenuse of △ABC.

If ∠B is the angle being observed, then side AC is the opposite side and side BC is the adjacent side in △ABC.

If ∠A is the angle being observed, then side BC is the opposite side and side AC is the adjacent side in △ABC.

Be very careful in naming the opposite and adjacent sides in a right angle triangle. Always ask yourself the question "Which acute angle am I working with?"

Recall that a ratio is a comparison of two quantities. The sine ratio in a right triangle, where ∠A is one of the acute angles, compares the length of the side opposite to ∠A to the length of the hypotenuse.

As an equation, the sine ratio is written as follows:

$$\text{sine } A = \frac{\text{length of the side opposite to } \angle A}{\text{length of the hypotenuse}}$$ or

$$\sin A = \frac{\text{opposite}}{\text{hypotenuse}}$$

Example

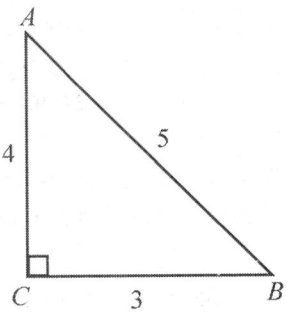

Write the ratio for sin A.

Solution

Step 1
Identify the hypotenuse for △ABC.
Side AB is across from the right angle, ∠C, so side AB is the hypotenuse for △ABC.

Step 2
Identify the side opposite to angle A.
The side opposite to angle A is side BC.

Step 3
Substitute the length of side BC, 3 units, and the length of side AB, 5 units, into the tangent ratio equation.

$$\sin A = \frac{\text{opposite}}{\text{hypotenuse}} = \frac{3}{5}$$

When given an exact acute angle, you can use your calculator to determine the sine ratio.

Example

Illustrate, with a possible diagram, the sine ratio, to three decimal places, for sin 35°.

Solution

Make sure your calculator is in degree mode.

Step 1

Determine the length of the side opposite to the angle measuring 35°.

Type in $\boxed{3}\boxed{5}$, and then press $\boxed{\sin}$ or type in $\boxed{\sin}\boxed{3}\boxed{5}\boxed{\text{ENTER}}$, depending on your calculator.

The screen will show 0.573576436. Therefore, the length of the opposite side, to three decimal places is 0.574 units.

Step 2

Determine the length of the hypotenuse.

When using your calculator to determine the sine ratio for a given angle measurement, the length of the hypotenuse is always 1 unit.

Step 3

Write the ratio for sin A.

The sine ratio is the ratio of the length of the side opposite the angle measuring 35° to the length of the hypotenuse.

$\sin 35° = \dfrac{\text{opposite}}{\text{hypotenuse}}$

$\sin 35° = \dfrac{0.574}{1}$

You can also say that the opposite side is 0.574 times as long as the hypotenuse.

Step 4

Illustrate the sine ratio for sin 35° with a diagram.

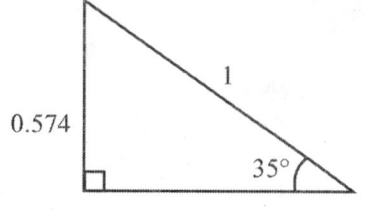

THE COSINE RATIO

One area of Trigonometry deals with the study of the relationships between the angles and sides of right triangles. A right angle triangle is a triangle that has one interior angle that measures 90°. This 90° angle is usually identified with a small square.

Each of the three sides in a right angle triangle is given a particular name. These names are:

1. **hypotenuse**—the longest side in the triangle, it is the side across from the right angle.
2. **opposite side**—the side across the angle you are observing.
3. **adjacent side**—the side, other than the hypotenuse, which is next to the angle you are observing.

Hint: When solving right triangle problems, it is helpful to first determine which side is the hypotenuse.

Example

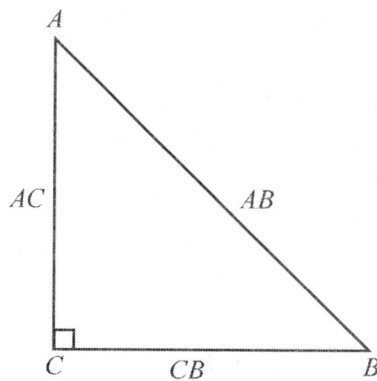

For $\triangle ABC$, identify the hypotenuse and then identify the opposite and adjacent side to each acute angle.

Solution

The side across from $\angle C$, (the right angle), is side AB. Therefore, side AB is the hypotenuse of $\triangle ABC$.

If $\angle B$ is the angle being observed, then side AC is the opposite side and side BC is the adjacent side in $\triangle ABC$.

If $\angle A$ is the angle being observed, then side BC is the opposite side and side AC is the adjacent side in $\triangle ABC$.

Be very careful in naming the opposite and adjacent sides in a right angle triangle. Always ask yourself the question "Which acute angle am I working with?"

A ratio is a comparison of two quantities. The cosine ratio in a right triangle, where $\angle A$ is one of the acute angle, compares the length of the side adjacent to $\angle A$ to the length of the hypotenuse.

As an equation, the cosine ratio is written as follows:

cosine A

$= \dfrac{\text{length of the side adjacent to } \angle A}{\text{length of the hypotenuse}}$ or

$\cos A = \dfrac{\text{adjacent}}{\text{hypotenuse}}$

Example
Write the ratio for cos A.

Solution

Step 1
Identify the hypotenuse of $\triangle ABC$.
Side AB is the hypotenuse of $\triangle ABC$ since side AB is across from the right angle, $\angle C$.

Step 2
Identify the side adjacent to angle A.
The side adjacent (next) to angle A is side AC.

Step 3
Substitute the length of side AB, 5 units, and the length of side AC, 4 units, into the cos ratio.

$\cos A = \dfrac{\text{adjacent}}{\text{hypotenuse}} = \dfrac{4}{5}$

When given an exact acute angle, you can use a calculator to determine the cosine ratio.

Example
Illustrate, with a possible diagram, the cos ratio, to three decimal places, for cos 35°.

Solution

Make sure your calculator is in degree mode.

Step 1
Determine the length of the side adjacent to the angle measuring 35°.

Type in $\boxed{3}\boxed{5}$, and then press $\boxed{\cos}$ or type in $\boxed{\cos}\boxed{3}\boxed{5}\boxed{\text{ENTER}}$, depending on your calculator.

The screen will show 0.8191520443. Therefore, the length of the adjacent side, to 3 decimal places is, 0.819.

Step 2
Determine the length of the hypotenuse.
When using your calculator to determine the sine ratio for a given angle measurement, the length of the hypotenuse is always 1 unit.

Step 3
Write the ratio for cos A.

In this case the cos ratio is the ratio of the length of the adjacent side to the angle measuring the 35° to the length of the hypotenuse.

$\cos A = \dfrac{\text{adjacent}}{\text{hypotenuse}}$

$\cos 35° = \dfrac{0.819}{1}$

You can also say that the adjacent side is 0.819 times as long as the hypotenuse.

Step 4
Illustrate the cos ratio for cos 35° with a diagram.

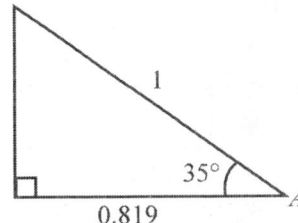

G-SRT.7 Explain and use the relationship between the sine and cosine of complementary angles.

VERIFYING EQUIVALENT TRIGONOMETRIC EXPRESSIONS

Trigonometric expressions that are equivalent can be verified algebraically or graphically.

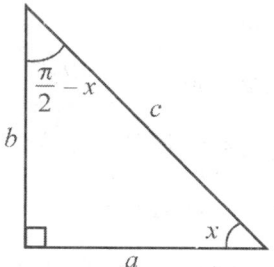

Since $90° = \frac{\pi}{2}$ rad, in a right triangle in which one of the acute angles has a measure of x rad, the other acute angle would have a measure of $\frac{\pi}{2} - x$ rad as shown in the triangle above.

The sides of the triangle are designated as a, b, and c as indicated in the diagram.

From the triangle,

$\sin x = \dfrac{\text{side opposite angle } x}{\text{hypotenuse}} = \dfrac{b}{c}$ and

$\cos\left(\dfrac{\pi}{2} - x\right) = \dfrac{\text{side adjacent angle }\left(\dfrac{\pi}{2} - x\right)}{\text{hypotenuse}} = \dfrac{b}{c}$.

Thus, $\sin x = \cos\left(\dfrac{\pi}{2} - x\right)$ is verified algebraically.

Consider the function $y = \cos\left(x + \dfrac{\pi}{2}\right)$.

This is a horizontal translation of the graph of $y = \cos x$ to the left $\dfrac{\pi}{2}$ units.

The graph of $y = \cos x$ is the lighter line, and the graph of $y = \cos\left(x + \dfrac{\pi}{2}\right)$ is the bold line in the diagram.

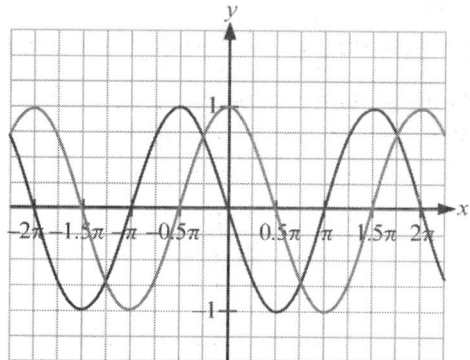

The graph of $y = -\sin x$ is shown below.

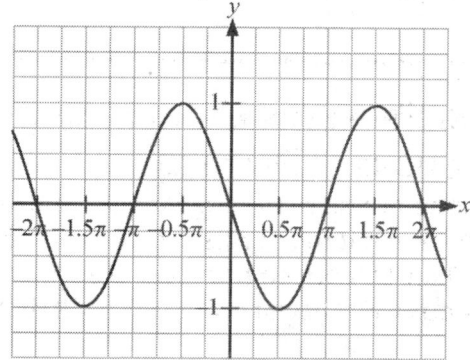

The function $y = -\sin x$ is a reflection of the graph of $y = \sin x$ in the x-axis. The result of translating $y = \cos x$ to the left $\frac{\pi}{2}$ units is equivalent to a reflection of the graph of $y = \sin x$ in the x-axis. Thus, $\cos\left(x + \frac{\pi}{2}\right) = -\sin x$ is verified graphically.

Example

Verify that $\sin\left(x - \frac{\pi}{2}\right) = -\cos x$ with a graphing calculator by graphing two different functions.

Solution

Graph $Y_1 = \sin\left(x - \frac{\pi}{2}\right)$ and $Y_2 = -\cos(x)$ with appropriate window settings such as $x:[-2\pi, 2\pi, \pi]$ and $y:[-2, 2, 1]$.

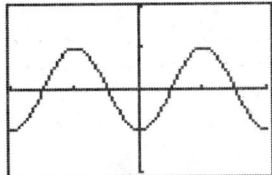

The fact that both graphs are the same verifies that $\sin\left(x - \frac{\pi}{2}\right) = -\cos x$.

SOLVING PROBLEMS USING PRIMARY COFUNCTIONS IN DEGREES

Cofunctions are pairs of functions that have an equal value when the inputs are complementary angles. The primary cofunctions are $\sin(\theta) = \cos(90° - \theta)$ and $\cos(\theta) = \sin(90° - \theta)$.

Example

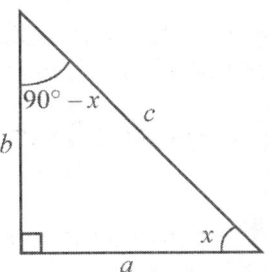

A right triangle is given.

From the triangle, $\sin x = \dfrac{\text{opposite}}{\text{hypotenuse}} = \dfrac{b}{c}$ and $\cos(90° - x) = \dfrac{\text{adjacent}}{\text{hypotenuse}} = \dfrac{b}{c}$. Therefore, the relationship $\sin(x) = \cos(90° - x)$ holds.

Example

Determine the value of θ which satisfies the relationship $\sin 42° = \cos \theta$, where $0° < \theta < 90°$.

Solution

Sine and cosine are cofunctions, so they are equal under complementary angles.
$\sin(\theta) = \cos(90° - \theta)$
$\sin(42°) = \cos(90° - 42°)$
$\sin(42°) = \cos(48°)$
The value of θ which satisfies $\sin 42° = \cos \theta$ is 48°.

Example

Determine a value of θ which satisfies the relationship $\cos(3\theta) = \sin(\theta + 300°)$.

Solution

Sine and cosine are cofunctions so they are equal under complementary angles.
$\cos(3\theta) = \sin(90° - 3\theta)$

It is also known that $\cos(3\theta) = \sin(\theta + 300°)$.
$\sin(90° - 3\theta) = \sin(\theta + 300°)$
$\quad 90° - 3\theta = \theta + 300°$
$\quad\quad -210° = 4\theta$
$\quad\quad -52.5° = \theta$
The value that satisfies the relationship $\cos(3\theta) = \sin(\theta + 300°)$ is −52.5°.

G-SRT.8 Use trigonometric ratios and the Pythagorean Theorem to solve right triangles in applied problems.

SOLVING PROBLEMS BY APPLYING THE PRIMARY TRIGONOMETRIC RATIOS AND THE PYTHAGOREAN THEOREM

The primary trigonometric ratios and the Pythagorean theorem can be used to solve problems involving the measures of sides and angles in real-life applications. When solving these types of problems, recall these key definitions:

- The **angle of elevation** is up from the horizontal.
- The **angle of depression** is down from the horizontal.

Example
A cat watches a bird in a tree. The bird is at an angle of elevation of 40° from the cat. If the cat is 7.1 m from the base of the tree, how high up in the tree is the bird?

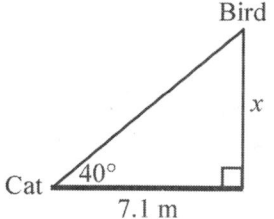

$\tan 40° = \dfrac{x}{7.1}$
$x = 7.1 \tan 40°$
$x \approx 6.0$ m

The bird is 6.0 m from the ground.

Example
Lexi is standing in her yard. She sees a cat sitting directly west of her. Directly east of her is a dog. Lexi's eye level is 1.48 m high. To look directly at where the cat is sitting, she looks down at an angle of depression of 30°. To the dog, the angle of depression is 25°. How far apart are the cat and dog?

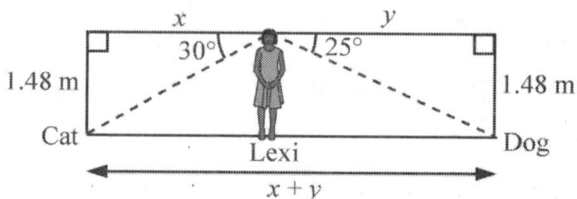

Notice that $x + y$ at eye level will be the same as $x + y$ on the ground.
The distance between the cat and dog = $x + y$.

$\tan 30° = \dfrac{1.48}{x}$

$x = \dfrac{1.48}{\tan 30°}$

$\tan 25° = \dfrac{1.48}{y}$

$y = \dfrac{1.48}{\tan 25°}$

distance = $x + y$
 $= \dfrac{1.48}{\tan 30°} + \dfrac{1.48}{\tan 25°}$
 ≈ 5.74 m

The cat and the dog are 5.74 m apart.

SOLVING A TRIANGLE USING TRIGONOMETRIC RATIOS AND THE PYTHAGOREAN THEOREM

Trigonometric problems often require solving a triangle. Solving a triangle means that the measures of all the unknown sides and all the unknown angles are calculated.

The following three procedures are often used to solve a triangle:

- Pythagorean theorem: $a^2 + b^2 = c^2$
- Property of angles in a triangle: the sum of the angles in a triangle equals 180°
- Trigonometric ratios: sine, cosine, and tangent

Example

One side and two angles are known for the given triangle.

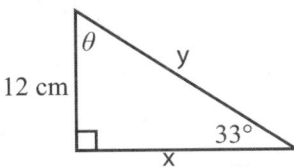

Solve the given triangle. Express the measures of the side lengths to the nearest tenth of a centimeter.

Solution

Step 1
Label the unknown sides and unknown angles using appropriate variables.

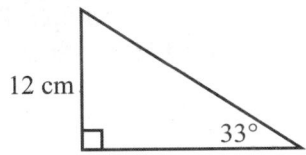

Step 2
Determine the measure of Φ.
Apply the rule that the sum of the measures of the angles in a triangle is 180°.
$$90° + 33° + \Phi = 180°$$
$$123° + \Phi = 180°$$
$$\Phi = 57°$$

Step 3
Determine the length of x by applying the tan ratio.
$$\tan 33° = \frac{12}{x}$$
$$x(\tan 33°) = 12$$
$$x = \frac{12}{\tan 33°}$$
$$x \approx 18.5 \text{ cm}$$

Step 4
Determine the length of y by applying the Pythagorean theorem or the sine ratio.
Use the Pythagorean theorem.
$$c^2 = a^2 + b^2$$
$$y^2 = 12^2 + x^2$$
When substituting for x, it is best to use the exact value, $\frac{12}{\tan 33°}$, rather than the approximate value of 18.5 cm.
$$y^2 = 12^2 + \left(\frac{12}{\tan 33°}\right)^2$$
$$y = \sqrt{12^2 + \left(\frac{12}{\tan 33°}\right)^2}$$
$$y \approx 22.0 \text{ cm}$$
Use the sine ratio.
$$\sin 33° = \frac{12}{y}$$
$$y(\sin 33°) = 12$$
$$y = \frac{12}{\sin 33°}$$
$$y \approx 22.0 \text{ cm}$$
The value of y is the same when using either the Pythagorean theorem or the trigonometric ratio.

CALCULATING UNKNOWN VALUES USING TWO RIGHT TRIANGLES

Many trigonometry questions require more than one calculation in order to determine the desired information. In some cases, the order of these calculations is not important, while in others, the order is crucial to determine the unknown values.

Some general problem-solving steps are as follows:

1. Read the problem carefully. Determine which measures are given and which measure needs to be calculated.
2. If a diagram is not given, draw a sketch to represent the situation presented in the problem.
3. Examine the diagram to decide which primary trigonometric ratio to apply.
4. Make substitutions into the appropriate formula, and use correct algebraic steps to solve for the unknown value. Avoid or minimize rounding until the last step.
5. Check your calculations.
6. Write a concluding statement.

Some of these problem-solving suggestions are used in the following problems.

Example

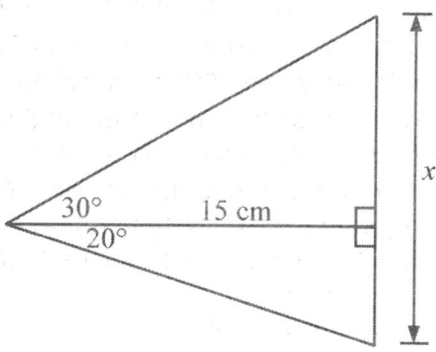

Calculate the value of x, to the nearest hundredth, in the given diagram.

Solution

In order to determine the entire length of x, the question must be broken down into two separate calculations. First, label (assign variables to) the first lengths that can be calculated.

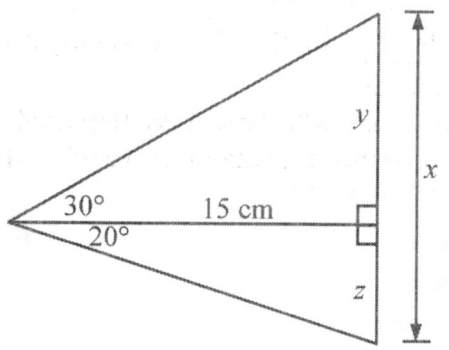

The value of x is equal to the sum of y and z.
$x = y + z$

It does not matter which length, y or z, is calculated first.

Use the tangent ratio to calculate the measure of y and z.

$\tan 30° = \dfrac{y}{15}$
$\quad y = 15(\tan 30°)$
$\quad y \approx 8.66 \text{ cm}$

$\tan 20° = \dfrac{z}{15}$
$\quad z = 15(\tan 20°)$
$\quad z \approx 5.46 \text{ cm}$

In order to avoid rounding errors, the expressions for y and z can be substituted into the equation $x = y + z$. Rounding will only need to be done at the end of the question.

$x = y + z$
$x = 15(\tan 30°) + 15(\tan 20°)$
$x \approx 14.12 \text{ cm}$

In the following problem, the use of two primary trigonometric ratios is applied.

Example

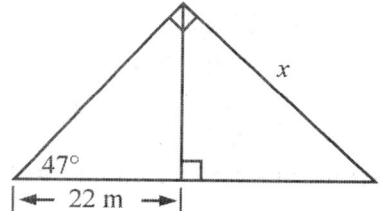

Calculate the value of x to the nearest tenth of a meter.

Solution

Step 1
Label the measures of the unknown angles. These can be determined by applying the fact that the sum of angles in a triangle total 180°.

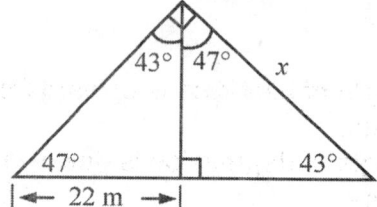

Right Angle Triangles in Trigonometry

Step 2
Calculate the measure of another unknown side so that the value of x can be determined. Label the two unknown sides y and z as shown.

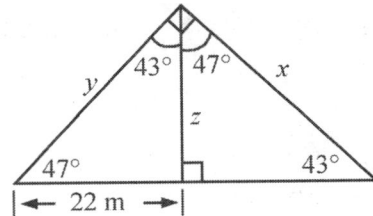

The value of x can be calculated once the measure of either y or z are known.
The measure of z will be calculated in this example.
Use the tangent ratio to calculate the length of z.

$$\tan 47° = \frac{z}{22}$$
$$z = 22(\tan 47°)$$
$$z \approx 23.6 \text{ m}$$

Step 3
Find the measure of x using the exact value of z or the expression for z.

$$\sin 43° = \frac{z}{x}$$
$$x(\sin 43°) = z$$
$$x = \frac{z}{\sin 43°}$$
$$x = \frac{22(\tan 47°)}{\sin 43°}$$
$$x \approx 34.6 \text{ m}$$

The length of side x is about 34.6 m.

SOLVING PROBLEMS USING THE TANGENT RATIO

The tangent ratio can be used to solve problems involving the measures of sides and angles in real-life applications. When solving these types of problems, the following definitions are helpful to remember:

- The **angle of elevation** is upward from the horizontal.
- The **angle of depression** is downward from the horizontal.

Example
A helicopter is involved in an air rescue mission of a sinking sailboat. The pilot determines that the angle of depression from the helicopter to the sailboat is 15°. The helicopter is flying at an altitude of 800 m.

What is the horizontal distance from the helicopter to the sailboat, to the nearest tenth of a meter?

Solution
Step 1
Draw a diagram that represents the information given in the problem.

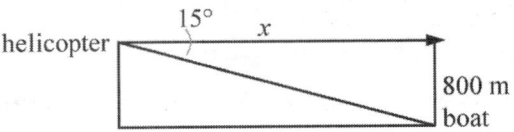

Step 2
Identify the ratio to use in order to solve for x. Start from the given angle which is 15°.
The side measuring 800 m is the opposite side since it is across from the given angle. The side labeled x is the adjacent side since it is next to the given angle and is not the hypotenuse. The trigonometric ratio that compares the length of the opposite side to the length of the adjacent is tangent.

$$\tan \theta = \frac{\text{opposite}}{\text{adjacent}}$$

Step 3
Substitute the known values from the triangle into the tangent ratio.

$$\tan 15° = \frac{800}{x}$$

Step 4
Find the decimal equivalent to tan 15°.
Type in $\boxed{1}\boxed{5}$, and then press $\boxed{\tan}$ or $\boxed{\text{TAN}}\boxed{1}\boxed{5}\boxed{\text{ENTER}}$, depending on your calculator.
The screen will show 0.2679491924.
The decimal equivalent, to 3 decimal places, for tan 15° is 0.268.

Step 5
Write the equivalent ratios.
Substitute 0.268 for tan 15° and place it over 1.
$$\frac{0.268}{1} = \frac{800}{x}$$

Step 6
Use cross products to solve for x.
$0.268 \times x = 800 \times 1$
$0.268x = 800$
Divide both sides by 0.268.
$$\frac{0.268x}{0.268} = \frac{800}{0.268}$$
$x = 2{,}985.074627$

Rounded to the nearest tenth of a meter, the horizontal distance from the helicopter to the sailboat is 2,985.1 m.

SOLVING PROBLEMS USING THE SINE RATIO

The sine ratio can be used to solve problems involving the measures of sides and angles in real-life applications. When solving these types of problems, the following definitions are helpful to remember:

- The **angle of elevation** is upward from the horizontal.
- The **angle of depression** is downward from the horizontal.

Example
A 12 m ladder is leaning against a building. The angle formed between the ladder and the ground is 40°.

Rounded to the nearest tenth, how far is the top of the ladder from the ground?

Solution

Step 1
Draw a diagram that represents the information given in the problem.

Use variables to indicate the measure of the sides you are trying to find.

The length of the ladder is represented by the hypotenuse of the triangle.

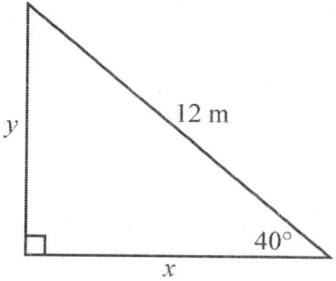

Step 2
Identify the ratio to use in order to solve for y.
Start from the given angle, which is 40°.
Side y is the opposite side since it is across from the given angle, and the side measuring 12 m is the hypotenuse.

The trigonometric ratio that compares the length of the opposite side to the length of the hypotenuse is sine.

$$\sin \theta = \frac{\text{opposite}}{\text{hypotenuse}}$$

Step 3
Substitute the known values from the triangle into the sine ratio.

$$\sin 40° = \frac{y}{12}$$

Step 4
Find the decimal equivalent to sin 40°.

Type in [4][0], and then press [sin] or type in [SIN][4][0][ENTER].

The screen will show 0.6427876097.
The decimal equivalent, to 3 decimal places, for sin 40° is 0.643.

Step 5
Write the equivalent ratios.
Substitute 0.643 for sin 40°, and place it over 1.
$$\frac{0.643}{1} = \frac{y}{12}$$

Step 6
Use cross products to solve for y.
0.643 × 12 = y × 1
7.716 = y

The value of y can also be determined by using your calculator and typing [4][0][sin][×][1][2][=] or typing [sin][(][4][0][)][×][1][2][ENTER], depending on your calculator.

Rounded to the nearest tenth, the top of the ladder is 7.7 m above the ground.

Example
To the nearest degree, find the angle of elevation of a ramp that is 15 m long if the top end of the ramp is 2 m above the ground.

Solution

Step 1
Draw a diagram that represents the information given in the problem.

Use a variable to indicate the measure of the angle you are trying to find.

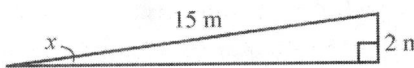

Step 2
Identify the ratio to use in order to solve for x.
Start from angle x.
The side measuring 2 m is the opposite side, since it is across angle x. The side measuring 15 m is the hypotenuse. The trigonometric ratio that compares the length of the opposite side to the length of the hypotenuse is sine.

$$\sin \theta = \frac{\text{opposite}}{\text{hypotenuse}}$$

Step 3
Substitute the known values from the triangle into the sine ratio.

$$\sin x = \frac{2}{15}$$

Step 4
Calculate the measure of angle x by using the $\sin^{-1}$ button on the calculator.
Type in [2][÷][1][5][=]
The screen will show $0.1\overline{3}$.
Then, type in [0][.][1][3][3][SHIFT][$\sin^{-1}$] or type in [2ND][$\sin^{-1}$][.][1][3][3][ENTER], depending on your calculator.
The screen will show 7.64298544.
To the nearest degree, the angle of elevation of the ramp is 8°.

SOLVING PROBLEMS USING THE COSINE RATIO

The cosine ratio can be used to solve problems involving the measures of sides and angles in real-life applications. When solving these types of problems, the following definitions are helpful to remember:

- The **angle of elevation** is upward from the horizontal.
- The **angle of depression** is downward from the horizontal.

Example
Rounded to the nearest tenth, how far is the base of the ladder from the building?

Solution

Step 1
Draw a diagram that represents the information given in the problem.
Use variables to indicate the measure of the sides you are trying to find.
The length of the ladder is represented by the hypotenuse of the triangle.

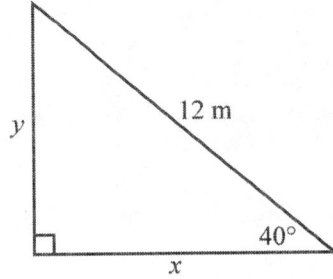

Step 2
Identify the ratio to use in order to solve for x.
Start from the given angle, which is 40°.
Side x is the adjacent side since it it next to the given angle, and the side measuring 12 m is the hypotenuse.
The trigonometric ratio that compares the length of the adjacent side to the length of the hypotenuse is cosine.

$\cos \theta = \dfrac{\text{adjacent}}{\text{hypotenuse}}$

Step 3
Substitute the known values from the triangle into the cosine ratio.

$\cos 40° = \dfrac{x}{12}$

Step 4
Find the decimal equivalent of cos 40°.
Type in $\boxed{4}\,\boxed{0}$, and then press $\boxed{\cos}$ or type in $\boxed{\text{COS}}\,\boxed{4}\,\boxed{0}\,\boxed{\text{ENTER}}$, depending on your calculator.
The screen will show 0.7660444431.
The decimal equivalent, to three decimal places, for cos 40° is 0.766.

Step 5
Write the equivalent ratios.
Substitute 0.766 for cos 40°, and place it over 1.

$\dfrac{0.766}{1} = \dfrac{x}{12}$

Step 6
Use cross products to solve for x.
$0.766 \times 12 = x \times 1$
$9.192 = x$

Note: The value of x can be determined in one step by using your calculator and typing $\boxed{4}\,\boxed{0}$ $\boxed{\cos}\,\boxed{\times}\,\boxed{12}\,\boxed{=}$ or typing $\boxed{\text{COS}}\,\boxed{(}\,\boxed{4}\,\boxed{0}\,\boxed{)}$ $\boxed{\times}\,\boxed{12}\,\boxed{\text{ENTER}}$, depending on your calculator.
The base of the ladder is 9.2 m from the building.

Applying the Cosine Ratio to Solve for a Missing Angle of a Right Triangle

The cosine ratio can be used to find the measure of an unknown angle when the lengths of the adjacent side and the hypotenuse are given.

Use the following steps to determine the missing angle of a right triangle using the cosine ratio:

1. Identify the hypotenuse and the side adjacent to the required angle, and then set up the cosine ratio.
2. Substitute the known values from the triangle into the cosine ratio.
3. Calculate the decimal equivalent of the cosine ratio.
4. Determine the measure of the required angle by using the $\cos^{-1}$ key on your calculator.

Example

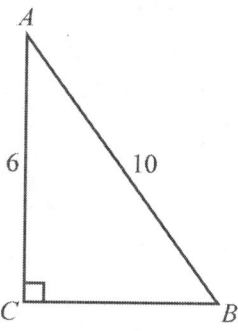

For $\triangle ABC$, find the measure of angle A to the nearest degree.

Solution

Step 1
Determine the hypotenuse and adjacent side of angle A, and set up the cosine ratio.
The hypotenuse of $\triangle ABC$ is AB, and the side adjacent to angle A is AC.

Therefore, $\cos A = \dfrac{AC}{AB}$.

Step 2
Substitute the known values from the triangle into the cosine ratio.

$\cos A = \dfrac{6}{10}$

Step 3
Calculate the decimal equivalent of the cos ratio.
Type in $\boxed{6}\boxed{\div}\boxed{1}\boxed{0}\boxed{ENTER}$.
The screen will show 0.6.

Step 4
Calculate the measure of angle A by using the $\cos^{-1}$ key on your calculator.
Type in $\boxed{0}\boxed{.}\boxed{6}\boxed{SHIFT}\boxed{COS^{-1}}$ or $\boxed{2nd}$ $\boxed{COS^{-1}}\boxed{.}\boxed{6}\boxed{ENTER}$, depending on your calculator.
The screen will show 53.13010235.
To the nearest degree, the measure of angle A is 53°.

APPLYING THE TANGENT RATIO TO SOLVE FOR A MISSING ANGLE OF A RIGHT TRIANGLE

The tangent ratio can be used to find the measure of an unknown angle when the lengths of the sides opposite and adjacent to the unknown angle are given.

Use the following steps to determine the missing angle of a right triangle using the tangent ratio:

1. Identify the sides opposite and adjacent to the required angle, and set up the tangent ratio.
2. Substitute the known values from the triangle into the tangent ratio.
3. Calculate the decimal equivalent of the tangent ratio.
4. Determine the measure of the unknown angle by using the $\tan^{-1}$ button on your calculator.

Example

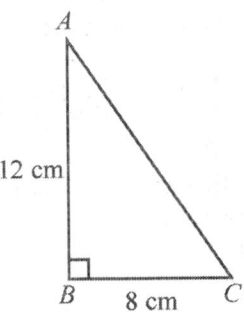

For triangle ABC, find the measure of angle A to the nearest degree.

Solution

Step 1
Determine the opposite and adjacent sides of angle A, and set up the tangent ratio.
The side opposite to angle A is BC, and the side adjacent to angle A is AB (side AC is the hypotenuse).
$$\tan A = \frac{BC}{AB}$$

Step 2
Substitute the known values from the triangle into the tangent ratio.
$$\tan A = \frac{8}{12}$$

Step 3
Calculate the decimal equivalent of the tangent ratio.
Type in $\boxed{8}\boxed{\div}\boxed{1}\boxed{2}$. The screen will show 0.666666666. Rounded to the nearest thousandth, this becomes 0.667.

Step 4
Calculate the measure of the angle A by using the $\tan^{-1}$ key on your calculator.
Type in $\boxed{.}\boxed{6}\boxed{6}\boxed{7}\boxed{SHIFT}\boxed{\tan^{-1}}$ or $\boxed{SHIFT}$ $\boxed{\tan^{-1}}\boxed{.}\boxed{6}\boxed{6}\boxed{7}\boxed{ENTER}$ depending on your calculator.
The screen will show 33.70328759.
To the nearest degree, the measure of angle A is 34°.

APPLYING THE SINE RATIO TO SOLVE FOR THE MISSING ANGLE OF A RIGHT TRIANGLE

The sine ratio can be used to find the measure of an unknown angle of a right triangle when the lengths of the opposite side and hypotenuse are given.

To determine the missing angle of a right triangle by using the sine ratio, follow these steps:

1. Identify the hypotenuse and the side opposite the required angle, and then set up the sine ratio.
2. Substitute the known values from the triangle into the sine ratio.
3. Calculate the decimal equivalent of the sine ratio.
4. Determine the measure of the required angle by using the $\sin^{-1}$ key on a calculator.

Example

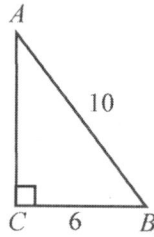

For $\triangle ABC$, find the measure of angle A to the nearest degree.

Solution

Step 1
Determine the hypotenuse and the opposite sides of angle A, and set up the sine ratio. The hypotenuse of $\triangle ABC$ is AB, and the side opposite to angle A is BC.
Therefore, $\sin A = \dfrac{BC}{AB}$.

Step 2
Substitute the known values from the triangle into the sine ratio.
$\sin A = \dfrac{6}{10}$

Step 3
Calculate the decimal equivalent of the sine ratio.
Type in $\boxed{6}\;\boxed{\div}\;\boxed{1}\,\boxed{0}\;\boxed{\text{ENTER}}$.
The screen will show 0.6.

Step 4
Calculate the measure of angle A using the $\sin^{-1}$ key on your calculator.
Type in $\boxed{0}\,\boxed{.}\,\boxed{6}\;\boxed{\text{shift}}\;\boxed{\sin^{-1}}\;\boxed{=}$, or type in $\boxed{\text{2nd}}\;\boxed{\sin^{-1}}\;\boxed{0}\,\boxed{.}\,\boxed{6}\;\boxed{\text{ENTER}}$.
The screen will show 36.86989765.
To the nearest degree, the measure of angle A is 37°.

APPLYING THE SINE RATIO TO SOLVE FOR A MISSING SIDE OF A RIGHT TRIANGLE

The sine ratio can be used to find the measure of an unknown side in a right triangle when the measures of one side and one angle are given.

To determine the missing side of a right triangle using the sine ratio, follow these steps:

1. Identify the hypotenuse and the opposite sides for the given angle, and then set up the sine ratio.
2. Substitute the known values from the triangle into the sine ratio.
3. Find the decimal equivalent for sine of the given angle.
4. Write the equivalent ratios.
5. Use cross multiplication to determine the length of the unknown side.

Example

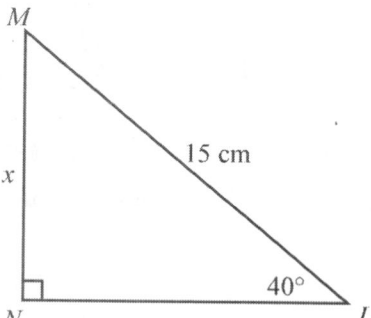

Right Angle Triangles in Trigonometry

For triangle LMN, find the length of side MN, to the nearest tenth of a centimeter.

Solution

Step 1
Identify the hypotenuse and opposite side of angle L, and set up the sine ratio.
The hypotenuse of △MNL is side ML and the side opposite to ∠L is MN.
Therefore, $\sin L = \dfrac{MN}{ML}$

Step 2
Substitute the known values from the triangle into the sine ratio.
$\sin 40° = \dfrac{x}{15}$

Step 3
Find the decimal equivalent of sin 40°.
Type in $\boxed{4}\boxed{0}$, and then press $\boxed{\sin}$ or type in $\boxed{\sin}\boxed{4}\boxed{0}\boxed{\text{ENTER}}$, depending on your calculator.
The screen will show 0.642787609.
The decimal equivalent for sin 40°, to three decimal places, is about 0.643.

Step 4
Write the equivalent ratios.
Substitute 0.643 in for sin 40°, and place it over 1.
$0.643 = \dfrac{x}{15}$
$\dfrac{0.643}{1} = \dfrac{x}{15}$

Step 5
Use cross products to solve for x.
$\dfrac{0.643}{1} = \dfrac{x}{15}$
$0.643 \times 15 = 1 \times x$
$9.6 \approx x$

Note: The value of x can be determined in one step by using your calculator and typing in $\boxed{4}\boxed{0}\boxed{\sin}\boxed{\times}\boxed{1}\boxed{5}$ or typing in $\boxed{\sin}\boxed{(}\boxed{4}\boxed{0}\boxed{)}\boxed{\text{ENTER}}\boxed{\times}\boxed{1}\boxed{5}\boxed{\text{ENTER}}$, depending on your calculator.
Rounded to the nearest tenth of a centimeter, the length of side MN is 9.6 cm.

A right triangle FGH is shown.

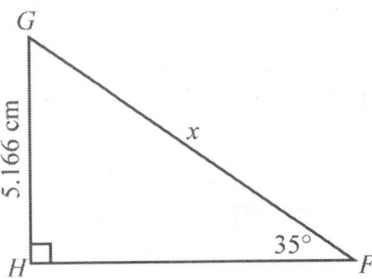

For triangle FGH, find the length of side GF, to the nearest whole number.

Solution

Step 1
Identify the hypotenuse and opposite side of angle F, and set up the sine ratio.
The hypotenuse of △FGH is GF and the side opposite to ∠F, is GH.
Therefore, $\sin F = \dfrac{GH}{GF}$.

Step 2
Substitute the known values from the triangle into the sine ratio.
$\sin 35° = \dfrac{5.166}{x}$

Step 3
Find the decimal equivalent of sin 35°.
Type in $\boxed{3}\boxed{5}$, and then press $\boxed{\sin}$ or type in $\boxed{\text{SIN}}\boxed{3}\boxed{5}\boxed{\text{ENTER}}$, depending on your calculator.
The screen will show 0.573576436.
The decimal equivalent for sin 35° to three decimal places is 0.574.

Step 4
Write the equivalent ratios.
Substitute 0.574 in for sin 35°, and place it over 1.
$0.574 = \dfrac{5.166}{x}$
$\dfrac{0.574}{1} = \dfrac{5.166}{x}$

Step 5
Use cross products to solve for x.
$$\frac{0.574}{1} = \frac{5.166}{x}$$
$0.574 \times x = 5.166 \times 1$
$0.574x = 5.166$

Divide both sides by 0.574.
$$\frac{0.574x}{0.574} = \frac{5.166}{0.574}$$
$x \approx 9.0$

The length of side GF, to the nearest whole number, is 9 cm.

APPLYING THE COSINE RATIO TO SOLVE FOR THE MISSING SIDE OF A RIGHT TRIANGLE

The cosine ratio can be used to find the measure of the unknown side of a right triangle when the measures of one side and one angle are given.

To determine the missing side of a right triangle using the cosine ratio, follow these steps:

1. Identify the hypotenuse and the adjacent side, and then set up the cosine ratio.
2. Substitute the known values from the triangle into the cosine ratio.
3. Find the decimal equivalent for the cosine of the given angle.
4. Write the equivalent ratios.
5. Use cross multiplication to determine the length of the unknown side.

Example

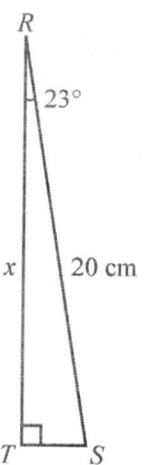

For triangle RST, find the length of side RT, to the nearest tenth of a centimeter.

Solution

Step 1
Identify the hypotenuse and adjacent side of angle R, and set up the cosine ratio.
The hypotenuse of $\triangle RST$ is side RS and the side adjacent to angle R is RT.
Therefore, $\cos R = \frac{RT}{RS}$

Step 2
Substitute the known values from the triangle into the cosine ratio.
$$\cos 23° = \frac{x}{20}$$

Step 3
Find the decimal equivalent for cos 23°.
Type in $\boxed{2}\boxed{3}$, and then press $\boxed{\cos}$ or type in $\boxed{\cos}\boxed{2}\boxed{3}\boxed{\text{ENTER}}$, depending on your calculator.
The screen will show 0.9205048535. A number to three decimal places is often sufficient. The decimal equivalent for cos 23° is about 0.921.

Step 4
Write the equivalent ratios.
Substitute 0.921 in for cos 23°, and place it over 1.
$$\frac{0.921}{1} = \frac{x}{20}$$

Step 5
Use cross products to solve for x.
$$\frac{0.921}{1} = \frac{x}{20}$$
$0.921 \times 20 = x \times 1$
$18.42 = x$

Note: The value of x can be determined in one step by using your calculator and typing $\boxed{2}\boxed{3}$ $\boxed{\cos}\boxed{\times}\boxed{2}\boxed{0}\boxed{=}$ or $\boxed{\cos}\boxed{(}\boxed{2}\boxed{3}\boxed{)}\boxed{\times}$ $\boxed{2}\boxed{0}\boxed{\text{ENTER}}$, depending on your calculator.
Rounded to a tenth of a centimeter, the length of side RT is 18.4 cm.

The right triangle JKL is shown.

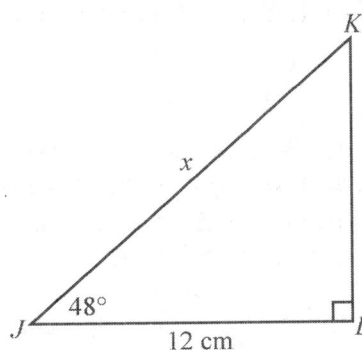

For triangle JKL, find the length of side JK, denoted by x, to the nearest tenth of a centimeter.

Solution

Step 1
Set up the cosine ratio for the given angle, angle J.
The hypotenuse of △JKL is JK and the side adjacent to angle J is JL.
Therefore, $\cos J = \dfrac{JL}{JK}$

Step 2
Substitute in the known values from the triangle into this cosine ratio.
The value of the adjacent side is 12 cm, and the measure of angle J is 48°
$\cos 48° = \dfrac{12}{x}$

Step 3
Find the decimal equivalent for cos 48°.
Type in $\boxed{4}\,\boxed{8}$, and then press $\boxed{\cos}$ or type in $\boxed{\cos}\,\boxed{4}\,\boxed{8}\,\boxed{\text{ENTER}}$, depending on your calculator.
The screen will show 0.6691306064.
The decimal equivalent, to 5 decimal places, for cos 48° is 0.66913.

Step 4
Write the equivalent ratios.
Substitute 0.66913 in for cos 48°, and place it over 1.
$\dfrac{0.66913}{1} = \dfrac{12}{x}$

Step 5
Use cross products to solve for x.
$0.66913 \times x = 12 \times 1$
$0.66913x = 12$
Divide both sides by 0.66913
$\dfrac{0.66913x}{0.66913} = \dfrac{12}{0.66913}$
$x = \cong 17.93373$
Rounded to the nearest tenth of a centimeter, the length of side JK is 17.9 cm.

APPLYING THE TANGENT RATIO TO SOLVE FOR A MISSING SIDE OF A RIGHT TRIANGLE

The tangent ratio can be used to find the measure of an unknown side in a right triangle when the measures of one side and one angle are given.

To determine the missing side of a right triangle using the tangent ratio, follow these steps:

1. Identify the opposite and adjacent sides for the given angle, and set up the tangent ratio.
2. Substitute the known values from the triangle into the tangent ratio.
3. Find the decimal equivalent for the tangent of the given angle.
4. Write the equivalent ratios.
5. Use cross multiplication to determine the length of the unknown side.

Example

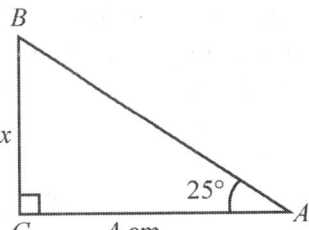

For triangle *ABC*, find the length of side *BC* to the nearest tenth of a centimeter.

Solution

Step 1
Identify the opposite and adjacent sides of angle *A*, and set up the tangent ratio.
The side opposite to angle *A* is *BC*, and the side adjacent to angle *A* is *AC* (side *AB* is the hypotenuse).
$\tan A = \dfrac{BC}{CA}$

Step 2
Substitute the known values from the triangle into the tangent ratio.
$\tan 25° = \dfrac{x}{4}$

Step 3
Find the decimal equivalent of tan 25°.
Type in $\boxed{2}\boxed{5}$, and then press $\boxed{\tan}$ or type in $\boxed{\tan}\boxed{2}\boxed{5}\boxed{\text{ENTER}}$, depending on your calculator.
The screen will show 0.466307658. A number to three decimal places is often sufficient. The decimal equivalent for tan 25° is about 0.466.

Step 4
Write the equivalent ratios.
Substitute 0.466 in for tan 25°, and place it over 1.
$0.466 = \dfrac{x}{4}$
$\dfrac{0.466}{1} = \dfrac{x}{4}$

Step 5
Use cross products to solve for *x*.
$\dfrac{0.466}{1} = \dfrac{x}{4}$
$0.466 \times 4 = 1x$
$1.9 \approx x$

Note: The value of *x* can be determined in one step by using your calculator and typing $\boxed{2}\boxed{5}$ $\boxed{\tan}\boxed{\times}\boxed{4}$ or $\boxed{\tan}\boxed{(}\boxed{2}\boxed{5}\boxed{)}\boxed{\times}\boxed{4}$ $\boxed{\text{ENTER}}$, depending on your calculator.
Rounded to the nearest tenth of a centimeter, the length of side *BC* is 1.9 cm.

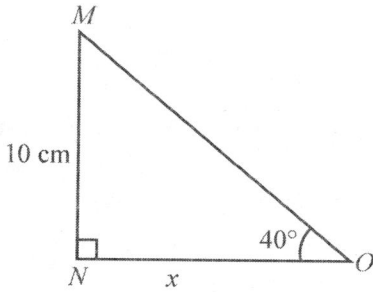

For triangle *MNO*, find the length of side *NO* to the nearest tenth of a centimeter.

Solution

Step 1
Identify the opposite and adjacent sides of angle *O*, and set up the tangent ratio.
The side opposite to angle *O* is *MN*, and the side adjacent to angle *O* is *NO* (side *MO* is the hypotenuse).
$\tan O = \dfrac{MN}{NO}$

Step 2
Substitute the known values from the triangle into the tangent ratio.
$\tan 40° = \dfrac{10}{x}$

Step 3

Find the decimal equivalent of tan 40°.

Type in $\boxed{4}\boxed{0}$, and then press $\boxed{\tan}$ or type in $\boxed{\text{TAN}}\boxed{4}\boxed{0}\boxed{\text{ENTER}}$, depending on your calculator.

The screen will show 0.8390996312. A number to three decimal places is often sufficient. The decimal equivalent for tan 40° is about 0.839.

Step 4

Write the equivalent ratios.

Substitute 0.839 for tan 40°, and place it over 1.

$$0.839 = \frac{10}{x}$$

$$\frac{0.839}{1} = \frac{10}{x}$$

Step 5

Use cross products to solve for x.

$$\frac{0.839}{1} = \frac{10}{x}$$
$$0.839 \times x = 10 \times 1$$
$$0.839x = 10$$

Divide both sides by 0.839 to solve for x.

$$\frac{0.839x}{0.839} = \frac{10}{0.839}$$
$$x \approx 11.9$$

Rounded to the nearest tenth of a centimeter, the length of side *NO* is 11.9 cm.

EXERCISE #1—RIGHT ANGLE TRIANGLES IN TRIGONOMETRY

Use the following information to answer the next question.

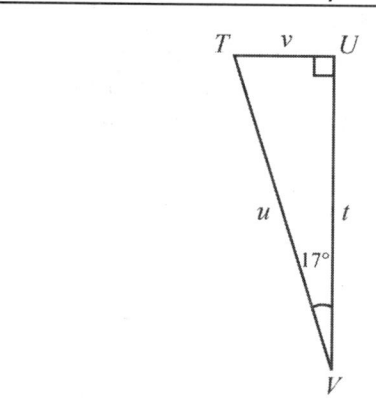

A diagram of a triangle is given.

114. What trigonometric ratio is represented by $\dfrac{t}{v}$ in the diagram?

A. sin 17°
B. tan 17°
C. sin 73°
D. tan 73°

115. Draw triangle *ABC* in which angle *B* is equal to 90° and sin *A* is equal to $\dfrac{2}{3}$.

Use the following information to answer the next question.

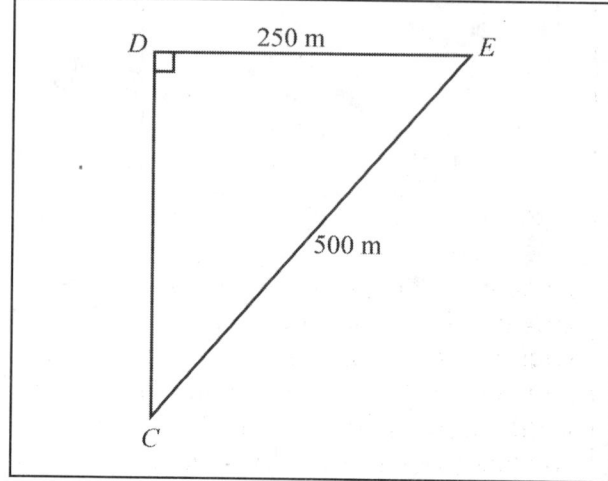

116. Expressed in lowest terms, the cosine ratio of ∠*E* is

A. $\dfrac{2}{1}$
B. $\dfrac{3}{2}$
C. $\dfrac{2}{3}$
D. $\dfrac{1}{2}$

117. The expression $\sin\left(\dfrac{\pi}{2} - x\right)$ is equivalent to

A. −sin *x*
B. cos *x*
C. $\cos\left(\dfrac{\pi}{2} + x\right)$
D. $\sin\left(x - \dfrac{\pi}{2}\right)$

118. If sin 4θ = cos θ, then a possible solution for θ is

A. 14°
B. 16°
C. 18°
D. 20°

Use the following information to answer the next question.

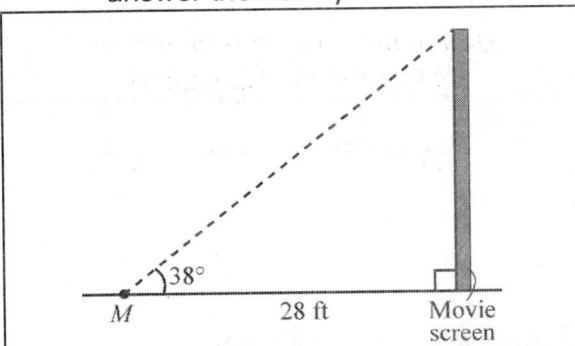

Michael is sitting in a movie theater at a certain point, *M*, as shown in the given diagram. With a clinometer, he measures the angle of elevation to the top of the screen as 38°. With a tape measure, he measures a distance of 28 ft from his seat to the bottom of the screen.

119. Rounded to the nearest foot, what is the height of the movie screen?

A. 45 ft
B. 35 ft
C. 22 ft
D. 17 ft

Use the following information to answer the next question.

Malcolm is asked to solve triangle *ACD*.

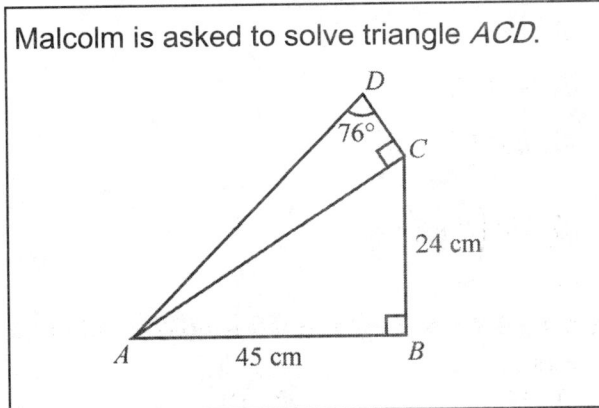

120. If Malcolm completes his work correctly, he will find that the length of the unknown side *CD*, to the nearest tenth, is

A. 12.3 cm
B. 12.7 cm
C. 13.2 cm
D. 13.6 cm

Use the following information to answer the next question.

Lexi is standing in her yard. She sees a cat sitting directly west of her position and a dog sitting directly east. Lexi's eye level is 1.48 m above the ground. For her to look directly at the cat, the angle of depression is 30°, and for her to look directly at the dog, the angle of depression is 25°.

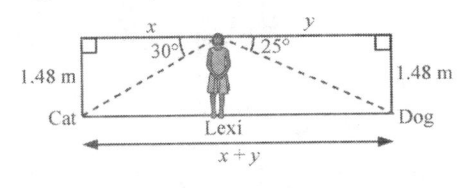

121. Calculate the distance between the cat and the dog.

Use the following information to answer the next question.

Matt spots an airplane flying at an angle of elevation of 42° from his position on the ground. The plane is flying at an altitude of 2.50 km.

122. The distance between Matt and the point on the ground directly below the plane is approximately

A. 1.67 km
B. 1.85 km
C. 2.25 km
D. 2.78 km

Use the following information to answer the next question.

A guy wire is to be attached halfway up a tower that is 48 m tall. The guy wire will make an angle of 58° with the ground. In order to secure the wire, an extra meter of wire is required at each end.

123. Expressed to the nearest tenth, what is the total length of wire required?
   A. 22.4 m
   B. 30.3 m
   C. 40.4 m
   D. 58.6 m

Use the following information to answer the next question.

The airport tower in Townsville is located 25.8 km from the closest edge of a nearby lake. At exactly 3:00, a plane is flying over the closest edge of the lake. The pilot measures the angle of depression to the airport tower in Townsville to be 22.5°.

124. Expressed to the nearest tenth, the distance between the airplane and the airport tower at 3:00 is _____ km.

Use the following information to answer the next question.

The diagram of a right triangle is shown.

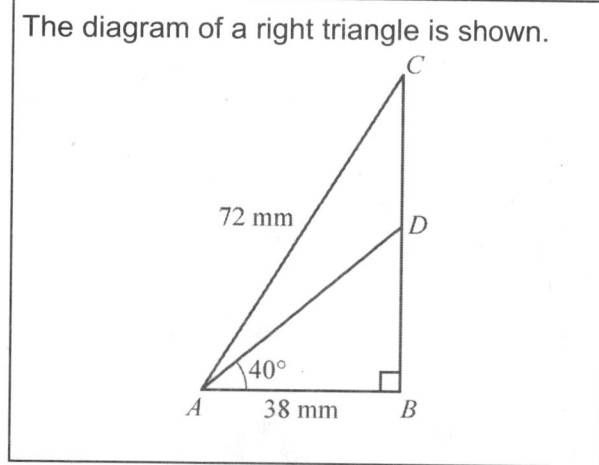

125. To the nearest degree, what is the measure of ∠CAD in the given triangle?
   A. 12°
   B. 18°
   C. 22°
   D. 26°

Use the following information to answer the next question.

In triangle MNP, $\angle N = 90°$, $MN = 42$ mm, and $NP = 65$ mm. Nadine is asked to determine the measure of $\angle P$ to the nearest tenth of a degree. Her solution is as shown.

1. $\tan P = \dfrac{NP}{MN}$
2. $\tan P = \dfrac{65}{42}$
3. $\tan P \approx 1.548$
4. $P \approx \tan^{-1} 1.548$
5. $P \approx 57.1°$
6. To the nearest tenth of a degree, the measure of $\angle P$ is 57.1°.

126. In which step of Nadine's solution did she make her first error?
   A. 1
   B. 2
   C. 3
   D. 4

Use the following information to answer the next question.

Carlita and Alvaro are asked to determine the measure of ∠A to the nearest hundredth of a degree.

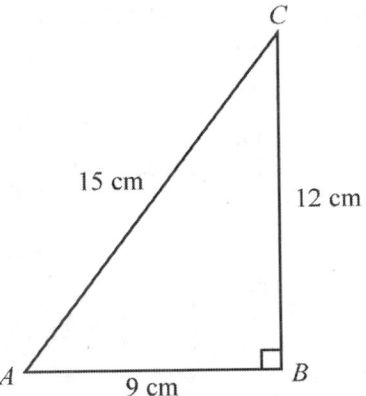

The following steps show Carlita's partial solution:

1. $\sin A = \dfrac{BC}{AC}$
2. $\sin A = \dfrac{12}{15}$
3. $A = \sin^{-1}(12 \div 15)$

The following steps show Alvaro's partial solution:

1. $\sin C = \dfrac{AB}{AC}$
2. $\sin C = \dfrac{9}{15}$
3. $\sin C = 0.6$
4. $C = \sin^{-1}(0.6)$
5. $A = 90° - \sin^{-1}(0.6)$

127. Which of the following statements about the two students' partial solutions is **true**?
  A. Both Carlita and Alvaro have correct partial solutions.
  B. Both Carlita and Alvaro have incorrect partial solutions.
  C. Carlita has a correct partial solution, and Alvaro has an incorrect partial solution.
  D. Carlita has an incorrect partial solution, and Alvaro has a correct partial solution.

Use the following information to answer the next question.

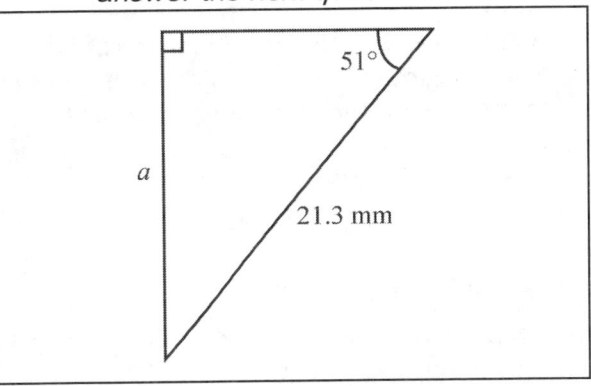

128. Rounded to the nearest tenth of a millimeter, the length of side *a* is
  A. 13.4 mm   B. 16.6 mm
  C. 26.3 mm   D. 27.4 mm

Use the following information to answer the next question.

Simon is pitching a tent that has walls that are 3.5 m long.

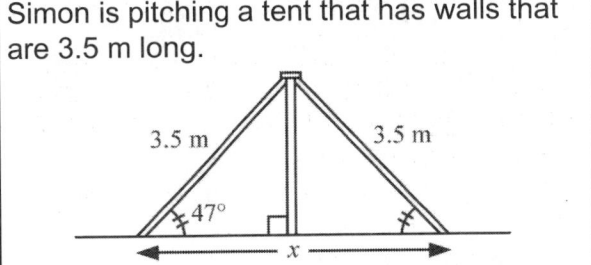

129. Rounded to the nearest tenth of a meter, the measure of length *x* is
  A. 2.4 m   B. 2.6 m
  C. 4.8 m   D. 5.2 m

Use the following information to answer the next question.

A rescue helicopter is at a height of 51 m from sea level. To save a drowning man at point C, the helicopter needs to carry him to point B, which is on the shore, with the help of a rope.

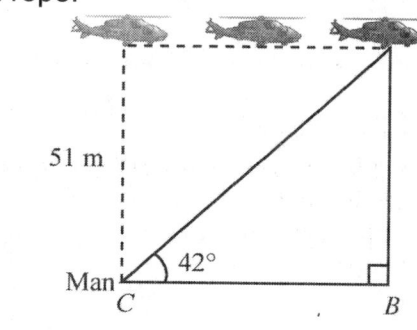

130. Rounded to the nearest hundredth of a meter, what is the distance the man travels?

A. 45.92 m
B. 56.67 m
C. 68.63 m
D. 76.22 m

EXERCISE #1—RIGHT ANGLE TRIANGLES IN TRIGONOMETRY
ANSWERS AND SOLUTIONS

114. D	119. C	124. 27.9	129. C
115. See solution	120. B	125. B	130. B
116. D	121. See solution	126. A	
117. B	122. D	127. A	
118. C	123. B	128. B	

114. D
Step 1
Determine which sides are represented in the triangle.
Sides t and v are the legs of the triangle. Since the hypotenuse is represented by u and the given ratio does not contain u, it is a tangent ratio.

Step 2
Determine the tan ratio when the reference angle is 17°.
When using 17° as the point of reference, t represents the adjacent side and v represents the opposite side.

The ratio is $\tan 17° = \dfrac{\text{opposite}}{\text{adjacent}} = \dfrac{v}{t}$.

Step 3
Determine the tan ratio for the other angle.
The third angle in the triangle is
$180° - 90° - 17° = 73°$.
When using 73° as the point of reference, t represents the opposite side and v represents the adjacent side.

The ratio is $\tan 73° = \dfrac{\text{opposite}}{\text{adjacent}} = \dfrac{t}{v}$.

Thus, the trigonometric ratio represented by $\dfrac{t}{v}$ is $\tan 73°$.

115.
Step 1
Identify angle A.
Make sure your calculator is in degree mode.

Type in 2 ÷ 3 = , then press SHIFT sin⁻¹
or SHIFT sin⁻¹ (2 ÷ 3) ENTER ,
depending on your calculator.
The screen will show 41.8103149. To the nearest degree, angle A equals 42°.

Step 2
Write the ratio for sin A.
sin 42° of a right triangle is a ratio of the side opposite the 42° angle to the hypotenuse.

$\sin 42° = \dfrac{\text{opposite}}{\text{hypotenuse}}$

$\sin 42° = \dfrac{2}{3}$

You can also say that the opposite side is 0.667 times as long as the hypotenuse.

Step 3
Label the lengths on the triangle.

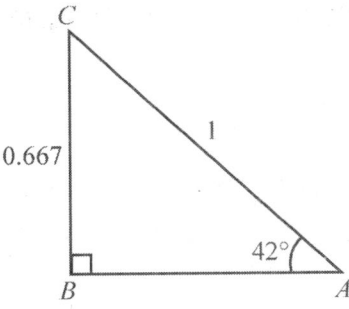

116. D
Step 1
Identify the side adjacent to $\angle E$.
The adjacent side is DE, which is equal to 250 m.

Step 2
Identify the hypotenuse.
The hypotenuse is the side opposite the right angle. It is side CE, which is equal to 500 m.

Step 3
Write the cosine ratio for $\angle E$.

$\cos \angle E = \dfrac{\text{adjacent}}{\text{hypotenuse}}$

$= \dfrac{250}{500}$

Step 4
Reduce the ratio to lowest terms.

$\cos \angle E = \dfrac{250 \div 250}{500 \div 250} = \dfrac{1}{2}$

117. B

The sum of the angles in a triangle is 180°. This is equivalent to π rad. In a right triangle, there is a 90° angle, which is equivalent to $\frac{\pi}{2}$ rad.

If a right triangle has one angle equal to $\frac{\pi}{2}$ rad, and another angle equal to $\frac{\pi}{2} - x$ rad, then the third angle in the triangle will be $\pi - \frac{\pi}{2} - \left(\frac{\pi}{2} - x\right) = x$ rad.

Draw a right triangle as shown.

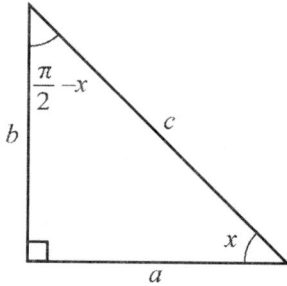

From the triangle, $\sin\left(\frac{\pi}{2} - x\right) = \frac{a}{c}$ and $\cos x = \frac{a}{c}$.

Therefore, $\sin\left(\frac{\pi}{2} - x\right) = \cos x$.

The expressions can also be shown to be equivalent by graphing the functions $y = \sin\left(\frac{\pi}{2} - x\right)$ and $y = \cos x$.

118. C

Sine and cosine are cofunctions, so they are equal under complementary angles $\cos(\theta) = \sin(90° - \theta)$.

Substitute $\sin(90° - \theta)$ for $\cos \theta$ in the equation $\sin 4\theta = \cos \theta$, and solve for θ.

$\sin 4\theta = \cos \theta$
$\sin 4\theta = \sin(90° - \theta)$
$\quad 4\theta = 90° - \theta$
$\quad 5\theta = 90°$
$\quad\ \theta = 18°$

119. C

Step 1
Draw a diagram representing the situation.
Label the triangle with a variable for the unknown measurement.

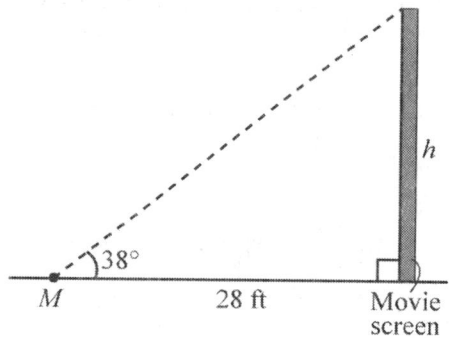

Step 2
Apply the appropriate trigonometric ratio to solve for the unknown height.

$\tan \theta = \dfrac{\text{opposite}}{\text{hypotenuse}}$

$\tan 38° = \dfrac{h}{28}$

$28 \times \tan 38° = h$

$21.88 \text{ ft} \approx h$

Therefore, the height of the movie screen is approximately 22 ft.

120. B

Step 1
Determine the length of the common side of the two right triangles shown (AC) by applying the Pythagorean theorem.

$(AB)^2 + (BC)^2 = (AC)^2$
$\quad 45^2 + 24^2 = (AC)^2$
$\quad 2{,}025 + 576 = (AC)^2$
$\quad\quad\ \ 2{,}601 = (AC)^2$
$\quad\quad \sqrt{2{,}601} = AC$
$\quad\quad\quad\ AC = 51 \text{ cm}$

Step 2
Determine the length of side CD by applying the tangent ratio.

$\tan 76° = \dfrac{AC}{CD}$

Substitute 51 for AC.

$\tan 76° = \dfrac{51}{CD}$

$CD \times \tan 76° = 51$

$CD = \dfrac{51}{\tan 76°}$

$CD \approx 12.7$

The length of side CD, to the nearest tenth, is 12.7 cm.

121.

The distance between the cat and the dog can be represented by $x + y$, where x represents the distance between Lexi and the cat and y represents the distance between Lexi and the dog.
Note that $x + y$ at eye level will be the same as $x + y$ on the ground.

Step 1
Determine the distance, x, between Lexi and the cat.
$$\tan 30° = \frac{1.48}{x}$$
$$x\tan 30° = 1.48$$
$$x = \frac{1.48}{\tan 30°}$$
$$x = 2.563435\ldots$$

Step 2
Determine the distance, y, between Lexi and the dog.
$$\tan 25° = \frac{1.48}{y}$$
$$y\tan 25° = 1.48$$
$$y = \frac{1.48}{\tan 25°}$$
$$y = 3.173870\ldots$$

Step 3
Determine the distance, $x + y$, between the cat and the dog.
$$x + y = 2.563435\ldots + 3.173870\ldots$$
$$x + y \approx 5.74$$
The cat and the dog are approximately 5.74 m apart.

122. D

Step 1
Draw a diagram to represent the given information.

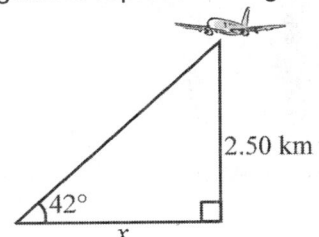

Step 2
Identify the trigonometric ratio to use to solve for x in the diagram, which represents the distance between Matt and the point on the ground directly below the plane.
The height 2.50 km is the side opposite the angle of elevation. The side adjacent to the angle of elevation is shown as x. This is the distance between Matt and the point on the ground directly below the plane. Since the opposite side and the adjacent side are involved, the tangent ratio should be used.
$$\tan \theta = \frac{O}{A}$$

Step 3
Substitute the variables into the equation, and solve for x.
$$\tan 42° = \frac{2.50}{x}$$
$$x\tan 42° = 2.50$$
$$x = \frac{2.50}{\tan 42°}$$
$$x \approx 2.78$$
The distance between Matt and the point on the ground directly below the plane is approximately 2.78 km.

123. B

Step 1
Draw a diagram to represent the given information. Let x represent the length of wire from the ground to the tower.

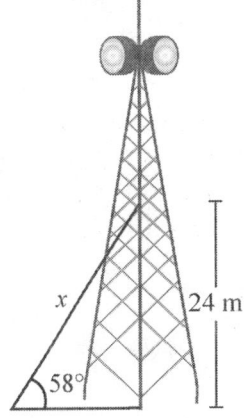

Step 2
Identify which trigonometric ratio to use to solve for x. The 24 m side, which is half the height of the tower, is opposite the 58° angle. The length of wire from the ground to the tower, x, is the hypotenuse. Since the opposite side and the hypotenuse are involved, the sine ratio should be used.
$$\sin \theta = \frac{O}{H}$$

Step 3
Substitute the variables into the equation, and solve for x.
$$\sin 58° = \frac{24}{x}$$
$$x\sin 58° = 24$$
$$x = \frac{24}{\sin 58°}$$
$$x \approx 28.3$$
Since an extra meter of wire is required at each end, the total length of wire required is
28.3 m + 2 m = 30.3 m.

124. 27.9

Step 1
Draw a diagram to represent the given information. The angle of depression from the airplane to the tower is equal to the angle of elevation from the tower to the airplane, since both angles are measured from the horizontal. Let x represent the distance of the airplane from the tower.

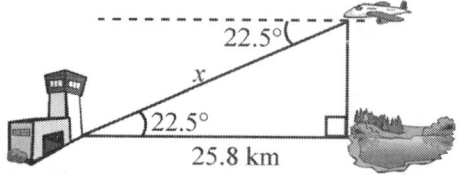

Step 2
Identify which trigonometric ratio to use to solve for x. The unknown side, x, is the hypotenuse, and the 25.8 km side is adjacent to the 22.5° angle. Since the adjacent side and the hypotenuse are involved, the cosine ratio should be used.
$$\cos \theta = \frac{A}{H}$$

Step 3
Substitute the variables into the equation, and solve for x.
$$\cos 22.5° = \frac{25.8}{x}$$
$$x\cos 22.5° = 25.8$$
$$x = \frac{25.8}{\cos 22.5°}$$
$$x \approx 27.9$$
At 3:00, the distance of the airplane from the tower is approximately 27.9 km.

125. B

The measure of ∠CAD is equal to the measure of ∠CAB minus the measure of ∠DAB.
∠CAD = ∠CAB − ∠DAB

Step 1
With respect to ∠CAB, identify the sides of △ABC (the right triangle) that have length measurements. The sides of △ABC that have length measurements are AB and AC. With respect to ∠CAB, side AB is the adjacent side and side AC is the hypotenuse of △ABC.

Step 2
Since the adjacent side (with respect to ∠CAB) and the hypotenuse of △ABC have length measurements, set up the cosine ratio in terms of these lengths and ∠CAB.
$$\cos(∠CAB) = \frac{\text{adjacent side}}{\text{hypotenuse}}$$
$$\cos(∠CAB) = \frac{AB}{AC}$$
$$\cos(∠CAB) = \frac{38}{72}$$

Step 3
Determine the measure of ∠CAB.
$$\cos(∠CAB) = \frac{38}{72}$$
$$∠CAB = \cos^{-1}(38 ÷ 72)$$
$$∠CAB \approx 58.14°$$
Note that the value of $\cos^{-1}(38 ÷ 72)$ can be obtained by using a calculator.

Step 4
Determine the measure of ∠CAD to the nearest degree by making use of the equation ∠CAD = ∠CAB − ∠DAB. Substitute 58.14° for ∠CAB and 40° for ∠DAB.
∠CAD = ∠CAB − ∠DAB
∠CAD = 58.14° − 40°
∠CAD = 18.14°
To the nearest degree, the measure of ∠CAD is 18°.

126. A

Step 1
Draw a sketch of △MNP.
A possible sketch of △MNP is shown here.

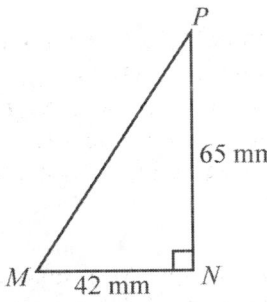

Step 2
Analyze Nadine's solution.
Nadine made an error in step 1 of her solution. Since $\tan P = \dfrac{\text{opposite side}}{\text{adjacent side}}$, $\tan P = \dfrac{MN}{NP}$ rather than $\tan P = \dfrac{NP}{MN}$.

Nadine's solution should have appeared as follows:

1. $\tan P = \dfrac{MN}{NP}$
2. $\tan P = \dfrac{42}{65}$
3. $\tan P \approx 0.6462$
4. $P \approx \tan^{-1} 0.6462$
5. $P \approx 32.87°$
6. To the nearest tenth of a degree, the measure of ∠P is 32.9°.

127. A

Step 1
Analyze Carlita's partial solution.
Carlita's partial solution is correct. Step 4 of Carlita's solution should be as follows.

4. To the nearest hundredth of a degree,
   $A = 53.13°$.

Step 2
Analyze Alvaro's partial solution.
Although Alvaro has not used the simplest method to determine the measure of ∠A, his partial solution is also correct.
Steps 6 and 7 of Alvaro's solution should be as follows:

6. $A \approx 90° - 36.87°$
7. To the nearest hundredth of a degree,
   $A = 53.13°$.

Therefore, both Carlita and Alvaro have correct partial solutions.

128. B

Step 1
Identify the sine ratio for 51°.
Substitute the known values from the triangle into the sine ratio.

$\sin \theta = \dfrac{\text{opposite}}{\text{hypotenuse}}$

$\sin 51° = \dfrac{a}{21.3}$

Step 3
Determine the length of side a.
Write the equivalent ratio, and solve for a using cross products.

$\dfrac{\sin 51°}{1} = \dfrac{a}{21.3}$
$(\sin 51°)(21.3) = a(1)$
$16.55 = a$

Step 4
Round answer to the nearest tenth of a millimeter.
$16.55 \to 16.6$ mm

129. C

Step 1
Draw a diagram to represent the given situation.
Since the tent is made up of two congruent right triangles, let y represent $\dfrac{1}{2} x$.

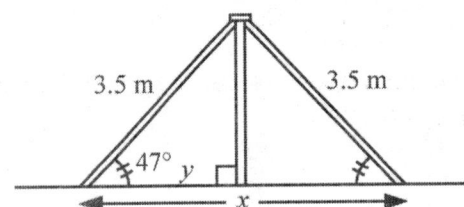

Step 2
Identify the cosine ratio for 47°.
Substitute the known values from the triangle into the cosine ratio.

$$\cos\theta = \frac{\text{adjacent}}{\text{hypotenuse}}$$

$$\cos 47° = \frac{y}{3.5}$$

Step 3
Determine the length of side y.
Write the equivalent ratio, and solve for y using cross products.

$$\frac{\cos 47°}{1} = \frac{y}{3.5}$$
$$(\cos 47°)(3.5) = y(1)$$
$$2.387 = y$$

Step 4
Calculate the value of x.
$x = 2y$
$= 2(2.387)$
$= 4.774$

Step 5
Round to nearest tenth of a meter.
$4.774 \to 4.8$
The width of the tent is 4.8 m.

130. **B**

Step 1
Identify the tan ratio.

$$\tan 42° = \frac{\text{opposite}}{\text{adjacent}}$$

Step 2
Substitute in the given values.
The value of the opposite side is 51 m.
Let x represent the adjacent side.

$$\tan 42° = \frac{51}{x}$$

Step 3
Find the value of tan 42° using your calculator.
Type [tan][4][2] or [4][2][tan] depending on your calculator.
The screen will show 0.900404044. Recording to three decimal places is sufficient: 0.900.

Step 4
Write the equivalent ratio.

$$\frac{0.900}{1} = \frac{51}{x}$$

Step 6
Use cross products to solve for x.

$$\frac{0.900}{1} = \frac{51}{x}$$
$$0.900(x) = 51(1)$$
$$\frac{0.900x}{0.900} = \frac{51}{0.900}$$
$$x = 56.667 \text{ m}$$

Rounded to the nearest hundredth of a meter, the man travels 56.67 m.

EXERCISE #2—RIGHT ANGLE TRIANGLES IN TRIGONOMETRY

Use the following information to answer the next question.

In the given triangle, tan 72° = 3.078.

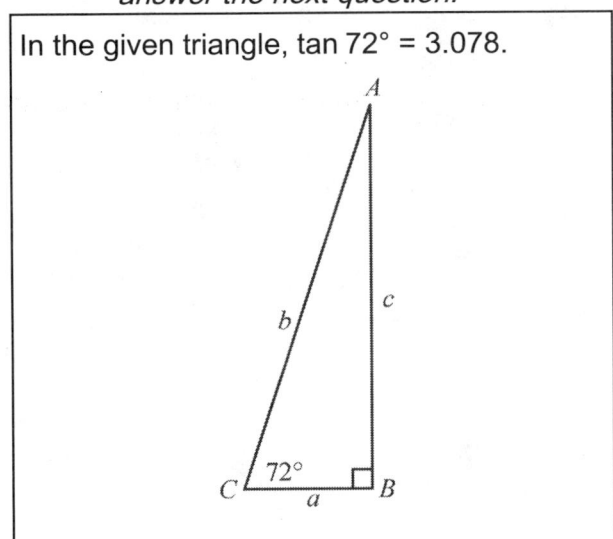

131. Which of the following ratios is equal to 3.078?

A. $\dfrac{a}{c}$ B. $\dfrac{c}{a}$

C. $\dfrac{a}{b}$ D. $\dfrac{b}{a}$

132. Diagram and solve sin 50° rounded to three decimal places.

133. Draw triangle *ABC* in which angle *B* is equal to 90° and cos *A* is equal to $\dfrac{2}{3}$.

134. Which of the following expressions is equivalent to $\sin\left(\dfrac{5\pi}{2} - x\right)$?

A. $\cos\left(x - \dfrac{\pi}{2}\right)$

B. $\sin\left(x - \dfrac{\pi}{2}\right)$

C. $\cos(x)$

D. $\sin(x)$

135. Since sine and cosine are cofunctions, if θ satisfies the equation $\cos\theta = \sin 8\theta$, a possible value of $\sin 3\theta$ is

A. –1   B. 0

C. 0.5   D. 1

136. A boy flying a kite decides to anchor the kite to the ground. If the string of the kite is 150 m long and makes an angle of 60° with the ground, then approximately how high is the kite above the ground (to the nearest tenth of a meter)? _____ m

Use the following information to answer the next question.

Dominika is asked to solve triangle *MNP*, where ∠*N* = 90°, ∠*P* = 48°, and *p* = 30 cm.

137. To the nearest tenth, what is the sum of the lengths of the two unknown sides, *m* and *n*? _____ cm

Use the following information to answer the next question.

Olivia looks out the window of her apartment building and sees a sports car parked down the street at an angle of depression of 18°. A little farther down the street, she sees a police car parked at an angle of depression of 15°. Her apartment window is 35 m above street level.

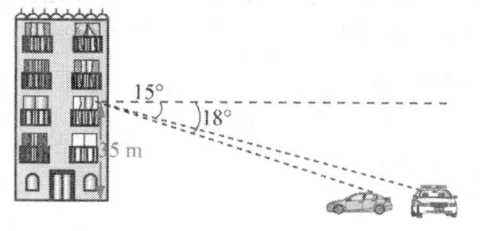

138. To the nearest tenth of a meter, how far apart are the sports car and the police car? _____ m

Use the following information to answer the next question.

John is at the top of a vertical cliff, 25 m directly above sea level. He spots a sailboat out on the sea at an angle of depression of 25° from the top of the cliff.

139. The distance of the sailboat from the base of the cliff is approximately
 A. 11.7 m B. 27.6 m
 C. 53.6 m D. 59.2 m

Use the following information to answer the next question.

From the crow's-nest of a ship, a sailor spots a lifeboat at an angle of depression of 25.5°. The crow's-nest is located 15.8 m above ocean level.

140. Expressed to the nearest tenth, the distance from the crow's-nest to the lifeboat is _____ m.

Use the following information to answer the next question.

Mikhail builds a shelter. A cross section of the shelter has the shape and dimensions shown in the diagram. The value of θ is equal to the measure of $\angle BDC$.

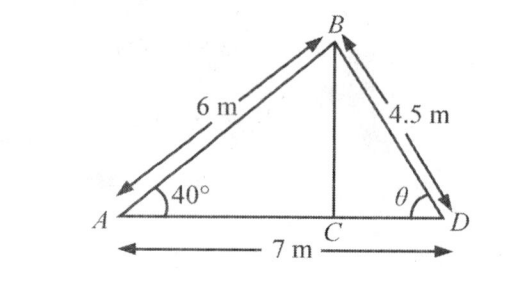

141. The value of θ is approximately
 A. 57.7° B. 48.6°
 C. 41.4° D. 32.3°

Use the following information to answer the next question.

In triangle RST, $\angle S = 90°$, $ST = 35$ mm, and $RT = 112$ mm.

142. To the nearest tenth of a degree, the measure of $\angle T$ is
 A. 17.4° B. 18.2°
 C. 71.8° D. 72.6°

Use the following information to answer the next question.

While on a fishing trip with his father, Julius casts a fishing line from his boat into the water. He is 105 cm from the surface of the water and casts the fishing line in a straight line 364 cm away from the boat.

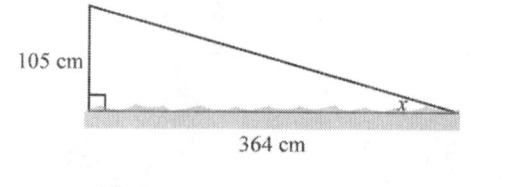

143. What angle does the fishing line make with the water rounded to the nearest degree?
 A. 16° B. 44°
 C. 52° D. 74°

Use the following information to answer the next question.

Triangle RST is shown.

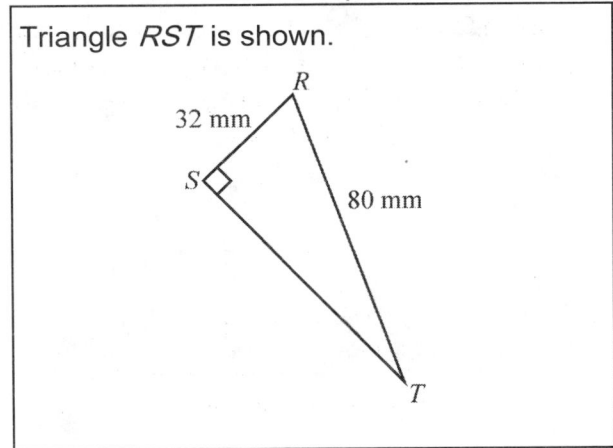

144. To the nearest tenth of a degree, what is the measure of angle T?

A. 21.8° B. 23.6°
C. 46.2° D. 66.4°

Use the following information to answer the next question.

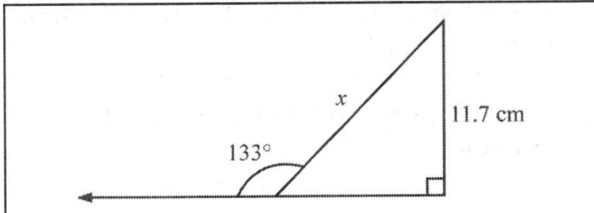

145. Rounded to the nearest tenth of a centimeter, what is the length of side x?

A. 8.0 cm B. 8.6 cm
C. 16.0 cm D. 17.2 cm

Use the following information to answer the next question.

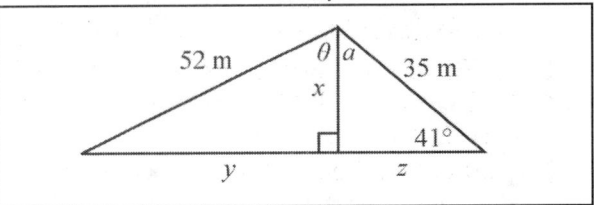

146. In order to calculate the value of z, which of the following ratios should be used?

A. $\cos\theta = \dfrac{z}{52}$

B. $\cos\alpha = \dfrac{z}{35}$

C. $\cos 41° = \dfrac{z}{35}$

D. $\cos 41° = \dfrac{35}{z}$

Use the following information to answer the next question.

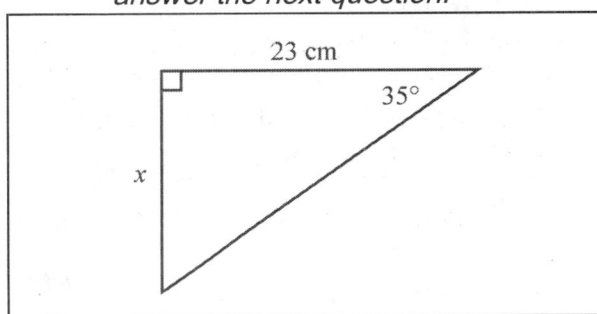

147. For the triangle, find the length of side x to the nearest tenth of a centimeter, then use $\tan^{-1}$ to find the remaining angle to the nearest degree.

EXERCISE #2—RIGHT ANGLE TRIANGLES IN TRIGONOMETRY
ANSWERS AND SOLUTIONS

131. B	136. 129.9	141. A	146. C
132. See solution	137. 67.4	142. C	147. See solution
133. See solution	138. 22.9	143. A	
134. C	139. C	144. B	
135. C	140. 36.7	145. C	

131. B

Step 1
Start from the given angle of 72° to identify the opposite and adjacent sides to this angle.
The length of the side opposite to the angle is c.
The length of the side adjacent to the angle is a.

Step 2
Write the ratio.

$\tan 72° = \dfrac{\text{opposite}}{\text{adjacent}} = \dfrac{c}{a}$, which means that this ratio is equal to 3.078.

132.

Make sure the calculator is in degree mode.

Step 1
Identify the length of the side opposite to angle 50°.
Type in $\boxed{5}\boxed{0}$, and then press $\boxed{\sin}$ or $\boxed{\text{SIN}}\boxed{5}\boxed{0}$ $\boxed{\text{ENTER}}$, depending on your calculator.
The screen will show 0.766044443. Since the question asks for a number rounded to three decimal places, the length of the side is 0.766.

Step 2
Identify the length of the hypotenuse.
When using your calculator to determine the sine ratio for a given angle measurement, the length of the hypotenuse is always 1 unit.

Step 3
Write the ratio for sin 50°.
The sine ratio is a ratio of the side opposite the angle measuring 50° to the length of the hypotenuse.

$\sin \theta = \dfrac{\text{opposite}}{\text{hypotenuse}}$

$\sin 50° = \dfrac{0.766}{1}$

You can also say that the opposite side is 0.766 times as long as the hypotenuse.

Step 4
Illustrate the sine ratio for sin 50° with a diagram by labeling the lengths on the triangle.

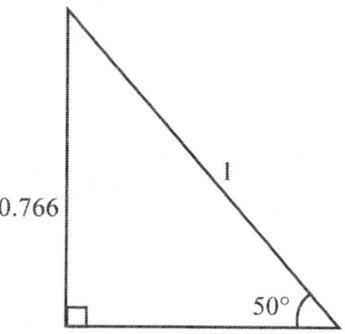

133.

Step 1
Draw a right triangle.
Angle B is the right angle. Assign A and C to the other two vertices.

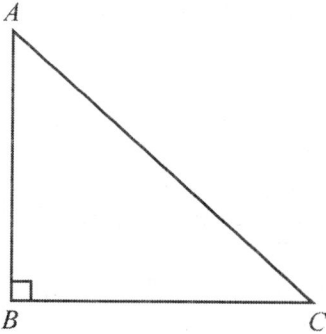

Step 2
Identify the ratio.

$\cos \theta = \dfrac{\text{adjacent}}{\text{hypotenuse}}$

Step 3
Identify the sides.
Angle B is the right angle. Its opposite side, line segment AC, is the hypotenuse. Angle A is formed by the joining of line segments AB and AC.
The adjacent side of angle A is line segment AB because line segment AC is the hypotenuse.

Step 4
Label the lengths on the sides to complete the required triangle.

$\cos A = \dfrac{\text{adjacent}}{\text{hypotenuse}} = \dfrac{AB}{AC} = \dfrac{2}{3}$

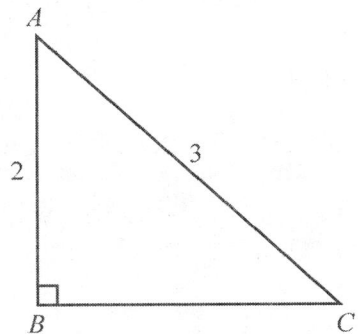

134. C

On a TI-83 graphing calculator, press $\boxed{Y=}$ and enter $\sin\left(\dfrac{5\pi}{2} - x\right)$ as $Y_1 = \sin((5\pi)/2 - X)$. Then, press $\boxed{\text{GRAPH}}$.

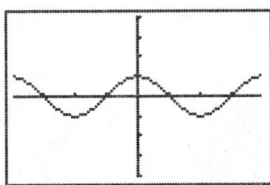

The graph shown is also the graph of $y = \cos x$, which can be verified by graphing $Y_2 = \cos X$.

Since both graphs are the same, it follows that $\sin\left(\dfrac{5\pi}{2} - x\right) = \cos x$.

135. C

Since sine and cosine are cofunctions, $\cos\theta = \sin(90° - \theta)$.

From the equation, θ also satisfies $\cos\theta = \sin 8\theta$.
$\sin(90° - \theta) = \sin 8\theta$
$90° - \theta = 8\theta$
$90° = 9\theta$
$30° = 3\theta$

Therefore, $\sin 3\theta = \sin 30° = 0.5$.

136. 129.9
Begin with a sketch for clarity.

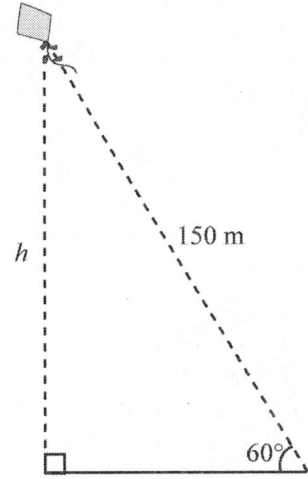

Recall,
$\sin\theta = \dfrac{\text{opposite}}{\text{hypotenuse}}$

$\sin 60° = \dfrac{h}{150}$

$150 \times \sin 60° = h$

$129.9\text{ m} \approx h$

137. 67.4

Step 1
Draw and label a diagram to represent the given information.
One possible triangle that can be drawn is shown here.

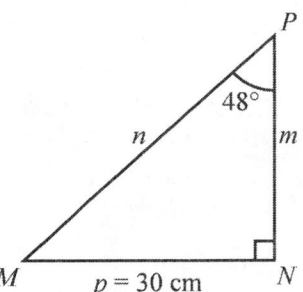

Step 2
Determine the value of m (the length of side NP) by applying the tangent ratio.

$\tan 48° = \dfrac{MN}{NP}$

$\tan 48° = \dfrac{p}{m}$

$\tan 48° = \dfrac{30}{m}$

$m \times \tan 48° = 30$

$m = \dfrac{30}{\tan 48°}$

$m \approx 27.0\text{ cm}$

Step 3
Determine the value of n by using the sine ratio, cosine ratio, or Pythagorean theorem.
Using the sine ratio, the value of n can be determined as follows:

$$\sin 48° = \frac{MN}{MP}$$
$$\sin 48° = \frac{p}{n}$$
$$\sin 48° = \frac{30}{n}$$
$$n \times \sin 48° = 30$$
$$n = \frac{30}{\sin 48°}$$
$$n \approx 40.4 \text{ cm}$$

Step 4
Determine the sum of m and n.
$m + n \approx 27.0 + 40.4$
$m + n \approx 67.4$ cm

138. 22.9
Step 1
Determine the sports car's horizontal distance, x_1, from the apartment building.

$$\tan \theta = \frac{\text{opposite}}{\text{adjacent}}$$
$$\tan 18° = \frac{35}{x_1}$$
$$(\tan 18°)x_1 = 35$$
$$(0.3249...)x_1 \approx 35$$
$$x_1 \approx \frac{35}{0.3249}$$
$$x_1 \approx 107.7 \text{ m}$$

Step 2
Determine the police car's horizontal distance, x_2, from the apartment building.

$$\tan \theta = \frac{\text{opposite}}{\text{adjacent}}$$
$$\tan 15° = \frac{35}{x_2}$$
$$(\tan 15°)x_2 = 35$$
$$(0.2679...)x_2 \approx 35$$
$$x_2 \approx \frac{35}{0.2679}$$
$$x_2 \approx 130.6 \text{ m}$$

Step 3
Subtract the sports car's horizontal distance from the police car's horizontal distance.
$x_2 - x_1 = 130.6 - 107.7$
$ = 22.9$ m
The sports car and the police car are 22.9 m apart.

139. C
Step 1
Draw a diagram to represent the given information.

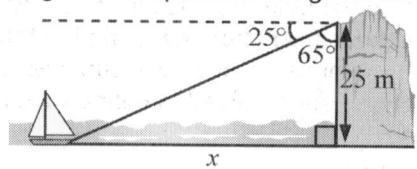

Since the angle of depression is measured relative to the horizontal, it is on the outside of the triangle. The angle between the cliff wall and the line of sight to the sailboat is $90° - 25° = 65°$.

Step 2
To solve for x in the diagram, identify the proper trigonometric ratio to use. As the diagram shows, x represents the distance of the sailboat from the base of the cliff.
The height of 25 m is the side adjacent to the 65° angle, and the distance of the sailboat from the base of the cliff, x, is the side opposite to the 65° angle. Since the opposite side and the adjacent side are involved, the tangent ratio should be used.

$$\tan \theta = \frac{O}{A}$$

Step 3
Substitute the variables into the equation, and solve for x.

$$\tan 65° = \frac{x}{25}$$
$$25 \tan 65° = x$$
$$53.6 \approx x$$

The sailboat is approximately 53.6 m from the base of the cliff.

140. 36.7
Step 1
Draw a diagram to represent the given information. Let x represent the distance from the crow's-nest to the lifeboat. The angle of depression from the crow's-nest is equal to the angle of elevation from the lifeboat since both angles are measured from the horizontal.

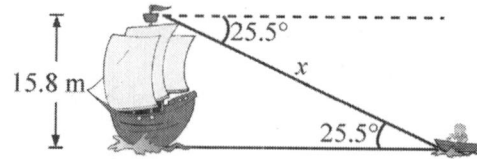

Step 2
Identify which trigonometric ratio to use to solve for x.
The height of the crow's-nest above the ocean, 15.8 m, is the side opposite to the 25.5° angle. The distance from the crow's-nest to the lifeboat, x, is the hypotenuse. Since the opposite side and hypotenuse are involved, the sine ratio should be used.

$$\sin \theta = \frac{O}{H}$$

Step 3
Substitute the variables into the equation, and solve for x.

$$\sin 25.5° = \frac{15.8}{x}$$
$$x \sin 25.5° = 15.8$$
$$x = \frac{15.8}{\sin 25.5°}$$
$$x \approx 36.7$$

The lifeboat is approximately 36.7 m from the crow's-nest.

141. A
Step 1
Determine the length of side AC of $\triangle ABC$.
Since side AC is adjacent to the 40° angle and side AB is the hypotenuse, the cosine ratio should be used.

$$\cos \theta = \frac{A}{H}$$
$$\cos 40° = \frac{AC}{6}$$
$$6\cos 40° = AC$$
$$4.596 \approx AC$$

Side AC is approximately 4.596 m long.

Step 2
Determine the length of side CD of $\triangle BCD$.

$$AC + CD = AD$$
$$4.596 + CD = 7$$
$$CD = 2.404$$

The length of side CD is approximately 2.404 m long.

Step 3
Determine the value of θ, which is the measure of $\angle BDC$.
Since side CD is adjacent to θ and side BD is the hypotenuse, the cosine ratio should be used.

$$\cos \theta = \frac{A}{H}$$
$$= \frac{CD}{BD}$$
$$\approx \frac{2.404}{4.5}$$
$$\theta \approx \cos^{-1}\left(\frac{2.404}{4.5}\right)$$
$$\approx 57.7°$$

The value of θ is approximately 57.7°.

142. C
Step 1
Draw and label a possible sketch of $\triangle RST$.
A possible sketch of $\triangle RST$ is as shown.

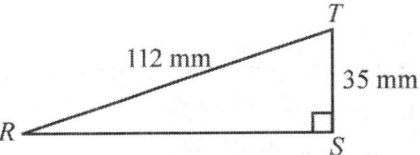

Step 2
Identify the hypotenuse and the side adjacent to the required angle, and then set up the cosine ratio.
With respect to $\angle T$, side ST is the adjacent side, and side RT is the hypotenuse of $\triangle RST$.
Since the side lengths of the adjacent side and hypotenuse are given, use the cosine ratio:

$$\cos T = \frac{ST}{RT}.$$

Step 3
Substitute the known values from the triangle into the cosine ratio.

$$\cos T = \frac{\text{adjacent side}}{\text{hypotenuse}}$$
$$= \frac{ST}{RT}$$
$$= \frac{35}{112}$$

Step 4
Calculate the decimal equivalent of the cosine ratio.
Type in $\boxed{3}\boxed{5}\boxed{\div}\boxed{1}\boxed{1}\boxed{2}\boxed{\text{ENTER}}$.
The screen will show 0.3125.

Step 5
Determine the measure of ∠T by using the $\cos^{-1}$ key on your calculator.
cos T = 0.3125
T = $\cos^{-1}$(0.3125)
T ≈ 71.79°

The value of $\cos^{-1}$(35 ÷ 112) can be obtained by using a graphing calculator and typing in [2nd] [COS] [(] [3] [5] [÷] [1] [1] [2] [)] [ENTER].

To the nearest tenth of a degree, the measure of ∠T is 71.8°.

143. A
Step 1
Draw a diagram to represent the given situation. Let x represent the unknown angle.

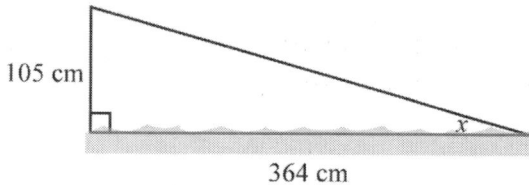

Step 2
Identify the tan ratio for angle x. Identify its opposite and adjacent sides, and substitute these values into the ratio.

tan = $\frac{\text{opposite}}{\text{adjacent}}$

tan x = $\frac{105}{364}$

Step 3
Calculate the decimal equivalent of the ratio.
tan x = $\frac{105}{364}$
tan x = 0.2885

Step 4
Calculate the angle using the [$\tan^{-1}$] button on the calculator.
$\tan^{-1}$(0.2885) = 16.09°

Step 5
Round to nearest degree.
16.09 = 16
The fishing line makes an angle of 16° with the water.

144. B
Step 1
With respect to ∠T, identify and name the sides of △RST that have given side lengths.

The sides of △RST with given side lengths are RS and RT. With respect to ∠T, side RS is the opposite side and side RT is the hypotenuse of △RST.

Step 2
Set up the sine ratio in terms of the given side lengths and ∠T.

sin T = $\frac{\text{opposite side}}{\text{hypotenuse}}$
 = $\frac{RS}{RT}$
 = $\frac{32}{80}$

Step 3
Determine the measure of ∠T.

sin T = $\frac{32}{80}$

T = $\sin^{-1}$(32 ÷ 80)
T ≈ 23.58°

Note that the value of $\sin^{-1}$(32 ÷ 80) can be obtained by using a graphing calculator and typing in [2nd] [sin] [(] [3] [2] [÷] [8] [0] [)] [ENTER].

To the nearest tenth of a degree, the measure of ∠T is 23.6°.

145. C
Step 1
Calculate the measure of the angle inside the triangle.
The angle inside the triangle is supplementary to 133°, so subtract 133° from 180°.
180° − 133° = 47°

Step 2
Identify the sine ratio for 47°.
Substitute the known values from the triangle into the sine ratio.

sin θ = $\frac{\text{opposite}}{\text{hypotenuse}}$

sin 47° = $\frac{11.7}{x}$

Step 3
Find the decimal equivalent of sin 47°, and write the equivalent ratio.

0.731 = $\frac{11.7}{x}$

$\frac{0.731}{1} = \frac{11.7}{x}$

Step 4
Use cross products to solve for x.
0.731(x) = 11.7(1)
$\frac{0.731(x)}{0.731} = \frac{11.7}{0.731}$
x = 16.00

To the nearest tenth, the length of side x is 16.0 cm.

146. C

In order to find the value of z, determine which measures of the sides and angles are given.

Side z is adjacent to 41°, and the hypotenuse of the triangle is 35 m. The ratio that uses the adjacent side and the hypotenuse is the cosine ratio.

The ratio will be $\cos 41° = \dfrac{z}{35}$.

147.

Step 1
Identify the tan ratio for the angle.

$\tan 35° = \dfrac{x}{23}$

Step 2
Find the decimal equivalent of $\tan 35°$.

Type in $\boxed{3}\boxed{5}$, then press $\boxed{\tan}$ or $\boxed{\text{TAN}}\boxed{3}\boxed{5}$ $\boxed{\text{ENTER}}$, depending on your calculator.

The screen will show 0.7002075382. A number to three decimal places is sufficient: 0.700.

Step 3
Write the equivalent ratio.
Substitute 0.700 in for $\tan 35°$, and place it over 1.

$\dfrac{0.700}{1} = \dfrac{x}{23}$

Step 4
Use cross products to solve for x.

$\dfrac{0.700}{1} = \dfrac{x}{23}$

$0.700 \times 23 = x \times 1$

$16.1 = x$

Rounded to the nearest tenth of a centimeter, the length of side x is 16.1 cm.

Step 5
Substitute the known values from the triangle into the tan ratio for the missing angle.

$\tan \theta = \dfrac{23}{16.1}$

Step 6
Calculate the decimal equivalent of the ratio.

Type in $\boxed{2}\boxed{3}\boxed{\div}\boxed{1}\boxed{6}\boxed{.}\boxed{1}\boxed{=}$. The screen will show 1.428571429. A number to three decimal places is sufficient: 1.429.

Step 7
Calculate the angle using the $\tan^{-1}$ button on your calculator.

Type in $\boxed{1}\boxed{.}\boxed{4}\boxed{2}\boxed{9}\boxed{\text{SHIFT}}\boxed{\tan^{-1}}\boxed{=}$ or $\boxed{\text{SHIFT}}\boxed{\text{TAN}^{-1}}\boxed{1}\boxed{.}\boxed{4}\boxed{2}\boxed{9}\boxed{\text{ENTER}}$.

The screen will show 55.01605342.

To the nearest degree, the measure of the angle is 55°.

NOTES

Applying Geometric Concepts

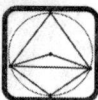

APPLYING GEOMETRIC CONCEPTS

Table of Correlations

Standard		Concepts	Exercise #1	Exercise #2
Unit2.4	Apply geometric concepts in modeling situations.			
G-MG.1	Use geometric shapes, their measures, and their properties to describe objects.	Solving Problems Involving the Volume of a Cylinder	148	159
		Solving Problems Involving the Volume of a Cone	149	160
		Solving Problems Involving the Volume of a Sphere	150	161
		Solving Problems Involving Volume of Pyramids	151	162
G-MG.3	Apply geometric methods to solve design problems.	Calculating Optimal Area given the Perimeter	152	163
		Calculating Optimal Area given Three or more Lengths	153	164
		Calculating Surface Area For Prisms and Cylinders given the Volume	154	165
		Solving Design Problems in Three Dimensions	155	166
		Calculating Optimal Volume For a Prism and a Cylinder given the Surface Area	156	167
		Calculating Optimal Perimeter Given the Area	157	168
		Calculating Optimal Perimeter with a Given Number of Lengths	158	169

G-MG.1 Use geometric shapes, their measures, and their properties to describe objects.

SOLVING PROBLEMS INVOLVING THE VOLUME OF A CYLINDER

To solve problems involving the volume of a cylinder, use the formula $V_{cylinder} = \pi r^2 \times h$, in which r is the radius of the circular base and h is the height.

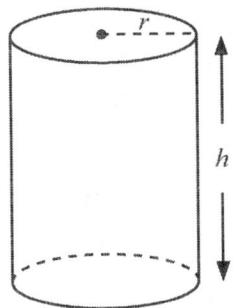

Example

The inner holding tank of an insulated container has a diameter of 10 cm and a height of 20 cm. The outer wall is 2 cm larger on either side and on the bottom.

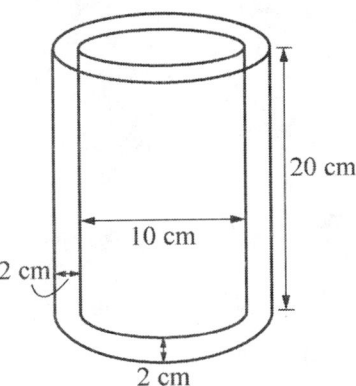

To the nearest unit, what is the volume of the space between the inner holding tank and the outer wall?

Solution

Step 1

Calculate the volume of the inner holding tank. The holding tank is in the shape of a cylinder. Substitute the given values into the volume formula for a cylinder, and simplify.

$$\begin{aligned} V_{cylinder} &= A_{base} \times h \\ &= A_{circle} \times h \\ &= \pi r^2 \times h \\ &= 3.14 \times \left(\frac{10}{2}\right)^2 \times 20 \\ &= 3.14 \times 25 \times 20 \\ &= 78.5 \times 20 \\ &= 1{,}570 \text{ cm}^3 \end{aligned}$$

Step 2

Calculate the dimensions of the outer wall of the insulated container.

The dimensions of the outer wall of the insulated container are 2 cm larger on either side and on the bottom than the inner wall. That means 4 cm must be added to the diameter and 2 cm must be added to the height.

$$\begin{aligned} d &= 10 + 4 \\ &= 14 \text{ cm} \\ h &= 20 + 2 \\ &= 22 \text{ cm} \end{aligned}$$

Step 3

Calculate the volume of the outer wall of the insulated container.

The outer wall is in the shape of a cylinder. Substitute the given values into the volume formula for a cylinder, and simplify.

$$\begin{aligned} V_{cylinder} &= A_{base} \times h \\ &= A_{circle} \times h \\ &= \pi r^2 \times h \\ &= 3.14 \times \left(\frac{14}{2}\right)^2 \times 22 \\ &= 3.14 \times 49 \times 22 \\ &= 153.86 \times 22 \\ &= 3{,}384.92 \text{ cm}^3 \end{aligned}$$

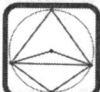

Step 4
Calculate the volume of the space in between the outer wall and the holding tank of the insulated container.

Subtract the volume of the holding tank from the volume of the outer wall.

$$V_{air\ space} = V_{outer\ wall} - V_{holding\ tank}$$
$$= 3{,}384.92 - 1{,}570$$
$$= 1{,}814.92\ cm^3$$

Rounded to the nearest unit, the difference in volume between the holding tank and the outer wall is 1,815 cm³.

SOLVING PROBLEMS INVOLVING THE VOLUME OF A CONE

To solve problems involving the volume of a cone, use the formula $V_{cone} = \dfrac{\pi r^2 h}{3}$, in which r is the radius of the circular base and h is the height.

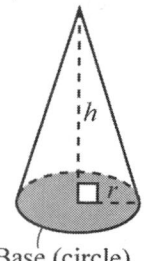
Base (circle)

Example

A snow cone has a diameter of 5.5 cm and a height of 13 cm.

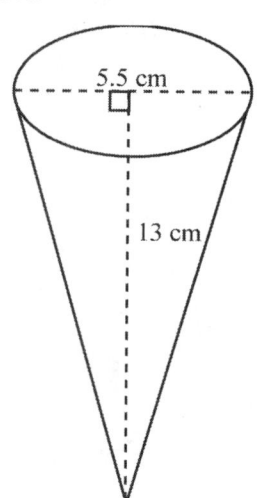

How much ice is needed to fill the snow cone to the brim?

Solution

Step 1
Determine the radius of the cone.
$$\frac{5.5\ cm}{2} = 2.75\ cm$$

Step 2
Calculate the volume of the cone.

The volume of a cone is one-third the volume of a cylinder with the same base and height.

$$V = \frac{\pi r^2 h}{3}$$

Use the volume formula for a cone, substitute in the values for radius and height, and evaluate.

$$V = \frac{\pi r^2 h}{3}$$
$$= \frac{\pi (2.75)^2 (13)}{3}$$
$$\approx 102.9526\ cm^3$$

To the nearest whole cubic centimeter, the amount of ice needed to fill the snow cone to the brim is 103 cm³.

SOLVING PROBLEMS INVOLVING THE VOLUME OF A SPHERE

To solve problems involving the volume of a sphere, use the formula $V_{sphere} = \dfrac{4\pi r^3}{3}$, in which r is the radius.

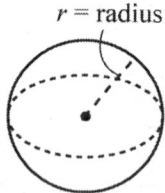
r = radius

Applying Geometric Concepts

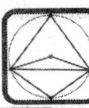

Example

A necklace is made up of 24 spherical silver beads. Each bead has a radius of 0.5 cm.

What is the total volume of silver in the necklace?

Solution

Step 1
Determine the volume of each bead.
Use 3.14 as the approximate value of π.

$$V_{sphere} = \frac{4\pi r^3}{3}$$
$$\approx \frac{4 \times 3.14 \times 0.5^3}{3}$$
$$\approx \frac{4 \times 3.14 \times 0.125}{3}$$
$$\approx \frac{1.57}{3}$$
$$\approx 0.52\overline{3} \text{ cm}^3$$

Each bead contains approximately $0.52\overline{3}$ cm³ of silver.

Step 2
Determine the total volume of silver in the entire necklace.
Multiply the volume of silver in one bead by the number of beads in the necklace.

$$V_{silver} \approx 0.52\overline{3} \text{ cm}^3 \times 24$$
$$\approx 12.56 \text{ cm}^3$$

The necklace contains 12.56 cm³ of silver.

SOLVING PROBLEMS INVOLVING VOLUME OF PYRAMIDS

Problems involving the volume of pyramids can be solved once the formulas have been determined.

To solve problems involving the volume of pyramids, use the formula $V_{pyramid} = \frac{1}{3}A_{base}h$, where A_{base} is the area of the base and h is the height.

Rectangular Pyramids

$a_{rectangle} = lw$

$V = \frac{1}{3}lwh$

OR

$V = \frac{lwh}{3}$

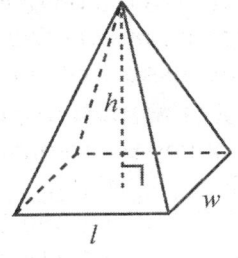

Square Pyramids

$a_{square} = s^2$

$V = \frac{1}{3}(s^2)h$

OR

$V = \frac{s^2 h}{3}$

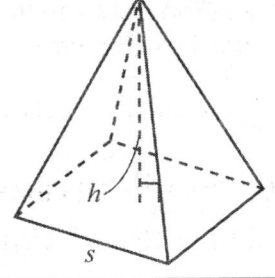

Triangular Pyramids

$a_{triangle} = \frac{1}{2}bh$

$V = c\frac{1}{3}h_{pyramid}\left(\frac{1}{2}bh_{triangle}\right)$

OR

$V = \frac{bh_{triangle}h_{pyramid}}{6}$

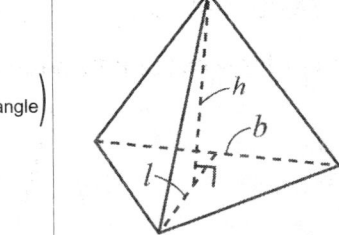

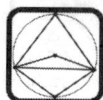

Example

For a class project, Yani plans to build two different models of pyramids. One of the models will be a square-based pyramid, and the other model will be a rectangular-based pyramid. The height of the square-based pyramid will be 60 cm, and each side length of the base will be 28 cm. The height of the rectangular-based pyramid will be 62 cm, and the base will be 25 cm by 30 cm.

Determine which pyramid will have a greater volume, and calculate how much greater the volume will be.

Solution

The volume, V, of a pyramid can be determined by applying the formula $V = \frac{1}{3}(A_{base} \times h)$, where A_{base} is the area of the base and h is the height of the pyramid.

Step 1

Determine the area of the base of the square-based pyramid.

The area, A, of the base of the square-based pyramid can be determined by applying the formula $A = s^2$, where s is the side length of the base.

Substitute 28 for s.

$A = s^2$
$A = 28^2$
$A = 784$ cm^2

Step 2

Determine the volume of the square-based pyramid.

Apply the formula $V = \frac{1}{3}(A_{base} \times h)$.

Substitute 784 for A_{base} and 60 for h.

$V = \frac{1}{3}(A_{base} \times h)$
$V = \frac{1}{3}(784 \times 60)$
$V = \frac{1}{3} \times 47{,}040$
$V = 15{,}680$ cm^3

Step 3

Determine the area of the base of the rectangular-based pyramid.

The area, A, of the base of the rectangular-based pyramid can be determined by applying the formula $A = lw$, where l is the length of the base and w is the width of the base.

Substitute 30 for l and 25 for w.

$A = lw$
$A = 30 \times 25$
$A = 750$ cm^2

Step 4

Determine the volume of the rectangular-based pyramid.

Apply the formula $V = \frac{1}{3}(A_{base} \times h)$.

Substitute 750 for A_{base} and 62 for h.

$V = \frac{1}{3}(A_{base} \times h)$
$V = \frac{1}{3}(750 \times 62)$
$V = \frac{1}{3} \times 46{,}500$
$V = 15{,}500$ cm^3

Step 5

Determine which pyramid has the greater volume by subtracting one volume from the other.

$15{,}680 - 15{,}500 = 180$ cm^3

The volume of the square-based pyramid will be 180 cm^3 greater than the volume of the rectangular-based pyramid.

G-MG.3 Apply geometric methods to solve design problems.

CALCULATING OPTIMAL AREA GIVEN THE PERIMETER

Optimal area occurs when the area is maximized within a given perimeter.

Problems involving perimeter and maximum area are present in everyday life. For example, Mr. Johnson purchased 42 m of building material to create the outside walls for a rectangular sandbox. He wants to build a sandbox with the greatest possible area using these materials.

There are two methods that can be used to determine optimal area: a table of values and the algebraic method.

To make a **table of values**, draw a three-column table with the following labels: width, length, and area. Use varying values for the width, and calculate the length using a rearranged perimeter formula. Finally, multiply these two values to calculate the area.

This method allows you to see all the possible measures of area so you can pick out the largest possible area.

Example

Use a table of values to determine the dimensions of a rectangle and its optimal area if its perimeter is 24 cm.

Solution

Use the following formula to calculate the length in each row of the table.

$$P = 2(l + w)$$
$$P = 2l + 2w$$
$$P - 2w = 2l$$
$$\frac{P - 2w}{2} = l$$

Step 1
Make a table of values to identify all the possible dimensions and areas of the rectangle.

Width (cm)	Length $= \frac{P - 2w}{2}$ (cm)	Area $A = l \times w$ (cm^2)
1	$l = \frac{24 - 2(1)}{2} = 11$	11
2	$l = \frac{24 - 2(2)}{2} = 10$	20
3	9	27
4	8	32
5	7	35
6	6	36
7	5	35
8	4	32
9	3	27
10	2	20
11	1	11

Step 2
Identify the maximum area.
Look at the values in the "area" column of the table of values. Notice the symmetry of the numbers. The maximum area occurs when the length and width of the rectangle are 6 cm.

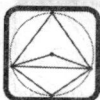

You can conclude that the maximum area of a four-sided rectangle with a fixed perimeter (P) occurs when the rectangle is a square.

Knowing this gives you another way to calculate maximum area when given a fixed perimeter: the **algebraic** method. The maximum area of a four-sided rectangle with a fixed perimeter (P) occurs when $w = l = \frac{P}{4}$.

Example

Use algebra to determine the dimensions of a rectangle and its optimal area if its perimeter is 24 cm.

Solution

Step 1
Calculate the length or width of the rectangle. Maximum area occurs when the rectangle is a square.
Substitute 24 in for P.
$w = l = \frac{P}{4} = \frac{24}{4} = 6$ cm

Step 2
Substitute 6 in for l and w in the area formula.
A = l × w
 = 6 × 6
 = 36 cm²

The optimal area of the rectangle is 36 cm².

Example

Joe has 20 m of fencing material with which to enclose a garden. Use algebra to determine the dimensions, in whole numbers, that will produce a rectangular garden with the maximum area.

Solution

Step 1
Calculate the length or width of the rectangle. Maximum area occurs when the rectangle is a square.
Substitute 20 in for P.
$w = l = \frac{P}{4} = \frac{20}{4} = 5$ m

Step 2
Substitute 5 in for l and w in the area formula.
A = l × w
 = 5 × 5
 = 25 m²

In order to produce a garden with an optimal area of 25 m², the side lengths of the rectangle must be 5 m.

Diagrams of the possible garden shapes verifies the largest area.

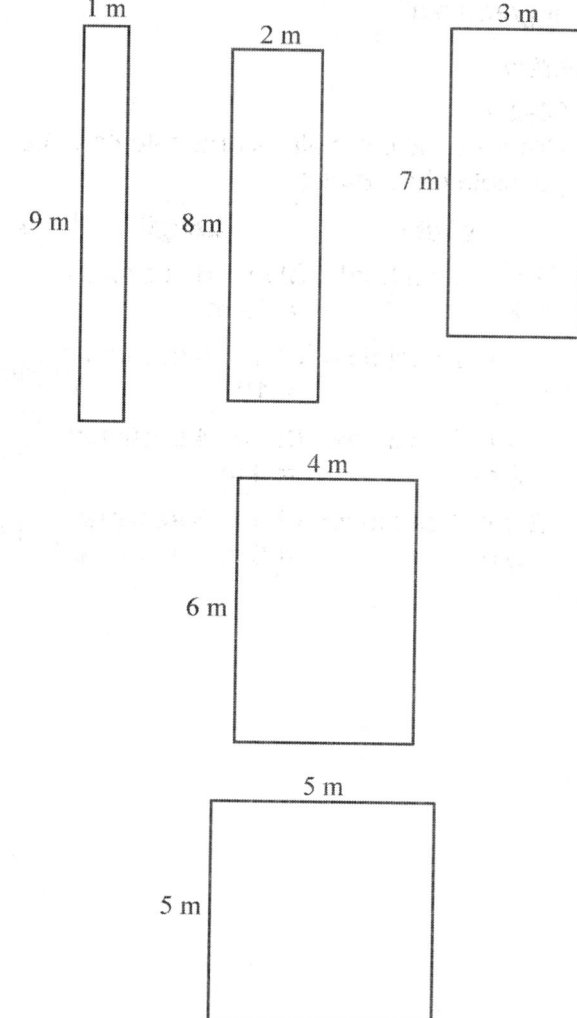

Applying Geometric Concepts

Sometimes a perfect square is not achievable. In this case, the dimensions that come closest to a square are the best.

Example

Colleen has 28 m of fencing material to make a pen for her chickens. The material comes in 2 m sections and cannot be cut.

List the possible dimensions of rectangular pens that Colleen could make.

Which dimensions would create a pen with the largest area?

Solution

Step 1

Create a table of values and calculate the possible dimensions.

Width	Length	Area
(2 m × 1 section) = 2 m	(2 m × 6 sections) = 12 m	24 m²
(2 m × 2 sections) = 4 m	(2 m × 5 sections) = 10 m	40 m²
(2 m × 3 sections) = 6 m	(2 m × 4 sections) = 8 m	48 m²
(2 m × 4 sections) = 8 m	(2 m × 3 sections) = 6 m	48 m²

Step 2

Identify the maximum area.

Look at the values in the "area" column of the table of values. The maximum area is 48 m².

The dimensions that would produce the maximum area are 3 sections by 4 sections or 6 m by 8 m.

A diagram can also be used to determine the various dimensions.

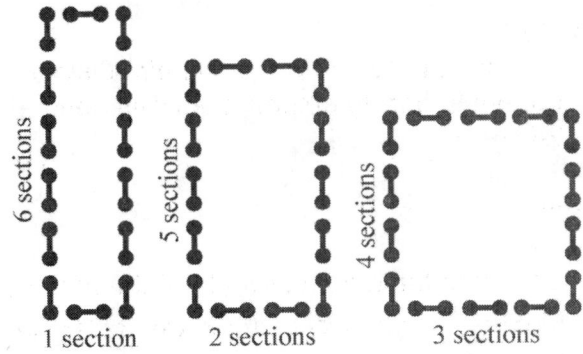

Notice that the rectangular shape closest to a square produced the largest area.

The maximum area of the rectangular pen is 48 m².

CALCULATING OPTIMAL AREA GIVEN THREE OR MORE LENGTHS

Optimal area occurs when the area is maximized within a given perimeter. Sometimes, one length or width is provided.

Problems involving perimeter and maximum area are present in everyday life. For example, Sheila purchased 36 meters of building material to build a bin next to her house. She wants to use these materials to build a bin with the greatest possible area.

Given a perimeter, the optimal area of a rectangle with one length and two widths occurs when the length is twice the width of the rectangle: $l = 2w$.

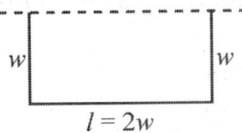

Example

Andre has 100 meters of fencing material to enclose a rectangular area for a snow-sculpture competition. One side of the area is bounded by a school. The fence is required for three sides of the rectangle.

In order to produce the maximum enclosed area with the 100 meters of fencing material, what dimensions should the three sides of the fence have? What is the optimal area?

Solution

A rectangle formed by adjusting the lengths of the three sides has an optimal area when its length (the long side) is twice its width (the two short sides).

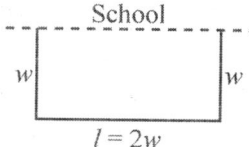

Step 1
Determine the width.
Use the formula for perimeter and substitute in the given value of the fencing material for perimeter.
$P = 2w + l$
In order to find the length of the sides for optimal area, use the formula $l = 2w$.
$P = 2w + 2w$
$P = 4w$
$100 = 4w$
$\frac{100}{4} = \frac{4w}{4}$
$25 = w$
$w = 25$ m

Step 2
Determine the length.
Substitute in the calculated value for width.
$l = 2(w)$
$= 2(25 \text{ m})$
$= 50$ m

Step 3
Determine the maximum area.
$A = l \times w$
$= 50 \text{ m} \times 25 \text{ m}$
$= 1{,}250 \text{ m}^2$

The fenced-off area has a maximum area of $1{,}250 \text{ m}^2$ when the side widths are 25 m and the length is 50 m.

The previous example illustrates the concept that a rectangle formed from a fixed dimension, containing one long side and two short sides, can be adjusted to give a maximum area when its length equals twice its width.

This concept extends to identical rectangular areas placed side by side against a fixed dimension.

A rectangle formed from a fixed dimension containing one long side and three identical short sides will have a maximum entire area when its length equals three times its width.

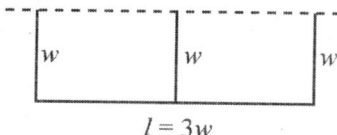

A rectangle formed from a fixed dimension containing one long side and four identical short sides will have a maximum entire area when its length equals four times its width.

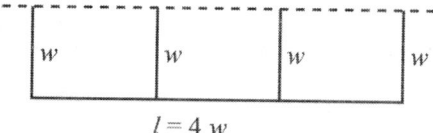

Example

Bill is building two animal pens side by side, as shown in the given diagram.

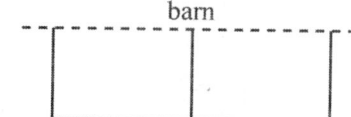

Applying Geometric Concepts

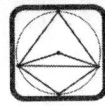

Determine the optimal area of the combined pens, given that Bill has 600 meters of fencing material available.

Solution

The maximum entire area occurs when the length (of the total area) equals three times the width: $l = 3w$.

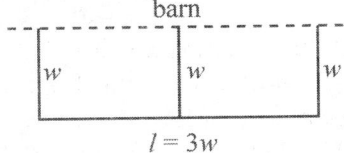

Step 1
Determine the width.

Use the perimeter formula and substitute in the given value of the fencing material for perimeter.
$P = 3w + l$

In order to determine the dimensions of the sides to find optimal area, use the formula $l = 3w$.

$$P = 3w + 3w$$
$$= 6w$$
$$600 = 6w$$
$$\frac{600}{6} = \frac{6w}{6}$$
$$w = 100 \text{ m}$$

Step 2
Determine the length.

Substitute in the calculated value for width.
$$l = 3w$$
$$= 3(100)$$
$$= 300 \text{ m}$$

The dimensions that produce the optimal area are a width of 100 meters and length of 300 meters.

Step 3
Determine the area.
$$A = l \times w$$
$$= 300 \times 100$$
$$= 30{,}000 \text{ m}^2$$

The maximum area of the two pens together is 30,000 m².

CALCULATING SURFACE AREA FOR PRISMS AND CYLINDERS GIVEN THE VOLUME

Optimal surface area occurs when surface area is minimized within a given volume.

Determining the optimal or minimal surface area is important for the development of consumer products. Manufacturers pay for the packaging of their products. To keep costs down, they want the smallest amount of surface area for their packaging. Also, containers that have insulating properties maintain the required temperature if there is less surface area from which heat can escape.

Two possible methods that can be used to determine the optimal surface area for a given volume are a table of values or an algebraic procedure.

When using a **table of values** to determine the optimal surface area for a square-based prism with a given volume, construct a three-column table with the following headings: side length, height, and surface area. Use different values for the side length and calculate the height using a rearranged volume formula. Lastly, substitute each side length and corresponding calculated height into the surface area formula to calculate each respective surface area.

Using this procedure it will hopefully be possible to determine a relationship between the side length and height of a square-based prism with a given volume and its optimal surface area.

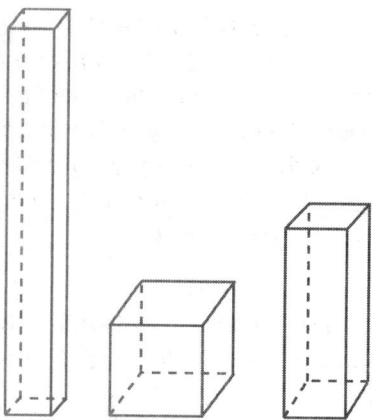

For example, to determine the optimal surface area of a square-based prism with a fixed volume determine the surface area of various square-based prisms with different side lengths and heights each with a volume of 27 cm³, using a table of values.

The volume of a rectangular prism can be determined by using the formula $V = lwh$. Since the length and width of a square-based prism are equal in measure, the volume of a square-based prism can be found by using the formula $V = s \times s \times h = s^2h$, where s is the side length. The surface area of a square-based prism can therefore be determined by applying the formula $SA = 2s^2 + 4sh$, where s is the side length and h is the height.

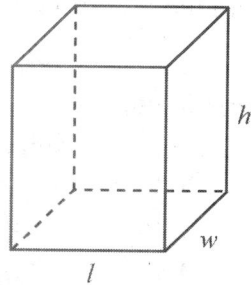

1. Start by rearranging the volume formula to solve for the height.

$$V = s^2h$$
$$\frac{V}{s^2} = \frac{s^2h}{s^2}$$
$$\frac{V}{s^2} = h$$

Use this formula to calculate the height in each row of the table.

2. Make a table of values to identify possible dimensions and corresponding surface areas of the square-based prism.

Side length in cm	Height in cm $h = \frac{V}{s^2}$	Surface Area in cm² $SA_{square\ prism} = 2s^2 + 4sh$
1	$\frac{27}{1^2} = \frac{27}{1} = 27$	$(2 \times 1^2) + (4 \times 1 \times 27) = 110$
2	$\frac{27}{2^2} = \frac{27}{4} = 6.75$	$(2 \times 2^2) + (4 \times 2 \times 6.75) = 62$
3	$\frac{27}{3^2} = \frac{27}{9} = 3$	$(2 \times 3^2) + (4 \times 3 \times 3) = 54$
4	$\frac{27}{4^2} = \frac{27}{16} = 1.6875$	$(2 \times 4^2) + (4 \times 4 \times 1.6875) = 59$

3. Identify the minimum surface area. Examine the values in the "surface area" column of the table of values. The minimum surface area occurs when the side length and height are each 3 cm.

The optimal surface area of a square-based prism with a given volume of 27 cm³ is 54 cm² when the side length and height are each 3 cm. In general, the optimal surface area of a square-based prism with a given volume occurs when the measure of the side length equals the measure of the height. Notice that the surface area of a box with a given volume is optimal when the box is in the shape of a cube.

The formula for determining the surface area of a cube is $SA = 6s^2$.

It follows that the side length of a square-based prism of optimal surface area for a given volume can be determined as follows:
The volume of a square-based prism is given by the formula $V = s^2h$. However, if $h = s$, the formula becomes $V = s^2 \times s = s^3$. Thus, $s = \sqrt[3]{V}$.

Applying Geometric Concepts

Example

Determine the dimensions and optimal surface area of a square-based prism if its volume must be 343 cm³.

Solution

The optimal surface area of a square-based prism with a given volume occurs when the prism is a cube.

Step 1

Calculate the side length of the cube.

Substitute 343 for V in the formula $s = \sqrt[3]{V}$ and solve for s as follows:

$s = \sqrt[3]{V}$
$= \sqrt[3]{343}$
$= 7$ cm

Step 2

Determine the surface area of the cube.

Substitute 7 for s in the formula $SA = 6s^2$.

$SA_{cube} = 6s^2$
$= 6(7^2)$
$= 294$ cm²

The optimal surface area of a square-based prism with a volume of 343 cm³ is 294 cm². The dimensions of the square-based prism are 7cm × 7cm × 7cm.

Many containers are in the shape of a cylinder, which means that their optimal surface area for a given volume must be calculated as well. Use the same procedure as calculating the optimal surface area of a square-based prism with a given volume in order to calculate the optimal surface-area for a cylinder with a given volume.

Example

Using a table of values, determine the optimal surface area of a cylinder with a volume of 50.24 cm³.

Solution

The volume and surface area of a cylinder can be calculated using the respective formulas $V_{cylinder} = \pi r^2 h$ and $SA_{cylinder} = 2(\pi r^2) + 2(\pi r h)$.

Step 1

Write the volume formula in terms of the height, h.

Isolate h by dividing both sides by πr^2.

$V = \pi r^2 h$
$\dfrac{V}{\pi \times r^2} = \dfrac{\pi r^2 h}{\pi r^2}$
$h = \dfrac{V}{\pi r^2}$

Step 2

Make a possible table of values.

Radius r in cm	Height in cm $h = \dfrac{V}{\pi r^2}$	Surface Area in cm² $SA_{cylinder} = 2(\pi r^2) + 2(\pi r h)$
1	$h = \dfrac{50.24}{3.14 \times 1^2} = 16$	$2(3.14 \times 1^2) + 2(3.14 \times 1 \times 16) = 106.76$
2	$h = \dfrac{50.24}{3.14 \times 2^2} = 4$	$2(3.14 \times 2^2) + 2(3.14 \times 2 \times 4) = 75.36$
3	$h = \dfrac{50.24}{3.14 \times 3^2} = 1.78$	$2(3.14 \times 3^2) + 2(3.14 \times 3 \times 1.78) = 90.06$

Note: If the π key on a scientific calculator or graphing calculator is used the values for the height and surface area will differ slightly from those in the given table of values.

Step 3
Identify the minimum surface area.

Examine the values in the "surface area" column of the table of values.

The optimal surface area of the cylinder with a given volume of 50.24 cm³ is 75.36 cm², when the height is 4 cm and the diameter is 4 cm (radius is 2 cm).

Notice that the surface area of a cylinder with a given volume is optimal when the height is equal to the diameter.

Therefore, when applying the volume formula, $V = \pi r^2 h$, to determine the radius of a cylinder with an optimal surface area for a given volume, substitute $2r$ for h.

$$\begin{aligned} V_{cylinder} &= \pi r^2 h \\ &= \pi r^2 (2r) \\ &= 2\pi r^3 \end{aligned}$$

When working with volume, be careful to keep all the units in your calculations the same.

Example
A manufacturer of juice crystals wants to package the crystals in a cylindrical container with a volume of 1 L.

Algebraically, determine the dimensions and the minimum surface area of the cylinder if its volume must be 1 L. Record your answer to the nearest tenth.

Solution
Minimum surface area occurs when the height of the cylinder is equal to the diameter or twice the radius of the cylinder.

Step 1
Make all the units the same.

Since volume is expressed in units cubed, one liter is equivalent to 1,000 cm³.

Step 2
Solve for r by substituting 1,000 for V in the formula $V = 2\pi r^3$.

$$\begin{aligned} V_{cylinder} &= 2\pi r^3 \\ 10 &= 2 \times 3.14 \times r^3 \\ \frac{10}{6.28} &= \frac{6.28 \times r^3}{6.28} \\ 159.2356688 &\approx r^3 \\ \sqrt[3]{159.2356688} &\approx \sqrt[3]{r^3} \\ 5.420176789 &\approx r \\ r &\approx 5.4 \text{ cm} \end{aligned}$$

Note: If the π key on a scientific or graphing calculator is used the value for r will be slightly different.

Step 3
Calculate the diameter and height.

The height is equal to the diameter, which is equal to $2r$.

$$\begin{aligned} h = d &= 2r \\ &= 2(5.4) \\ &= 10.8 \text{ cm} \end{aligned}$$

The juice-crystal cylinder will have a height and diameter of 10.8 cm.

Step 4
Substitute the values for the radius and height into the surface area formula for a cylinder.

$$\begin{aligned} SA_{cylinder} &= 2(\pi r^2) + 2(\pi r h) \\ &= 2(3.14 \times 5.4^2) \\ &\quad + 2(3.14 \times 5.4 \times 10.8) \\ &= 2(3.14 \times 29.16) \\ &\quad + 2(3.14 \times 5.4 \times 10.8) \\ &= 2(91.5624) + 2(183.1248) \\ &= 183.1248 + 366.2496 \\ &= 549.3744 \\ &= 549.4 \text{ cm}^2 \end{aligned}$$

The optimal surface area of a cylinder with a volume of 1 L is 549.4 cm². This cylinder will have a radius of 5.4 cm and a height of 10.8 cm.

Applying Geometric Concepts

Solving Design Problems in Three Dimensions

When shipping companies need to ship items, they often pack small items into large containers. In order to know how many small items can be placed into a large container, the companies first need to calculate the volume of the large container and the volume of each small item being put into the large container. After the two volumes have been determined, the number of small items that can be placed in a large container can be determined by dividing the larger volume by the smaller volume.

Example
What is the maximum number of boxes measuring 6 cm by 3 cm by 2 cm that can be packed into a shipping crate measuring 24 cm by 9 cm by 12 cm?

Solution

Step 1
Calculate the volume of the larger container, the shipping crate.
$V_{shipping\ crate} = lwh$
$= 24 \times 9 \times 12$
$= 2,592\ cm^3$

Step 2
Calculate the volume of the smaller container, the box.
$V_{box} = lwh$
$= 6 \times 3 \times 2$
$= 36\ cm^3$

Step 3
Divide the volume of the larger container by the volume of the smaller container.
$\frac{2,592}{36} = 72$

A maximum of 72 boxes will fit in the shipping crate.

Sometimes a company decides to change the size of the shipping container they want to use to ship their items. In this instance, the volume of the larger container must be recalculated and divided by the volume of each small item. This will determine how many items will fit inside it.

For example, if the dimensions of the shipping crate in the previous example doubled, how many boxes will fit inside?

1. Double each dimension of the shipping crate.
   $l = 24 \times 2 = 48\ cm$
   $w = 9 \times 2 = 18\ cm$
   $h = 12 \times 2 = 24\ cm$

2. Find the volume of the shipping crate with the new dimensions.
   $V_{shipping\ crate} = 48 \times 18 \times 24$
   $= 20,736\ cm^3$

3. Divide the volume of the larger container by the volume of the smaller container.
   $\frac{20,736}{36} = 576$

When the dimensions of the shipping crate are doubled, 576 small boxes will fit into the shipping crate.

Example
A company wants to package marbles in a cylindrical container that has a maximum volume and a minimum surface area. Each marble has a volume of 11.4 cm³. The company has determined that the diameter of the cylindrical container must be 12.2 cm.

How many marbles would fit into the cylindrical container?

Solution

Step 1
Calculate the volume of the container.
Recall that a cylinder with a maximum volume and minimum surface area will have the same height as its diameter. Therefore, the height of the cylinder is also 12.2 cm.
$V_{cylinder} = \pi r^2 h$
$= 3.14 \times 6.1^2 \times 12.2$
$= 3.14 \times 37.21 \times 12.2$
$\approx 1,425.44\ cm^3$

The maximum volume of the container is about 1,425.44 cm³.

Note that if the π key on a scientific or graphing calculator is used, the maximum volume will be about 1,426.34 cm³.

Step 2
Divide the volume of the container by the volume of each marble in order to determine the number of marbles that fit into the cylindrical container.

$$\frac{1{,}425.44}{11.4} = 125.03$$

A total of 125 marbles will fit into the cylindrical container.

Example

A movie theater is redesigning the shape of its small popcorn container and is trying to choose between a rectangular prism and a cylinder for the shape of the container. The container must have a volume of 1.5 L and the smallest surface area possible because the theater manager wants to save on printing costs.

Which of the two possible containers would have the **smallest** surface area?

Solution

The maximum volume and minimum surface area for a rectangular prism is a cube.
A cylinder has a maximum volume and minimum surface area when its height and diameter are equal.

Step 1
Convert 1.5 L into cubic centimeters.
1.5 L = 1,500 mL = 1,500 cm³

Step 2
Calculate the length, s, of each side of the cube. Substitute 1,500 for V in the volume of a cube formula and solve for s.

$$V_{cube} = s^3$$
$$1{,}500 = s^3$$
$$\sqrt[3]{1{,}500} = \sqrt[3]{s^3}$$
$$11.44714243 = s$$
$$s \approx 11.45 \text{ cm}$$

Step 3
Calculate the surface area of the cube using the calculated value for the side length.
Since a cube has six equal sized faces, the surface area of a cube can be calculated using the formula $SA_{cube} = 6s^2$. However, a cube shaped popcorn container has five equal sized faces because it does not have a top. Therefore, use the formula $SA_{cube} = 5s^2$.
Substitute 11.45 for s.

$$SA_{cube} = 5s^2$$
$$= 5(11.45)^2$$
$$\approx 655.51 \text{ cm}^2$$

Step 4
Calculate the diameter and height of the cylinder with maximum volume and minimum surface area.
Substitute 1,500 for V in the volume of a cylinder formula and solve for the radius, r.

$$V_{cylinder} = 2\pi r^3$$
$$1{,}500 = 2 \times 3.14 \times r^3$$
$$\frac{1{,}500}{6.28} = \frac{6.28 \times r^3}{6.28}$$
$$238.8535032 = r^3$$
$$\sqrt[3]{238.8535032} = \sqrt[3]{r^3}$$
$$6.204553568 = r$$
$$r \approx 6.2 \text{ cm}$$

The diameter is two times the radius, and since the height and diameter of the cylinder must be equal, the diameter and height of the of the cylinder are about 2 × 6.2 = 12.4 cm.

Step 5
Calculate the surface area of the cylinder using the calculated values for the height and radius. A cylindrical popcorn container will have one lateral face and a bottom, but no top.

$SA_{cylinder} = A_{cylinder\ base} + A_{lateral\ face}$

$A_{cylinder\ base} = \pi r^2$
$\approx 3.14 \times 6.2^2$
$\approx 3.14 \times 38.44$
≈ 120.7016
$\approx 120.7\ cm^2$

$A_{lateral\ face} = 2(\pi rh)$
$\approx 2(3.14 \times 6.2 \times 12.4)$
$\approx 2 \times 241.4032$
≈ 482.8064
$\approx 482.8\ cm^2$

$SA_{cylinder} = A_{cylinder\ base} + A_{lateral\ face}$
$\approx 120.7 + 482.8$
$\approx 603.5\ cm^2$

Note: If the π button on a scientific or a graphing calculator is used, the surface area of the cylinder may be slightly different.

The cylinder has less surface area (603.5 cm²) than the rectangular prism (655.51 cm²). As a result, the cost to print cylindrical popcorn containers would be less.

CALCULATING OPTIMAL VOLUME FOR A PRISM AND A CYLINDER GIVEN THE SURFACE AREA

Optimal volume occurs when the volume is maximized within a given surface area.

Sometimes manufacturers have a limited amount of material to create a package. If the maximum volume for a given surface area is known, manufacturers can determine the maximum amount of goods a package can hold.

Two possible methods that can be used to determine the optimal volume for a given surface area are: a table of values or an algebraic procedure.

To make a **table of values**, construct a three-column table of values with the following headings: side length, height, and volume. Use different values for the side length and calculate each corresponding height using a rearranged surface area formula. Finally, substitute each side length and corresponding height into the volume formula to calculate the volume.

This procedure will allow you to determine a relationship between the side length and height of a square-based prism with a given surface area and its optimal volume.

For example, to determine the optimal volume of a square-based prism with a fixed surface area of 54 cm², determine the volume of various square-based prisms with different side lengths and heights each with a surface area of 54 cm². Use a table of values to organize the results.

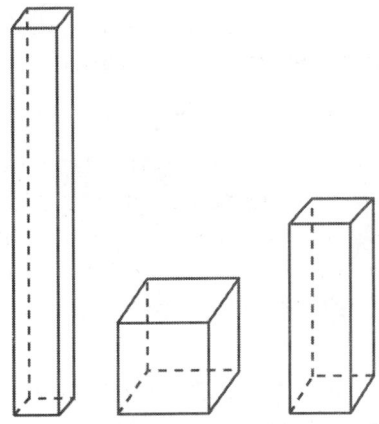

The formula for the surface area of a rectangular prism is $SA_{rectangular\ prism} = 2(lw) + 2(wh) + 2(lh)$.

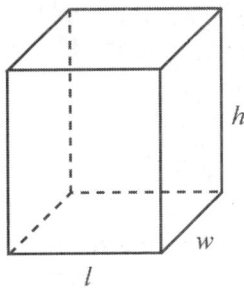

When the base is a square, the formula changes to $SA_{square-based\ prism} = 2(s \times s) + 2(s \times h) + 2(s \times h)$ or $SA_{square-based\ prism} = 2s^2 + 4sh$.

1. Rearrange the equation $SA_{\text{square-based prism}} = 2s^2 + 4sh$ to solve for the height, h.

   Use this formula to calculate the height in each row of the table of values.

   $$SA = 2s^2 + 4sh$$
   $$SA - 2s^2 = 4sh$$
   $$\frac{SA - 2s^2}{4s} = h$$

2. Make a table of values to identify possible dimensions and volumes of the square-based prism.

Side length (cm) s	Height (cm) $h = \dfrac{SA - 2s^2}{4s}$	Volume (cm³) $V_{\text{square-based prism}} = s^2 h$
1	$\dfrac{54 - 2 \times 1^2}{4 \times 1} = 13$	$1^2 \times 13 = 13$
2	$\dfrac{54 - 2 \times 2^2}{4 \times 2} = 5.75$	$2^2 \times 5.75 = 23$
3	$\dfrac{54 - 2 \times 3^2}{4 \times 3} = 3$	$3^2 \times 3 = 27$
4	$\dfrac{54 - 2 \times 4^2}{4 \times 4} = 1.375$	$4^2 \times 1.375 = 22$

3. Identify the optimal volume.

Examine the values in the volume column of the table of values. The optimal volume occurs when the side length and height are each 3 cm.

Thus, the optimal volume of a square-based prism with a given surface area of 54 cm² is 27 cm³.

In general, the optimal volume of a square-based prism with a given surface area occurs when the measure of the side length equals the measure of the height.

Notice that the volume of a box with a given surface area is optimal when the box is in the shape of a cube.

The formula for the surface area of a cube is $SA = 6s^2$ and the formula for the volume of a cube is $V = s^3$. Applying the surface area of a cube formula and the volume of a cube formula allows you to calculate the optimal volume, given a fixed surface area, using an algebraic approach.

Example

Determine the dimensions and the maximum volume of a square-based prism if its surface area must be 96 cm².

Solution

The optimal volume of a square-based prism with a given surface are occurs when the prism is a cube.

Step 1

Calculate the side length of the cube.

Substitute 96 for SA in the formula $SA = 6s^2$ and then solve for s as follows:

$$SA_{\text{cube}} = 6s^2$$
$$96 = 6s^2$$
$$\frac{96}{6} = \frac{6s^2}{6}$$
$$16 = s^2$$
$$\sqrt{16} = \sqrt{s^2}$$
$$4 = s$$

The length of each side of the cube is 4 cm.

Step 2

Calculate the optimal volume.

Substitute 4 for s in the formula $V = s^3$ in order to determine the optimal volume.

$$V_{\text{cube}} = s^3$$
$$= 4^3$$
$$= 64 \text{ cm}^3$$

The optimal volume of a square-based prism with a surface area of 96 cm² is 64 cm³.

The dimensions of the square-based prism are 4 cm × 4 cm × 4 cm.

Many containers are in the shape of a cylinder, which means that their optimal volume for a given surface area must be calculated as well. Use a similar procedure as calculating the optimal volume of a square-based prism with a given surface area in order to calculate the optimal volume for a cylinder with a given surface area.

Example

Use a table of values to determine the optimal volume of a cylinder that has a surface area of 75.36 cm².

Solution

The surface area of a cylinder can be determined by applying the formula $SA_{cylinder} = 2(\pi r^2) + 2(\pi rh)$ and the volume of a cylinder can be determined by applying the formula $V = \pi r^2 h$.

Step 1

Rearrange the surface area formula to solve for the height, h.

$$SA = 2(\pi r^2) + 2(\pi rh)$$
$$SA - 2(\pi r^2) = 2(\pi rh)$$
$$\frac{SA - 2(\pi r^2)}{2(\pi r)} = \frac{2(\pi rh)}{2(\pi r)}$$
$$\frac{SA - 2(\pi r^2)}{2(\pi r)} = h$$

Use this formula to calculate the height in each row of the table of values.

Step 2

Make a possible table of values.

Radius (cm) r	Height (cm) $\frac{SA - 2(\pi r^2)}{2(\pi r)} = h$	Volume (cm³) $V_{cylinder} = \pi r^2 h$
1	$\frac{75.36 - 2(3.14 \times 1^2)}{2(3.14 \times 1)}$ = 11	$3.14 \times 1^2 \times 11$ = 34.54
2	$\frac{75.36 - 2(3.14 \times 2^2)}{2(3.14 \times 2)}$ = 4	$3.14 \times 2^2 \times 4$ = 50.24
3	$\frac{75.36 - 2(3.14 \times 3^2)}{2(3.14 \times 3)}$ = 1	$3.14 \times 3^2 \times 1$ = 28.26

Note: If the π key on a scientific or graphing calculator is used the values for the height and surface area will differ slightly from those in the given table of values.

Examine the values in the volume column of the table of values.

The optimal volume of a cylinder with a given surface area of 75.36 cm² is 50.24 cm³ when the height is 4 cm and the diameter is 4 cm (radius is 2 cm).

Notice that the volume of a cylinder with a given surface area is optimal when the height is twice the radius. In other words, a cylinder has a maximum volume when the height equals the diameter.

Therefore, when applying the surface area formula, $SA_{cylinder} = 2(\pi r^2) + 2(\pi rh)$, to determine the radius of a cylinder with an opitmal volume for a given surface area, substitute $2r$ in for h. The formula can be rewritten as follows:

$$SA_{cylinder} = 2(\pi r^2) + 2(\pi rh)$$
$$= 2(\pi r^2) + 2(\pi r 2r)$$
$$= 2(\pi r^2) + 4(\pi r^2)$$
$$= 6(\pi r^2)$$

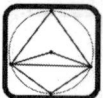

Example

Algebraically determine the dimensions and the optimal volume of a cylinder if its surface area must be 96 cm². Record your answers to the nearest tenth.

Solution

A cylinder with a given surface area of 96 cm² has an optimal volume when the diameter and the height are equal.

Step 1

Calculate the radius.
Substitute 96 for the surface area in the formula $SA = 6\pi r^2$, and solve for the radius, r.

$$SA_{cylinder} = 6\pi r^2$$
$$96 = 6(3.14 \times r^2)$$
$$96 = 18.84 \times r^2$$
$$\frac{96}{18.84} = \frac{18.84 \times r^2}{18.84}$$
$$5.1 \approx r^2$$
$$\sqrt{5.1} \approx \sqrt{r^2}$$
$$2.3 \approx r$$

The cylinder has an optimal volume when the radius is 2.3 cm.

Note: If the $\boxed{\pi}$ key on a scientific or graphing calculator is used the value for r will be slightly different.

Step 2

Calculate the height.
The height is equal to the diameter.
$$h = d = 2r$$
$$= 2 \times 2.3$$
$$= 4.6 \text{ cm}$$

The cylinder will have a height of 4.6 cm.

Step 3

Calculate the optimal volume.
Substitute the values for the radius and height into the volume formula for a cylinder.

$$V_{cylinder} = \pi r^2 h$$
$$= 3.14 \times 2.3^2 \times 4.6$$
$$= 3.14 \times 5.29 \times 4.6$$
$$\approx 76.4 \text{ cm}^3$$

The optimal volume of a cylinder with a surface area of 96 cm² is 76.4 cm³.

The cylinder will have a radius of 2.3 cm and a height of 4.6 cm.

CALCULATING OPTIMAL PERIMETER GIVEN THE AREA

Optimal perimeter occurs when the perimeter is minimized within a given area.

There are three methods that can be used to determine optimal area:

1. A table of values
2. A graphing calculator
3. And the algebraic method.

To make a **table of values**:

1. Draw a three-column table with the following labels: width, length, and perimeter.
2. Use varying values for the width, and calculate the length using a rearranged area formula.
3. Apply the perimeter formula to calculate the perimeter.

The table of values allows you to see all the possible measures of perimeter so you can pick out the smallest possible perimeter.

Example
Determine the minimum perimeter of a rectangle with an area of 25 m.

Solution
Method 1: Table of Values
Because the area is given rather than the perimeter, solve for the length as follows:

$$A = l \times w$$
$$\frac{A}{w} = \frac{l \times w}{w}$$
$$l = \frac{A}{w}$$

Use a table of values to find the perimeter, $P = 2l + 2w$, for different widths.

Width	Length = $\frac{A}{w}$	$P = 2l + 2w$
1	$\frac{25}{1} = 25$	$2(25) + 2(1) = 52$
2	$\frac{25}{2} = 12.5$	$2(12.5) 2(2) + = 29$
3	$\frac{25}{3}$	$2\left(\frac{25}{3}\right) + 2(3) = \frac{68}{3} = 22.7$
4	$\frac{25}{4} = 6.25$	$2(6.25) + 2(4) = 20.5$
5	$\frac{25}{5} = 5$	$2(5) + 2(5) = 20$
6	$\frac{25}{6}$	$2\left(\frac{25}{6}\right) + 2(6) = \frac{61}{3} = 20.3$
7	$\frac{25}{7}$	$2\left(\frac{25}{7}\right) + 2(7) = \frac{148}{7} = 21.1$

Look at the values in the "perimeter" column of the table of values. Notice that the minimum value for perimeter occurs when the length and width are 5 m.

Method 2: Graphic Calculator
Define the terms that will be substituted in the equation $P = 2w + 2l$.

$$l = \frac{25}{w}$$
$$w = x$$
$$P = y$$

Substitute the values into the equation for perimeter.

$$P = 2w + 2l$$
$$P = 2w + 2 \times \frac{25}{w}$$
$$y = 2x + 2 \times \frac{25}{x}$$

Enter the expression $2x + 2 \times \frac{25}{x}$ into the [Y =] menu of the graphing calculator.

Choose an appropriate window setting, such as the following:

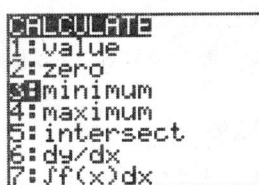

To find the minimum value of y, press [2nd] [TRACE] to access the CALC menu. Select 3:minimum.

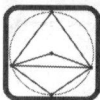

Move the cursor to the left of the low point on the line of the graph and press [ENTER]. Then, move the cursor to the right of the low point on the line of the graph and press [ENTER]. Press [ENTER] one more time to have the calculator determine the minimum value of y.

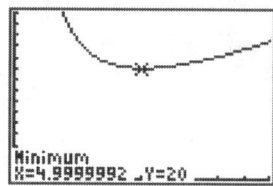

Since $y = P$, the minimum perimeter, 20 m, occurs when the length and width are 5 m. You can conclude that the minimum perimeter of a four-sided rectangle with a fixed area occurs when the rectangle is a square. Knowing this gives you a third way to calculate the minimum perimeter when given a fixed area.

Method 3: Algebraically

The minimum perimeter of a four-sided rectangle with a fixed area occurs when $w = l = \sqrt{A}$.

Substitute 25 in for A.

$w = l = \sqrt{25} = 5$ m

Substitute l and w into the perimeter formula.

$P = 2l + 2w$
$= 2(5) + 2(5)$
$= 10 + 10$
$= 20$ m

Since $l = w = \sqrt{A}$, another way to calculate the optimal perimeter (P) is as follows:

$P = 2w + 2l$
$= 2(\sqrt{A}) + 2(\sqrt{A})$
$= 4\sqrt{A}$

Substitute 25 in for the area and solve for P.

$P = 4\sqrt{A}$
$= 4\sqrt{25}$
$= 4 \times 5$
$= 20$ m

Example

Amy is a lifeguard at a swimming pool. She has been instructed to enclose a rectangular area of 90 m² in the pool where a group of children will receive a swimming lesson.

Determine the minimum length of rope required, to the nearest tenth meter, to enclose this rectangular area.

Solution

Method 1: Table of Values

Width	Length = $\frac{A}{w}$	$P = 2l + 2w$
1	$\frac{90}{1} = 90$	$2(90) + 2(1) = 182$
2	$\frac{90}{2} = 45$	$2(45) + 2(2) = 94$
3	$\frac{90}{3} = 30$	$2(30) + 2(3) = 66$
4	$\frac{90}{4} = 22.5$	$2(22.5) + 2(4) = 53$
5	$\frac{90}{5} = 18$	$2(18) + 2(5) = 46$
6	$\frac{90}{6} = 15$	$2(15) + 2(6) = 42$
7	$\frac{90}{7}$	$2\left(\frac{90}{7}\right) + 2(7) = \frac{278}{7} = 39.7$
8	$\frac{90}{8} = 11.25$	$2(11.25) + 2(8) = 38.5$
9	$\frac{90}{9} = 10$	$2(10) + 2(9) = 38$
10	$\frac{90}{10} = 9$	$2(9) + 2(10) = 38$
11	$\frac{90}{11}$	$2\left(\frac{90}{11}\right) + 2(11) = \frac{400}{11} = 38.4$

Applying the symmetry of this question, the minimum perimeter occurs midway between the lines at which the width is 9 m and 10 m. In this case width and length of the enclosed swimming pool area are 9.5 m.

Method 2: Graphing Calculator

Enter the expression $2x + 2 \times \dfrac{90}{x}$ into the [Y =] menu of your graphing calculator. Turn STATS PLOT on.

Choose an appropriate window setting, such as the following:

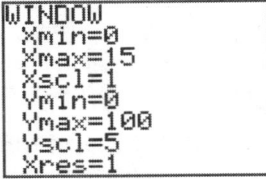

To find the minimum value of y, press [2nd][TRACE] to access the CALC menu. Select 3:minimum.

Move the cursor to the left of the low point on the line of the graph and press [ENTER]. Then, move the cursor to the right of the low point on the line of the graph and press [ENTER]. Press [ENTER] one more time to have the calculator determine the minimum value of y.

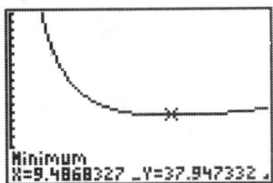

Method 3: Algebraically

The minimum perimeter occurs when
$w = l = \sqrt{A}$
$= \sqrt{90}$
$= 9.5$ m

The value of the minimum perimeter is 38 m.
$P = 2w + 2l$
$= 2(9.5) + 2(9.5)$
≈ 38 m

OR

$P = 4\sqrt{A}$
$= 4\sqrt{90}$
$= 37.9$ m
≈ 38 m

CALCULATING OPTIMAL PERIMETER WITH A GIVEN NUMBER OF LENGTHS

Optimal perimeter occurs when the perimeter is minimized for a given area. For a rectangular region that is divided into one or more sections the minimum perimeter occurs when the measure of a long side (the length) is equal to the product of the measure of a short side (the width) and the number of short sides. For example, a rectangular area formed from a fixed area containing one long side (l) and three identical short sides (w) will have a minimum total perimeter when its length equals three times its width.

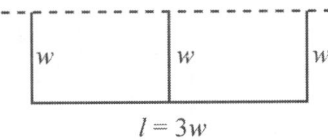

Let A = the fixed area
$A = lw$
Since $l = 3w$,
$A = (3w)w$
$A = 3w^2$

Therefore, $w^2 = \dfrac{A}{3}$ or $w = \sqrt{\dfrac{A}{3}}$.

The minimum perimeter, P, for one length, l, and three widths, w, is $P = 3w + l$, and since $l = 3w$,
$P = 3w + 3w = 6w$.

Example

Bryn is building three identical animal pens along one side of her barn, as shown in the given diagram.

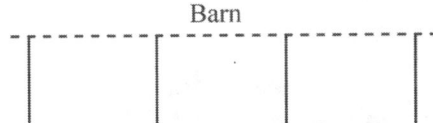

The total area of the rectangle formed by the three pens must be 1,600 m².

Determine the dimensions that will minimize the fencing material Bryn needs for the four short sides and one long side of the rectangular area.

Solution

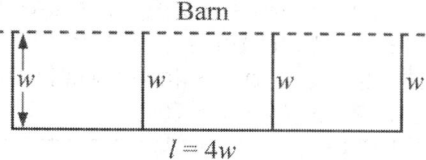

Since there are 4 short sides, the minimum perimeter of the rectangular region occurs when the length of the rectangular region equals four times the width of the rectangular region: $l = 4w$.

Step 1

Determine the measure of the width.
Use the formula for area. Substitute the given area, 1,600 for A and $4w$ for l.

$A_{total} = lw$
$1,600 = 4w \times w$
$1,600 = 4w^2$
$\dfrac{1,600}{4} = w^2$
$w^2 = 400$
$\sqrt{w^2} = \sqrt{400}$
$w = 20$ m

Step 2

Determine the measure of the length. Since $l = 4w$, substitute 20 for w.
$l = 4w$
$l = 4 \times 20$
$l = 80$ m

To achieve minimum perimeter, the dimensions of the animal pens will be 20 m by 80 m.

What is the minimum amount of fencing material that she can use?

Solution

The dimensions of the total rectangular area with a minimum perimeter are $l = 80$ m by $w = 20$ m.

$P = l + 4w$
$ = 80 + (4 \times 20)$
$ = 160$ m

The minimum amount of fencing material that Bryn can use is 160 m.

EXERCISE #1—APPLYING GEOMETRIC CONCEPTS

Use the following information to answer the next question.

Greg is building a sandcastle and uses a pail in the shape of a cylinder with the given dimensions to gather the sand.

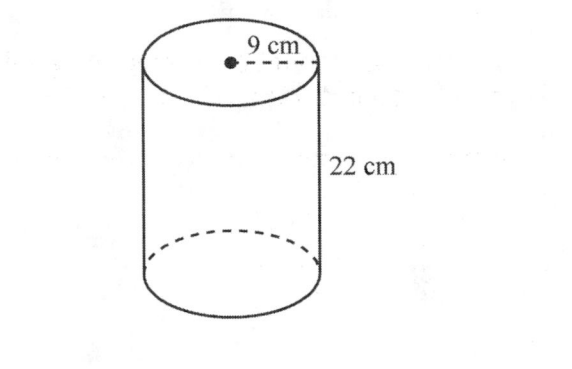

148. If Greg fills the pail with sand 6 times, the amount of sand he uses to build his castle is _____ cm³.

Use the following information to answer the next question.

A conical container with a diameter of 1.4 m and a height of 3.7 m is used to transport rocks.

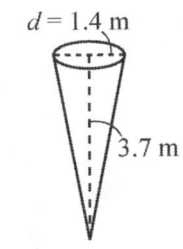

149. If the rocks are sold at a rate of $22.00/m³ and 3.14 is used as the value of π, what will be the cost to the nearest cent to fill the container completely?

   A. $39.52   B. $41.75
   C. $44.38   D. $46.93

Use the following information to answer the next question.

Sharon wants to fill two identical flower pots with dirt. The flower pots have an attached base, but the pots themselves are spherical in shape with a radius of 40 cm. Through an opening at the top, Sharon will fill each flower pot 90% full of dirt.

150. If Sharon uses 3.14 as the value of π and rounds her answer to the nearest whole number, how much dirt will she require to fill the two flower pots? _____ cm³

Use the following information to answer the next question.

At a gardening store, two different types of a particular style of flower pot are available. Each type is in the shape of an inverted pyramid, as illustrated in the given diagrams.

Type One

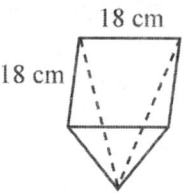
18 cm
18 cm

Type Two

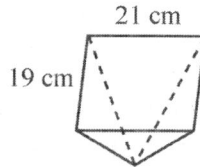
21 cm
19 cm

151. If the depth (height) of the type-one flower pot is 20 cm and the depth (height) of the type-two flower pot is 16 cm, which of the following statements about the volumes of the two flower pots is **true**?
   A. The volume of a type-two flower pot is 24 cm³ more than the volume of a type-one flower pot.
   B. The volume of a type-two flower pot is 75 cm³ more than the volume of a type-one flower pot.
   C. The volume of a type-one flower pot is 32 cm³ more than the volume of a type-two flower pot.
   D. The volume of a type-one flower pot is 96 cm³ more than the volume of a type-two flower pot.

Use the following information to answer the next question.

Andrew wants to make a new rectangular garden at his farm. To enclose the garden, he will use a 480 m piece of wire fencing.

152. Determine the dimensions of the fence that would enclose the largest garden, and calculate that garden's area.

153. Optimal area occurs when the
   A. area is minimized within a given perimeter
   B. perimeter is minimized within a given area
   C. area is maximized within a given perimeter
   D. perimeter is maximized within a given area

Use the following information to answer the next question.

A carton must be designed to hold 6 packages of golf balls. Each package of golf balls is 6 cm by 6 cm by 18 cm.

154. What is the minimum amount of cardboard needed to make the carton?
   A. 1,065.4 cm²   B. 1,133.9 cm²
   C. 1,221.7 cm²   D. 1,482.7 cm²

155. Which of the following formulas could be used to determine how many small boxes will fit into a larger box?

A. $\dfrac{V_{\text{large box}}}{V_{\text{small box}}}$

B. $\dfrac{V_{\text{small box}}}{V_{\text{large box}}}$

C. $V_{\text{large box}} \times V_{\text{small box}}$

D. $\dfrac{1}{V_{\text{large box}} \times V_{\text{small box}}}$

Use the following information to answer the next question.

> Alexandria's company makes cylindrical glass liners for thermoses, which use up 515 cm² of material.

156. If a manufacturer decides to use Alexandria's glass liners for their thermoses, then what is the maximum volume of these thermoses rounded to the nearest milliliter?

A. 718 mL   B. 785 mL
C. 875 mL   D. 898 mL

157. If the area of a rectangle is 900 m², what is its smallest possible perimeter?

A. 30 m   B. 60 m
C. 120 m   D. 450 m

Use the following information to answer the next question.

> Jed needs to construct a rectangular enclosure with fencing behind his chicken coop. One of the four sides will border the back wall of the coop so it will not require fencing. The enclosure will be divided into four smaller rectangular sections by erecting three fences perpendicular to the chicken coop, as shown (the sketch is not to scale).

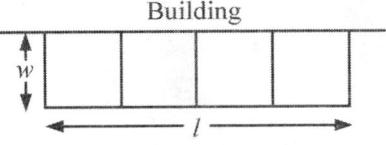

158. If Jed purchased 1,000 m of fencing for the enclosure, what should be the width (w) and length (l) for the enclosure to have a maximum area?

A. $w = 200$ m, $l = 800$ m
B. $w = 167$ m, $l = 167$ m
C. $w = 100$ m, $l = 500$ m
D. $w = 80$ m, $l = 600$ m

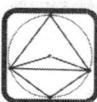

EXERCISE #1—APPLYING GEOMETRIC CONCEPTS
ANSWERS AND SOLUTIONS

148. 33572.88	151. C	154. D	157. C
149. B	152. See solution	155. A	158. C
150. 482304	153.	156. D	

148. 33572.88

Step 1
Calculate the volume of the cylinder.
The shape of the base is a circle. The height is the measured distance between the parallel circles (bases).

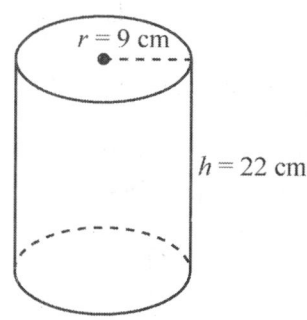

Substitute 3.14 for π, 9 for r, and 22 for h.
$$V_{cylinder} = A_{base} \times h$$
$$= A_{circle} \times h$$
$$= \pi r^2 \times h$$
$$= 3.14 \times 9^2 \times 22$$
$$= 3.14 \times 81 \times 22$$
$$= 5{,}595.48 \text{ cm}^3$$

Step 2
Multiply the volume of the cylinder by 6.
$6 \times 5{,}595.48 = 33{,}572.88 \text{ cm}^3$
Greg's sandcastle contains 33,572.88 cm³ of sand.

149. B

Step 1
Determine the radius of the cone.
$$r = \frac{d}{2}$$
$$r = \frac{1.4}{2}$$
$$r = 0.7$$

Step 2
Calculate the volume of the cone.
$$V_{cone} = \frac{\pi r^2 h}{3}$$
$$V_{cone} \approx \frac{(3.14)(0.7)^2(3.7)}{3}$$
$$V_{cone} \approx \frac{(3.14)(0.49)(3.7)}{3}$$
$$V_{cone} \approx \frac{5.69282}{3}$$
$$V_{cone} \approx 1.8976 \text{ m}^3$$

Step 3
Determine the cost of the rocks.
Multiply the volume of the cone by the rate that the rocks are being sold.
cost = $V_{cone} \times 22.00$
cost $\approx 1.8976 \times 22.00$
cost $\approx \$41.75$
Therefore, the cost of the rocks to fill the conical container will be $41.75.

150. 482304

Step 1
Determine the volume of one flower pot by applying the formula for the volume of a sphere, $V = \frac{4}{3}\pi r^3$ or $V = \frac{4\pi r^3}{3}$.

Substitute 3.14 for π and 40 for r in the formula $V = \frac{4}{3}\pi r^3$, and solve for V.

$$V \approx \frac{4 \times 3.14 \times 40^3}{3}$$
$$V \approx \frac{4 \times 3.14 \times 64{,}000}{3}$$
$$V \approx \frac{803{,}840}{3}$$
$$V \approx 267{,}946.67$$

The volume of one flower pot is approximately 267,946.67 cm³.

Step 2
Determine the total volume of the two flower pots.
267,946.67 × 2 ≈ 535,893.34
The total volume of the two flower pots is approximately 535,893.34 cm³.

Step 3
Determine the amount of dirt required to fill the two flower pots.
Since each flower pot is to be filled 90% full of dirt, the amount of dirt required to fill the two flower pots can be determined as follows:
90% × 535,893.34
≈ 0.90 × 535,893.34
≈ 482,304.006
To the nearest whole number, Sharon will require 482,304 cm³ of dirt to fill the two flower pots.

151. C

The volume, V, of each flower pot can be determined by applying the formula $V = \frac{1}{3}(A_{base} \times h)$, in which A_{base} is the area of the base and h is the height of the flower pot.

Step 1
Determine the volume of a type-one flower pot.
The area of the top (base), A_{base}, of a type-one flower pot is 18 × 18 = 324 cm², and the height, h, of a type-one flower pot is given as 20 cm. The volume of a type-one flower pot can now be determined by applying the formula $V = \frac{1}{3}(A_{base} \times h)$.

Substitute 324 for A_{base} and 20 for h, and then solve for V.
$V = \frac{1}{3}(324 \times 20)$
$V = \frac{1}{3} \times 6,480$
$V = 2,160$
The volume of a type-one flower pot is 2,160 cm³.

Step 2
Determine the volume of a type-two flower pot.
The area of the top (base), A_{base}, of a type-two flower pot is 21 × 19 = 399 cm², and the height of a type-two flower pot is given as 16 cm. The volume of a type-two flower pot can now be determined by applying the formula $V = \frac{1}{3}(A_{base} \times h)$.

Substitute 399 for A_{base} and 16 for h, and then solve for V.
$V = \frac{1}{3}(399 \times 16)$
$V = \frac{1}{3} \times 6,384$
$V = 2,128$
The volume of a type-two flower pot is 2,128 cm³.

Step 3
Determine the correct statement from the given alternatives.
The volume of a type-one flower pot is 2,160 − 2,128 = 32 cm³ more than the volume of a type-two flower pot.

152.

Step 1
Calculate the length or width of the rectangular garden.
Maximum area occurs when the rectangle becomes a square.
$w = l = \frac{P}{4} = \frac{480}{4} = 120$ m
The dimensions required for maximum area are $w = 120$ m and $l = 120$ m.

Step 2
Substitute in this value for length and width in the area formula.
$A = l \times w$
$= 120 \times 120$
$= 14,400$ m²
The garden will have a maximum area of 14,400 m² when the sides are 120 m long.

153.

154. D

Step 1
Calculate the volume of each box of golf balls.
$V = lwh$
$= 6 \times 6 \times 18$
$= 648$ cm³

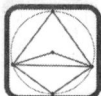

Step 2
Calculate the total volume of the 6 packages of golf balls.
Multiply the volume of one package by the total that can fit inside the carton.
$V_{total} = 648 \times 6$
$= 3,888 \text{ cm}^3$

Step 3
To determine the side length of the carton, substitute the volume into the formula, and take the cube root.
$s = \sqrt[3]{V}$
$= \sqrt[3]{3,888}$
$= 15.72 \text{ cm}$

Step 4
Substitute the side length into the surface area formula for a cube, and solve.
$SA_{cube} = 6s^2$
$= 6 \times (15.72)^2$
$= 1,482.7 \text{ cm}^2$

The minimum surface area of the carton will be 1,482.7 cm² when the length of each side is 15.72 cm.

155. A

The formula $\dfrac{V_{large\ box}}{V_{small\ box}}$ could be used to determine how many small boxes will fit into a larger box.

Dividing the volume of the larger box by the volume of the smaller box will give a constant since the units will cancel. This constant indicates how many smaller components the larger box can be grouped into.

156. D

A cylinder with a given surface area has a maximum volume when the diameter and the height are equal.

Step 1
Calculate the radius.
Substitute the surface area into the formula, and solve for the radius.
$SA = 6\pi r^2$
$515 = 6(3.14)r^2$
$515 = 18.84r^2$
$\dfrac{515}{18.84} = \dfrac{18.84r^2}{18.84}$
$27.34 = r^2$
$\sqrt{27.34} = \sqrt{r^2}$
$5.23 = r$

Step 2
Calculate the height.
The height is equal to the diameter.
$d = 2r$
$= 2(5.23)$
$= 10.46$

Step 3
Calculate the volume the liner can hold.
Substitute the radius and height into the volume formula.
$V = \pi r^2 h$
$= (3.14)(5.23)^2(10.46)$
$= (3.14)(27.3529)(10.46)$
$= 898.39 \text{ cm}^3$

Step 4
Convert cubic centimeters (cm³) to milliliters (mL).
$898.39 \text{ cm}^3 = 898.39 \text{ mL}$

Step 5
Round to the nearest milliliter.
$898.39 \to 898 \text{ mL}$
Each thermos can hold 898 mL of liquid.

157. C

The smallest possible perimeter, P, for a given area, A, occurs when the length, l, is equal to the width, w ($l = w$).
$A = (l)(w)$

Replace l with w.
$A = (w)(w)$
$A = w^2$
$\sqrt{A} = \sqrt{w^2}$
$\sqrt{A} = w$

Substitute 900 for A.
$w = \sqrt{A}$
$w = \sqrt{900}$
$w = 30 \text{ m}$

Since $l = w$, the length of the rectangle is also 30 m.

Calculate the perimeter of the rectangle.
$P = 2l + 2w$
$= 2(30) + 2(30)$
$= 60 + 60$
$= 120 \text{ m}$

The smallest possible perimeter of this rectangle is 120 m.

158. C

The rectangular enclosure is divided into four rectangular sections with equal areas. Therefore, the length and width of each smaller rectangular area will be equal. Since one length of the enclosure is made from the wall of the chicken coop, the fencing will make up one length of the enclosure (l) and five widths (w) of equal measure.

$P = l + 5w$

The total perimeter, P, formed by the fencing is 1,000 m.

Recall that a rectangular region divided into one or more sections has a maximum area when the measure of its the length is equal to the product of the measure of a short side and the number of short sides. Therefore, the maximum area, A, of the rectangular enclosure occurs when the length is five times the width ($l = 5w$).

Substitute $5w$ for l in the perimeter equation.

$P = 5w + 5w$
$P = 10w$
$w = \dfrac{P}{10}$

Substitute 1,000 m for P.

$w = \dfrac{1{,}000}{10}$
$w = 100$ m

Since $l = 5w$, the length of the rectangular fence can be found as follows.

$l = 5 \times 100 = 500$ m

The maximum area of the rectangular enclosure occurs with a width of 100 m and a length of 500 m.

EXERCISE #2—APPLYING GEOMETRIC CONCEPTS

Use the following information to answer the next question.

A cylindrical water tower is 30 m high with a radius of 10 m.

159. Rounded to the nearest whole number, how many cubic meters of water can be stored in the tower?
 A. 892 m³
 B. 3,140 m³
 C. 9,420 m³
 D. 28,260 m³

Use the following information to answer the next question.

The top section of a model rocket is made up of two geometric shapes: a cylinder and a cone.

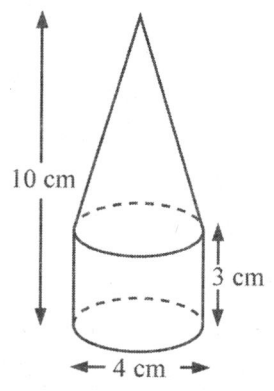

160. If the cone at the top of the model rocket is filled with sand to help stabilize its flight, how much sand could it hold, rounded to the nearest tenth of a cubic centimeter?
 A. 27.6 cm³
 B. 28.5 cm³
 C. 29.3 cm³
 D. 30.1 cm³

Use the following information to answer the next question.

Kurt built a snowman by placing three spherical snowballs on top of each other.

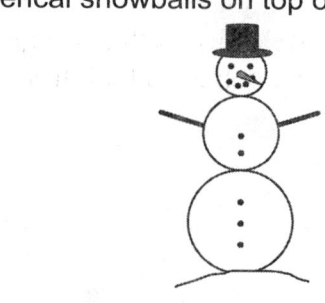

161. If the diameter of the bottom snowball is 90 cm, then the volume, V, in cm³ can be expressed as
 A. $V = 108{,}000\pi$
 B. $V = 121{,}500\pi$
 C. $V = 143{,}500\pi$
 D. $V = 172{,}000\pi$

Use the following information to answer the next question.

Ariel built a model of a square-based Egyptian pyramid for a school science fair project.

162. If the height of the pyramid is 36 cm and the volume of the pyramid is 21,168 cm³, then the side length of the base of the pyramid is _____ cm.

Use the following information to answer the next question.

> The Wong family buys 60 m of chain link fencing to make a pen for their new puppy. They want to build a pen with the greatest possible area.

163. Determine the dimensions that will give the optimal area, and calculate that area.

Use the following information to answer the next question.

> The promoters of a rock concert fence off a rectangular area directly in front of the stage for a VIP area. They use 16 sections of fence. Each section is 1 m long. They use the fence for three sides of the rectangular area. The front of the stage makes up the fourth side.

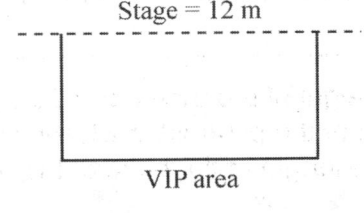

164. If the length of the stage is 12 m, what are the dimensions of the largest VIP area that can be enclosed using 16 m of fence?

Use the following information to answer the next question.

> Maria has been asked to design an insulated cylinder to transport cold liquids. To keep heat gain to a minimum, the total surface area must be minimized.

165. What is the minimum amount of material needed to build a cylindrical container that will hold 6 L of liquid?
 A. 904.7 cm^2
 B. 1,809.4 cm^2
 C. 2,714.1 cm^2
 D. 3,618.8 cm^2

166. What is the maximum number of boxes measuring 5 cm by 4 cm by 3 cm that can be packed into a shipping crate measuring 30 cm by 10 cm by 20 cm?

Use the following information to answer the next question.

> Leroy has a company that sells golf balls to retailers. Each shipping box contains 10 packages of golf balls. Leroy wants to maximize the volume of golf balls he ships out to retailers while keeping the shipping material to a minimum.

167. What must the dimensions of the packages of golf balls be in order for all of them to fit in a box that contains 1,177.68 cm^2 of cardboard?
 A. 3 cm × 3 cm × 13 cm
 B. 4 cm × 4 cm × 10 cm
 C. 5 cm × 5 cm × 11 cm
 D. 6 cm × 6 cm × 12 cm

168. Ana is a lifeguard at a swimming pool. She needs to rope off a 60 m² rectangular area of the pool for swimming lessons. To the nearest tenth of a meter, what is the minimum length of rope needed to enclose this area?

   A. 15.5 m
   B. 16.0 m
   C. 31.0 m
   D. 32.0 m

Use the following information to answer the next question.

A rectangular field is to be fenced off against one side of a school as illustrated.

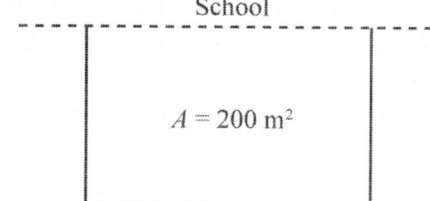

The cost of labor and materials to construct the three sides of the fence is $30/m.

169. If the area of the rectangular field must be 200 m², then the minimum cost of building the fence is

   A. $900
   B. $1,200
   C. $3,000
   D. $6,000

EXERCISE #2—APPLYING GEOMETRIC CONCEPTS
ANSWERS AND SOLUTIONS

159. C	162. 42	165. B	168. C
160. C	163. See solution	166. See solution	169. B
161. B	164. See solution	167. C	

159. C

Calculate the volume of the cylindrical water tower. The formula for determining the volume of a cylinder is $V_{cylinder} = \pi r^2 \times h$. Substitute 3.14 for π, 10 for r, 30 for h, and then solve.

$V_{cylinder} = \pi r^2 \times h$
$V_{cylinder} = 3.14(10)^2 \times 30$
$V_{cylinder} = 314 \times 30$
$V_{cylinder} = 9,420$

The cylindrical water tower can hold 9,420 m³ of water.

160. C

Step 1
Determine the radius of the cone's circular base.
$r = \dfrac{d}{2}$
$= \dfrac{4}{2}$
$= 2$ cm

Step 2
Determine the height of the cone.
$h_{cone} = h_{rocket} - h_{cylinder}$
$= 10 - 3$
$= 7$ cm

Step 3
Calculate the volume of the cone. Use 3.14 as an approximation to π.

$V_{cone} = \dfrac{\pi r^2 h}{3}$
$\cong \dfrac{(3.14)(2)^2(7)}{3}$
$\cong \dfrac{(3.14)(4)(7)}{3}$
$\cong \dfrac{87.92}{3}$
$\cong 29.3$ cm³

The cone at the top of the model rocket could be filled with 29.3 cm³ of sand.

161. B

Step 1
Determine the radius of the bottom snowball. Since the radius is equal to one-half the length of the diameter, the radius is $\dfrac{90}{2} = 45$ cm.

Step 2
Determine the volume, V, of the bottom snowball in terms of π by applying the formula for the volume of a sphere.

Substitute 45 for r in the formula $V = \dfrac{4}{3}\pi r^3$, and then solve for V.

$V = \dfrac{4}{3}\pi r^3$
$V = \dfrac{4}{3}\pi(45)^3$
$V = \dfrac{4}{3}\pi(91,125)$
$V = \dfrac{364,500\pi}{3}$
$V = 121,500\pi$

162. 42

The volume, V, of a pyramid can be determined by applying the formula $V = \dfrac{1}{3}(A_{base} \times h)$, where A_{base} is the area of the base and h is the height of the pyramid.

Step 1
Determine an expression for the area of the base of the pyramid.
If x represents the side length of the base of the pyramid, then the area of the base of the pyramid would be represented by the expression $x \times x$, or x^2.

Step 2
Determine the value of x.
Apply the formula $V = \frac{1}{3}(A_{base} \times h)$. Substitute 21,168 for V, x^2 for A_{base}, and 36 for h. Then, solve for x.

$$21{,}168 = \frac{1}{3}(x^2 \times 36)$$
$$21{,}168 = \frac{1}{3}(36x^2)$$
$$21{,}168 = 12x^2$$
$$\frac{21{,}168}{12} = x^2$$
$$1{,}764 = x^2$$
$$\sqrt{1{,}764} = x$$
$$42 = x$$

The side length of the base of the pyramid is 42 cm.

163.

Step 1
Calculate the length or width of the rectangle. Maximum area occurs when the rectangle becomes a square.
$$l = w = \frac{P}{4} = \frac{60}{4} = 15 \text{ m}$$

Step 2
Substitute in this value for length and width in the area formula.
$$A = l \times w$$
$$= 15 \times 15$$
$$= 225 \text{ m}^2$$

In order to produce a pen with an optimal area of 225 m², the sides must be 15 m long.

164.

A rectangle formed by adjusting the lengths of three sides has an optimal area when its length is twice its width.

Step 1
Determine the width.
Use the perimeter formula $P = 2w + l$, and substitute 16 for P and $2w$ for l.
$$P = 2w + l$$
$$16 = 2w + 2w$$
$$16 = 4w$$
$$16 = 4w$$
$$\frac{16}{4} = w$$
$$w = 4 \text{ m}$$

Step 2
Determine the length.
Substitute in the calculated value for width, $w = 4$.
$$l = 2w$$
$$l = 2(4)$$
$$l = 8 \text{ m}$$

The dimensions that produce the largest VIP area are a width of 4 m and a length of 8 m.

165. B

Minimum surface area occurs when the height of the cylinder is equal to the diameter of the cylinder.

Step 1
Convert all the units to the same measure.
Since volume is in units cubed, convert 6 L to 6,000 cm³.

Step 2
Substitute the given volume into the volume formula for a cylinder, and solve for the radius.
$$V_{cylinder} = 2\pi r^3$$
$$6{,}000 = 2 \times 3.14 \times r^3$$
$$\frac{6{,}000}{6.28} = \frac{6.28 \times r^3}{6.28}$$
$$955.4140127 = r^3$$
$$\sqrt[3]{955.4140127} = \sqrt[3]{r^3}$$
$$9.849 = r$$
$$r = 9.8 \text{ cm}$$

Step 3
Determine the height of the cylinder.
The height is equal to the diameter, which is equal to $2r$.
$$d = 2r$$
$$= 2 \times 9.8$$
$$= 19.6 \text{ cm}$$

The cylinder will have a height of 19.6 cm and a radius of 9.8 cm.

Step 4
Substitute the radius and height into the surface area formula for a cylinder.
$$SA_{cylinder} = 2\pi r^2 + 2\pi rh$$
$$= (2 \times 3.14 \times 9.8^2) + (2 \times 3.14 \times 9.8 \times 19.6)$$
$$= 603.1312 + 1{,}206.2624 = 1{,}809.4 \text{ cm}^2$$

The minimum surface area for the cylindrical container is 1,809.4 cm².

166.

Step 1
Calculate the volume of the larger item.
The shipping crate is the larger item.
$$V_{\text{shipping crate}} = lwh$$
$$= 30 \times 10 \times 20$$
$$= 6{,}000 \text{ cm}^3$$

Step 2
Calculate the volume of the smaller items.
The boxes are the smaller items.
$$V_{\text{box}} = lwh$$
$$= 5 \times 4 \times 3$$
$$= 60 \text{ cm}^3$$

Step 3
Divide the volume of the larger container by the volume of the smaller container.
$$\frac{6{,}000}{60} = 100$$
The maximum number of boxes that can fit into the shipping crate is 100.

167. C

Step 1
To determine s when the surface area is given, substitute the surface area into the surface area formula for a cube.
$$SA = 6s^2$$
$$1{,}177.68 = 6s^2$$
$$\frac{1{,}177.68}{6} = \frac{6s^2}{6}$$
$$196.28 = s^2$$
$$\sqrt{196.28} = \sqrt{s^2}$$
$$14.01 = s$$

Step 2
Determine the volume. Substitute the side length into the volume formula for a cube.
$$V = s^3$$
$$= (14.01)^3$$
$$= 2{,}749.9 \text{ cm}^3$$
$$= 2{,}750 \text{ cm}^3$$

Step 3
Calculate the volume of the individual package. Divide the volume of the shipping box by the number of packages that can fit inside it.
$$\frac{2{,}750}{10} = 275$$

Step 4
To determine which of the given alternatives contains the correct dimensions, calculate the volume of each alternative to see which has a volume of 275 cm³.
$3 \times 3 \times 13 = 117 \text{ cm}^3$
$4 \times 4 \times 10 = 160 \text{ cm}^3$
$5 \times 5 \times 11 = 275 \text{ cm}^3$
$6 \times 6 \times 12 = 432 \text{ cm}^3$
The dimensions of the packages of golf balls should be 5 cm × 5 cm × 11 cm.

168. C

The perimeter is represented by the rope needed to enclose the rectangular swimming area.
The minimum length of rope required to enclose the given area occurs when $P = 4\sqrt{A}$.

Substitute the area $(A = 60 \text{ m}^2)$ into the equation.
$$P = 4\sqrt{60}$$
$$\approx 4(7.746)$$
$$\approx 31.0 \text{ m}$$

The shortest rope required to enclose the given swimming area is 31.0 m.

169. B

The perimeter of the required fencing material is given by $P = 2w + l$ since there are only three sides of the fence that need to be built.

When the sum of the length of three sides of a rectangle is fixed, the minimum perimeter occurs when the length is two times the width ($l = 2w$).

Step 1
Determine the value of w by substituting the known values into the area formula for a rectangle and simplifying.
$$A = (l)(w)$$
Substitute $2w$ for l.
$$A = (2w)(w)$$
$$A = 2w^2$$
$$w^2 = \frac{A}{2}$$
$$w = \sqrt{\frac{A}{2}}$$

Substitute 200 m² for A.
$$w = \sqrt{\frac{200 \text{ m}^2}{2}}$$
$$w = \sqrt{100 \text{ m}^2}$$
$$w = 10 \text{ m}$$

Step 2
Determine the value of l.
Since $l = 2w$, then $l = 2(10 \text{ m}) = 20 \text{ m}$.

Step 3
Determine the perimeter of the fence by substituting the known values into the perimeter formula.
$P = 2w + l$
$= 2(10) + 20$
$= 20 + 20$
$= 40$ m

Step 4
Calculate the cost of building the fence.
$C = \$30/\text{m} \times 40 \text{ m} = \$1{,}200$
The minimum cost, C, to build this fence is $1,200.

General Triangles in Trigonometry

GENERAL TRIANGLES IN TRIGONOMETRY

Table of Correlations

Standard		Concepts	Exercise #1	Exercise #2
Unit2.5	Apply trigonometry to general triangles.			
G-SRT.9	*Derive the formula A = 1/2 ab sin(C) for the area of a triangle by drawing an auxiliary line from a vertex perpendicular to the opposite side.*	Calculating the Area of a Triangle Given One Angle and Two Adjacent Sides	170	179
G-SRT.10	*Prove the Laws of Sines and Cosines and use them to solve problems.*	Applying the Sine Law Using Acute Triangles	171	180
		Applying the Cosine Law Using Acute Triangles	172	181
		Applying the Sine Law Using Obtuse Triangles	173	182
		Applying the Cosine Law to Obtuse Triangles	174	183
G-SRT.11	*Understand and apply the Law of Sines and the Law of Cosines to find unknown measurements in right and non-right triangles.*	Solving Problems Using the Sine Law for Acute Triangles	175	184
		Solving Problems Using the Cosine Law for Acute Triangles	176	185
		Solving Problems Using Sine Laws for Obtuse Triangles	177	186
		Solving Problems Using Cosine Laws for Obtuse Triangles	178	187

G-SRT.9 Derive the formula A = 1/2 ab sin(C) for the area of a triangle by drawing an auxiliary line from a vertex perpendicular to the opposite side.

CALCULATING THE AREA OF A TRIANGLE GIVEN ONE ANGLE AND TWO ADJACENT SIDES

Sometimes, the area of a triangle is required, but the height of the triangle is not given or readily available. Without knowing the height (h) of the triangle, the usual area formulas $A = \dfrac{bh}{2}$ or $A = \dfrac{1}{2}bh$ (where b is the base) cannot be used.

With trigonometry, however, it is possible to derive another formula for the area of a triangle.

A NEW AREA FORMULA

A new formula for the area of the following triangle can be derived.

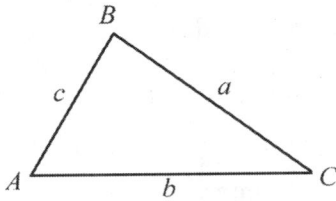

The object is to find an expression for the area of $\triangle ABC$ in terms of C, a, and b only.

Let h be the height of the triangle from vertex B to side AC.

$\sin C = \dfrac{h}{a}$

$a\sin C = h$

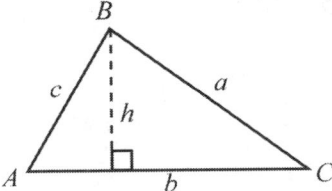

Use the area formula $A = \dfrac{1}{2}bh$, and substitute $h = a\sin C$ for h to derive a new area formula.

$A = \dfrac{1}{2}bh$

$ = \dfrac{1}{2}b(a\sin C)$

$ = \dfrac{1}{2}ab\sin C$

The area of a triangle can be found using the formula $A = \dfrac{1}{2}ab\sin C$, where a and b are side lengths of a triangle, and C is the included angle.

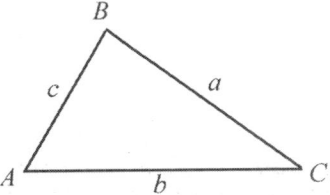

The area formula works using any two known sides and the included angle, as shown in the following formulas:

$A = \dfrac{1}{2}ab\sin C$

$A = \dfrac{1}{2}ac\sin B$

$A = \dfrac{1}{2}bc\sin A$

This particular version of the area formula is not frequently used because of the potential for confusion caused by the use of A to mean area on the left side of formula and to refer to angle A on the right side of the formula.

Example

A seamstress has been commissioned to create 500 mini-pennants for a local sports team. The pennant is designed to have one side measuring 8 cm, another side measuring 10 cm, and the angle between the two sides measuring 50°, as illustrated in the diagram.

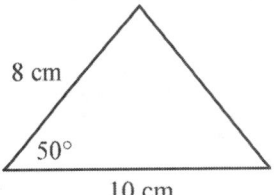

To the nearest square centimeter, what is the minimum amount of fabric required to create the 500 pennants?

Solution

Step 1

Calculate the area of one pennant.
Because the height of the triangle is not given but the lengths of two sides and the included angle are known, use the formula

$A = \frac{1}{2}ac\sin(B)$.

$A = \frac{1}{2}ac\sin(B)$
$= \frac{1}{2}(8 \text{ cm})(10 \text{ cm})\sin(50°)$
$\approx 30.6 \text{ cm}^2$

Step 2

Calculate the amount of material required to create 500 pennants.
Multiply the area of one pennant by 500.
$500 \times 30.6 \text{ cm}^2 = 15,320.1 \text{ cm}^2$

Since 15,320 cm^2 will not be enough fabric for the pennants, the amount must be rounded up. To the nearest square centimeter, the minimum amount of fabric required to create 500 mini-pennants is 15,321 cm^2.

G-SRT.10 Prove the Laws of Sines and Cosines and use them to solve problems.

APPLYING THE SINE LAW USING ACUTE TRIANGLES

The sine law can be used to calculate the measures of unknown side lengths or angles in non-right triangles provided that at least three other measures are given.

Since the sine law uses two ratios at a time, only one unknown and three known quantities must be given.

Either of the following triangles gives enough information to determine the measure of side *a*.

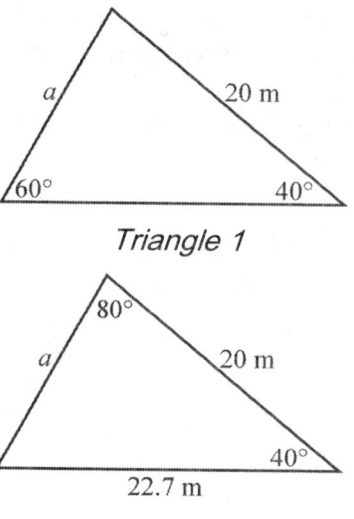

Triangle 1

Triangle 2

In triangle 1, the measure of the angle opposite to side *a* is 40°, and the angle-side pair is 60° and 20 m.

In triangle 2, the measure of the angle opposite to side *a* is 40°, and the angle-side pair is 80° and 22.7 m.

In order to solve any problems involving triangles, it is helpful to label the triangle first.

For example, once triangle 1 has been labeled with its known values, make the appropriate substitutions into the sine law, and solve for *a*.

$$\frac{a}{\sin A} = \frac{b}{\sin B}$$
$$\frac{a}{\sin 40°} = \frac{20}{\sin 60°}$$
$$a = \frac{20\sin 40°}{\sin 60°}$$
$$\approx 14.8 \text{ m}$$

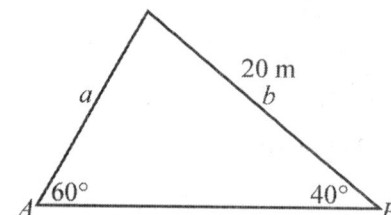

The sine law can be used to calculate the measure of an unknown angle in an acute triangle.

In order to determine the measure of an unknown angle, the following information is required:

- The measure of the side opposite the unknown angle
- Another complete angle-side pair

Example

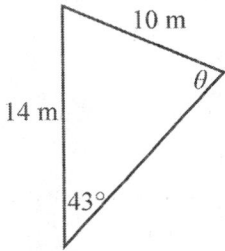

Determine the measure of the unknown angle θ, rounded to the nearest tenth of a degree. _____°

Solution

Step 1
Label the diagram with the appropriate variables.

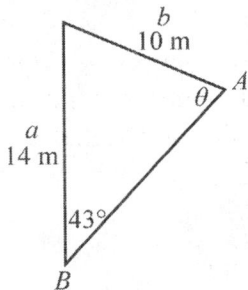

Step 2
Apply the sine law and solve for θ.
$$\frac{\sin A}{a} = \frac{\sin B}{b}$$
$$\frac{\sin \theta}{14} = \frac{\sin 43°}{10}$$
$$\sin \theta = \frac{14 \sin 43°}{10}$$
$$\theta = \sin^{-1}(0.9548)$$
$$\theta = 72.71°$$

Rounded to the nearest tenth of a degree, the measure of θ is 72.7°.

The sine law can be used to calculate the measure of a side length in an acute triangle.

In order to determine the measure of a side length, the following information is required:

- The angle opposite to the unknown side
- Another complete angle-side pair

Example
The following triangle is given.

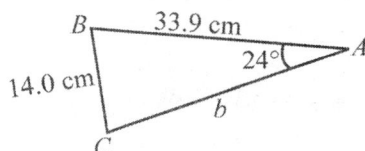

Determine the length of side b, to the nearest tenth centimeter.

Solution

Since a known pair (a side with its corresponding opposite angle) is given, use the sine law.

Step 1
Find $\angle C$ using its corresponding opposite side.
$$\frac{a}{\sin A} = \frac{c}{\sin C}$$
$$\frac{14.0}{\sin 24°} = \frac{33.9}{\sin C}$$
$$14.0(\sin C) = 33.9(\sin 24°)$$
$$\sin C = \frac{33.9(\sin 24°)}{14.0}$$
$$\sin C = 0.9848837286...$$
$$\angle C = \sin^{-1}(0.9848837286...)$$
$$\angle C \approx 80.0°$$

Step 2
Find $\angle B$.
Since the sum of the measures of all three angles within a triangle is equal to 180°, the measure of $\angle B$ can be calculated as follows:
$$\angle B = 180° - 80.0° - 24°$$
$$\angle B = 76°$$

Step 3

Find side b by using its corresponding opposite angle B.

$$\frac{a}{\sin A} = \frac{b}{\sin B}$$
$$\frac{14.0}{\sin 24°} = \frac{b}{\sin 76°}$$
$$14.0(\sin 76°) = b(\sin 24°)$$
$$\frac{14.0(\sin 76°)}{\sin 24°} = b$$
$$33.39787649\ldots = b$$
$$b \approx 33.4$$

Therefore, the length of side b, to the nearest tenth centimeter, is 33.4 cm.

APPLYING THE COSINE LAW USING ACUTE TRIANGLES

The cosine law can be used to calculate either the measures of unknown side lengths or unknown angles in non-right triangles, provided that at least three other measures are given. Use the cosine law primarily when the measures of an angle-side pair are not given.

The measure to be calculated depends on the following information:

- If the measures of all three sides of the triangle are given, the measures of any of the angles can be calculated using the cosine law in the form of $\cos A = \frac{b^2 + c^2 - a^2}{2bc}$.

- If the measures of two sides of the triangle and the measure of the angle contained between those sides are given, the measure of the unknown side can be calculated using the cosine law in the form of $a^2 = b^2 + c^2 - 2bc\cos A$.

Example

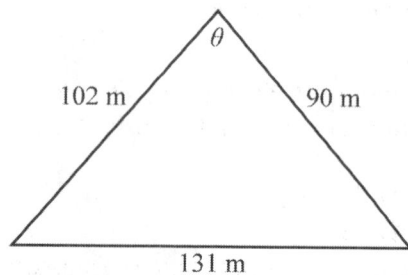

Rounded to the nearest tenth of a degree, calculate the measure of the unknown angle on the given triangle.

Solution

The value of $\angle A$ is θ, the measure of side a is 131 m, and sides b and c are interchangeable.

Substitute the known values into the cosine law and solve for θ:

$$\cos A = \frac{b^2 + c^2 - a^2}{2bc}$$
$$\cos \theta = \frac{102^2 + 90^2 - 131^2}{2(102)(90)}$$
$$\cos \theta = \frac{1,343}{18,360}$$
$$\theta = \cos^{-1}\left(\frac{1,343}{18,360}\right)$$
$$\theta \approx 85.805°$$

Rounded to the nearest tenth of a degree, the measure of θ is 85.8°.

APPLYING THE SINE LAW USING OBTUSE TRIANGLES

The sine law states that in triangle ABC, $\frac{\sin A}{a} = \frac{\sin B}{b} = \frac{\sin C}{c}$, where a, b, and c represent the sides of the triangle. The sine law can also be written as $\frac{a}{\sin A} = \frac{b}{\sin B} = \frac{c}{\sin C}$.

In order to solve any problems that involve triangles, it is helpful to label the triangle first.

Since the sine law uses two ratios at a time, three known quantities and only one unknown must be given.

Use the sine law when the measures of two angles and the length of one side are supplied.

The measure of the third angle must first be determined using the property that the sum of the measures of the angles in a triangle is 180°. Then, use the sine law to determine the length of either missing side. The length of the third side can be determined from either the sine law or the cosine law. If the length of the side between the angles is given, the situation is called angle-side-angle (ASA). If the length of one of the sides that is not between the two angles is given, the situation is called angle-angle-side (AAS).

In order to determine the measure of a side length, you need to know the measure of the angle opposite to the unknown side and another complete angle-side pair.

Example

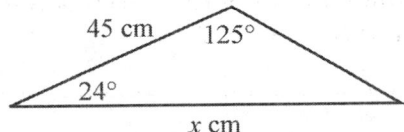

Determine the measure of the missing side, x, rounded to the nearest tenth of a centimeter.

Solution

The angle opposite the unknown side length is given, but the measure of the angle opposite 45 cm is not.

Step 1
Calculate the measure of the unknown angle by subtracting the known angles from 180°.
$180° - 125° - 24° = 31°$

Step 2
Apply the sine law.
$$\frac{\sin A}{a} = \frac{\sin B}{b}$$
$$\frac{\sin 125°}{x} = \frac{\sin 31°}{45}$$
$x \sin 31° = 45 \sin 125°$
$$x = \frac{45 \sin 125°}{\sin 31°}$$
$x \approx 71.57 \text{ cm}$

Rounded to the nearest tenth of a centimeter, the measure of side x is 71.6 cm.

Use the sine law when the lengths of two sides and the measure of one of the angles that is not between the two given sides are supplied. This is called side-side-angle (SSA). The sine law must be used as the first step to find the measure of a missing angle. However, the solution may not be unique, or there may be no solution. This situation is called the ambiguous case.

In order to determine the measure of an unknown angle, you need to know the measure of the side opposite the unknown angle and another complete angle-side pair.

Example

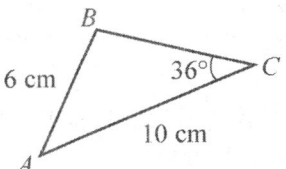

Triangle *ABC* is given.

Determine the measure of ∠*A*, rounded to the nearest degree.

Solution

Step 1
Apply the sine law to determine the measure of ∠*B*.

The side that measures 6 cm is opposite the angle that measures 36°. The side that measures 10 cm is opposite ∠*B*.
$$\frac{6}{\sin 36°} = \frac{10}{\sin \angle B}$$
$6 \sin \angle B = 10 \sin 36°$
$$\sin \angle B = \frac{10 \sin 36°}{6}$$
$$\angle B = \sin^{-1}\left(\frac{5 \sin 36°}{3}\right)$$
$\angle B \approx 78.42°$

The value determined for ∠*B*, 78.42°, is too small because according to the given diagram ∠*B* is an obtuse angle.

Step 2
Determine the other possible value for ∠*B*. Subtract 180° by 78.42° to find the other value of ∠*B*.
$\angle B \approx 180° - 78.42°$
$\angle B \approx 101.58°$

This is a more reasonable measurement for the given diagram.

Step 3
Determine the measure of $\angle A$.
Apply the property that the sum of the interior angles of a triangle is equal to 180°.
$\angle A = 180° - (\angle B + \angle C)$
$\angle A \approx 180° - (101.58° + 36°)$
$\angle A \approx 180° - (137.58°)$
$\angle A \approx 42.42°$

Therefore, rounded to the nearest degree, the measure of $\angle A$ is 42°.

APPLYING THE COSINE LAW TO OBTUSE TRIANGLES

The cosine law can be used to calculate either the measures of unknown side lengths or the measures of unknown angles in non-right triangles, provided that at least three other measures are given. You can use the cosine law primarily when the measures of an angle-side pair are not given.

The measure to be calculated depends on the following information:

- If the measures of all three sides of the triangle are given, the measures of any of the angles can be calculated by using the cosine law in the form $\cos A = \dfrac{b^2 + c^2 - a^2}{2bc}$.

- If the measures of two sides of the triangle and the measure of the angle contained between those sides are given, the measure of the unknown side can be calculated by using the cosine law in the form $a^2 = b^2 + c^2 - 2bc\cos A$.

Example
Expressing all values to the nearest tenth, solve triangle ABC if $a = 15$ cm, $b = 8$ cm, and $\angle C = 55°$.

Solution
Step 1
Sketch the triangle.
The sketch of the triangle shows that this situation is SAS. The lengths of two sides and the measure of the included angle are given.

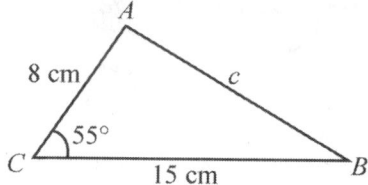

Step 2
Determine the measure of the third side using the cosine law.
$c^2 = a^2 + b^2 - 2ab\cos C$
$c^2 = (15)^2 + (8)^2 - 2(15)(8)\cos 55°$
$c^2 \approx 151.34$
$c \approx 12.3$

Step 3
Determine the measure of either $\angle A$ or $\angle B$.
$\angle A$ will be determined using the cosine law.
$\cos A = \dfrac{b^2 + c^2 - a^2}{2bc}$
$\cos A = \dfrac{(8)^2 + (12.3)^2 - (15)^2}{2(8)(12.3)}$
$\cos A \approx -0.049$
$A \approx \cos^{-1}(-0.049)$
$A \approx 92.8°$

Step 4
Determine the measure of $\angle B$.
$\angle A + \angle B + \angle C = 180°$
$92.8° + \angle B + 55° \approx 180°$
$\angle B \approx 32.2°$

The missing measures of triangle ABC are $\angle A = 92.8°$, $\angle B = 32.2°$, and $c = 12.3$ cm.

Example

Expressing all values to the nearest tenth, solve triangle ABC if a = 13 cm, b = 22 cm, and c = 11 cm.

Solution

Step 1
Sketch the triangle.
Since the lengths of all three sides are given, this situation is side-side-side (SSS).

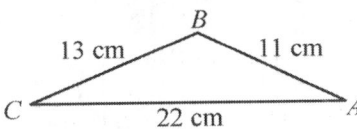

Step 2
Determine the measure of any angle using the cosine law.
∠A will be determined.

$$\cos A = \frac{b^2 + c^2 - a^2}{2bc}$$
$$\cos A = \frac{(22)^2 + (11)^2 - (13)^2}{2(22)(11)}$$
$$\cos A \approx 0.9008$$
$$A \approx \cos^{-1}(0.9008)$$
$$A \approx 25.7°$$

Step 3
Determine the measure of either ∠B or ∠C.
∠B will be determined using the cosine law.

$$\cos B = \frac{a^2 + c^2 - b^2}{2ac}$$
$$\cos B = \frac{(13)^2 + (11)^2 - (22)^2}{2(13)(11)}$$
$$\cos B \approx -0.6783$$
$$B \approx \cos^{-1}(-0.6783)$$
$$B \approx 132.7°$$

Step 4
Determine the measure of ∠C.
$$\angle A + \angle B + \angle C = 180°$$
$$25.7° + 132.7° + \angle C \approx 180°$$
$$\angle C \approx 21.6°$$

The measures of the missing angles are ∠A = 25.7°, ∠B = 132.7°, and ∠C = 21.6°.

G-SRT.11 Understand and apply the Law of Sines and the Law of Cosines to find unknown measurements in right and non-right triangles.

SOLVING PROBLEMS USING THE SINE LAW FOR ACUTE TRIANGLES

Problems involving acute triangles can be solved by following these general steps:

1. Read the problem carefully. Determine which measures are given and which measure needs to be calculated.
2. If a diagram is not given, draw a sketch to represent the situation presented in the problem.
3. Make substitutions into the sine law, and use correct algebraic steps to solve for the unknown value. Avoid or minimize rounding until the last step.
4. Check your calculations.
5. Write a concluding statement.

Example

During hockey practice, players performed the following drill: Player A passed the puck to player B, who was 12 m away. Player B redirected the puck at an angle of 40° to player C. Player C then passed the puck back to player A, who was standing 9 m away.

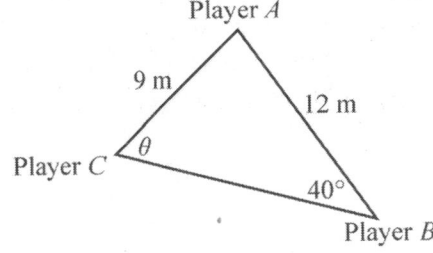

To the nearest degree, determine the measure of angle θ.

Solution

Since it is not a side-side-side situation, apply the sine law. The side measuring 9 m is opposite the 40° angle, and the side measuring 12 m is opposite angle θ. Solve for θ as follows:

$$\frac{9}{\sin 40°} = \frac{12}{\sin \theta}$$
$$9\sin \theta = 12\sin 40°$$
$$\frac{9\sin \theta}{9} = \frac{12\sin 40°}{9}$$
$$\sin \theta = \frac{12\sin 40°}{9}$$
$$\theta \approx 58.99°$$

The measure of angle θ, to the nearest degree, is 59°.

Example

A surveyor needs to find the length, b, of a bridge across a pond in a park.

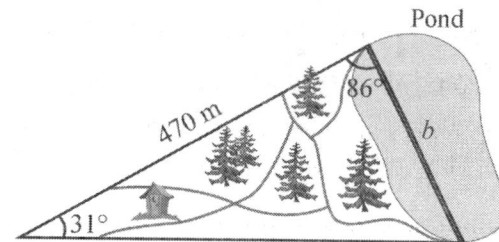

Explain which trigonometric law you would use to find the length of the bridge, b. Then, use the trigonometric law to find the length of the bridge, to the nearest whole meter.

Solution

The missing angle in the triangle can be easily determined, since the sum of the measures of the angles must be equal to 180°. This will provide a known pair with the side 470 m. Therefore, the sine law would be the correct formula to use to find the length of the bridge, b.

First, find the missing angle, A.
$\angle A = 180° - 86° - 31° = 63°$

Next, let side $a = 470$ m and $\angle B = 31°$ in the given triangle. Then, use the sine law to find the value of b.

$$\frac{a}{\sin A} = \frac{b}{\sin B}$$
$$\frac{470}{\sin 63°} = \frac{b}{\sin 31°}$$
$$\frac{470(\sin 31°)}{\sin 63°} = b$$
$$b = 271.6791501$$

The length of the bridge, b, to the nearest whole meter, is 272 m.

SOLVING PROBLEMS USING THE COSINE LAW FOR ACUTE TRIANGLES

Problems involving acute triangles can be solved by following these general steps:

1. Read the problem carefully. Determine which measures are given and which measure needs to be calculated.
2. If a diagram is not given, draw a sketch to represent the situation presented in the problem.
3. Make substitutions into the cosine law formula, and use correct algebraic steps to solve for the unknown value. Avoid or minimize rounding until the last step.
4. Check your calculations.
5. Write a concluding statement.

Example

A radar tracking station locates two boats: a fishing boat at a distance of 3.4 km from the tracking station, and a passenger ferry at a distance of 5.6 km from the tracking station. From the tracking station, the angle between the line of sight to the two boats is 86°. Determine the distance between the two boats to the nearest tenth of a kilometer.

Solution

Draw a diagram representing the situation. Let x represent the distance between the two boats.

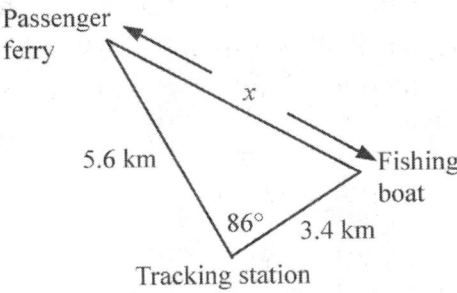

Since the problem is a side-angle-side situation, apply the cosine law. Side x is opposite the 86° angle; therefore, solve for x as follows:

$a^2 = b^2 + c^2 - 2bc\cos A$
$x^2 = 5.6^2 + 3.4^2 - 2(5.6)(3.4)\cos 86°$
$x^2 \approx 31.36 + 11.56 - 2.66$
$x^2 \approx 40.26$
$x \approx \sqrt{40.26}$
$x \approx 6.345$ km

The distance between the fishing boat and the passenger ferry, to the nearest tenth of a kilometer, is 6.3 km.

Example

To display the Stanley Cup, staff at a hockey arena roped off a triangular area and installed a security camera, as illustrated in the given diagram.

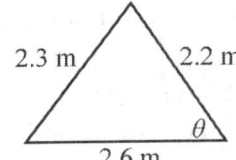

The security camera, located at θ, moves continuously between the two ropes, which measure 2.2 m and 2.6 m, respectively.

To the nearest tenth of a degree, determine the measure of angle θ.

Solution

Since this is a side-side-side situation, apply the cosine law. Angle θ is opposite the side measuring 2.3 m, so solve for θ as follows:

$\cos A = \dfrac{b^2 + c^2 - a^2}{2bc}$

$\cos \theta = \dfrac{2.6^2 + 2.2^2 - 2.3^2}{2(2.6)(2.2)}$

$\cos \theta = \dfrac{6.76 + 4.84 - 5.29}{11.44}$

$\cos \theta = \dfrac{6.31}{11.44}$

$\theta \approx 56.525°$

To the nearest tenth of a degree, the measure of angle θ is 56.5°.

Solving Problems Using Sine Laws for Obtuse Triangles

Problems involving obtuse triangles can be solved by following these general steps:

1. Read the problem carefully. Determine what measures are given and what measure needs to be calculated.
2. If a diagram is not given, draw a sketch to represent the situation presented in the problem.
3. Make substitutions into the sine law, and use correct algebraic steps to solve for the unknown value. Avoid or minimize rounding until the last step.
4. Check your calculations for the ambiguous case.
5. Write a concluding statement.

Example

The given image shows where three basketball players were standing as they performed a practice drill. One player stood at point *A* and passed the ball to another player standing at point *B*, which was 6 m away. The player standing at *B* then passed it at an angle of 20° to a player standing at point *C*. The player standing at *C* then passed the ball back to the player standing at point *A*, which was 3 m away.

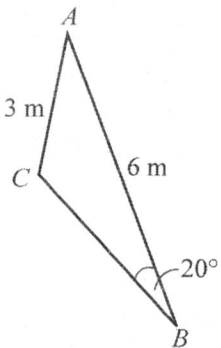

To the nearest degree, determine the measure of ∠*A*.

Solution

Step 1
Apply the sine law to determine the measure of ∠*C*.

The side measuring 3 m is opposite the 20° angle, and the side measuring 6 m is opposite ∠*C*. Solve for ∠*C*.

$$\frac{3}{\sin 20°} = \frac{6}{\sin \angle C}$$
$3\sin \angle C = 6\sin 20°$
$\sin \angle C = 2\sin 20°$
$\angle C = \sin^{-1}(2\sin 20°)$
$\angle C \approx 43.16°$

Looking at the given diagram, the value determined for ∠*C* is too small because an obtuse angle is shown in the diagram. This is a scenario where the ambiguous case is possible.

Step 2
Determine the other possible value of ∠*C*.
Subtract 180° by 43.16° to find the other value of ∠*C*.
$\angle C \approx 180° - 43.16°$
$\angle C \approx 136.84°$
This is a more reasonable measurement for the given diagram.

Step 3
Determine the measure of ∠*A*.
Apply the property that the sum of the interior angles of a triangle is equal to 180°.
$\angle A = 180° - (\angle B + \angle C)$
$\angle A \approx 180° - (20° + 136.84°)$
$\angle A \approx 180° - (156.84°)$
$\angle A \approx 23.16°$
Rounded to the nearest degree, the measure of ∠*A* is 23°.

Example

A golfer at point *T* on the given diagram wishes to sink his golf ball in a hole directly on the other side of a pond at point *H*. The golfer has two options. He can play two low-risk shots (one from point *T* to point *A* and another from point *A* to point *H*) or he can play a high-risk shot and attempt to shoot directly from point *T* to point *H*. The golfer estimates that the distance from point *T* to point *A* is 175 m, the measure of angle *ATH* is 45°, and the measure of angle *TAH* is 95°.

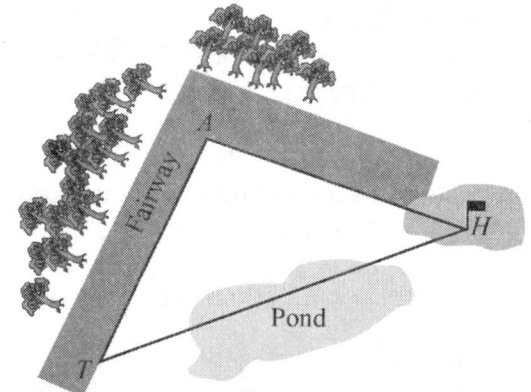

To the nearest meter, what is the distance from point *T* to point *H*?

Solution

Step 1
Determine the measure of angle *AHT*.
$\angle AHT = 180° - (\angle ATH + \angle TAH)$
$\angle AHT = 180° - (45° + 95°)$
$\angle AHT = 40°$

Step 2
Use the sine law to determine the distance from point T to point H.

$$\frac{TH}{\sin TAH} = \frac{TA}{\sin AHT}$$

$$\frac{TH}{\sin 95°} = \frac{175}{\sin 40°}$$

$$TH = \frac{175\sin 95°}{\sin 40°}$$

$$TH = 271.2156699\ldots$$

Step 3
Round the answer to the neatest meter.
The distance from point T to point H is about 271 m.

SOLVING PROBLEMS USING COSINE LAWS FOR OBTUSE TRIANGLES

Problems that involve obtuse triangles can be solved by following these general steps:

1. Read the problem carefully. Determine which measures are given and which measure needs to be calculated.
2. If a diagram is not given, draw a sketch to represent the situation presented in the problem.
3. Make substitutions into the cosine law formula, and use correct algebraic steps to solve for the unknown value. Avoid or minimize rounding until the last step.
4. Write a concluding statement.

Example
To navigate his sailboat home at night, a sailor uses a lighthouse as a reference point. He is 1 km away from the lighthouse, and the lighthouse is 2 km away from the harbor, as shown.

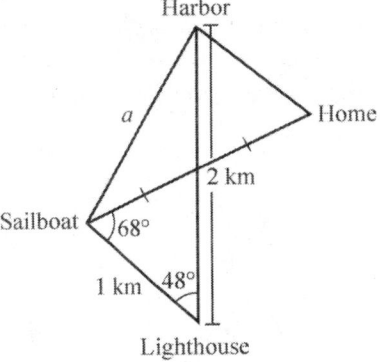

To the nearest tenth of a kilometer, calculate the distance from the sailboat to the harbor.

Solution
Step 1
Draw a diagram.
The sailboat is denoted as B, the lighthouse as A, and the harbor as C.

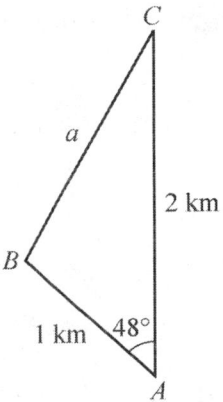

Step 2
Since the triangle is not a right triangle and the measures of two sides and an included angle are known, use the cosine law to solve for a.

$$a^2 = b^2 + c^2 - 2bc(\cos A)$$
$$a^2 = 2^2 + 1^2 - 2(2)(1)\cos 48°$$
$$a^2 \approx 2.3235$$
$$a \approx 1.5 \text{ km}$$

The distance from the sailboat to the harbor is approximately 1.5 km.

Example

From the top of a 100 m fire tower, a fire ranger at point *R* observes smoke coming from two separate fires. The angle of elevation from Fire *A* is 5° and from Fire *B* it is 3°. The angle that the two fires make with the base of the tower, *T*, is 87°.

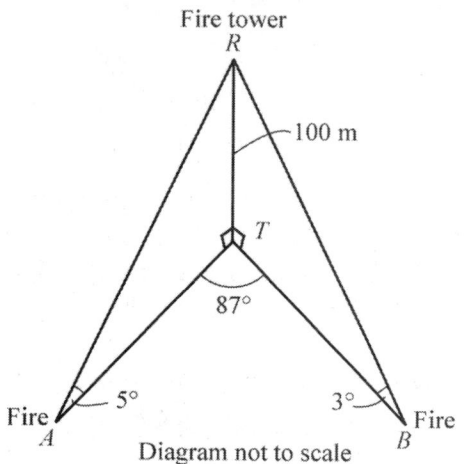

To the nearest meter, what is the distance from Fire *A* to Fire *B*?

Solution

Step 1
Draw a diagram, and label it as shown.

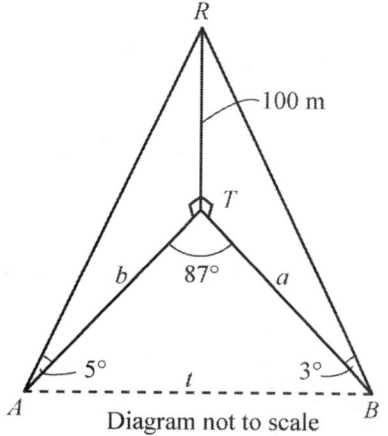

Step 2
Solve for sides *a* and *b*.
Since $\triangle ART$ and $\triangle BRT$ are right triangles, use the primary trigonometric ratios to solve for *a* and *b*.

Solve for *a* using the tangent ratio.

$$\tan \theta = \frac{\text{opposite}}{\text{adjacent}}$$

$$\tan 3° = \frac{100}{a}$$

$$a = \frac{100}{\tan 3°}$$

$$a \approx 1{,}908 \text{ m}$$

Solve for *b* using the tangent ratio.

$$\tan \theta = \frac{\text{opposite}}{\text{adjacent}}$$

$$\tan 5° = \frac{100}{b}$$

$$b = \frac{100}{\tan 5°}$$

$$b \approx 1{,}143 \text{ m}$$

Step 3
Since two sides and the angle between the two sides are known, solve for *t* in $\triangle ATB$ using the cosine law $t^2 = a^2 + b^2 - 2ab(\cos T)$.

$$t^2 = a^2 + b^2 - 2ab(\cos T)$$
$$t^2 \approx 1{,}908^2 + 1{,}143^2 - 2(1{,}908)(1{,}143)\cos 87°$$
$$t^2 \approx 4{,}946{,}913 - 228{,}273.1123$$
$$t^2 \approx 4{,}718{,}639.888$$
$$t \approx 2{,}172 \text{ m}$$

The distance from Fire *A* to Fire *B* is 2,172 m.

EXERCISE #1—GENERAL TRIANGLES IN TRIGONOMETRY

Use the following information to answer the next question.

> Along a straight stretch of highway, there are two access roads that lead to a general store. The distance from the highway to the general store along one of the access roads is 3.7 mi. The distance from the highway to the general store along the other access road is 5.4 mi.

170. If the area of the region bordered by the highway and the two access roads is 9.5 mi^2, what is the angle between the two access roads, expressed to the nearest tenth of a degree?

  A. 28.4°
  B. 36.0°
  C. 68.4°
  D. 72.0°

Use the following information to answer the next question.

> The measure of side p of $\triangle PQR$ is 25 cm long. The measure of $\angle P$ is 55°, and the measure of $\angle R$ is 40°.

171. The measure of the longest side in $\triangle PQR$, expressed to the nearest tenth, is about _____ cm.

Use the following information to answer the next question.

> A student is asked to solve $\triangle ABC$. In $\triangle ABC$, a = 15 cm, b = 18 cm, and $\angle C$ = 48°.

172. After sketching the triangle, the next step in the student's solution is to determine the measure of

  A. side AB using the cosine law
  B. angle A using the cosine law
  C. side AB using the sine law
  D. angle A using the sine law

Use the following information to answer the next question.

> Triangle ABC is shown.

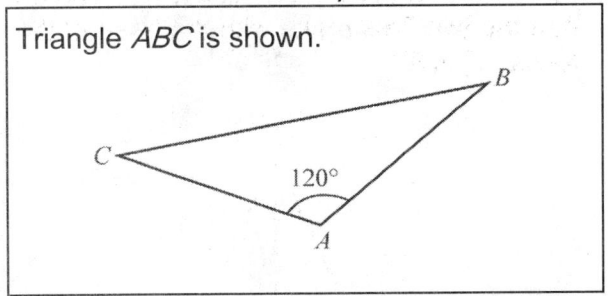

173. If the length of BC is 52 cm and the length of AB is 30 cm, the measure of $\angle B$, to the nearest tenth of a degree, is _____°.

Use the following information to answer the next question.

> Triangle ABC is shown.

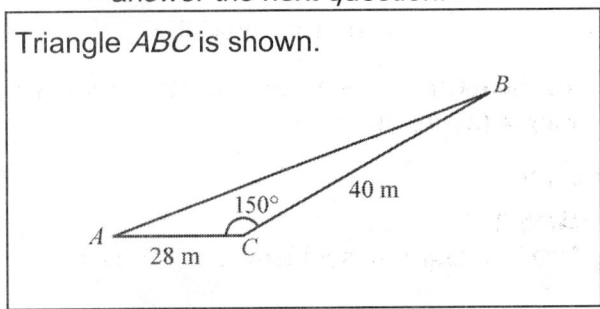

174. What is the length of AB?

  A. 65.8 m
  B. 68.2 m
  C. 70.7 m
  D. 73.1 m

Use the following information to answer the next question.

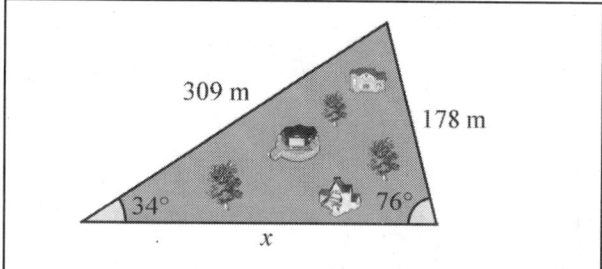

175. An equation that could be used to solve for the length, in meters, of side x in the given diagram is

A. $x = \dfrac{(309)\sin 70°}{\sin 76°}$

B. $x = \dfrac{(178)\sin 70°}{\sin 76°}$

C. $x = \sqrt{309^2 + 178^2 - 2(309)(178)\cos 34°}$

D. $x = \sqrt{309^2 + 178^2 - 2(392)(178)\cos 76°}$

Use the following information to answer the next question.

A weather balloon is flying in a field outside of London, Ontario. One end of a lightweight rope is attached to the base of the weather balloon, and the other end of the rope is anchored to the ground at point P. On a windy day, Rachel decides to determine the length of the rope, x, between P and the connection point located at the base of the weather balloon. She locates two points, A and B, that are 200 m apart, and records the measurements shown in the diagram.

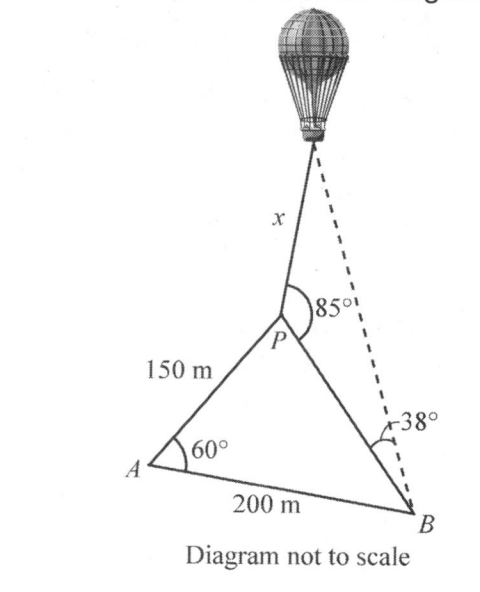

Diagram not to scale

176. The value of x, to the nearest meter, is

A. 128 m B. 132 m
C. 136 m D. 140 m

Use the following information to answer the next question.

At 4:00 P.M., the distance between the tip of the minute hand and the tip of the hour hand on a clock is 20 cm.

177. If the length of the minute hand is 15 cm, then the approximate length of the hour hand is

A. 5.00 cm B. 7.71 cm
C. 13.23 cm D. 15.00 cm

Use the following information to answer the next question.

The given diagram shows a triangle in three dimensions.

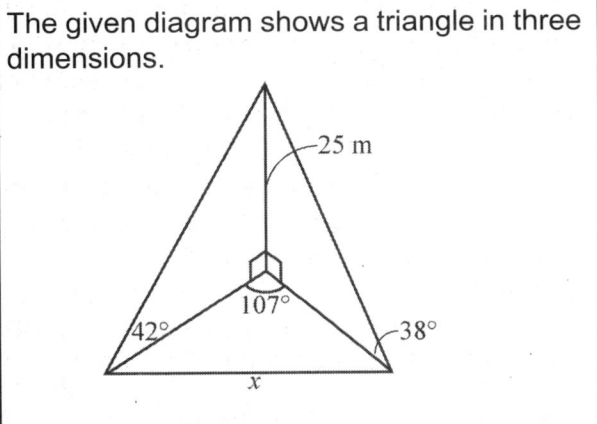

178. To the nearest tenth of a meter, the length of x is _____ m.

EXERCISE #1—GENERAL TRIANGLES IN TRIGONOMETRY
ANSWERS AND SOLUTIONS

170. D	173. 30.0	176. B
171. 30.4	174. A	177. B
172. A	175. A	178. 48.1

170. D

Draw a sketch to represent the triangle.

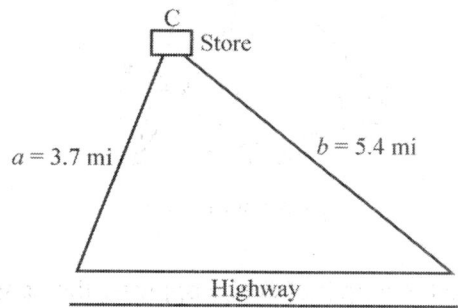

The area and lengths of two sides of a triangle are given. The angle, C, between the two known sides, a and b, can be calculated using the area formula $A = \frac{1}{2}ab\sin C$.

$$A = \frac{1}{2}ab\sin C$$
$$9.5 = \frac{1}{2}(3.7)(5.4)\sin C$$
$$\frac{9.5}{\frac{1}{2}(3.7)(5.4)} = \sin C$$
$$72.0° \approx C$$

The angle between the two access roads is approximately 72.0°.

171. 30.4

Step 1
Sketch the triangle.
The sketch of the triangle shows that this situation is Angle-Angle-Side (AAS). The measures of two angles and the length of a non-included side are given.

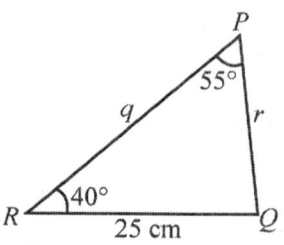

Step 2
Determine the measure of ∠Q.
∠P + ∠Q + ∠R = 180°
55° + ∠Q + 40° = 180°
∠Q = 180° − 55° − 40°
∠Q = 85°

Step 3
Determine the length of the longest side using the sine law. The longest side is opposite the largest angle. Since ∠Q is the largest angle, PR is the longest side.

$$\frac{q}{\sin Q} = \frac{p}{\sin P}$$
$$\frac{q}{\sin 85°} = \frac{25}{\sin 55°}$$
$$q = \frac{25\sin 85°}{\sin 55°}$$
$$q \approx 30.4$$

The longest side has a measure of about 30.4 cm.

172. A

Step 1
Sketch the triangle.

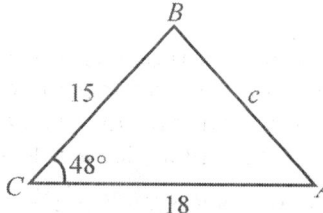

The sketch shows that the situation is side-angle-side (SAS).

Step 2
Determine the next step in the solution.
When the situation is SAS, the next step is to determine the length of the missing side using the cosine law. In this case, side AB will be determined using the cosine law.

173. 30.0

Step 1
Determine the measure of ∠C by applying the sine law.
$$\frac{\sin \angle C}{30 \text{ cm}} = \frac{\sin 120°}{52 \text{ cm}}$$
$$\sin \angle C = \frac{(30 \text{ cm})(\sin 120°)}{52 \text{ cm}}$$
$$\angle C = \sin^{-1}\left(\frac{(30 \text{ cm})(\sin 120°)}{52 \text{ cm}}\right)$$
$$\angle C = \sin^{-1}(0.49963...)$$
$$\angle C \approx 29.9755°$$

Step 2
Determine the measure of ∠B.
Since the sum of all angles in a triangle is 180°, subtract the sum of the two known angles from 180°.
$\angle B = 180° - (\angle A + \angle C)$
$\angle B \approx 180° - (120° + 29.9755°)$
$\angle B \approx 180° - 149.9755°$
$\angle B \approx 30.0245°$
$\angle B \approx 30.0°$
To the nearest tenth of a degree, the measure of ∠B is 30.0°.

174. A

Determine the length of AB by using the cosine law.
$AB^2 = BC^2 + AC^2 - 2(BC)(AC)\cos C$
$AB^2 = (40)^2 + (28)^2 - 2(40)(28)\cos 150°$
$AB^2 \approx 4,323.8969$
$AB \approx 65.8 \text{ m}$

175. A

Alternative C and D make incorrect use of the Cosine Law because there is no contained angle in between the given sides. To find side x using the Sine Law, the angle opposite of x, plus a side and its opposite angle are used. Therefore, $\frac{309}{\sin 76°} = \frac{x}{\sin 70°}$.

Then, solving for x:
$$x = \frac{(309)\sin 70°}{\sin 76°}$$

176. B

Step 1
Label the diagram as shown:

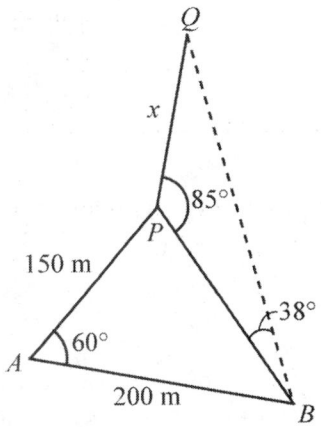

Diagram not to scale

Step 2
Determine the length of BP by applying the cosine law as follows:
$a^2 = b^2 + c^2 - 2bc\cos A$
$(BP)^2 = 150^2 + 200^2 - 2(150)(200)\cos 60$
$(BP)^2 = 22,500 + 40,000 - 30,000$
$(BP)^2 = 32,500$
$BP \approx 180.28 \text{ m}$

Step 3
Calculate the measure of ∠Q.
$180° - 85° - 38° = 57°$

Step 4
Calculate the value of x by applying the sine law as follows:
$$\frac{x}{\sin B} = \frac{BP}{\sin Q}$$
$$\frac{x}{\sin 38°} = \frac{180.28}{\sin 57°}$$
$$x = \frac{180.28(\sin 38°)}{\sin 57°}$$
$$x \approx 132.34 \text{ m}$$

The value of x, rounded to the nearest meter, is 132 m.

177. B

Step 1
Draw and label a diagram that represents the situation.

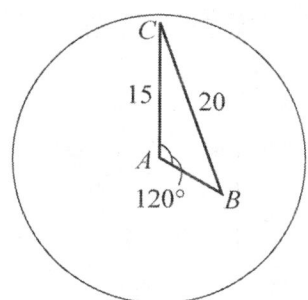

Step 2
Find the measures of angles B and C.
Since two sides and an angle opposite to one of the sides are given, apply the law of sines.

$$\frac{a}{\sin A} = \frac{b}{\sin B}$$

$$\frac{20}{\sin 120°} = \frac{15}{\sin B}$$

$$\frac{\sin 120°}{20} \times 15 = \sin B$$

$$\sin^{-1}\left(\frac{\sin 120°}{20} \times 15\right) = B$$

$$40.5° \approx B$$

The sum of all the interior angles in a triangle is 180°.
$\angle C \approx 180° - (120° + 40.5°)$
$\approx 19.5°$

Step 3
Use the law of sines to determine the side length AB.

$$\frac{a}{\sin A} = \frac{c}{\sin C}$$

$$\frac{20}{\sin 120°} \approx \frac{AB}{\sin 19.5°}$$

$$\frac{20}{\sin 120°} \times \sin 19.5° \approx AB$$

$$7.71 \approx AB$$

The approximate length of the hour hand is 7.71 cm.

178. 48.1

Step 1
Determine the lengths of the bases of the vertical triangles using the tangent ratio.

$$\tan 42° = \frac{25}{y}$$

$$y = \frac{25}{\tan 42°}$$

$$y \approx 27.77$$

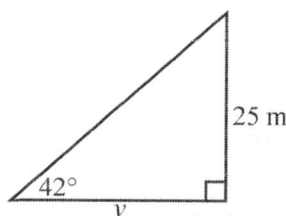

$$\tan 38° = \frac{25}{z}$$

$$z = \frac{25}{\tan 38°}$$

$$z \approx 32.00$$

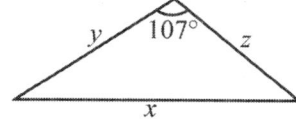

Step 2
Determine x using the cosine law.

$a^2 = b^2 + c^2 - 2bc\cos A$
$x^2 = y^2 + z^2 - 2(y)(z)\cos 107°$
$x \approx \sqrt{(27.77)^2 + (32.00)^2 - 2(27.77)(32.00)\cos 107°}$
$x \approx 48.1$

EXERCISE #2—GENERAL TRIANGLES IN TRIGONOMETRY

Use the following information to answer the next question.

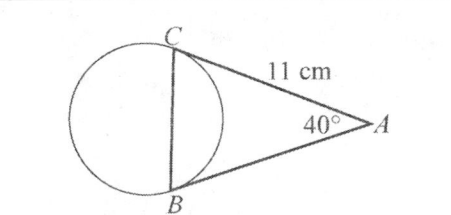

Chord BC and line segments AB and AC, which are tangent to the circle, form △ABC.

179. Determine the area of △ABC.
  A. 30.25 cm²
  B. 38.89 cm²
  C. 60.50 cm²
  D. 77.78 cm²

Use the following information to answer the next question.

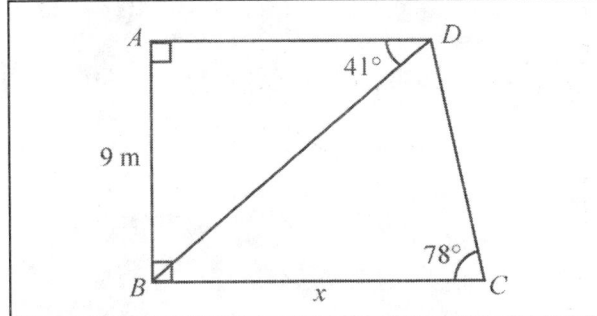

180. Correct to the nearest tenth, what is the length of side x in the given diagram?
  A. 9.2 m
  B. 11.2 m
  C. 12.3 m
  D. 13.7 m

Use the following information to answer the next question.

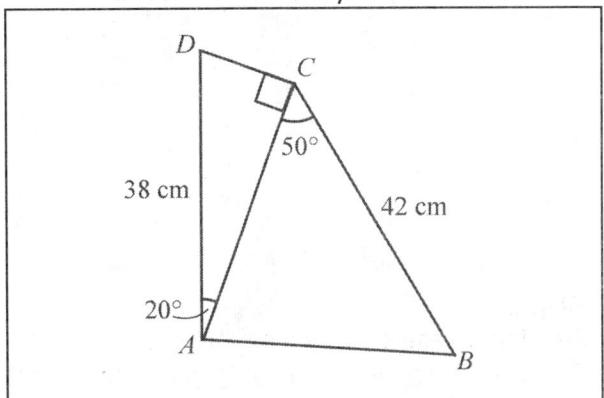

181. Correct to the nearest centimeter, the perimeter of △ABC is _____ cm.

182. Expressed to the nearest tenth, the perimeter of △ABC, if ∠A = 40°, ∠B = 35°, and c = 15 cm, is
  A. 32.3 cm
  B. 32.8 cm
  C. 33.6 cm
  D. 33.9 cm

Use the following information to answer the next question.

The measures of the sides of △ABC are a = 6, b = 8, and c = 13.

183. Expressed to the nearest tenth, the ratio of the measure of the largest angle in △ABC to the sum of the measures of the two smallest angles is _____.

Use the following information to answer the next question.

An engineer needs to calculate the distance across a deep canyon. She takes a sighting from a point A and then from a point C, which are both on the same side of the canyon, to a point B on the opposite side of the canyon, as shown in the diagram.

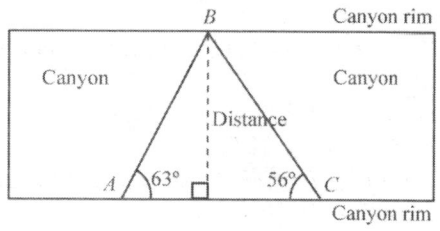

184. If points A and C are 70 m apart, then the distance across the canyon, correct to the nearest tenth of a meter, is
A. 51.9 m   B. 59.1 m
C. 60.3 m   D. 68.7 m

Use the following information to answer the next question.

To display a valuable trophy, the staff at a hockey arena roped off a triangular area and installed a security camera. The security camera was installed so that it rotated continually between the two longest ropes through the angle θ, as shown in the given diagram.

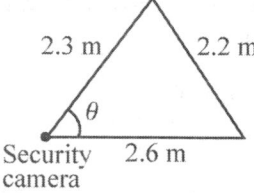

185. The measure of angle θ, rounded to the nearest degree, is
A. 53°   B. 57°
C. 64°   D. 70°

Use the following information to answer the next question.

From a particular point, Jennifer determined that the angle of elevation to the top of her school was 18°. When she walked 12.5 m closer to the school, she determined that the angle of elevation to the top of the school was 29°, as illustrated in the diagram.

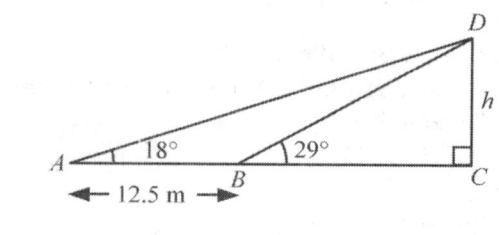

186. Correct to the nearest meter, the height of the school, h, is _____ m.

Use the following information to answer the next question.

A golf course engineer designs a fairway that curves to the right. In golf terms, this is called a dog-leg right. The designer places four reference points on his sketch of the hole. Reference point T is at the starting location, A and B are at each side of the dog leg, and point G is where the hole is, as shown in the diagram.

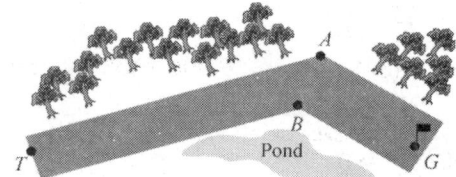

In the sketch, distance TA = 240 m, distance TB = 210 m, ∠ATB = 10°, ∠GAB = 68°, and ∠GBA = 84°.

187. Rounded to the nearest meter, the distance of BG is
A. 46 m   B. 53 m
C. 97 m   D. 104 m

EXERCISE #2—GENERAL TRIANGLES IN TRIGONOMETRY ANSWERS AND SOLUTIONS

179. B	182. D	185. A
180. C	183. 3.1	186. 10
181. 111	184. B	187. C

179. B

Step 1
Apply properties of tangents.
Two tangent segments from one external point are equal in length.
$AB = AC = 11$ cm

Step 2
Find the area of $\triangle ABC$.
The height of the triangle is not given. The lengths of two sides and the included angle are known, so use the formula Area $= \frac{1}{2}bc\sin(A)$.

Area $= \frac{1}{2}bc\sin(A)$
$= \frac{1}{2}(11 \text{ cm})(11 \text{ cm})\sin(40°)$
$\approx 38.89 \text{ cm}^2$

180. C

Step 1
Determine the length of side BD.
Use the sine ratio to determine the length of side BD in $\triangle BAD$.
$\sin \angle ADB = \frac{AB}{BD}$
Substitute 41° for $\angle ADB$ and 9 for AB. Solve for BD.
$\sin 41° = \frac{9}{BD}$
$BD\sin 41° = 9$
$BD = \frac{9}{\sin 41°}$
$BD = 13.72$ m

Step 2
Determine the measure of $\angle D$ in $\triangle CBD$.
In $\triangle BAD$, $\angle ABD = 180° - 90° - 41° = 49°$.
In $\triangle CBD$, $\angle CBD = 90° - 49° = 41°$.
In $\triangle CBD$, $\angle BDC = 180° - 41° - 78° = 61°$.

Step 3
Solve for x.
In $\triangle CBD$, since it is not a side-angle-side situation, use the sine law.
$\frac{BC}{\sin \angle BDC} = \frac{BD}{\sin \angle BCD}$
Substitute x for BC, 13.72 for BD, 61° for $\angle BDC$, and 78° for $\angle BCD$.
$\frac{x}{\sin 61°} = \frac{13.72}{\sin 78°}$
$x\sin 78° = 13.72\sin 61°$
$x = \frac{13.72\sin 61°}{\sin 78°}$
$x = 12.27$ m
Correct to the nearest tenth, the length of side x is 12.3 m.

181. 111

In order to determine the perimeter of $\triangle ABC$, find the length of each of the three sides of the triangle. The length of side BC is given, but the lengths of side AC and AB must be calculated.

Step 1
Calculate the measure of side AC in $\triangle DAC$.
Use the cosine ratio to solve for side AC.
$\cos \angle DAC = \frac{AC}{AD}$
Substitute 20° for $\angle DAC$ and 38 for AD.
$\cos 20° = \frac{AC}{38}$
$AC = 38\cos 20°$
$AC = 35.71$ cm

Step 2
Calculate the measure of side AB in $\triangle ABC$.
Use the law of cosines to determine AB as follows:
$(AB)^2 = (AC)^2 + (BC)^2 - 2(AC)(BC)\cos \angle ACB$
Substitute 35.71 for AC, 42 for BC, and 50° for $\angle ACB$. Then, solve for side AB.
$(AB)^2 = (35.71)^2 + (42)^2 - 2(35.71)(42)\cos 50°$
$(AB)^2 = 1,111.07$
$AB = 33.33$ cm

Step 3
Calculate the perimeter of $\triangle ABC$.
The perimeter of $\triangle ABC$ is
$42 + 35.71 + 33.33 = 111.04$ cm.
Rounded to the nearest centimeter, the perimeter of $\triangle ABC$ is 111 cm.

182. D

Step 1
Sketch the triangle.
The sketch of the triangle shows that this situation is ASA, where the measures of two angles and the length of the included side are given.

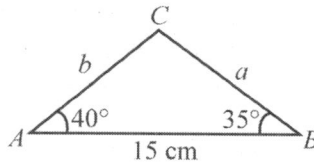

Step 2
Determine the measure of $\angle C$.
$\angle A + \angle B + \angle C = 180°$
$40° + 35° + \angle C = 180°$
$\angle C = 105°$

Step 3
Determine the length of one of the missing sides by using the sine law.
The length of $\overline{BC}$ will be determined.
$$\frac{a}{\sin A} = \frac{c}{\sin C}$$
$$\frac{a}{\sin 40°} = \frac{15}{\sin 105°}$$
$$a = \frac{15\sin 40°}{\sin 105°}$$
$$a \approx 9.98$$

Step 4
Determine the length of $\overline{AC}$.
$$\frac{b}{\sin B} = \frac{c}{\sin C}$$
$$\frac{b}{\sin 35°} = \frac{15}{\sin 105°}$$
$$b = \frac{15\sin 35°}{\sin 105°}$$
$$b \approx 8.91$$

Step 5
Determine the perimeter.
$P = a + b + c$
$P \approx 9.98 + 8.91 + 15$
$P \approx 33.89$
To the nearest tenth, the perimeter of the triangle is approximately 33.9 cm.

183. 3.1

Since the lengths of all three sides are given, the measure of any angle can be determined using the cosine law.

Step 1
Determine the measure of $\angle A$.
$$\cos A = \frac{b^2 + c^2 - a^2}{2bc}$$
$$\cos A = \frac{(8)^2 + (13)^2 - (6)^2}{2(8)(13)}$$
$$\cos A \approx 0.9471$$
$$A \approx \cos^{-1}(0.9471)$$
$$A \approx 18.7°$$

Step 2
Determine the measure of either $\angle B$ or $\angle C$.
The measure of $\angle B$ is determined using the cosine law.
$$\cos B = \frac{a^2 + c^2 - b^2}{2ac}$$
$$\cos B = \frac{(6)^2 + (13)^2 - (8)^2}{2(6)(13)}$$
$$\cos B \approx 0.9038$$
$$B \approx \cos^{-1}(0.9038)$$
$$B \approx 25.3°$$

Note that the sine law could also have been used to solve for the measure of either angle.

Step 3
Determine the measure of $\angle C$.
$\angle A + \angle B + \angle C = 180°$
$18.7° + 25.3° + \angle C = 180°$
$\angle C = 136.0°$

Step 4
Determine the ratio of the measure of the largest angle to the sum of the measures of the two smallest angles.
$$\text{ratio} = \frac{136°}{18.7° + 25.3°}$$
$$= \frac{136°}{44.0°}$$
$$= 3.0909$$

Expressed to the nearest tenth, the ratio is 3.1.

184. B

Step 1
Label the diagram.
The given diagram can be labeled as shown.

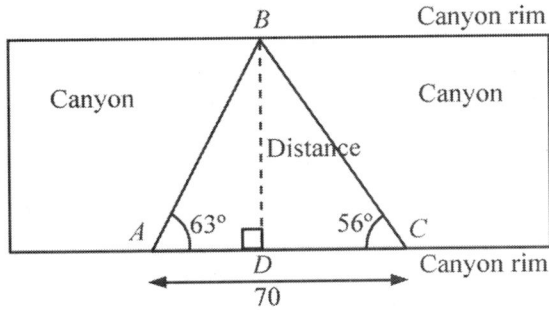

Step 2
Calculate the measure of $\angle B$.
$\angle B = 180° - 63° - 56° = 61°$

Step 3
Determine the length of either side AB or CB by applying the sine law with respect to $\triangle ABC$.
The length of AB can be determined as follows:
$$\frac{AB}{\sin C} = \frac{AC}{\sin B}$$
Substitute 56° for C, 70 for AC, and 61° for B. Solve for AB.
$$\frac{AB}{\sin 56°} = \frac{70}{\sin 61°}$$
$AB \times \sin 61° = 70 \times \sin 56°$
$$AB = \frac{70 \times \sin 56°}{\sin 61°}$$
$AB \approx 66.35$ m

Step 4
Solve for BD by examining $\triangle ADB$.
In $\triangle ADB$, $\sin A = \dfrac{BD}{AB}$

Substitute 63° for A and 66.35 for AB.
$\sin 63° = \dfrac{BD}{66.35}$
$BD = 66.35 \times \sin 63°$
$BD = 59.12$ m

To the nearest tenth, the distance across the canyon BD is 59.1 m.
A similar procedure can be used to determine the length of side BC, and then the sine ratio can be used with respect to $\triangle BCD$.

185. A

Substitute the known values into the cosine formula, and solve for θ:
$$\cos A = \frac{b^2 + c^2 - a^2}{2bc}$$
$$\cos \theta = \frac{2.3^2 + 2.6^2 - 2.2^2}{2(2.3)(2.6)}$$
$$\cos \theta = \frac{7.21}{11.96}$$
$$\theta = \cos^{-1}\left(\frac{7.21}{11.96}\right)$$
$\theta \approx 52.926°$

Rounded to the nearest degree, the measure of θ is 53°.

186. 10

Step 1
Determine the length of side BD by applying the sine law.
In $\triangle ABD$, observe that $\angle ABD = 180° - 29° = 151°$. Thus, the measure of $\angle ADB$ is
$180° - 151° - 18° = 11°$.
$$\frac{BD}{\sin \angle A} = \frac{AB}{\sin \angle ADB}$$
Substitute 18° for $\angle A$, 12.5 for AB, and 11° for $\angle ADB$.
$$\frac{BD}{\sin 18°} = \frac{12.5}{\sin 11°}$$
$BD \times \sin 11° = 12.5 \times \sin 18°$
$$BD = \frac{12.5 \times \sin 18°}{\sin 11°}$$
$BD \approx 20.24$ m

Step 2
Solve for h in right triangle BCD.
Substitute 29° for $\angle DBC$, h for DC, and 20.24 for BD.
$$\sin \angle DBC = \frac{DC}{BD}$$
$$\sin 29° = \frac{h}{20.24}$$
$h = 20.24 \times \sin 29°$
$h \approx 9.81$ m

The height of the school, to the nearest meter, is 10 m.

187. C

Step 1
Label the diagram.
The given diagram can be labeled as follows:

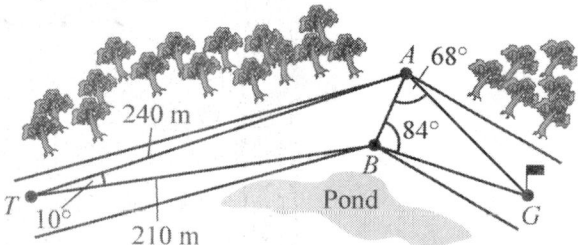

Step 2
Determine the distance from point A to point B.
In $\triangle ATB$, it is a side-angle-side situation; therefore, solve for AB by applying the cosine law.
$(AB)^2 = (TA)^2 + (TB)^2 - 2(TA)(TB)\cos \angle T$
Substitute 240 for TA, 210 for TB, and 10° for $\angle T$, and solve for AB.
$(AB)^2 = 240^2 + 210^2 - 2(240)(210)\cos 10°$
$(AB)^2 \approx 57{,}600 + 44{,}100 - 99{,}268.62$
$(AB)^2 \approx 2{,}431.38$
$AB \approx \sqrt{2{,}431.38}$
$AB \approx 49.31$

Step 3
Use $\triangle GAB$, and apply the sine law in order to determine the distance of BG.
$$\frac{BG}{\sin \angle GAB} = \frac{AB}{\sin \angle G}$$
Calculate the measure of $\angle G$ by subtracting the known angle measures of $\triangle ABG$ from 180°.
$\angle G = 180° - 68° - 84° = 28°$
Substitute 68° for $\angle GAB$, 49.31 for AB, and 28° for $\angle G$, and solve for BG.
$$\frac{BG}{\sin 68°} = \frac{49.31}{\sin 28°}$$
$BG \times \sin 28° = 49.31 \times \sin 68°$
$$BG = \frac{49.31 \times \sin 68°}{\sin 28°}$$
$BG \approx 97.38$ m

To the nearest meter, the distance of BG is 97 m.

Volume Formulas

VOLUME FORMULAS

Table of Correlations

Standard		Concepts	Exercise #1	Exercise #2
Unit3.1	Explain volume formulas and use them to solve problems.			
G-GMD.3	Use volume formulas for cylinders, pyramids, cones, and spheres to solve problems.	Solving Problems Involving the Volume of a Cylinder	148	159
		Solving Problems Involving the Volume of a Cone	149	160
		Solving Problems Involving the Volume of a Sphere	150	161
		Solving Problems Involving Volume of Pyramids	151	162
		Calculating the Volume of Cylinders	188	192
		Calculating the Volume of a Sphere	189	195
		Calculating the Volume of a Cone	190	193
		Calculating the Volume of a Pyramid	191	194

G-GMD.3 Use volume formulas for cylinders, pyramids, cones, and spheres to solve problems.

CALCULATING THE VOLUME OF CYLINDERS

Cylinders are three-dimensional figures with two congruent and parallel circular bases connected by a curved rectangular face. In a right cylinder, the parallel circular bases are perpendicular (⊥) to the curved rectangular face (side).

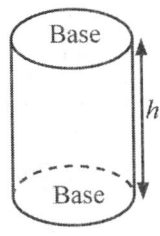 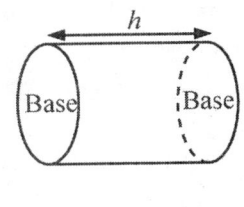

Volume is the space found inside a three-dimensional object. To calculate the volume of a right cylinder, take the area of one of the bases and multiply it by the perpendicular (⊥) distance to the other end of the cylinder. The perpendicular (⊥) distance between the parallel circular bases is equal to the height of the cylinder.

The general formula for volume is $V = A_{base} \times h$.

The general formula for the volume of a cylinder becomes $V = A_{circle} \times h$.

The A_{circle} is replaced with πr^2.

Therefore, the formula for the volume of a cylinder is $V = \pi r^2 \times h$.

To calculate the volume of a cylinder, substitute the known values into the volume formula and simplify.

Example

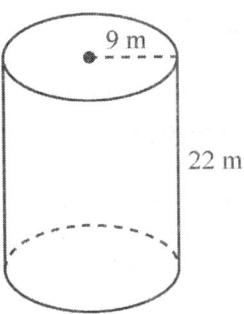

Calculate the volume of the given cylinder.

Solution

Step 1
Determine the formula to use to calculate the volume of the cylinder.

The volume of a cylinder can be calculated by multiplying the area of the base by its height.

The shape of the base is a circle. The height is the measured distance between the parallel circles (bases), so the formula is as follows:

$V_{cylinder} = A_{base} \times h$
$= A_{circle} \times h$
$= \pi r^2 \times h$

Step 2
Substitute in the known values, and evaluate the equation following the order of operations.

$V_{cylinder} = \pi r^2 \times h$
$= 3.14 \times 9^2 \times 22$
$= 3.14 \times 81 \times 22$
$= 5\ 595.48 \text{ m}^3$

When given a cylinder with a diameter, first calculate the **radius**.

Example

A cylindrical-shaped tank has a diameter of 8 ft and a height of 10 ft, as shown in the given diagram.

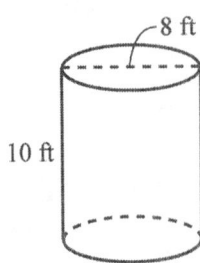

Determine the volume of the tank, to the nearest cubic foot.

Solution

Step 1
Find the radius, r, of the cylinder.
$$r = \frac{1}{2}d$$
$$= \frac{1}{2}(8)$$
$$= 4 \text{ ft}$$

Step 2
Determine the volume of the cylinder using the appropriate formula.
$$V_{cylinder} = \pi r^2 h$$
$$= \pi(4)^2(10)$$
$$= \pi(16)(10)$$
$$\approx 502.6548 \text{ ft}^3$$

The volume of the tank, to the nearest cubic foot, is 503 ft³.

Use the same process to solve volume problems in everyday situations.

Example
A paint can has a diameter of 25 cm and is 40 cm tall.

How many milliliters of paint are there in the can if it is one-half full?

Solution

The shape of the base is a circle. The height is the measured distance between the parallel circles.

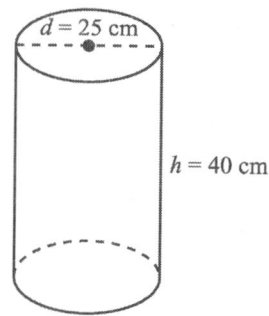

Step 1
Calculate the radius.
$$r = \frac{d}{2} = \frac{25}{2} = 12.5 \text{ cm}$$

Step 2
Calculate the volume.
$$V_{cylinder} = A_{circle} \times h$$
$$= \pi r^2 \times h$$
$$= 3.14 \times 12.5^2 \times 40$$
$$= 3.14 \times 156.25 \times 40$$
$$= 490.625 \times 40$$
$$= 19{,}625 \text{ cm}^3$$

Step 3
Divide the volume by 2 because the can is only one-half full.
$$19{,}625 \div 2 = 9{,}812.5 \text{ cm}^3$$

Step 4
Convert centimeters cubed into milliliters.
$$9{,}812.5 \text{ cm}^3 = 9{,}812.5 \text{ mL}$$
The can, which is one-half full, contains 9812.5 mL of paint.

CALCULATING THE VOLUME OF A SPHERE

The volume of a **sphere** is two-thirds the volume of a cylinder with the same dimensions.

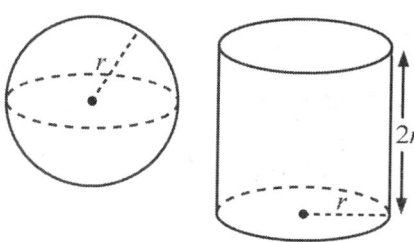

That is, the radius of the sphere is the same as the radius of the base of the cylinder and the height of the cylinder is equal to the diameter of the sphere.

Since the height of the cylinder is equal to the diameter of the sphere, $h = 2r$. The formula for the volume of a sphere can now be derived from the formula for the volume of a cylinder:

$$V_{cylinder} = (A_{base})(\text{height})$$
$$= (\pi r^2)h$$
$$V_{sphere} = \frac{2}{3}(A_{base})(\text{height})$$
$$V_{sphere} = \frac{2}{3}(\pi r^2)(2r)$$
$$V_{sphere} = \frac{2 \times 2\pi r^3}{3}$$
$$V_{sphere} = \frac{4\pi r^3}{3}$$

Example

Calculate the volume of the given sphere rounded to the nearest tenth of a cm^3.

$$V_{sphere} = \frac{4\pi r^3}{3}$$
$$= \frac{4 \times 3.14 \times 7^3}{3}$$
$$= \frac{4 \times 3.14 \times 343}{3}$$
$$= \frac{4,308.08}{3}$$
$$= 1,436.02\bar{6}$$
$$= 1,436.0 \text{ cm}^3$$

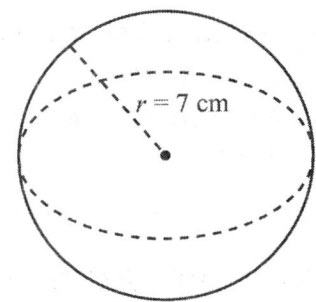

Calculate the volume of the given sphere to the nearest cm^3.

$$V_{sphere} = \frac{4\pi r^3}{3}$$
$$= \frac{4 \times 3.14 \times 4^3}{3}$$
$$= \frac{4 \times 3.14 \times 64}{3}$$
$$= \frac{803.84}{3}$$
$$= 267.94\bar{6}$$
$$= 268 \text{ cm}^3$$

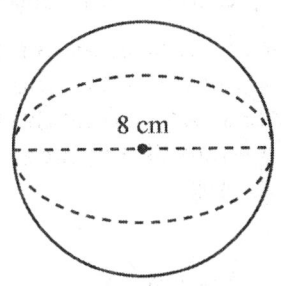

Often, the size of a ball is specified by its circumference instead of its radius or diameter. The following illustrates one way to find the volume of the ball, if only the circumference is known.

Example

The circumference of a baseball is 22 cm.

Determine the volume of the baseball rounded to the nearest tenth of a cubic centimeter (cm^3).

Solution

Determine the radius of the baseball rounded to the nearest hundredth of cm.

$$C = \pi d$$
$$22 = 3.14d$$
$$\frac{22}{3.14} = \frac{3.14d}{3.14}$$
$$7.00636943 = d$$
$$d = 7.00636943 \text{ cm}$$
$$r = \frac{d}{2} = \frac{7.00636943}{2}$$
$$= 3.5031847 \text{ cm}$$
$$= 3.50 \text{ cm}$$

Now, substitute the known values into the volume formula, and solve.

$$V_{sphere} = \frac{4\pi r^3}{3}$$
$$= \frac{4 \times 3.14 \times 3.50^3}{3}$$
$$= \frac{4 \times 3.14 \times 42.875}{3}$$
$$= \frac{538.51}{3}$$
$$= 179.50$$
$$= 179.5 \text{ cm}^3$$

The volume of the baseball is 179.5 cm^3.

CALCULATING THE VOLUME OF A CONE

The volume of a cone can be found using the formula $V_{cone} = \frac{A_{base}h}{3}$, where A_{base} is the area of the base and h is the height. The equation can also be expressed as $V_{cone} = \frac{\pi r^2 h}{3}$.

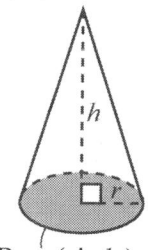
Base (circle)

Example

Determine the volume of a cone, rounded to the nearest tenth of a centimeter, with a base radius of 6 cm and height of 4 cm.

Solution

Step 1
Substitute the known values into the volume formula for a cone.
$$V_{cone} = \frac{\pi r^2 h}{3}$$
$$= \frac{\pi (6)^2 (4)}{3}$$

Step 2
Solve for the missing variable.
Follow the order of operations when solving questions.
$$V_{cone} = \frac{3.14(36)(4)}{3}$$
$$= \frac{452.16}{3}$$
$$= 150.72$$

Volume is always calculated in cubic units or units^3. Rounded to the tenths position, the volume of the cone is 150.7 cm^3.

Example

A cone has a base radius of 11.5 cm and height of 7.4 cm.

To the nearest tenth of a centimeter, determine the volume of the cone.

Solution

Step 1
Substitute the known values into the volume formula for a cone.
$$V_{cone} = \frac{(\pi r^2)h}{3}$$
$$= \frac{(3.14 \times 11.5^2)(7.4)}{3}$$

Step 2
Solve for the missing variable.
Follow the order of operations when solving equations.
$$V_{cone} = \frac{(3.14 \times 132.25)(7.4)}{3}$$
$$= \frac{3,072.961}{3}$$
$$\approx 1,024.3$$

Volume is always calculated in cubic units or units^3. Rounded to the tenths position, the volume of the cone is 1,024.3 cm^3.

CALCULATING THE VOLUME OF A PYRAMID

The general formula for the volume of a pyramid is $V_{pyramid} = \frac{1}{3} A_{base} h$, where A_{base} is the area of the base and h is the height. The volume of any pyramid is $\frac{1}{3}$ the volume of a prism with the same base and height.

The formula for the volume of a pyramid with a rectangular base is $V_{pyramid} = \frac{1}{3} lwh$ or $V_{pyramid} = \frac{lwh}{3}$.

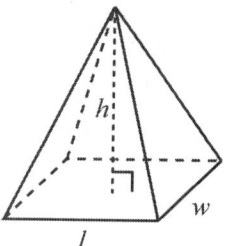

Example

A pyramid has a base measuring 15 m by 12 m and a height of 9 m.

Determine the volume of the pyramid.

Solution

Step 1

Substitute the known values into the volume formula for a pyramid.

$$V_{pyramid} = \frac{(lw)h}{3}$$
$$= \frac{(15 \times 12) \times 9}{3}$$

Step 2

Solve for the volume.
Follow the order of operations when solving equations.

$$V_{pyramid} = \frac{1{,}620}{3}$$
$$= 540 \text{ m}^3$$

Volume is always calculated in cubic units or units^3. The volume of the pyramid is 540 m^3.

Example

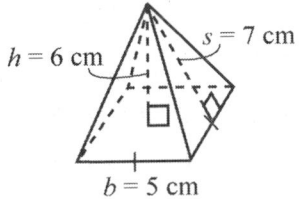

Calculate the volume of the given square pyramid.

Solution

Pyramids have one-third the volume of rectangular prisms with the same dimensions. Therefore, the formula for the volume of a square pyramid can be expressed as the volume formula for a rectangular prism divided by 3.

$$V_{square\ pyramid} = \frac{A_{base} \times h}{3}$$
$$= \frac{b^2 \times h}{3}$$
$$= \frac{5^2 \times 6}{3}$$
$$= \frac{25 \times 6}{3}$$
$$= \frac{150}{3}$$
$$= 50$$

The volume of the given square pyramid is 50 cm^3.

EXERCISE #1—VOLUME FORMULAS

Use the following information to answer the next question.

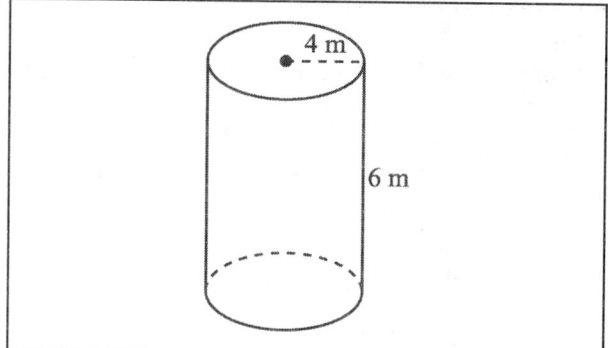

188. Calculate the volume of the cylinder.

189. What is the volume of a ball that has a diameter of 24 cm? Use $\pi = 3.14$.
   A. 1,848.12 cm³
   B. 3,240.28 cm³
   C. 7,234.56 cm³
   D. 9,472.84 cm³

Use the following information to answer the next question.

The volume of a right cylinder is 1,056 cm³.

190. What is the volume of a right cone with the same base and height?
   A. 176 cm³
   B. 352 cm³
   C. 528 cm³
   D. 704 cm³

191. What is the volume of a pyramid with a base of 15 m by 12 m that is 14 m high?
   A. 840 m³
   B. 1,470 m³
   C. 2,520 m³
   D. 2,856 m³

EXERCISE #1—VOLUME FORMULAS ANSWERS AND SOLUTIONS

| 188. See solution | 189. C | 190. B | 191. A |

188.
In order to calculate the volume of a cylinder, you need to know the area of the base and the height of the cylinder. The shape of the base is a circle. The height is the measured distance between the parallel circles.

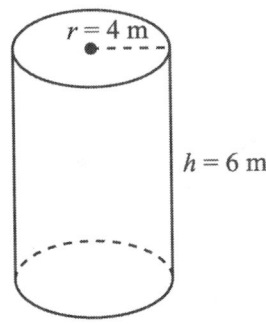

Step 1
In order to calculate the area of the base, you need to know the radius of the base, which in this case, is given to you.
$r = 4$ m

Step 2
Calculate the volume.
$V_{cylinder} = A_{base} \times h$
$V_{cylinder} = A_{circle} \times h$
$= \pi r^2 \times h$
$= 3.14 \times 4^2 \times 6$
$= 3.14 \times 16 \times 6$
$= 301.44$
$= 301.44$ m^3

189. C
Step 1
Find the radius of the ball.
The radius of the ball is half the diameter.
$r = \dfrac{d}{2} = \dfrac{24}{2} = 12$ cm

Step 2
Use the radius of the ball to calculate the volume of the ball.
$V_{sphere} = \dfrac{4\pi r^3}{3}$
$= \dfrac{4 \times 3.14 \times 12^3}{3}$
$= \dfrac{4 \times 3.14 \times 1{,}728}{3}$
$= \dfrac{21{,}703.68}{3}$
$= 7{,}234.56$ cm^3

The volume of the ball is 7,234.56 cm^3.

190. B
The volume of a right cone is one-third the volume of a right cylinder that has the same base and height.

Divide the volume of the cylinder by 3.
$\dfrac{1{,}056}{3} = 352$

The volume of the cone is 352 cm^3.

191. A
Step 1
Substitute the given values into the volume formula for a pyramid.
$V = \dfrac{lwh}{3}$
$= \dfrac{(15)(12)(14)}{3}$

Step 2
Calculate the volume of the pyramid.
$V = \dfrac{2{,}520}{3}$
$= 840$ m^3

EXERCISE #2—VOLUME FORMULAS

Use the following information to answer the next question.

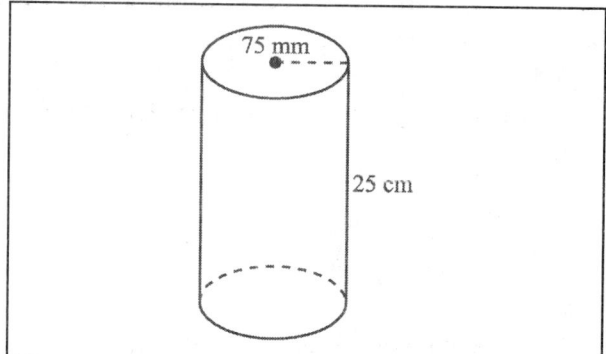

192. Calculate the volume of the cylinder.

Use the following information to answer the next question.

Grain is piled in a grain bin in the shape of a cone. The pile has a base radius of 20 m and a height of 5.5 m.

193. What is the volume of grain, to the nearest hundred cubic meters? _____ m³

194. A pyramid has a base measuring 20 cm by 30 cm and a height of 36 cm. What is the volume of the pyramid?
   A. 21,600 cm³
   B. 7,200 cm³
   C. 600 cm³
   D. 28.7 cm³

195. The formula for the volume of a sphere is $V = \frac{4}{3}\pi r^3$. If the volume of a ball is 36π cm³, then the radius of the sphere is _____ cm.

EXERCISE #2—VOLUME FORMULAS ANSWERS AND SOLUTIONS

| 192. See solution | 193. 2300 | 194. B | 195. 3 |

192.

Step 1
Convert millimeters to centimeters.
1 mm = 0.1 cm
75 mm = 7.5 cm

Step 2
Calculate the volume.
The shape of the base is a circle. The height is the measured distance between the parallel circles.

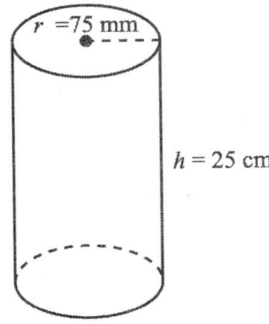

Substitute the known values into the formula and solve following order of operations.
$V = A_{base} \times h$
$V = A_{circle} \times h$
$= \pi r^2 \times h$
$= 3.14 \times 7.5^2 \times 25$
$= 3.14 \times 56.25 \times 25$
$= 4,415.63 \text{ cm}^3$

193. 2300

Step 1
Substitute the known values into the formula
$V_{cone} = \dfrac{(\pi r^2)h}{3}$.
$V_{cone} \approx \dfrac{(3.14 \times 20^2)(5.5)}{3}$

Step 2
Solve for the unknown variable.
$V_{cone} \approx \dfrac{(3.14 \times 400)(5.5)}{3}$
$V_{cone} \approx \dfrac{6,908}{3}$
$V_{cone} \approx 2,302.66$

Rounded to the nearest hundred cubic meters, the volume of grain is 2,300 m³.

194. B

Step 1
Substitute the given values in the volume formula for a pyramid.
$V = \dfrac{lwh}{3}$
$= \dfrac{(20)(30)(36)}{3}$

Step 2
Calculate the volume of the pyramid.
$V = \dfrac{21,600}{3}$
$= 7,200 \text{ cm}^3$

195. 3

The formula for the volume of a sphere is
$V = \dfrac{4}{3}\pi r^3$.

To find the radius of the ball, substitute $V = 36\pi$ into the formula.
$36\pi = \dfrac{4}{3}\pi r^3$

Divide both sides by π.
$36 = \dfrac{4}{3}r^3$

Multiply both sides by 3.
$108 = 4r^3$

Divide both sides by 4.
$r^3 = 27$
$r = 3$

NOTES

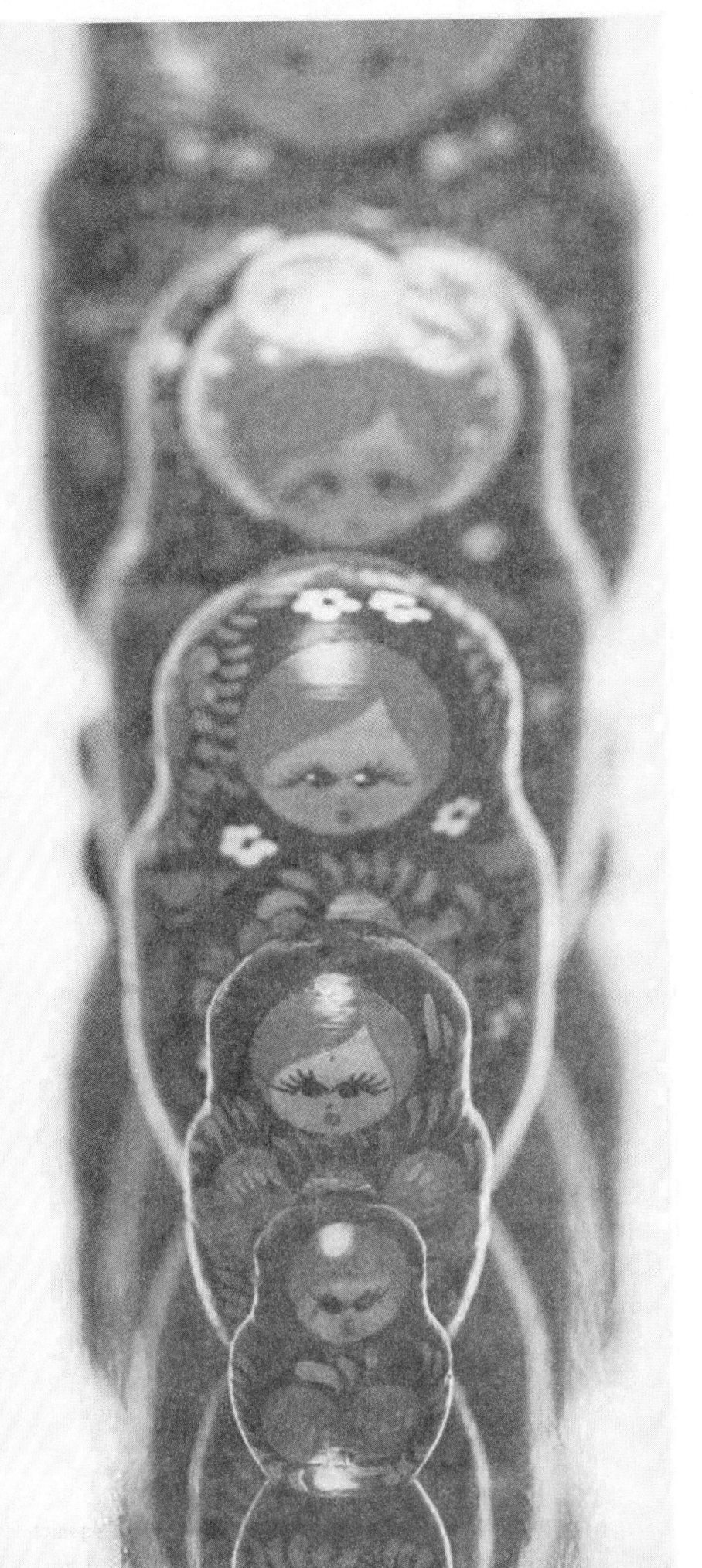

Two and Three-Dimensional Objects

TWO AND THREE-DIMENSIONAL OBJECTS

Table of Correlations

Standard		Concepts	Exercise #1	Exercise #2
Unit3.2	Visualize the relation between two-dimensional and three-dimensional objects.			
G-GMD.4	*Identify the shapes of two-dimensional cross-sections of threedimensional objects, and identify three-dimensional objects generated by rotations of two-dimensional objects.*	Sketching Plan and Elevation Views from 3-D Objects	196	200
		Sketching 3-D Objects Given Plan and Elevation Views	197	201
		Classifying Conics	198	202
		Identifying and Sketching Three-Dimensional Cross Sections	199	203

G-GMD.4 Identify the shapes of two-dimensional cross-sections of three-dimensional objects, and identify three-dimensional objects generated by rotations of two-dimensional objects.

SKETCHING PLAN AND ELEVATION VIEWS FROM 3-D OBJECTS

Three-dimensional objects have three dimensions: length, width, and height. Three-dimensional objects can be drawn in two-dimensions from a plan view or elevation view. **Plan view** is drawing the object as seen from the top or bottom. **Elevation view** is drawing the object from the front, rear, or side view.

Example

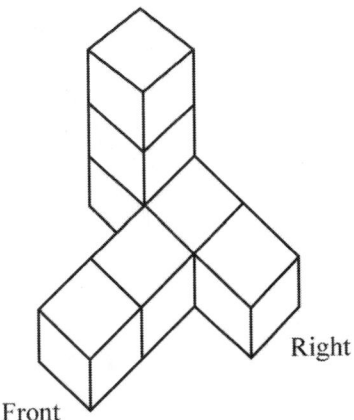

For this three-dimensional diagram, draw the two-dimensional diagram from a top plan view and from the front and right elevation views.

Solution

Step 1
Draw the plan view.
Identify the tiles that are on the top of the drawing.
To make it clear, shade the tiles that are on the top.

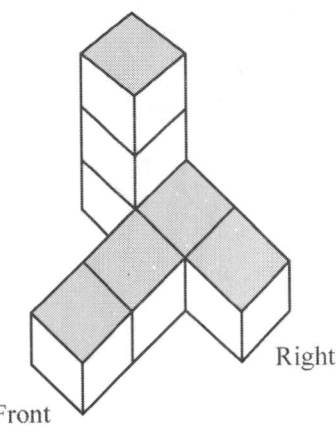

Step 2
Draw the shaded tiles in two-dimensions.

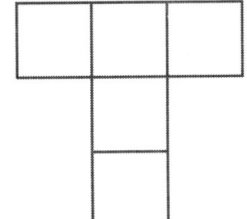

Step 3
Draw the front elevation view.

Identify the tiles you would see if standing in front of the object.

To make it clear, shade the tiles that are seen from the front.

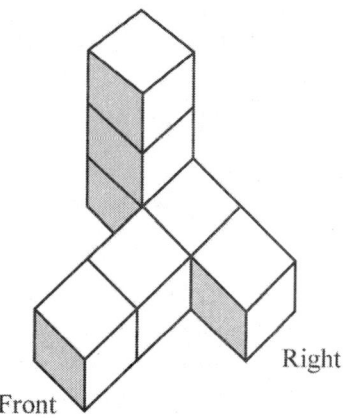

Step 4
Draw the shaded tiles in two-dimensions.

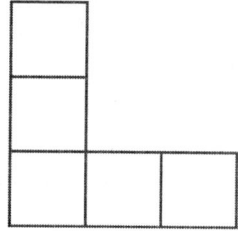

Step 5
Draw the right side elevation view.

Identify the tiles you would see if standing on the right side of the object.

To make it clear, shade the tiles that are seen from the right.

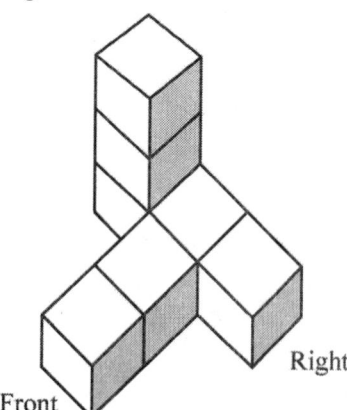

Step 6
Draw the shaded tiles in two-dimensions.

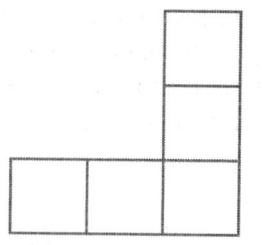

SKETCHING 3-D OBJECTS GIVEN PLAN AND ELEVATION VIEWS

Three-dimensional objects have three dimensions: length, width, and height. Three-dimensional objects can be drawn when given the plan view and elevation view.

Plan view is drawing the object as seen from the top or bottom of the object. **Elevation view** is drawing the object from the front, rear, or side view.

Example

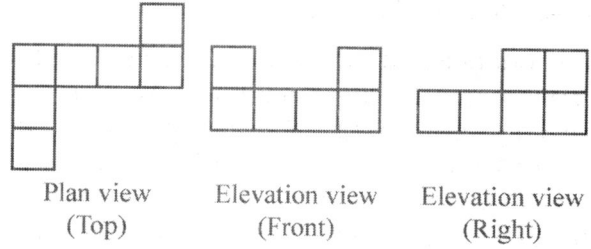

Plan view (Top)   Elevation view (Front)   Elevation view (Right)

Given these views, draw a three-dimensional diagram.

Solution

Step 1
Determine the heights of each view.

Use the plan view to label the front of each square with the height of the blocks indicated by the front view.

Use the plan view to label the right side of each square with the height as indicated by the right side view.

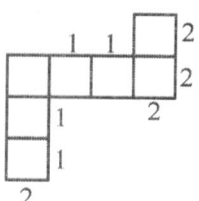

Two and Three-Dimensional Objects

Step 2

Draw the three-dimensional figure. Cross-reference the number from the front view and the right side view for each block in the plan view. If the two numbers are the same, that is the height of the block in that square of the plan view.

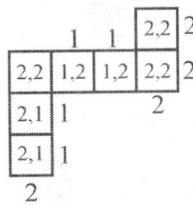

If the two numbers are different, the height of the block in that square (on the plan view) is the smaller number.

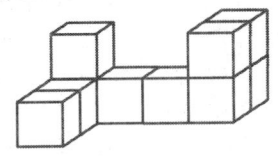

CLASSIFYING CONICS

The connection between the shape of a section of a cone and a quadratic relation in two variables was first studied by the Greek mathematician Apollonius in approximately 200 BC when he examined the intersection of a plane and a double-napped cone. The following will reveal some of these connections.

Rotating a right-angled triangle about one of its legs will generate a cone.

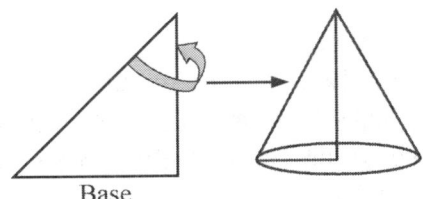

Rotating an oblique line about a fixed point will generate what is known as a **double-napped cone**.

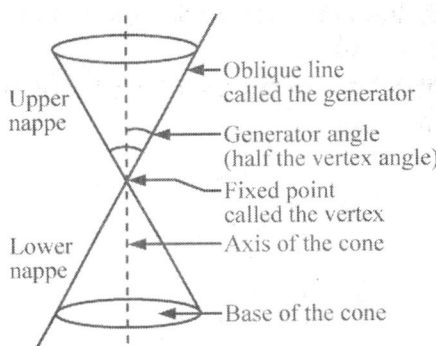

The line that goes through the vertex and is perpendicular to the base is called the **axis** of the cone. The angle between this axis and the generator is the **generator angle**. The measure of the generator angle is half the measure of the **vertex angle**.

When a plane intersects this double-napped cone, either a circle, parabola, ellipse, or hyperbola is produced. These are known as the **primary conic sections**.

The size of the angle between the intersecting plane and the cone or cylinder determines which of the four primary conics is produced.

CIRCLES

A **circle** is produced if the plane intersects the cone at a point that is perpendicular to the axis.

As the plane moves farther from the vertex, the size of the circle increases.

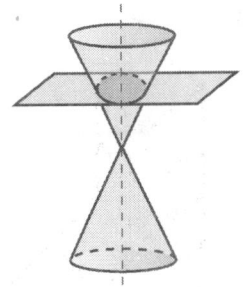

Hence, as the plane moves closer to the vertex, the circle becomes smaller. If the plane intersects the vertex, the circle is said to degenerate to a point.

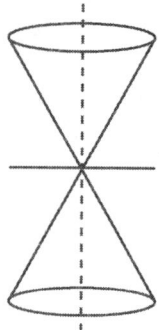

ELLIPSES

An **ellipse** is produced if the plane intersects the axis at an angle that is greater than the generator angle but less than 90°.

As the plane maintains a given angle with the axis and moves in relation to the vertex, the size of the ellipse changes. It gets larger as it moves away from the vertex and smaller as it moves toward the vertex.

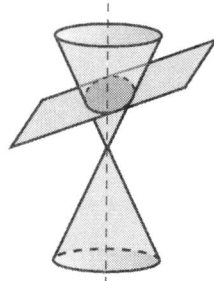

If the plane passes through the vertex, the ellipse degenerates to a point.

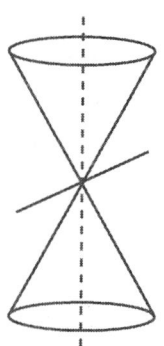

PARABOLAS

A **parabola** is produced if the plane intersects the cone at a point that is parallel to the generator. Thus, the plane intersects the axis at an angle that is equal to the generator angle.

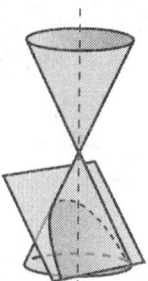

As the plane moves away from the vertex, the parabola becomes wider. As the plane moves closer to the vertex, the parabola becomes narrower.

If the plane passes through the vertex, the parabola degenerates to a line.

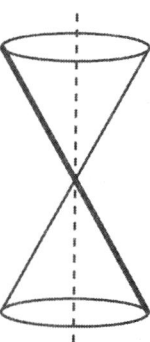

HYPERBOLAS

A plane may intersect both nappes of the cone. A **hyperbola** is produced if the plane is parallel to the axis or intersects the axis at an angle that is greater than or equal to 0° but less than the generator angle.

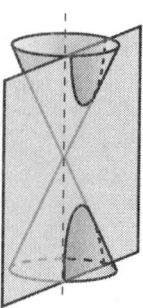

The graph of a hyperbola has two separate sections.

As the plane moves to a place where it intersects the vertex, the hyperbola degenerates to a pair of intersecting lines.

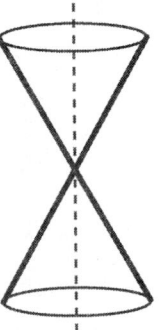

Conic Sections Produced by a Plane Intersecting a Cylinder

Consider the result when a cone with a fixed base is stretched by moving the vertex farther and farther from the base.

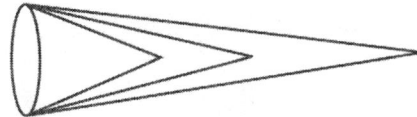

As can be seen, the shape of the cone approaches a cylinder.

It follows that a cylinder can be considered to be a cone that has its vertex extended infinitely.

A cylinder can also be produced by rotating a generator around and parallel to an axis.

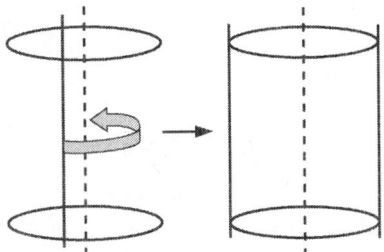

Circles and ellipses can be produced by a plane intersecting a cylindrical region.

In a circle, the plane intersects the axis (and generator) at 90°.

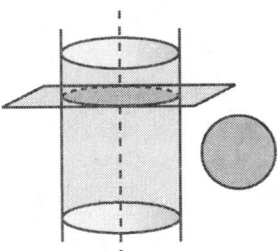

In an ellipse, the plane intersects the axis and the generator at an angle that is not equal to 90° or 0°.

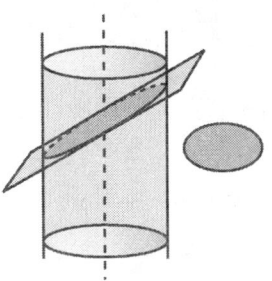

DEGENERATE PARABOLAS FROM A CYLINDER

If the plane is parallel to the generator, by definition, the result is a form of a parabola, of which there are three possibilities:

1. The plane intersects the cylinder resulting in two parallel lines.

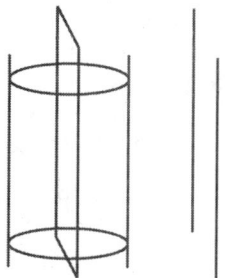

2. The plane intersects the cylinder resulting in one line.

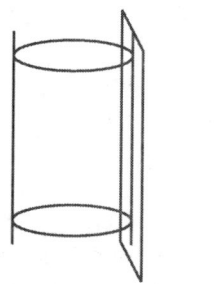

3. The plane misses the cylinder so that there is no graph.

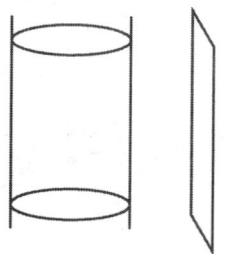

Thus, a parabola can degenerate into a pair of parallel lines, one line, or no graph.

The following table summarizes the degenerate cases.

Primary Conic	Degenerate Conic
Circle	Point or no graph
Ellipse	Point or no graph
Hyperbola	Two intersecting lines
Parabola	Two parallel lines, one line, or no graph

Example

This diagram illustrates a double-napped cone with a vertex angle of 60° and a plane intersecting this cone. The measure of the angle between the plane and the axis of the cone is represented by θ.

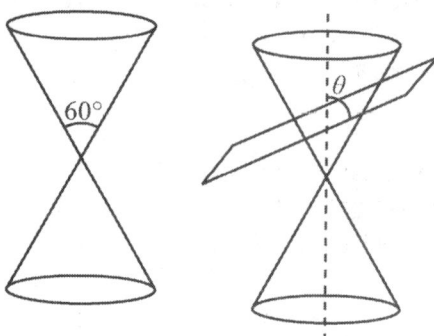

What values of θ, where $0° \leq \theta \leq 90°$, will produce each of the four conics?

Solution

For a circle, the plane must be perpendicular to the axis. Therefore, θ must equal 90°.

For an ellipse, the plane can intersect only one nappe. Therefore, θ must be greater than 30° but less than 90° $(30° < \theta < 90°)$.

For a parabola, the plane must be parallel to the generator. Therefore, θ must equal 30° ($\frac{1}{2}$ of the vertex angle).

For a hyperbola, the plane must intersect both nappes. Therefore, θ must be greater than or equal to 0° but less than 30° $(0° \leq \theta < 30°)$.

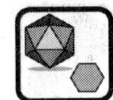

This same approach can be used for other cones with different vertex angles.

Example

The vertex angle of a double-napped cone is 72°.

At what angles ($0° \leq \theta \leq 90°$) would a plane intersect the axis of the cone to create a hyperbola?

Solution

Half the vertex angle is 36°. If θ is the angle between the cutting plane and the axis, then to create a hyperbola, $0° \leq \theta < 36°$.

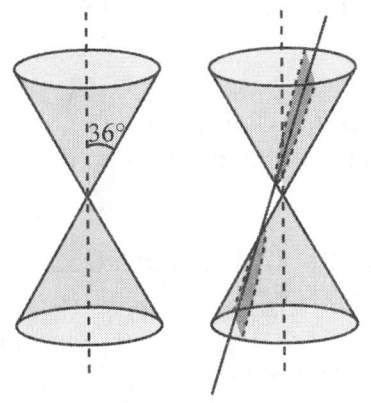

IDENTIFYING AND SKETCHING THREE-DIMENSIONAL CROSS SECTIONS

A **cross section** is the image of the intersection of a plane and a three-dimensional figure. A cross section is also known as a plane section. This results in a two-dimensional image of a three-dimensional figure. This image can either be on the inside of a figure or on the surface.

One way to visualize a cross section is to imagine cutting an object into two pieces with a knife. In this case, the knife is comparable to the plane, and the newly exposed inside is comparable to the cross section.

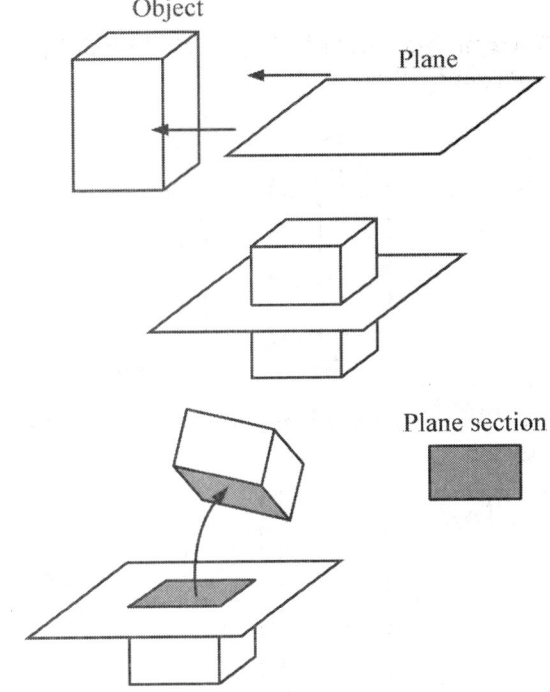

For many objects, moving the plane that intersects the object will change the appearance of the cross section.

A **torus** is an object formed by rotating a circle about a line.

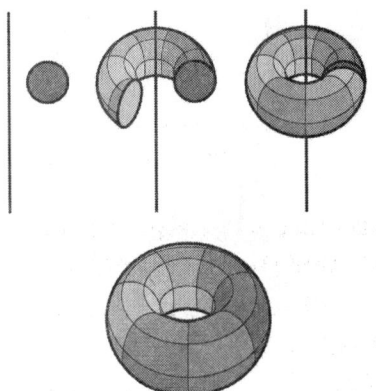

A real-life object that is torus-shaped is a doughnut.

Moving a plane across a torus produces different cross sections.

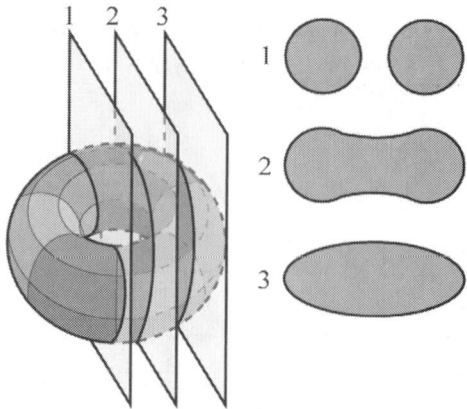

Cross sections are usually taken perpendicular to the base of an object, although different orientations are possible.

Example

Cross sections can be taken from this square pyramid at different orientations.

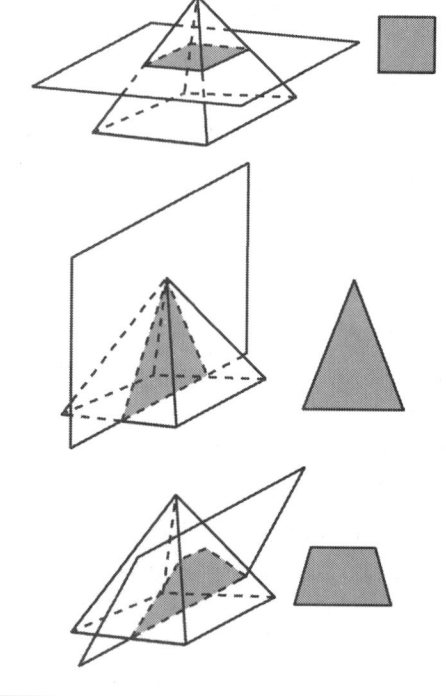

It is important to visualize the entire three-dimensional figure. Sometimes, it is useful to imagine how many edges or vertices of the object are intersected. This will determine how many corners are found on the cross-sectional image.

Example

A cross section is taken out of the given cube.

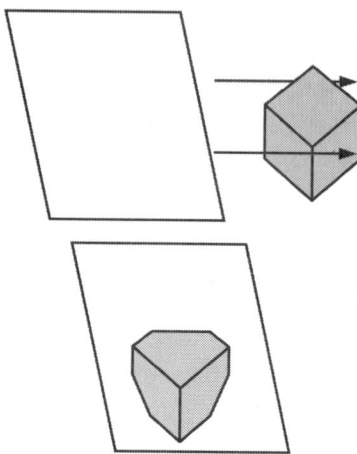

Determine the shape of the cross section.

Solution

By considering the entire object, it can be seen that the plane intersects the cube along six edges.

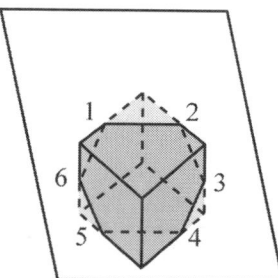

The resulting cross section is a hexagon.

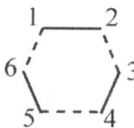

Two and Three-Dimensional Objects

EXERCISE #1—TWO AND THREE-DIMENSIONAL OBJECTS

Use the following information to answer the next question.

Mike made this structure out of building blocks.

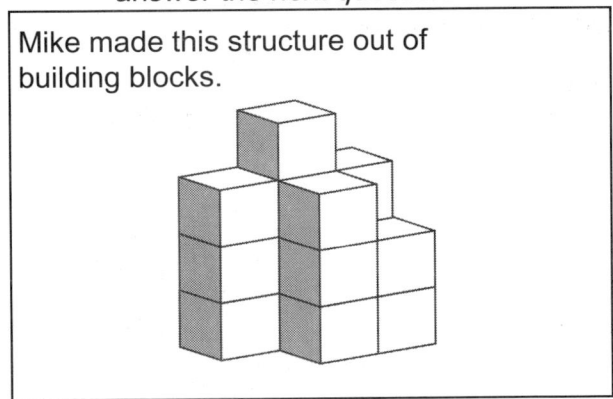

196. Which of the following sets of views is correct for this structure?

A.
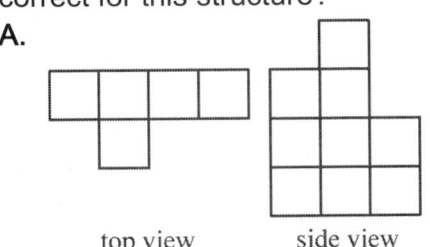
top view   side view

B.
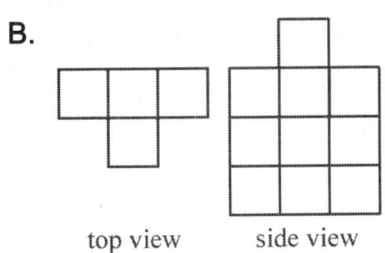
top view   side view

C.
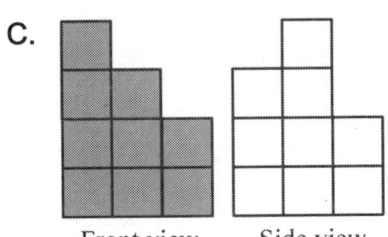
Front view   Side view

D.
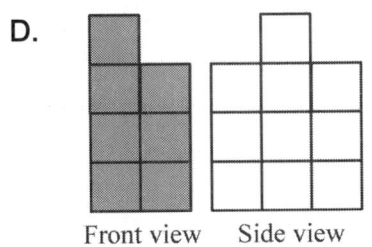
Front view   Side view

Use the following information to answer the next question.

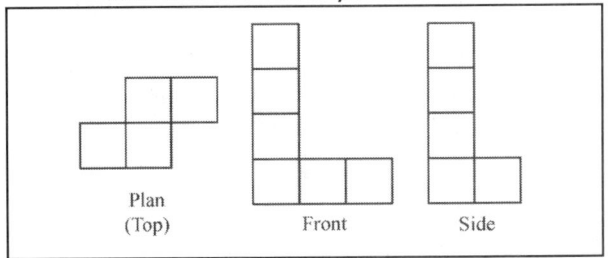
Plan (Top)   Front   Side

197. Which of the following diagrams shows the three-dimensional view of the object?

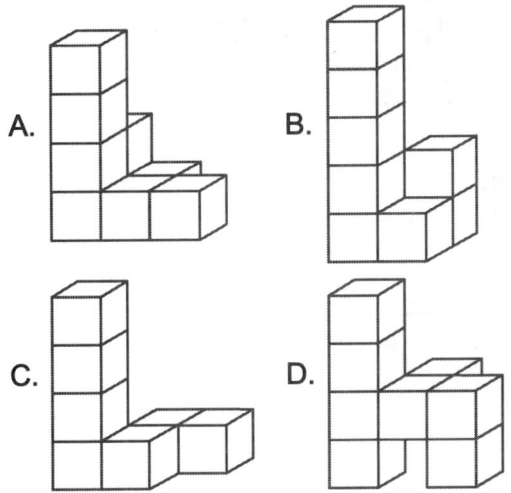

A.   B.   C.   D.

198. What happens to the shape of a parabola produced by the intersection of a plane and a cone as the plane of intersection moves closer to the cone's vertex?
   A. The parabola widens.
   B. The parabola narrows.
   C. The parabola remains unchanged.
   D. The parabola degenerates to a point.

Use the following information to answer the next question.

A machine part with three cylindrical holes is intersected by a plane, as shown.

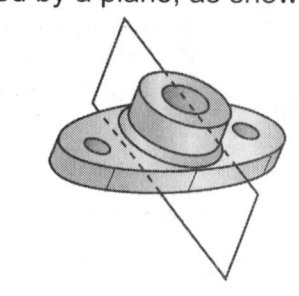

199. If the plane is perpendicular to the base of the machine part, which of the following diagrams illustrates the shape of the resulting cross section?

A.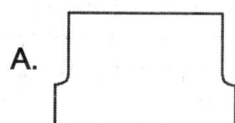

B.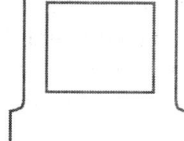

C.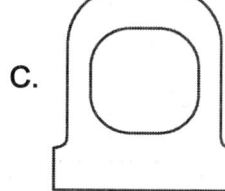

D.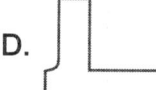

Not for Reproduction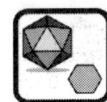

EXERCISE #1—TWO AND THREE-DIMENSIONAL OBJECTS ANSWERS AND SOLUTIONS

| 196. D | 197. C | 198. B | 199. D |

196. D

Step 1
Draw the front view.
Identify the tiles that are on the front of the drawing.

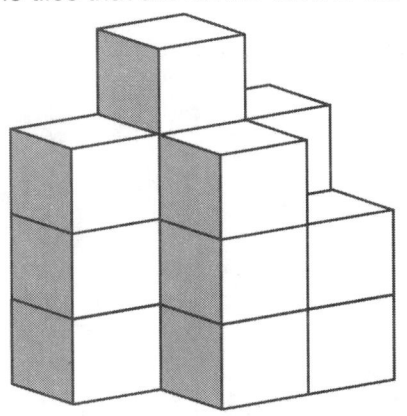

Step 2
Draw the two-dimensional view of the front.

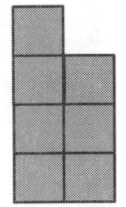
Front view

Step 3
Draw the side view.
Identify the tiles that are on the side of the drawing.

Step 4
Draw the two-dimensional view of the side.

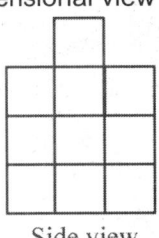
Side view

197. C

Step 1
Determine the height of the front and right view.
Label each of the front squares with the height of the blocks as indicated by the front view. Label each of the right side views with the height of the blocks as indicated by the right side view.

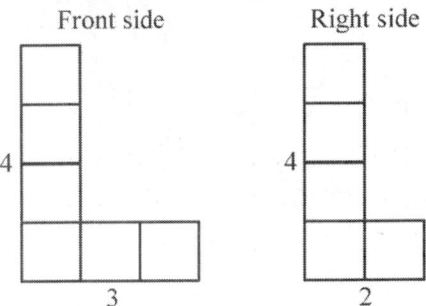

Step 2
Draw the three-dimensional view.
Cross-reference the number from the front view and the right side view. If the two numbers are the same, that is the height of the object in that square of the plan view.

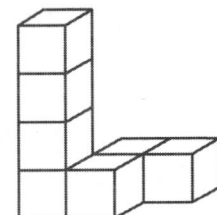

SOLARO Study Guide – Geometry   337   Two and Three-Dimensional Objects

198. B

When the plane intersects the double-napped cone parallel to the generator, a parabola is formed. As the plane moves away from the vertex, the parabola becomes wider. As the plane moves closer to the vertex, the parabola becomes narrower, as shown in the following diagram.

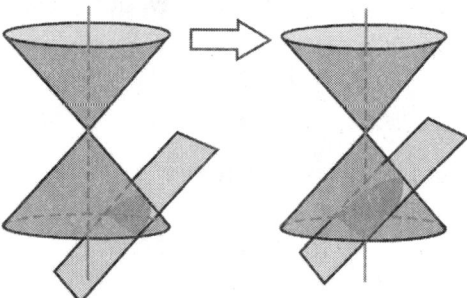

199. D

The following diagram illustrates the two sections of the machine part after the part is cut by the plane.

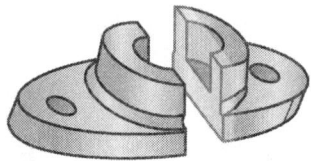

The shape of the resulting cross section is highlighted in the following diagram.

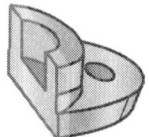

The resulting cross section therefore has the shape shown here.

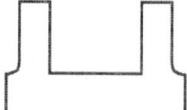

EXERCISE #2—TWO AND THREE-DIMENSIONAL OBJECTS

Use the following information to answer the next question.

Manjit stacked some boxes in his basement.

200. Which of the following sets of views represents the layout for the boxes?

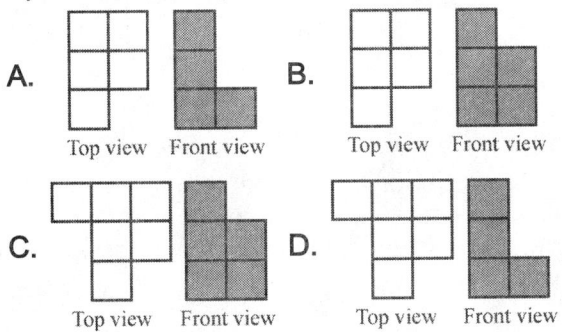

201. Which of the following groups of blocks is **best** represented by the given diagrams?

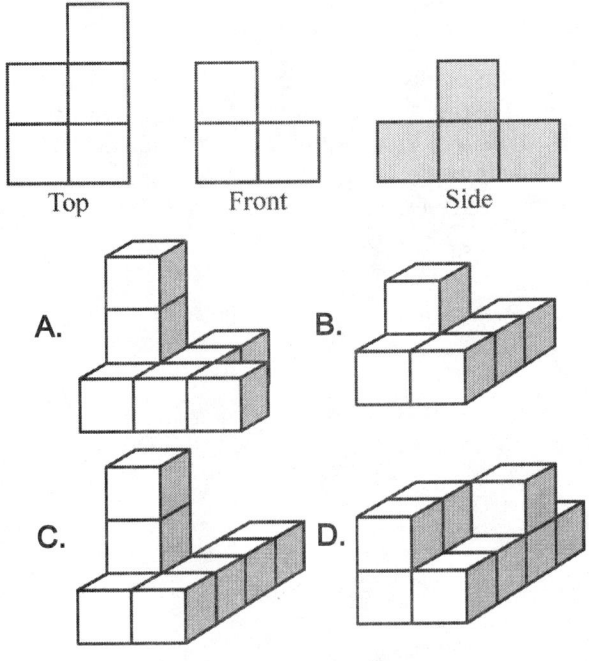

202. A plane intersects a double-napped cone such that it is parallel to the cone's axis of symmetry. If the plane does **not** pass through the vertex of the cone, the conic section that is produced is
   A. an ellipse
   B. a parabola
   C. a hyperbola
   D. a pair of parallel lines

Use the following information to answer the next question.

A plane intersects a cone as shown.

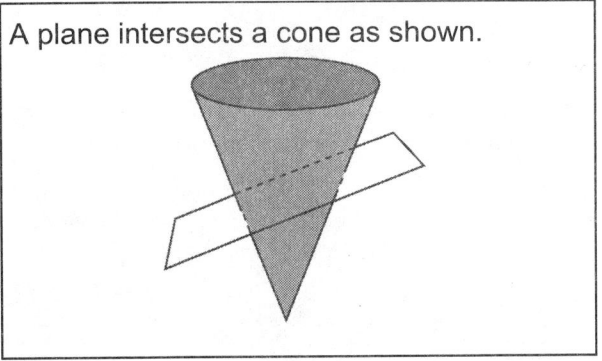

203. Which of the following images shows the shape of the resulting cross section?

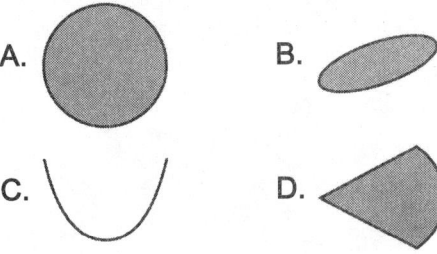

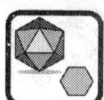

EXERCISE #2—TWO AND THREE-DIMENSIONAL OBJECTS ANSWERS AND SOLUTIONS

| 200. A | 201. B | 202. C | 203. B |

200. A

Step 1
Identify the tiles that are on the top of the drawing.

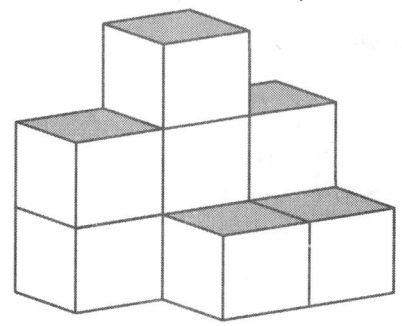

Step 2
Draw the top view in two-dimensions.

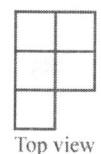
Top view

Step 3
Identify the tiles that are on the front of the object.

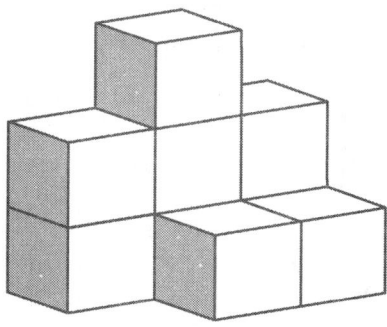

Step 4
Draw the front view in two-dimensions.

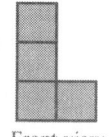
Front view

201. B

Step 1
Determine the height of the front and side views. Label each of the front squares with the number of blocks tall the shape can be as indicated by the front view. Label each of the right side views with the number of blocks tall the shape can be as indicated by the right side view.

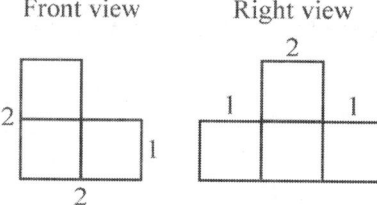

Step 2
Draw the three dimensional figure.
Cross reference the number from the front view and the right side view. If the two numbers are the same, that is the height of the object in that square of the plan view.

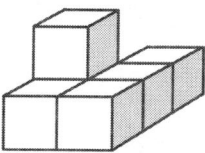

202. C

When the plane intersects a double-napped cone parallel to the axis or intersects the axis at an angle that is greater than or equal to 0° but less than the generator angle, a hyperbola is produced. Since the plane does not pass through the vertex, the parabola will not degenerate.

203. B

The shape of the resulting cross section is highlighted in the diagram shown here.

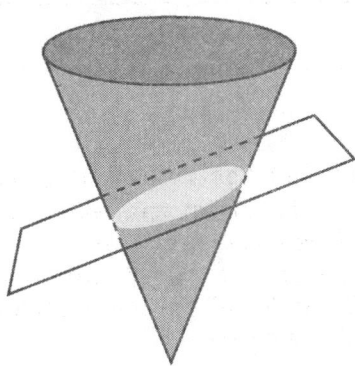

The shape of the cross section is an ellipse.

NOTES

Using Coordinates

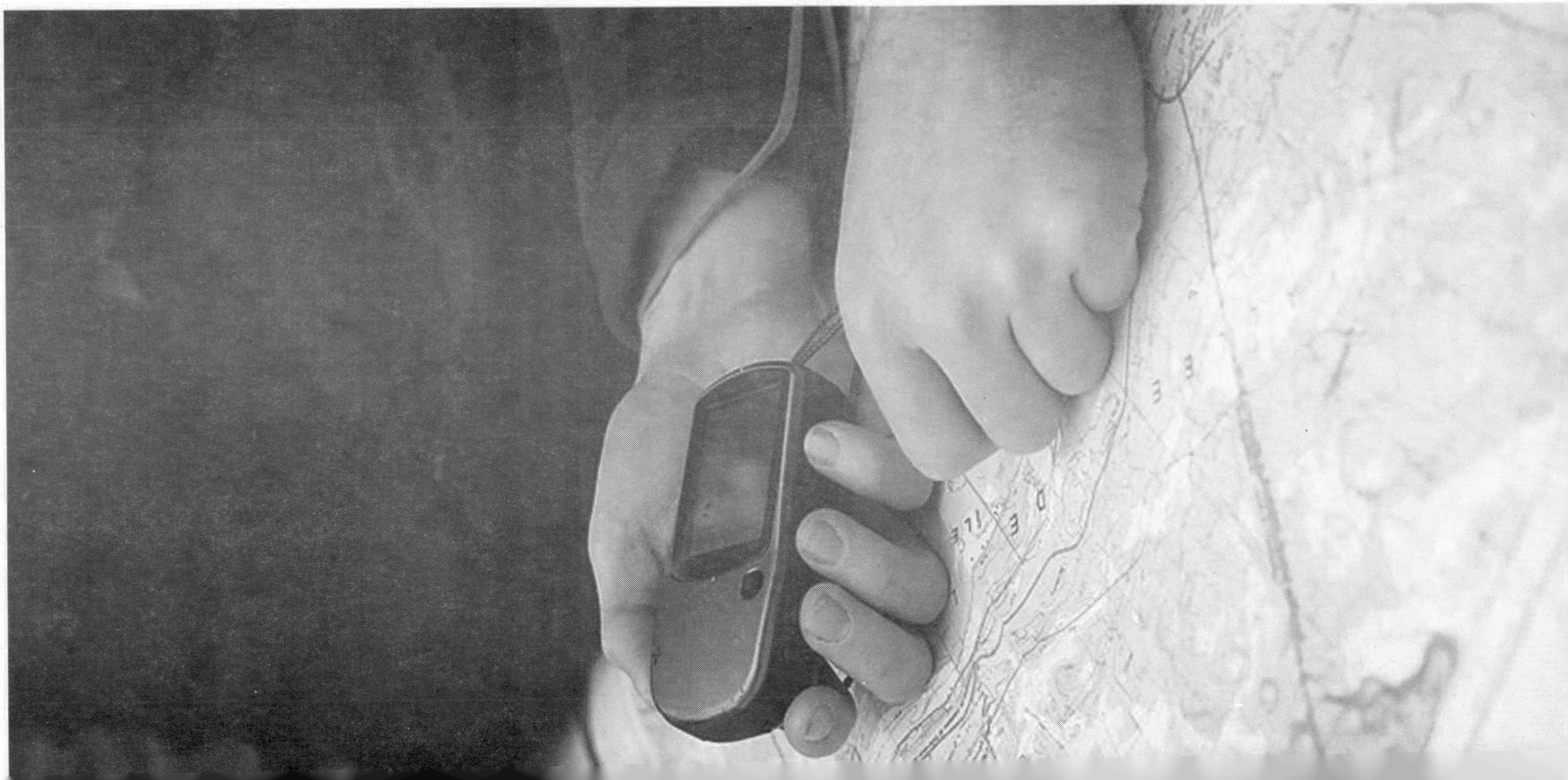

USING COORDINATES

Table of Correlations

Standard		Concepts	Exercise #1	Exercise #2
Unit4.1	Use coordinates to prove simple geometric theorems algebraically.			
G-GPE.4	Use coordinates to prove simple geometric theorems algebraically.	Using Coordinate Geometry to Prove Two Quadrilaterals Are Congruent	31	36
		Using Coordinate Geometry to Prove Two Quadrilaterals Are Similar	93	101
		Determining the Shape of Geometric Figures Using Analytical Geometry	204	218
		Verifying Properties of Triangles and Quadrilaterals	205	219
		Proving Conjectures Using Coordinate Geometry	206	220
		Determining the Midpoint of Line Segments	207	221
		Applying the Distance Formula	208	222
		Using Coordinate Geometry to Prove a Given Polygon Is Regular	209	223
		Problem Solving Using the Distance Formula	210	224
G-GPE.5	Prove the slope criteria for parallel and perpendicular lines and uses them to solve geometric problems.	Slopes of Parallel and Perpendicular Lines	211	225
		Applications of Parallel and Perpendicular Slopes	212	226
		Determining the Equation of a Line when Given a Point and the Equation of a Perpendicular Line	213	227
		Determining the Equation of a Line When Given a Point and an Equation of a Parallel Line	214	228
G-GPE.6	Find the point on a directed line segment between two given points that partitions the segment in a given ratio.	Determining the Midpoint of Line Segments	207	221
		Applying the Distance Formula	208	222
		Problem Solving Using the Distance Formula	210	224
G-GPE.7	Use coordinates to compute perimeters of polygons and areas of triangles and rectangles.	Determining the Shape of Geometric Figures Using Analytical Geometry	204	218
		Applying the Distance Formula	208	222
		Using Coordinate Geometry to Prove a Given Polygon Is Regular	209	223
		Problem Solving Using the Distance Formula	210	224
		Solving Problems with Areas of Triangles	215	229
		Solving Problems Involving the Area of a Rectangle	216	230

| | | Understanding and Applying the Perimeter Formula for Irregular Polygons | 217 | 231 |

G-GPE.4 Use coordinates to prove simple geometric theorems algebraically.

Determining the Shape of Geometric Figures Using Analytical Geometry

The shapes of geometric figures can be determined and verified using both algebraic and geometric techniques. An algebraic verification may require the use of previously developed definitions, formulas, or theorems. Geometric verification often involves sketching by hand or using dynamic geometric software.

Example

Verify that triangle *ABC* with vertices $A(2, 3)$, $B(6, 1)$, and $C(5, 4)$ is an isosceles triangle.

Solution

To verify that triangle *ABC* is isosceles, determine the lengths of each of the three sides of the triangle, and show that exactly two sides have the same length. Recall the distance formula $d = \sqrt{(x_2 - x_1)^2 + (y_x - y_1)^2}$.

Length of side *AB*:
$d_{AB} = \sqrt{(6-2)^2 + (1-3)^2}$
$= \sqrt{16 + 4}$
$= \sqrt{20}$ units

Length of side *BC*:
$d_{BC} = \sqrt{(5-6)^2 + (4-1)^2}$
$\sqrt{1 + 9}$
$\sqrt{10}$ units

Length of side *AC*:
$d_{AC} = \sqrt{(5-2)^2 + (4-3)^2}$
$= \sqrt{9 + 1}$
$= \sqrt{10}$ units

Since the length of side *BC* is equal to the length of side *AC*, triangle *ABC* is isosceles. It is important to note that if all three sides of triangle *ABC* were the same length, triangle *ABC* would be an equilateral triangle.

Example

Verify that the quadrilateral with vertices $A(1, 1)$, $B(6, 1)$, $C(9, 5)$, and $D(4, 5)$ is a rhombus.

Solution

In order to verify that quadrilateral *ABCD* is a rhombus, determine the length and then the slope of each side of the quadrilateral.

Step 1

Calculate the length of each side of the quadrilateral. Apply the distance formula $d = \sqrt{(x_2 - x_1)^2 + (y_2 - y_1)^2}$.

$d_{AB} = \sqrt{(6-1)^2 + (1-1)^2}$
$= \sqrt{5^2 + 0^2}$
$= \sqrt{25}$
$= 5$ units

$d_{BC} = \sqrt{(9-6)^2 + (5-1)^2}$
$= \sqrt{3^2 + 4^2}$
$= \sqrt{9 + 16}$
$= \sqrt{25}$
$= 5$ units

$d_{CD} = \sqrt{(4-9)^2 + (5-5)^2}$
$= \sqrt{(-5)^2 + 0^2}$
$= \sqrt{25}$
$= 5$ units

$d_{AD} = \sqrt{(4-1)^2 + (5-1)^2}$
$= \sqrt{3^2 + 4^2}$
$= \sqrt{9 + 16}$
$= \sqrt{25}$
$= 5$ units

Notice that all four sides of the quadrilateral are equal.

Using Coordinates

Step 2
Determine the slope of each side of the quadrilateral by applying the slope formula $m = \dfrac{y_2 - y_1}{x_2 - x_1}$.

$m_{AB} = \dfrac{1 - 1}{6 - 1}$
$= \dfrac{0}{5}$
$= 0$

$m_{DC} = \dfrac{5 - 5}{9 - 4}$
$= \dfrac{0}{5}$
$= 0$

Observe that $m_{AB} = m_{DC}$.

$m_{BC} = \dfrac{5 - 1}{9 - 6}$
$= \dfrac{4}{3}$

$m_{AD} = \dfrac{5 - 1}{4 - 1}$
$= \dfrac{4}{3}$

Observe that $m_{BC} = m_{AD}$.

The quadrilateral has sides of equal length, and its opposite sides are parallel (opposite sides have equal slopes). Since its adjacent sides are not perpendicular (slopes are not negative reciprocals of each other), the quadrilateral is a rhombus.

Example
Verify that quadrilateral *KLMN* with vertices $K(1, 3)$, $L(5, -1)$, $M(1, -5)$, and $N(-3, -1)$ is a square.

Solution
In order to verify that quadrilateral *KLMN* is a square, determine the length of each side, the slope of each side, and whether adjacent sides are perpendicular.

Step 1
Calculate the length of each side of the quadrilateral by applying the distance formula $d = \sqrt{(x_2 - x_1)^2 + (y_2 - y_1)^2}$.

Length of side *KL*:
$d_{KL} = \sqrt{(5 - 1)^2 + (-1 - 3)^2}$
$= \sqrt{(4)^2 + (-4)^2}$
$= \sqrt{16 + 16}$
$= \sqrt{32}$

Length of *LM*:
$d_{LM} = \sqrt{((1 - 5)^2) + (-5 - (-1))^2}$
$= \sqrt{(-4)^2 + (-4)^2}$
$= \sqrt{16 + 16}$
$= \sqrt{32}$

Length of *MN*:
$d_{MN} = \sqrt{(-3 - 1)^2 + (-1 - (-5))^2}$
$= \sqrt{(-4)^2 + 4^2}$
$= \sqrt{16 + 16}$
$= \sqrt{32}$

Length of *KN*:
$d_{KN} = \sqrt{(-3 - 1)^2 + (-1 - 3)^2}$
$= \sqrt{(-4)^2 + (-4)^2}$
$= \sqrt{16 + 16}$
$= \sqrt{32}$

All four sides of the quadrilateral are equal.

Step 2
Determine the slope of each side of the quadrilateral by applying the slope formula
$m = \dfrac{y_2 - y_1}{x_2 - x_1}$.

$m_{KL} = \dfrac{-1 - 3}{5 - 1}$
$= -\dfrac{4}{4}$
$= -1$

$m_{LM} = \dfrac{-5 - (-1)}{1 - 5}$
$= \dfrac{-4}{-4}$
$= 1$

$m_{MN} = \dfrac{-1 - (-5)}{-3 - 1}$
$= \dfrac{4}{-4}$
$= -1$

$m_{KN} = \dfrac{-1 - 3}{-3 - 1}$
$= \dfrac{-4}{-4}$
$= 1$

Since line segments *KL* and *MN* have the same slope, they are parallel. As well, line segments *LM* and *KN* have the same slope, so they are parallel.

Step 3
Determine if the adjacent sides are perpendicular.
Perpendicular lines have negative reciprocal slopes: $m_1 \times m_2 = -1$.
KL and *LM* are adjacent sides.
$m_{KL} \times m_{LM} = -1 \times 1$
$= -1$
MN and *KN* are adjacent sides.
$m_{MN} \times m_{KN} = -1 \times 1$
$= -1$
The adjacent line segments are perpendicular. Therefore, quadrilateral *KLMN* is a square since all its sides are equal, the opposite sides are parallel, and the adjacent sides are perpendicular.

Example
Verify that triangle *DEF* with vertices *D*(3, 5), *E*(5, 2), and *F*(8, 4) is a right triangle.

Solution
To verify that triangle *DEF* is a right triangle, show that either ∠*D*, ∠*E*, or ∠*F* is a right angle. An angle is a right angle when the two sides forming the angle are perpendicular to one another. If two sides of a triangle are perpendicular to one another, their respective slopes are negative reciprocals of each other ($m_1 \times m_2 = -1$). Therefore, determine the slope of each side of triangle *DEF*, and show that one side of the triangle is perpendicular to another side of the triangle.

Determine the slope of each side of triangle *DEF* by applying the slope formula
$m = \dfrac{y_2 - y_1}{x_2 - x_1}$.

Slope of *DE*:
$m = \dfrac{2 - 5}{5 - 3}$
$m = \dfrac{-3}{2}$

Slope of *DF*:
$m = \dfrac{4 - 5}{8 - 3}$
$m = \dfrac{-1}{5}$

Slope of *EF*:
$m = \dfrac{4 - 2}{8 - 5}$
$m = \dfrac{2}{3}$

The slope of side *DE* is the negative reciprocal of the slope of side *EF* $\left(\dfrac{-3}{2} \times \dfrac{2}{3} = \dfrac{-6}{6} = -1\right)$.

Therefore, side *DE* is perpendicular to side *EF*. It follows that ∠*E* = 90° and triangle *DEF* is a right triangle.

Verifying Properties of Triangles and Quadrilaterals

The use of analytical geometry to verify properties of triangles and quadrilaterals often requires a multi-step approach.

Use these general steps to verify properties in any given problem:

1. Sketch the given information on a Cartesian plane.
2. Apply the appropriate formulas such as distance, midpoint, and slope.
3. State the solution to the given problem.

Example

The vertices of $\triangle ABC$ are $A(2, 5)$, $B(-4, -1)$, and $C(1, -1)$. Segment DE is formed by connecting the midpoint D of side AB and the midpoint E of side AC.

In the given triangle, verify that segment DE is parallel to and half the length of segment BC.

Solution

Step 1
Draw a sketch to represent the given information.

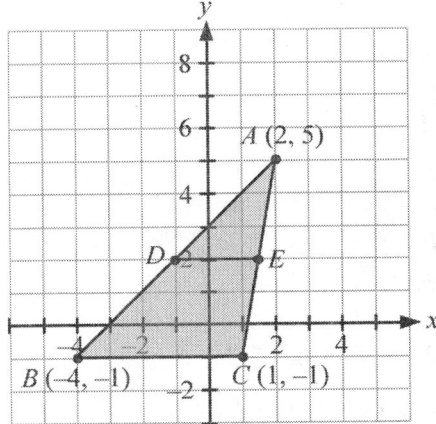

Step 2
Determine the coordinates of the midpoints D and E.

Apply the midpoint formula
$$M = \left(\frac{x_1 + x_2}{2}, \frac{y_1 + y_2}{2}\right).$$

$$D = M_{AB} = \left(\frac{2 + (-4)}{2}, \frac{5 + (-1)}{2}\right)$$
$$= \left(\frac{-2}{2}, \frac{4}{2}\right)$$
$$= (-1, 2)$$

$$E = M_{AC} = \left(\frac{2 + 1}{2}, \frac{5 + (-1)}{2}\right)$$
$$= \left(\frac{3}{2}, \frac{4}{2}\right)$$
$$= \left(\frac{3}{2}, 2\right)$$

Step 3
Determine the slope of segment DE and segment BC.

Apply the slope formula $m = \frac{y_2 - y_1}{x_2 - x_1}$.

$$m_{DE} = \frac{2 - 2}{-1 - \left(\frac{3}{2}\right)}$$
$$= \frac{0}{-\frac{5}{2}}$$
$$= 0$$

$$m_{BC} = \frac{-1 - (-1)}{1 - (-4)}$$
$$= \frac{0}{5}$$
$$= 0$$

Therefore, $m_{DE} = m_{BC} = 0$.

Step 4
Determine the length of segments DE and BC. Apply the distance formula
$d = \sqrt{(x_2 - x_1)^2 + (y_2 - y_1)^2}$.

$d_{DE} = \sqrt{\left(\dfrac{3}{2} - (-1)\right)^2 + (2 - 2)^2}$

$= \sqrt{\left(\dfrac{5}{2}\right)^2 + (0)^2}$

$= \sqrt{\dfrac{25}{4}}$

$= \dfrac{5}{2}$ units

$d_{BC} = \sqrt{(1 - (-4))^2 + (-1 - (-1))^2}$

$= \sqrt{(5)^2 + (0)^2}$

$= \sqrt{25}$

$= 5$ units

Notice that $d_{DE} = \dfrac{1}{2} d_{BC}$.

Since the slope of DE is equal to the slope of BC and the length of DE is one-half the length of BC, it is verified that segment DE is parallel to and half the length of segment BC.

Example
The vertices of a parallelogram are A(−2, 4), B(2, −1), C(−2, −4), and D(−6, 1).

Verify that the diagonals of the given parallelogram ABCD bisect each other.

Solution

Step 1
Draw a sketch to represent the given information.

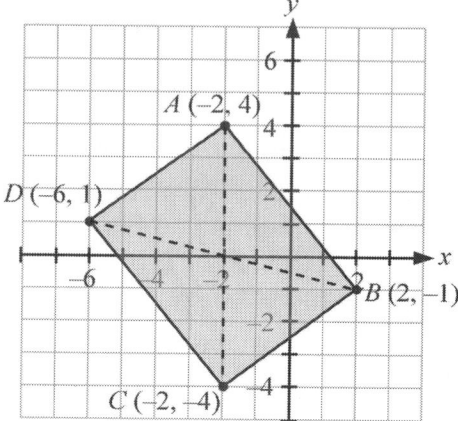

The diagonals of the parallelogram are line segments AC and BD.

If the diagonals bisect each other, then line segments AC and BD will have the same midpoint.

Step 2
Determine the coordinates of the midpoint of AC and the coordinates of the midpoint of BD.

Apply the midpoint formula
$M = \left(\dfrac{x_1 + x_2}{2}, \dfrac{y_1 + y_2}{2}\right)$.

$M_{AC} = \left(\dfrac{-2 + (-2)}{2}, \dfrac{4 + (-4)}{2}\right)$

$= \left(\dfrac{-4}{2}, \dfrac{0}{2}\right)$

$= (-2, 0)$

$M_{BD} = \left(\dfrac{2 + (-6)}{2}, \dfrac{-1 + 1}{2}\right)$

$= \left(\dfrac{-4}{2}, \dfrac{0}{2}\right)$

$= (-2, 0)$

Since line segments AC and BD have the same midpoint (−2, 0), the diagonals of quadrilateral ABCD bisect each other.

Proving Conjectures Using Coordinate Geometry

A conjecture may have been verified for a specific case, or even for many cases, but this does not mean that the conjecture is true for all cases.

Did You Know?
There are many interesting examples of this from the history of mathematics. One such example involves prime numbers. Prior to the 1500s, most mathematicians believed that numbers of the form $2^n - 1$ were prime numbers as long as n was a prime number. For example, the number $2^7 - 1 = 31$ is prime. In 1536, the mathematician Hudalricus Regius showed that $2^{11} - 1 = 2{,}047$ is not prime (it is 23×89), thus disproving the conjecture that numbers of the form $2^n - 1$ are prime as long as n is prime.

To **prove a conjecture** means to show that the general case is true. When the conjecture is provable, the conjecture becomes a **theorem**. Proving a theorem depends on agreed-upon definitions, postulates (statements), and previously proven theorems.

Example
Show for all points (x_1, y_1) and (x_2, y_2) in the Cartesian plane that the distance between the points is given by the formula
$d = \sqrt{(x_2 - x_1)^2 + (y_2 - y_1)^2}$.

Solution

Step 1
Draw a Cartesian plane, and show any two points $A(x_1, y_1)$ and $B(x_2, y_2)$.

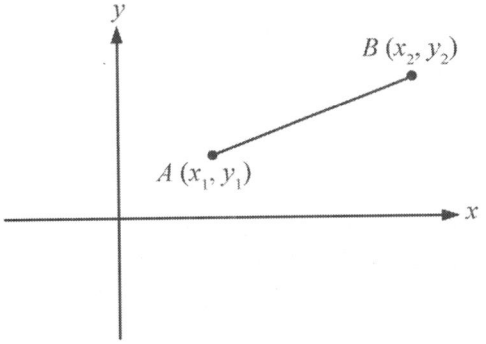

Step 2
Show that the distance representing the length of line segment AB is
$d = \sqrt{(x_2 - x_1)^2 + (y_2 - y_1)^2}$.
Draw a vertical segment from B so that it intersects a horizontal segment from A at point C.

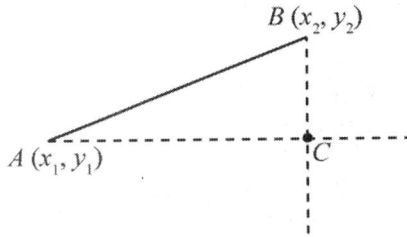

Since vertical lines have the same x-coordinate and horizontal lines have the same y-coordinate, label C in terms of x_1, y_1, x_2, and y_2.
Thus, $BC = y_2 - y_1$ and $AC = x_2 - x_1$ as shown in the diagram.

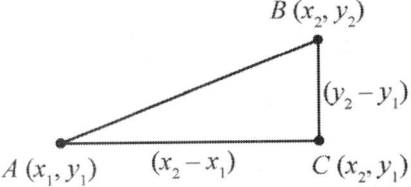

Step 3
Use the Pythagorean theorem.
$d^2 = (x_2 - x_1)^2 + (y_2 - y_1)^2$
$d = \sqrt{(x_2 - x_1)^2 + (y_2 - y_1)^2}$
It has been shown for all points (x_1, y_1) and (x_2, y_2) in the Cartesian plane that the distance between the points, and not simply two specific points, is given by the formula
$d = \sqrt{(x_2 - x_1)^2 + (y_2 - y_1)^2}$.

Example

For any parallelogram ABCD, prove that M, the midpoint of AC, is equidistant from D and B.

Solution

Step 1

Draw a parallelogram ABCD in the Cartesian plane, and label the vertices.

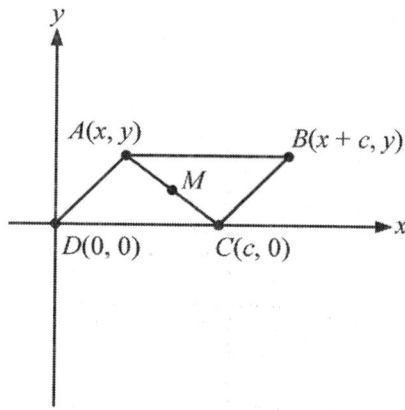

In this case, B is the point $(x + c, y)$ so that AB is parallel and equal in length to DC. It is usually convenient to draw the polygon (in this case, a parallelogram) with one vertex at (0, 0) and one side along one of the axes.

Step 2

Identify the coordinates of point M.
From the midpoint formula, M has coordinates of $\left(\dfrac{x+c}{2}, \dfrac{y+0}{2}\right) = \left(\dfrac{x+c}{2}, \dfrac{y}{2}\right)$.

Step 3

Use the distance formula to find the length of DM.

$DM = \sqrt{(x_2 - x_1)^2 + (y_2 - y_1)^2}$
$= \sqrt{\left(\dfrac{x+c}{2} - 0\right)^2 + \left(\dfrac{y}{2} - 0\right)^2}$
$= \sqrt{\left(\dfrac{x+c}{2}\right)^2 + \left(\dfrac{y}{2}\right)^2}$

Step 4

Use the distance formula to find the length of BM.

$BM = \sqrt{(x_2 - x_1)^2 + (y_2 - y_1)^2}$
$= \sqrt{\left(\dfrac{x+c}{2} - (x+c)\right)^2 + \left(\dfrac{y}{2} - y\right)^2}$

Give each squared expression a common denominator of 2.

$BM = \sqrt{\left(\dfrac{x+c}{2} - \dfrac{2(x+c)}{2}\right)^2 + \left(\dfrac{y}{2} - \dfrac{2y}{2}\right)^2}$
$= \sqrt{\left(\dfrac{-x-c}{2}\right)^2 + \left(\dfrac{-y}{2}\right)^2}$

Factor –1 from each term to simplify the expression.

$BM = \sqrt{\left(\dfrac{-1(x+c)}{2}\right)^2 + \left(\dfrac{-1y}{2}\right)^2}$
$= \sqrt{\left(\dfrac{x+c}{2}\right)^2 + \left(\dfrac{y}{2}\right)^2}$

Step 5

Prove that M is equidistant from D and B.
Since DM = BM, M is equidistant from D and B.

Example

Triangle ABC is drawn on the Cartesian plane, where M is the midpoint of side AB and N is the midpoint of side BC.

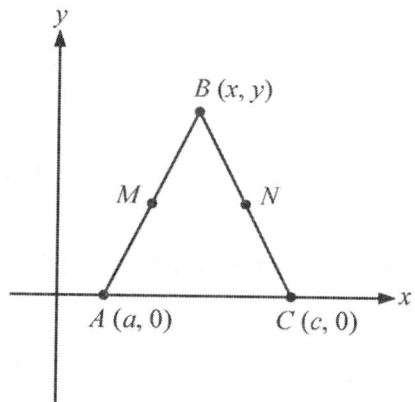

Prove that a line joining points M and N is parallel to side AC.

Solution

To prove that MN is parallel to AC, show that the two lines have the same slope.

Step 1
Determine the coordinates of M and N.
Find the coordinates of M.
$$\left(\frac{a+x}{2}, \frac{0+y}{2}\right) \Rightarrow \left(\frac{a+x}{2}, \frac{y}{2}\right)$$
Find the coordinates of N.
$$\left(\frac{c+x}{2}, \frac{0+y}{2}\right) \Rightarrow \left(\frac{c+x}{2}, \frac{y}{2}\right)$$

Step 2
Determine the slopes of AC and MN.

The slope of AC is 0 since it is a horizontal line segment on the x-axis.

Find the slope of MN.
$$\frac{\frac{y}{2} - \frac{y}{2}}{\left(\frac{c+x}{2} - \frac{a+x}{2}\right)} = \frac{0}{\frac{c-a}{2}} = 0$$

Therefore, since both AC and MN have a slope of 0, they are parallel.

DETERMINING THE MIDPOINT OF LINE SEGMENTS

The midpoint is a point that divides a line segment into two equal parts.

In the given line segment, point C is the midpoint of segment AB.

The distance from point C to point A is the same as the distance from point C to point B. To determine the location of point C on a coordinate grid, determine the mean of the two endpoint coordinates. If the line is horizontal, the midpoint is calculated by adding the values of the x-coordinates and dividing by 2. If the line is vertical, the midpoint is calculated by adding the values of the y-coordinates and dividing by 2.

MIDPOINT OF A HORIZONTAL LINE SEGMENT

The point that is halfway between points A(−2, 2) and B(4, 2) is labeled M.

Using the x-values of A and B, the x-value of the midpoint can be determined.

$$x\text{-value} = \frac{-2+4}{2}$$
$$= \frac{2}{2}$$
$$= 1$$

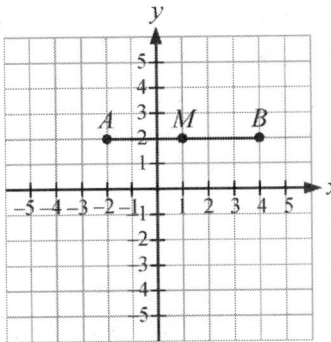

The coordinates of the midpoint of AB are (1, 2).

MIDPOINT OF A VERTICAL LINE SEGMENT

The point that is halfway between points C(3, 4) and D(3, −4) is labeled N.

Using the y-values of C and D, the y-value of the midpoint can be determined.

$$y\text{-value} = \frac{4+-4}{2}$$
$$= \frac{0}{2}$$
$$= 0$$

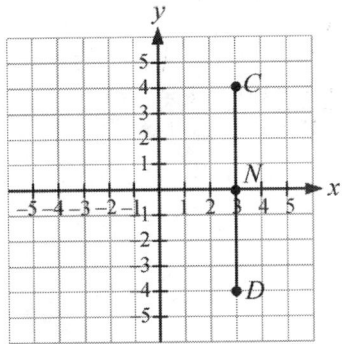

The coordinates of N are (3, 0).

MIDPOINT OF AN OBLIQUE LINE SEGMENT

You can calculate the midpoint of any line segment. If point A has coordinates (x_1, y_1) and point B has coordinates (x_2, y_2), then the midpoint of the x-values = $\dfrac{x_1 + x_2}{2}$ and the midpoint of the y-values = $\dfrac{y_1 + y_2}{2}$.

Therefore, the formula for the midpoint, (x, y), of a line segment with endpoints $A(x_1, y_1)$ and $B(x_2, y_2)$ is given as: $(x, y) = \left(\dfrac{x_1 + x_2}{2}, \dfrac{y_1 + y_2}{2}\right)$.

For example, the midpoint formula can be used to determine the midpoint (x, y) of the given line segment AB.

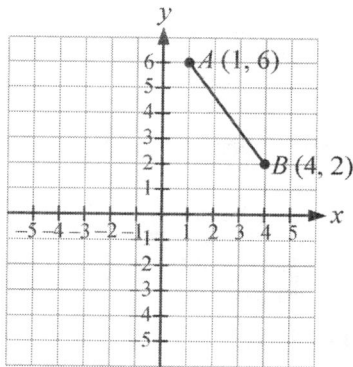

In the midpoint formula, let $(x_1, y_1) = (1, 6)$ and $(x_2, y_2) = (4, 2)$.

Substitute the values into the formula, and simplify.

$(x, y) = \left(\dfrac{x_1 + x_2}{2}, \dfrac{y_1 + y_2}{2}\right)$

$= \left(\dfrac{1 + 4}{2}, \dfrac{6 + 2}{2}\right)$

$= \left(\dfrac{5}{2}, \dfrac{8}{2}\right)$

$= \left(\dfrac{5}{2}, 4\right)$ or $(2.5, 4)$

Example
Determine the midpoint between points $U(-2.5, -3.4)$ and $V(-1.1, 0)$.

Solution
Determine the midpoint (x, y), using the midpoint formula $(x, y) = \left(\dfrac{x_1 + x_2}{2}, \dfrac{y_1 + y_2}{2}\right)$.

Let $(x_1, y_1) = (-2.5, -3.4)$ and $(x_2, y_2) = (-1.1, 0)$.

Substitute the values into the midpoint formula, and simplify.

$(x, y) = \left(\dfrac{x_1 + x_2}{2}, \dfrac{y_1 + y_2}{2}\right)$

$= \left(\dfrac{-2.5 - 1.1}{2}, \dfrac{-3.4 + 0}{2}\right)$

$= \left(-\dfrac{3.6}{2}, -\dfrac{3.4}{2}\right)$

$= (-1.8, -1.7)$

To determine an endpoint of a line segment when the other endpoint and the midpoint are given, follow these steps:

1. Apply the midpoint formula $(x, y) = \left(\dfrac{x_1 + x_2}{2}, \dfrac{y_1 + y_2}{2}\right)$, substituting the coordinates of the midpoint for (x, y) and the coordinates of the endpoint for (x_1, y_1).

2. Solve for (x_2, y_2) by separating the equation into two equations: one to solve for x_2 and one to solve for y_2.

Example
For line segment CD, with one endpoint C at $(2, 1)$, the midpoint is $(0, -6)$.

What are the coordinates of the other endpoint D?

Solution

Step 1
Apply the midpoint formula $(x, y) = \left(\dfrac{x_1 + x_2}{2}, \dfrac{y_1 + y_2}{2}\right)$.

Substitute $(2, 1)$ for (x_1, y_1) and $(0, -6)$ for (x, y).

$(0, -6) = \left(\dfrac{2 + x_2}{2}, \dfrac{1 + y_2}{2}\right)$

Step 2
Solve for (x_2, y_2) by separating the equation into two equations: one to solve for x_2 and one to solve for y_2.

$$\left(\frac{2 + x_2}{2}\right) = 0 \text{ and } \left(\frac{1 + y_2}{2}\right) = -6$$

Solve for x_2.
$$\left(\frac{2 + x_2}{2}\right) = 0$$
$$2 + x_2 = 0$$
$$x_2 = -2$$

Solve for y_2.
$$\left(\frac{1 + y_2}{2}\right) = -6$$
$$1 + y_2 = -12$$
$$y_2 = -13$$

Since $x_2 = -2$ and $y_2 = -13$, the coordinates of endpoint D are $(-2, -13)$.

PROBLEM SOLVING WITH THE MIDPOINT FORMULA

The idea of a midpoint can be integrated into problems that model real-life situations or applications of geometry problems. The methods of solving the problems stay the same.

Example
A store is located midway between Stephen's house and Bryce's house. The locations of their houses are represented by points $(-6, -1)$ and $(4, 10)$, respectively.

What point represents the store's location?

Solution
Determine the midpoint (x, y) representing the store's location, by using the midpoint formula

$$(x, y) = \left(\frac{x_1 + x_2}{2}, \frac{y_1 + y_2}{2}\right).$$

Let $(x_1, y_1) = (-6, -1)$ and $(x_2, y_2) = (4, 10)$.

Substitute the values into the midpoint formula, and simplify.

$$(x, y) = \left(\frac{x_1 + x_2}{2}, \frac{y_1 + y_2}{2}\right)$$
$$= \left(\frac{-6 + 4}{2}, \frac{-1 + 10}{2}\right)$$
$$= \left(-\frac{2}{2}, \frac{9}{2}\right)$$
$$= \left(-1, \frac{9}{2}\right)$$

The point representing the store's location is $\left(-1, \frac{9}{2}\right)$.

Applying the Distance Formula

The **distance formula**, $d_{AB} = \sqrt{(x_2 - x_1)^2 + (y_2 - y_1)^2}$, can be used to calculate the distance, d_{AB}, between two points, $A(x_1, y_1)$ and $B(x_2, y_2)$, on a coordinate grid. To use the formula, begin by subtracting the *x*-coordinates of both points from each other and the *y*-coordinates from each other. Then, square both results, add the squared values together, and calculate the square root of the sum.

There are a couple of common mistakes to avoid when using the distance formula. The most common mistake is accidentally mismatching the *x*- and *y*-values, so ensure that the numbers are paired correctly. Another common problem is found in the square root operation. Often, the very last step of finding the square root of the sum of the squared values will be forgotten.

Example
Determine the distance between point $D(4, -3)$ and point $E(-1, -9)$.

Solution
To determine the length of the line segment joining points *D* and *E*, use the distance formula $d = \sqrt{(x_2 - x_1)^2 + (y_2 - y_1)^2}$.

Let $E(-1, -9)$ represent the point (x_2, y_2), and let $D(4, -3)$ represent the point (x_1, y_1). Substitute -1 for x_2, 4 for x_1, -9 for y_2, and -3 for y_1.

$d_{DE} = \sqrt{(x_2 - x_1)^2 + (y_2 - y_1)^2}$
$d_{DE} = \sqrt{((-1) - 4)^2 + ((-9) - (-3))^2}$
$d_{DE} = \sqrt{(-5)^2 + (-6)^2}$
$d_{DE} = \sqrt{25 + 36}$
$d_{DE} = \sqrt{61}$
$d_{DE} \approx 7.81$

To the nearest hundredth, the distance between points *D* and *E* is approximately 7.81 units.

Using Coordinate Geometry to Prove a Given Polygon Is Regular

All sides and angles of a regular polygon are congruent. For example, a square and an equilateral triangle are regular polygons. The slope and distance formulas can be used to prove a polygon is regular. The distance between two points $A(x_A, y_A)$ and $B(x_B, y_B)$ can be calculated using the formula $d_{AB} = \sqrt{(x_A - x_B)^2 + (y_A - y_B)^2}$. The slope between two points $A(x_A, y_A)$ and $B(x_B, y_B)$ can be found by using the formula $m_{AB} = \dfrac{y_B - y_A}{x_B - x_A}$.

Example
A figure is drawn on a Cartesian plane.

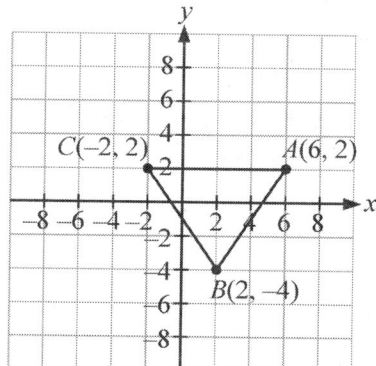

Determine if the given figure is an equilateral triangle.

Solution
All sides of an equilateral triangle are congruent.

Step 1
Determine the distance between $A(6, 2)$ and $B(2, -4)$.
$d_{AB} = \sqrt{(x_A - x_B)^2 + (y_A - y_B)^2}$
$d_{AB} = \sqrt{(6 - 2)^2 + (2 - (-4))^2}$
$d_{AB} = \sqrt{(4)^2 + (6)^2}$
$d_{AB} = \sqrt{16 + 36}$
$d_{AB} = \sqrt{52}$
$d_{AB} \approx 7.211$

Step 2
Determine the distance between $B(2, -4)$ and $C(-2, 2)$.
$d_{BC} = \sqrt{(x_B - x_C)^2 + (y_B - y_C)^2}$
$d_{BC} = \sqrt{(2 - (-2))^2 + (-4 - 2)^2}$
$d_{BC} = \sqrt{(4)^2 + (-6)^2}$
$d_{BC} = \sqrt{16 + 36}$
$d_{BC} = \sqrt{52}$
$d_{BC} \approx 7.211$

Step 3
Determine the distance between $A(6, 2)$ and $C(-2, 2)$.
$d_{AC} = \sqrt{(x_A - x_C)^2 + (y_A - y_C)^2}$
$d_{AC} = \sqrt{(6 - (-2))^2 + (2 - 2)^2}$
$d_{AC} = \sqrt{(8)^2 + (0)^2}$
$d_{AC} = \sqrt{64}$
$d_{AC} = 8$

Since $8 \neq 7.211$, all three side lengths are not equal. Therefore, the given figure is not an equilateral triangle.

Example
A polygon is formed by the points $A(2, 4)$, $B(-2, 7)$, $C(-5, 3)$, and $D(-1, 0)$. Prove that the given points form a square.

Solution
All sides of a square are congruent, and adjacent sides are perpendicular. Recall that perpendicular line segments have slopes that are negative reciprocals of each other.
To prove that the given points form a square, determine the length of each side and show that at least two pairs of adjacent sides are perpendicular.

Step 1
Determine the distance between $A(2, 4)$ and $B(-2, 7)$.
$d_{AB} = \sqrt{(x_A - x_B)^2 + (y_A - y_B)^2}$
$d_{AB} = \sqrt{(2 - (-2))^2 + (4 - 7)^2}$
$d_{AB} = \sqrt{(4)^2 + (-3)^2}$
$d_{AB} = \sqrt{16 + 9}$
$d_{AB} = \sqrt{25}$
$d_{AB} = 5$

Step 2
Determine the distance between $B(-2, 7)$ and $C(-5, 3)$.
$d_{BC} = \sqrt{(x_B - x_C)^2 + (y_B - y_C)^2}$
$d_{BC} = \sqrt{((-2) - (-5))^2 + (7 - 3)^2}$
$d_{BC} = \sqrt{(3)^2 + (4)^2}$
$d_{BC} = \sqrt{9 + 16}$
$d_{BC} = \sqrt{25}$
$d_{BC} = 5$

Step 3
Determine the distance between $C(-5, 3)$ and $D(-1, 0)$.
$d_{CD} = \sqrt{(x_C - x_D)^2 + (y_C - y_D)^2}$
$d_{CD} = \sqrt{((-5) - (-1))^2 + (3 - 0)^2}$
$d_{CD} = \sqrt{(-4)^2 + (3)^2}$
$d_{CD} = \sqrt{16 + 9}$
$d_{CD} = \sqrt{25}$
$d_{CD} = 5$

Step 4
Determine the distance between $D(-1, 0)$ and $A(2, 4)$.
$d_{DA} = \sqrt{(x_D - x_A)^2 + (y_D - y_A)^2}$
$d_{DA} = \sqrt{((-1) - 2)^2 + (0 - 4)^2}$
$d_{DA} = \sqrt{(-3)^2 + (-4)^2}$
$d_{DA} = \sqrt{9 + 16}$
$d_{DA} = \sqrt{25}$
$d_{DA} = 5$

Step 5
Determine if sides AB and BC are perpendicular.
Calculate the slope of AB.

$m_{AB} = \dfrac{y_B - y_A}{x_B - x_A}$

$m_{AB} = \dfrac{7 - 4}{-2 - 2}$

$m_{AB} = -\dfrac{3}{4}$

Calculate the slope of BC.

$m_{BC} = \dfrac{y_C - y_B}{x_C - x_B}$

$m_{BC} = \dfrac{3 - 7}{-5 - (-2)}$

$m_{BC} = \dfrac{4}{3}$

Since the slopes of AB and BC are negative reciprocals of each other, the sides are perpendicular.

Step 6
Determine if sides AD and CD are perpendicular.
Calculate the slope of AD.

$m_{AD} = \dfrac{y_D - y_A}{x_D - x_A}$

$m_{AD} = \dfrac{0 - 4}{-1 - 2}$

$m_{AD} = \dfrac{4}{3}$

Calculate the slope of CD.

$m_{CD} = \dfrac{y_D - y_C}{x_D - x_C}$

$m_{CD} = \dfrac{0 - 3}{-1 - (-5)}$

$m_{CD} = -\dfrac{3}{4}$

The slopes of AD and CD are negative reciprocals of each other; therefore, the sides are perpendicular.

The lengths of all four sides sides are equal, and two pairs of adjacent sides are perpendicular. Therefore, the given vertices form a square.

PROBLEM SOLVING USING THE DISTANCE FORMULA

To solve a problem where you have to calculate the distance between two points, use the distance formula, $d_{AB} = \sqrt{(x_2 - x_1)^2 + (y_2 - y_1)^2}$, for two points, $A(x_1, y_1)$ and $B(x_2, y_2)$, on a coordinate grid.

Example
A ship is 5 km east and 7 km south of a lighthouse. Assuming that (1 grid unit = 1 kilometer) the location of the ship can be expressed as (5, −7) and the light house as (0, 0) on a Cartesian plane.

What is the distance, to the nearest tenth kilometer, between the ship and the lighthouse?

Solution
Apply the distance formula. In terms of the formula, the coordinates of the lighthouse, (0, 0), would provide values for (x_1, y_1), and the coordinates of the ship, (5, −7), would provide the values for (x_2, y_2).

$d = \sqrt{(x_2 - x_1)^2 + (y_2 - y_1)^2}$
$= \sqrt{(5 - 0)^2 + (-7 - 0)^2}$
$= \sqrt{(5)^2 + (-7)^2}$
$= \sqrt{(25) + (49)}$
$= \sqrt{74}$
≈ 8.6

Therefore, the ship is approximately 8.6 km from the lighthouse.

Example

The corners of a square garden are located at (0, 0), (5, −2), (3, −7), and (−2, −5).

What is the area of the garden?

Solution

Step 1

Determine the length of each side of the square garden.

Since it is given that the garden is a square, all the sides are of equal length. Therefore, the length of only one side has to be found.

Use the points (0, 0) and (5, −2), and substitute them into the distance formula $d = \sqrt{(x_2 - x_1)^2 + (y_2 - y_1)^2}$.

$$d = \sqrt{(x_2 - x_1)^2 + (y_2 - y_1)^2}$$
$$= \sqrt{(5 - 0)^2 + ((-2) - 0)^2}$$
$$= \sqrt{(5)^2 + (-2)^2}$$
$$= \sqrt{25 + 4}$$
$$= \sqrt{29} \text{ units}$$

The length of each side of the square garden is $\sqrt{29}$ units.

Step 2

Calculate the area of the garden.

$$A_{square} = b \times h$$
$$= \sqrt{29} \times \sqrt{29}$$
$$= 29 \text{ units}^2$$

Therefore, the area of the square garden is 29 units².

G-GPE.5 Prove the slope criteria for parallel and perpendicular lines and uses them to solve geometric problems.

SLOPES OF PARALLEL AND PERPENDICULAR LINES

Parallel lines are straight lines that do not intersect; they remain the same distance apart. In order to be parallel, lines must rise and run the same amount over the same space. In other words, the lines must have equal slopes. Conversely, lines with equal slopes are parallel.

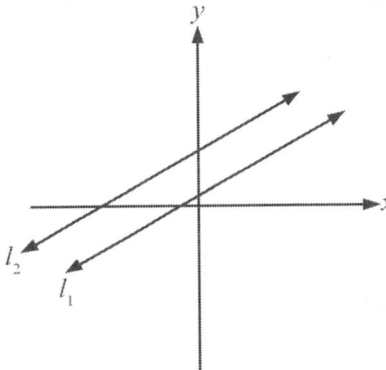

Example

Find the slope of a line that is parallel to a line with a slope of $-\frac{2}{3}$.

Solution

If two lines are parallel, they must have the same slope. Therefore, the slope of a parallel line will be $-\frac{2}{3}$.

Perpendicular lines are lines that intersect to form a 90° angle.

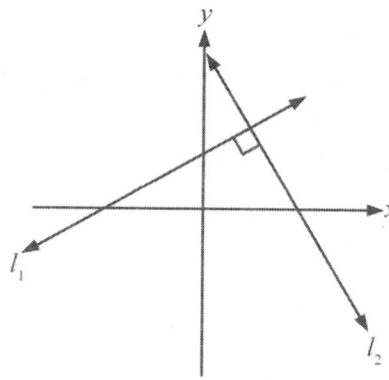

In order for line l_1 to be perpendicular to line l_2, the product of their respective slopes must equal −1. In other words, the slope of line l_1 must be the negative reciprocal of the slope of line l_2 for lines l_1 and l_2 to be perpendicular. For example, if the slope of line l_1 is $\frac{2}{3}$, the slope of line l_2 must be $-\frac{3}{2}$ for lines l_1 and l_2 to be perpendicular.

$$\frac{2}{3} \times -\frac{3}{2} = -1$$

Example
Find the slope of a line that is perpendicular to a line that has a slope of 5.

Solution
When two lines are perpendicular, their slopes will be negative reciprocals of each other. The slope of a line that is perpendicular to the given line will be $-\frac{1}{5}$.

If the slope of the original line is not given, its slope must be calculated before determining the slope of a line that is parallel or perpendicular to the original line by applying the slope formula $m = \frac{y_2 - y_1}{x_2 - x_1}$.

Example
The points $A(2, -6)$ and $B(4, -3)$ lie on a line. Determine the slope of a line parallel to this line and the slope of a line perpendicular to this line.

Solution
First, find the slope of the original line.
$$m = \frac{-3 - (-6)}{4 - 2} = \frac{3}{2}$$

Since parallel lines have equal slopes, the slope of a line parallel to the original line would be $\frac{3}{2}$.

Since perpendicular lines have slopes that are negative reciprocals of one another, the slope of a line perpendicular to the original line would be $-\frac{2}{3}$.

APPLICATIONS OF PARALLEL AND PERPENDICULAR SLOPES

The ability to classify lines as parallel or perpendicular is helpful when classifying geometric shapes as parallelograms, right triangles, or rectangles. Each of these shapes contains lines that are either parallel or perpendicular:

- Parallelograms have opposite sides that are parallel.
- Right triangles have two adjacent sides that are perpendicular.
- Rectangles contain four right angles and have opposite sides that are parallel.

Consider a triangle.

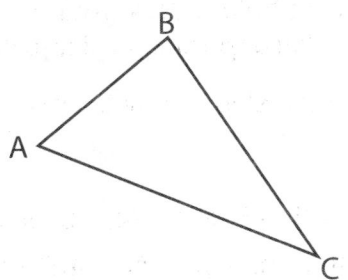

To determine whether this is a right triangle with ∠B = 90°, calculate the slopes of AB and BC. If they are negative reciprocals of each other, then △ABC is a right triangle with ∠B = 90°. If they are not, it is not a right triangle with ∠B = 90°.

Now consider this quadrilateral.

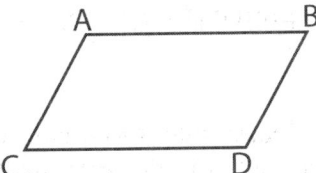

To determine whether this quadrilateral is a parallelogram, calculate the slopes of AB, BD, CD, and AC. If the slope of AB is equal to the slope of CD and the slope of BD is equal to the slope of AC, then the figure is a parallelogram.

Example

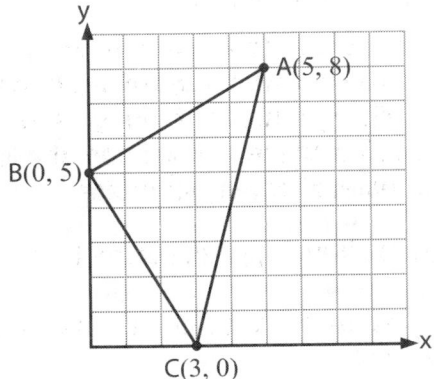

Prove whether or not the given triangle ABC is a right triangle.

Solution

The only angle that looks as though it could be a right angle is ∠B.

Calculate the slope of AB.
$$m = \frac{y_2 - y_1}{x_2 - x_1}$$
$$m = \frac{8 - 5}{5 - 0}$$
$$m = \frac{3}{5}$$

Calculate the slope of BC.
$$m = \frac{0 - 5}{3 - 0}$$
$$= -\frac{5}{3}$$

Since the slope of BC is the negative reciprocal of the slope of AB, the line segments are perpendicular and therefore, △ABC is a right triangle with ∠B = 90°.

Determining the Equation of a Line when Given a Point and the Equation of a Perpendicular Line

It is possible to determine the equation of a line if the equation of another line that is perpendicular to it is given. Perpendicular lines have slopes that are negative reciprocals of each other. In order to determine the equation of the required line, a point that passes through it must also be given.

If you have the necessary information, you can determine the equation of the required line using the following steps:

1. Determine the slope, *m*, of the line that is perpendicular to the required line.
2. Determine the slope of the required line.
3. Apply the slope formula, and determine the equation of the required line using the calculated value for its slope and the point it passes through.

Example

Write the equation of the line, in general form, that is perpendicular to the line defined by the equation $4x - 3y - 1 = 0$ and passes through the point $(-4, -1)$.

Solution

Step 1

Determine the slope of the line that is perpendicular to the required line.
Write the equation $4x - 3y - 1 = 0$ in slope-intercept form ($y = mx + b$).

$$4x - 3y - 1 = 0$$
$$-3y = -4x + 1$$
$$\frac{-3y}{-3} = \frac{-4x}{-3} + \frac{1}{-3}$$
$$y = \frac{4}{3}x - \frac{1}{3}$$

The slope, m, is $\frac{4}{3}$.

Step 2

Determine the slope of the required line.
The slope of the required perpendicular line is the negative reciprocal of the slope of the given line.

The negative reciprocal of $\frac{4}{3}$ is $-\frac{3}{4}$. Therefore, the slope, m, of the required line is $-\frac{3}{4}$.

Step 3

Apply the slope formula using the calculated value for m and the given point to determine the equation of the required line.

The slope, m, of the required line is $-\frac{3}{4}$ and it passes through the point $(-4, -1)$.
Substitute the known values into the slope formula.

$$m = \frac{y_2 - y_1}{x_2 - x_1}$$
$$-\frac{3}{4} = \frac{y - (-1)}{x - (-4)}$$
$$-\frac{3}{4} = \frac{y + 1}{x + 4}$$

Simplify by using cross multiplication and write the equation in standard form.

$$-\frac{3}{4} = \frac{y + 1}{x + 4}$$
$$-3(x + 4) = 4(y + 1)$$
$$-3x - 12 = 4y + 4$$
$$-3x - 12 - 4y - 4 = 0$$
$$-3x - 4y - 16 = 0$$

The equation $-3x - 4y - 16 = 0$ can also be written as $3x + 4y + 16 = 0$.

DETERMINING THE EQUATION OF A LINE WHEN GIVEN A POINT AND AN EQUATION OF A PARALLEL LINE

It is possible to determine the equation of a line if the equation of another line that is parallel to it is given. Parallel lines have the same slope. In order to determine the equation of the required line, a point that it passes through must also be given.

Provided that you have the necessary information, you can determine the equation of the required line by following these steps:

1. Determine the slope, m, of the line that is parallel to the required line.
2. Determine the slope of the required line.
3. Determine the equation of the required line by applying the slope formula. In the formula, use the calculated value of its slope and the point it passes through.

Example

Write the equation of the line, in standard form, that is parallel to the line defined by the equation $2x - 3y - 5 = 0$ and that passes through the point $(2, -4)$.

Solution

Step 1

Determine the slope of the line that is parallel to the required line.
Write the equation $2x - 3y - 5 = 0$ in slope-intercept form ($y = mx + b$).

$$2x - 3y - 5 = 0$$
$$-3y = -2x + 5$$
$$\frac{-3y}{-3} = \frac{-2x}{-3} + \frac{5}{-3}$$
$$y = \frac{2}{3}x - \frac{5}{3}$$

The slope, m, is $\frac{2}{3}$.

Step 2

Determine the slope of the required line.
Since parallel lines have the same slope, the slope of the required line is $\frac{2}{3}$.

Step 3

Apply the slope formula using the calculated value for m and the given point to determine the equation of the required line.

The value of m is $\frac{2}{3}$, and the given point is $(2, -4)$.

$$m = \frac{y_2 - y_1}{x_2 - x_1}$$
$$\frac{2}{3} = \frac{y - (-4)}{x - 2}$$
$$\frac{2}{3} = \frac{y + 4}{x - 2}$$

Simplify by using cross product, and write the equation in standard form.

$$2(x - 2) = 3(y + 4)$$
$$2x - 4 = 3y + 12$$
$$2x - 4 - 3y - 12 = 0$$
$$2x - 3y - 16 = 0$$

G-GPE.7 Use coordinates to compute perimeters of polygons and areas of triangles and rectangles.

SOLVING PROBLEMS WITH AREAS OF TRIANGLES

When solving problems involving finding the area of a triangle, draw a diagram of the triangle if one is not already provided for you. Include the dimensions on the diagram.

To solve problems with areas of triangles, follow these steps:

1. Start with the area formula $A = \frac{b \times h}{2}$.
2. Substitute in the known values.
3. Simplify to get the answer.

Example

Taran needs to resod part of his backyard. This diagram illustrates the dimensions of the part he needs to resod.

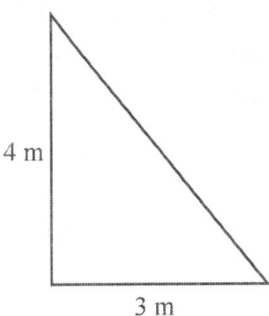

How much sod will Taran need to purchase to completely cover the part of the yard he is resodding?

Solution

In order to determine how much sod Taran will need, you must calculate the area of the part of the backyard that he is resodding.

Step 1

Determine the shape of the part of the backyard that needs to be resodded.

The part that will be resodded is in the shape of a triangle.

The area formula for a triangle is
$A = \frac{b \times h}{2}$.

Step 2

Substitute the length of the base (3 m) and the height of the triangle (4 m) into the formula.

$$A = \frac{b \times h}{2}$$

$$A = \frac{3 \times 4}{2} = \frac{12}{2} = 6 \text{ m}^2$$

Taran will need 6 m² of sod to cover the triangular shape of the part of the backyard that needs resodding.

SOLVING PROBLEMS INVOLVING THE AREA OF A RECTANGLE

To solve problems involving the area of a rectangle, follow these steps:

1. Start with the area formula for a rectangle, $A = l \times w$.
2. Substitute in the known values.
3. Simplify to get the answer.

Example

Callie's teacher asked her to draw a rectangle on the board by using decimal measurements for the length and width. This is the rectangle Callie drew.

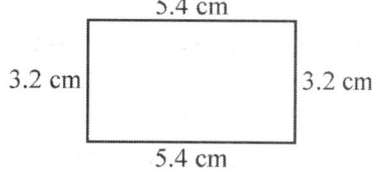

What is the area of the rectangle Callie drew?

Solution

The area of the rectangle is equal to the number of square centimeters that are needed to cover the surface of the rectangle. To determine the area of Callie's rectangle, multiply the length of 5.4 cm by the width of 3.2 cm.

Use the formula of Area = length × width to determine the area. Be sure to include the appropriate unit of measure with your answer.

$A = l \times w$
$A = 5.4 \times 3.2$
$A = 17.28 \text{ cm}^2$

The area of the rectangle Callie drew is 17.28 cm².

Example

The floor of a room is covered by eight square tiles. Each square tile has a side length of 4 m.

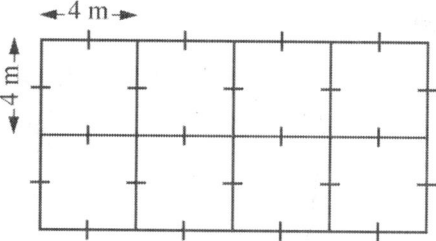

What is the total area of the tiled floor?

Solution

Step 1

Determine the length and width of the tiled floor.

The length of the tiled floor is 16 m.
4 m × 4 = 16 m

The width of the tiled floor is 8 m.
4 m × 2 = 8 m

Step 2

Calculate the area of the tiled floor.
$A = l \times w$
$= 16 \times 8$
$= 128 \text{ m}^2$

The total area of the tiled floor is 128 m².

UNDERSTANDING AND APPLYING THE PERIMETER FORMULA FOR IRREGULAR POLYGONS

An **irregular polygon** is a two-dimensional closed figure with sides that are not equal and angles that are not all congruent. The **perimeter** of an irregular polygon is the total distance around the shape, or the sum of the lengths of all the sides.

The formula for the perimeter of a polygon is $P = s_1 + s_2 + \ldots + s_n$, where n is the total number of sides of the polygon. For example, the quadrilateral shown here is an irregular polygon. Since it has four sides, the formula for the perimeter would be $P = s_1 + s_2 + s_3 + s_4$.

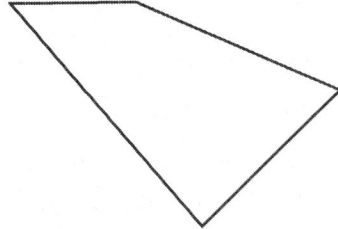

Example

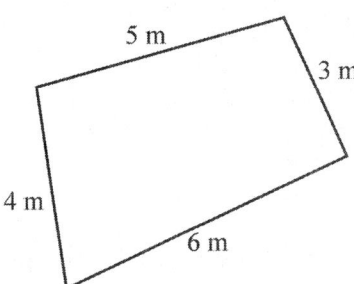

Calculate the perimeter of the given polygon.

Solution

The formula for the perimeter of a polygon is $P = s_1 + s_2 + \ldots + s_n$. This polygon has four sides, so $n = 4$.
$P = s_1 + s_2 + s_3 + s_4$
$P = 5\text{ m} + 3\text{ m} + 6\text{ m} + 4\text{ m}$
$P = 18\text{ m}$

The perimeter of the given polygon is 18 m.

The image is a polygon with the different lengths given.

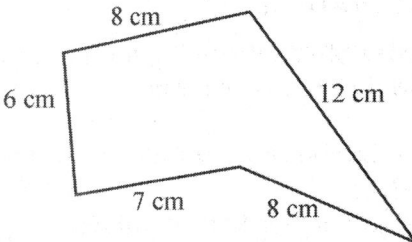

What is the perimeter of the polygon? _____ cm

Solution

The formula for the perimeter of a polygon is $P = s_1 + s_2 + \ldots + s_n$. Since this polygon has five sides, $n = 5$.

Substitute the side lengths of the polygon into the formula.
$P = s_1 + s_2 + s_3 + s_4 + s_5$
$P = 8\text{ cm} + 12\text{ cm} + 8\text{ cm} + 7\text{ cm} + 6\text{ cm}$
$P = 41\text{ cm}$

The perimeter of the given polygon is 41 cm.

EXERCISE #1—USING COORDINATES

Use the following information to answer the next question.

Triangle ABC has the points A(−3, 3), B(3, 2), and C(−1, −4).

204. Classify triangle ABC as scalene, isosceles, or equilateral.

Use the following information to answer the next question.

The vertices of a rectangle are A(1, 1), B(1, 5), C(9, 5), and D(9, 1). Four line segments are drawn joining the midpoints of the adjacent sides of this rectangle.

205. The shape that the line segments form in the given rectangle is a
   A. square
   B. triangle
   C. rhombus
   D. trapezoid

206. If triangle PQR has vertices at points P(2, 4), Q(6, 1), and R(−1, 0), what type of triangle is it?
   A. Acute
   B. Scalene
   C. Isosceles
   D. Equilateral

Use the following information to answer the next question.

A triangle has vertices of (−6, −7), (4, 9), and (8, −1).

207. Which of the following ordered pairs does **not** represent the midpoint of one of the sides of the triangle?
   A. (6, 4)
   B. (2, 1)
   C. (1, −4)
   D. (−1, 1)

208. A line passes through the points A(−4, −7), B(−1, 2), and C(4, 17). Which of the following expressions does **not** represent the length of segment AC?
   A. $\sqrt{640}$ units
   B. $\sqrt{90}+\sqrt{250}$ units
   C. $(3\sqrt{10})^2+(5\sqrt{10})^2$ units
   D. $\sqrt{(-3)^2 + (-9)^2}+\sqrt{(-5)^2 + (-15)^2}$ units

Use the following information to answer the next question.

The vertices of polygon MNPQ are M(−4, −5), N(4, 3), P(12, −5), and Q(4, −13). The four statements shown here may or may not apply to polygon MNPQ.
I. Each side is 8 units long.
II. Each side is $8\sqrt{2}$ units long.
III. Sides NP and QM are parallel to each other.
IV. Sides MN and QM are perpendicular to each other.

209. Which of the given statements are **true**?
   A. II and IV only
   B. I and IV only
   C. II, III, and IV
   D. I, III, and IV

Use the following information to answer the next question.

Points $A(-2, 2)$, $B(1, -4)$, and $C(2, 6)$ are shown on the given coordinate plane.

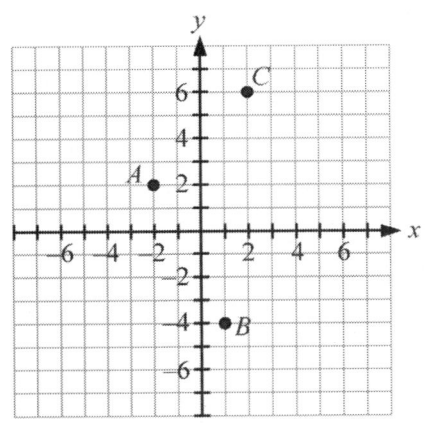

210. The perimeter of triangle ABC is equal to
    A. $\sqrt{178}$
    B. $\sqrt{784}$
    C. $\sqrt{5} + \sqrt{13} + 8$
    D. $3\sqrt{5} + 4\sqrt{2} + \sqrt{101}$

211. The line defined by which of the following equations is parallel to the line defined by the equation $y = x + 5$?
    A. $y = -x - \frac{1}{5}$
    B. $x + y = \frac{1}{5}$
    C. $x - y = 5$
    D. $y = 5 - x$

Use the following information to answer the next question.

The vertices of square ABCD are $A(-5, -9)$, $B(-10, 3)$, $C(2, y)$, and $D(7, -4)$, where y represents a whole number.

212. If the diagonals AC and BD are perpendicular to each other, the value of y is _____.

213. The equation of the line that is perpendicular to line $y = -3x + 5$ and has the same y-intercept as line $y = 2x - 8$ is
    A. $y - 3x - 8 = 0$
    B. $y + 3x + 8 = 0$
    C. $3y + x - 24 = 0$
    D. $3y - x + 24 = 0$

214. The equation of a line that passes through point $(6, 1)$ and is parallel to the line $4y - 2x - 1 = 0$ is
    A. $x - 2y + 4 = 0$
    B. $x - 2y - 4 = 0$
    C. $2x + y - 13 = 0$
    D. $2x + y + 11 = 0$

Use the following information to answer the next question.

A triangle is shown on the grid.

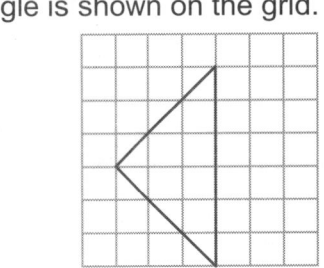

215. Estimate the area of the given triangle, and then evaluate the estimate by comparing it to the actual area of the triangle.

Use the following information to answer the next question.

A lifeguard at a beach has 300 m of heavy cord to rope off a rectangular swimming area, with the beach forming one side of the rectangle.

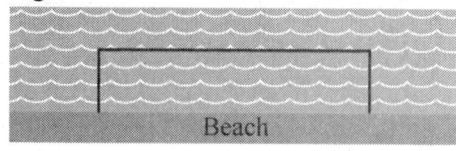

216. What is the area of the roped-off section when the side parallel to the beach has a measure of 200 m?

   A. 2,500 m^2
   B. 5,000 m^2
   C. 10,000 m^2
   D. 20,000 m^2

Use the following information to answer the next question.

A triangle is given.

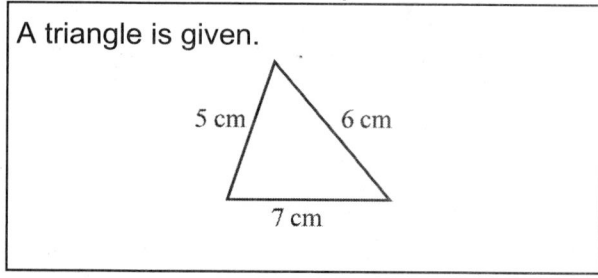

217. What is the perimeter of this triangle?

   A. 11 cm
   B. 13 cm
   C. 18 cm
   D. 22 cm

EXERCISE #1—USING COORDINATES ANSWERS AND SOLUTIONS

204. See solution	208. C	212. 8	216. C
205. C	209. C	213. D	217. C
206. C	210. D	214. B	
207. B	211. C	215. See solution	

204.

Calculate the lengths of the sides of triangle ABC.

Step 1
Calculate the length of AB.
$AB = \sqrt{(3-(-3))^2 + (2-3)^2}$
$AB = \sqrt{37}$

Step 2
Calculate the length of BC.
$BC = \sqrt{((-1)-3)^2 + (-4-2)^2}$
$BC = \sqrt{52}$

Step 3
Calculate the length of CA.
$CA = \sqrt{(-3-(-1))^2 + (3-(-4))^2}$
$CA = \sqrt{53}$

Since all three sides have different lengths, the triangle is scalene.

205. C

Step 1
Determine the midpoints (E, F, G, and H) of each side of the rectangle using the midpoint formula
$M = \left(\dfrac{x_1 + x_2}{2}, \dfrac{y_1 + y_2}{2}\right)$.

$E = M_{AB} = \left(\dfrac{1+1}{2}, \dfrac{1+5}{2}\right)$
$= \left(\dfrac{2}{2}, \dfrac{6}{2}\right)$
$= (1, 3)$

$F = M_{BC} = \left(\dfrac{1+9}{2}, \dfrac{5+5}{2}\right)$
$= \left(\dfrac{10}{2}, \dfrac{10}{2}\right)$
$= (5, 5)$

$G = M_{CD} = \left(\dfrac{9+9}{2}, \dfrac{1+5}{2}\right)$
$= \left(\dfrac{18}{2}, \dfrac{6}{2}\right)$
$= (9, 3)$

$H = M_{AD} = \left(\dfrac{1+9}{2}, \dfrac{1+1}{2}\right)$
$= \left(\dfrac{10}{2}, \dfrac{2}{2}\right)$
$= (5, 1)$

Step 2
Determine the length of the line segments joining the midpoints of the rectangle using the distance formula
$d = \sqrt{(x_2 - x_1)^2 + (y_2 - y_1)^2}$.

$d_{EF} = \sqrt{(5-1)^2 + (5-3)^2}$
$= \sqrt{(4)^2 + (2)^2}$
$= \sqrt{16 + 4}$
$= \sqrt{20}$

$d_{FG} = \sqrt{(9-5)^2 + (3-5)^2}$
$= \sqrt{(4)^2 + (-2)^2}$
$= \sqrt{16 + 4}$
$= \sqrt{20}$

$d_{GH} = \sqrt{(5-9)^2 + (1-3)^2}$
$= \sqrt{(-4)^2 + (-2)^2}$
$= \sqrt{16 + 4}$
$= \sqrt{20}$

$d_{HE} = \sqrt{(1-5)^2 + (3-1)^2}$
$= \sqrt{(-4)^2 + (2)^2}$
$= \sqrt{16 + 4}$
$= \sqrt{20}$

Since the lengths of all line segments are the same, namely $\sqrt{20}$, the shape formed by these sides is a square or a rhombus.

Step 3
Determine whether the adjacent line segments of the shape EFGH are perpendicular.
Line segments are perpendicular if their slopes are negative reciprocals of one another.
Use the slope formula $m = \dfrac{y_2 - y_1}{x_2 - x_1}$ to determine the slopes of the line segments EF, FG, GH, and HE.

$m_{EF} = \dfrac{5-3}{5-1}$
$= \dfrac{2}{4}$
$= \dfrac{1}{2}$

$m_{FG} = \dfrac{3-5}{9-5}$
$= \dfrac{-2}{4}$
$= -\dfrac{1}{2}$

$m_{GH} = \dfrac{1-3}{5-9}$
$= \dfrac{-2}{-4}$
$= \dfrac{1}{2}$

$m_{HE} = \dfrac{3-1}{1-5}$
$= \dfrac{2}{-4}$
$= -\dfrac{1}{2}$

Since the slope $m = \dfrac{1}{2}$ is not the negative reciprocal to the slope of $m = -\dfrac{1}{2}$, the slopes of each pair of adjacent sides are not perpendicular to one another.
Note that the negative reciprocal of $m = \dfrac{1}{2}$ is $m = \dfrac{-1}{\frac{1}{2}} = -2$ and the negative reciprocal of $m = -\dfrac{1}{2}$ is $m = \dfrac{-1}{-\frac{1}{2}} = 2$.

Since the slopes of the adjacent sides of the shape EFGH are not perpendicular, the shape cannot be a square.
Therefore, the line segments joining the midpoints of the adjacent sides of the given rectangle form a rhombus.

206. C
Step 1
Determine the lengths PQ, QR, and PR using the distance formula $d = \sqrt{(x_2 - x_1)^2 + (y_2 - y_1)^2}$.

$PQ = \sqrt{(6-2)^2 + (1-4)^2}$
$= \sqrt{25}$
$= 5$

$QR = \sqrt{(-1-6)^2 + (0-1)^2}$
$= \sqrt{(-7)^2 + (-1)^2}$
$= \sqrt{50}$

$PR = \sqrt{(-1-2)^2 + (0-4)^2}$
$= \sqrt{25}$
$= 5$

Step 2
Classify the triangle.
A triangle with exactly two sides of equal length is an isosceles triangle.
Here, PQ = PR.
Therefore, triangle PQR is an isosceles triangle.

207. B
Step 1
Sketch the triangle on a coordinate plane.
Label the vertices of the triangle A(–6, –7), B(4, 9), and C(8, –1).

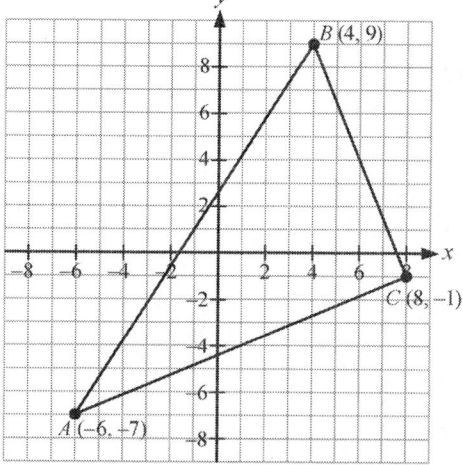

Exercise #1 Answers and Solutions

Step 2
Apply the midpoint formula to determine midpoint M_{AB} of side AB of the triangle.
The midpoint (x, y) of the points (x_1, y_1) and (x_2, y_2) is given by
$(x, y) = \left(\dfrac{x_1 + x_2}{2}, \dfrac{y_1 + y_2}{2}\right)$.
Substitute $(-6, -7)$ for (x_1, y_1) and $(4, 9)$ for (x_2, y_2).
$M_{AB} = \left(\dfrac{-6 + 4}{2}, \dfrac{-7 + 9}{2}\right)$
$= \left(\dfrac{-2}{2}, \dfrac{2}{2}\right)$
$= (-1, 1)$
The midpoint of side AB is $(-1, 1)$.

Step 3
Apply the midpoint formula to determine midpoint M_{BC} of side BC of the triangle.
Substitute $(4, 9)$ for (x_1, y_1) and $(8, -1)$ for (x_2, y_2) in the formula
$(x, y) = \left(\dfrac{x_1 + x_2}{2}, \dfrac{y_1 + y_2}{2}\right)$
$M_{BC} = \left(\dfrac{4 + 8}{2}, \dfrac{9 - 1}{2}\right)$
$= \left(\dfrac{12}{2}, \dfrac{8}{2}\right)$
$= (6, 4)$
The midpoint of side BC is $(6, 4)$.

Step 4
Apply the midpoint formula to determine midpoint M_{AC} of side AC of the triangle.
Substitute $(-6, -7)$ for (x_1, y_1) and $(8, -1)$ for (x_2, y_2) in the formula
$(x, y) = \left(\dfrac{x_1 + x_2}{2}, \dfrac{y_1 + y_2}{2}\right)$
$M_{AC} = \left(\dfrac{-6 + 8}{2}, \dfrac{-7 + (-1)}{2}\right)$
$= \left(\dfrac{2}{2}, \dfrac{-8}{2}\right)$
$= (1, -4)$
The midpoint of side AC is $(1, -4)$.
Therefore, the ordered pair $(2, 1)$ does not represent the midpoint of one of the sides of the triangle.

208. C
Apply the distance formula
$d = \sqrt{(x_2 - x_1)^2 + (y_2 - y_1)^2}$.
Use the points $(4, 17)$ for P_2 and $(-4, -7)$ for P_1 in the formula. Substitute 4 for x_2, -4 for x_1, 17 for y_2, and -7 for y_1.
$d = \sqrt{(4 - (-4))^2 + (17 - (-7))^2}$
$= \sqrt{64 + 576}$
$= \sqrt{640}$ units

The expression $\sqrt{640}$ units does represent the length of segment AC.

Alternatively, the length of segment AC can be determined by adding the length of AB and the length of BC. Determine the length of AB using the distance formula.
$d_{AB} = \sqrt{(x_A - x_B)^2 + (y_A - y_B)^2}$
$= \sqrt{(-4 - (-1))^2 + (-7 - (2))^2}$
$= \sqrt{(-3)^2 + (-9)^2}$ units

Determine the length of BC using the distance formula.
$d_{BC} = \sqrt{(x_B - x_C)^2 + (y_B - y_C)^2}$
$= \sqrt{(-1 - (4))^2 + (2 - 17)^2}$
$= \sqrt{(-5)^2 + (-15)^2}$ units

Calculate the length of AC by adding the lengths of AB and BC.
$d_{AC} = d_{AB} + d_{BC}$
$= \sqrt{(-3)^2 + (-9)^2} + \sqrt{(-5)^2 + (-15)^2}$
$= \sqrt{90} + \sqrt{250}$ units

The expressions $\sqrt{90} + \sqrt{250}$ units and $\sqrt{(-3)^2 + (-9)^2} + \sqrt{(-5)^2 + (-15)^2}$ units also represent the length of segment AC.

209. C

Step 1

Determine the length of each side of polygon MNPQ by applying the distance formula, $d = \sqrt{(x_2 - x_1)^2 + (y_2 - y_1)^2}$.

$d_{MN} = \sqrt{(4 - (-4))^2 + (3 - (-5))^2}$
$d_{MN} = \sqrt{(8)^2 + (8)^2}$
$d_{MN} = \sqrt{64 + 64}$
$d_{MN} = \sqrt{128}$
$d_{MN} = 8\sqrt{2}$

$d_{NP} = \sqrt{(12 - 4)^2 + (-5 - 3)^2}$
$d_{NP} = \sqrt{(8)^2 + (-8)^2}$
$d_{NP} = \sqrt{64 + 64}$
$d_{NP} = \sqrt{128}$
$d_{NP} = 8\sqrt{2}$

$d_{PQ} = \sqrt{(4 - 12)^2 + (-13 - (-5))^2}$
$d_{PQ} = \sqrt{(-8)^2 + (-8)^2}$
$d_{PQ} = \sqrt{64 + 64}$
$d_{PQ} = \sqrt{128}$
$d_{PQ} = 8\sqrt{2}$

$d_{QM} = \sqrt{((-4) - 4)^2 + (-5 - (-13))^2}$
$d_{QM} = \sqrt{(-8)^2 + (8)^2}$
$d_{QM} = \sqrt{64 + 64}$
$d_{QM} = \sqrt{128}$
$d_{QM} = 8\sqrt{2}$

The length of each side of polygon MNPQ is $8\sqrt{2}$ units.

Step 2

Determine the slope of each side of polygon MNPQ by applying the slope formula, $m = \dfrac{y_2 - y_1}{x_2 - x_1}$.

$m_{MN} = \dfrac{3 - (-5)}{4 - (-4)}$
$m_{MN} = \dfrac{8}{8}$
$m_{MN} = 1$

$m_{NP} = \dfrac{-5 - 3}{12 - 4}$
$m_{NP} = \dfrac{-8}{8}$
$m_{NP} = -1$

$m_{PQ} = \dfrac{-13 - (-5)}{4 - 12}$
$m_{PQ} = \dfrac{-8}{-8}$
$m_{PQ} = 1$

$m_{QM} = \dfrac{-5 - (-13)}{-4 - 4}$
$m_{QM} = \dfrac{8}{-8}$
$m_{QM} = -1$

The slope of side NP is −1, and the slope of side QM is also −1. Since parallel lines have equal slopes, sides NP and QM are parallel to each other. (Note that sides MN and PQ are also parallel to each other.)

The slope of side MN is 1, and the slope of side QM is −1. Since perpendicular lines have slopes that are negative reciprocals of each other (−1 is the negative reciprocal of 1), sides MN and QM are perpendicular to each other. (Note that sides MN and NP are also perpendicular to each other, as are sides PQ and NP, and PQ and QM.)

Step 3

Determine which of the given statements are true. From the derived information, statements II, III, and IV are true.

Since the sides of polygon MNPQ are equal in length, the opposite sides are parallel, and the adjacent sides are perpendicular, polygon MNPQ is a regular polygon (a square).

210. D

Step 1
Using the distance formula
$d = \sqrt{(x_2 - x_1)^2 + (y_2 - y_1)^2}$, find the distances d_{AC}, d_{AB}, and d_{BC}.

$$d_{AC} = \sqrt{(-2-2)^2 + (2-6)^2}$$
$$= \sqrt{(-4)^2 + (-4)^2}$$
$$= \sqrt{16 + 16}$$
$$= \sqrt{32}$$
$$= \sqrt{16(2)}$$
$$d_{AC} = 4\sqrt{2}$$

$$d_{AB} = \sqrt{(-2-1)^2 + [2-(-4)]^2}$$
$$= \sqrt{(-3)^2 + 6^2}$$
$$= \sqrt{9 + 36}$$
$$= \sqrt{45}$$
$$= \sqrt{9(5)}$$
$$d_{AB} = 3\sqrt{5}$$

$$d_{BC} = \sqrt{(1-2)^2 + (-4-6)^2}$$
$$= \sqrt{(-1)^2 + (-10)^2}$$
$$= \sqrt{1 + 100}$$
$$d_{BC} = \sqrt{101}$$

Step 2
Find the perimeter by adding the distances d_{AC}, d_{AB}, and d_{BC}.
$d_{AC} + d_{AB} + d_{BC} = 4\sqrt{2} + 3\sqrt{5} + \sqrt{101}$
The perimeter is equal to $3\sqrt{5} + 4\sqrt{2} + \sqrt{101}$.

211. C

Step 1
Determine the relationship between the slopes of two lines that are parallel.
Two lines are parallel if their slopes are equal.

Step 2
Apply the slope y-intercept formula to identify the slope of the line defined by the equation $y = x + 5$.
The slope-intercept form is $y = mx + b$, where m is the slope and b is the y-intercept.
Thus, the slope of the line defined by the equation $y = x + 5$ is 1.

Step 3
Determine the slope of the line defined by the equation in each of the given alternatives.
- The slope of the line defined by the equation $y = -x - \frac{1}{5}$ is -1.
- The slope of the line defined by the equation $x + y = \frac{1}{5}$, which can be written as $y = -x + \frac{1}{5}$, is -1.
- The slope of the line defined by the equation $x - y = 5$, which can be written as $x - 5 = y$, is 1.
- The slope of the line defined by the equation $y = 5 - x$, which can be written as $y = -x + 5$, is -1.

Therefore, the line defined by the equation $x - y = 5$ is parallel to the line defined by the equation $y = x + 5$.

212. 8

The slope, m, of a line or a line segment can be determined by applying the formula $m = \frac{y_2 - y_1}{x_2 - x_1}$.

Step 1
Determine an expression for the slope of diagonal AC, m_{AC}.
Apply the slope formula.
$$m = \frac{y_2 - y_1}{x_2 - x_1}$$
$$m_{AC} = \frac{y - (-9)}{2 - (-5)}$$
$$m_{AC} = \frac{y + 9}{2 + 5}$$
$$m_{AC} = \frac{y + 9}{7}$$

Step 2
Determine an expression for the slope of diagonal BD, m_{BD}.
Apply the slope formula.
$$m = \frac{y_2 - y_1}{x_2 - x_1}$$
$$m_{BD} = \frac{-4 - 3}{7 - (-10)}$$
$$m_{BD} = \frac{-7}{17}$$

Step 3
Determine the value of y.
Since diagonals AC and BD are perpendicular to each other, their respective slopes must be negative reciprocals of each other. Thus, $\dfrac{y+9}{7}$ must be the negative reciprocal of $-\dfrac{7}{17}$. In other words, $\dfrac{y+9}{7} = \dfrac{17}{7}$. The value of y can now be determined.

$$\dfrac{y+9}{7} = \dfrac{17}{7}$$
$$7(y+9) = 7(17)$$
$$7y + 63 = 119$$
$$7y = 56$$
$$y = 8$$

213. D

Lines that are perpendicular have slopes that are inverse reciprocals of each other. Thus, since the line $y = -3x + 5$ has a slope of -3, the perpendicular line will have a slope of $\dfrac{1}{3}$.

If the line has the y-intercept -8, then the equation for the perpendicular line can be written $y = \dfrac{1}{3}x - 8$.

This equation can be converted to standard form as follows.

$$y = \dfrac{1}{3}x - 8$$
$$y - \dfrac{1}{3}x + 8 = 0$$
$$3y - 1x + 24 = 0$$

The equation of the perpendicular line with a y-intercept equal to the intercept of $y = 2x - 8$ is $3y - x + 24 = 0$.

214. B

Step 1
Write the equation $4y - 2x - 1 = 0$ in slope y-intercept form.
$$4y - 2x - 1 = 0$$
$$4y = 2x + 1$$
$$\dfrac{4y}{4} = \dfrac{2}{4}x + \dfrac{1}{4}$$
$$y = \dfrac{1}{2}x + \dfrac{1}{4}$$

Step 2
Identify the slope of the equation $y = \dfrac{1}{2}x + \dfrac{1}{4}$.
The slope-intercept form of the line is $y = mx + b$, where m is the slope and b is the y-intercept.
Therefore, the slope of the line is $\dfrac{1}{2}$.
Since parallel lines have the same slope, the equation of the new line will also have a slope of $\dfrac{1}{2}$.

Step 3
Substitute the coordinates of point $(6, 1)$ into the slope formula.
$$m = \dfrac{y_2 - y_1}{x_2 - x_1}$$
$$\dfrac{1}{2} = \dfrac{y - 1}{x - 6}$$

Step 4
Simplify.
$$x - 6 = 2(y - 1)$$
$$x - 6 = 2y - 2$$
$$x - 2y - 4 = 0$$

215.

Step 1
Estimate the area by counting the number of squares and half squares.
There are 6 squares and 6 half squares.
Two half squares equal one full square.
$6 + 3 = 9$
A good estimate of the area is 9 square units.

Step 2
Count the number of squares in the base and the height.
It may help to rotate the triangle 90° to see the base and height more easily.

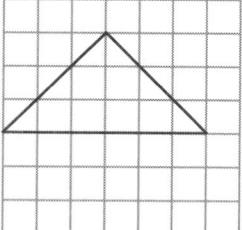

There are 6 squares in the base.
The triangle is 3 squares high.

Step 3
Use the area formula to determine the area of the triangle.
$A = \frac{1}{2}(\text{base} \times \text{height})$
$A = \frac{1}{2}(6 \times 3)$
$A = \frac{1}{2}(18)$
$A = 9 \text{ units}^2$

Step 4
Compare the estimated area to the calculated area. The calculation of the area (9 units²) is the same as the estimate (9 square units).

216. C

Step 1
Calculate the length and width of the roped-off section.
The length (l) is equal to the side parallel to the beach, so $l = 200$ m.
To find the width (w), subtract the length from the total amount of cord, and divide by 2.
$w = \frac{300 - 200}{2}$
$= \frac{100}{2}$
$= 50$ m

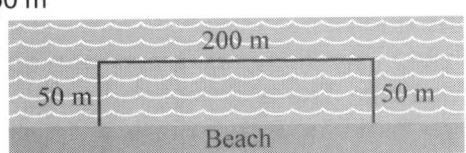

Step 2
Determine the area of the roped-off section.
Substitute 200 for l and 50 for w.
$A = l \times w$
$= 200 \times 50$
$= 10{,}000$
The area of the roped-off swimming section is 10,000 m².

217. C

Step 1
Decide which formula to use.
The triangle is an irregular polygon with three sides, so you will use the formula $P = s_1 + s_2 + s_3$.

Step 2
Apply the formula.
$P = s_1 + s_2 + s_3$
$P = 5 + 6 + 7$
$P = 18$
Remember to include the unit when you write your answer.
The perimeter of the triangle is 18 cm.

EXERCISE #2—USING COORDINATES

Use the following information to answer the next question.

Jody and Brittany are asked to verify that $\triangle ABC$ with vertices $A(-3, 1)$, $B(-1, 5)$, and $C(5, 2)$ is a right triangle with $\angle ABC = 90°$. Each student's partial solution is shown below.

Jody's Partial Solution
It is given that $\angle ABC = 90°$. In order to verify that $\triangle ABC$ is a right triangle, it is necessary to verify that segments AB and BC are perpendicular.

Step 1:
Slope of $AB = \dfrac{5-1}{-1-(-3)} = \dfrac{4}{2} = 2$

Step 2:
Slope of $BC = \dfrac{2-5}{5-(-1)} = \dfrac{-3}{6}$

Brittany's Partial Solution
It is given that $\angle ABC = 90°$. In order to verify that $\triangle ABC$ is a right triangle, it is necessary to show that $(AB)^2 + (BC)^2 = (AC)^2$.

Step 1:
$AB = \sqrt{(-1-(-3))^2 + (5-1)^2}$
$AB = \sqrt{(2)^2 + (4)^2}$
$AB = \sqrt{20}$

Step 2:
$BC = \sqrt{(5-(-1))^2 + (2-5)^2}$
$BC = \sqrt{(6)^2 + (-3)^2}$
$BC = \sqrt{45}$

Step 3:
$AC = \sqrt{(5-(-3))^2 + (2-1)^2}$

218. Which of the following statements is **true** with respect to the partial solution obtained by each of the two students?
 A. Both girls have a correct partial solution.
 B. Both girls have an incorrect partial solution.
 C. Jody has a correct partial solution, and Brittany has an incorrect partial solution.
 D. Jody has an incorrect partial solution, and Brittany has a correct partial solution.

Use the following information to answer the next question.

The vertices of a square are $A(0, 0)$, $B(3, 4)$, $C(7, 1)$, and $D(4, -3)$.
Four students made the following statements about the diagonals of the given square.

- Ted: The diagonals are equal in length.
- Ruth: The diagonals are perpendicular to one another.
- Tyler: The diagonals bisect one another.
- Jasmine: The length of one side is two-thirds the length of each diagonal.

219. Which student made an incorrect statement?
 A. Ted
 B. Ruth
 C. Tyler
 D. Jasmine

Use the following information to answer the next question.

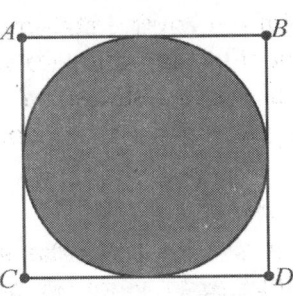

Line segments AB, CD, AC, and BD are each tangent to the circle, as illustrated in the given diagram. The endpoints of $\overline{AB}$ are at (–2, 2) and (4, 2).

220. If $\overline{AB}$ is parallel to $\overline{CD}$ and perpendicular to both $\overline{AC}$ and $\overline{BD}$, then the area of the circle, to the nearest tenth, is _____ square units.

221. A rectangle has vertices (–12, 4), (–2, –10), (–2, 4), and (–12, –10). The midpoint of one of the diagonals of the rectangle is located at which of the following ordered pairs?
   A. (–7, –3)
   B. (–2, –3)
   C. (–7, 4)
   D. (–2, 4)

222. The length of the line segment that joins point P(–6, 7) and point Q(9, –11), correct to the nearest tenth, is _____ units.

Use the following information to answer the next question.

A particular polygon has vertices $M\left(-\frac{1}{2}, \frac{\sqrt{3}}{2}\right)$, N(1, 0), and $P\left(-\frac{1}{2}, -\frac{\sqrt{3}}{2}\right)$.

223. Which of the following statements about polygon MNP is **true**?
   A. Polygon MNP is not a regular polygon because not every side has the same length.
   B. Polygon MNP is not a regular polygon because not every interior angle has the same measure.
   C. Polygon MNP is a regular polygon because each side is $\sqrt{3}$ units in length and each interior angle has a measure of 60°.
   D. Polygon MNP is a regular polygon because each side is $\frac{\sqrt{3}}{4}$ units in length and each interior angle has a measure of 120°.

224. What is the perimeter of a triangle with vertices at points (2, 3), (6, 0), and (5, 7)?
   A. $(10 + 5\sqrt{3})$ units
   B. $(5 + 10\sqrt{3})$ units
   C. $(10 + 5\sqrt{2})$ units
   D. $(5 + 10\sqrt{2})$ units

Use the following information to answer the next question.

A particular line has a slope of $-\frac{3}{4}$. A line that is parallel to the first line has a slope of $\frac{K}{10}$.

225. The value of K is
   A. $-\frac{40}{3}$
   B. $-\frac{15}{2}$
   C. $\frac{40}{3}$
   D. $\frac{15}{2}$

Use the following information to answer the next question.

Hunter applies the slope formula $m = \dfrac{y_2 - y_1}{x_2 - x_1}$, to determine if $\triangle DEF$, with vertices $D(-2, 3)$, $E(8, -2)$ and $F(4, 6)$, is a right triangle.

226. According to this calculation, $\triangle DEF$ is
   A. an isosceles triangle, since line segment EF is parallel to line segment FD
   B. an isosceles triangle, since line segment FD is parallel to line segment DE
   C. a right triangle, since line segment DE is perpendicular to line segment EF
   D. a right triangle, since line segment EF is perpendicular to line segment FD

227. What is the equation of the line that is perpendicular to the line $2x + y - 7 = 0$ and has the same x-intercept as the line $3x + 4y + 24 = 0$?
   A. $2x + y + 16 = 0$
   B. $x - 2y - 8 = 0$
   C. $x + 2y + 8 = 0$
   D. $x - 2y + 8 = 0$

228. The equation of the line that is parallel to the line $y = 4x - 7$ and has the same x-intercept as the line $y = -3x + 6$ is
   A. $4y + x - 2 = 0$
   B. $4y + x + 2 = 0$
   C. $4x - y + 8 = 0$
   D. $4x - y - 8 = 0$

Use the following information to answer the next question.

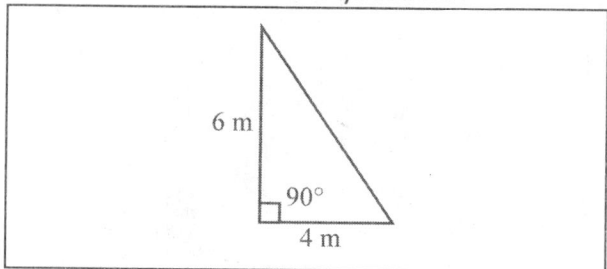

229. What is the area of the given triangle?
   A. 4 m^2 B. 10 m^2
   C. 12 m^2 D. 24 m^2

Use the following information to answer the next question.

The floor of a room contains 8 square tiles. Each square tile has a side length of 4 m.

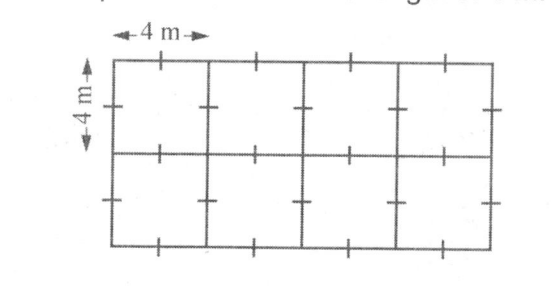

230. What is the total area of the tiled floor?
   A. 128 m^2 B. 130 m^2
   C. 132 m^2 D. 140 m^2

Use the following information to answer the next question.

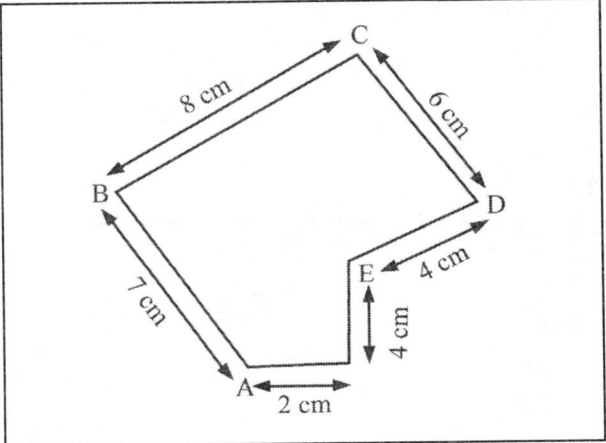

231. What is the perimeter of the given irregular polygon? _____ cm

EXERCISE #2—USING COORDINATES ANSWERS AND SOLUTIONS

218. A	222. 23.4	226. D	230. A
219. D	223. C	227. D	231. 31
220. 28.3	224. C	228. D	
221. A	225. B	229. C	

218. A

In order to verify that $\triangle ABC$ is a right triangle using the fact that $\angle ABC = 90°$, there are two main methods.

Method 1:
Verify that segments AB and BC are perpendicular by using the slope formula $m = \dfrac{y_2 - y_1}{x_2 - x_1}$ to determine the slopes of line segments AB and BC.

Step 1
Determine the slope of $AB = \dfrac{5-1}{-1-(-3)} = \dfrac{4}{2} = 2$

Step 2
Determine the slope of $BC = \dfrac{2-5}{5-(-1)} = \dfrac{-3}{6} = -\dfrac{1}{2}$

Note that $2 \times -\dfrac{1}{2} = -1$. Since $m_1 \times m_2 = -1$, line segments AB and BC are perpendicular.

Method 2:
Verify the Pythagorean theorem for this triangle, such that $(AB)^2 + (BC)^2 = (AC)^2$.

Use the distance formula
$d = \sqrt{(x_2 - x_1)^2 + (y_2 - y_1)^2}$ to determine the distance of each of the line segments.

Step 1
$AB = \sqrt{(-1-(-3))^2 + (5-1)^2}$
$AB = \sqrt{(2)^2 + (4)^2}$
$AB = \sqrt{20}$

Step 2
$BC = \sqrt{(5-(-1))^2 + (2-5)^2}$
$BC = \sqrt{(6)^2 + (-3)^2}$
$BC = \sqrt{45}$

Step 3
$AC = \sqrt{(5-(-3))^2 + (2-1)^2}$
$AC = \sqrt{(8)^2 + (1)^2}$
$AC = \sqrt{65}$

Step 4
Substitute the distance values into $(AB)^2 + (BC)^2 = (AC)^2$.
$(\sqrt{20})^2 + (\sqrt{45})^2 = (\sqrt{65})^2$
$20 + 45 = 65$
$65 = 65$

Since the Pythagorean theorem has been verified for this triangle, it is a right triangle.

When the full solutions are compared with the partial student solutions, both girls have a correct partial solution.

219. D

Step 1
Determine whether the diagonals AC and BD bisect one another.

Line segments bisect one another if they share the same midpoint.

Use the midpoint formula $M = \left(\dfrac{x_1 + x_2}{2}, \dfrac{y_1 + y_2}{2}\right)$ to determine the midpoint of each diagonal.

$M_{AC} = \left(\dfrac{7+0}{2}, \dfrac{1+0}{2}\right)$
$= \left(\dfrac{7}{2}, \dfrac{1}{2}\right)$

$M_{BD} = \left(\dfrac{4+3}{2}, \dfrac{-3+4}{2}\right)$
$= \left(\dfrac{7}{2}, \dfrac{1}{2}\right)$

Since the midpoint of both diagonals is the same, $\left(\dfrac{7}{2}, \dfrac{1}{2}\right)$, the diagonals bisect one another.

Therefore, Tyler's statement is correct.

Step 2
Determine whether the diagonals AC and BD are perpendicular to one another.
Lines are perpendicular if their slopes are negative reciprocals of one another.
Use the slope formula $m = \dfrac{y_2 - y_1}{x_2 - x_1}$ to determine the slopes of the diagonals AC and BD.

$$m_{AC} = \frac{1-0}{7-0}$$
$$= \frac{1}{7}$$

$$m_{BD} = \frac{-3-4}{4-3}$$
$$= \frac{-7}{1}$$
$$= -7$$

Since the slope of diagonal AC, $m_{AC} = \dfrac{1}{7}$, is the negative reciprocal of the slope of diagonal BD, $m_{BD} = -7$, the diagonals are perpendicular to one another. Therefore, Ruth's statement is correct.

Step 3
Determine the lengths of the diagonals AC and BD using the formula $d = \sqrt{(x_2 - x_1)^2 + (y_2 - y_1)^2}$.

$$d_{AC} = \sqrt{(7-0)^2 + (1-0)^2}$$
$$= \sqrt{49+1}$$
$$= \sqrt{50}$$
$$= \sqrt{25 \times 2}$$
$$= 5\sqrt{2}$$

$$d_{BD} = \sqrt{(4-3)^2 + (-3-4)^2}$$
$$= \sqrt{(1)^2 + (-7)^2}$$
$$= \sqrt{1+49}$$
$$= \sqrt{50}$$
$$= \sqrt{25 \times 2}$$
$$= 5\sqrt{2}$$

Since $d_{AC} = d_{AB} = 5\sqrt{2}$, the diagonals are equal in length. Therefore, Ted's statement is correct.

Step 4
Determine the length of one of the sides of the square, such as AB.

$$d_{AB} = \sqrt{(3-0)^2 + (4-0)^2}$$
$$= \sqrt{9+16}$$
$$= \sqrt{25}$$
$$= 5$$

Step 5
Determine if the length of the side AB is two-thirds the length of each diagonal, such as BD.

$$\frac{2}{3}(d_{AB}) = d_{BD}$$
$$\frac{2}{3}(5) = 5\sqrt{2}$$
$$\frac{10}{3} \neq 5\sqrt{2}$$

Since the length of the side is not two-thirds the length of each diagonal, Jasmine's statement is incorrect.

220. **28.3**

The given information indicates that there is a circle inscribed in a square. The diameter of the circle is equal to the length of one of the sides of the square, such as AB.

$$AB = \sqrt{(x_2 - x_1)^2 + (y_2 - y_1)^2}$$
$$= \sqrt{((-2) - 4)^2 + (2-2)^2}$$
$$= \sqrt{(-6)^2 + (0)^2}$$
$$= \sqrt{36}$$
$$= 6$$

Therefore, the radius of the circle is 3.

The area of a circle can be determined using the formula $A = \pi r^2$.

$$A = \pi r^2$$
$$A = \pi(3)^2$$
$$A \approx 28.3$$

The area of the circle is approximately 28.3 square units.

221. A

Step 1
Determine the diagonals of the rectangle by sketching the rectangle on a coordinate plane. Label the vertices $A(-12, 4)$, $B(-2, 4)$, $C(-2, -10)$, and $D(-12, -10)$.

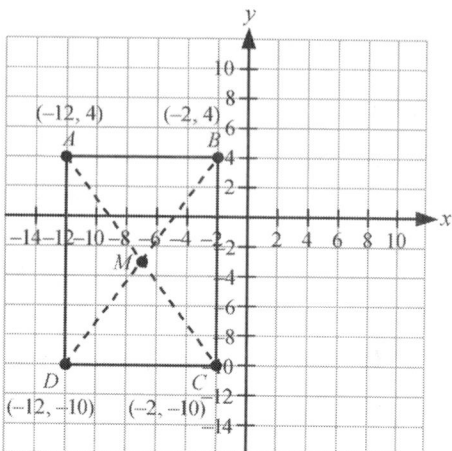

According to the property of diagonals of a quadrilateral, the diagonals of a quadrilateral bisect each other. Therefore, segments AC and BD are the diagonals of the rectangle, and M is the midpoint of the diagonals.

Step 2
Apply the midpoint formula to determine the midpoint, M, of one of the diagonals.
The midpoint (x, y) of the points (x_1, y_1) and (x_2, y_2) is given by the equation

$(x, y) = \left(\dfrac{x_1 + x_2}{2}, \dfrac{y_1 + y_2}{2}\right)$.

Substitute $(-12, 4)$ for (x_1, y_1) and $(-2, -10)$ for (x_2, y_2).

$M_{AC} = \left(\dfrac{-12 - 2}{2}, \dfrac{4 - 10}{2}\right)$
$= \left(\dfrac{-14}{2}, \dfrac{-6}{2}\right)$
$= (-7, -3)$

The midpoint of the diagonals is $(-7, -3)$.
Note: If the diagonal BD would have been used instead, the midpoint would also be $(-7, -3)$.

222. 23.4

The length of the line segment is the distance between the two points.

Apply the distance formula
$d = \sqrt{(x_2 - x_1)^2 + (y_2 - y_1)^2}$ using the points $(-6, 7)$ and $(9, -11)$.

$d = \sqrt{(9 - (-6))^2 + ((-11) - 7)^2}$
$d = \sqrt{(15)^2 + (-18)^2}$
$d = \sqrt{(15)^2 + (-18)^2}$
$d = \sqrt{549}$
$d \approx 23.4$

Correct to the nearest tenth, the length of the line segment that joins point $P(-6, 7)$ and point $Q(9, -11)$ is 23.4 units.

223. C

All sides and angles of a regular polygon are congruent.

Step 1
Determine the length of each side of polygon MNP by applying the distance formula,
$d_{AB} = \sqrt{(x_B - x_A)^2 + (y_B - y_A)^2}$.

$d_{MN} = \sqrt{\left(1 - \left(-\dfrac{1}{2}\right)\right)^2 + \left(0 - \dfrac{\sqrt{3}}{2}\right)^2}$
$d_{MN} = \sqrt{\left(1 + \dfrac{1}{2}\right)^2 + \left(-\dfrac{\sqrt{3}}{2}\right)^2}$
$d_{MN} = \sqrt{\left(\dfrac{3}{2}\right)^2 + \left(-\dfrac{\sqrt{3}}{2}\right)^2}$
$d_{MN} = \sqrt{\dfrac{9}{4} + \dfrac{3}{4}}$
$d_{MN} = \sqrt{\dfrac{12}{4}}$
$d_{MN} = \sqrt{3}$

$d_{NP} = \sqrt{\left(-\dfrac{1}{2} - 1\right)^2 + \left(-\dfrac{\sqrt{3}}{2} - 0\right)^2}$
$d_{NP} = \sqrt{\left(-\dfrac{3}{2}\right)^2 + \left(-\dfrac{\sqrt{3}}{2}\right)^2}$
$d_{NP} = \sqrt{\dfrac{9}{4} + \dfrac{3}{4}}$
$d_{NP} = \sqrt{\dfrac{12}{4}}$
$d_{NP} = \sqrt{3}$

$d_{PM} = \sqrt{\left(\left(-\dfrac{1}{2}\right) - \left(-\dfrac{1}{2}\right)\right)^2 + \left(\dfrac{\sqrt{3}}{2} - \left(-\dfrac{\sqrt{3}}{2}\right)\right)^2}$
$d_{PM} = \sqrt{(0)^2 + \left(\dfrac{2\sqrt{3}}{2}\right)^2}$
$d_{PM} = \sqrt{(0)^2 + (\sqrt{3})^2}$
$d_{PM} = \sqrt{0 + 3}$
$d_{PM} = \sqrt{3}$

Exercise #2 Answers and Solutions

Step 2
Determine the measure of each interior angle of polygon MNP.
Since polygon MNP has three sides and the length of each side is the same, $\sqrt{3}$ units, polygon MNP is an equilateral triangle. The measure of each interior angle of an equilateral triangle is 180° ÷ 3 = 60°.
Thus, polygon MNP is a regular polygon because each side is $\sqrt{3}$ units in length and each interior angle has a measure of 60°.

224. C

Let the triangle be △ABC, and let A(2, 3), B(6, 0), and C(5, 7) be the vertices of the triangle.

Step 1
Calculate the length of each side using the distance formula $d = \sqrt{(x_2 - x_1)^2 + (y_2 - y_1)^2}$.
Calculate the length of side AB.
$AB = \sqrt{(6-2)^2 + (0-3)^2}$
$AB = \sqrt{4^2 + (-3)^2}$
$AB = \sqrt{16 + 9}$
$AB = \sqrt{25}$
$AB = 5$ units
Calculate the length of BC.
$BC = \sqrt{(5-6)^2 + (7-0)^2}$
$BC = \sqrt{(-1)^2 + 7^2}$
$BC = \sqrt{1 + 49}$
$BC = \sqrt{50}$
$BC = 5\sqrt{2}$ units
Calculate the length of CA.
$CA = \sqrt{(2-5)^2 + (3-7)^2}$
$CA = \sqrt{(-3)^2 + (-4)^2}$
$CA = \sqrt{9 + 16}$
$CA = \sqrt{25}$
$CA = 5$ units

Step 2
Determine the perimeter of △ABC.
△ABC = AB + BC + CA
△ABC = $5 + 5\sqrt{2} + 5$
△ABC = $(10 + 5\sqrt{2})$ units
The perimeter of the given triangle is $(10 + 5\sqrt{2})$ units.

225. B

Step 1
Determine the relationship between the slopes of two lines that are parallel.
Since the lines are parallel, they have the same slope.
Therefore, $-\dfrac{3}{4} = \dfrac{K}{10}$

Step 2
Solve for K.
$-30 = 4K$
$-\dfrac{30}{4} = \dfrac{4K}{4}$
$-\dfrac{15}{2} = K$

226. D

The slope, m, of a line or a line segment can be determined by applying the formula $m = \dfrac{y_2 - y_1}{x_2 - x_1}$.

Step 1
Determine the slope of line segment DE, m_{DE}, in △DEF.
Apply the slope formula.
$m = \dfrac{y_2 - y_1}{x_2 - x_1}$
$m_{DE} = \dfrac{-2 - 3}{8 - (-2)}$
$m_{DE} = \dfrac{-5}{10}$
$m_{DE} = -\dfrac{1}{2}$

Step 2
Determine the slope of line segment EF, m_{EF}, in △DEF.
Apply the slope formula.
$m = \dfrac{y_2 - y_1}{x_2 - x_1}$
$m_{EF} = \dfrac{6 - (-2)}{4 - 8}$
$m_{EF} = \dfrac{8}{-4}$
$m_{EF} = -2$

Step 3
Determine the slope of line segment FD, m_{FD}, in $\triangle DEF$.
Apply the slope formula.
$$m = \frac{y_2 - y_1}{x_2 - x_1}$$
$$m_{FD} = \frac{6 - 3}{4 - (-2)}$$
$$m_{FD} = \frac{3}{6}$$
$$m_{FD} = \frac{1}{2}$$

Since the number $\frac{1}{2}$ is the negative reciprocal of the number −2, line segment FD is perpendicular to line segment EF. Since the two line segments are perpendicular, $\triangle DEF$ is a right triangle.

227. D
Step 1
Determine the slope of the required line.
The required line is perpendicular to the line defined by the equation $2x + y - 7 = 0$. Thus, the slope of the required line is the negative reciprocal of the slope of the given line. Determine the slope of the given line by rearranging the equation of the line into slope-intercept form:
$$2x + y - 7 = 0$$
$$y = -2x + 7$$
The slope of the given line is −2, so the slope of the perpendicular line is $m = \frac{1}{2}$.

Step 2
Determine a point on the required line.
The required line has the same x-intercept as the line defined by the equation $3x + 4y + 24 = 0$. Determine the x-intercept of the given line to determine the point on the required line.
Substitute 0 for y in $3x + 4y + 24 = 0$ and solve for x.
$$3x + 4(0) + 24 = 0$$
$$3x = -24$$
$$x = -8$$
Therefore, a point on the required line is (−8, 0).

Step 3
Determine the equation of the line by applying the slope formula, using $m = \frac{1}{2}$ and point (−8, 0).
Substitute $\frac{1}{2}$ for m, −8 for x_1 and 0 for y_1 in the equation $m = \frac{y - y_1}{x - x_1}$.
$$\frac{1}{2} = \frac{y - 0}{x - (-8)}$$
$$\frac{1}{2} = \frac{y}{x + 8}$$
Use the cross products to find the equation of the perpendicular line.
$$x + 8 = 2y$$
Rearrange the equation into the standard form of the equation.
$$x - 2y + 8 = 0$$

228. D
Parallel lines have the same slope.
Step 1
Determine the slope of the required line.
Identify the slope of the line $y = 4x + 7$.
The slope intercept form of the line is $y = mx + b$, where m is the slope and b is the y-intercept.
The slope of the line $y = 4x + 7$ is 4. Since the new line is to be parallel to $y = 4x + 7$, its slope will also be 4.

Step 2
Determine the x-intercept of the line $y = -3x + 6$.
Substitute 0 for y, and solve for x.
$$0 = -3x + 6$$
$$3x = 6$$
$$\frac{3x}{3} = \frac{6}{3}$$
$$x = 2$$
The x-intercept of the line $y = -3x + 6$ is (2, 0). Since the new line is to have the same x-intercept as $y = -3x + 6$, its x-intercept will also be (2, 0).

Step 3
Substitute the slope of 4 and the coordinates of the point (2, 0) into the slope formula to determine the equation of the new line.
$$m = \frac{y_2 - y_1}{x_2 - x_1}$$
$$4 = \frac{y - 0}{x - 2}$$

Step 4
Simplify.
$$4(x-2) = y$$
$$4x - 8 = y$$
$$4x - y - 8 = 0$$

229. C

Base of the triangle = 4 m

Height of the triangle = 6 m

The area of a triangle = $\frac{1}{2}$ × base × height

$A = \frac{1}{2} \times 4\,m \times 6\,m$

$A = \frac{1}{2} \times 24\,m^2$

$A = 12\,m^2$

230. A

Step 1
Determine the length and width of the tiled floor.
The length of the tiled floor is 16 m.
4 m × 4 = 16 m
The width of the tiled floor is 8 m.
4 m × 2 = 8 m

Step 2
Calculate the area of the tiled floor.
$A = l \times w$
$A = 16 \times 8 = 128\,m^2$

The total area of the floor covered by the tiles is 128 m².

231. 31

To determine the perimeter of an irregular polygon like the given shape, add all six side lengths.

If the letter *s* represents a side length, you could use a formula such as the following to determine the perimeter.
$P = s + s + s + s + s + s$
$P = 7 + 8 + 6 + 4 + 4 + 2$
$P = 31$ cm

The perimeter of the irregular polygon is 31 cm.

NOTES

Equations for Conic Sections

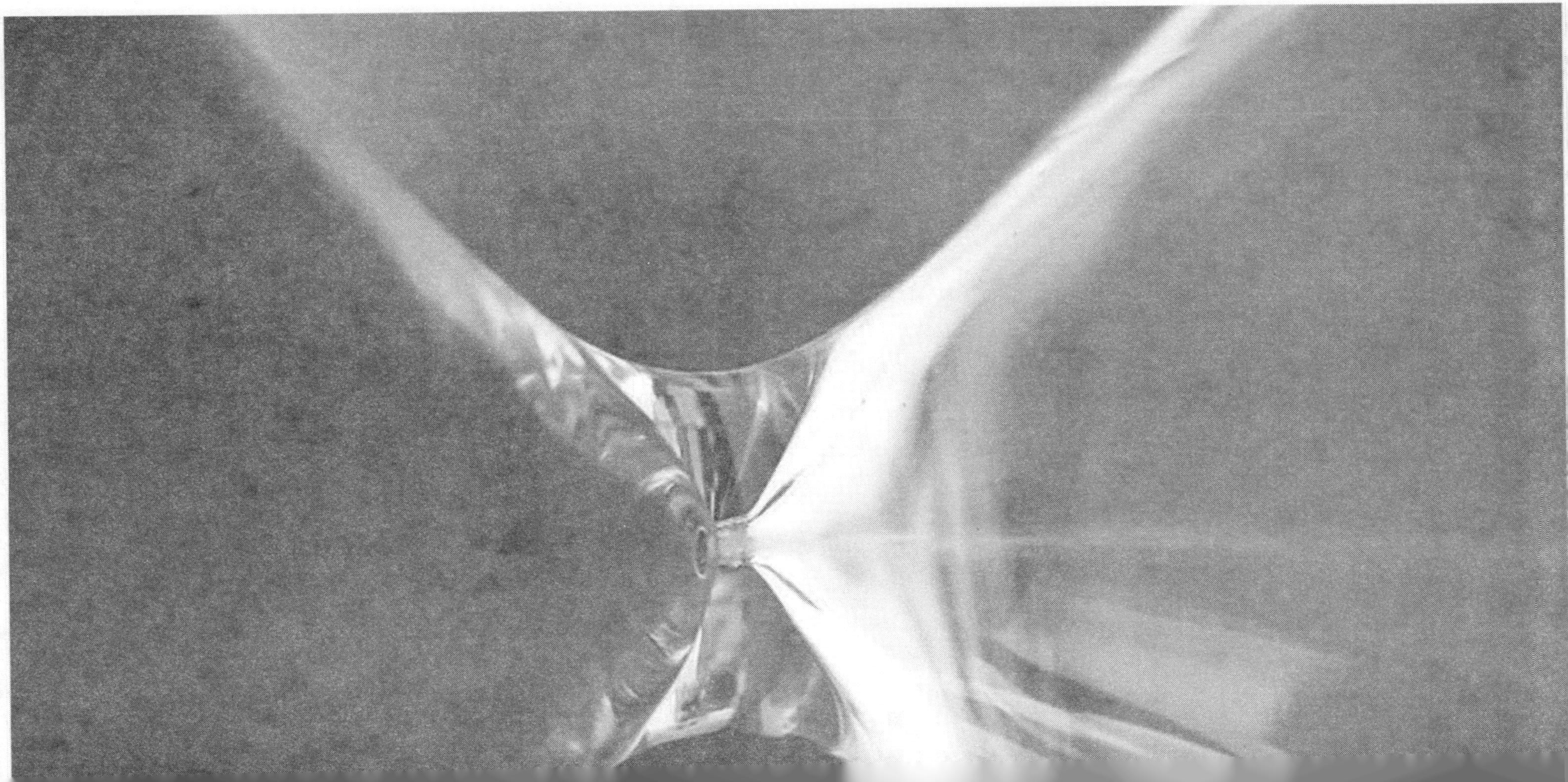

EQUATIONS FOR CONIC SECTIONS

Table of Correlations

Standard		Concepts	Exercise #1	Exercise #2
Unit4.2	Translate between the geometric description and the equation for a conic section.			
G-GPE.2	Derive the equation of a parabola given a focus and directrix.	Defining Foci and Eccentricity of Conic Sections	232	234
		Deriving the Equation of a Parabola from its Locus Definition	233	235

G-GPE.2 Derive the equation of a parabola given a focus and directrix.

Defining Foci and Eccentricity of Conic Sections

Every conic section can be defined by a constant e called the eccentricity. In the diagram shown, L is a fixed line in the plane called a directrix and F is a fixed point that is not on the line called the focus. The constant e is ≥ 0.

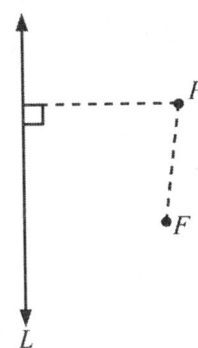

In general, a conic section consists of the set of all points P, such that the ratio of the distance between P and the focus (PF) to the distance between P and the directrix (PL) is e.

In other words, a conic section with F as one focus consists of the set of all points P in the plane, which satisfies the following equation:

$$\frac{\text{the distance between } P \text{ and the focus}}{\text{the distance between } P \text{ and the directrix}} = e, \text{ or}$$

$e = \dfrac{PF}{PL}$.

The conic section is an ellipse if $0 < e < 1$.

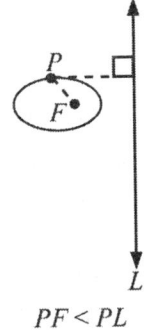

$PF < PL$

The conic section is a parabola if $e = 1$.

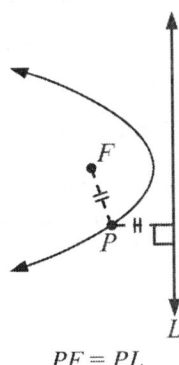

$PF = PL$

The conic section is a hyperbola if $e > 1$.

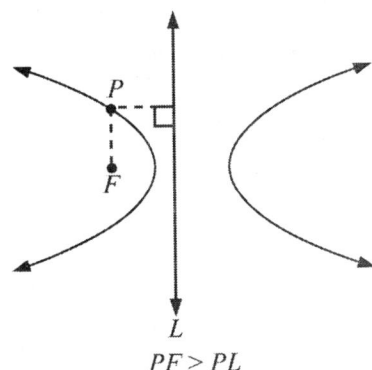

$PF > PL$

The eccentricity of a circle is zero.

Because of the symmetry of both the ellipse and the hyperbola, each conic section has two foci, F_1 and F_2, and two directrices L_1 and L_2.

The shape of ellipses and hyperbolas is determined by the size of the eccentricity.

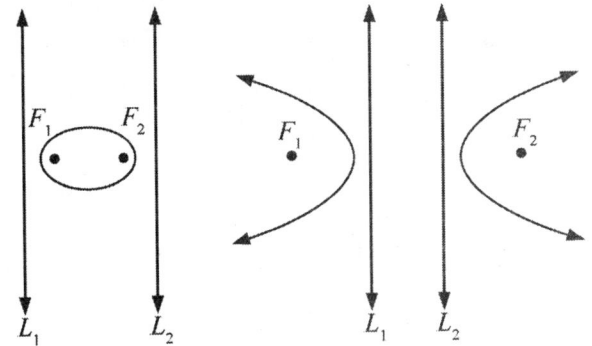

For ellipses, if *e* is close to zero, the ellipse is nearly circular. If *e* is close to 1, the ellipse is very narrow and elongated.

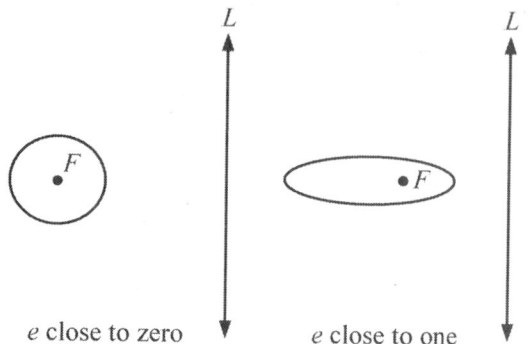

e close to zero   e close to one

For hyperbolas, when *e* is close to 1, the branches of the hyperbola are very narrow and get wider as the eccentricity increases.

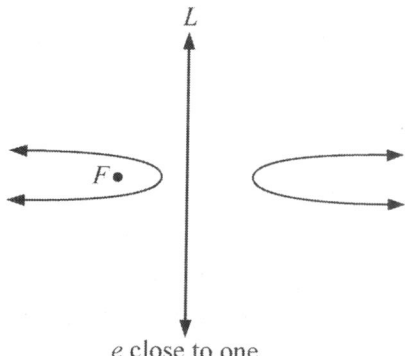

e close to one

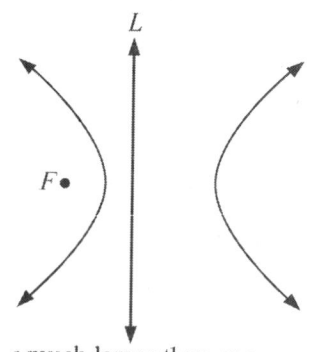

e much larger than one

Example

A certain conic section has a focus at the point $F(3, -2)$ and a directrix of $y = 4$.

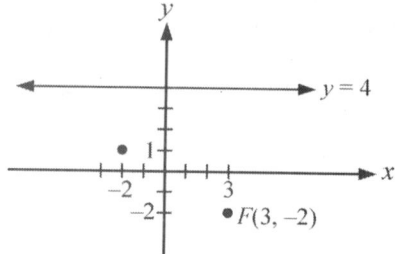

The point $P(-2, 1)$ is on the locus of the conic section.

Determine the eccentricity of the conic section expressed to the nearest hundredth, and specify whether it is an ellipse, parabola, or hyperbola.

Solution

Step 1

Determine the distance from point *P* to the focus using the distance formula $d = \sqrt{(x_2 - x_1)^2 + (y_2 - y_1)^2}$.

$PF = \sqrt{(3 - -2)^2 + (-2 - 1)^2}$
$= \sqrt{25 + 9}$
$= \sqrt{34}$

Step 2

Determine the distance from point *P* to the directrix.

Since the directrix is a horizontal line, the distance from point *P* can be determined from the absolute value of the difference in the *y*-coordinates.

$PL = |y_2 - y_1|$
$= |4 - 1|$
$= 3$

Step 3

Determine the eccentricity using $e = \dfrac{PF}{PL}$.

$e = \dfrac{\sqrt{34}}{3}$

$e \approx 1.94$

Step 4

Specify the type of conic section.

Since the eccentricity is larger than 1, the conic section is a hyperbola.

Deriving the Equation of a Parabola from its Locus Definition

Like all conic sections, a parabola can be defined by using the set of all points that create its particular shape. This is known as its locus definition.

The given diagram shows the directrix, L, which is a fixed line in the plane. The focus, F, is a fixed point that is not on the line.

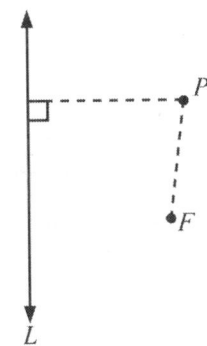

A parabola is defined as a locus of points equidistant from the focus and the directrix. In other words, the length of PF is equal to the length of PL.

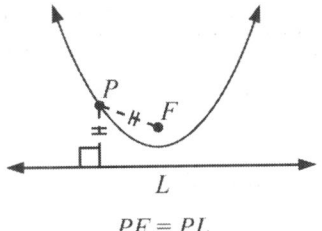

$PF = PL$

Example

Using its locus definition, determine the equation of a parabola with a vertical orientation and its vertex at the origin.

Solution

Step 1
Sketch and label a parabola with a vertical orientation and its vertex at the origin.

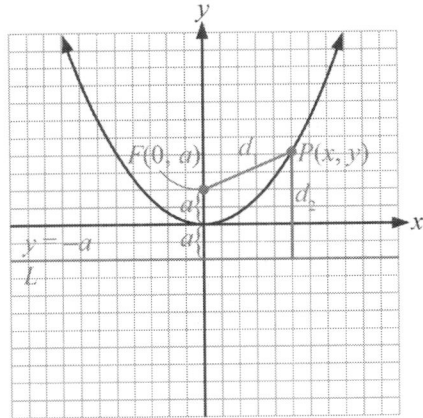

- The focus of the parabola is located at $(0, a)$.
- The directrix is the line $y = -a$.
- The distance from the origin to the focus and the distance from the origin to the directrix is a.
- Point $P(x, y)$ represents any point on the curve of the parabola.
- The distance from point P to the focus is d_1.
- The distance from point P to the directrix is d_2.

Step 2
Determine the length of d_1 and d_2.

Using the formula for distance, the length of $d_1 = \sqrt{(x-0)^2 + (y-a)^2}$.

Using the diagram as reference, the length of $d_2 = y + a$.

Step 3
Derive the equation.

According to the locus definition of a parabola, the distance from any point to the focus is equal to the distance from that same point to the directrix.

$$d_1 = d_2$$
$$\sqrt{x^2 + (y-a)^2} = y + a$$

Simplify the equation by squaring both sides.

$$\sqrt{x^2 + (y-a)^2} = y + a$$
$$x^2 + (y-a)^2 = (y+a)^2$$
$$x^2 + y^2 - 2ay + a^2 = y^2 + 2ay + a^2$$
$$x^2 = 4ay$$

Thus, the equation of a parabola with a vertical orientation and its vertex at the origin is $x^2 = 4ay$.

In general, to shift the vertex of a vertically orientated parabola from the origin (0, 0) to any point, (h, k), replace each x-value with $(x - h)$ and each y-value with $(y - k)$. The resulting formula for a vertical parabola with its vertex at (h, k) is $(x - h)^2 = 4a(y - k)$.

Example
The given vertically orientated parabola has its vertex at (5, 2).

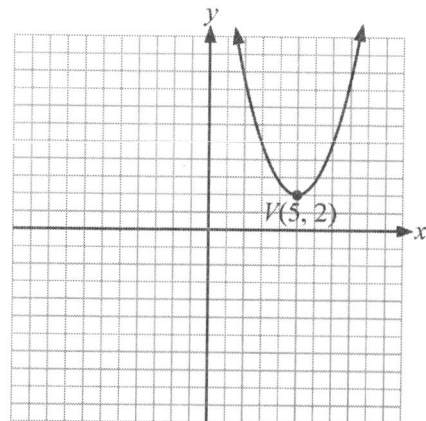

If you were to derive the equation of the vertically orientated parabola with its vertex at (5, 2), the equation would be $(x - 5)^2 = 4a(y - 2)$.

Example
From its locus definition, derive the equation of a parabola with a horizontal orientation and its vertex at the origin.

Solution
Step 1
Sketch and label a parabola with a horizontal orientation and its vertex at the origin.

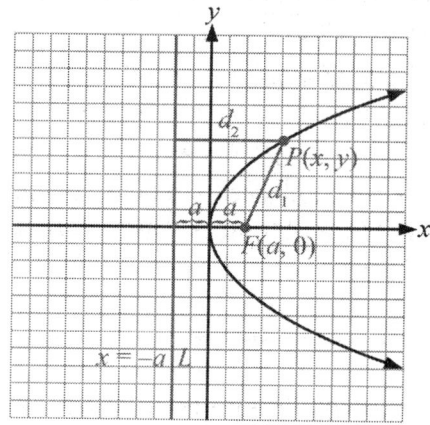

- The focus of the parabola is located at $(a, 0)$.
- The directrix is the line $x = -a$.
- The distance from the origin to the focus and the distance from the origin to the directrix is a.
- Point $P(x, y)$ represents any point on the curve of the parabola.
- The distance from point P to the focus is d_1.
- The distance from point P to the directrix is d_2.

Step 2
Determine the length of d_1 and d_2.

Using the formula for distance, the length of $d_1 = \sqrt{(x-a)^2 + (y-0)^2}$.

Using the diagram as reference, the length of $d_2 = x + a$.

Step 3
Derive the equation.

According to the locus definition of a parabola, the distance from any point on the parabola to the focus is equal to the distance from that same point to the directrix.

$$d_1 = d_2$$
$$\sqrt{(x-a)^2 + y^2} = x + a$$

Simplify the equation by squaring both sides.

$$\sqrt{(x-a)^2 + y^2} = x + a$$
$$(x-a)^2 + y^2 = (x+a)^2$$
$$x^2 - 2ax + a^2 + y^2 = x^2 + 2ax + a^2$$
$$y^2 = 4ax$$

Thus, the equation of a parabola with a horizontal orientation and its vertex at the origin is $y^2 = 4ax$.

In general, to shift the vertex of a horizontally orientated parabola from the origin $(0, 0)$ to any point, (h, k), replace each x-value with $(x - h)$ and each y-value with $(y - k)$. Thus, the resulting formula for a horizontal parabola with its vertex at (h, k) is $(y - k)^2 = 4a(x - h)$.

Example
The given horizontally orientated parabola has its vertex at $(-8, 3)$.

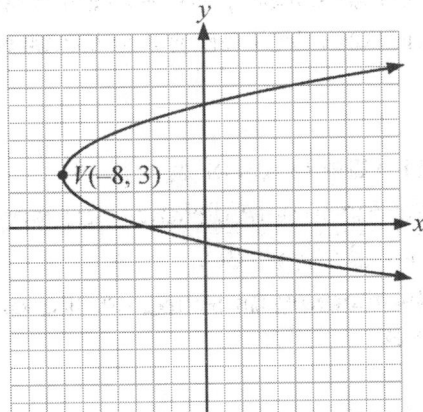

If you were to derive the equation of the horizontally orientated parabola with its vertex at $(-8, 3)$, the equation would be $(y - 3)^2 = 4a(x + 8)$.

EXERCISE #1—EQUATIONS FOR CONIC SECTIONS

Use the following information to answer the next question.

A certain conic section has a focus at the point $F(2, -5)$ and a directrix at $y = 4$. The point $P(5, -1)$ is on the locus of the conic section.

232. What is the conic section defined by the given information?
   A. Circle
   B. Ellipse
   C. Parabola
   D. Hyperbola

233. If the focus of a parabola is at $(0, 4)$ and the vertex is at $(0, 0)$, what is the equation of the parabola?
   A. $x^2 = 16y$
   B. $y^2 = 16x$
   C. $x^2 = 4y$
   D. $y^2 = 4x$

EXERCISE #1—EQUATIONS FOR CONIC SECTIONS
ANSWERS AND SOLUTIONS

| 232. C | 233. A |

232. C

Determine the eccentricity of the conic section.

Step 1
Determine the distance from point P to the focus by using the distance formula
$d = \sqrt{(x_2 - x_1)^2 + (y_2 - y_1)^2}$.
$PF = \sqrt{(2-5)^2 + ((-5)-(-1))^2}$
$PF = \sqrt{(-3)^2 + (-4)^2}$
$PF = \sqrt{9 + 16}$
$PF = \sqrt{25}$
$PF = 5$

Step 2
Determine the distance from point P to the directrix. Since the directrix is a horizontal line, the distance from point P can be determined from the absolute value of the difference in the y-coordinates.
$PL = |y_2 - y_1|$
$PL = |4 - (-1)|$
$PL = 5$

Step 3
Determine the eccentricity by using $e = \dfrac{PF}{PL}$.
$e = \dfrac{PF}{PL}$
$e = \dfrac{5}{5}$
$e = 1$

Step 4
Specify the type of conic section.
Since the eccentricity equals 1, the conic section is a parabola.

233. A

Step 1
Determine the equation of the directrix.
Given the symmetry of the parabola, the directrix must be perpendicular to the line drawn from the focus to the vertex at (0, 0). Thus, in this case, the directrix is a horizontal line 4 units from the origin. Therefore, the equation of the directrix is $y = -4$.

Step 2
Let $P(x, y)$ be any point on the parabola, and write equations that represent the distance from $P(x, y)$ to the focus, d_1, and from $P(x, y)$ to the directrix, d_2.
The distance from $P(x, y)$ to (0, 4) is
$d_1 = \sqrt{(x-0)^2 + (y-4)^2} = \sqrt{x^2 + (y-4)^2}$.
The distance from $P(x, y)$ to line $y = -4$ is
$d_2 = \sqrt{(x-x)^2 + (y-(-4))^2} = \sqrt{(y+4)^2}$.

Step 3
Derive the equation.
According to the locus definition of a parabola, the distance from any point to the focus is equal to the distance from that same point to the directrix. Set the equations so that they equal each other, and simplify.
$d_1 = d_2$
$\sqrt{x^2 + (y-4)^2} = \sqrt{(y+4)^2}$
$x^2 + (y-4)^2 = (y+4)^2$
$x^2 + y^2 - 8y + 16 = y^2 + 8y + 16$
$x^2 - 8y = 8y$
$x^2 = 16y$

The equation of the parabola is $x^2 = 16y$.

EXERCISE #2—EQUATIONS FOR CONIC SECTIONS

Use the following information to answer the next question.

A conic section has an eccentricity of 1.75, and there is a focus that is 7 units away from a point, P, on the conic.

234. Which of the following statements about the conic section is **true**?
   A. The conic is an ellipse, and point P is 4 units from the directrix.
   B. The conic is a hyperbola, and point P is 4 units from the directrix.
   C. The conic is an ellipse, and point P is 12.25 units from the directrix.
   D. The conic is a hyperbola, and point P is 12.25 units from the directrix.

Use the following information to answer the next question.

The directrix and focus of a parabola are shown in the given image.

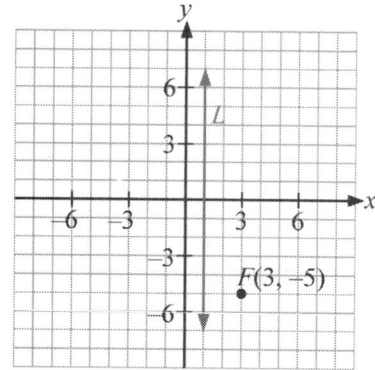

235. What is the equation of the parabola?
   A. $\dfrac{(y+5)^2}{4} + 2 = x$
   B. $\dfrac{(y-5)^2}{4} - 2 = x$
   C. $(y-5)^2 - 3 = x$
   D. $(y+5)^2 + 3 = x$

EXERCISE #2—EQUATIONS FOR CONIC SECTIONS
ANSWERS AND SOLUTIONS

234. B	235. A

234. B

Step 1
Determine the type of conic.
Since the eccentricity is greater than 1, the conic is a hyperbola.

Step 2
Determine the distance between point P and the directrix.
Let PF be the distance from point P to the focus and PL be the distance from point P to the directrix.
Substitute 1.75 for e and 7 for PF in the equation $e = \dfrac{PF}{PL}$.

$$e = \dfrac{PF}{PL}$$
$$1.75 = \dfrac{7}{PL}$$
$$PL = \dfrac{7}{1.75}$$
$$PL = 4 \text{ units}$$

235. A

Step 1
Determine the orientation of the parabola.
Since the directrix is along the y-axis, the parabola must have a horizontal orientation; therefore, it will have an equation of the form $(y - k)^2 = 4a(x - h)$.

Step 2
Determine the coordinates of the vertex (h, k).
The vertex is located halfway between the focus and directrix. Since the focus is at $(3, -5)$ and the directrix is $x = 1$, the vertex is $\left(\dfrac{1+3}{2}, -5\right)$, or $(2, -5)$.

Step 3
Determine the value of a.
The value of a is the distance between the vertex and focus or between the vertex and directrix. It can be seen that the distance between the focus $(3, -5)$ and the vertex $(2, -5)$ is 1, so $a = 1$.

Step 4
Substitute the values into the equation.
Be careful not to confuse the focus and the vertex.

$$(y - k)^2 = 4a(x - h)$$
$$(y + 5)^2 = 4(1)(x - 2)$$
$$\dfrac{(y + 5)^2}{4} = x - 2$$
$$\dfrac{(y + 5)^2}{4} + 2 = x$$

NOTES

Circle Theorems

CIRCLE THEOREMS

Table of Correlations

Standard		Concepts	Exercise #1	Exercise #2
Unit5.1	Understand and apply theorems about circles.			
G-C.2	Identify and describe relationships among inscribed angles, radii, and chords. Include the relationship between central, inscribed, and circumscribed angles; inscribed angles on a diameter are right angles; the radius of a circle is perpendicular to the tangent where the radius intersects the circle.	Applying the Properties of Angles between Tangent Lines and Chords	236	240
		Proving the Property of Inscribed Angles		
		Solving Problems Involving Tangents to a Circle from the Same External Point	237	241
		Understanding Circle Terminology	238	242
G-C.3	Construct the inscribed and circumscribed circles of a triangle, and prove properties of angles for a quadrilateral inscribed in a circle.	Cyclic Quadrilaterals	239	243
		Solving Problems Involving Cyclic Quadrilaterals	239	243

G-C.2 Identify and describe relationships among inscribed angles, radii, and chords. Include the relationship between central, inscribed, and circumscribed angles; inscribed angles on a diameter are right angles; the radius of a circle is perpendicular to the tangent where the radius intersects the circle.

APPLYING THE PROPERTIES OF ANGLES BETWEEN TANGENT LINES AND CHORDS

Property: The measure of the angle formed between a tangent line and a chord at the point of tangency is equal to the measure of the inscribed angle subtended by the chord and is half the measure of the central angle subtended by the chord.

The following diagram illustrates the property:

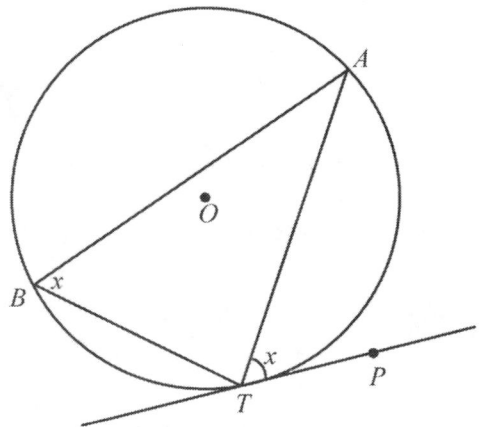

In the given diagram,

- Line TP is a tangent line; point T is the point of tangency; and line segment TA is a chord.
- The measure of the angle $\angle ATP$ formed between chord TA and tangent line TP is x.
- $\angle ABT$ is an inscribed angle subtended by arc AT (and chord AT). The chord–tangent line property states that the measure of angle $\angle ABT$ is x.

Note: There are two angles formed between a chord and a tangent line at the point of tangency. The following diagram illustrates the property for the second of the two angles:

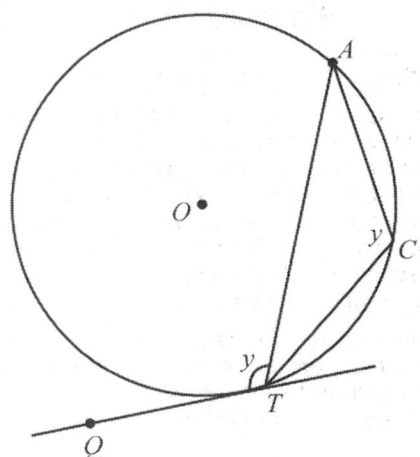

- Angle $\angle QTA$ is the angle between tangent line QT and chord TA at the point of tangency T.
- The measure of the angle is y (also $180° - x$).
- The inscribed angle, $\angle ACT$, is equal to $\angle ATQ$. Both have the measure of y.

By applying this property, the measure of unknown angles can be determined.

Example

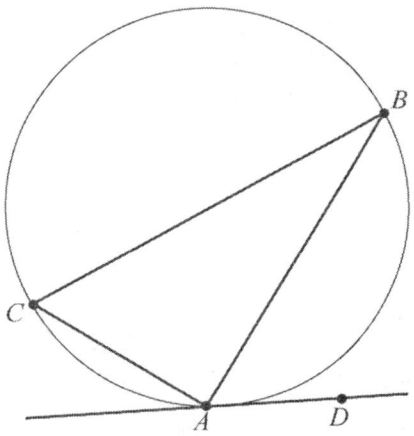

Given that *A* is the point of tangency and ∠*BAD* = 65°, determine the measure of ∠*C*.

Solution

Step 1
Interpret the diagram.

- Line *AD* is a tangent line. (Point *A* is the point of tangency, as given.)
- Line segment *AB* is a chord at the point of tangency.
- ∠*BAD* is the angle formed by a chord and a tangent line.
- ∠*ACB* is an inscribed angle subtended by chord *AB*.

Step 2
Apply properties of chords and tangent lines. Determine the required angle.

By the properties of tangent lines and chords at the point of tangency, the measure of angle ∠*BAD* is equal to the measure of angle ∠*ACB*. Therefore, ∠*C* = 65°.

Example

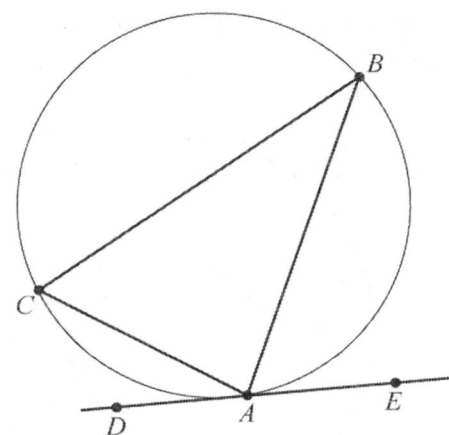

Given that *A* is the point of tangency and ∠*BAD* = 125°, determine the measure of ∠*BCA*.

Solution

Step 1
Interpret the diagram.

- Angle ∠*BCA* is subtended by chord *AB*.
- By the properties of tangent lines and of chords at the point of tangency, angle ∠*EAB* is the angle formed between chord *AB* and tangent line *DAE* and thus has the same measure as angle ∠*BCA*.
- Angles ∠*EAB* and ∠*BAD* are supplementary.

Step 2
Determine the measure of angle ∠*EAB*.
∠*EAB* = 180° − ∠*BAD*
= 180° − 125°
= 55°

Step 3
Determine the measure of angle ∠*BCA*.
∠*BCA* = ∠*EAB*
= 55°

Sometimes, more than one property must be applied to determine the measure of an unknown angle.

Example

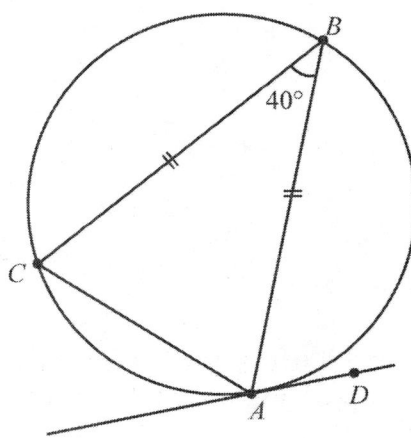

Given that A is the point of tangency, determine the measure of ∠BAD.

Solution

Step 1
Interpret the diagram.

- ∠BCA is an inscribed angle subtended by minor arc AB (chord AB).
- ∠BAD is the angle between chord AB and tangent line AD.
- △ABC is an isosceles triangle (two equal sides).

Step 2
Apply known properties.

- Since △ABC is an isosceles triangle, the measure of ∠C = ∠A and ∠A + ∠B + ∠C = 180°.
- Since ∠C = ∠A, this relationship can be rewritten as 2∠C + ∠B = 180°.

Rearrange the formula to isolate ∠C.
$$2\angle C + \angle B = 180°$$
$$\angle C = \frac{180° - \angle B}{2}$$
$$\angle BCA = \frac{180° - \angle B}{2}$$

Step 3
Determine the measure of angle ∠BAD.
According to the chord-tangent line property, ∠BAD = ∠BCA.
$$\angle BAD = \angle BCA$$
$$= \frac{180° - \angle B}{2}$$
$$= \frac{180° - 40°}{2}$$
$$= \frac{140°}{2}$$
$$= 70°$$

PROVING THE PROPERTY OF INSCRIBED ANGLES

An **inscribed angle** is formed when two chords of a circle share an endpoint. A **central angle** is formed between two radii of a circle.

An arc that is formed opposite an inscribed angle or a central angle is said to **subtend** the angle.

The reflex central angle is subtended by a major arc. If a minor arc subtends an inscribed angle, the vertex for the inscribed angle must be on the major arc. If a major arc subtends an inscribed angle, the vertex for the inscribed angle must be on the minor arc.

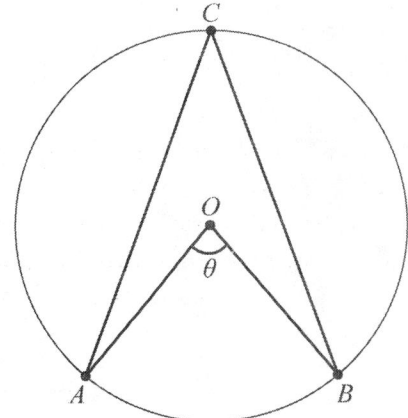

In the given diagram, angle θ is a central angle subtended by minor arc AB. The vertex for the inscribed angle, C, is on major arc ACB.

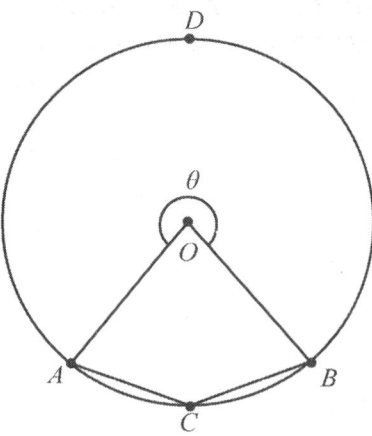

In the given diagram, angle θ is a reflex central angle, and $\angle ACB$ is an inscribed angle subtended by major arc ADB.

PROOFS OF PROPERTIES OF INSCRIBED AND CENTRAL ANGLES

There are three properties of inscribed and central angles.

The first property states that the measure of the central angle is twice the measure of the inscribed angle subtended by the same arc. This property is illustrated in the given diagram.

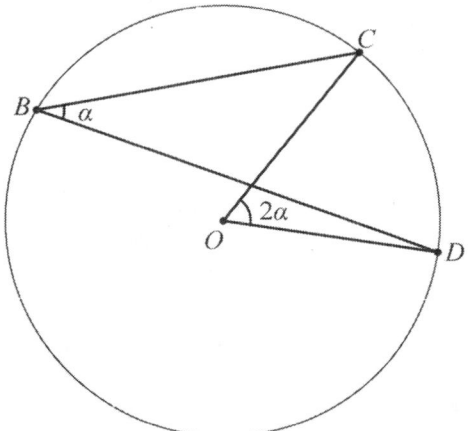

Example

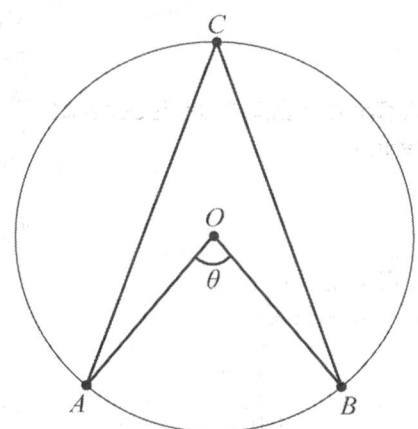

Point O is the center of the given circle.

Prove that $\angle AOB = 2\angle ACB$ in the given diagram.

Solution

Draw the radius, CO.

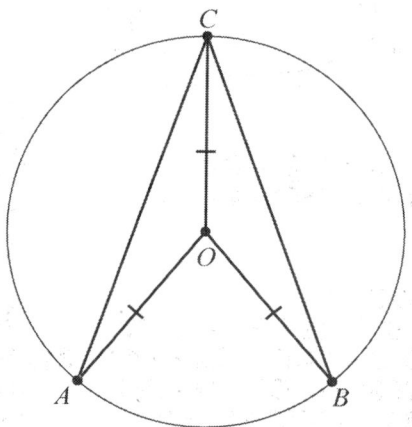

Statement	Reason
△AOC and △BOC are isosceles triangles.	AO, BO, and CO are all radii; therefore, they are all the same length.
∠ACO = ∠CAO and ∠CBO = ∠BCO *(diagram: circle with center O, points A, B, C on circle, with angles x at A and ACO, and y at B and BCO)*	In isosceles triangles, the angles opposite the congruent sides are equal.
∠AOC = 180° − 2x ∠BOC = 180° − 2y	The sum of all interior angles in a triangle is 180°.
∠AOB = 360° − (∠AOC − ∠BOC) = 360° − (180° − 2x + 180° − 2y) = 360° − (360° − 2x − 2y) = 360° − 360° + 2x + 2y = 2x + 2y = 2(x + y)	The angles around the center of a circle add up to 360°.
∠ACB = ∠ACO + ∠BCO = x + y	∠ACB is the sum of its interior angles.
∠AOB = 2(x + y) = 2∠ACB	Result

The second property states that all inscribed angles subtended by the same arc are equal in measure.

Example

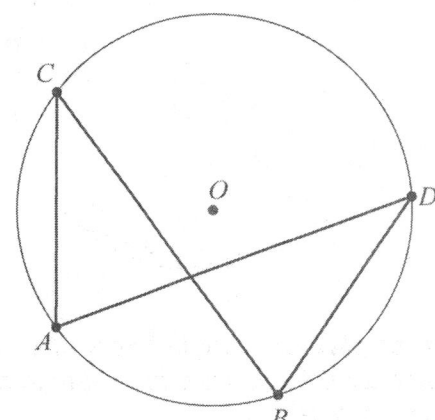

Point O is the center of the given circle.

Prove that ∠ACB = ∠ADB in the given diagram.

Solution

Draw the radii, AO and BO.

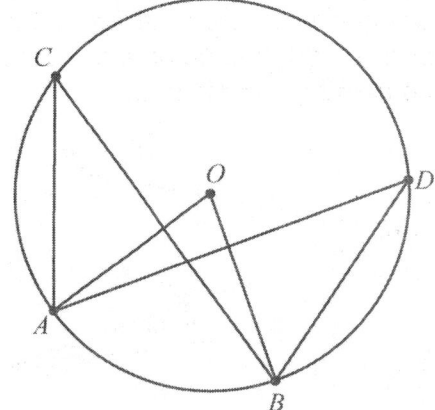

Statement	Reason
∠ACB is an inscribed angle subtended by arc AB.	Formed by chords AC and CB
∠ADB is an inscribed angle subtended by arc AB.	Formed by chords AD and BD
∠AOB is a central angle subtended by arc AB.	Formed by radii OA and OB
∠ACB = $\frac{1}{2}$∠AOB	Property of inscribed and central angles
∠AOB = 2∠ADB	Property of inscribed and central angles
∠ACB = $\frac{1}{2}$∠AOB = $\frac{1}{2}$(2∠ADB) = ∠ADB	Result

The third property states that an angle inscribed in a semicircle is a right angle.

Example

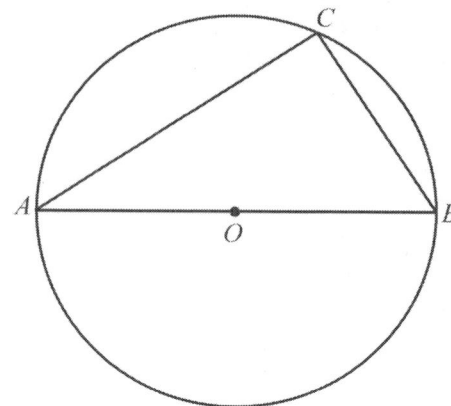

Line segment AB is a diameter.

Use the given diagram and the properties of inscribed angles to prove that any angle subtended by a diameter is a right angle.

Solution

Statement	Reason
Line segment AB contains point O.	Diameter of the circle
∠ACB is an inscribed angle subtended by arc AB.	Formed by chords AC and CB
∠AOB is a central angle subtended by arc AB.	Formed by radii OA and OB
∠ACB = $\frac{1}{2}$∠AOB	Property of inscribed and central angles
∠AOB = 180°	Straight line
∠ACB = $\frac{1}{2}$ · 180° = 90°	Result

SOLVING PROBLEMS INVOLVING TANGENTS TO A CIRCLE FROM THE SAME EXTERNAL POINT

When solving problems using the properties of tangents to a circle, first interpret the information, and then apply the correct property. Use this information to answer the question.

Example

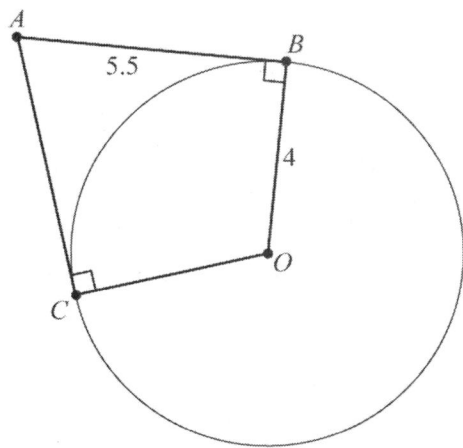

A quadrilateral is formed with two vertices, B and C, lying on the circumference of a circle. O is the center of the circle.

Determine the length of line segment AC.

Solution

Step 1
Interpret the given information.

- Line segments OB and OC are radii of the circle since O is the center point and B and C are points on the circumference of the circle.
- Radii OB and OC are perpendicular to line segments AB and AC, respectively.

Step 2
Apply properties of tangent lines and radii.
Since radii OB and OC are perpendicular to line segments AB and AC, line segments AB and AC are contained by tangent lines from external point A.

Step 3
Two tangent segments from one external point are equal in length; therefore, since AB and AC are two tangent line segments from the same external point, $AB = AC$.
$AC = 5.5$ units

Example

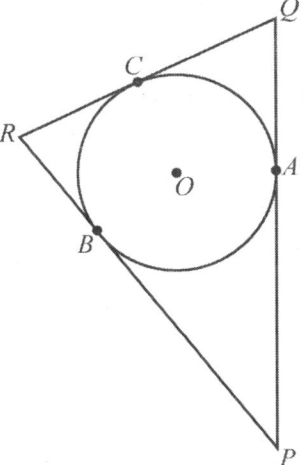

Points C, A, and B are points of tangency.

Given that $PA = 9$, $QA = 3$, and $RC = 2$, the perimeter of triangle PRQ is _____.

Solution

Step 1
Interpret the diagram, and apply the properties of tangent lines and tangent distances.
Since tangent distances from the same external point are equal, $PA = PB = 9$, $QA = QC = 3$, and $RC = RB = 2$.

Step 2
Determine the perimeter.
= $PA + QA + QC + RC + RB + PB$
= $9 + 3 + 3 + 2 + 2 + 9$
= 28

Understanding Circle Terminology

A **circle** is a set of points in a plane that are equidistant from a given point. The given point is called the **center** of the circle, and the distance from the center to any point on the circumference of the circle is called the **radius** of the circle.

A **chord** of a circle is a line segment with endpoints on the circumference of the circle. A chord passing through the center of the circle is called the **diameter**.

Example

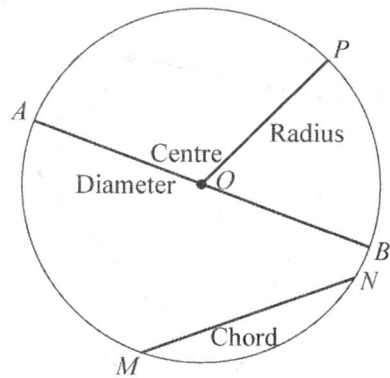

The given circle has the following characteristics:

- *O* is the center of the circle.
- $\overline{OP}$ is a radius because it extends from the center to the circumference of the circle.
- $\overline{MN}$ is a chord because it has endpoints on the circumference of the circle.
- $\overline{AB}$ is a diameter because it has endpoints on the circumference of the circle and passes through the center of the circle.

Arcs

An **arc** is part of the circumference of a circle. Arcs can be classified as follows:

- A minor, or smaller, arc takes up less than half the circumference of the circle.
- A major, or larger, arc takes up more than half the circumference of the circle.
- A semicircle is an arc that makes up exactly half the circumference of the circle.

Example

Minor arc, major arc, semi-circle

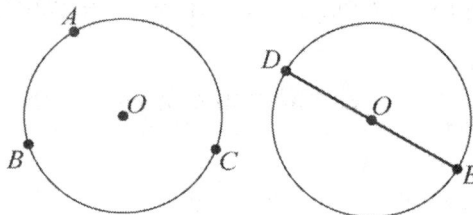

These circles have the following characteristics:

- *AB* is a minor arc because it is less than half the circle.
- *ACB* is a major arc because it is more than half the circle.
- *DE* is a semicircle because it is exactly half the circle.

Angles

There are two types of angles found in circles: **inscribed angles** and **central angles**. The vertex of an inscribed angle is on the circumference of the circle, and the arms of the angle are chords. The vertex of a central angle is at the center of the circle, and the arms of the angle are radii.

Example

Central and Inscribed angle

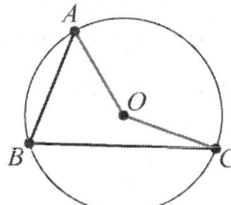

The given circle has the following characteristics:

- ∠*ABC* is an inscribed angle.
- ∠*AOC* is a central angle.

To **subtend** means to enclose or extend under. Central and inscribed angles can be subtended by both minor and major arcs, as well as by chords.

Example

Subtended angles

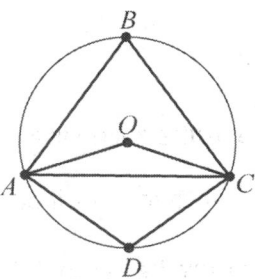

The given circle has the following characteristics:

- ∠ADC is an inscribed angle subtended by the major arc ABC.
- ∠AOC is a central angle subtended by the minor arc ADC.
- ∠ABC is an inscribed angle subtended by the chord AC.

Tangents and Secants

A **secant line** (or secant) is a line that passes through a circle. A **tangent line** (or tangent) to a circle is a straight line that touches the circle at one point but does not intersect it. The point where the tangent line and the circle touch is called the **point of tangency** or the point of contact.

In this diagram, point A is the point of tangency.

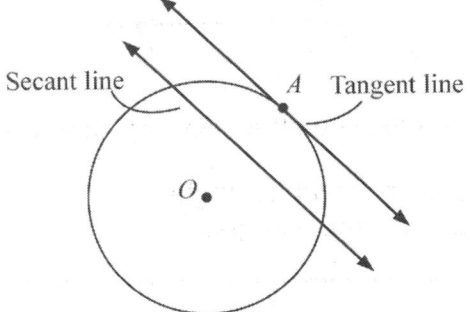

G-C.3 Construct the inscribed and circumscribed circles of a triangle, and prove properties of angles for a quadrilateral inscribed in a circle.

Cyclic Quadrilaterals
Defining and Identifying Cyclic Quadrilaterals

A **cyclic quadrilateral** is a quadrilateral with vertices on the circumference of a circle. A cyclic quadrilateral contains four inscribed angles.

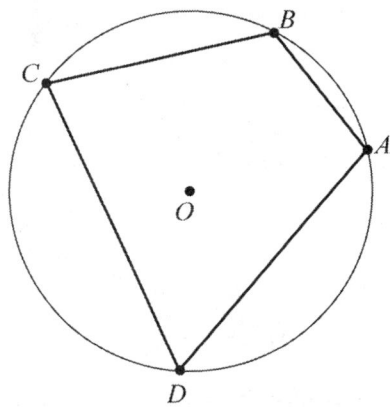

In the diagram, ABCD is a cyclic quadrilateral. Angles ∠ABC, ∠BCD, ∠CDA, and ∠DAB are inscribed angles.

Example

Two cyclic quadrilaterals are shown in the given diagram.

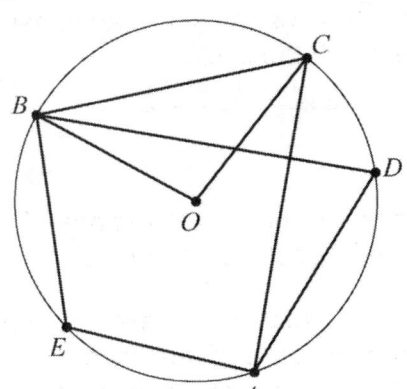

Identify all cyclic quadrilaterals.

Solution

A cyclic quadrilateral is a quadrilateral with vertices on the circumference of a circle. A cyclic quadrilateral contains four inscribed angles.

By definition, the two cyclic quadrilaterals shown in the given diagram are *ACBE* and *ADBE*.

One property of cyclic quadrilaterals is that the opposite angles are supplementary.

The converse of this property is also true: If opposite angles of a quadrilateral are supplementary, the quadrilateral is a cyclic quadrilateral.

Example

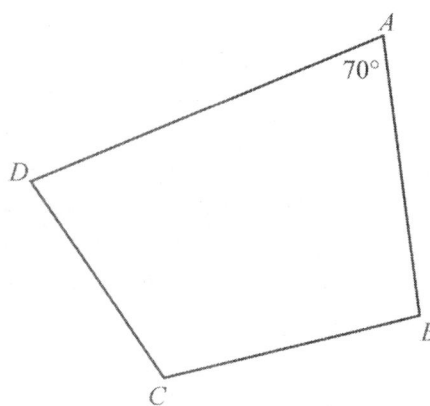

Quadrilateral ABCD

Given that quadrilateral *ABCD* is cyclic, the measure of angle *BCD* is _____°.

Solution

Apply properties of cyclic quadrilaterals.

Opposite angles in a cyclic quadrilateral are supplementary.
$\angle BCD = 180° - 70°$
$\qquad = 110°$

Example

Determine whether quadrilateral *ABCD* is cyclic if angle *BCD* measures 110°, angle *ADC* measures 85°, and angle *CBA* measures 95°.

Solution

A quadrilateral is cyclic if opposite angles are supplementary.
$\angle BAD + \angle BCD = 70° + 110°$
$\qquad\qquad\qquad = 180°$
$\angle ADC + \angle CBA = 85° + 95°$
$\qquad\qquad\qquad = 180°$

Since opposite angles are supplementary, the quadrilateral is cyclic.

SOLVING PROBLEMS INVOLVING CYCLIC QUADRILATERALS

Numerous applications of cyclic quadrilaterals exist in fields such as construction, design, and engineering. Since some problems require a unique approach, the following techniques may be helpful:

- Work with a diagram.
- Identify line segments, lines, and angles as chords, tangent lines, and inscribed and central angles.
- Look for relationships (properties) between what is required (unknown) and what is given (known).

It is often necessary to determine an intermediate value before solving a problem.

Example

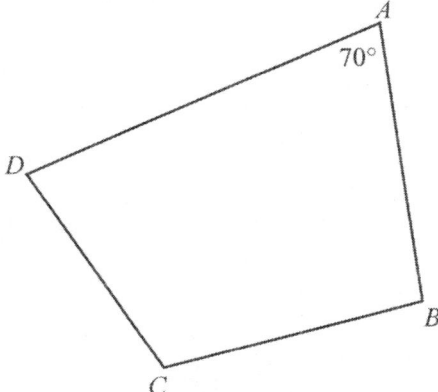

Quadrilateral ABCD

Given that quadrilateral *ABCD* is cyclic, the measure of angle *BCD* is _____°.

Solution

Apply properties of cyclic quadrilaterals.

Opposite angles in a cyclic quadrilateral are supplementary.
∠*BCD* = 180° − 70°
= 110°

Determine whether quadrilateral *ABCD* is cyclic if angle *BCD* measures 110°, angle *ADC* measures 85°, and angle *CBA* measures 95°.

Solution

A quadrilateral is cyclic if opposite angles are supplementary.
∠*BAD* + ∠*BCD* = 70° + 110°
= 180°
∠*ADC* + ∠*CBA* = 85° + 95°
= 180°

Since opposite angles are supplementary, the quadrilateral is cyclic.

Example

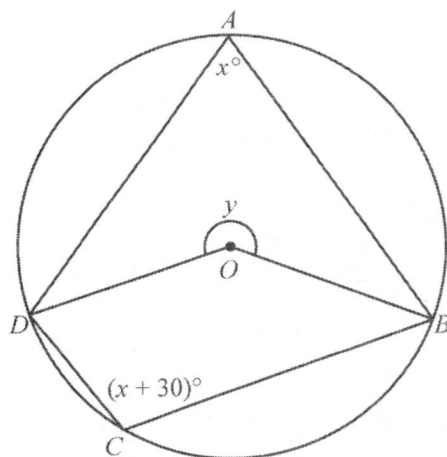

Determine the value of *y* to the nearest whole degree. _____

Solution

Step 1
Interpret the diagram.

Quadrilateral *ABCD* is inscribed in a circle. It is a cyclic quadrilateral. Angle *y* is the measure of reflex central angle *BOD*, which is subtended by major arc *BAD*. Angle *BCD* is an inscribed angle subtended by the same major arc *BAD*.

Step 2
Determine the value of *x* by applying properties of cyclic quadrilaterals.

Opposite angles in cyclic quadrilaterals are supplementary.
∠*BAD* + ∠*BCD* = 180°
$x + (x + 30°) = 180°$
$2x = 180° - 30°$
$x = \frac{1}{2} \cdot 150°$
$x = 75°$

Step 3
Determine the value of *y* by applying properties of inscribed and central angles.

The measure of a central angle is twice the measure of an inscribed angle subtended by the same arc.
reflex ∠*BOD* = 2∠*BCD*
$y = 2(x + 30)°$
$= 2(75 + 30)°$
$= 210°$

Example

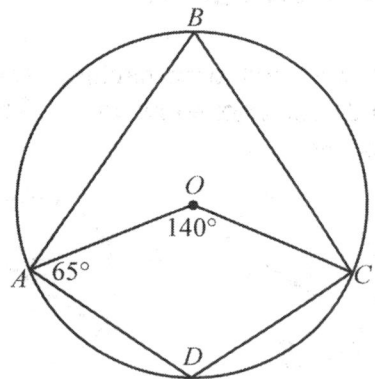

In the diagram, the circle has a center O. Determine ∠ADC. _____

Solution

Statement	Reason
∠ABC is an inscribed angle.	Angle between two chords with a shared endpoint
∠AOC is a central angle.	Angle between two radii
$\angle ABC = \frac{1}{2}(\angle AOC)$ $= \frac{1}{2}(140°)$ $= 70°$	Measure of an inscribed angle is half the measure of a central angle subtended by the same arc.
∠ADC + ∠ABC = 180° ∠ADC = 180° − ∠ABC = 180° − 70° = 110°	Opposite angles in a cyclic quadrilateral are supplementary.

EXERCISE #1—CIRCLE THEOREMS

Use the following information to answer the next question.

The measure of the angle between a tangent line, through point of tangency A, and chord AC is $(3x + 10)°$. The measure of the angle subtended by arc AC is $(7x - 22)°$.

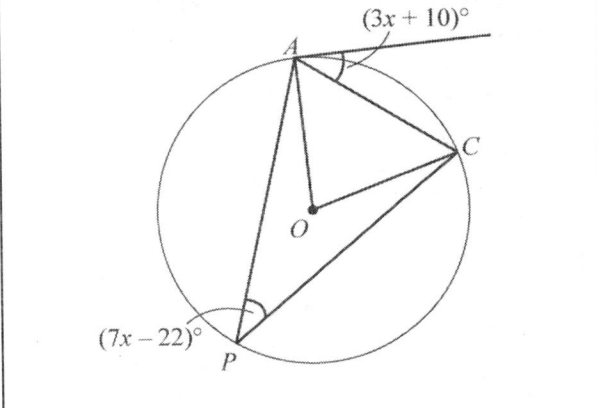

236. The measure of the central angle, ∠AOC, subtended by arc AC is _____°.

Use the following information to answer the next question.

AB, BC, and AC are tangents to the circle at points D, E, and F, respectively.

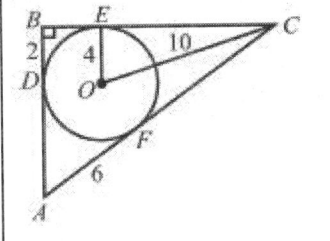

237. Rounded to the nearest tenth, what is the perimeter of triangle ABC? _____ units

238. Which of the following circles, each with center O, does **not** show arc ABC defined as a major arc?

A. 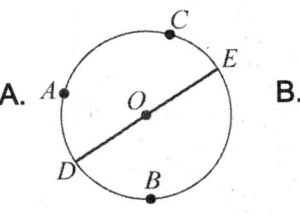   B.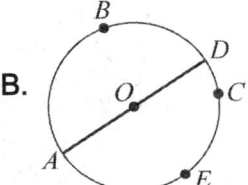

C. 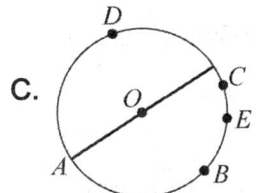   D.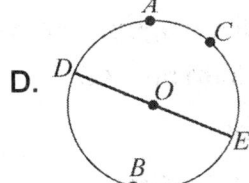

Use the following information to answer the next question.

Point O is at the center of the circle.

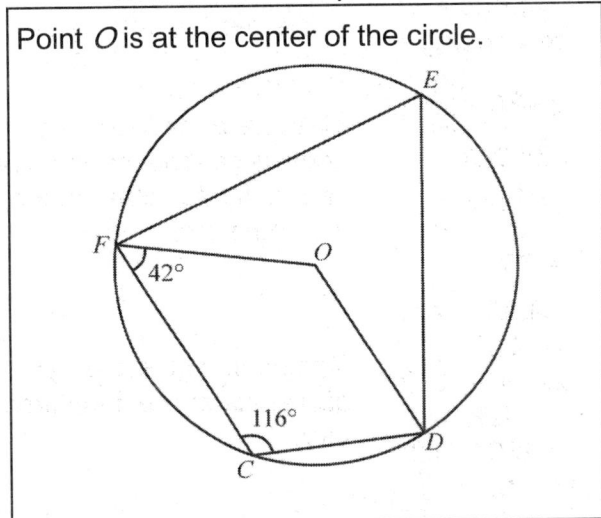

239. The measure of angle FED is
 A. 128°   B. 116°
 C. 64°   D. 58°

EXERCISE #1—CIRCLE THEOREMS ANSWERS AND SOLUTIONS

| 236. 68 | 237. 34.3 | 238. C | 239. C |

236. 68

Step 1
Calculate the value of x.
Apply the following property of tangent lines and chords:
The measure of the angle formed between a tangent line and a chord at the point of tangency is equal to the measure of the inscribed angle subtended by the chord and is half the measure of the central angle subtended by the chord.
This property specifies that $(7x - 22)° = (3x + 10)°$.
$7x - 22 = 3x + 10$
$\quad 4x = 32$
$\quad\ \ x = 8$

Step 2
Determine the measure of ∠APC.
Substitute 8 into $(7x - 22)°$.
∠APC = $(7x - 22)°$
      = $7(8) - 22$
      = $56 - 22$
      = $34°$

Step 3
Determine the measure of ∠AOC.
The measure of the central angle, ∠AOC is double the measure of the inscribed angle ∠APC.
∠AOC = 2 × ∠APC
      = 2 × 34°
      = 68°

237. 34.3

Step 1
Since OE is a radius and BC is a tangent, ∠OEC = 90°. Therefore, triangle OEC is a right triangle.

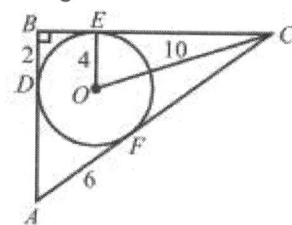

Let CE = x.
$a^2 + b^2 = c^2$
$x^2 + 4^2 = 10^2$
$x^2 + 16 = 100$
$\sqrt{x^2} = \sqrt{84}$
$\quad x \approx 9.165$

Step 2
According to the properties of circles, two tangent segments meeting at an external point are equal.
AD = AF = 6
BC = BE = 2
CE = CF ≈ 9.165

Step 3
Calculate the perimeter of the triangle.
$P \approx 2(2) + 2(6) + 2(9.165) \approx 34.33$
Rounded to the nearest tenth, the perimeter of triangle ABC is 34.3 units.

238. C

To be defined as a major arc, the arc must take up more than half the circumference of the circle.

In this circle, arc ABC is defined as a minor arc because it takes up less than half the circumference of the circle.

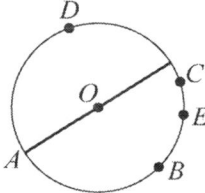

239. C

Apply the theorem of cyclic quadrilaterals, which states that the opposite angles in a cyclic quadrilateral are supplementary.
Quadrilateral FEDC is cyclic.
∠FED + ∠FCD = 180°
     ∠FED = 180° − ∠FCD
          = 180° − 116°
          = 64°

EXERCISE #2—CIRCLE THEOREMS

Use the following information to answer the next question.

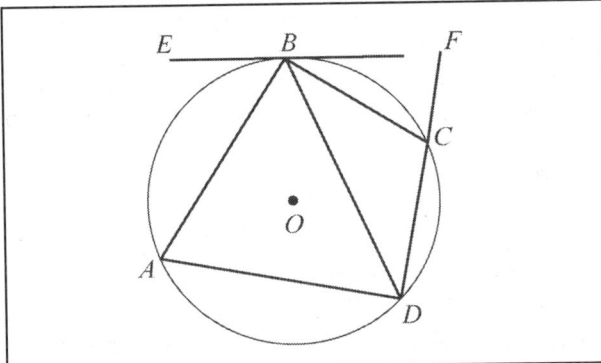

240. If the value of ∠BCF = 68° and ∠ABE = 58°, what is the value of ∠ABD?

Use the following information to answer the next question.

Point O is the center of the circle shown.

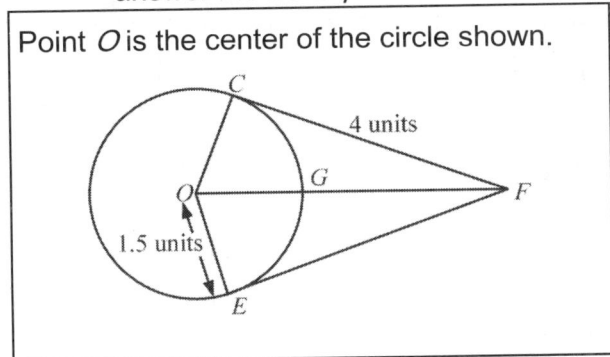

241. To the nearest tenth, the length of segment FG is
 A. 2.8 units
 B. 3.7 units
 C. 4.3 units
 D. 5.5 units

Use the following information to answer the next question.

A circle with center O and various points around its circumference is shown.

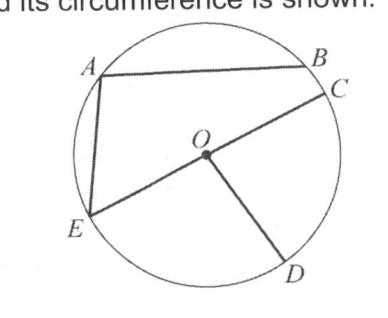

242. Which segment in the given circle **cannot** be classified as a chord?
 A. $\overline{AB}$
 B. $\overline{AE}$
 C. $\overline{EC}$
 D. $\overline{OD}$

Use the following information to answer the next question.

A polygon is inscribed in a circle as illustrated.

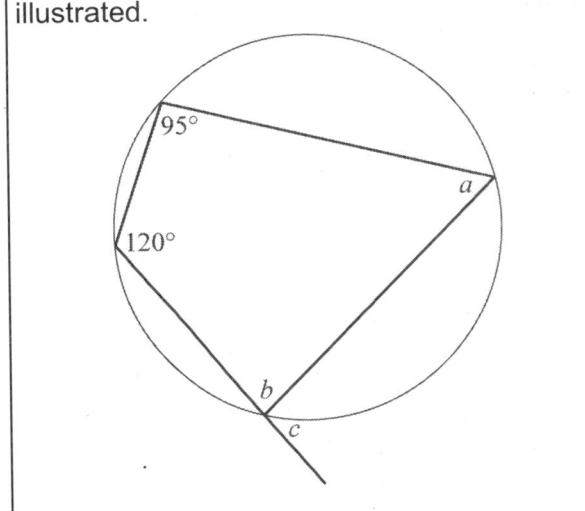

243. The measures of angles a, b, and c are
 A. a = 120°, b = 95°, and c = 85°
 B. a = 120°, b = 95°, and c = 95°
 C. a = 60°, b = 85°, and c = 85°
 D. a = 60°, b = 85°, and c = 95°

EXERCISE #2—CIRCLE THEOREMS ANSWERS AND SOLUTIONS

240. 54	241. A	242. D	243. D

240. 54

Step 1
Calculate the value of ∠BCD.
∠BCF and ∠BCD are supplementary angles.
If ∠BCF = 68°, then the measure of ∠BCD is as follows:
∠BCD = 180° − 68°
= 112°

Step 2
Calculate the value of ∠BAD.
In cyclic quadrilaterals, opposite angles have a sum of 180°.
∠BAD + ∠BCD = 180°
∠BAD + 112° = 180°
∠BAD = 68°

Step 3
Calculate the value of ∠ADB.
Apply the following property of tangent lines and chords: The measure of the angle formed between a tangent line and a chord at the point of tangency is equal to the measure of the inscribed angle subtended by the chord.
If ∠ABE = 58°, then ∠ADB = 58°.

Step 4
Calculate the value of ∠ABD.
The interior angles of a triangle have a sum of 180°.
∠ABD + ∠ADB + ∠BAD = 180°
∠ABD + 58° + 68° = 180°
∠ABD + 126° = 180°
∠ABD = 54°

241. A

Step 1
Apply property of tangent segments from an external point to determine the length of line segment EF.
The two tangent segments from an external point are equal in length.
EF = CF
Therefore, EF = 4.

Step 2
Apply properties of tangents and radii at the point of tangency and the Pythagorean Theorem to determine the length of the segment OF.
A tangent to a circle is perpendicular to the radius at the point of tangency. Therefore, △OEF is a right-angled triangle.
Apply the Pythagorean theorem to determine the length of segment OF.
$OF^2 = OE^2 + EF^2$
Substitute 1.5 for OE and 4 for EF.
$OF^2 = 1.5^2 + 4^2$
$OF^2 = 2.25 + 16$
$OF^2 = 18.25$
$\sqrt{OF^2} = \sqrt{18.25}$
OF ≈ 4.3

Step 3
Determine the length of the segment GF.
OF = OG + GF
GF = OF − OG
Since OG is the length of the radius, substitute 1.5 for OG and 4.3 for OF.
GF = 4.3 − 1.5
= 2.8

Therefore, the length of segment FG, correct to the nearest tenth, is 2.8 units.

242. D

A chord of a circle is a line segment with end points on the circumference of the circle.

Segments AB, AE, and EC can all be classified as chords in the given circle. (Although $\overline{EC}$ is usually referred to as a diameter of the given circle, it is, by definition, a chord.) Segment OD is not a chord; it is a radius of the given circle.

243. D

Step 1
Determine the measures of angles a and b.
Apply the property that opposite angles in a cyclic quadrilateral are supplementary.
∠a + 120° = 180°
∠a = 180° − 120°
∠a = 60°
∠b + 95° = 180°
∠b = 180° − 95°
∠b = 85°

Step 2
Determine the measure of angle c.
The measure of angle b and the measure of angle c are supplementary.
$\angle c + \angle b = 180°$
$\quad \angle c = 180° - 85°$
$\quad \angle c = 95°$
Therefore, $a = 60°$, $b = 85°$, and $c = 95°$.

NOTES

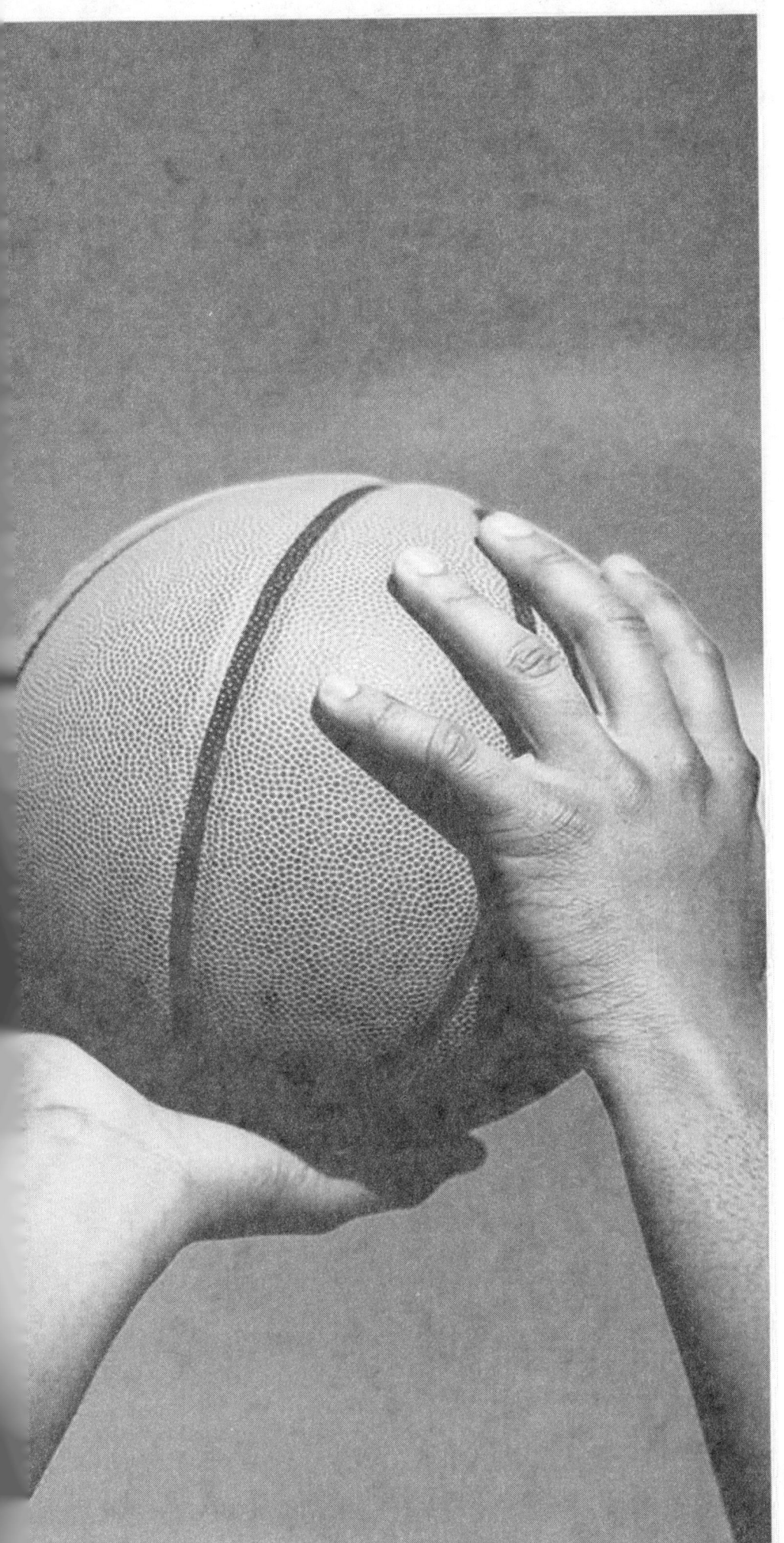

Arc Lengths and Sector Areas of Circles

ARC LENGTHS AND SECTOR AREAS OF CIRCLES

Table of Correlations

Standard		Concepts	Exercise #1	Exercise #2
Unit5.2 Find arc lengths and areas of sectors of circles.				
G-C.5	Derive using similarity the fact that the length of the arc intercepted by an angle is proportional to the radius, and define the radian measure of the angle as the constant of proportionality; derive the formula for the area of a sector.	Calculating Arc Lengths	1	15
		Understanding Radian Measure	244	247
		Determining the Area of Sectors of a Circle	245	248
		Finding the Area of a Sector of a Circle	246	249

G-C.5 Derive using similarity the fact that the length of the arc intercepted by an angle is proportional to the radius, and define the radian measure of the angle as the constant of proportionality; derive the formula for the area of a sector.

UNDERSTANDING RADIAN MEASURE

Although angles are most commonly measured in degrees, there are other units that can be used to measure angles, just as there are several units that can be used to measure quantities like temperature, length, and volume.

Did You Know?
The history of measuring angles in degrees can be traced back to the Babylonians, who believed that there were 360 days in each year.
The Babylonians lived from about 5000 BC to 500 BC in the area of present-day Iraq.

WHAT IS A RADIAN?

The ratio that compares the length of an arc on the circumference of a circle to the circle's radius gives the radian measure of the angle at the center of the circle subtended by that arc.

One radian is the measure of the angle at the center of the circle subtended by an arc of length equal to the circle's radius.

Consider taking a circle with radius r and measuring an arc of length r on the circumference of the circle.

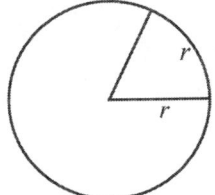

The angle formed at the center of the circle, when the ends of the arc are joined to the center, has a measure of 1 rad.

In a circle with radius r, the angle formed at the center of a circle (central angle) resting on (*subtended* by) the arc of length $2r$ has a measure of 2 rad.

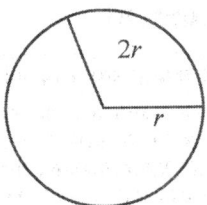

The relationship between the radian measure of an angle, the arc length, and the radius of a circle is given by the formula $\theta = \dfrac{a}{r}$, where θ is measured in radians, a is the arc length, and r is the radius.

HOW MANY RADIANS ARE IN A CIRCLE?

If an arc with a length equal to one radius ($1r$) forms an angle measuring 1 rad, how many arcs of length r are required to form an entire circle's circumference?

The formula for calculating the circumference, C, of a circle is $C = 2\pi r$, where r is the radius. This means that exactly 2π radii can fit around the circumference of a circle. Since each arc of length r subtends an angle of 1 rad and 2π radii can fit around the circumference of a circle, there are 2π rad in one complete revolution. In other words, there are approximately 6.28 rad ($2 \times \pi$) in one revolution.

Note the following important angle measures in radians:

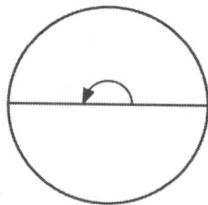

If one complete circular revolution is 2π rad (360°), then half a revolution is π rad (180°).

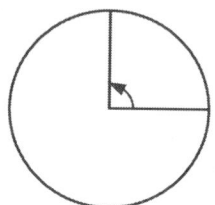

One-quarter of a revolution is $\dfrac{\pi}{2}$ rad (90°).

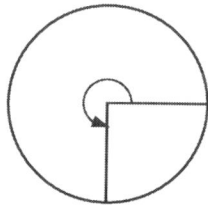

Three-quarters of a revolution is $\dfrac{3\pi}{2}$ rad (270°).

DETERMINING THE AREA OF SECTORS OF A CIRCLE

Given the radius, r, the area of a circle can be determined with the formula $A = \pi r^2$. This formula is also useful for finding the area of a sector of a circle. A sector is formed by two radii and an arc. In general, any sector of a circle will have an area that is a fraction of the full area of the circle.

A semicircle is half of a circle. The area of this shape is half the area of a full circle.

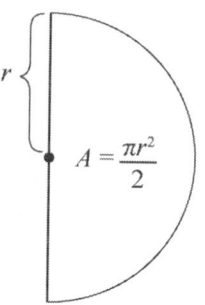

A quarter circle is one-quarter of a circle. The area of this shape is one-quarter of the area of a full circle.

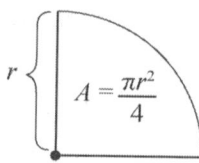

Example

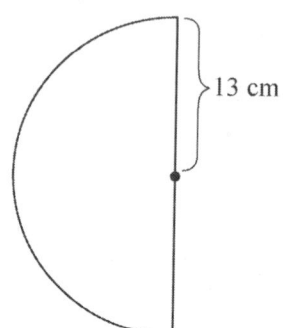

Determine the area of the given semicircle to the nearest centimeter.

Solution

Step 1
Determine what fraction of the circle is given.
One-half $\left(\dfrac{1}{2}\right)$ of a circle is given.

Step 2
Determine the area of the sector.
The sector has an area that is half that of a full circle of the same radius.

$A = \dfrac{\pi r^2}{2}$

$A = \dfrac{\pi 13^2}{2}$

$A \approx 265.4645792$

To the nearest centimeter, the area of the semicircle is 265 cm².

Arc Lengths and Sector Areas of Circles

FINDING THE AREA OF A SECTOR OF A CIRCLE

A sector of a circle is an enclosed portion of a circle formed between two radii and an arc. In the diagram, r is the radius of the circle, AB is an arc on the circle, O is the center of the circle, and θ is the central angle.

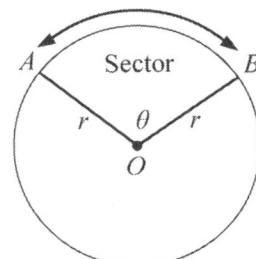

You can find the area of the sector of a circle if you are given the length of the radius and the measure of the central angle.

Use the ratio $\dfrac{\theta°}{360°}$, where $\theta°$ represents the measure of the central angle, to find the area of a sector.

The formula for calculating the area of a circle is $A = \pi r^2$. A formula for finding the area of a sector of a circle is $\dfrac{\theta°}{360°} \times \pi r^2$.

Use the following steps to calculate the area of a sector of a circle:

1. Substitute all known values into the formula.
2. Calculate the area of the sector.
3. Clearly state the area, remembering to include the proper units.

Example

The radius of the circle is 4 cm. The central angle is 108°.

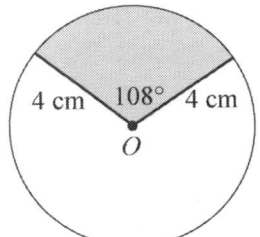

Calculate the area of the shaded region.

Solution

To calculate the area of the shaded sector of the circle, use the formula $\dfrac{\theta°}{360°} \times \pi r^2$.

Substitute the known values into the formula and simplify. Use 3.14 as an approximation for π.

Step 1
Substitute all known values into the formula.
$$\dfrac{\theta°}{360°} \times \pi r^2 \approx \dfrac{108°}{360°} \times (3.14)(4)^2$$

Step 2
Calculate the area of the sector.
$$\dfrac{\theta°}{360°} \times \pi r^2 \approx \dfrac{108°}{360°} \times (3.14)(4)^2$$
$$\approx (0.3)(3.14)(16)$$
$$\approx 15.072$$

Step 3
Clearly state the area, remembering to include the proper units.
The shaded region has an area of approximately 15.072 cm².

EXERCISE #1—ARC LENGTHS AND SECTOR AREAS OF CIRCLES

244. Expressed to the nearest hundredth, the value of $\dfrac{11\pi}{6}$ is _____ rad.

Use the following information to answer the next question.

The given circle is split into 10 equal sectors.

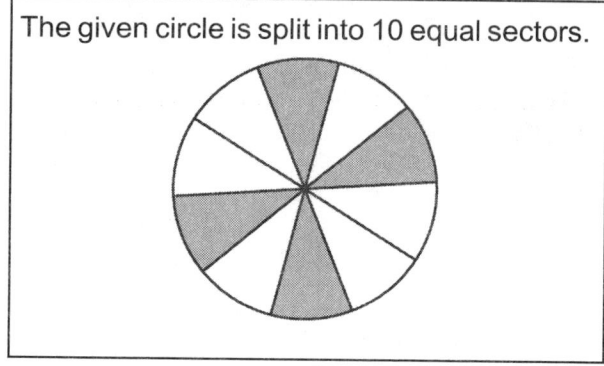

245. If the radius of the circle is 3.7 cm, what is the area of the shaded region?
  A. 17.2 cm²
  B. 23.4 cm²
  C. 27.5 cm²
  D. 38.3 cm²

Use the following information to answer the next question.

A circle with a shaded sector is shown.

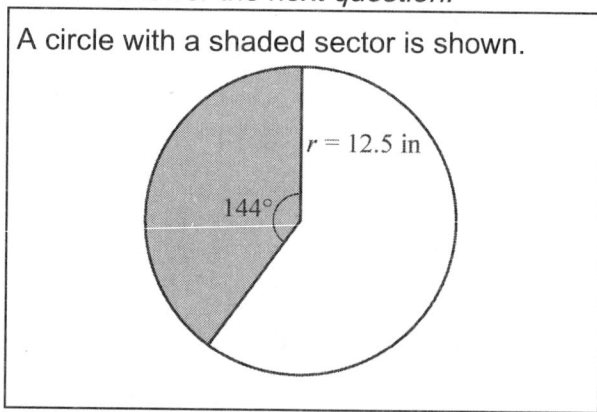

$r = 12.5$ in, $144°$

246. What is the area of the shaded sector?
  A. 31.4 in²
  B. 98.13 in²
  C. 196.25 in²
  D. 1,226.56 in²

EXERCISE #1—ARC LENGTHS AND SECTOR AREAS OF CIRCLES ANSWERS AND SOLUTIONS

| 244. 5.76 | 245. A | 246. C |

244. 5.76

Convert $\frac{11\pi}{6}$ to a decimal by using a calculator to divide 11π by 6.

$\frac{11\pi}{6} \approx 5.76$

Expressed to the nearest hundredth, the value of $\frac{11\pi}{6}$ is 5.76 rad.

245. A

Step 1
Determine the fraction of the circle represented by one sector.

One sector is one-tenth $\left(\frac{1}{10}\right)$ of the given circle.

Step 2
Determine the area of one sector.
The area of one sector is one-tenth of the area of the full circle.

$A = \frac{\pi r^2}{10}$

$A = \frac{\pi (3.7)^2}{10}$

$A \approx 4.300840343$

Step 3
Determine the area of the shaded region.
Since four parts of the circle are shaded, the area of the shaded region is $4 \times 4.300840343 \approx 17.2$ cm^2.

246. C

Step 1
To calculate the area of the shaded sector of the circle, use the formula $\frac{x°}{360°} \times \pi r^2$.

Substitute the known values into the formula. Use 3.14 for π.

$\frac{x°}{360°} \times \pi r^2 = \frac{144°}{360°} \times 3.14 \times 12.5^2$

Step 2
Calculate the area of the sector.

$\frac{x°}{360°} \times \pi r^2 = \frac{144°}{360°} \times 3.14 \times 12.5^2$

$\frac{x°}{360°} \times \pi r^2 = 0.4 \times 3.14 \times 156.25$

$\frac{x°}{360°} \times \pi r^2 = 196.25$

The area of the shaded sector of the circle is 196.25 in^2.

EXERCISE #2—ARC LENGTHS AND SECTOR AREAS OF CIRCLES

Use the following information to answer the next question.

A triangle is shown.

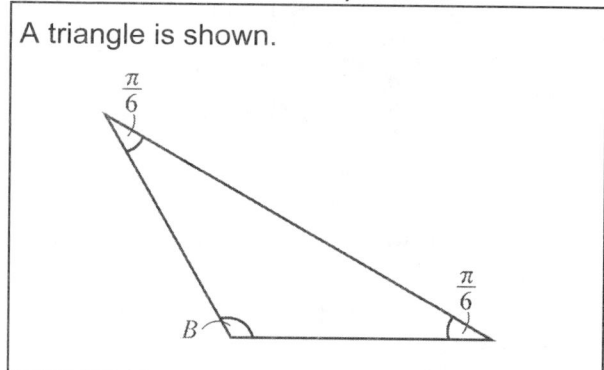

247. Calculated to the nearest hundredth, the approximate value in radian measure of ∠B is _____.

Use the following information to answer the next question.

Irene is baking a pizza for a birthday party. She splits the pizza into six equal slices as shown in the given diagram.

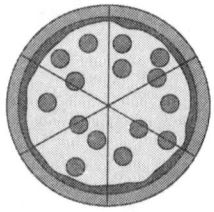

248. If the diameter of the pizza is 42.5 cm, what is the area of one slice of pizza to the nearest tenth of a centimeter?
- A. 133.2 cm²
- B. 236.4 cm²
- C. 584.6 cm²
- D. 945.8 cm²

Use the following information to answer the next question.

A circle has a radius of 42 cm and a central angle of 54°.

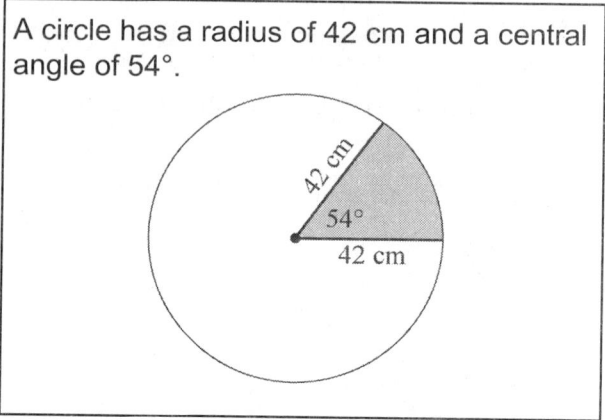

249. Rounded to the nearest unit, what is the area of the shaded sector of the circle?
- A. 13 cm²
- B. 103 cm²
- C. 831 cm²
- D. 7,213 cm²

EXERCISE #2—ARC LENGTHS AND SECTOR AREAS OF CIRCLES ANSWERS AND SOLUTIONS

| 247. 2.09 | 248. B | 249. C |

247. 2.09

Step 1
Determine the value of ∠B. Since the sum of the angles is equal to π, subtract the two $\frac{\pi}{6}$ angles from π.

$$\angle B = \pi - \frac{\pi}{6} - \frac{\pi}{6}$$
$$= \frac{6\pi}{6} - \frac{\pi}{6} - \frac{\pi}{6}$$
$$= \frac{4\pi}{6}$$
$$= \frac{2\pi}{3}$$

Step 2
Convert $\frac{2\pi}{3}$ to decimal form. Use a calculator to divide 2π by 3.
$$\frac{2\pi}{3} \approx 2.09 \text{ rad}$$
The approximate value of ∠B is 2.09 rad.

248. B

Step 1
Determine the fraction of one slice of pizza.
Since the pizza is cut into six equal slices, one slice of pizza is $\frac{1}{6}$ of the whole pizza.

Step 2
Determine the area of one slice of pizza.
Since the radius of the pizza is
42.5 ÷ 2 = 21.25 cm, the area of one slice of pizza can be calculated as follows:
$$A = \frac{\pi r^2}{6}$$
$$A = \frac{\pi (21.25)^2}{6}$$
$$A \approx 236.4375721$$
To the nearest tenth of a centimeter, the area of one slice of pizza is 236.4 cm².

249. C

Step 1
Substitute all known values into the formula.
$$\frac{\theta°}{360°} \times \pi r^2 \approx \frac{54°}{360°} \times 3.14 \times 42^2$$

Step 2
Calculate the area of the sector.
$$\frac{\theta°}{360°} \times \pi r^2 \approx \frac{54°}{360°} \times 3.14 \times 42^2$$
$$\approx 0.15 \times 3.14 \times 1,764$$
$$\approx 830.844$$
$$\approx 831$$

Step 3
Clearly state the area, remembering to include the proper units.
The approximate area of the sector of the circle is 831 cm².

NOTES

Relating Conic Sections to Their Equation

RELATING CONIC SECTIONS TO THEIR EQUATION

Table of Correlations

Standard		Concepts	Exercise #1	Exercise #2
Unit5.3	Translate between the geometric description and the equation for a conic section.			
G-GPE.1	Derive the equation of a circle of given center and radius using the Pythagorean Theorem; complete the square to find the center and radius of a circle given by an equation.	The Equation of a Circle	250	255
		Converting the Equation of a Circle from General to Standard Form by Completing the Square	251	256
		Determining the Key Characteristics of a Circle from the Standard Form Equation	252	257
		Determining the Equation of a Circle when Given Key Characteristics	253	258
		Determining the Equation of a Circle from a Graph	254	259

G-GPE.1 Derive the equation of a circle of given center and radius using the Pythagorean Theorem; complete the square to find the center and radius of a circle given by an equation.

THE EQUATION OF A CIRCLE

A circle is a set of points in a plane that are equidistant from a given point called the center.

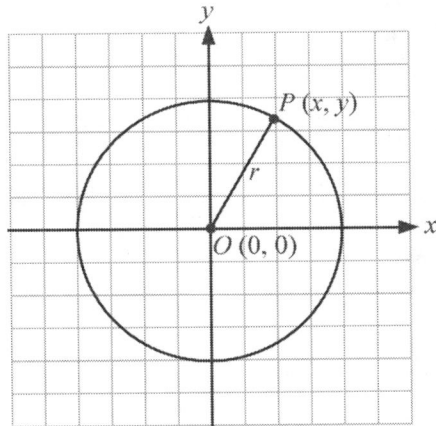

Since any point on the circle can be represented by the ordered pair $P(x, y)$, the distance from P to the center O, $(0, 0)$, is the radius r.

The distance formula yields the following result for the length of line segment PO which also represents the radius, r.

$d_{PO} = \sqrt{(x_2 - x_1)^2 + (y_2 - y_1)^2}$
$d_{PO} = \sqrt{(x_2 - 0)^2 + (y_2 - 0)^2}$
$d_{PO} = \sqrt{x^2 + y^2} = r$

Therefore, when both sides of the equation $\sqrt{x^2 + y^2} = r$ are squared, the result is $x^2 + y^2 = r^2$.

The equation of a circle with center $(0, 0)$ and radius r is $x^2 + y^2 = r^2$.

Example
Using the distance formula, determine the equation of the circle with center $(0, 0)$ that passes through the point $(-2, 7)$.

Solution

Step 1
Determine the measure of the radius of the circle using the distance formula.
$d = r = \sqrt{(x_2 - x_1)^2 + (y_2 - y_1)^2}$
$= \sqrt{(-2 - 0)^2 + (7 - 0)^2}$
$= \sqrt{4 + 49}$
$= \sqrt{53}$

Step 2
Determine the equation of the circle. Substitute $\sqrt{53}$ for r in the equation $x^2 + y^2 = r^2$.
$x^2 + y^2 = (\sqrt{53})^2$
$x^2 + y^2 = 53$

Therefore, the equation $x^2 + y^2 = 53$ describes a circle with center $(0, 0)$ that passes through the point $(-2, 7)$.

If you use the equation of a circle with center $(0, 0)$ and radius r, which is $x^2 + y^2 = r^2$, you are able to do several things:

- You can determine the radius r of a particular circle written in the form $x^2 + y^2 = r^2$.
- You can write the equation of a circle with center $(0, 0)$ given its radius r.
- On a Cartesian plane, you can sketch a given circle written in the form $x^2 + y^2 = r^2$.

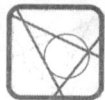

For example, it is possible to determine the radius of the circle defined by the equation $x^2 + y^2 = 81$.

Since the equation $x^2 + y^2 = r^2$ represents a circle with center (0, 0) and radius r, you can calculate the radius of the circle.
$r^2 = 81$
$r = \sqrt{81}$
$= 9$

Thus, the radius of the circle $x^2 + y^2 = 81$ is 9 units.

Example

A circle has its center at (0, 0) and a diameter of 6 units.

Write the equation of the circle, and then sketch the circle on a Cartesian plane.

Solution

Since the diameter is twice the length of the radius, the radius of the circle is 3 units. In order to write the equation of the circle, substitute 3 for r in the equation $x^2 + y^2 = r^2$.
$x^2 + y^2 = (3)^2$
$x^2 + y^2 = 9$

Thus, the equation of the circle with center (0, 0) and a diameter of 6 units is $x^2 + y^2 = 9$.

The circle defined by the equation $x^2 + y^2 = 9$ has a center at (0, 0) and a radius of 3 units. You can choose the ordered pairs (0, 3), (0, −3), (3, 0), and (−3, 0) to help you sketch the circle.

The circle is sketched here on a Cartesian plane.

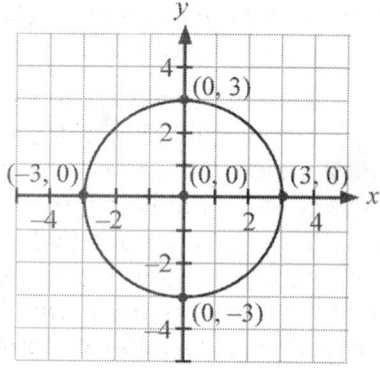

CONVERTING THE EQUATION OF A CIRCLE FROM GENERAL TO STANDARD FORM BY COMPLETING THE SQUARE

The standard form of the equation of a circle is convenient for identifying the basic characteristics of the circle (center, radius, domain, and range), and it makes sketching the graph of the circle easy. Converting from general to standard form usually involves **completing the square**.

The following steps can be taken to convert the equation of a circle from general to standard form by completing the square:

1. Factor out any common factors.
2. Move all terms with x or y in them to one side of the equation and the constants to the other side.
3. Rearrange the equation by grouping terms with x-variables and y-variables in brackets and leaving spaces to complete each square.
4. Fill in the blanks to create perfect square trinomials, thus completing the square.
5. Factor the perfect square trinomials produced, and add the numbers on the right side of the equation.

Example

Convert the equation $x^2 + y^2 - 6x + 2y - 6 = 0$ to standard form, and state the center and radius of the circle.

Solution

The given equation defines a circle since $A = C$. It is also possible that it is the degenerate form of a circle.

Converting to standard form involves completing the square for the x-terms and for the y-terms.

Step 1
Add 6 to each side of the equation.
$x^2 + y^2 - 6x + 2y = 6$

Step 2
Rearrange the equation by grouping terms with x-variables and y-variables in brackets and leaving spaces to complete each square.
$(x^2 - 6x + \underline{}) + (y^2 + 2y + \underline{}) = 6$

Step 3
Fill in the blanks to create perfect square trinomials, thus completing the squares.

Complete the square by adding $\left(-\frac{6}{2}\right)^2 = 9$ and $\left(\frac{2}{2}\right)^2 = 1$ to both sides of the equation.

$(x^2 - 6x + \underline{9}) + (y^2 + 2y + \underline{1}) = 6 + 9 + 1$

Step 4
Factor the perfect square trinomials produced, and add the numbers on the right side of the equation.

$(x - 3)^2 + (y + 1)^2 = 16$

Step 5
Identify the center and radius of the circle using the standard form of the equation $(x - 3)^2 + (y + 1)^2 = 16$.

The center is at $(3, -1)$ and the radius, r, is $\sqrt{16} = 4$ units.

Example

Convert the equation $3x^2 + 3y^2 + 12x - 24y + 60 = 0$ to standard form, and state the center and radius of the conic.

Solution

Since $A = C$, the equation defines a circle.
$3x^2 + 3y^2 + 12x - 24y + 60 = 0$

Step 1
Divide each side of the equation by 3.
$x^2 + y^2 + 4x - 8y + 20 = 0$

Step 2
Add -20 to each side of the equation.
$x^2 + y^2 + 4x - 8y = -20$

Step 3
Rearrange the equation by grouping terms with x-variables and y-variables in separate brackets, leaving spaces to complete the squares.

$(x^2 + 4x + \underline{\hspace{0.5cm}}) + (y^2 - 8y + \underline{\hspace{0.5cm}}) = -20$

Step 4
Complete the squares by adding 4 and 16 to each side of the equation.

$\left(\frac{4}{2}\right)^2 = 2^2 = 4$ and $\left(-\frac{8}{2}\right)^2 = (-4)^2 = 16$.

$(x^2 + 4x + \underline{4}) + (y^2 - 8y + \underline{16}) = -20 + 4 + 16$

Step 5
Factor the perfect square trinomials produced, and add the numbers on the right side of the equation.

$(x + 2)^2 + (y - 4)^2 = 0$

Step 6
Identify the center and radius of the circles using the standard form of the equation $(x + 2)^2 + (y - 4)^2 = 0$.

The circle appears to have a center at $(-2, 4)$ and a radius of 0. Therefore, the equation defines a degenerate form of a circle since it represents a point. The only point that satisfies the equation is $(-2, 4)$. The physical representation is a plane intersecting the vertex of a cone.

Example

Convert the equation $x^2 + y^2 - 2x + 10y + 30 = 0$ to standard form, and state the center and radius of the resulting conic.

Solution

Since $A = C$, the equation defines a circle.

Step 1
Complete the square.

$x^2 + y^2 - 2x + 10y = -30$
$(x^2 - 2x + \underline{\hspace{0.3cm}}) + (y^2 + 10y + \underline{\hspace{0.3cm}}) = -30$
$(x^2 - 2x + \underline{1}) + (y^2 + 10y + \underline{25}) = -30 + 1 + 25$
$(x - 1)^2 + (y + 5)^2 = -4$

Step 2
Identify the center and the radius of the circle using the standard form of the equation $(x - 1)^2 + (y + 5)^2 = -4$.

The circle appears to have a center at $(1, -5)$, but the -4 on the right side of the equation makes it impossible to solve. Substituting any numbers for x and y makes the left side of the equation positive; it cannot equal -4. Also, the square of the radius cannot be a negative number, so there is no graph and the given equation defines a degenerate form of a circle.

Determining the Key Characteristics of a Circle from the Standard Form Equation

A circle with a center (0, 0) is defined by an equation of the form $x^2 + y^2 = r^2$, where r represents the radius of the circle. For example, the circle defined by the equation $x^2 + y^2 = 9$ has its center at (0, 0) and a radius of $\sqrt{9} = 3$ units.

Generally, the standard form equation for a circle is $(x - h)^2 + (y - k)^2 = r^2$. The standard form equation is useful for determining the key characteristics of the graph of the circle, such as the center, radius, domain, and range.

The characteristics of the graph of the circle defined by $(x - h)^2 + (y - k)^2 = r^2$ are as follows:

- The center is at (h, k).
- The radius is r units.
- The domain is $h - r \leq x \leq h + r$.
- The range is $k - r \leq y \leq k + r$.

Example

What is the center and the radius of the circle defined by the equation $(x - 1)^2 + (y + 6)^2 = 49$?

Solution

The standard form for a circle is $(x - h)^2 + (y - k)^2 = r^2$, where the center of the circle is at (h, k) and the radius is r units. Therefore, the center is at (1, −6), and the radius, r, is $r = \sqrt{49} = 7$ units.

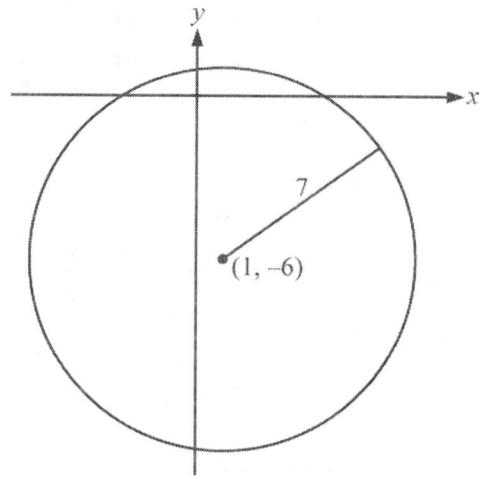

Determine the domain for the graph defined by the equation $(x - 1)^2 + (y + 6)^2 = 49$.

Solution

The resulting graph of the equation $(x - 1)^2 + (y + 6)^2 = 49$ is a circle with its center at (1, −6) and a radius of 7 units. To determine the domain, use the center (1, −6) and the radius of 7 units to determine the endpoints of a horizontal diameter.

The endpoints of the horizontal diameter are $(1 - 7, -6) = (-6, -6)$ and $(1 + 7, -6) = (8, -6)$. Therefore, the domain is $-6 \leq x \leq 8$.

Determine the range for the graph defined by the equation $(x - 1)^2 + (y + 6)^2 = 49$.

Solution

The resulting graph of the equation $(x - 1)^2 + (y + 6)^2 = 49$ is a circle with its center at (1, −6) and a radius of 7 units.

To determine the range, use the center (1, −6) and the radius of 7 units to find the endpoints of the vertical diameter.

The endpoints of the vertical diameter are $(1, -6 - 7) = (1, -13)$ and $(1, -6 + 7) = (1, 1)$.

Thus, the range is $-13 \leq y \leq 1$.

Determining the Equation of a Circle when Given Key Characteristics

The equation of a circle in standard or general form can be determined from given characteristics of the circle, such as the center and the radius.

Use the following steps to determine the equation of a circle when given particular characteristics:

1. Determine the center, (h, k), and the radius, r, of the circle. Recall that the center of a circle can be determined by calculating the midpoint of the diameter of the circle, and the radius can be calculated by halving the distance of the diameter or by determining the distance between the center and a point that lies on the circle.
2. Substitute those values into the standard form equation of a circle, $(x - h)^2 + (y - k)^2 = r^2$, and simplify.
3. If required, convert to general form.

Example
Determine the equation of a circle with its center at $(-5, 2)$ and a radius of 6.

Solution
A circle is defined by the equation $(x - h)^2 + (y - k)^2 = r^2$, where (h, k) is the center of the circle and r is the radius.

Substitute the given information into the circle equation.
$(x - h)^2 + (y - k)^2 = r^2$
$(x + 5)^2 + (y - 2)^2 = 6^2$
$(x + 5)^2 + (y - 2)^2 = 36$

The equation of a circle with its center at $(-5, 2)$ and a radius of 6 is
$(x + 5)^2 + (y - 2)^2 = 36$.

Example
Given that point $(-3, -5)$ lies on a circle with center $(-7, -8)$, determine the equation of the circle.

Solution

Step 1
Determine the radius of the circle.
The radius of the circle is equal to the distance between the center $(-7, -8)$ and a point on the circumference $(-3, -5)$.
Apply the distance formula.
$r = \sqrt{(-7 - (-3))^2 + (-8 - (-5))^2}$
$ = \sqrt{16 + 9}$
$ = \sqrt{25}$
$ = 5$

Step 2
Determine the equation of the circle.
Substitute the values for the radius and the coordinates of the center into the equation $(x - h)^2 + (y - k)^2 = r^2$.
$(x - (-7))^2 + (y - (-8))^2 = (5)^2$
$(x + 7)^2 + (y + 8)^2 = 25$

DETERMINING THE EQUATION OF A CIRCLE FROM A GRAPH

Given the graph of a circle, you can determine the equation of the circle in standard or general form by identifying some of the key characteristics of the circle directly from the graph.

To determine the equation of a circle from a graph, follow these general steps:

1. Look at the graph to determine the center, (h, k), and the radius, r.
2. Substitute these values into the standard form of the equation of a circle, $(x - h)^2 + (y - k)^2 = r^2$.
3. Convert to general form if required.

Example

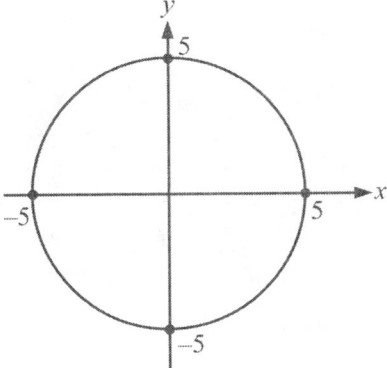

Write an equation in standard form for the given circle.

Solution

The center of the circle is at $(0, 0)$, and the radius is equal to 5.

Thus, the equation is $x^2 + y^2 = 5^2$ or $x^2 + y^2 = 25$.

Example

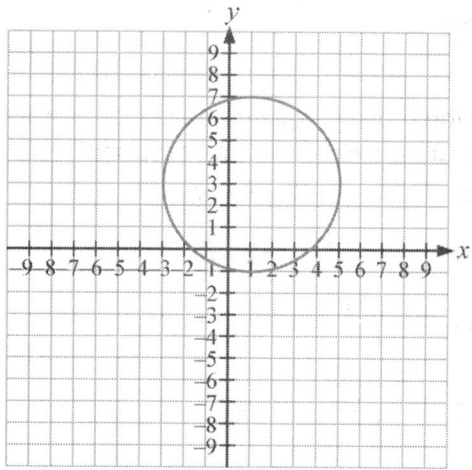

Determine the equation in general form for the given circle.

Solution

Step 1
From the given graph, determine the center, (h, k), and the radius, r, of the circle.
The center of the circle is at $(1, 3)$, and the radius is 4 units.

Step 2
Substitute 1 for h, 3 for k, and 4 for r into the standard form of the equation of a circle, $(x - h)^2 + (y - k)^2 = r^2$.
$(x - 1)^2 + (y - 3)^2 = 4^2$
$(x - 1)^2 + (y - 3)^2 = 16$

Step 3
Convert to the general form
$Ax^2 + Cy^2 + Dx + Ey + F = 0$.
$$(x - 1)^2 + (y - 3)^2 = 16$$
$$(x^2 - 2x + 1) + (y^2 - 6y + 9) = 16$$
$$x^2 + y^2 - 2x - 6y + 1 + 9 - 16 = 0$$
$$x^2 + y^2 - 2x - 6y - 6 = 0$$
The general form of the equation of the circle is $x^2 + y^2 - 2x - 6y - 6 = 0$.

EXERCISE #1—RELATING CONIC SECTIONS TO THEIR EQUATION

Use the following information to answer the next question.

A circle with center (0, 0) and a diameter with endpoints (*a*, *b*) and (*c*, *d*) is shown.

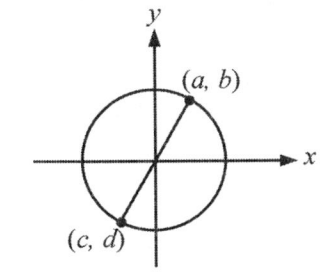

250. The equation of this circle could be written as

   A. $x^2 + y^2 = \dfrac{(a-b)+(c-d)}{2}$

   B. $x^2 + y^2 = \dfrac{(a-b)+(c-d)}{4}$

   C. $x^2 + y^2 = \dfrac{(a-c)^2+(b-d)^2}{2}$

   D. $x^2 + y^2 = \dfrac{(a-c)^2+(b-d)^2}{4}$

Use the following information to answer the next question.

The equation of a circle is
$x^2 + y^2 - 10x - 12y - 3 = 0$.

251. When the equation is converted into the form $(x-h)^2 + (y-k)^2 = r^2$, the values of *k* and *r* are

   A. $k = 6$ and $r = 8$
   B. $k = 6$ and $r = 5$
   C. $k = -6$ and $r = 8$
   D. $k = -6$ and $r = 5$

252. Which of the following equations represents a circle with a radius of 3 units?

   A. $2x^2 + 2(y+1)^2 = 6$

   B. $3(x-2)^2 + 3(y+1)^2 = 9$

   C. $\dfrac{(x+1)^2}{3} + \dfrac{(y-2)^2}{3} = 1$

   D. $\dfrac{(x+4)^2}{9} + \dfrac{(y-7)^2}{9} = 1$

253. Which equation defines a circle centered at point (2, −5) with a diameter of 12 units?

   A. $x^2 + y^2 - 4x + 10y - 115 = 0$
   B. $x^2 + y^2 + 4x - 10y - 115 = 0$
   C. $x^2 + y^2 + 4x - 10y - 7 = 0$
   D. $x^2 + y^2 - 4x + 10y - 7 = 0$

Use the following information to answer the next question.

The graph of a circle is shown.

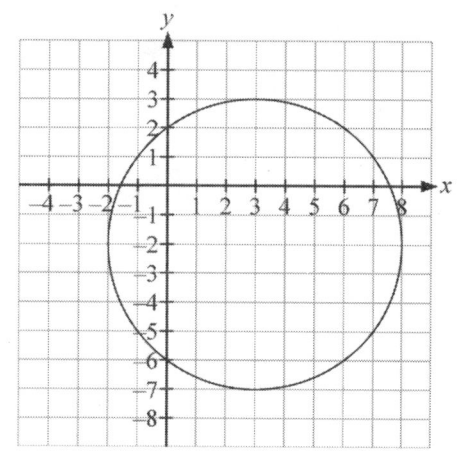

254. What is the equation of the given circle in standard form?

A. $(x-3)^2 + (y+2)^2 = 5^2$

B. $(x+3)^2 + (y-2)^2 = 5^2$

C. $(x-2)^2 + (y+3)^2 = 5^2$

D. $(x+2)^2 + (y-3)^2 = 5^2$

EXERCISE #1—RELATING CONIC SECTIONS TO THEIR EQUATION ANSWERS AND SOLUTIONS

| 250. D | 252. D | 254. A |
| 251. A | 253. D | |

250. D

Determine an expression for the radius, r, in the equation of a circle given by the equation $x^2 + y^2 = r^2$.

Recall that the radius of a circle is $\frac{1}{2}$ the diameter.

Use the distance formula to determine the diameter of this circle.

$d = \sqrt{(x_2 - x_1)^2 + (y_2 - y_1)^2}$
$d = \sqrt{(a - c)^2 + (b - d)^2}$

Therefore, the radius will be $= \dfrac{\sqrt{(a - c)^2 + (b - d)^2}}{2}$

If $x^2 + y^2 = r^2$ is the equation of a circle with its center at (0, 0), substitute the expression for the radius into this equation.

$x^2 + y^2 = \left(\dfrac{\sqrt{(a - c)^2 + (b - d)^2}}{2}\right)^2$

$x^2 + y^2 = \dfrac{(a - c)^2 + (b - d)^2}{4}$

Therefore, the equation of this circle could be

$x^2 + y^2 = \dfrac{(a - c)^2 + (b - d)^2}{4}$.

251. A

Step 1
Isolate the constant.
$x^2 + y^2 - 10x - 12y - 3 = 0$
$x^2 + y^2 - 10x - 12y = 3$

Step 2
Group the terms with the same variable.
$x^2 - 10x + y^2 - 12y = 3$

Step 3
Complete the square.
$\left(\begin{array}{l}(x^2 - 10x + 25) \\ + (y^2 - 12y + 36)\end{array}\right) = 3 + 25 + 36$

$\left(\begin{array}{l}(x^2 - 10x + 25) \\ + (y^2 - 12y + 36)\end{array}\right) = 64$

Step 4
Factor the perfect square trinomials, and rewrite the constant as a perfect square.
$(x - 5)^2 + (y - 6)^2 = 8^2$

Step 5
Determine the values of k and r.
By comparing the equation $(x - 5)^2 + (y - 6)^2 = 8^2$ to $(x - h)^2 + (y - k)^2 = r^2$, observe that $k = 6$ and $r = 8$.

252. D

Step 1
Identify the standard form of the equation of a circle.
The standard form of the equation of a circle is $(x - h)^2 + (y - k)^2 = r^2$, where (h, k) is the center and r is the radius.

Step 2
Write the equation $2x^2 + 2(y + 1)^2 = 6$ in standard form to determine the radius of the circle defined by the equation.
Divide both sides of the equation by 2.
$x^2 + (y + 1)^2 = 3$
$x^2 + (y + 1)^2 = (\sqrt{3})^2$
The radius of the circle defined by the equation $2x^2 + 2(y + 1)^2 = 6$ is $\sqrt{3}$ units.

Step 3
Write the equation $3(x - 2)^2 + 3(y + 1)^2 = 9$ in standard form to determine the radius of the circle defined by the equation.
Divide both sides of the equation by 3.
$(x - 2)^2 + (y + 1)^2 = 3$
$(x - 2)^2 + (y + 1)^2 = (\sqrt{3})^2$
The radius of the circle defined by the equation $3(x - 2)^2 + 3(y + 1)^2 = 9$ is $\sqrt{3}$ units.

Step 4
Write the equation $\dfrac{(x + 1)^2}{3} + \dfrac{(y - 2)^2}{3} = 1$ in standard form to determine the radius of the circle defined by the equation.
Multiply both sides of the equation by 3.
$(x + 1)^2 + (y - 2)^2 = 3$
$(x + 1)^2 + (y - 2)^2 = (\sqrt{3})^2$
The radius of the circle defined by the equation $\dfrac{(x + 1)^2}{3} + \dfrac{(y - 2)^2}{3} = 1$ is $\sqrt{3}$ units.

Step 5

Write the equation $\frac{(x+4)^2}{9} + \frac{(y-7)^2}{9} = 1$ in standard form to determine the radius of the circle defined by the equation.

Multiply both sides of the equation by 9.

$(x+4)^2 + (y-7)^2 = 9$
$(x+4)^2 + (y-7)^2 = 3^2$

The radius of the circle defined by the equation $\frac{(x+4)^2}{9} + \frac{(y-7)^2}{9} = 1$ is 3 units.

253. D

Step 1

Determine the standard form of the equation of the circle, $(x-h)^2 + (y-k)^2 = r^2$, where (h, k) is the center of the circle and r is the radius.

The center of the circle is at $(2, -5)$ and the diameter is 12 units, so the radius is $\frac{12}{2}$, or 6 units. Substitute 2 for h, -5 for k, and 6 for r in the equation $(x-h)^2 + (y-k)^2 = r^2$.

Therefore, the standard form of the equation of the circle is $(x-2)^2 + (y+5)^2 = 6^2$.

Step 2

Expand the binomials.

$(x^2 - 4x + 4) + (y^2 + 10y + 25) = 36$

Step 3

Collect the like terms, and set the right-hand side of the equation equal to 0.

$x^2 + y^2 - 4x + 10y - 7 = 0$

254. A

Step 1

Determine the center, (h, k), and the radius, r, of the circle from the given graph.

The center of the circle is at $(3, -2)$, and the radius is 5 units.

Step 2

Substitute 3 for h, -2 for k, and 5 for r into the standard form of the equation of a circle, $(x-h)^2 + (y-k)^2 = r^2$.

$(x-3)^2 + (y-(-2))^2 = 5^2$
$\quad (x-3)^2 + (y+2)^2 = 5^2$

EXERCISE #2—RELATING CONIC SECTIONS TO THEIR EQUATION

Use the following information to answer the next question.

A circle with a center of (0, 0) and passing through the point (3, 4) is shown.

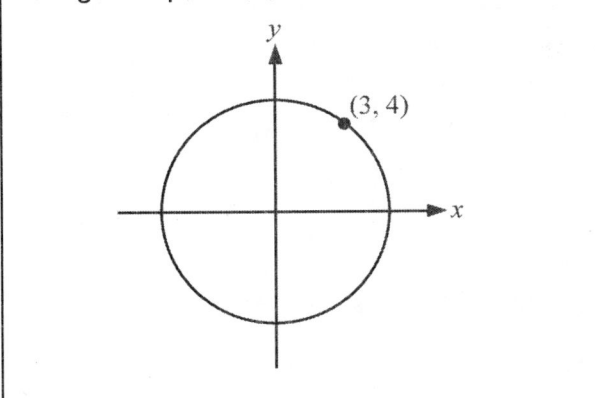

255. Another point that this circle will pass through is
 A. (−5, 5)
 B. (0, 25)
 C. (4, −5)
 D. (−4, −3)

256. The equation of a circle is $x^2 + y^2 - 8x + 2y + 1 = 0$. What is the equation when converted into standard form?
 A. $(x-4)^2 + (y+1)^2 = 4^2$
 B. $(x-4)^2 + (y+1)^2 = 2^2$
 C. $(x-4)^2 + y^2 = 4^2$
 D. $(x-4)^2 + y^2 = 2^2$

257. The range of the graph of the quadratic relation defined by the equation $(x+3)^2 + (y-1)^2 = 4$ is
 A. $-1 \le y \le 3$
 B. $-3 \le y \le 1$
 C. $-5 \le y \le -1$
 D. $-7 \le y \le 1$

258. The general form equation that defines a circle that is centered at point (−3, 5) and has a diameter of 10 units is
 A. $x^2 + y^2 + 6x - 10y + 59 = 0$
 B. $x^2 + y^2 - 6x + 10y + 41 = 0$
 C. $x^2 + y^2 + 6x - 10y + 9 = 0$
 D. $x^2 + y^2 - 6x + 10y - 9 = 0$

Use the following information to answer the next question.

The graph of a circle is shown.

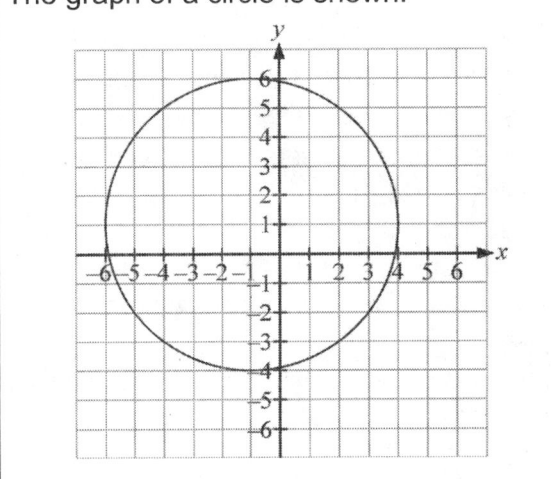

259. If an equation for the given circle is written in the general form $Ax^2 + Cy^2 + Dx + Ey + F = 0$, the value of $|A + C + D + E + F|$ is _____.

EXERCISE #2—RELATING CONIC SECTIONS TO THEIR EQUATION ANSWERS AND SOLUTIONS

| 255. D | 257. A | 259. 21 |
| 256. A | 258. C | |

255. D

The distance between the center (0, 0) and the point (3, 4) is the radius of the circle. Find the length of the radius using the distance formula.

$d = \sqrt{(x_2 - x_1)^2 + (y_2 - y_1)^2}$
$= \sqrt{(3-0)^2 + (4-0)^2}$
$= \sqrt{9 + 16}$
$= \sqrt{25}$
$= 5$

Since the radius of the circle is 5 units, the distance from the center to any other point on the circle must also be 5 units.

Determine the distance from the center to each of the other points provided in each choice.

Choice A: For the point (−5, 5):
$d = \sqrt{(-5-0)^2 + (5-0)^2}$
$= \sqrt{25 + 25}$
$= \sqrt{50}$
$\cong 7.1$

Choice B: For the point (0, 25):
$d = \sqrt{(0-0)^2 + (25-0)^2}$
$= \sqrt{0 + 625}$
$= \sqrt{625}$
$= 25$

Choice C: For the point (4, −5):
$d = \sqrt{(4-0)^2 + (-5-0)^2}$
$= \sqrt{16 + 25}$
$= \sqrt{41}$
$\cong 6.4$

Choice D: For the point (−4, −3):
$d = \sqrt{(-4-0)^2 + (-3-0)^2}$
$= \sqrt{16 + 9}$
$= \sqrt{25}$
$= 5$

Since the point (−4, −3) is 5 units from the center, it is another point that this circle will pass through.

256. A

Step 1
Isolate the constant.
$x^2 + y^2 - 8x + 2y + 1 = 0$
$x^2 + y^2 - 8x + 2y = -1$

Step 2
Group the terms with the same variable.
$x^2 - 8x + y^2 + 2y = -1$

Step 3
Complete the square.
$\begin{pmatrix} (x^2 - 8x + 16) \\ + (y^2 + 2y + 1) \end{pmatrix} = -1 + 16 + 1$
$\begin{pmatrix} (x^2 - 8x + 16) \\ + (y^2 + 2y + 1) \end{pmatrix} = 16$

Step 4
Factor the perfect square trinomials, and rewrite the constant as a perfect square.
$(x - 4)^2 + (y + 1)^2 = 4^2$

257. A

Step 1
Determine the center and the radius of the circle defined by the equation $(x + 3)^2 + (y - 1)^2 = 4$.

Rewrite the equation $(x + 3)^2 + (y - 1)^2 = 4$ so that 4 is a power of 2.
$(x + 3)^2 + (y - 1)^2 = 2^2$

The equation represents a circle with a radius of 2 units and a center at (−3, 1).

Step 2
Determine the endpoints of the vertical diameter of the circle using the center and the radius of 2 units.
The endpoints of the vertical diameter are
(−3, 1 − 2) = (−3, −1) and (−3, 1 + 2) = (−3, 3).
The range is −1 ≤ y ≤ 3.

258. C

Step 1
Identify the standard form of the equation of a circle.
The standard form of the equation of a circle is
$(x - h)^2 + (y - k)^2 = r^2$, where (h, k) is the center of the circle and r is the radius.

Given that the center of the circle is at (−3, 5) and the diameter is 10 units, the radius is $\frac{10}{2}$, or 5 units.

Substitute −3 for h, 5 for k, and 5 for r in the equation $(x - h)^2 + (y - k)^2 = r^2$.

The standard form of the equation of the circle is $(x + 3)^2 + (y - 5)^2 = 5^2$.

Step 2
Expand the binomials.
$(x^2+6x+9)+(y^2-10y+25)=25$

Step 3
Collect the like terms, and set the right side of the equation equal to 0.
$x^2+y^2+6x-10y+9=0$

259. 21

Step 1
From the given graph, determine the center, (h, k), and the radius, r, of the circle.
The center of the circle is at $(-1, 1)$, and the radius is 5 units.

Step 2
Substitute -1 for h, 1 for k, and 5 for r into the standard form of the equation of a circle, $(x-h)^2+(y-k)^2=r^2$.
$(x-(-1))^2+(y-1)^2=5^2$
$(x+1)^2+(y-1)^2=25$

Step 3
Convert to the general form, $Ax^2+Cy^2+Dx+Ey+F=0$.
$(x+1)^2+(y-1)^2=25$
$(x^2+2x+1)+(y^2-2y+1)=25$
$x^2+y^2+2x-2y+1+1-25=0$
$x^2+y^2+2x-2y-23=0$
The general form of the equation of the circle is $x^2+y^2+2x-2y-23=0$.

Step 4
Determine the value of $|A+C+D+E+F|$.
$|A+C+D+E+F|$
$=|1+1+2+(-2)+(-23)|$
$=|1+1+2-2-23|$
$=|-21|$
$=21$

NOTES

Independence and Conditional Probability

INDEPENDENCE AND CONDITIONAL PROBABILITY

Table of Correlations

Standard		Concepts	Exercise #1	Exercise #2
Unit6.1	Understand independence and conditional probability and use them to interpret data.			
S-CP.1	Describe events as subsets of a sample space (the set of outcomes) using characteristics (or categories) of the outcomes, or as unions, intersections, or complements of other events ("or," "and," "not").	Sample Space	260	266
		Using Logic and the Words *And*, *Or*, and *Not*	261	267
S-CP.2	Understand that two events A and B are independent if the probability of A and B occurring together is the product of their probabilities, and use this characterization to determine if they are independent.	Identifying Sample Space for Two Independent Events	262	268
		Understanding the Difference between Independent and Dependent Events		
		Calculating the Theoretical Probability of Independent Events	263	269
S-CP.3	Understand the conditional probability of A given B as P(A and B)/P(B), and interpret independence of A and B as saying that the conditional probability of A given B is the same as the probability of A, and the conditional probability of B given A is the same as the probability of B.	Identifying Conditional Probability	264	270
S-CP.4	Construct and interpret two-way frequency tables of data when two categories are associated with each object being classified. Use the two-way table as a sample space to decide if events are independent and to approximate conditional probabilities.	Finding Conditional Probability Given a Frequency Table	265	271
S-CP.5	Recognize and explain the concepts of conditional probability and independence in everyday language and everyday situations.	Identifying Conditional Probability	264	270

S-CP.1 Describe events as subsets of a sample space (the set of outcomes) using characteristics (or categories) of the outcomes, or as unions, intersections, or complements of other events ("or," "and," "not").

SAMPLE SPACE

A **sample space** is a data set that contains all possible outcomes of an experiment. There are two types of sample spaces: discrete and continuous.

In a **discrete sample space**, the outcomes can be counted, so it has a finite number of possible outcomes.

Example

This chart illustrates the possible outcomes when two standard six-sided dice are rolled together.

	Die A					
Die B	1	2	3	4	5	6
1	(1, 1)	(1, 2)	(1, 3)	(1, 4)	(1, 5)	(1, 6)
2	(2, 1)	(2, 2)	(2, 3)	(2, 4)	(2, 5)	(2, 6)
3	(3, 1)	(3, 2)	(3, 3)	(3, 4)	(3, 5)	(3, 6)
4	(4, 1)	(4, 2)	(4, 3)	(4, 4)	(4, 5)	(4, 6)
5	(5, 1)	(5, 2)	(5, 3)	(5, 4)	(5, 5)	(5, 6)
6	(6, 1)	(6, 2)	(6, 3)	(6, 4)	(6, 5)	(6, 6)

Determine the number of possible outcomes in the sample space, and classify the sample space as discrete or continuous.

Solution

The outcomes are the ordered pairs, so there are 36 outcomes.

The sample space is discrete because the outcomes can be counted.

In a **continuous sample space**, the outcomes must be measured, so it has an infinite number of possible outcomes.

Example

Four girls participate in the final shot put event at Blue Ridge School. The following chart gives their results.

Participant	Sarah	Leah	Eva	Suri
Distance (m)	5.65	6.53	4.98	6.01

Determine the number of possible outcomes in the sample space, and classify the sample space as discrete or continuous.

Solution

The number of possible outcomes is infinite because the four girls could have putted their shot puts any number of distances.

The sample space is continuous because the number of possible outcomes cannot be defined. This inability to give a finite number is because the outcomes are measured rather than counted.

Example

A toy manufacturer makes a stuffed toy using the following choices of colors:

- Head—red (R), green (G), or white (W)
- Body—blue (B) or orange (O)
- Arms—yellow (Y) or purple (P)

Classify the data as discrete or continuous, and determine the size of the sample space.

Solution

Step 1
Build a table showing all possible outcomes.

Head	Body	Arms	Outcome
R	B	Y	RBY
R	B	P	RBP
R	O	Y	ROY
R	O	P	ROP
G	B	Y	GBY
G	B	P	GBP
G	O	Y	GOY
G	O	P	GOP
W	B	Y	WBY
W	B	P	WBP
W	O	Y	WOY
W	O	P	WOP

Step 2
Classify the sample space, and determine its size.

The sample space is discrete because the 12 outcomes can be counted.

USING LOGIC AND THE WORDS *AND*, *OR*, AND *NOT*

Mathematics uses very specific language. Some of the mathematical language that is related to formal reasoning and logic has become a common part of day-to-day activities when doing searches on the computer and the Internet. It is common to use the words *and*, *or*, and *not* to expand or limit the regions or sites for a search. In fact, the computer itself is built upon the logic associated with these three words. This logic is based on the mathematics known as Boolean algebra, which was developed by the British mathematician George Boole (1815-1864).

These three words are also used to make mathematical statements. However, a statement has its own definition in logic. A statement in logic is a sentence that is either true or false. If the sentence is not accepted or proven to be either true or false, then the sentence may simply be an opinion.

A **compound statement** is a larger statement formed from two or more statements connected with the logic operators *and*, *or*, or *not*. For example, a compound statement is "Prince Edward Island is on the east coast and is Canada's most densely populated province." It is a compound statement because it is made up of these two statements:

i. Prince Edward Island is on the East Coast.
ii. Prince Edward Island is Canada's most densely populated province.

Example
  i. Maria's new car is a hatchback.
  ii. Maria's new car is built in Germany.

Form a compound statement from the given two statements.

Solution
  Maria's new car is a hatchback and is built in Germany.

USE OF THE WORD *NOT* IN MATHEMATICS AND LOGIC

Negating a statement has the opposite meaning of the original statement. The word *not* is often used to form the negation of a statement. For example, Calgary is not in Eastern Canada.

In mathematics, negations are often formed by using the symbols $\neq$, $\not>$, and $\not<$. These symbols are read as "not equal to," "not greater than," and "not less than," respectively.

Example

On a number line, graph $x \not> 7$, where $x \in \mathbb{R}$.

Solution

Since numbers that are not greater than 7 are all numbers less than 7 inclusive, the graph of $x \not> 7$ is the same as the graph of $x \leq 7$.

The graph of $x \leq 7$ is shown.

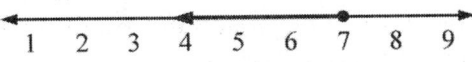

USE OF THE WORD *OR* IN MATHEMATICS AND LOGIC

In the English language, the word *or* may be exclusive or inclusive. For example, the statement "Brian is going to ride his bicycle or drive his mom's car to school today" indicates that he is only going to use one of the two modes of transportation to get to school. The use of *or* is exclusive in this case.

Now, consider the following statement:
To travel to a particular country, Alesha requires a passport or a birth certificate.

In this situation, if Alesha has either a passport, a birth certificate, or both, she would be able to travel to this particular country. The use of *or* is inclusive in this case.

In mathematics and logic, the use of *or* is always inclusive.

Example

On a number line, graph $x > -3$ or $x \geq 2$, where $x \in \mathbb{R}$.

Solution

Since the values for x that satisfy the inequality $x \geq 2$ also satisfy the inequality $x > -3$, the solution can be written as the single statement $x > -3$.

The graph of $x > -3$ is as shown.

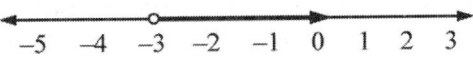

Example

On a number line, graph $x < -1$ or $x \geq 2$, where $x \in \mathbb{R}$.

Solution

In this case, there are no numbers that satisfy both inequalities. However, satisfying at least one of the inequalities is all that is required to satisfy the operator *or*.

The resulting graph is shown.

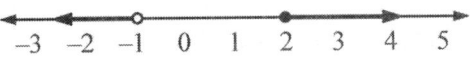

USE OF THE WORD *AND* IN MATHEMATICS AND LOGIC

The use of the word *and* in mathematics and logic is consistent with its use in common English. For example, Deon is a football player and a baseball player.

For this statement to be true, Deon must participate in both sports. When the word *and* is used in mathematics, both conditions must also apply.

Example

On a number line, graph the values of x that satisfy the compound statement $x \geq -5$ and $x < 3$, where $x \in \mathbb{R}$.

Solution

Since both conditions $x \geq -5$ and $x < 3$ must be satisfied, they can be written as $-5 \leq x < 3$.

The resulting graph is shown.

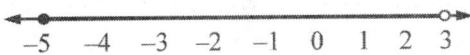

VENN DIAGRAMS

Venn diagrams are diagrams of closed loops (usually circles) that illustrate the relationships between sets. A set is a collection of particular objects (or elements).

Example

In a particular sports school for boys, every boy participates in at least one of the two sports being offered: hockey and football.

Use shading in a Venn diagram to illustrate the set of boys who play football but not hockey.

Solution

This operator describes the set of boys who play one sport only, which is football in this case. The region to be shaded is the circle representing the set of football players without shading the region that is also part of the hockey circle.

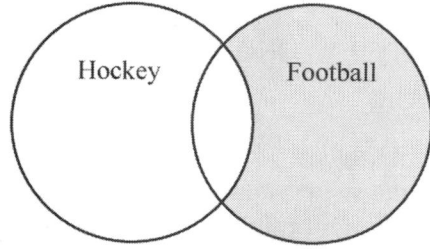

Venn diagrams can be used to represent sets that may have common elements.

Use shading in a Venn diagram to illustrate the boys who play hockey or football.

Solution

This Venn diagram consists of two overlapping circles that illustrate the two sets of boys who play each sport. The overlapping region represents the set of boys who play both sports.

The set of boys who play hockey or football consists of all the boys who play only one of the two sports plus the boys who play both sports. All three regions shaded represent the set of boys who play both sports.

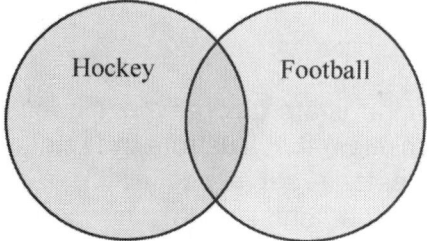

Use shading in a Venn diagram to illustrate the boys who play hockey and football.

Solution

The set of boys who play hockey and football is illustrated in the Venn diagram by the overlapping region of the two circles, so only this region is shaded.

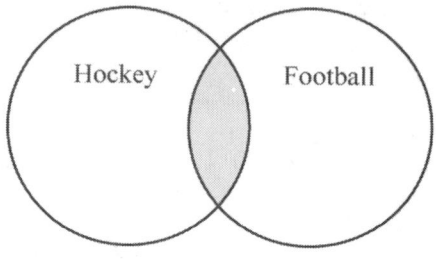

Venn diagrams can also be used to solve problems involving sets that may or may not have common elements. The method involves determining the number of elements in a particular region by subtracting the number in an overlapping region from the number in a larger region.

Example

In a particular class of twelfth grade students, 14 students are taking chemistry, 11 students are taking physics, 8 students are taking chemistry and physics, and 5 students are taking neither chemistry nor physics.

Use a Venn diagram to determine how many students are in the class.

Solution

Step 1

Draw two overlapping circles representing each group of students taking the two subjects, and label the circles.

Put a boundary around these circles because there are students taking neither of the subjects that need to be counted.

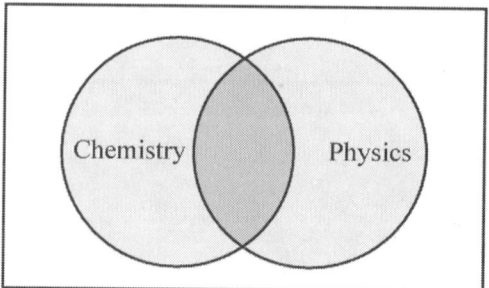

Independence and Conditional Probability

Step 2
Label the regions representing the information in the problem appropriately.

- Begin with the portion overlapped by the two circles. This region represents 8 students, so label this region with an 8.
- Since 14 students are taking chemistry, the region for students taking chemistry only is labeled with 14 − 8 = 6. Similarly, the region for students taking physics only is labeled with 11 − 8 = 3.
- Label the region outside of the two circles with the number of students taking neither subject, which is 5.

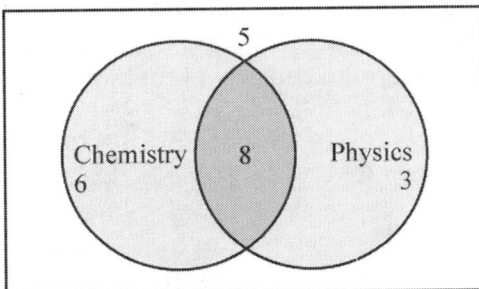

Step 3
Determine the number of students in the class. The total number of students in the class is the sum of all the number labels for each region. This is 8 + 6 + 3 + 5 = 22.

Example
At a dinner party for 26 people, 14 people order an appetizer, and 18 people order dessert. Five people order neither an appetizer nor dessert.

How many people order both an appetizer and dessert?

Solution
Step 1
Draw two overlapping circles representing each group of people ordering the two items, and label the circles.

Put a boundary around these circles because there are people that order neither of the items that need to be counted.

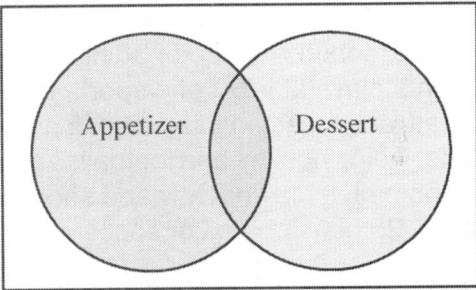

Step 2
Label the regions representing the information in the problem appropriately.

Let the number of people who order both an appetizer and a dessert be represented by x.

- Begin with the region overlapped by the two circles. The number of people in this region is required. Label this region as x.
- Since 14 people order an appetizer, the number of people that order only an appetizer can be labeled with 14 − x. Similarly, the region for students that order only a dessert is labeled with 18 − x.
- Label the region outside of the two circles with the number of people that order neither item, which is 5.

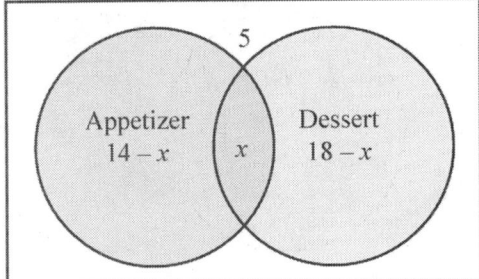

Step 3

Determine the number of people that order both an appetizer and a dessert.

Since the total number of people, 26, is the sum of all the number labels for each region, the equation that represents this sum is
$x + (14 - x) + (18 - x) + 5 = 26$.

Solve the equation for x.
$$x + 14 - x + 18 - x + 5 = 26$$
$$-x + 37 = 26$$
$$-x = -11$$
$$x = 11$$

Therefore, 11 people order both an appetizer and a dessert.

Example

Every person in a group of 30 high school students plays at least one sport: hockey, football, or soccer. In this group, 5 play all three sports, 7 play hockey and football, 8 play soccer and football, 9 play hockey and soccer, 20 play soccer, 25 play football or soccer, and 22 play hockey or football.

How many students play hockey only? _____

Solution

Step 1

Draw three overlapping circles representing each group of players, and label the circles.

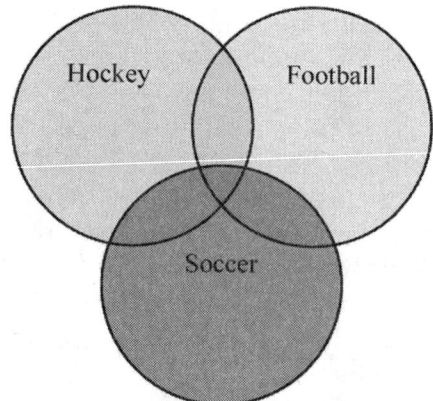

Step 2

Label the regions representing the information in the problem appropriately.

- Begin with the portion overlapped by all three circles. This region represents 5 students, so label this region with a 5.
- Move onto the areas overlapped by only two circles.

  To represent 7 students playing hockey and football, the remaining portion of this overlapped region is labeled with $7 - 5 = 2$.
  To represent 8 students playing soccer and football, the remaining portion of this overlapped region is labeled with $8 - 5 = 3$.
  To represent 9 students playing hockey and soccer, the remaining portion of this overlapped region is labeled with $9 - 5 = 4$

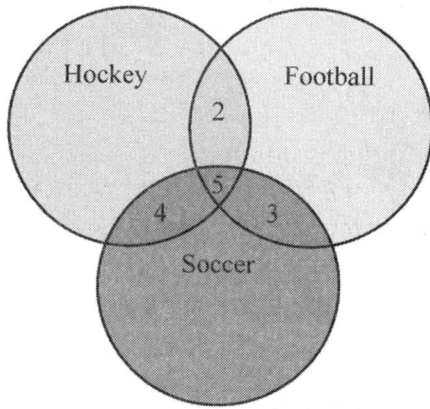

Now, move onto the outermost regions.

- Since 20 students play soccer, then the number of students that play soccer only is $20 - 4 - 5 - 3 = 8$.
- Since 25 students play football or soccer, subtract all the numbers within the two circles representing football and soccer from 25 to obtain the number of students that play football only. The result is
$25 - 8 - 4 - 5 - 3 - 2 = 3$.

- Finally, to obtain the number of students that play hockey only, subtract all the numbers within the two circles representing hockey and football from 22. The result is 22 − 4 − 5 − 3 − 2 − 3 = 5.

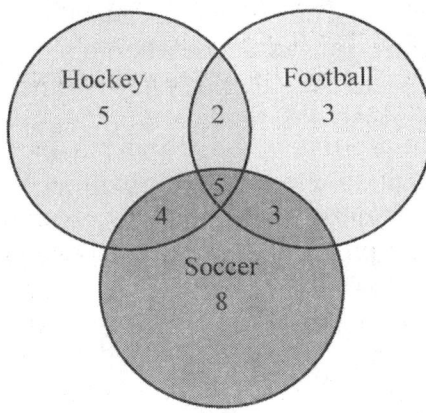

Therefore, 5 students play hockey only.

S-CP.2 Understand that two events A and B are independent if the probability of A and B occurring together is the product of their probabilities, and use this characterization to determine if they are independent.

IDENTIFYING SAMPLE SPACE FOR TWO INDEPENDENT EVENTS

Independent events are events in which one outcome has no effect on the next outcome. An example of independent events would be the tossing of two coins. The first coin could have the outcomes of heads or tails, and the second coin could have the same two outcomes of heads or tails. The outcome of the first event has no effect on the second event.

Sample space is a data set that contains all possible outcomes of an experiment.

To identify sample space, follow these steps:

1. Identify the two events.
2. Display outcomes of each event.
3. Add up all the outcomes.

Sample space can be displayed using tables or tree diagrams.

Example

Glynn has a four-sided die and a spinner with the colors red, blue, green, and yellow on it.

Use a table to determine the sample space for the outcomes of the two independent events.

Solution

Step 1
Identify the two events.

Event 1: The result of rolling a die.
Event 2: The result of spinning the spinner.

Step 2
Display outcomes of each event.

The table headers are the objects being used in the experiment. Combine the side outcomes with the top outcomes.

		Spinner			
		Red (R)	Blue (B)	Green (G)	Yellow (Y)
	1	1R	1B	1G	1Y
Die	2	2R	2B	2G	2Y
	3	3R	3B	3G	3Y
	4	4R	4B	4G	4Y

Step 3
Add up all the outcomes.

Write each outcome only once.

The sample space according to the table is {1R, 1B, 1G, 1Y, 2R, 2B, 2G, 2Y, 3R, 3B, 3G, 3Y, 4R, 4B, 4G, 4Y}.

Example

Glynn has a four-sided die and a spinner with the colors red, blue, green, and yellow on it.

Use a tree diagram to determine the sample space for the outcomes of the two independent events.

Solution

Step 1
Identify the two events.

Event 1: The result of rolling a die.
Event 2: The result of spinning the spinner.

Step 2

Display outcomes of each event.

Start with one of the objects being used (die), and list the outcomes (1, 2, 3, 4). Draw a branch from each of these outcomes for each of the next outcomes (red, blue, green, yellow) of the second object.

```
Roll        Spin      Possible outcomes
        ┌─ Red          1R
   1 ───┼─ Blue         1B
        ├─ Green        1G
        └─ Yellow       1Y
        ┌─ Red          2R
   2 ───┼─ Blue         2B
        ├─ Green        2G
        └─ Yellow       2Y
        ┌─ Red          3R
   3 ───┼─ Blue         3B
        ├─ Green        3G
        └─ Yellow       3Y
        ┌─ Red          4R
   4 ───┼─ Blue         4B
        ├─ Green        4G
        └─ Yellow       4Y
```

Step 3

Add up all the outcomes.

Write each outcome only once.

The sample space according to the tree diagram is {1R, 1B, 1G, 1Y, 2R, 2B, 2G, 2Y, 3R, 3B, 3G, 3Y, 4R, 4B, 4G, 4Y}.

UNDERSTANDING THE DIFFERENCE BETWEEN INDEPENDENT AND DEPENDENT EVENTS

Two events are **independent** if the result of one event does not affect the probability of the other event. For example, when two cards are pulled out of the deck one after the other and the first card is replaced before the second card is drawn, the events are independent. The reason for this is that the deck is complete for each card that is drawn. In other words, 52 cards is the sample space for each event. The following examples are all independent events:

- Rolling two number cubes
- Flipping a coin and spinning a spinner
- Drawing a marble out of a bag, replacing it, then drawing another marble

Events are **dependent** when the result of one event does affect the probability of the other event. In the previous example of drawing two cards from a deck, if the first card drawn is not replaced before the second card is drawn, the two events are dependent. The reason for this is that the second card is drawn from a deck containing only 51 cards, so the sample space has been changed. The following examples are all dependent events:

- Drawing two marbles out of a bag without replacing the first marble
- Drawing two coins out of a pocket without replacing the first coin

When you are calculating the probability of dependent and independent events, it is important to use the correct notation. In the case of independent events, the probability that event A will occur is called $P(A)$. The probability of event B is $P(B)$.

In the case of dependent events, you need to show that the probability of event B changes. The notation used to express the probability of B if A has already happened is $P(B|A)$.

Example

Suresh performs a probability experiment by rolling a ten-sided die and then pulling a card out of a deck of cards.

Are these two events dependent or independent?

Solution

The result of one event does not affect the result of the second event. In other words, no matter what Suresh rolls on the ten-sided die, the probability of pulling a certain card out of the deck will be exactly the same. The events are independent.

Example

Candace has a bag of eight differently colored pencils that she wants to share with her friends. Each of her friends picks one pencil from the bag without looking.

Are these events dependent or independent?

Solution

As each pencil gets taken out of the bag, it changes the probability for the next draw. For instance, if the first friend pulls out a yellow pencil, then it is still possible for the second friend to pull out a red pencil. If the first friend pulls out a red pencil, though, then it is impossible for the second friend to pull out a red pencil. These events are dependent.

CALCULATING THE THEORETICAL PROBABILITY OF INDEPENDENT EVENTS

Two events A and B are independent only if $P(A \text{ and } B) = P(A) \times P(B)$, where $P(A \text{ and } B)$ is the probability that both events occur simultaneously.

There are two methods that can be used to find the probability of two or more independent events occurring.

Method 1:

1. Determine the possible outcomes for each independent event.
2. Determine the sample space.
3. Calculate the probability of the desired combination of independent events.

Example

When two coins are tossed, what is the probability of obtaining two heads?

Solution

Step 1
Determine the possible outcomes for each independent event.

Each coin has a possible outcome of heads (H) or tails (T).

Step 2
Determine the sample space.
List each of the possible combinations of outcomes for the event.

A tree diagram is often useful for calculating the probability of an experiment involving independent events.

```
Coin 1    Coin 2    Outcomes
            H         HH
   H <
            T         HT

            H         HT
   T <
            T         TT
```

Step 3
Calculate the probability of the desired event.
There are four different possible outcomes. Only one outcome has both coins being heads. Substitute the values 1 and 4 appropriately into the probability formula.

$P_{\text{(favorable outcome)}}$
$= \dfrac{\text{number of favorable outcomes}}{\text{total number of possible outcomes}}$

$P_{(HH)} = \dfrac{1}{4}$

The probability of obtaining two heads is $\dfrac{1}{4}$.

Method 2:

1. Determine the probability of each separate outcome.
2. Calculate the probability of the desired combination of independent events by multiplying the separate probabilities together.

Example

Find the probability of rolling a die and getting a 4 followed by tossing a coin and obtaining heads.

Solution

Step 1

Determine the probability of each separate outcome.

The probability of rolling a 4 is $P_{(4)} = \frac{1}{6}$.

The probability of obtaining heads is $P_{(heads)} = \frac{1}{2}$.

Step 2

Calculate the probability of the desired event. Multiply the separate probabilities together.

$P_{(AB)} = P_A \times P_B$

$P_{(4, heads)} = \frac{1}{6} \times \frac{1}{2}$

$= \frac{1}{12}$

The probability of rolling a 4 and obtaining heads is $\frac{1}{12}$.

Example

What is the probability of drawing two black cards from a standard deck of 52 cards, where the first card is replaced before the second is drawn?

Solution

These events are independent because the sample space remains unchanged.

$P(B_1 \text{ and } B_2) = P(B_1) \times P(B_2)$

$= \frac{26}{52} \times \frac{26}{52}$

$= \frac{1}{2} \times \frac{1}{2}$

$= \frac{1}{4}$

The probability that both cards will be black is $\frac{1}{4}$ if the first card is replaced.

Example

What is the probability of drawing a queen, followed by a four, from a standard deck of 52 cards, where the first card is replaced before the second is drawn?

Solution

Because of replacement, these events are independent.

Let Q be the event of drawing a queen and F be the event of drawing a four.

Calculate the probability of drawing a queen followed by a four, when the first card is replaced before the second card is drawn.

$P(Q_1 \text{ and } F_2) = P(Q_1) \times P(F_2)$

$= \frac{4}{52} \times \frac{4}{52}$

$= \frac{1}{13} \times \frac{1}{13}$

$= \frac{1}{169}$

The probability that the first card drawn will be a queen and the second card will be a four is $\frac{1}{169}$ if the first card is replaced before the second is drawn.

Independence and Conditional Probability

Example

What is the probability of drawing a queen and a four, in either order, from a standard deck of 52 cards, where the first card is replaced before the second card is drawn.

Solution

In this case, there are two different sets of outcomes: either the first card is a four and the second card is a queen or the first card is a queen and the second card is a four.
The presence of the word **or** suggests that the probabilities of the two separate pairs of independent events must be added.

Calculate the probability of drawing a queen and a four (in either order), when the first card is replaced before the second card is drawn.

$P(Q \text{ and } F) = P(Q_1 \text{ and } F_2) + P(F_1 \text{ and } Q_2)$
$= P(Q_1) \times P(F_2) + P(F_1) \times P(Q_2)$
$= \dfrac{4}{52} \times \dfrac{4}{52} + \dfrac{4}{52} \times \dfrac{4}{52}$
$= \dfrac{1}{13} \times \dfrac{1}{13} + \dfrac{1}{13} \times \dfrac{1}{13}$
$= \dfrac{1}{169} + \dfrac{1}{169}$
$= \dfrac{2}{169}$

Therefore, the probability that one card is a queen and the other is a four is $\dfrac{2}{169}$ if the first card is replaced before the second is drawn.

S-CP.3 Understand the conditional probability of A given B as P(A and B)/P(B), and interpret independence of A and B as saying that the conditional probability of A given B is the same as the probability of A, and the conditional probability of B given A is the same as the probability of B.

IDENTIFYING CONDITIONAL PROBABILITY

When events are dependent, the occurrence of one event affects the probability of the occurrence of the other.

For example, when drawing cards from a standard deck of 52, if the first card drawn is not replaced before the second card is drawn, then the two events are dependent. The second card is drawn from 51 cards, so the sample space has been altered.

When the probability of event B depends directly on the outcome of event A, the conditional probability of B, denoted by $P(B|A)$, is the probability that event B occurs given that event A has already occurred.

Example

A student was given a list of events and was asked to classify them as independent or dependent events. His work is shown:

1. A fair coin is tossed and a standard 6-sided die is rolled. The result is Heads and a 4. INDEPENDENT
2. Two queens are drawn from a standard deck of 52 cards, one after the other without replacement. INDEPENDENT
3. A blue marble is drawn from a bag of marbles, replaced and then a red marble is drawn from the same bag. INDEPENDENT
4. A student sinks four out of ten basketball shots on Monday and then sinks five out of ten basketball shots on Tuesday. INDEPENDENT

What is the student's error?

Solution

When the probability of event B depends directly on the outcome of event A, the conditional probability of B, denoted by $P(B|A)$, is the probability that event B occurs given that event A has already occurred.

Tossing a coin and rolling a die are independent events because neither event's probability depends on the other.

When the two queens are drawn from a standard deck, without replacement, the sample space changes for the second event (second queen). As such, the probability that the second queen is drawn depends on the fact that the first queen was already drawn. The student should have classified this pair of events as dependent.

When two marbles are drawn from a bag, one after the other with replacement, the sample space for each draw is the same and the probability of drawing the red marble has nothing to do with whether a blue marble was drawn first. The events are independent.

Sinking five shots on Tuesday does not depend on sinking four on Monday. The events are independent.

Example

Two cards are drawn from a standard deck of 52, without replacement.

What is the probability that the second card is a queen given that the first card was a king?

Solution

When the probability of event B depends directly on the outcome of event A, the conditional probability of B, denoted by $P(B|A)$, is the probability that event B occurs given that event A has already occurred.

Given that the first card was a king and it was not replaced before the second card was drawn, the sample space from which the queen could be drawn is now just 51 cards.

$P(\text{Queen}|\text{King}) = \dfrac{4}{51}$

S-CP.4 Construct and interpret two-way frequency tables of data when two categories are associated with each object being classified. Use the two-way table as a sample space to decide if events are independent and to approximate conditional probabilities.

FINDING CONDITIONAL PROBABILITY GIVEN A FREQUENCY TABLE

Conditional probability is used when two events are dependent. This means that the occurrence of one event affects the probability of the occurrence of the other.

When the probability of event B depends directly on the outcome of event A, the conditional probability of B, denoted by $P(B|A)$, is the probability that event B occurs given that event A has already occurred.

Conditional probability is defined as

$P(B|A) = \dfrac{P(A \text{ and } B)}{P(A)}$, where $P(A \text{ and } B)$ is the probability of event A and B occurring, and $P(A)$ is the probability of event A occurring.

Two-way frequency tables are a useful tool for examining conditional probability between categorical variables.

In a two-way frequency table, the probabilities $P(A \text{ and } B)$ and $P(A)$ will be the number of occurrences under each event in the table divided by the total number of occurrences. When calculating $\dfrac{P(A \text{ and } B)}{P(A)}$, the total number of occurrences will cancel out. To determine $P(B|A)$, divide the number of occurrences under events A and B by the number of occurrences under event A.

Example

A teacher surveyed 205 students in junior high. One of the questions on the survey was whether the students preferred playing sports or watching television after school. A frequency table of the results is given.

Activities

Gender	Television	Sports	Total
Girl	25	70	95
Boy	44	66	110
Total	69	136	205

Determine the probability that a boy randomly selected from the total students surveyed prefers playing sports.

Solution

Step 1
Determine if the event that a randomly selected boy prefers playing sports is dependent or independent.

Let A represent the event that a boy is selected. Let B represent the event that the student selected prefers to play sports.

The event is dependent because the probability that a randomly selected boy prefers playing sports depends on the probability that a boy was chosen. This can be denoted by $P(B|A) = \dfrac{P(A \text{ and } B)}{P(A)}$.

Step 2
Determine the value of $P(A \text{ and } B)$.

The probability of selecting a boy and a student who prefers sports is $P(A \text{ and } B) = \dfrac{66}{205}$.

Step 3
Determine the value of $P(A)$.

The probability of selecting a boy out of all the surveyed students is $P(A) = \dfrac{110}{205}$.

Step 4
Determine the probability that a randomly selected boy prefers playing sports using the formula $P(B|A) = \dfrac{P(A \text{ and } B)}{P(A)}$.

$P(B|A) = \dfrac{P(A \text{ and } B)}{P(A)}$

$P(B|A) = \dfrac{\frac{66}{205}}{\frac{110}{205}}$

$P(B|A) = \left(\dfrac{66}{205}\right)\left(\dfrac{205}{110}\right)$

$P(B|A) = \dfrac{66}{110}$

$P(B|A) = 0.6$

The probability that a randomly selected boy prefers playing sports is 0.6.

EXERCISE #1—INDEPENDENCE AND CONDITIONAL PROBABILITY

Use the following information to answer the next question.

A restaurant is offering 3 choices of starters, 4 choices of main dishes, and 2 different desserts as shown in the chart.

Menu Items

Starter	Main Course	Dessert
Greek salad (GS)	Stir fry (SF)	Apple pie (AP)
Tossed salad (TS)	Salmon with side rice (SR)	Mixed fruit bowl (MB)
Soup of the day (SD)	Shepherd's pie (SP)	
	Hungarian stew (HS)	

260. Determine the size of the sample space that represents a random selection of one starter, one main course, and one dessert.

Use the following information to answer the next question.

y is a factor of 24 and 36.

261. The values of y that satisfy this statement are
    A. 1 and 36
    B. 2, 3, 4, 6, and 12
    C. 1, 2, 3, 4, 6, and 12
    D. 1, 2, 3, 4, 6, 8, 9, 12, and 36

Use the following information to answer the next question.

Jack and Selma play a game in which a coin is tossed and a six-sided number cube is rolled. The player who gets a tail on the coin and a four on the number cube is the winner.

262. How many outcomes are there in Jack and Selma's game?
    A. 6
    B. 8
    C. 12
    D. 24

263. When tossing two coins, what is the probability of obtaining two heads?

264. Which of the following sets of events can be classified as dependent?
    A. A fair coin is tossed twice in a row. The result is heads both times.
    B. A black card is drawn from a deck and replaced. A red card is then drawn from the same deck.
    C. A six-sided die is rolled, and a spinner with four equal-sized color sections is spun. The result is 3 and yellow.
    D. Two game tiles are drawn from a bag one after the other without replacement. The first tile drawn is red, and the second is blue.

Use the following information to answer the next question.

A class of 33 students was surveyed by their teacher to find out who took the bus to school and who did not. The results were arranged in a table according to the gender of the student.

Form of Transport

Gender	Bus	Other	Total
Girl	8	7	15
Boy	12	6	18
Total	20	13	33

265. What is the probability to the nearest hundredth that a girl selected randomly from the total group of students takes the bus to school?

A. 0.53
B. 0.60
C. 0.61
D. 0.67

EXERCISE #1—INDEPENDENCE AND CONDITIONAL PROBABILITY ANSWERS AND SOLUTIONS

260. 24	262. C	264. D
261. C	263. See solution	265. A

260. 24

Step 1
Build a table showing all possible outcomes.

Starter	Main Course	Dessert	Outcome
GS	SF	AP	GS, SF, AP
		MB	GS, SF, MB
	SR	AP	GS, SR, AP
		MB	GS, SR, MB
	SP	AP	GS, SP, AP
		MB	GS, SP, MB
	HS	AP	GS, HS, AP
		MB	GS, HS, MB
TS	SF	AP	TS, SF, AP
		MB	TS, SF, MB
	SR	AP	TS, SR, AP
		MB	TS, SR, MB
	SP	AP	TS, SP, AP
		MB	TS, SP, MB
	HS	AP	TS, HS, AP
		MB	TS, HS, MB
SD	SF	AP	SD, SF, AP
		MB	SD, SF, MB
	SR	AP	SD, SR, AP
		MB	SD, SR, MB
	SP	AP	SD, SP, AP
		MB	SD, SP, MB
	HS	AP	SD, HS, AP
		MB	SD, HS, MB

Step 2
Count the outcomes to determine the size of the sample space.
The size of the sample space is 24.

261. C

Step 1
Determine the factors of 24.
The factors of 24 are 1, 2, 3, 4, 6, 8, 12, and 24.

Step 2
Determine the factors of 36.
The factors of 36 are 1, 2, 3, 4, 6, 12, and 36.

Step 3
Determine the numbers that satisfy the given statement.
Since the connecting word "and" is used in the given statement, the numbers that are factors of both 24 and 36 must be included.
Therefore, the values of y that satisfy the given statement are 1, 2, 3, 4, 6, and 12.

262. C

Tossing a coin has two outcomes: head and tails. Rolling a number cube has six outcomes: 1, 2, 3, 4, 5, and 6. You can use a tree diagram or a table to find out how many different outcomes there are.

Using a tree diagram:

There are 12 outcomes for flipping a coin and rolling a six-sided number cube.

- Make a tree with the outcomes for flipping a coin on the left side. Make a branch for each of the outcomes for rolling a number cube.

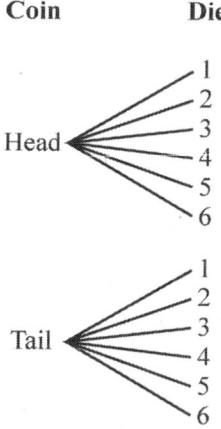

- Write all of the outcomes on the right side of the tree. The letter H means *heads* and the letter T means *tails*.

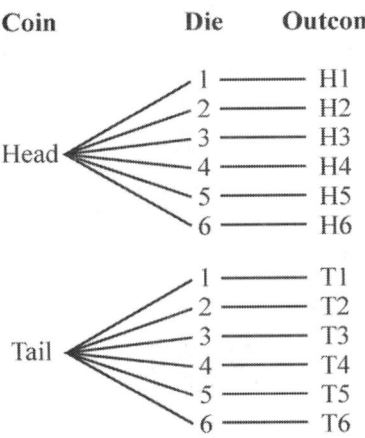

- There are 12 outcomes for flipping a coin and rolling a six-sided number cube.

Making a table:

- Write the outcomes for flipping a coin on the left side of the table and the outcomes for rolling a number cube across the top. There are 12 outcomes for flipping a coin and rolling a six-sided number cube.

		Die					
		1	2	3	4	5	6
Coin	H						
	T						

- Combine the outcomes from the top and side to fill in the table. The letter H means *heads* and the letter T means *tails*. There are 12 outcomes for flipping a coin and rolling a six-sided number cube.

		Die					
		1	2	3	4	5	6
Coin	H	1H	2H	3H	4H	5H	6H
	T	1T	2T	3T	4T	5T	6T

- There are 12 outcomes for flipping a coin and rolling a six-sided number cube.

263.

Step 1
Determine the probability of each separate outcome. The probability of obtaining heads on the first coin is $P_{H_1} = \frac{1}{2}$.

The probability of obtaining heads on the second coin is $P_{H_2} = \frac{1}{2}$.

Step 2
Calculate the probability of the event happening. Multiply the separate probabilities together.
$$P_{(AB)} = P_A \times P_B$$
$$P_{(H_1 H_2)} = \frac{1}{2} \times \frac{1}{2}$$
$$= \frac{1}{4}$$

The probability of obtaining two heads is $\frac{1}{4}$.

264. D

Two events are dependent if the outcome of the first event affects the probability that the second event will occur.

When the two game tiles are drawn from the same bag without replacement, the sample space changes for the second event (blue tile). As such, the probability that the second tile drawn will be blue depends on the fact that a red tile was already drawn and removed from the bag. These events are dependent.

The probability of tossing heads on the second toss of a fair coin does not depend on the result of the first toss. These events are independent.

When two cards are drawn from a deck one after the other with replacement, the sample space for each draw is the same; therefore, the probability of drawing a red card has nothing to do with whether a black card was drawn first. These events are independent.

Rolling a die and spinning a spinner are independent events because neither event's probability depends on the other.

265. A

Step 1
Determine if the event that a randomly selected girl takes the bus is dependent or independent.

Let event A be the selection of a girl and event B be the selection of a student who takes the bus to school. The event is dependent because the probability that a randomly selected girl takes the bus depends on the probability that a girl was selected, A. This is denoted by
$$P(B|A) = \frac{P(A \text{ and } B)}{P(A)}.$$

Step 2
Determine the value of $P(A)$.

From the chart, $P(A) = \frac{15}{33}$, since there are 15 girls in the class of 33.

Step 3
Determine the value of $P(A \text{ and } B)$.
Since there are 8 students in the class of 33 who are girls that take the bus, $P(A \text{ and } B) = \frac{8}{33}$.

Step 4
Determine the probability of randomly selecting a girl who takes the bus from the total students, using the formula $P(B|A) = \frac{P(A \text{ and } B)}{P(A)}$.

$P(B|A) = \frac{P(A \text{ and } B)}{P(A)}$

$P(B|A) = \frac{\frac{8}{33}}{\frac{15}{33}}$

$P(B|A) = \frac{8}{15}$

$P(B|A) \approx 0.53$

The probability that a randomly selected girl takes the bus is 0.53.

There is an alternate, less formal method for finding the solution to this problem. If it is known that the selected student is a girl and it is known that there are 15 girls and 8 of them take the bus, it is possible to create a fraction.

$\frac{8}{15} \approx 0.53$

EXERCISE #2—INDEPENDENCE AND CONDITIONAL PROBABILITY

Use the following information to answer the next question.

During an industrial accident, a petroleum product spills into a lake. A team of scientists is sent to assess the level of pollution of the lake water. The scientists decide to take samples of the water and test each sample for the presence of a particular chemical. The given table shows the concentration measurements of 10 samples.

Sample Number	Measurement (ppm)
1	12
2	14
3	10
4	11
5	12
6	13
7	12
8	11
9	16
10	12

Use the following information to answer the next question.

Shea and Dana are planning a probability experiment with the spinner shown and a four-sided number cube.

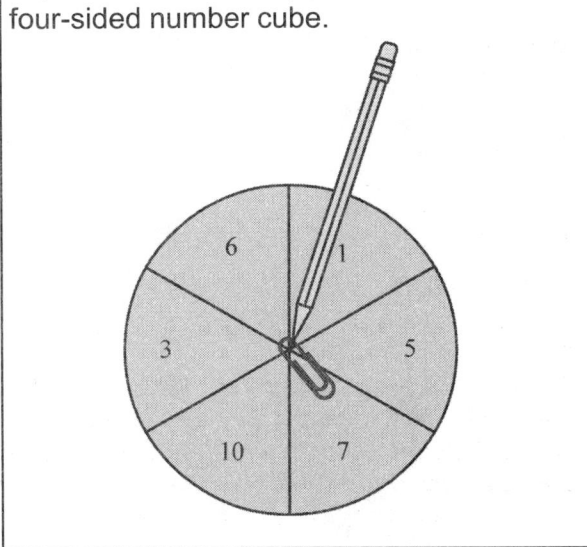

266. Describe the sample space for the measurements, and classify it as discrete or continuous.

267. Which of the following number lines illustrates the solution described by the compound statement "$x > -1$ and $x \leq 4$"?

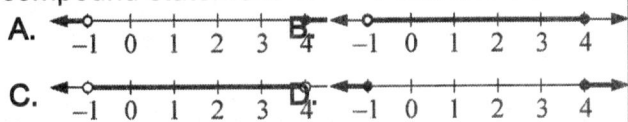

268. Which of the following tables could be used to show the possible outcomes?

A.

	1	2	3	4
1				
2				
3				
4				
5				
6				

B.

	1	5	7	10
1				
2				
3				
4				
5				
6				

C.

	1	2	3	4
1				
3				
5				
6				
7				
10				

D.

	1	5	7	10
1				
3				
5				
6				
7				
10				

Use the following information to answer the next question.

Pat and Kathy are starting a family and hope to have four children.

269. What is the probability that they will have four boys?

Use the following information to answer the next question.

Two cards are drawn from a standard deck of 52 cards. The first card is a 10 of diamonds.

270. Rounded to the nearest thousandth, the probability that the second card is a 10 of hearts is _____.

Exercise #2

Use the following information to answer the next question.

A psychologist randomly surveyed 135 students in a high school. One of the survey questions asked whether the student purchased lunch or packed a lunch to school on a regular basis. The given frequency table shows the results.

Types of Lunches

Gender	Packed	Purchased	Total
Girl	30	37	67
Boy	21	47	68
Total	51	84	135

271. Rounded to the nearest tenth, what is the probability of selecting a student who purchases lunch on a regular basis, given that a boy is selected?

A. 0.3
B. 0.4
C. 0.6
D. 0.7

EXERCISE #2—INDEPENDENCE AND CONDITIONAL PROBABILITY ANSWERS AND SOLUTIONS

| 266. See solution | 268. C | 270. 0.020 |
| 267. B | 269. See solution | 271. D |

266.

Although the measurements from the 10 samples are reported as whole numbers, {10, 11, 12, 13, 14, 16}, it is probable that future additional measurements could result in any value. Measurements of this sort can be reported to any number of significant digits, depending on the precision of the measurement instrument and the reporting standards.

Since the outcomes must be measured and they have an infinite number of possible outcomes, the sample space is continuous and may contain any non-negative value.

267. B

Step 1
State the solution set to the inequality $x > -1$.
The values of x that satisfy the inequality $x > -1$ are all the numbers that are greater than but not equal to -1.

Step 2
State the solution set to the inequality $x \leq 4$.
The values of x that satisfy the inequality $x \leq 4$ are all the numbers that are less than or equal to 4.

Step 3
Identify the number line that represents the solution to the compound statement "$x > -1$ and $x \leq 4$."
Since the connecting word "and" is used in the given compound statement, both the conditions $x > -1$ and $x \leq 4$ must be satisfied.
The statement "$x > -1$ and $x \leq 4$" can also be written as $-1 < x \leq 4$. The solution is all the numbers that lie between -1 and 4. The solution does not include -1, which is indicated on a number line by an open circle. The solution does include 4, which is indicated on a number line by a closed circle.
The following number line illustrates the values for x that are greater than -1 and less than or equal to 4:

268. C

In a table, put the four numbers from the number cube in the row across the top and the six numbers from the spinner in the column on the left.

	1	2	3	4
1				
3				
5				
6				
7				
10				

If you want to list the outcomes, you can fill in the table. In each square, write one number from the spinner and one number from the number cube.

	1	2	3	4
1	1, 1	1, 2	1, 3	1, 4
3	3, 1	3, 2	3, 3	3, 4
5	5, 1	5, 2	5, 3	5, 4
6	6, 1	6, 2	6, 3	6, 4
7	7, 1	7, 2	7, 3	7, 4
10	10, 1	10, 2	10, 3	10, 4

269.

Step 1
Determine the probability of each separate outcome.
- The probability of having a boy first is
  $P(\text{boy}) = \frac{1}{2}$.
- The probability of having a boy second is
  $P(\text{boy}) = \frac{1}{2}$.
- The probability of having a boy third is
  $P(\text{boy}) = \frac{1}{2}$.
- The probability of having a boy fourth is
  $P(\text{boy}) = \frac{1}{2}$.

Step 2
Calculate the probability of the event happening.
Multiply the separate probabilities together.
$P(A, B, C, \text{ and } D) = P(A) \times P(B) \times P(C) \times P(D)$
$P(\text{all boys}) = \dfrac{1}{2} \times \dfrac{1}{2} \times \dfrac{1}{2} \times \dfrac{1}{2}$
$= \dfrac{1}{16}$

The probability of having four children that are all boys is $\dfrac{1}{16}$.

270. 0.020

When the probability of event B depends directly on the outcome of event A, the conditional probability of B, denoted by $P(B|A)$, is the probability that event B will occur given that event A has already occurred.

Given that the first card was a 10 of diamonds (D) and it was not replaced before the second card was drawn, the sample space from which the 10 of hearts (H) could be drawn is now 51 cards.

$P(D|H) = \dfrac{1}{51}$
≈ 0.020

271. D

Step 1
Determine if the events are dependent.
These events are dependent because the probability of selecting a student who purchases lunch, B, depends on the event of first selecting a boy, A. This can be denoted by $P(B|A)$.

Step 2
Determine the value of $P(A \text{ and } B)$.
The probability of selecting a student who is a boy who purchases lunch is $P(A \text{ and } B) = \dfrac{47}{135}$.

Step 3
Determine the value of $P(A)$.
The probability of selecting a boy out of all the students is $P(A) = \dfrac{68}{135}$.

Step 4
Use the formula $P(B|A) = \dfrac{P(A \text{ and } B)}{P(A)}$ to determine the probability that a randomly selected boy purchases lunch.

$P(B|A) = \dfrac{P(A \text{ and } B)}{P(A)}$

$P(B|A) = \dfrac{\frac{47}{135}}{\frac{68}{135}}$

$P(B|A) = \left(\dfrac{47}{135}\right)\left(\dfrac{135}{68}\right)$

$P(B|A) = \dfrac{47}{68}$

$P(B|A) \approx 0.691$

Rounded to the nearest tenth, the probability that a randomly selected boy purchases lunch on a regular basis is 0.7.

NOTES

Probabilities of Compound Events

PROBABILITIES OF COMPOUND EVENTS

Table of Correlations

Standard		Concepts	Exercise #1	Exercise #2
Unit6.2	Use the rules of probability to compute probabilities of compound events in a uniform probability model.			
S-CP.6	Find the conditional probability of A given B as the fraction of B's outcomes that also belong to A, and interpret the answer in terms of the model.	Calculating the Theoretical Probability of Independent Events	263	269
		Finding Conditional Probability Given a Frequency Table	265	271
		Calculating the Probability of Dependent Events	272	291, 305
S-CP.7	Apply the Addition Rule, P(A or B) = P(A) + P(B) − P(A and B), and interpret the answer in terms of the model.	Calculating Probabilities of Mutually Exclusive Events	273	292
		Calculating Probabilities of Non-Mutually Exclusive Events	274	293
S-CP.8	Apply the general Multiplication Rule in a uniform probability model, P(A and B) = P(A)P(B|A) = P(B)P(A|B), and interpret the answer in terms of the model.	Calculating the Probability of Dependent Events	272	291, 305
S-CP.9	Use permutations and combinations to compute probabilities of compound events and solve problems.	Classifying Counting Problems and Solving Permutation Problems Using Certain Techniques	275, 280	294, 307
		Combinations	276	306, 309
		Using the Combinations Formula When Solving Problems Involving Special Cases	284, 290	295, 310
		Simplifying Expressions and Solving Problems Using Both Permutations and Combinations	277, 289	296, 311
		Using Combinations to Solve Probability Problems	278	297
		Solving Problems Involving Permutations of n Objects	279	294, 298
		Solving Problems Involving Permutations of n Objects Taken r at a Time	280	307
		Calculating Permutations with Non-Distinct Objects	288	308
		Calculating Permutations with Objects in Order or out of Order	281	299
		Calculating Permutations with Grouping	282	300
		Calculating Permutations with Separation	283	301, 302
		Calculate Single Combinations	284, 285	303, 310
		Calculating Complex Combinations	276	309
		Problem Solving with Combinations	286	304
		Solving Combination Problems Involving Special Cases	284	310
		Calculating Combinations in Situations with Upper or Lower Limits	290	295

		Solving Problems Using Both Permutations and Combinations	289	311
		Using Permutations to Solve Probability Problems	272, 287	305

S-CP.6 Find the conditional probability of A given B as the fraction of B's outcomes that also belong to A, and interpret the answer in terms of the model.

CALCULATING THE PROBABILITY OF DEPENDENT EVENTS

When events are dependent, the occurrence of one event affects the probability of the other.

When the probability of event B depends directly on the outcome of event A, then the conditional probability of B, denoted by $P(B|A)$, is the probability that event B occurs given that event A has already occurred.

To calculate probabilities of dependent events A and B, use the formula
$P(A \text{ and } B) = P(A) \times P(B|A)$ if event A occurs first or $P(B \text{ and } A) = P(B) \times P(A|B)$ if event B occurs first.

Example

Determine the probability of drawing two black cards from a standard deck of 52 when the first card is not replaced before the second card is drawn.

Solution

These events are dependent because the sample space changes for the second draw.

Calculate the probability of drawing two black cards, when the first card is not replaced before the second card is drawn.

$$P(B_1 \text{ and } B_2) = P(B_1) \times P(B_2|B_1)$$
$$= \frac{26}{52} \times \frac{25}{51}$$
$$= \frac{1}{2} \times \frac{25}{51} = \frac{25}{102}$$

Note that the numerator and denominator of the second fraction differ from the first because if the first card drawn is a black card, then the second card drawn will come from only 25 (instead of 26) black cards in an incomplete deck of 51 (instead of 52) cards.

The probability that both cards will be black is $\frac{25}{102}$ if the first card is not replaced.

Example

Determine the probability of drawing a queen, followed by a four, from a standard deck of 52 cards, when the first card is not replaced before the second card is drawn.

Solution

Let Q be the event of drawing a queen and F be the event of drawing a four.

Calculate the probability of drawing a queen followed by a four, when the first card is not replaced before the second card is drawn.

$$P(Q_1 \text{ and } F_2) = P(Q_1) \times P(F_2|Q_1)$$
$$= \frac{4}{52} \times \frac{4}{51}$$
$$= \frac{1}{13} \times \frac{4}{51}$$
$$= \frac{4}{663}$$

Note that only the denominator of the second fraction differs from the first because if the first card drawn is a queen, then there are still 4 fours remaining in the deck. However, the deck is incomplete with only 51 instead of 52 cards.

The probability that the first card drawn will be a queen and the second card will be a four is $\frac{4}{663}$ if the first card is not replaced.

Example

When two cards are drawn from a standard deck of 52 without replacement, determine the probability that one card drawn is a queen and the other is a four.

Solution

Calculate the probabilities that one of the cards drawn is a queen and the other is a four.

In this case, there are two different sets of outcomes: either the first card is a four and the second card is a queen or the first card is a queen and the second card is a four.
The presence of the word **or** suggests that the probabilities of the two separate events must be added.

Calculate the probability of drawing a queen and a four (in either order), when the first card is not replaced before the second card is drawn.

$$P(Q \text{ and } F) = P(Q_1 \text{ and } F_2) + P(F_1 \text{ and } Q_2)$$
$$= P(Q_1) \times P(F_2 | Q_1) + P(F_1) \times P(Q_2 | F_1)$$
$$= \frac{4}{52} \times \frac{4}{51} + \frac{4}{52} \times \frac{4}{51}$$
$$= \frac{1}{13} \times \frac{4}{51} + \frac{1}{13} \times \frac{4}{51}$$
$$= \frac{4}{663} + \frac{4}{663}$$
$$= \frac{8}{663}$$

The probability that one card is a queen and the other is a four is $\frac{8}{663}$ if the first card is not replaced.

S-CP.7 Apply the Addition Rule, P(A or B) = P(A) + P(B) − P(A and B), and interpret the answer in terms of the model.

CALCULATING PROBABILITIES OF MUTUALLY EXCLUSIVE EVENTS

Probabilities can be calculated for events that are mutually exclusive or non-mutually exclusive.

Mutually exclusive events are events that do not have any common outcomes. For example, in a standard deck of 52 cards, the set of hearts and the set of diamonds are mutually exclusive because there is no card that is both a heart and a diamond.

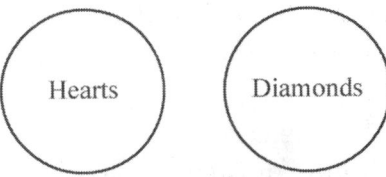

Mutually Exclusive Events

Related questions typically ask for the probability of event *A* OR event *B* happening. To calculate probabilities of mutually exclusive events, use the formula $P(A \text{ or } B) = P(A) + P(B)$.

The following example illustrates the computation of probability involving mutually exclusive events.

Example

A candy manufacturer produces packages of assorted chocolate candy. Each candy contains hazelnut (*H*), caramel (*C*), or fudge (*F*) filling, and dark chocolate (*D*), milk chocolate (*M*), or white chocolate (*W*) coating. A typical bag contains 300 candies: 108 are dark chocolate, 108 are milk chocolate, and 84 are white chocolate. One-third of all the chocolates are hazelnut, one-third are caramel, and one-third are fudge filled.

Jessica only likes a dark chocolate candy with caramel filling (*CD*) or a white chocolate candy with fudge filling (*FW*). Determine the probability that a randomly selected candy is one that Jessica likes.

Solution

Step 1
Determine the probability of randomly selecting a dark chocolate candy with caramel filling. One-third of the dark chocolate candies are caramel filled.

$\frac{1}{3} \times 108 = 36$

$P(DC) = \frac{36}{300}$
$= \frac{3}{25}$

The probability of selecting a dark chocolate with caramel filling is $\frac{3}{25}$.

Step 2
Determine the probability of selecting a white chocolate candy with fudge filling. One-third of the white chocolate candies are fudge filled.

$\frac{1}{3} \times 84 = 28$

$P(WF) = \frac{28}{300}$
$= \frac{7}{75}$

The probability of selecting a white chocolate candy with fudge filling is $\frac{7}{75}$.

Step 3
Determine the probability that a randomly selected candy is dark chocolate with caramel (*DC*) or white chocolate with fudge (*WF*).

These events are mutually exclusive as you can have one type of candy or another.

$P(DC \text{ or } WF) = P(DC) + P(WF)$
$= \frac{3}{25} + \frac{7}{75}$
$= \frac{9}{75} + \frac{7}{75}$
$= \frac{16}{75}$

The probability that Jessica randomly selects a candy that she likes from a new bag of candies is $\frac{16}{75}$.

CALCULATING PROBABILITIES OF NON-MUTUALLY EXCLUSIVE EVENTS

Probabilities can be calculated for events that are mutually exclusive or non-mutually exclusive.

Non-mutually exclusive events have at least one common outcome. For example, the set of hearts and the set of queens are not mutually exclusive because the queen of hearts is both a heart and a queen.

Non-Mutually Exclusive Events

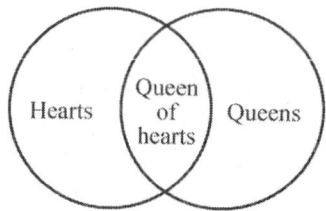

Notice that some of the hearts are queens (there is one card in the suit of hearts that is also a queen) and some of the queens are hearts (there is one card that is a queen that is also in the suit of hearts). Since this is the same card, it should not be counted twice (once as a heart and once as a queen).

To calculate probabilities of non-mutually exclusive events, use the formula
$P(A \text{ or } B) = P(A) + P(B) - P(A \text{ and } B)$.

Subtracting $P(A \text{ and } B)$ eliminates the double counting of a single outcome.

The following example illustrates the computation of probability involving non-mutually exclusive events.

Example

Larson likes any dark chocolate candy and any candy that is hazelnut filled. Determine the probability that from a bag of 300 candies, Larson randomly selects a candy he likes.

Solution

Since it is possible to select a dark chocolate candy with hazelnut filling, these events are not mutually exclusive.

Step 1
Determine the probability of randomly selecting a dark chocolate candy.

There are 108 dark chocolate candies in a bag of 300 candies.

$$P(D) = \frac{108}{300} = \frac{9}{25}$$

Step 2
Determine the probability of selecting a candy with hazelnut filling.

One-third of all of the chocolate candies are hazelnut filled.

$$P(H) = \frac{1}{3}$$

Step 3
Determine the probability that a randomly selected candy is dark chocolate with hazelnut filling.

Since one-third of all candies have hazelnut filling, one-third of 108 dark chocolate candies have hazelnut filling.

$$\frac{1}{3} \times 108 = 36$$

$$P(DH) = \frac{36}{300} = \frac{3}{25}$$

The probability of selecting a dark chocolate candy with hazelnut filling is $\frac{3}{25}$.

Step 4
Determine the probability that Larson randomly chooses a candy that he likes.

This is the same as the probability that Larson selects a dark chocolate candy or a candy with hazelnut filling.

$$P(D \text{ or } H) = P(D) + P(H) - P(D \text{ and } H)$$
$$= \frac{9}{25} + \frac{1}{3} - \frac{3}{25}$$
$$= \frac{27}{75} + \frac{25}{75} - \frac{9}{75}$$
$$= \frac{43}{75}$$

The probability that Larson randomly chooses a candy that he likes is $\frac{43}{75}$.

S-CP.9 Use permutations and combinations to compute probabilities of compound events and solve problems.

CLASSIFYING COUNTING PROBLEMS AND SOLVING PERMUTATION PROBLEMS USING CERTAIN TECHNIQUES

Counting problems can be classified according to whether they involve selections in which order is important or selections in which order is not important.

In order to correctly classify a counting problem, consider the following three questions:

1. How many objects are there to begin with?
2. How many objects are selected from them?
3. Does the order of the selected objects matter?

It is not difficult to tell how many objects there are in total and how many of them are to be selected. Determining if the order of the selected objects matters (question 3) is more complex.

To understand question 3 better, examine the following two examples, and decide whether order matters in each case.

Example

Three swimmers will be selected for the school team from a group of five swimmers. How many possible selections of swimmers are there?
To decide if order matters in this case, answer the three given questions:

1. How many objects are there to begin with?
   - There are five swimmers to begin with.
2. How many objects are selected from them?
   - Three swimmers are selected for the school team.
3. Does the order of the selected objects matter?
   - Let's call the selected swimmers Ann, Bob, and Charlie.
   - Does their order matter? If Ann, Bob, and Charlie were ordered differently, would it result in a different selection? For example, if the swimmers were ordered as Bob, Charlie, and Ann, would that order result in a different selection than the previous order? No, it makes no difference how the swimmers are ordered—they are all on the school team.

Therefore, the answer to question 3 is no—the order of the selected objects does not matter in this case.

Now, compare this problem to a problem that appears to be very similar.

Example

There are five swimmers who compete at a swim meet. Gold, silver, and bronze medals are awarded to the top three swimmers. How many different medal distributions are possible?

To decide if order matters in this case, answer the three given questions:

1. How many objects are there to begin with?
   - There are five swimmers to begin with.
2. How many objects are selected from them?
   - There are three swimmers who win medals.
3. Does the order of the selected objects matter?
   - Let's call the selected swimmers Ann, Bob, and Charlie. The swimmers are now assigned gold, silver, and bronze medals. Does the order in which the swimmers are assigned their medals matter?

Consider the following two scenarios:

Scenario 1	Scenario 2
Gold: Ann Silver: Bob Bronze: Charlie	Gold: Charlie Silver: Ann Bronze: Bob

The final outcome of the tournament is different if Ann wins the gold medal than if Bob wins the gold medal. The answer to question 3 is yes—the order of the three selected swimmers matters for the purpose of assigning medals.

Example 1 and Example 2 are very similar, except that order does not matter in Example 1, whereas it does matter in Example 2.

When the order of the selected objects matters in a counting problem, the problem is considered to be a **permutation** problem.

When the order of the selected objects does not matter, the problem is considered to be a **combination** problem.

TECHNIQUES FOR SOLVING PERMUTATION PROBLEMS

PERMUTATIONS OF n OBJECTS

The permutation of n objects refers to counting permutations in which all the n objects are to be selected.

Example

In how many different arrangements can five children be seated in a row?

Solution

To begin, answer the following three questions:

1. How many objects are there to begin with?
   There are five children to begin with.
2. How many objects are selected from them?
   Since all five children are to be arranged, all five children are selected.
3. Does the order of the selected objects matter? Since it is required to determine the number of different seating arrangements for the five children, the order in which the five children are arranged matters.

To illustrate this problem, label the five chairs 1 to 5, then fill each chair one by one.

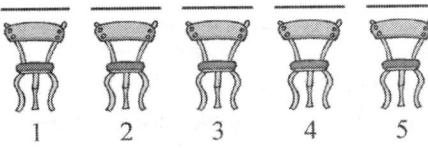

The process of seating the five children consists of five stages.

1. There are five children from which to choose, so there are five ways to complete stage 1.
2. Once one of the children has been seated in chair 1, there are only four children left to be seated, so there are four choices for seat 2.
3. Since there are three children left to be seated, there are three choices for seat 3.
4. There are only two children left, so there are only two choices for seat 4.
5. At this stage there is only one child left to be seated, so there is only one choice for seat 5.

Since a child is placed in each seat, by the fundamental counting principle, the required results can be determined by multiplying the numbers from each stage.

The number of arrangements for seating all five children is $5 \times 4 \times 3 \times 2 \times 1 = 120$.

There are 120 possible arrangements for seating five children in a row.

This result can be generalized as illustrated in the following example.

Example

How many arrangements are possible for seating n children in a row?

Solution

The process of seating the n children consists of n stages:

1. There are n different children who could be seated in chair 1.
2. There are $n - 1$ different children who could be seated in chair 2.
3. There are $n - 2$ different children who could be seated in chair 3.

This process continues in the same manner until the nth seat.

Stage $n - 1$ (the second last stage): There are two different children left to be seated in chair $n - 1$.

Stage n (the last stage): There is only one child left to be seated in chair n.

To complete the task of seating all n children, all the stages must be completed (i.e., a child must be placed in chair 1, chair 2, chair 3, chair $n - 1$, and chair n).

Therefore, the total number of possible arrangements is as follows:
$n \times (n - 1) \times (n - 2) \times \ldots \times 2 \times 1 = n!$

The word *distinct* implies that each object is different than any other object. In general, $n!$ represents the number of permutations of n distinct objects. This rule applies when all n objects are permuted or, in other words, all of the n objects are selected and their order matters. The solution to each of the following problems illustrates this rule.

Example

How many different six-letter arrangements can be made using all the letters in the word OBJECT?

Solution

There are six letters to arrange, and all six letters must be selected. The order in which the letters are arranged matters. For instance, the arrangement CETJOB is different than the arrangement JTBOEC because the ordering of the letters is different.

Since the six letters in the word OBJECT are all different (or distinct), the number of different permutations of the six distinct letters is $6!$ or 720.

Thus, 720 different six-letter arrangements can be made using all the letters in the word OBJECT.

Example

There are 11 positions on a soccer team, and a particular team has 11 players.

How many different arrangements are possible when all 11 players are put into a position? _____

Solution

Since there are 11 different players and each of the 11 is to be assigned a different position, the order matters.

Assuming that each of the 11 players can play any of the 11 positions, the number of permutations of the 11 players is $11! = 39,916,800$.

There are 39,916,800 different arrangements for the 11 players.

PERMUTATIONS OF n OBJECTS TAKEN r AT A TIME

"Permutations of n objects taken r at a time" refers to counting permutations in which only some of the n objects are selected.

Example

If there are six children, how many different arrangements are possible for seating four of them in a row?

Solution

Start by answering the following three questions:

1. How many objects are there to begin with? There are six children to begin with.
2. How many objects are selected from them? Four children are selected to be seated in a row.
3. Does the order of the selected objects matter? It is required to determine the number of different seating arrangements of the four children.

This can be illustrated by labeling the four chairs.

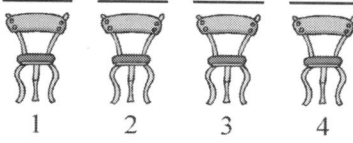

The process of seating four of the children consists of four stages:

1. There are six children to choose from, so there are six ways to complete stage 1.
2. Once a child has been seated in chair 1, there are five children left. This means that there are five choices for chair 2.
3. Now there are only four children remaining; therefore, stage 3 can be completed in four ways.
4. Since only three children remain, stage 4 can be completed in three ways.

Since a child is placed in seat 1, seat 2, seat 3, and seat 4, by the fundamental counting principle, the required result can be determined by multiplying the numbers in each of the stages.

The number of arrangements for seating the four children is 6 × 5 × 4 × 3 = 360.

In the previous example, there is a sequence of descending numbers that are multiplied together. Although the numbers get smaller, they do not reach 1.

If you wish to eliminate factors from the previous multiplying sequence, you need to divide by those factors.

$$\frac{6 \times 5 \times 4 \times 3 \times (2 \times 1)}{(2 \times 1)} = 6 \times 5 \times 4 \times 3$$

The expression $\frac{6 \times 5 \times 4 \times 3 \times 2 \times 1}{2 \times 1}$ is equivalent to $\frac{6!}{(6-4)!}$.

The mathematical notation used for this is $_nP_r$, which stands for "the number of permutations of n things taken r at a time."

The definition of $_nP_r$ is $_nP_r = \frac{n!}{(n-r)!}$.

Example
Evaluate $_{10}P_3$.

Solution

Step 1
Substitute 10 for n and 3 for r in the formula
$_nP_r = \frac{n!}{(n-r)!}$.

$_{10}P_3 = \frac{10!}{(10-3)!}$
$= \frac{10!}{7!}$

Step 2
Rewrite $\frac{10!}{7!}$ as a quotient of products, then reduce the numerator and denominator.

$\frac{10!}{7!} = \frac{10 \times 9 \times 8 \times (7!)}{7!}$
$= 10 \times 9 \times 8$
$= 720$

The following example illustrates how the $_nP_r$ notation is used to calculate the number of permutations of n objects taken r at a time.

Example
How many different five-letter arrangements can be made using the letters from the word CHAMPION?

Solution
There are eight letters available, from which five are to be selected and used to form different letter arrangements. The order of the letters does matter, so the problem is a permutation problem.

To permute five letters out of eight letters, use the notation $_8P_5$.

Step 1
Substitute 8 for n and 5 for r in the formula
$_nP_r = \frac{n!}{(n-r)!}$.

$_8P_5 = \frac{8!}{(8-5)!}$
$= \frac{8!}{3!}$

Step 2
Evaluate $\frac{8!}{3!}$.

$\frac{8!}{3!} = 6,720$

Thus, 6,720 different five-letter arrangements can be made using the letters in the word CHAMPION.

Example

How many different letter arrangements can be made using one or more of the letters from the word WIND?

Solution

It is necessary to count the number of letter arrangements that can be made when one or more of the letters are selected. Thus, count the number of letter arrangements using 1 letter, 2 letters, 3 letters, or 4 letters.

Step 1
Determine the number of one-letter arrangements.
To make a one-letter arrangement, select one letter from the four available letters.
The number of permutations of four letters taken one at a time is $_4P_1$.

Step 2
Determine the number of two-letter arrangements.
There are $_4P_2$ different two-letter arrangements.

Step 3
Determine the number of three-letter arrangements.
There are $_4P_3$ different three-letter arrangements.

Step 4
Determine the number of four-letter arrangements.
There are $_4P_4$ different four-letter arrangements.

Step 5
Determine the total number of different letter arrangements that can be formed.
Since it is required to count the number of letter arrangements with 1 letter, 2 letters, 3 letters, or 4 letters, it is necessary to determine the sum of $_4P_1$, $_4P_2$, $_4P_3$, and $_4P_4$.
$_4P_1 + {_4P_2} + {_4P_3} + {_4P_4}$
$= 4 + 12 + 24 + 24$
$= 64$
Thus, there are 64 different letter arrangements that can be formed using one or more letters from the word WIND.

COMBINATIONS

Problems involving combinations are problems in which order does not matter. The following examples illustrate the procedure for counting combinations in which the order of the selected objects does not matter.

The number of permutations of *n* objects taken *r* at a time is $_nP_r = \dfrac{n!}{(n-r)!}$.

The number of combinations of *n* objects taken *r* at a time is $_nC_r = \dfrac{n!}{(n-r)!\,r!}$.

Notice the similarities and differences in the two formulas. The only difference is that the combination formula has an additional *r*! in the denominator. This factor represents the number of arrangements of *r* objects, so dividing by this factor eliminates the arranging that is part of the permutations formula.

Example

Jane wants to order a three-topping pizza. If there are 8 toppings from which to choose, then how many different three-topping pizzas are possible?

Solution

Start by answering the following three questions:

1. How many objects are there to begin with?
   There are eight toppings to begin with.
2. How many objects are selected from them?
   Three toppings are to be selected.
3. Does the order of the selected objects matter?
   No, the order does not matter. For example, a pizza with pepperoni, mushrooms, and green peppers is the same as a pizza with mushrooms, pepperoni, and green peppers. Since the order of the selected objects does not matter, this is a combination problem.
   To solve combination problems, a formula that is similar to the formula for permutations can be used.

The question asks for the number of combinations of 3 toppings selected from 8 toppings. Therefore, the number of combinations is $_8C_3$.

Evaluate $_8C_3$.

Substitute 8 for n and 3 for r in the formula $_nC_r = \dfrac{n!}{(n-r)!\,r!}$.

$_nC_r = \dfrac{n!}{(n-r)!\,r!}$

$= \dfrac{8!}{5!\,3!}$

Rewrite factorials as products.

$= \dfrac{8 \times 7 \times 6 \times (5!)}{(5!) \times 3 \times 2 \times 1}$

Cancel, or divide, common factors.

$= \dfrac{8 \times 7 \times 6}{3 \times 2 \times 1}$

Evaluate.
= 56

There are 56 different three-topping pizzas.

Example

How many selections of a four-member committee are possible if there are 10 people from which to choose?

Solution

The question asks for the number of selections of 4 people from 10, and order does not matter. This can be represented by the expression $_{10}C_4$.

Evaluate $_{10}C_4$ as follows:

Substitute 10 for n and 4 for r in the formula $_nC_r = \dfrac{n!}{(n-r)!\,r!}$.

$_{10}C_4 = \dfrac{10!}{(10-4)!\,4!}$

Simplify.

$= \dfrac{10!}{6!\,4!}$

Evaluate.
= 210

There are 210 different selections of a four-person committee that can be made from 10 people.

Many calculators have an $_nC_r$ button that will calculate combinations.

To obtain $_{10}C_4$ from a TI graphing calculator, press the following combination of buttons:

| 10 |

| MATH | → → → | PRB |

| 3 |

| 4 |

| ENTER |

Example

Mr. Fraser has been asked to donate 2 of his sculptures to the local art gallery. If Mr. Fraser owns 25 sculptures, how many different donations of 2 sculptures are possible?

Solution

Since order does not matter, this is a combination question.

Two sculptures must be selected from 25 sculptures, and order does not matter. Therefore, there are $_{25}C_2$ combinations.

Evaluate $_{25}C_2$.

$_{25}C_2 = 300$

There are 300 different combinations for selecting two sculptures from 25 sculptures. Therefore, Mr. Fraser can make 300 different donations.

Example

Mrs. Klemke has 10 paintings. She wants to give 4 of them to her son and 3 to her granddaughter. How many different distributions of the paintings are possible?

Solution

This problem consists of two stages:

1. Give 4 paintings to her son.
2. Give 3 paintings to her granddaughter.

Stage 1

Mrs. Klemke begins with 10 paintings, and selects 4 of them to give to her son. Since the order in which she gives the paintings to her son does not matter, this is a combination question. There are $_{10}C_4 = 210$ combinations for selecting 4 out of the 10 paintings.

Now that she has selected 4 paintings for her son, it is possible to move to stage 2 to determine how she can select 3 paintings for her granddaughter.

Stage 2

Since Mrs. Klemke has already selected 4 paintings for her son, there are only 6 paintings remaining to select from. She will select 3 paintings from these 6. There are $_6C_3 = 20$ combinations for selecting 3 out of 6 paintings.

In order to solve this problem, both stages 1 and 2 must be completed. There are 210 combinations in stage 1 and 20 combinations in stage 2.

By the fundamental counting principle, there are 210 × 20 or 4,200 combinations for both stages.

Mrs. Klemke has 4,200 possible distributions for giving 4 paintings to her son and 3 paintings to her granddaughter.

Example

A mixed volleyball team consists of 3 girls and 3 boys. If 7 girls and 8 boys try out for the team, how many different selections for the team are possible?

Solution

This problem consists of two stages:

1. Select the 3 girls.
2. Select the 3 boys.

Stage 1

Select 3 girls from the 7 who tried out for the team. Since the order in which the girls are selected does not matter, this is a combination question.

There are $_7C_3 = 35$ combinations for selecting 3 out of 7 girls.

Stage 2

Select 3 boys from the 8 who tried out for the team. Since the order in which the boys are selected does not matter, this is a combination question. There are $_8C_3 = 56$ combinations for selecting 3 out of 8 boys.

In order to solve this problem, stages 1 and 2 must be combined. There are 35 combinations for completing stage 1, and 56 combinations for completing stage 2.

By the fundamental counting principle, there are $35 \times 56 = 1,960$ combinations for completing both stages.

Thus, there are 1,960 possible teams.

Example

The general staff in a hospital consists of 3 doctors and 12 nurses. How many different teams of 2 doctors and 5 nurses can be formed, if a particular doctor must be included on each team and 2 particular nurses are on vacation and cannot be part of the teams?

Solution

Step 1
Determine if the problem involves a permutation or a combination.

The order in which the doctors and nurses are selected does not matter; therefore, the given question is a combination problem.

Step 2
Determine the number of possible selections for the doctors.

Since one particular doctor must be included, the other doctor on the team must be selected from the two remaining doctors. This can be represented by $_1C_1 \times {_2C_1}$, which simplifies to $_2C_1$.

Step 3
Determine the number of possible selections for the nurses.

Since two nurses cannot be part of the team, the 5 required nurses must be selected from the 10 available nurses. This can be represented by $_{10}C_5$.

Step 4
Determine the number of possible doctor-nurse teams that can be formed.

The number of possible doctor-nurse teams can be determined by applying the fundamental counting principle.

$_2C_1 \times {_{10}C_5} = 504$

Thus, there are 504 different doctor-nurse teams that can be formed.

Example

There are 120 ways of choosing a committee of 2 students from a certain math class. Determine the number of students in the class.

Solution

Step 1
Determine if the problem involves a permutation or a combination.

The order in which the students are chosen does not matter; therefore, the given question is a combination problem.

Step 2
Let n represent the number of students in the class. Write an expression that represents the number of selections of 2 students out of n students.

The number of selections of 2 students out of n students can be represented by $_nC_2$.

Step 3

Solve for n in the equation $_nC_2 = 120$, given that there are 120 ways of choosing 2 students out of n students.

$_nC_2 = 120$

Write $_nC_2$ in factorial form.

$$\frac{n!}{(n-2)!\,2!} = 120$$

Write out the factorials until the numerators and the denominator have overlapping factors.

$$\frac{(n)(n-1)(n-2)(n-3)\ldots \times 2 \times 1}{(n-2)(n-3)\ldots \times 2 \times 1 \times (2 \times 1)} = 120$$

Reduce by common factors and solve for n.

$$\frac{n(n-1)}{2} = 120$$

$n(n-1) = 120(2)$
$n^2 - n = 240$
$n^2 - n - 240 = 0$

Factor $n^2 - n - 240$.
$(n-16)(n+15) = 0$
$n = 16, n = -15$

Since -15 is an inadmissible answer, it follows that there are 16 students in the math class.

USING THE COMBINATIONS FORMULA WHEN SOLVING PROBLEMS INVOLVING SPECIAL CASES

SITUATIONS INVOLVING THE PHRASES "AT LEAST" OR "AT MOST"

The phrases "at least" or "at most" set up situations that must be considered separately. First, calculate the possibility of each selection separately, then add them together.

For example, a question asks "How many different selections are possible when at least 4 books are selected from 6 books?"

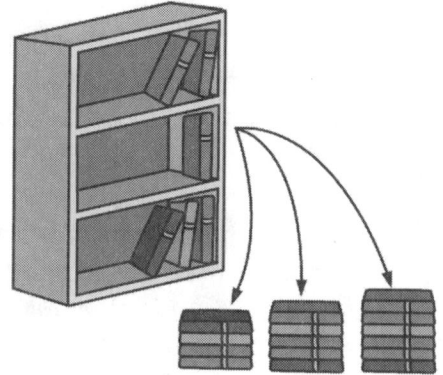

The phrase "at least 4" means 4 or more books are selected. Therefore, each situation must be calculated separately.

- 4 books selected from 6 results in $_6C_4$ selections
- 5 books selected from 6 results in $_6C_5$ selections
- 6 books selected from 6 results in $_6C_6$ selections

Since the selection is either 4 books, 5 books, or 6 books, the answer is the **sum** of the number of selections:

$= {_6C_4} + {_6C_5} + {_6C_6}$
$= 15 + 6 + 1$
$= 22$

A question might ask "How many 5-card poker hands are there with at most 2 clubs?"

The phrase "at most 2 clubs" means either 0 clubs, 1 club, or 2 clubs. Consider each of these three cases separately.

- If there are no clubs selected, then the 5 cards are chosen from the 39 other cards, represented by $_{39}C_5$.
- If there is 1 club selected, then it is chosen from the 13 clubs, and the 4 other cards are chosen from the 39 non-clubs. This is represented by $_{13}C_1 \times {_{39}C_4}$.
- If there are 2 clubs selected, then they are chosen from the 13 clubs, and the 3 other cards are chosen from the 39 non-clubs. This is represented by $_{13}C_2 \times {_{39}C_3}$.

Since the hands have either 0 clubs, 1 club, or 2 clubs, the answer is the sum of the different hand types:

$= {}_{39}C_5 + ({}_{13}C_1 \times {}_{39}C_4) + ({}_{13}C_2 \times {}_{39}C_3)$

$= 575{,}757 + 1{,}069{,}263 + 712{,}842$

$= 2{,}357{,}862$

In summary, restrictions that involve the phrases "at least" or "at most" often require breaking the problem down into different cases, then summing up each case.

However, if the number of cases that satisfy the requirements is large, it may be better to calculate the numbers of cases that do not satisfy the requirements, then subtract these from the total number of cases with no restrictions.

SOLVING COMBINATION PROBLEMS INVOLVING SPECIAL CASES

When solving problems that involve combinations, make sure the order of selections does not matter. Then, look for key words such as "at least" or "at most," and solve the problem using the combinations formula.

The following examples illustrate special cases involving handshakes, sports leagues, lines, and polygons. These events involve two events that are codependent of one another.

For example, when dealing with handshakes, it takes two people to create one handshake. Therefore, in a room of 9 people, ${}_9C_2$ handshakes are possible. In other words, 36 handshakes are possible.

In general, in a group of *n* people in which every person shakes hands with every other person, there are ${}_nC_2$ handshakes possible.

Example

In a 10-team soccer league, each team plays every other team 3 times. How many games are played in total? _____

Solution

Two teams are required to play one game of soccer. Therefore, it is necessary to count the number of combinations of 10 teams taken 2 at a time.

There are ${}_{10}C_2 = 45$ such combinations.

If each team were to play every other team once, there would be 45 games. However, each team plays 3 games, so the total number of games played is $3 \times 45 = 135$.

Example

There are 6 points on the circumference of a circle. How many lines can be drawn by connecting any 2 of these points? _____

Solution

In this case, a line can be drawn by selecting any 2 points from the 6 and connecting them.

It does not matter in what order the points are selected, since connecting point A to point B is the same as connecting point B to point A.

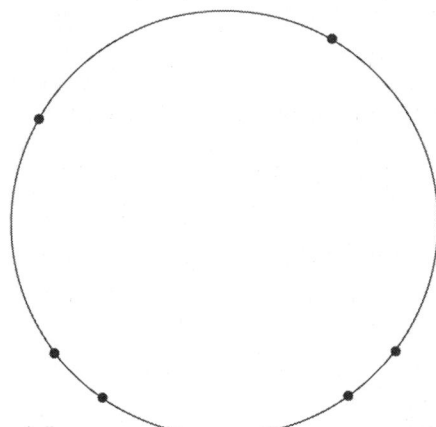

Count the number of combinations of 2 points selected from 6.

There are ${}_6C_2 = 15$ such combinations.

Therefore, 15 lines can be drawn using 6 points on the circumference of a circle.

In general, if there are *n* points on the circumference of a circle, a total of ${}_nC_2$ lines can be drawn by connecting any two of them.

To generalize even further, given n points with no 3 points being collinear, the following apply:

- the number of lines = $_nC_2$
- the number of triangles = $_nC_3$
- the number of quadrilaterals = $_nC_4$
- the number of pentagons = $_nC_5$

This continues as the number of sides on a shape increases.

SIMPLIFYING EXPRESSIONS AND SOLVING PROBLEMS USING BOTH PERMUTATIONS AND COMBINATIONS

SIMPLIFYING EXPRESSIONS WITH $_nP_r$ AND $_nC_r$

The formula for counting permutations is
$$_nP_r = \frac{n!}{(n-r)!}.$$

The formula for counting combinations is
$$_nC_r = \frac{n!}{(n-r)!\, r!}.$$

The formula for $_nC_r$ has an extra $r!$ factor in the denominator compared to the $_nP_r$ formula.

This leads to the following identity: $_nC_r = \dfrac{_nP_r}{r!}$.

Example

If $n = 6$ and $r = 2$, then the expression $_nP_r + {_nC_r}$ is equal to _____.

Solution

Step 1

Evaluate $_nP_r$ when $n = 6$ and $r = 2$.

Substitute 6 for n and 2 for r in the permutations formula.

$$_nP_r = \frac{n!}{(n-r)!}$$
$$_6P_2 = \frac{6!}{(6-2)!}$$
$$= \frac{6!}{4!}$$
$$= \frac{6 \times 5 \times 4!}{4!}$$
$$= 30$$

Step 2

Evaluate $_nC_r$ using the identity.

Substitute the value of $_nP_r$ into the identity $_nC_r = \dfrac{_nP_r}{r!}$.

$$_nC_r = \frac{_nP_r}{r!}$$
$$_6C_2 = \frac{_6P_2}{r!}$$
$$_6C_2 = \frac{30}{2!}$$
$$_6C_2 = 15$$

Step 3

Determine the sum of $_6P_2$ and $_6C_2$.

$$_6P_2 + {_6C_2} = 30 + 15$$
$$= 45$$

When simplifying expressions involving permutations and combinations, the factorials need to be written out only as far as is necessary to create common factors in the numerator and denominator.

Example

Simplify the expression $_{n+1}C_{n-1}$.

Solution

Step 1

Apply the formula for $_nC_r$, and simplify the expression.

$$_nC_r = \frac{n!}{(n-r)!\, r!}$$
$$_{n+1}C_{n-1} = \frac{(n+1)!}{((n+1)-(n-1))!\,(n-1)!}$$
$$= \frac{(n+1)!}{(n+1-n+1)!\,(n-1)!}$$
$$= \frac{(n+1)!}{(2)!\,(n-1)!}$$

Step 2
Simplify the expression.

Write out the factorials until the numerator and the denominator have an equal factorial.

Cancel out common factorials.

$$\frac{(n+1)!}{(2)!(n-1)!} = \frac{(n+1)(n)(n-1)!}{(2)!(n-1)!}$$
$$= \frac{(n+1)(n)}{2!}$$

Apply the distributive property.

$$\frac{(n+1)n}{2!} = \frac{(n+1)n}{2}$$
$$= \frac{n^2+n}{2}$$

Sometimes, it is necessary to multiply or divide both sides of an equation by a common factor when simplifying the equations. The following example illustrates this process.

Example
The value of n in the equation $_nP_3 = 2(_nC_4)$ is _____.

Solution

Step 1
Apply the formulas for $_nP_r$ and $_nC_r$.

$$_nP_r = \frac{n!}{(n-r)!} \text{ and } _nC_r = \frac{n!}{(n-r)!\,r!}$$

$$_nP_3 = 2(_nC_4)$$
$$\frac{n!}{(n-3)!} = 2\left(\frac{n!}{(n-4)!\,4!}\right)$$

Step 2
Simplify the equation.

Divide both sides of the equation by $n!$, where $n \neq 0$.

$$\frac{1}{(n-3)!} = 2\left(\frac{1}{(n-4)!\,4!}\right)$$

Write out factorials until the denominators have an equal factorial and simplify.

$$\frac{1}{(n-3)(n-4)!} = \frac{2}{(n-4)!(4 \times 3 \times 2 \times 1)}$$
$$\frac{1}{(n-3)(n-4)!} = \frac{2}{24(n-4)!}$$

Multiply both sides of the equation by $(n-4)!$

$$\frac{1}{(n-3)} = \frac{2}{24}$$

Step 3
Solve the equation.

Equate the cross products.
$$24(1) = 2(n-3)$$
$$24 = 2n - 6$$
$$30 = 2n$$
$$15 = n$$

Solving Problems Involving Both a Permutation and a Combination

When solving problems that involve permutations and combinations, it may be necessary to calculate the different number of combinations first, and then calculate the permutations. Most problems will ask for the different ways in which particular items can be chosen and then arranged or displayed. When choosing the items, order does not matter, so the combinations formula can be applied. When arranging the items, order does matter, so the permutations formula must be applied.

Example
A clothing store owner is assembling a window display. The store owner will choose two outfits from a collection of six spring outfits and three outfits from a collection of seven summer outfits to make a display of five outfits arranged in a row.

The number of possible arrangements of outfits in the window display is _____.

Solution

This problem involves both a combination (selecting the outfits) and a permutation (arranging the outfits in the store window).

Step 1
Determine the number of possible selections for the spring outfits.

There are $_6C_2 = 15$ combinations for selecting 2 out of 6 spring outfits.

Step 2
Determine the number of possible selections for the summer outfits.

There are $_7C_3 = 35$ combinations for selecting 3 out of 7 summer outfits.

Step 3
Determine the number of possible arrangements of the 5 selected outfits in the store window.

Since order matters, the number of arrangements of the 5 selected outfits in the store window can be displayed in $_5P_5$, or $5!$, ways.

$5! = 120$

Step 4
Determine the total number of possible arrangements of outfits.

The total number of possible displays can be determined by applying the fundamental counting principle.

There are $15 \times 35 \times 120 = 63\,000$ possible arrangements of outfits.

Using Combinations to Solve Probability Problems

Applying the skills used to solve combination problems can be helpful in solving probability problems. When solving probability problems that involve combinations, first determine the different combinations, and then apply the formula $P(E) = \dfrac{S}{N}$. In this formula, $P(E)$ represents the probability of an event E, S represents the number of successful outcomes, and N represents the number of equally likely outcomes.

Example
A bag contains 8 white golf balls and 5 yellow golf balls. Two balls are drawn from the bag at random.

What is the probability that both balls drawn from the bag are white?

Solution

Step 1
Determine an expression for the number of successful outcomes.

Since there are 8 white golf balls in the bag, the number of selections of 2 white golf balls from 8 white golf balls can be represented by the expression $_8C_2$.

Step 2
Determine an expression for the number of equally likely outcomes.

Since there are 13 golf balls in the bag, the number of selections of 2 golf balls from 13 golf balls can be represented by the expression $_{13}C_2$.

Step 3
Determine the probability that both golf balls are white.

Apply the formula $P(E) = \dfrac{S}{N}$.

Substitute $_8C_2$ for S and $_{13}C_2$ for N.

$P(\text{white, white}) = \dfrac{_8C_2}{_{13}C_2}$

$= \dfrac{28}{78}$

$= \dfrac{14}{39}$

Therefore, the probability that both balls drawn from the bag are white is $\dfrac{14}{39}$.

After the balls are drawn from the bag, what is the probability that one ball is white and one ball is yellow?

Solution

Step 1
Determine an expression for the number of successful outcomes.

Since there are 8 white golf balls in the bag, the number of selections of 1 white golf ball from 8 white golf balls can be represented by the expression $_8C_1$.

Since there are 5 yellow golf balls in the bag, the number of selections of 1 yellow golf ball from 5 yellow golf balls can be represented by the expression $_5C_1$.

According to the fundamental counting principle, the number of selections of 1 white golf ball and 1 yellow golf ball can be represented by the expression $_8C_1 \times _5C_1$.

Step 2
Determine an expression for the number of equally likely outcomes.
Since there are 13 golf balls in the bag, the number of selections of 2 golf balls from 13 golf balls can be represented by the expression $_{13}C_2$.

Step 3
Determine the probability that 1 white golf ball and 1 yellow golf ball are chosen.
Apply the formula $P(E) = \dfrac{S}{N}$.

Substitute $_8C_1 \times {}_5C_1$ for S and $_{13}C_2$ for N.

$$P(\text{white, yellow}) = \dfrac{{}_8C_1 \times {}_5C_1}{{}_{13}C_2}$$
$$= \dfrac{8 \times 5}{78}$$
$$= \dfrac{40}{78}$$
$$= \dfrac{20}{39}$$

Therefore, the probability that one ball is white and one ball is yellow is $\dfrac{20}{39}$.

The sum of the probability of an event happening and the probability of an event not happening is equal to 1. The probability of event E not happening is denoted by $P(\overline{E})$.

Thus, $P(E) + P(\overline{E}) = 1$ or $P(E) = 1 - P(\overline{E})$.

What is the probability that at least one ball drawn from the bag is yellow?

Solution

The answer could be obtained directly by calculating the sum of the probabilities of 1 yellow ball and of 2 yellow balls; however, another approach is to calculate the probability of no yellows and subtract from 1.

$P(\text{at least one yellow}) = 1 - P(\text{no yellow})$
$$= 1 - \dfrac{{}_8C_2}{{}_{13}C_2}$$
$$= 1 - \dfrac{14}{39}$$
$$= \dfrac{25}{39}$$

Notice that the probability of no yellow balls is the same as the probability of both balls being white.

Therefore, the probability that at least one ball is yellow is $\dfrac{25}{39}$.

Apply the same strategy when solving probability problems involving combinations in real-life situations.

Example
In a box of 8 calculators, 3 have dead batteries.

If 2 calculators are randomly drawn from the box, what is the probability that both have good batteries?

Solution

Step 1
Determine an expression for the number of successful outcomes.

In a box of 8 calculators, if 3 have dead batteries, then there are 5 calculators with good batteries in the box.

The number of selections of 2 good calculators from 5 good calculators can be represented by the expression $_5C_2$.

Step 2

Determine an expression for the number of equally likely outcomes.

The selection of 2 calculators from 8 calculators can be represented by the expression $_8C_2$.

Step 3

Determine the probability that 2 good calculators are selected

Apply the formula $P(E) = \dfrac{S}{N}$.

Substitute $_5C_2$ for S and $_8C_2$ for N.

$$P(\text{2 good calculators}) = \dfrac{_5C_2}{_8C_2}$$
$$= \dfrac{10}{28}$$
$$= \dfrac{5}{14}$$

Therefore, the probability that both calculators have good batteries is $\dfrac{5}{14}$.

SOLVING PROBLEMS INVOLVING PERMUTATIONS OF *n* OBJECTS

When the order of selected objects matters in a counting problem, the problem is considered to be a permutation problem. The permutation of *n* objects refers to counting permutations in which all the *n* objects are to be selected.

As in any counting problem, consider these three questions:

1. How many objects are there to begin with?
2. How many objects are to be selected?
3. Does the order of the selected objects matter?

Example

In how many different arrangements can five children be seated in a row?

Solution

To begin, answer the following three questions:

1. How many objects are there to begin with? There are five children to begin with.
2. How many objects are selected from them? Since all five children are to be arranged, all five children are selected.
3. Does the order of the selected objects matter? Since it is required to determine the number of different seating arrangements for the five children, the order in which the five children are arranged matters.

To illustrate this problem, label the five chairs 1 to 5, then fill each chair one by one.

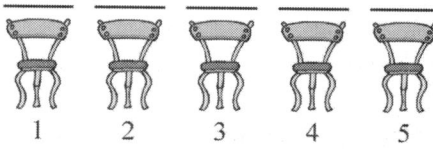

Probabilities of Compound Events

The process of seating the five children consists of five stages.

1. There are five children from which to choose, so there are five ways to complete stage 1.
2. Once one of the children has been seated in chair 1, there are only four children left to be seated, so there are four choices for seat 2.
3. Since there are three children left to be seated, there are three choices for seat 3.
4. There are only two children left, so there are only two choices for seat 4.
5. At this stage there is only one child left to be seated, so there is only one choice for seat 5.

Since a child is placed in each seat, by the fundamental counting principle, the required results can be determined by multiplying the numbers from each stage.

The number of arrangements for seating all five children is $5 \times 4 \times 3 \times 2 \times 1 = 120$.

There are 120 possible arrangements for seating five children in a row.

Example
How many arrangements are possible for seating n children in a row?

Solution
The process of seating the n children consists of n stages:

1. There are n different children who could be seated in chair 1.
2. There are $n - 1$ different children who could be seated in chair 2.
3. There are $n - 2$ different children who could be seated in chair 3.

This process continues in the same manner until the nth seat.

Stage $n - 1$ (the second last stage): There are two different children left to be seated in chair $n - 1$.

Stage n (the last stage): There is only one child left to be seated in chair n.

To complete the task of seating all n children, all the stages must be completed (i.e., a child must be placed in chair 1, chair 2, chair 3, chair $n - 1$, and chair n).

Therefore, the total number of possible arrangements is as follows:
$n \times (n - 1) \times (n - 2) \times \ldots \times 2 \times 1 = n!$

The word *distinct* implies that each object is different from any other object.

In general, $n \times (n - 1) \times (n - 2) \times \ldots \times 2 \times 1 = n!$ represents the number of permutations of n distinct objects. This rule applies when all n objects are permuted or, in other words, all n objects are selected and their order matters.

Example
There are 11 positions on a soccer team, and a particular team has 11 players.

How many different arrangements are possible when all 11 players are put into a position? _____

Solution
Since there are 11 different players and each of the 11 is to be assigned a different position, the order matters.

Assuming that each of the 11 players can play any of the 11 positions, the number of permutations of the 11 players is
$11! = 39,916,800$.

There are 39,916,800 different arrangements for the 11 players.

Solving Problems Involving Permutations of *n* Objects Taken *r* at a Time

The phrase "permutations of *n* objects taken *r* at a time" refers to counting permutations in which only some of the *n* objects are selected.

Example

If there are six children, how many different arrangements are possible for seating four of them in a row?

Solution

Start by answering the following three questions:

1. How many objects are there to begin with? There are six children to begin with.
2. How many objects are selected from them? Four children are selected to be seated in a row.
3. Does the order of the selected objects matter? It is required to determine the number of different seating arrangements of the four children.

This can be illustrated by labeling the four chairs.

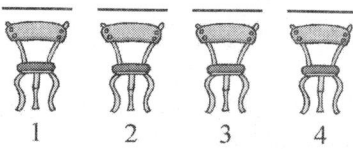

The process of seating four of the children consists of four stages:

1. There are six children to choose from, so there are six ways to complete stage 1.
2. Once a child has been seated in chair 1, there are five children left. This means that there are five choices for chair 2.
3. Now there are only four children remaining; therefore, stage 3 can be completed in four ways.
4. Since only three children remain, stage 4 can be completed in three ways.

Since a child is placed in seat 1, seat 2, seat 3, and seat 4, by the fundamental counting principle, the required result can be determined by multiplying the numbers in each of the stages.

The number of arrangements for seating the four children is $6 \times 5 \times 4 \times 3 = 360$.

In the given example, there is a sequence of numbers in descending order that are multiplied together. Although the numbers get smaller, they do not reach 1.

For the sake of developing the formula for the number of permutations of *n* objects taken *r* at a time, consider if the product of numbers in descending order continued all the way to 1. The result would be that the product of the *n* numbers could be simplified to the expression $n!$. However, if the product were extended to 1, some values would be multiplied unnecessarily. As such, the unnecessary product must be divided out.

Example

Express the product $6 \times 5 \times 4 \times 3$ using factorial notation.

Solution

Express the solution as a fraction, in which the numerator is the product of descending whole number values starting at 6 and ending at 1 and the denominator is the product of any of the unnecessary values from the numerator.

$$6 \times 5 \times 4 \times 3 = \frac{6 \times 5 \times 4 \times 3 \times (2 \times 1)}{(2 \times 1)}$$

The expression $\frac{6 \times 5 \times 4 \times 3 \times 2 \times 1}{2 \times 1}$ is equivalent to $\frac{6!}{2!} = \frac{6!}{(6-4)!}$.

The definition of $_nP_r$ is $_nP_r = \dfrac{n!}{(n-r)!}$, in which $_nP_r$ stands for the number of permutations of n objects taken r at a time.

Example
Evaluate $_{10}P_3$.

Solution

Step 1
Substitute 10 for n and 3 for r in the formula
$$_nP_r = \dfrac{n!}{(n-r)!}.$$
$$_{10}P_3 = \dfrac{10!}{(10-3)!}$$
$$= \dfrac{10!}{7!}$$

Step 2
Rewrite $\dfrac{10!}{7!}$ as a quotient of products, then reduce the numerator and denominator.
$$\dfrac{10!}{7!} = \dfrac{10 \times 9 \times 8 \times (7!)}{7!}$$
$$= 10 \times 9 \times 8$$
$$= 720$$

Example
How many different five-letter arrangements can be made using the letters from the word CHAMPION?

Solution

There are eight letters available, from which five are to be selected and used to form different letter arrangements. The order of the letters does matter, so the problem is a permutation problem.

To permute five letters out of eight letters, use the notation $_8P_5$.

Step 1
Substitute 8 for n and 5 for r in the formula
$$_nP_r = \dfrac{n!}{(n-r)!}.$$
$$_8P_5 = \dfrac{8!}{(8-5)!}$$
$$= \dfrac{8!}{3!}$$

Step 2
Evaluate $\dfrac{8!}{3!}$.
$$\dfrac{8!}{3!} = 6{,}720$$

Thus, 6,720 different five-letter arrangements can be made using the letters in the word CHAMPION.

Many calculators have a button that can be used to evaluate expressions such as $_{10}P_3$ or $_6P_2$.

To evaluate $_{10}P_3$ using a TI-83 Plus graphing calculator, type 10, followed by $\boxed{\text{MATH}} \to \to \to \boxed{\text{2:nPr}}$, and then type 3 $\boxed{\text{ENTER}}$.

Example
How many different letter arrangements can be made using one or more of the letters from the word WIND?

Solution

It is necessary to count the number of letter arrangements that can be made when one or more of the letters are selected. Thus, count the number of letter arrangements using 1 letter, 2 letters, 3 letters, or 4 letters.

Step 1
Determine the number of one-letter arrangements.

To make a one-letter arrangement, select one letter from the four available letters.
The number of permutations of four letters taken one at a time is $_4P_1$.

Step 2
Determine the number of two-letter arrangements.
There are $_4P_2$ different two-letter arrangements.

Step 3
Determine the number of three-letter arrangements.
There are $_4P_3$ different three-letter arrangements.

Step 4
Determine the number of four-letter arrangements.
There are $_4P_4$ different four-letter arrangements.

Step 5
Determine the total number of different letter arrangements that can be formed.
Since it is required to count the number of letter arrangements with 1 letter, 2 letters, 3 letters, or 4 letters, it is necessary to determine the sum of $_4P_1$, $_4P_2$, $_4P_3$, and $_4P_4$.
$_4P_1 + {_4P_2} + {_4P_3} + {_4P_4}$
$= 4 + 12 + 24 + 24$
$= 64$

Thus, there are 64 different letter arrangements that can be formed using one or more letters from the word WIND.

CALCULATING PERMUTATIONS WITH NON-DISTINCT OBJECTS

Permutations with non-distinct objects occur when there is a set of objects in which some of the objects are the same.

Example
In the word BELL, there are four objects, but two of the objects are the same. If the letters were all distinct, the number of different arrangements that could be made using all the letters from the word BELL would be 4! (or 24). However, the letters are not all distinct since the letter L occurs twice.

Consider naming the letters L_1 and L_2 to make them distinct. Accordingly, one possible word is BEL_1L_2 and another possible word is BEL_2L_1. In reality, however, two identical letters are not distinct. As such, there are duplications in the list of words that can be assembled. For example, EL_1BL_2 and EL_2BL_1 have been counted as two different words even though they both spell ELBL. When the objects are non-distinct, there is only one permutation instead of two.

Similarly, the words L_1EBL_2 and L_2EBL_1 are different words when the two Ls are distinct; when they are non-distinct, however, there is only one permutation: LEBL. Consequently, there are fewer permutations with repeated letters than there are when all the letters are distinct. In this example, the letter L occurs twice, so every two permutations when the two Ls are distinct correspond to only one permutation when the Ls are identical.

If all the letters are distinct, the number of permutations is 4!, or 24. Because of the two Ls, there is half the number of distinct permutations, so divide 4! by 2.
$$\frac{4!}{2} = \frac{24}{2} = 12$$

Therefore, 12 different arrangements can be made using all the letters from the word BELL.

Example
How many different 5-letter arrangements can be made using all the letters from the word POPPY? _____

Solution
Start by treating the 3 Ps as if they were distinct. Label them P_1, P_2, and P_3. Thus, one possible word is $P_1OP_2P_3Y$.

If all 5 letters are distinct, there are 5! = 120 permutations. Instead of listing all 120 words, just examine those that begin with the letters OY.

If the O and the Y are fixed in the first and second positions, it is only necessary to permute the 3 distinct Ps. There are 3! or 6 ways to permute the 3 distinct Ps. However, if the designations P_1, P_2, and P_3 are ignored and the Ps become non-distinct, the 6 permutations all become the same. Thus, only one word (OYPPP) is possible. The same result will occur for every other situation with the O and Y in certain positions, such as OPYPP and POPYP.

If all 5 letters were distinct, there would be 5! permutations. However, since there are 3 identical Ps, 5! must be divided by 3! or 6.

$$\frac{5!}{3!} = \frac{120}{6} = 20$$

Therefore, there are 20 different 5-letter arrangements that can be made.

In general, when some of the objects to be arranged are identical, the number of distinct permutations of n objects taken n at a time can be calculated by $\frac{n!}{a!\,b!\,c!\,...}$, where a objects are one kind, b objects are a second kind, c objects are a third kind, and so on.

The numerator $n!$ is the number of permutations if all n objects are distinct. The denominator $a!$, $b!$, $c!$ ... accounts for the various permutations of the repeated objects.

Example

Julia wants to plant a row of 10 trees in front of her farmhouse. She has 3 identical pine trees, 4 identical elm trees, 2 identical birch trees, and 1 willow tree.

How many different arrangements are possible for planting the distinct trees in a row? _____

Solution

If you were to determine how many arrangements for planting 10 distinct trees, there would be 10! orderings. However, not all the trees are distinct.

Tree	Frequency
Pine	3
Elm	4
Birch	2
Willow	1
Total	10

If each tree is represented by its first letter (P = pine, E = elm, B = birch, and W = willow), the arrangement consists of 3 Ps, 4 Es, 2 Bs, and 1 W.

For example, one possible order to plant the trees would be EEBWPEPPBE, and another order would be PEPEEEBPBW.

The number of possible arrangements for planting the trees is $\frac{10!}{4!\,3!\,2!} = 12{,}600$.

Example

How many permutations of all the letters of RED DEER begin with a letter R? _____

Solution

This problem deals not only with permutations of non-distinct objects, but also with the added restriction that the permutations begin with an R.

Step 1

Sort the letters.

Letter	Frequency
R	2
E	3
D	2
Total	7

Step 2

Determine the number of permutations of the letters in RED DEER that begin with a letter R.

Consider all the letters as being different, two of which could be selected for the first position.

The result would be 2 letter choices for the first position from which one is chosen, leaving 6! arrangements for the remaining positions.

Thus, if the letters were all different, the answer would be 2 × 6!. Since there are 2 Rs, 3 Es, and 2 Ds, the effect of ordering these letters must be eliminated. The result is

$$\frac{2 \times 6!}{2!\,3!\,2!} = 60.$$

There are 60 permutations of the letters in RED DEER in which each new word begins with the letter R.

CALCULATING PERMUTATIONS WITH OBJECTS IN ORDER OR OUT OF ORDER

Occasionally, arrangements are made that require a few of the objects to be kept in order or out of order.

Example

There are 5 vehicles waiting to cross a bridge one at a time. Of the 5 vehicles, 3 of them cross in order, but not necessarily together.

How many arrangements are possible? _____

Solution

Label the vehicles A, B, C, D, and E, and require A, B, and C to be in order.

One possible arrangement is A, B, E, D, C. Another one is D, A, E, B, C, and so forth.

Notice that given particular positions for A, B, and C, they cannot be rearranged in those positions.

For example, for the arrangement A, B, E, D, C, the other arrangements with A, B, and C in positions 1, 2, and 5 and also with E and D in positions 3 and 4 respectively, that cannot be counted are as follows:
A, C, E, D, B
B, A, E, D, C
B, C, E, D, A
C, A, E, D, B
C, B, E, D, A

Therefore, there are 5 arrangements that cannot be counted here—only 1 out of 6 can be counted.

The same situation will apply when A, B, and C are in different positions, such as 2, 4, and 5, as in D, A, E, B, C. Again, 5 arrangements would be eliminated, and only 1 out of 6 would be counted.

As a result, only 1 out of 6 of all the possible arrangements would be counted. Notice that $6 = 3!$, which is the number of possible arrangements for the letters A, B, and C.

$$\frac{\text{number of arrangements of all 5 cars}}{\text{number of arrangements of the 3 cars that are kept in order}} = \frac{5!}{3!} = 20$$

Thus, the number of arrangements for the cars about to cross the bridge is 20.

In general, the number of permutations of n objects with a of them in order is $\frac{n!}{a!}$.

Notice that the approach to "things in order" is the same as the approach to "things alike", such as repetitive letters in a word.

If objects are not to be in order, the approach is as follows: Number of permutations not in order = total number of permutations − number of permutations in order

In the previous example, the number of arrangements of the 5 vehicles with the 3 vehicles (A, B, C) not in order is

$$5! - \frac{5!}{3!} = 120 - 20$$
$$= 100$$

Example

How many arrangements of 7 volumes of an encyclopedia on a shelf are possible if volumes 1, 3, 5, and 7 are to be kept in order? _____

Solution

The number of arrangements of the 7 books with volumes 1, 3, 5, and 7 in order is
$\frac{7!}{4!} = 7 \times 6 \times 5 = 210$.

Example

How many arrangements of 7 volumes of an encyclopedia on a shelf are possible if volumes 1 and 2 are **not** to be in order? _____

Solution

The number of arrangements of the 7 books with volumes 1 and 2 out of order is equal to the total number of arrangements of all books minus the total number of arrangements of books with volumes 1 and 2 in order.

$$7! - \frac{7!}{2!} = 5{,}040 - 2{,}520$$
$$= 2{,}520$$

CALCULATING PERMUTATIONS WITH GROUPING

Sometimes, it is necessary to deal with permutations where certain objects must be grouped together.

In general, follow these steps to solve problems where objects are grouped together:

1. Create the groups.
2. Count the number of permutations of the groups.
3. Count the number of permutations of the objects within the groups.
4. Multiply these numbers together.

When objects must be grouped together, but not placed in any particular order within the group, it is important to consider the ways of arranging the group of objects with all other objects or groups involved AND the number of ways in which the grouped objects themselves can be arranged within the group.

Example

Ann, Bob, Carl, David, Emma, and Fran are seated in a row.

How many different arrangements are possible if Ann, Bob, and Emma must sit next to each other? _____

Solution

This is a permutation problem where some objects are grouped together.

Step 1

Create the different groups, with Ann, Bob, and Emma all in one group.

| ABE | C | D | F |

Altogether, there are 4 distinct groups.
One possible arrangement of these groups is as follows:

| D | F | C | ABE |

There are 4! permutations of these 4 distinct groups and 3! permutations of Ann, Bob, and Emma within their group.

Step 2

Use the fundamental counting principle.
$4! \times 3! = 24 \times 6 = 144$

The number of permutations is 144.

CALCULATING PERMUTATIONS WITH SEPARATION

The general procedure for solving problems in which the restriction is that the objects must be separated is as follows:

Number of permutations with objects separated = total number of permutations − number of permutations with objects together.

Example

How many different arrangements of all the letters in the word CALCULUS are possible so that the 2 C's are **not** together?

Solution

The restriction is that the 2 C's cannot be together.

Step 1
Determine the number of possible arrangements without the restriction.

Since the letters of the word CALCULUS are not all distinct, it is necessary to sort out the letters to see how much duplication exists.

There are 8 letters with 2 C's, 1 A, 2 L's, 2 U's, and 1 S.

$$\frac{8!}{2!\,2!\,2!} = 5{,}040$$

The number of arrangements of the letters in the word CALCULUS is 5,040.

Step 2
Determine how many arrangements have the 2 C's together.

Create a box with 2 C's and six more blocks for each of the remaining letters.

| CC | A | L | L | U | U | S |

There are 7 boxes altogether, but not all the blocks are distinct. There are 2 boxes with L's and 2 boxes with U's.

Thus, the number of permutations of the 7 boxes is $\frac{7!}{2!\,2!} = 1{,}260$.

It then follows that there are 1,260 permutations of the letters such that the 2 C's are together.

Step 3
Determine the number of arrangements where the 2 C's are not together.

Subtract the 1,260 arrangements from the 5,040 arrangements.
5,040 − 1,260 = 3,780

The number of arrangements where the 2 C's are not together is 3,780.

CALCULATE SINGLE COMBINATIONS

Problems involving combinations are problems in which order does not matter.

The number of permutations of n objects taken r at a time is $_nP_r = \frac{n!}{(n-r)!}$.

The number of combinations of n objects taken r at a time is $_nC_r = \frac{n!}{(n-r)!\,r!}$.

Notice the similarities and differences in the two formulas. The only difference is that the combination formula has an additional factor of $r!$ in the denominator. This factor represents the number of arrangements of r objects, so dividing by this factor eliminates the arranging that is part of the permutations formula.

To correctly classify a counting problem, consider the following three questions:

1. How many objects are there to begin with?
2. How many objects are selected from them?
3. Does the order of the selected objects matter?

Example

Jane wants to order a three-topping pizza. If there are 8 toppings from which to choose, then how many different three-topping pizzas are possible?

Solution

Start by answering the following three questions:

1. How many objects are there to begin with?
   There are eight toppings to begin with.
2. How many objects are selected from them?
   Three toppings are to be selected.
3. Does the order of the selected objects matter?
   No, the order does not matter. For example, a pizza with pepperoni, mushrooms, and green peppers is the same as a pizza with mushrooms, pepperoni, and green peppers. Since the order of the selected objects does not matter, this is a combination problem.

To solve combination problems, a formula that is similar to the formula for permutations can be used.

The question asks for the number of combinations of 3 toppings selected from 8 toppings. Therefore, the number of combinations is $_8C_3$.

Evaluate $_8C_3$.

Substitute 8 for n and 3 for r in the formula $_nC_r = \dfrac{n!}{(n-r)!\,r!}$.

$$_nC_r = \dfrac{n!}{(n-r)!\,r!}$$
$$= \dfrac{8!}{5!\,3!}$$

Rewrite factorials as products.
$$= \dfrac{8 \times 7 \times 6 \times (5!)}{(5!) \times 3 \times 2 \times 1}$$

Cancel, or divide, common factors.
$$= \dfrac{8 \times 7 \times 6}{3 \times 2 \times 1}$$

Evaluate.
$$= 56$$

There are 56 different three-topping pizzas.

With practice, it becomes easier to identify problems that can be solved using the combination formula.

Example

How many selections of a four-member committee are possible if there are 10 people from which to choose?

Solution

The question asks for the number of selections of 4 people from 10, and order does not matter. This can be represented by the expression $_{10}C_4$.

Evaluate $_{10}C_4$ as follows:

Substitute 10 for n and 4 for r in the formula $_nC_r = \dfrac{n!}{(n-r)!\,r!}$.

$$_{10}C_4 = \dfrac{10!}{(10-4)!\,4!}$$

Simplify.
$$= \dfrac{10!}{6!\,4!}$$

Evaluate.
$$= 210$$

There are 210 different selections of a four-person committee that can be made from 10 people.

Many calculators have an $_nC_r$ button that will calculate combinations.

To obtain $_{10}C_4$ from a TI graphing calculator, press the following combination of buttons:

| 10 |
| MATH | → → → | PRB |
| 3 |
| 4 |
| ENTER |

Example

Mr. Fraser has been asked to donate 2 of his sculptures to the local art gallery. If Mr. Fraser owns 25 sculptures, how many different donations of 2 sculptures are possible?

Solution

Since order does not matter, this is a combination question.

Two sculptures must be selected from 25 sculptures, and order does not matter. Therefore, there are $_{25}C_2$ combinations.

Evaluate $_{25}C_2$.

$_{25}C_2 = 300$

There are 300 different combinations for selecting two sculptures from 25 sculptures. Therefore, Mr. Fraser can make 300 different donations.

CALCULATING COMPLEX COMBINATIONS

With permutations, order matters.
With combinations, order does not matter—different orders are not counted as additional combinations.

The number of combinations of *n* objects taken *r* at a time is $_nC_r = \dfrac{n!}{(n-r)!\,r!}$.

The fundamental counting principle can be applied with combinations to calculate complex combinations.

Example

Mrs. Klemke has 10 paintings. She wants to give 4 of them to her son and 3 to her granddaughter. How many different distributions of the paintings are possible?

Solution

This problem consists of two stages:

1. Give 4 paintings to her son.
2. Give 3 paintings to her granddaughter.

Stage 1
Mrs. Klemke begins with 10 paintings, and selects 4 of them to give to her son. Since the order in which she gives the paintings to her son does not matter, this is a combination question. There are $_{10}C_4 = 210$ combinations for selecting 4 out of the 10 paintings.
Now that she has selected 4 paintings for her son, it is possible to move to stage 2 to determine how she can select 3 paintings for her granddaughter.

Stage 2
Since Mrs. Klemke has already selected 4 paintings for her son, there are only 6 paintings remaining to select from. She will select 3 paintings from these 6. There are $_6C_3 = 20$ combinations for selecting 3 out of 6 paintings.
In order to solve this problem, both stages 1 and 2 must be completed. There are 210 combinations in stage 1 and 20 combinations in stage 2.
By the fundamental counting principle, there are 210 × 20 or 4,200 combinations for both stages.
Mrs. Klemke has 4,200 possible distributions for giving 4 paintings to her son and 3 paintings to her granddaughter.

Example

A mixed volleyball team consists of 3 girls and 3 boys. If 7 girls and 8 boys try out for the team, how many different selections for the team are possible?

Solution

This problem consists of two stages:

1. Select the 3 girls.
2. Select the 3 boys.

Stage 1
Select 3 girls from the 7 who tried out for the team. Since the order in which the girls are selected does not matter, this is a combination question.
There are $_7C_3 = 35$ combinations for selecting 3 out of 7 girls.

Stage 2

Select 3 boys from the 8 who tried out for the team. Since the order in which the boys are selected does not matter, this is a combination question. There are $_8C_3 = 56$ combinations for selecting 3 out of 8 boys.

In order to solve this problem, stages 1 and 2 must be combined. There are 35 combinations for completing stage 1, and 56 combinations for completing stage 2.

By the fundamental counting principle, there are $35 \times 56 = 1,960$ combinations for completing both stages.

Thus, there are 1,960 possible teams.

Example

The general staff in a hospital consists of 3 doctors and 12 nurses. How many different teams of 2 doctors and 5 nurses can be formed, if a particular doctor must be included on each team and 2 particular nurses are on vacation and cannot be part of the teams?

Solution

Step 1

Determine if the problem involves a permutation or a combination.

The order in which the doctors and nurses are selected does not matter; therefore, the given question is a combination problem.

Step 2

Determine the number of possible selections for the doctors.

Since one particular doctor must be included, the other doctor on the team must be selected from the two remaining doctors. This can be represented by $_1C_1 \times {_2C_1}$, which simplifies to $_2C_1$.

Step 3

Determine the number of possible selections for the nurses.

Since two nurses cannot be part of the team, the 5 required nurses must be selected from the 10 available nurses. This can be represented by $_{10}C_5$.

Step 4

Determine the number of possible doctor-nurse teams that can be formed.

The number of possible doctor-nurse teams can be determined by applying the fundamental counting principle.

$_2C_1 \times {_{10}C_5} = 504$

Thus, there are 504 different doctor-nurse teams that can be formed.

PROBLEM SOLVING WITH COMBINATIONS

Problems involving combinations are problems in which order does not matter.

Sometimes, instead of asking you to calculate the number of possible combinations of *n* objects taken *r* at a time, a problem will give you the number of combinations and ask you to determine the value of *n* or *r*.

In such a situation, use the formula for the number of combinations of *n* objects taken *r* at a time,

$$_nC_r = \frac{n!}{(n-r)!\,r!}.$$

Example

There are 120 ways of choosing a committee of 2 students from a certain math class. Determine the number of students in the class.

Solution

Step 1

Determine if the problem involves a permutation or a combination.

The order in which the students are chosen does not matter; therefore, the given question is a combination problem.

Step 2

Let *n* represent the number of students in the class. Write an expression that represents the number of selections of 2 students out of *n* students.

The number of selections of 2 students out of *n* students can be represented by $_nC_2$.

Step 3

Solve for n in the equation $_nC_2 = 120$, given that there are 120 ways of choosing 2 students out of n students.

$_nC_2 = 120$

Write $_nC_2$ in factorial form.

$$\frac{n!}{(n-2)!\,2!} = 120$$

Write out the factorials until the numerators and the denominator have overlapping factors.

$$\frac{(n)(n-1)(n-2)(n-3)\ldots \times 2 \times 1}{(n-2)(n-3)\ldots \times 2 \times 1 \times (2 \times 1)} = 120$$

Reduce by common factors and solve for n.

$$\frac{n(n-1)}{2} = 120$$
$$n(n-1) = 120(2)$$
$$n^2 - n = 240$$
$$n^2 - n - 240 = 0$$

Factor $n^2 - n - 240$.

$(n-16)(n+15) = 0$

$n = 16, n = -15$

Since -15 is an inadmissible answer, it follows that there are 16 students in the math class.

It is always important to consider the solutions within the context of the given problem. In a situation that deals with objects, as in $_nC_r$, n must be positive ($n > 0$), and r must be greater than or equal to zero ($r \geq 0$).

SOLVING COMBINATION PROBLEMS INVOLVING SPECIAL CASES

One special type of combination problem involves events that are codependent of one another. Examples of such events could include handshakes and sports leagues.

For a combination involving handshakes, in a group of n people with every person shaking hands with every other person, there are $_nC_2$ handshakes possible.

Example

In a room of 9 people, how many handshakes are possible?

Solution

Step 1

Interpret the given information.

Each handshake is formed by selecting 2 people from 9 where the order of the 2 people does not matter.

There are $_9C_2$ such selections, so $_9C_2$ handshakes can be formed in total.

Step 2

Calculate the number of handshakes.

$_9C_2 = 36$

Therefore, 36 handshakes are possible in the room.

For a combination problem involving sports leagues, if there are n teams with every team playing every other team, a total of $_nC_2$ games will be played.

Example

In a 10-team soccer league, each team plays every other team 3 times. How many games are played in total? _____

Solution

Two teams are required to play one game of soccer. Therefore, it is necessary to count the number of combinations of 10 teams taken 2 at a time.

There are $_{10}C_2 = 45$ such combinations.

If each team were to play every other team once, there would be 45 games. However, each team plays 3 games, so the total number of games played is $3 \times 45 = 135$.

There are many other examples of combination problems involving codependent events that apply to figures and shapes. In a particular shape, for instance, if you are given n points with no three points being collinear, the following generalizations apply:

- The number of line segments = $_nC_2$.
- The number of triangles = $_nC_3$.
- The number of quadrilaterals = $_nC_4$.
- The number of pentagons = $_nC_5$, and so on.

For a combination problem involving line segments, if there are n points on the circumference of a circle, a total of $_nC_2$ line segments can be drawn by connecting any two points.

Example
There are 6 points on the circumference of a circle. How many lines can be drawn by connecting any 2 of these points? _____

Solution
In this case, a line can be drawn by selecting any 2 points from the 6 and connecting them.

It does not matter in what order the points are selected, since connecting point A to point B is the same as connecting point B to point A.

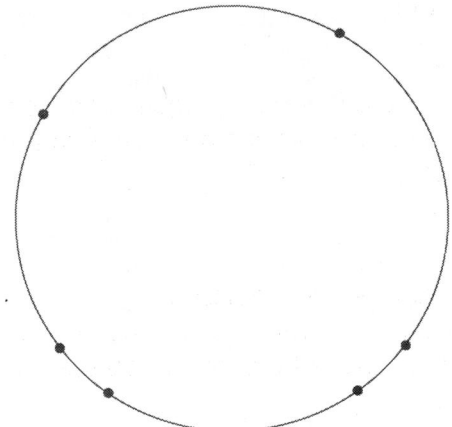

Count the number of combinations of 2 points selected from 6.

There are $_6C_2 = 15$ such combinations.

Therefore, 15 lines can be drawn using 6 points on the circumference of a circle.

In general, if there are n points on the circumference of a circle, a total of $_nC_2$ lines can be drawn by connecting any two of them.

Calculating Combinations in Situations with Upper or Lower Limits

Some combination problems involve situations with upper or lower limits of selections. The key phrases *at least* or *at most* set up situations that must be considered separately. Look for these key phrases, and solve the problem using the combinations formula or technology ($_nC_r$ button on a calculator). Whenever you are solving problems that involve calculating combinations, it is important to make sure that the order of selections does not matter.

Follow these steps to calculate combinations with upper or lower limits:

1. Break the problem down into different selection situations.
2. Calculate the number of combinations for each selection.
3. Find the sum of the number of combinations for each selection.

Example
Calculate how many different selections are possible when at least 4 books are selected from 6 books.

Solution
Step 1
Break the problem down into different selection situations.

The phrase *at least 4* means that 4 or more books are selected. The selection situation is for 4 books, 5 books, or 6 books.

Step 2

Since the problem has a lower limit, calculate the number of combinations for each selection situation separately.

- The situation in which 4 books are selected from 6 results in $_6C_4$ selections.
- The situation in which 5 books are selected from 6 results in $_6C_5$ selections.
- The situation in which 6 books are selected from 6 results in $_6C_6$ selections.

Step 3

Find the sum of the number of combinations.

Since the selection is either 4 books, 5 books, or 6 books, the answer is the sum of the number of combinations of each selection situation.

$_6C_4 + {}_6C_5 + {}_6C_6$
$= 15 + 6 + 1$
$= 22$

There are 22 different selections that are possible for the given situation.

Example

How many 5-card hands have at most 2 clubs?

Solution

A standard deck of 52 cards consists of 13 clubs, 13 spades, 13 hearts, and 13 diamonds.

The phrase *at most 2 clubs* means either 0 clubs, 1 club, or 2 clubs are in the hand.

Since there is an upper limit, each selection situation must be calculated separately.

- If there are no clubs selected, then the 5 cards are chosen from the 39 other cards, represented by $_{39}C_5$.
- If there is 1 club selected, then it is chosen from the 13 clubs, and the 4 other cards are chosen from the 39 non-clubs. This is represented by $_{13}C_1 \times {}_{39}C_4$.
- If there are 2 clubs selected, then they are chosen from the 13 clubs, and the 3 other cards are chosen from the 39 non-clubs. This is represented by $_{13}C_2 \times {}_{39}C_3$.

Since the hands have either 0 clubs, 1 club, or 2 clubs, the answer is the sum of combinations of each selection situation.

$_{39}C_5 + ({}_{13}C_1 \times {}_{39}C_4) + ({}_{13}C_2 \times {}_{39}C_3)$
$= 575,757 + 1,069,263 + 712,842$
$= 2,357,862$

There are 2,357,862 possible 5-card hands with at most 2 clubs.

If the number of selection situations that satisfy the *at most* or *at least* requirements is large, it might be easier to calculate the number of selection situations that do not satisfy the requirements and subtract that number from the total number of possible selections with no restrictions.

SOLVING PROBLEMS USING BOTH PERMUTATIONS AND COMBINATIONS

When solving problems that involve permutations and combinations, it may be necessary to calculate the different number of combinations first, followed by the permutations.

Most problems ask for the different ways in which particular items can be chosen and then arranged or displayed. When choosing the items, order does not matter, so the combinations formula can be applied. When arranging the items, order does matter, so the permutations formula must be applied.

Example

A clothing store owner is assembling a window display. The store owner will choose two outfits from a collection of six spring outfits and three outfits from a collection of seven summer outfits to make a display of five outfits arranged in a row.

The number of possible arrangements of outfits in the window display is _____.

Solution

This problem involves both a combination (selecting the outfits) and a permutation (arranging the outfits in the store window).

Step 1
Determine the number of possible selections for the spring outfits.
There are $_6C_2 = 15$ combinations for selecting 2 out of 6 spring outfits.

Step 2
Determine the number of possible selections for the summer outfits.
There are $_7C_3 = 35$ combinations for selecting 3 out of 7 summer outfits.

Step 3
Determine the number of possible arrangements of the 5 selected outfits in the store window.
Since order matters, the number of arrangements of the 5 selected outfits in the store window can be displayed in $_5P_5$, or 5!, ways.
5! = 120

Step 4
Determine the total number of possible arrangements of outfits.
The total number of possible displays can be determined by applying the fundamental counting principle.
There are 15 × 35 × 120 = 63,000 possible arrangements of outfits.

Using Permutations to Solve Probability Problems

Applying the skills used to solve permutation problems can be very helpful in solving probability problems. When solving probability problems that involve permutations, the order of events is important.

First, determine the different permutations, then apply the formula $P(E) = \dfrac{S}{N}$, in which $P(E)$ represents the probability of an event (E), S represents the number of successful outcomes, and N represents the number of equally likely outcomes.

While certain common techniques are followed to solve most probability problems, more than one method can usually be used to arrive at the correct solution.

Example

After a championship game, there are 10 hockey players that randomly line up for a picture.

Rounded to the nearest thousandth, what is the probability that the captain and the two assistant captains stand together in the picture?

Solution

Step 1
Determine an expression for the number of equally likely outcomes.
Since there are no restrictions with respect to the location of the players in the line, there are $_{10}P_{10}$ or 10! = 3,628,800 possible arrangements.

Step 2
Determine the number of successful outcomes.
Let the letter C represent the captain, and let A_1 and A_2 represent the two assistant captains. Let the remaining players be represented by P_1, P_2, P_3, P_4, P_5, P_6, and P_7.
The following lineup is one possible arrangement:

$\boxed{C, A_1, A_2}, P_1, P_2, P_3, P_4, P_5, P_6, P_7$

The block $\boxed{C, A_1, A_2}$ can be placed in any location in the arrangement. As well, the letters C, A_1, and A_2 can be placed in any order in the block.

Thus, the number of possible arrangements with the captain and two assistant captains standing together is $_8P_8 \times {_3P_3}$ or $8! \times 3! = 241{,}920$.

Step 3
Determine the probability that the captain and the two assistant captains stand together.

Apply the formula $P(E) = \dfrac{S}{N}$.

Substitute 241,920 for S and 3,628,800 for N.

$P(C, A_1, A_2) = \dfrac{241{,}920}{3{,}628{,}800}$

≈ 0.0667

The probability that the captain and the two assistant captains stand together for the picture is approximately 0.067.

The sum of the probability of an event happening and the probability of an event not happening is equal to 1. The probability of event E not happening is denoted by $P(\overline{E})$.
Therefore, $P(E) + P(\overline{E}) = 1$, and $P(E) = 1 - P(\overline{E})$.

Example
After a championship game, there are 10 hockey players that randomly line up for a picture.

Expressed as a fraction, what is the probability that the captain and the two assistant captains do **not** stand together in the picture?

Solution
Step 1
Determine an expression for the number of equally likely outcomes.
Since there are no restrictions with respect to the location of the players in the line, there are $_{10}P_{10}$ or $10! = 3{,}628{,}800$ possible arrangements.

Step 2
Determine the number of outcomes in which the captain and assistant captains stand together.
Let the letter C represent the captain, and let A_1 and A_2 represent the two assistant captains. Let the remaining players be represented by P_1, P_2, P_3, P_4, P_5, P_6, and P_7.
The following lineup is one possible arrangement:

$\boxed{C, A_1, A_2}, P_1, P_2, P_3, P_4, P_5, P_6, P_7$

The block $\boxed{C, A_1, A_2}$ can be placed in any location in the arrangement. As well, the letters C, A_1, and A_2 can be placed in any order in the block.
Thus, the number of possible arrangements with the captain and two assistant captains standing together is $_8P_8 \times {_3P_3}$ or $8! \times 3! = 241{,}920$.

Step 3
Determine the probability that the captain and the two assistant captains stand together.

Apply the formula $P(E) = \dfrac{S}{N}$.

Substitute 241,920 for S and 3,628,800 for N.

$$P(C, A_1, A_2) = \dfrac{241{,}920}{3{,}628{,}800}$$

The probability that the captain and the two assistant captains stand together for the picture is approximately 0.067.

Step 4
Determine the probability that the captain and the two assistant captains do not stand together.

$$\begin{aligned} P(\overline{E}) &= 1 - P(E) \\ &= 1 - \dfrac{241{,}920}{3{,}628{,}800} \\ &= \dfrac{3{,}386{,}880}{3{,}628{,}800} \\ &= \dfrac{14}{15} \end{aligned}$$

EXERCISE #1—PROBABILITIES OF COMPOUND EVENTS

272. Ashley draws three cards successively without replacement, from a standard deck of 52 cards. The probability, to the nearest millionth, that all three cards are aces is
   A. 0.000171
   B. 0.000177
   C. 0.000181
   D. 0.000455

273. What is the probability of randomly drawing a heart or an even, non-face spade card from a standard deck of 52 cards?
   A. $\dfrac{1}{4}$
   B. $\dfrac{4}{13}$
   C. $\dfrac{9}{26}$
   D. $\dfrac{19}{52}$

Use the following information to answer the next question.

> Sam has a bag of assorted jellybeans. Each jellybean is either red (R), blue (B), or green (G) and is fruit flavored (F) or cinnamon flavored (C). Each bag typically contains 100 jellybeans: 40 are red, 40 are green, and 20 are blue. Three-quarters of all the jellybeans are fruit flavored, and one-quarter of all the jellybeans are cinnamon flavored. Sam likes red jellybeans and fruit-flavored jellybeans.

274. What is the probability that Sam randomly selects a jellybean he likes from a bag of 100?
   A. $\dfrac{3}{10}$
   B. $\dfrac{2}{5}$
   C. $\dfrac{17}{20}$
   D. $\dfrac{23}{20}$

275. Which of the following problems can be solved by using permutations?
   A. Determine the number of 5 letter arrangements of the letters in the word COUNTRY.
   B. Determine the number of 5 card hands that can be made using a standard deck of 52 cards.
   C. Determine the number of quadrilaterals that can be formed using the vertices of an octagon.
   D. Determine the number of 4 member committees that can be selected from a group of 12 people.

Use the following information to answer the next question.

> Terry and 19 of his friends are being considered for a trip.

276. If only 3 people can go on this trip, then the number of groups of 3 that would include Terry is
   A. 171
   B. 190
   C. 969
   D. 1,140

277. A simplified form of the expression $_{n-1}P_2 + {}_{n+1}C_2$ is
   A. $n^2 - n + 1$
   B. $2n^2 - 2n + 2$
   C. $\dfrac{3n^2 - 2n + 2}{2}$
   D. $\dfrac{3n^2 - 5n + 4}{2}$

Exercise #1 Castle Rock Research

278. A committee of three students is to be selected from a group of six female students and four male students. What is the probability that Tanjay, one of the male students, and Mary, one of the female students, will both be selected?

   A. $\dfrac{1}{15}$ B. $\dfrac{2}{15}$

   C. $\dfrac{3}{20}$ D. $\dfrac{1}{120}$

Use the following information to answer the next question.

> Jen is having a party at her house and is expecting 7 friends to come. She wants to give each friend a gift. She has 8 gifts to give away, but decides she really likes 1 particular gift and keeps it for herself.

279. How many different ways can Jen randomly give each friend a gift?

   A. 5,040
   B. 40,320
   C. $7! \times 6! \times 5! \times 4! \times 3! \times 2! \times 1!$
   D. $8! \times 7! \times 6! \times 5! \times 4! \times 3! \times 2! \times 1!$

280. A ship has 6 different colored flags on board. To send signals, the ship's crew arranges some or all of the flags vertically on a flagpole. How many different signals can be made if at **least** 4 flags must be used at a time?

   A. 15   B. 360
   C. 516   D. 1,800

281. A 10-volume set of encyclopedias is randomly placed on a shelf. If the first 3 volumes are not in order, then the number of possible arrangements of the encyclopedias on the shelf is

   A. 201,600   B. 604,800
   C. 3,024,000 D. 3,628,800

Use the following information to answer the next question.

> The members of the Smith family are going to stand in line for a family portrait. The family consists of 4 sons, 3 daughters, 2 parents, and 1 dog.

282. If the sons must stand together, the daughters must stand together, and the parents must stand together, what is the number of possible arrangements of the family members for the portrait?

   A. $10!$
   B. 576
   C. 6,912
   D. $(2!)(4!)(3!)(1!)$

283. What is the number of possible arrangements of the letters in the word POPPY that do **not** have O and Y placed together?

   A. 10   B. 12
   C. 16   D. 18

284. Zach draws 20 points on the circumference of a circle. Using these points as vertices, how many different triangles can Zach draw?

   A. $17!$ B. $20!$
   C. $_{20}P_3$ D. $_{20}C_3$

Use the following information to answer the next question.

> A restaurant offers ice cream sundaes with 9 different topping choices.

285. Which of the following expressions represents the number of three-topping sundaes a customer could order?

   A. $\dfrac{9!}{6!\,3!}$ B. $\dfrac{9!}{6!}$

   C. $\dfrac{9!\,3!}{6!}$ D. $\dfrac{9!}{3!}$

Use the following information to answer the next question.

During the regular season of a recreational soccer league, each team plays every other team only once. The total number of games in the regular season is 45.

286. How many teams are in this league?
   A. 6
   B. 8
   C. 10
   D. 12

287. Jack's mother randomly placed four blocks labeled J, A, C, and K on a shelf. The probability that she placed them on the shelf so they spell JACK is
   A. $\dfrac{1}{4}$
   B. $\dfrac{1}{6}$
   C. $\dfrac{1}{24}$
   D. $\dfrac{1}{256}$

Use the following information to answer the next question.

A car dealership manager wants to line up 9 cars in a row along one side of the dealership. All the cars are identical except for color: 2 are red, 3 are blue, and 4 are black.

288. If the manager wishes to park a black car on each end of the row, then the number of different possible arrangements of the 9 cars is
   A. 210
   B. 1,260
   C. 5,040
   D. 60,480

Use the following information to answer the next question.

The owner of a video store has 4 posters of recent releases of different comedy movies and 5 posters of recent releases of different drama movies. From these posters, the owner decides to choose 2 comedy movie posters and 3 drama movie posters to display in a row on the front window of his store.

289. The number of different displays that the owner can make from these posters is
   A. 60
   B. 120
   C. 7,200
   D. 86,400

Use the following information to answer the next question.

A team of 6 volleyball players is to be chosen from among 6 boys and 7 girls.

290. How many different teams could be formed with at least one boy? _____

Exercise #1

Castle Rock Research

EXERCISE #1—PROBABILITIES OF COMPOUND EVENTS
ANSWERS AND SOLUTIONS

272. C	277. D	282. C	287. C
273. C	278. A	283. B	288. A
274. C	279. A	284. D	289. C
275. A	280. D	285. A	290. 1709
276. A	281. C	286. C	

272. C
Since the cards are not replaced in the deck after being drawn, the events are dependent.
P (drawing 3 aces)
$= P(A_1) \times P(A_2/A_1) \times P[A_3/(A_1 \text{ and } A_2)]$
$= \dfrac{4}{52} \times \dfrac{3}{51} \times \dfrac{2}{50}$
$= \dfrac{1}{13} \times \dfrac{1}{17} \times \dfrac{1}{25}$
$= \dfrac{1}{5,525} \approx 0.000181$

273. C
Step 1
Determine the probability of drawing a heart.
Hearts are one of the four equally represented suits in a deck.
$P(H) = \dfrac{1}{4}$

Step 2
Determine the probability of drawing an even, non-face spade card.
Ten cards in a suit are non-face cards, and half of those cards are even.
$\dfrac{1}{2} \times 10 = 5$
$P(ENFCS) = \dfrac{5}{52}$

Step 3
Determine the probability of drawing a heart or an even, non-face spade card.
The two events are mutually exclusive.
$P(H \text{ or } ENFCS)$
$= P(H) + P(ENFCS)$
$= \dfrac{1}{4} + \dfrac{5}{52}$
$= \dfrac{13}{52} + \dfrac{5}{52}$
$= \dfrac{18}{52}$
$= \dfrac{9}{26}$

274. C
Since it is possible to select a red jellybean that is fruit flavored, these two events are not mutually exclusive.

Step 1
Determine the probability of randomly selecting a red jellybean.
There are 40 red jellybeans in a bag of 100.
$P(R) = \dfrac{40}{100}$

Step 2
Determine the probability of randomly selecting a fruit-flavored jellybean.
Three-quarters of all the jellybeans are fruit flavored.
$P(F) = \dfrac{3}{4}$

Step 3
Determine the probability that a randomly selected jellybean is red and fruit flavored.
Since three-quarters of all the jellybeans are fruit flavored, three-quarters of 40 red jellybeans are fruit flavored.
$\dfrac{3}{4} \times 40 = 30$
$P(RF) = \dfrac{30}{100}$

Step 4
Determine the probability that Sam randomly selects a jellybean he likes.
$P(R \text{ or } F)$
$= P(R) + P(F) - P(R \text{ and } F)$
$= \dfrac{40}{100} + \dfrac{3}{4} - \dfrac{30}{100}$
$= \dfrac{40}{100} + \dfrac{75}{100} - \dfrac{30}{100}$
$= \dfrac{85}{100}$
$= \dfrac{17}{20}$

The probability that Sam randomly selects a jellybean he likes is $\dfrac{17}{20}$.

275. A

"Determining the number of 5 letter arrangements of the letters in the word COUNTRY" is the only problem in which order is important. Different arrangements of the 5 letters form different "words."

The other problems are examples of combinations, where the order of selection does not make a difference.

276. A

If Terry is one of the 3 members of the group, then there are 2 other members to be selected from the group of 19.

Step 1
The order of selection does not matter, so use combinations.
The number of ways to select 2 people from a group of 19 is $_{19}C_2$.

Use $_nC_r = \dfrac{(n!)}{(n-r)!\,r!}$ to calculate $_{19}C_2$.

$$_{19}C_2 = \dfrac{(19!)}{(19-2)!\,2!}$$

Step 2
Simplify.

$$_{19}C_2 = \dfrac{19 \times 18 \times 17}{17!\times 2}$$
$$= \dfrac{19 \times 18}{2}$$
$$= 171$$

Therefore, there are 171 groups of 3 that would include Terry.

277. D

Step 1
Evaluate $_nP_r$ when $n = n-1$ and $r = 2$.
Substitute $n-1$ for n and 2 for r in the formula $_nP_r = \dfrac{n!}{(n-r)!}$.

$$_nP_r = \dfrac{(n-1)!}{((n-1)-2)!}$$
$$= \dfrac{(n-1)!}{(n-3)!}$$
$$= \dfrac{(n-1)(n-2)(n-3)!}{(n-3)!}$$
$$= (n-1)(n-2)$$
$$= n^2 - 3n + 2$$

Step 2
Evaluate $_nC_r$ when $n = n+1$ and $r = 2$.
Substitute $n+1$ for n and 2 for r in the formula $_nC_r = \dfrac{n!}{(n-r)!\,r!}$.

$$_{n+1}C_2 = \dfrac{(n+1)!}{((n+1)-2)!\,2!}$$
$$= \dfrac{(n+1)!}{(n-1)!\,2!}$$
$$= \dfrac{(n+1)n(n-1)!}{(n-1)!\,2!}$$
$$= \dfrac{(n+1)n}{2}$$
$$= \dfrac{n^2 + n}{2}$$

Step 3
Determine the sum of $_{n-1}P_2$ and $_{n+1}C_2$.

$$_{n-1}P_2 + {}_{n+1}C_2 = \dfrac{n^2 - 3n + 2}{1} + \dfrac{n^2 + n}{2}$$
$$= \dfrac{2n^2 - 6n + 4}{2} + \dfrac{n^2 + n}{2}$$
$$= \dfrac{3n^2 - 5n + 4}{2}$$

278. A

Step 1
Determine the number of possible outcomes.
The number of ways in which r objects can be chosen from n distinct objects is represented by the equation $_nC_r = \dfrac{n!}{(n-r)!\,r!}$.

A three-member committee can be selected from 10 students, of whom six are female and four are male, in $_{10}C_3$ different ways.

Evaluate $_{10}C_3$.

$$_{10}C_3 = \dfrac{10!}{(10-3)!\,3!}$$
$$= 120$$

The possible number of outcomes is 120.

Step 2
Determine the number of favorable outcomes. That is, determine the number of committees that contain Mary, Tanjay, and one other person.

Since the committee is made up of three students, the third member has to be selected from these eight people.

One student can be chosen from eight in $_8C_1 = 8$ different ways.

There are eight possible three-member committees that include both Mary and Tanjay. Therefore, the number of favorable outcomes is eight.

Step 3
Calculate the probability.
The probability that Tanjay and Mary will both be selected is

$$\text{probability} = \frac{\text{committees with Mary and Tanjay}}{\text{all possible committees}}$$

$$= \frac{8}{120}$$

$$= \frac{1}{15}$$

279. A

In general, $n \times (n-1) \times (n-2) \times \ldots \times 2 \times 1 = n!$ represents the number of permutations of n distinct objects.

Since Jen is keeping 1 specific item, there are only 7 items to give to 7 people.
$7! = 7 \times 6 \times 5 \times 4 \times 3 \times 2 \times 1 = 5,040$

There are 5,040 possible arrangements that Jen can use to give the gifts to her friends.

280. D

Recognize this problem as a permutation, since the order of flags in a vertical line on the pole matters.

Also, to make signals with at **least** 4 flags means that the signals could consist of 4, 5, or 6 flags.

Step 1
Determine the expressions describing each possible flag set.
To make a signal with 4 flags, select 4 flags from the given 6. The number of permutations of 6 objects taken 4 at a time is $_6P_4$.

To make a signal with 5 flags, select 5 flags from the given 6. This can be expressed as $_6P_5$.

To make a signal with 6 flags, select 6 flags from the given 6. This can be expressed as $_6P_6$.

Step 2
Determine the total number of different signals that could be made.
Since signals can be made with 4 or 5 or 6 flags, the permutations must be added together.
$_6P_4 + {_6P_5} + {_6P_6} = 360 + 720 + 720$
$= 1,800$

Therefore, the total number of different signals that can be made is 1,800.

281. C

In general, the number of permutations of n objects with a of the objects in order is $\frac{n!}{a!}$. If a of the objects are out of order, there are $n! - \frac{n!}{a!}$ permutations.

If there are 10 volumes of which 3 are not in order, there are $10! - \frac{10!}{3!} = 3,024,000$ possible arrangements of the encyclopedias.

282. C

Step 1
Create the groups.
There are 4 groups to arrange in this case.

Step 2
Determine the number of permutations of the groups.
Since there are 4 groups, there are 4! permutations of these groups.

Step 3
Determine the number of permutations of the members within the groups.
The number of possible arrangements is 2! for the parents, 4! for the sons, 3! for the daughters, and 1! for the dog.

Step 4
Apply the fundamental counting principle to determine the total number of arrangements.
There are $(4!)(2!)(4!)(3!)(1!) = 6,912$ possible arrangements of the family members under the given restrictions.

283. B

Step 1
Determine the total number of possible arrangements.
Find the number of arrangements of 5 letters such that 3 of the letters are identical.

$$\frac{5!}{3!} = \frac{120}{6}$$

$$= 20$$

Step 2
Determine the number of arrangements that have O and Y placed together.
The O and Y are grouped together and arranged with the other 3 letters. Therefore, 4 objects are being arranged, which gives 4! arrangements.
The number of arrangements of O and Y is 2!, and there is duplication of the 3 letters, so the product of 4! × 2! must be divided by 3!.

$$\frac{(4!)(2!)}{3!} = \frac{(24)(2)}{6} = 8$$

Step 3
Determine the number of arrangements that do not have O and Y placed together.
The total number of arrangements minus the number of arrangements that have O and Y placed together gives the number of arrangements that do not have O and Y placed together.
20 − 8 = 12
There are 12 arrangements of the letters in the word POPPY that do not have O and Y placed together.

284. D

Since the order in which the points are chosen for the vertices of the triangle is not important, this is a combinations problem.

Out of 20 points, the number of different choices of 3 points for vertices is $_{20}C_3$.

285. A

The formula $_nC_r = \frac{n!}{(n-r)!\,r!}$ can be used to calculate the different ways of selecting r objects from a group of n objects.

$$_9C_3 = \frac{9!}{(9-3)!\,3!} = \frac{9!}{6!\,3!}$$

The expression $\frac{9!}{6!\,3!}$ represents the number of three-topping sundaes a customer could order.

286. C

Step 1
Determine how to find the number of games for n teams if each team plays every other team only once.
The order in which the teams are chosen does not matter; therefore, this problem is a combination problem. In this case, a game is determined by choosing two teams from n. Therefore, the total number of games will be $_nC_2$.

Step 2
Find n by using $_nC_2$.
Solve for n, given that the total number of games is 45.

$$_nC_2 = 45$$
$$\frac{n!}{(n-2)!\,(2)!} = 45$$
$$\frac{n(n-1)(n-2)!}{(n-2)!\,2} = 45$$
$$\frac{(n)(n-1)}{2} = 45$$
$$(n)(n-1) = 90$$
$$n^2 - n - 90 = 0$$
$$(n-10)(n+9) = 0$$

Therefore, $n = 10$ or $n = -9$. However, because -9 cannot be the number of teams in a league, the answer is 10 teams.

287. C

The total number of different arrangements of the 4 blocks on the shelf is 4! = 24. Since only one of these arrangements spells JACK, the probability of this placement occurring is

$$\frac{1}{4!} = \frac{1}{24}$$

288. A

Step 1
Determine the number of ways to fill the first and last places.
Each end of the row has to have a black car. Therefore, the first place can be filled in 4 different ways and the last place can be filled in 3 different ways.

Step 2
Determine the number of ways to fill the middle 7 places.
The remaining seven places can be filled by the remaining 7 cars in 7! ways.

Step 3
Determine the total number of permutations with 4, 3, and 2 identical objects.
Since there are 4 black cars, 3 blue cars, and 2 red cars, the total number of permutations is given by

$$\frac{4 \times 7! \times 3}{4!\,3!\,2!} = 210.$$

289. C

Step 1

Apply the combinations formula $_nC_r = \dfrac{n!}{(n-r)!\,r!}$ to determine how many different ways comedy movie posters can be chosen.

Two comedy movie posters can be chosen from 4 comedy movie posters in $_4C_2$ ways.

$$_4C_2 = \dfrac{4!}{(4-1)!\,2!} = 6$$

Step 2

Apply the combinations formula $_nC_r = \dfrac{n!}{(n-r)!\,r!}$ to determine how many different ways drama movie posters can be chosen.

Three drama movie posters can be chosen from 5 drama movie posters in $_5C_3$ different ways.

$$_5C_3 = \dfrac{5!}{(5-3)!\,3!} = 10$$

Step 3

Apply the fundamental counting principle to determine the total number of ways in which the choices can be made.

The two comedy movie posters can be chosen in 6 ways, and the three drama movie posters can be chosen in 10 ways.

Two comedy movie posters and three drama movie posters can be chosen in $6 \times 10 = 60$ different ways.

Step 4

Determine the total number of different ways the posters can be displayed.

Each of the chosen five posters can be displayed in $_5P_5$ or $5!$ ways.

Therefore, the total number of different displays is $5! \times 60 = 7{,}200$.

290. 1709

Step 1

Break the problem down into different selection situations.

The number of different teams formed with at least one boy will be equal to the total number of possible teams minus the total number of different teams formed without any boys.

Step 2

Determine the number of choices in each selection situation.

- The total number of different teams of 6 players that can be chosen from the 13 possible players is $_{13}C_6 = 1{,}716$.
- The total number of all-girl teams of 6 players that can be chosen from 7 possible girls is $_7C_6 = 7$.

Step 3

Subtract the total number of all-girl teams, $_7C_6$, from the total number of teams, $_{13}C_6$.

$$_{13}C_6 - {_7C_6} = 1{,}716 - 7 = 1{,}709$$

The number of teams that could be formed with at least one boy is 1,709.

EXERCISE #2—PROBABILITIES OF COMPOUND EVENTS

291. The probabilities that Xavier will pass twelfth grade math and twelfth grade physics this semester are 0.82 and 0.78, respectively. If these events are independent, what is the probability, to the nearest hundredth, that Xavier will pass math but not physics?

292. What is the probability of randomly drawing an ace or a face card from a standard deck of 52 cards?
   A. $\dfrac{2}{13}$
   B. $\dfrac{4}{13}$
   C. $\dfrac{9}{52}$
   D. $\dfrac{15}{52}$

Use the following information to answer the next question.

> Judy wrote the numbers 1 to 15 on pieces of paper and placed them in a draw box. She randomly picked one piece of paper from the box.

293. If K represents the event of selecting a number greater than 5 and M represents the event of selecting an odd number, what is the probability of K or M?
   A. $\dfrac{13}{15}$
   B. $\dfrac{8}{15}$
   C. $\dfrac{7}{15}$
   D. $\dfrac{5}{15}$

Use the following information to answer the next question.

> There are 7 students standing in line for ice cream. Bradley, Maureen, and Tim are the first three students in line.

294. If the remainder of the students line up behind Bradley, Maureen, and Tim, how many different orders can they line up in?
   A. 24
   B. 144
   C. 840
   D. 5,040

Use the following information to answer the next question.

> From a group of 20 football players and 10 basketball players, a group of 4 is chosen to represent the school at a banquet.

295. The number of possible four-member groups consisting of at least one football player that can be formed can be determined by evaluating
   A. $_{30}C_4 - _{10}C_1$
   B. $_{30}C_4 - _{20}C_1$
   C. $_{30}C_4 - _{10}C_4$
   D. $_{30}C_4 - _{20}C_4$

296. If $_nP_3 = 30(_nC_2)$, then the value of n is _____.

Use the following information to answer the next question.

> In a particular group of 20 people, 5 are married.

297. If 3 people are randomly selected from the group, what is the probability that all three of the people chosen are married?
   A. $\dfrac{1}{6,840}$
   B. $\dfrac{1}{684}$
   C. $\dfrac{1}{342}$
   D. $\dfrac{1}{114}$

Use the following information to answer the next question.

Six friends are running in a 5 km race. Jerry finished first, Lee was second, and Lewis was third. Stevie, Ray, and Vaughan are still running.

298. In how many different orders can the race finish?
 A. $6! \times 5! \times 4! \times 3! \times 2! \times 1!$
 B. $6 \times 5 \times 4 \times 3 \times 2 \times 1$
 C. $3 \times 2 \times 1$
 D. $3! \times 2! \times 1!$

Use the following information to answer the next question.

Scott has a week-long vacation and selects 8 movies that he plans on watching during the week. Four of these movies are a series, and he wants to watch them in the correct order but not necessarily all together.

299. If Scott watches the series in the correct order, what is the number of possible arrangements in which he can watch the movies?
 A. 40,320
 B. 38,640
 C. 5,040
 D. 1,680

Use the following information to answer the next question.

Remi has 2 different English books, 3 different math books, and 4 different chemistry books. She arranges the books on a shelf so that an English book is always first and last and the other books are kept together according to subject.

300. The total number of possible arrangements of Remi's books is
 A. 4
 B. 288
 C. 576
 D. 10,080

Use the following information to answer the next question.

A volleyball coach asks 6 players to sit on a bench.

301. If 2 particular players are not allowed to sit side by side, then the number of different possible seating arrangements on the bench is
 A. 240
 B. 480
 C. 600
 D. 718

302. What is the number of possible arrangements of the letters in the word *mister* that do **not** include two vowels written beside each other?
 A. 220
 B. 360
 C. 480
 D. 620

Use the following information to answer the next question.

At a garage sale, Marcie finds a box containing 7 old records. She decides to purchase 3 of the records. She pays for the records and puts them in her bag.

303. How many different groups of 3 records can Marcie possibly have in her bag?
 A. 21
 B. 35
 C. 210
 D. 420

Use the following information to answer the next question.

At Vinny's Pizzeria, customers can order the "left-overs special," where a random assortment of 2 different toppings of any of the toppings used in the restaurant are added to a pizza. Vinny claims that there are 190 different possible "left-overs special" pizzas that can be made. In other words, there are 190 different possible mixtures of toppings.

304. How many different toppings are used at the restaurant? _____

Use the following information to answer the next question.

> Shawna has two bags (bag A and bag B) containing colored marbles. Bag A contains 2 white and 2 green marbles. Bag B contains 3 white, 5 red, and 4 green marbles.

305. If Shawna draws one marble at random from each bag, the probability of her drawing 1 white marble and 1 green marble is

   A. $\dfrac{1}{6}$ B. $\dfrac{1}{8}$

   C. $\dfrac{5}{24}$ D. $\dfrac{7}{24}$

306. The number of 8-member committees that can be selected from 10 men and 15 women can be determined by evaluating

   A. $8!$

   B. $_{25}P_8$

   C. $\dfrac{25!}{17!\,8!}$

   D. $_{10}C_8 + {}_{15}C_8$

Use the following information to answer the next question.

> A teacher must form an executive committee consisting of a president, a vice president, a treasurer, and a secretary from 16 available student council members.

307. The number of different executive committees that can be formed can be determined by evaluating

   A. $\dfrac{16!}{4!}$

   B. $\dfrac{16!}{12!}$

   C. $\dfrac{16!}{4!\,2!}$

   D. $\dfrac{16!}{12!\,4!}$

308. Given the word NANAIMO, how many different combinations can be made using all the letters if all the combinations must begin with N?

309. A tennis club has 40 members, of whom 18 are men and 22 are women. The club is going to choose three members to serve on the board of directors. The number of different boards that can be formed if exactly two women are chosen can be determined by evaluating

   A. $_{22}C_2 \times {}_{18}C_1$

   B. $_{22}P_2 \times {}_{18}P_1$

   C. $_{22}C_2$

   D. $_{22}P_2$

310. There are 8 points on the circumference of a circle. The number of lines that can be formed using any 2 of these points is the same as

   A. the number of handshakes in a room of 8 persons, where each person shake every other person's hand once.

   B. the number of handshakes in a room of 8 persons, where each person shake every other person's hand twice.

   C. the number of gifts given in a gift-exchange of 8 members, where each member gives 1 gift to every other member.

   D. the number of gifts given in a gift-exchange of 8 members, where each member gives 2 gifts to every other member.

Use the following information to answer the next question.

> The owner of a travel agency has 3 different posters advertising vacations to Cuba and 4 different posters advertising vacations to Mexico. From these posters, the owner decides to choose 1 Cuba poster and 2 Mexico posters to display in a row on the front window of his travel agency.

311. The number of different displays that the owner can make from these posters is

   A. 6   B. 18

   C. 108   D. 216

EXERCISE #2—PROBABILITIES OF COMPOUND EVENTS
ANSWERS AND SOLUTIONS

291. 0.18	297. D	303. B	309. A
292. B	298. C	304. 20	310. A
293. A	299. D	305. D	311. C
294. A	300. C	306. C	
295. C	301. B	307. B	
296. 17	302. C	308. 360	

291. 0.18

Not passing physics is the complement of passing physics.
P(pass math and not pass physics)
$= P$(pass math) $\times P$(not pass physics)
$= 0.82 \times (1 - 0.79)$
$= 0.82 \times 0.22$
≈ 0.18

292. B

Step 1
Determine the probability of randomly selecting an ace.
Four of the 52 cards are aces.
$\frac{4}{52} = \frac{1}{13}$

Step 2
Determine the probability of randomly selecting a face card.
There are three different face cards: jacks, queens, and kings.
There are four of each of these types of cards.
$4 \times 3 = 12$
Therefore, 12 of the 52 cards are face cards.
$\frac{12}{52} = \frac{3}{13}$

Step 3
Determine the probability that a randomly drawn card will be an ace or a face card.
The two events are mutually exclusive.
$P(A \text{ or } FC) = P(A) + P(FC)$
$= \frac{1}{13} + \frac{3}{13}$
$= \frac{4}{13}$

293. A

There are 15 numbers in the sample space: 1 to 15 inclusive.

- K is the set of numbers greater than 5.
  {6, 7, 8, 9, 10, 11, 12, 13, 14, 15}
- M is the set of odd numbers.
  {1, 3, 5, 7, 9, 11, 13, 15}

Step 1
Determine the probability of event K.
There are 10 numbers greater than 5.
$P(K) = \frac{10}{15}$

Step 2
Determine the probability of event M.
There are 8 odd numbers.
$P(M) = \frac{8}{15}$

Step 3
Determine the probability of K or M.
K and M are non-mutually exclusive events because they have 5 outcomes in common (7, 9, 11, 13, and 15).
$P(K \text{ and } M) = \frac{5}{15}$
$P(K \text{ or } M) = P(K) + P(M) - P(K \text{ and } M)$
$= \frac{10}{15} + \frac{8}{15} - \frac{5}{15}$
$= \frac{13}{15}$

The probability of K or M is $\frac{13}{15}$.

294. A

This is a permutation problem because order is involved. Find the total number of possible arrangements by using the formula
$n \times (n-1) \times (n-2) \times \ldots \times 2 \times 1 = n!$.
$4! = 4 \times 3 \times 2 \times 1$
$4! = 24$

The number of different orders of the remaining 4 students is 24.

295. C

There are 30 players of whom 20 are football players and 10 are basketball players.

Since the order of selection is not important, use combinations.

Step 1
Determine the number of ways to choose a group of 4 players.
Four players can be selected from 30 players in $_{30}C_4$ ways.

Step 2
Selecting a four-member group without a football player is the same as selecting a four-member group that consists of only basketball players.
Determine the number of ways to choose a four-member group of only basketball players.
Four basketball players can be selected from 10 basketball players in $_{10}C_4$ ways.

Step 3
Determine the number of groups with at least one football player.
Subtract the number of groups with 4 basketball players from the total number of possible groups.
$_{30}C_4 - {}_{10}C_4$

296. 17

Step 1
Apply the formulas for $_nP_r$ and $_nC_r$.
$$\frac{n!}{(n-3)!} = 30\left(\frac{n!}{(n-2)!\,2!}\right)$$

Step 2
Divide both sides by $n!$, where $n \neq 0$.
$$\frac{1}{(n-3)!} = 30\left(\frac{1}{(n-2)!\,2!}\right)$$

Step 3
Write out the factorials until the denominators have an equal factorial, and simplify.
$$\frac{1}{(n-3)!} = \frac{30}{(n-2)(n-3)!\,(2\times 1)}$$
$$\frac{1}{(n-3)!} = \frac{15}{(n-2)(n-3)!}$$

Step 4
Multiply both sides of the equation by $(n-3)!$.
$$1 = \frac{15}{n-2}$$

Step 5
Solve the equation $1 = \frac{15}{n-2}$.
Equate the cross products.
$n - 2 = 15$
$n = 17$

297. D

Step 1
Determine the number of favorable outcomes.
Use combinations to determine the number of selections of 3 out of 5 choices.
$_5C_3 = 10$

Step 2
Determine the number of possible outcomes.
Use combinations to determine the number of selections of 3 out of 20 choices.
$_{20}C_3 = 1{,}140$

Step 3
Determine the probability of randomly selecting 3 married people.
Divide the number of favorable outcomes by the number of total possible outcomes to find the probability that all three people are married.
$$P = \frac{10}{1{,}140} = \frac{1}{114}$$
The probability of selecting three married people from the group is $\frac{1}{114}$.

298. C

In general, $n \times (n-1) \times (n-2) \times \ldots \times 2 \times 1 = n!$ represents the number of permutations of n distinct objects. Since the first three positions have already been determined, the solution needs to consider only how the last three runners could finish. The race can therefore finish in $3 \times 2 \times 1$, or $3!$, different orders.

299. D

In general, the number of permutations of n objects with a of them in order is $\frac{n!}{a!}$. Since there are 8 objects with 4 of them in order, there are $\frac{8!}{4!} = 1{,}680$ possible arrangements in which Scott can watch the movies.

300. C

Step 1
Determine the number of different ways the English books can be arranged.
The English books have to be on either ends.
Therefore, the first place can be filled in 2 ways and the last place can be filled in 1 way.

Step 2
Determine the number of different ways the other books can be arranged.
Since the other books are to be kept together according to the subject, consider the books of the same subject as a block.

- The number of different arrangements of the chemistry books among themselves is 4!, or 24.
- The number of different arrangements of the math books among themselves is 3!, or 6.
- The blocks of math and chemistry books can be arranged in 2!, or 2 ways.

Step 2
Apply the fundamental counting principle.
$2 \times 6 \times 24 \times 1 \times 2 = 576$
The total number of possible arrangements of Remi's books is 576.

301. B

Step 1
Determine the total number of arrangements of the six players without any restrictions.
The total number of arrangements of the six players without any restriction is 6!.
However, there are 6 volleyball players of which 2 are not allowed to sit side by side.

Step 2
Determine the number of permutations in which the 2 particular players will sit together.
For the time being, consider them as a single person. This person together with the other 4 players makes 5 people. These five people can be seated in 5! ways.
Now, the two particular players can be arranged within themselves in 2! or 2 ways.
Therefore, the number of arrangements where the 2 particular players sit together is $5! \times 2$.

Step 3
Determine the total number of arrangements of the six players with the restriction that 2 particular players are not allowed to sit side by side.
Subtract the number of arrangements where the 2 particular players sit together from the total number of possible arrangements of the 6 players.
$6! - (5! \times 2) = 5!(6-2)$
$\qquad\qquad\qquad\quad = 480$

302. C

Step 1
Determine the total number of possible arrangements of the six letters without any restrictions.
The total number of possible arrangements of the six letters is 6!.

Step 2
Determine the number of arrangements that include the two vowels written beside each other.
When the two vowels are treated as one group that can be arranged with the other four letters, there are five objects being arranged, so the number of possible arrangements is 5!. The number of arrangements of the two vowels is 2!. Thus, if the vowels are grouped together, the number of possible arrangements of the letters is $(5!)(2!)$.

Step 3
Determine the number of arrangements that do not include the two vowels written beside each other.
Subtracting the number of arrangements with the two vowels written beside each other from the total number of arrangements gives the number of arrangements where the two vowels are not written beside each other.
$6! - (5!)(2!) = 720 - (120)(2)$
$\qquad\qquad\qquad = 720 - 240$
$\qquad\qquad\qquad = 480$

There are 480 possible arrangements of the letters that do not include two vowels written beside each other.

303. B

The number of possible arrangements for selecting r objects from a group of n objects is given by the formula $_nC_r = \dfrac{n!}{(n-r)!\,r!}$.

Substitute the given information into the combination formula, and solve.

$$_7C_3 = \frac{7!}{(7-3)!\,3!}$$
$$= \frac{7 \times 6 \times 5 \times 4!}{4! \times 3!}$$
$$= \frac{7 \times 6 \times 5}{3!}$$
$$= 35$$

Marcie can possibly have 35 different groups of 3 records in her bag.

304. 20

Step 1
Determine if the problem involves a permutation or a combination.
The order in which the toppings are chosen does not matter, so the given question is a combination problem.

Step 2
Let n represent the number of possible toppings used in the restaraunt. Write an expression that represents the number of selections of 2 toppings out of n toppings.
The number of selections of 2 toppings out of n toppings can be represented by $_nC_2$.

Step 3
Solve for n in the equation $_nC_2 = 190$ given that there are 190 ways of choosing 2 toppings out of n toppings.

$$_nC_2 = 190$$

Write $_nC_2$ in factorial form.

$$\frac{n!}{(n-2)!\,2!} = 190$$

Write the factorials until the numerators and the denominator have overlapping factors.

$$\frac{(n)(n-1)(n-2)(n-3)\ldots \times 2 \times 1}{(n-2)(n-3)\ldots \times 2 \times 1 \times (2 \times 1)} = 190$$

Reduce by common factors, and solve for n.

$$\frac{(n)(n-1)}{2} = 190$$
$$(n)(n-1) = 380$$
$$n^2 - n = 380$$
$$n^2 - n - 380 = 0$$

Factor $n^2 - n - 380$.
$(n-20)(n+19) = 0$
$n = 20$ or $n = -19$

Since -19 is not a possible number of toppings, it follows that there are 20 toppings used at Vinny's Pizzeria.

305. D

In order to select 1 white and 1 green marble, Shawna could select a white (W) marble from bag A and a green (G) marble from bag B. This probability is calculated as follows:

$$P(W_A \text{ and } G_B) = \frac{2}{4} \times \frac{4}{12}$$
$$= \frac{1}{2} \times \frac{1}{3}$$
$$= \frac{1}{6}$$

She could also select a green marble from bag A and a white marble from bag B. The probability of this is calculated as follows:

$$P(G_A \text{ and } W_B) = \frac{2}{4} \times \frac{3}{12}$$
$$= \frac{1}{2} \times \frac{1}{4}$$
$$= \frac{1}{8}$$

Therefore, the probability of selecting 1 white marble and 1 green marble is calculated as follows:

$P(W \text{ and } G)$
$= P(W_A \text{ and } G_B) + P(G_A \text{ and } W_B)$
$= \frac{1}{6} + \frac{1}{8}$
$= \frac{4}{24} + \frac{3}{24}$
$= \frac{7}{24}$

306. C

Step 1
Determine the expression for the number of committees.
There are $10 + 15 = 25$ people, from which 8 members have to be selected for the committee. Since there are no restrictions on the number of men or women on the committees, the information about gender is extraneous.
There are $_{25}C_8$ ways in which an 8-member committee can be chosen from 25 people.

Step 2
Evaluate the expression for the number of committees.
The number of combinations of n objects taken r at a time is given by $_nC_r = \frac{n!}{(n-r)!\,r!}$.

Therefore, $_{25}C_8 = \frac{25!}{(25-8)!\,8!}$.

Simplify.
$$= \frac{25!}{17!\,8!}$$

307. B

Since the students are given specific positions on the committee, permutations must be used to account for the different possible orders. Of the 16 student council members, 4 must be arranged.

This can be calculated as follows:
$$_{16}P_4 = \frac{16!}{(16-4)!} = \frac{16!}{12!}$$

308. 360

Recognize this problem as a permutation with non-distinct objects.

Step 1
Determine the number of letters that can be used for the restricted position.
The first letter must be N, so there is 1 choice for the first letter since both N's are identical.

Step 2
Determine the number choices that can be made for the other places in the word.
For the other six places, there are 6 letters to arrange, of which 2 are identical A's.
When some of the objects to be arranged are identical, the number of distinct permutations of n objects taken r at a time can be calculated by the formula $\frac{n!}{a!\,b!\,c!\,\ldots}$, where $a!\,b!\,c!\,\ldots$ accounts for the various permutations of the repeated objects.
Substitute 6 for n, 6 for r, and 2 for a, and simplify.
$$\frac{6!}{2!} = 360$$
Therefore, the number of different formations of the words that begin with the letter N is 360.

309. A

Step 1
Interpret the question and identify the procedure.
To select three members with exactly two women means the third member is a male. Since the three members will all sit on the same board of directors, the order of selection is not important. Therefore, use combinations.
Total number of selections, by fundamental counting principle, is the product of the number of possible selections of two women and the number of possible selections of one man.

Step 2
Determine the number of possible selections of 2 women.
There need to be exactly two women members on the board. They can be chosen from 22 women in $_{22}C_2$ different ways.

Step 3
Determine the number of possible selections of one male.
One male from 18 men may be selected in $_{18}C_1$ different ways.

Step 4
Apply the fundamental counting principle to determine the total number.
The total number of different boards with exactly two women is $_{22}C_2 \times _{18}C_1$.

310. A

Step 1
Interpret the given information.
Each line is formed by selecting 2 points from 8 where the order of the 2 points does not matter. There are $_8C_2$ such selections, so $_8C_2$ lines can be formed in total.

Step 2
Interpret the answer choices.
In the gift exchange, each gift is a selection of 2 members from 8 where the order of the 2 members matters (because a gift given by A to B is different from a gift given by B to A). There are $_8P_2$ such selections, so if each member gives 1 gift, there $_8P_2$ gifts are given altogether.

If each member gives 2 gifts, the number of gifts doubles to $2 \times _8P_2$.

Each handshake is a selection of 2 people from 8 where the order of the 2 people does not matter (because a handshake between A and B is the same as a handshake between B and A. There are $_8C_2$ such selections, so there are $_8C_2$ handshakes altogether. This is the same as the number of lines formed.

If each pair shakes hands twice, the number of handshakes doubles to $2 \times _8C_2$.

Step 3
Compare the choices and state the answer.
The number of lines drawn between any of the eight points on the circumference is the same as the number of handshakes amongst eight people, where each person shakes every other person's hand once.

311. C

Step 1

Apply the combinations formula $_nC_r = \dfrac{n!}{(n-r)!\,r!}$ to determine how many different ways posters of Cuba can be chosen.

One poster has to be chosen from 3 different Cuba posters.

This can be done in $_3C_1 = \dfrac{3!}{(3-1)!\,1!} = 3$ different ways.

Step 2

Apply the combinations formula $_nC_r = \dfrac{n!}{(n-r)!\,r!}$ to determine how many different ways posters of Mexico can be chosen.

Two posters have to be chosen from 4 different Mexico posters.

This can be done in $_4C_2 = \dfrac{4!}{(4-2)!\,2!} = 6$ different ways.

Step 3

Apply the fundamental counting principle to determine the total number of ways in which the choices can be made.

One Cuba poster can be chosen in 3 ways, and two Mexico posters can be chosen in 6 ways.

There are 3 × 6 = 18 different ways to select the posters.

Step 4

Determine the total number of different ways the posters can be displayed.

Each of the chosen three posters can be displayed in $_3P_3$ ways.

$_3P_3 = 3! = 6$

Therefore, the total number of different displays is 6 × 18 = 108.

Evaluating Outcomes Using Probability

EVALUATING OUTCOMES USING PROBABILITY

Table of Correlations

Standard		Concepts	Exercise #1	Exercise #2
Unit6.3	Use probability to evaluate outcomes of decisions.			
S-MD.6	*Use probabilities to make fair decisions.*	Making Decisions Based on Probability	312	315
		Using Probability to Support Opposing Views	313	316
		Making Decisions Based on Theoretical Probability, Experimental Probability, and Subjective Judgment	314	317
S-MD.7	*Analyze decisions and strategies using probability concepts.*	Making Decisions Based on Probability	312	315
		Using Probability to Support Opposing Views	313	316
		Making Decisions Based on Theoretical Probability, Experimental Probability, and Subjective Judgment	314	317

S-MD.6 Use probabilities to make fair decisions.

Making Decisions Based on Probability

Probability is used to make decisions. When there is a certain chance of an event happening, it may influence your decision to go somewhere, to purchase an item, or even to wear something. For example, while you are deciding what clothing to wear for the day, you hear the local weather station say that there is a 30% chance of rain. When you go outside, it is humid and you see a solid dark sky. Even though the probability is low, according to the weather report, that there will be rain, you may dress for rain or bring an umbrella. You are using your own judgement to conclude that there is a much higher probability of rain than 30%.

Statistics can also be used to make decisions. Companies use statistics when it comes to making marketing decisions. They want to make sure their advertising money is put to good use.

For example, an owner of a company that makes razors for men is deciding where to direct advertising dollars. The owner wants to direct the money toward events that attract men.

His advertising department uses available statistics about the gender of the spectators at events to determine where to put their advertisements. These are their findings:

Sport	Male Spectators (%)	Female Spectators (%)
Football	68	32
Boxing	82	18
Volleyball	35	65
Field hockey	15	85

Based on these statistics, the company needs to focus their advertising dollars on the football and boxing events.

Using Probability to Support Opposing Views

There are often two views when considering an event. One view will be a favorable view, while the other will be a non-favorable view.

Probability can be used to support opposing viewpoints depending on how an event is interpreted.

For example, if someone has a 2 in 5 chance of completing a marathon, an athlete may decide not to compete because there is a 3 in 5 chance of not finishing the competition. However, another athlete may decide to compete in the marathon because there is still a chance of finishing the competition, even if the chances are less than not finishing.

Example

The morning weather report shows a 35% chance of afternoon snow and possible whiteout conditions on highways. Mr. Cory has to drive from Edmonton to Calgary for a meeting. However, from this weather report, his son advises him not to go.

How can Mr. Cory and his son use this information to support their views?

Solution

Mr. Cory can argue that 35% is not a high enough percentage to guarantee snow and unsafe highway conditions. He can argue that there is a 65% chance that these conditions will not occur and he can still drive to Calgary for his meeting. His son can argue that this percentage is very high, and in the past, such a percentage has guaranteed snow. He can argue that this means that it will snow, causing the highways to be unsafe for driving.

Making Decisions Based on Theoretical Probability, Experimental Probability, and Subjective Judgment

Every day you are asked to make decisions, and you base your decisions on many different factors. Theoretical probability, experimental probability, and subjective judgment are three common techniques used for making decisions in everyday life.

Theoretical probability is based on the chance of an outcome happening under ideal circumstances. When decisions are based on theoretical probability, they are based on mathematical calculations about the likelihood of an outcome occurring. Mathematical calculations of theoretical probability are made using the following formula:

$$\text{probability} = \frac{\text{\# desired outcomes}}{\text{\# possible outcomes}}$$

Example

At a carnival, 2 out of 3 spaces on a spinner are blue, while 1 space is red. Jen can will a prize if she correctly guesses the color the spinner will land on. Based on theoretical probability, she selects blue because she has a 66% chance of being correct.

$$P = \frac{2}{3} \times 100$$
$$P \approx 66\%$$

Experimental probability is the probability of an event occurring based on observations or the results of an experiment. When decisions are based on experimental probability, they are based on past experiences and the likelihood of the same outcome occurring.

Example

Sue frequently visits the mall. She observes that the lower half of the parkade often has more available parking spots than the upper half. She makes the decision, based on experimental probability, to look for a parking spot in the lower half of the parkade first.

Subjective judgment is based on feelings, emotions, or beliefs. When decisions are based on subjective judgment, they are based on a particular feeling or sense about an event.

Example

A basketball team has won 10 games wearing its blue jerseys, but it has lost 10 games wearing its white jerseys. If given a choice, the team would choose to wear its blue jerseys because the players feel they are more likely to win in the blue jerseys. This is a decision based on subjective judgment.

Example

Wesley, Bolun, and Myra go to a football game where they are asked by a vendor if they want to buy raffle tickets for a student fund-raiser. Bolun decides not to buy a raffle ticket because he has never won anything from a raffle before. Wesley decides not to buy a raffle ticket because he believes all raffles are rigged. Myra decides to buy 20 raffle tickets to increase her chances of winning.

Identify who uses theoretical probability, who uses experimental probability, and who uses subjective judgment to make a decision about the raffle tickets.

Solution

Myra decides to buy 20 raffle tickets because she wants to increase her chances of winning. Making a decision based on the likelihood of an event occurring is an example of theoretical probability. Myra makes her decision to purchase raffle tickets based on theoretical probability.

Bolun decides not to buy a raffle ticket because he has never won anything in the past. Making a decision based on past experiences is an example of experimental probability. Bolun makes his decision not to purchase a raffle ticket based on experimental probability.

Wesley decides not to buy a raffle ticket because he believes raffles are rigged. Making a decision based on a particular belief or feeling is an example of subjective judgment. Wesley makes his decision not to purchase a raffle ticket based on subjective judgment.

EXERCISE #1—EVALUATING OUTCOMES USING PROBABILITY

Use the following information to answer the next question.

> When shooting baskets, a person can either get the ball in the basket or miss. In theory, a player has a fifty-fifty chance of getting the ball in the basket.

312. Is this an accurate assessment of probability regarding the success of a basketball shot?

Use the following information to answer the next question.

> Gordon and Jill are choosing between buying a cat or a dog. Jill would like to buy a dog. She recently found a study in which 60% of dog owners report that their dogs help them stay in shape. Gordon, on the other hand, would like to buy a cat. According to a recent statistic he found, 60% of cat owners feel that their cats increase their happiness.

313. To support her position, Jill would most likely **most likely** argue that
   A. 40% of dog owners report that their dogs do not help them stay in shape
   B. 60% of dog owners report that their dogs help them stay in shape
   C. 60% of cat owners feel that their cats increase their happiness
   D. 40% of dog owners are out of shape

Use the following information to answer the next question.

> Anton believes that every time he steps on a spider, it will rain the next day. He is going on a picnic tomorrow and is hoping for a sunny day. He found a spider in the basement, but instead of stepping on it, he picked it up and placed it outside.

314. Anton's decision to avoid killing the spider was **most likely** based on
   A. experimental probability
   B. theoretical probability
   C. deductive reasoning
   D. subjective judgment

EXERCISE #1—EVALUATING OUTCOMES USING PROBABILITY ANSWERS AND SOLUTIONS

| 312. See solution | 313. B | 314. D |

312.

This is not a realistic probability assessment. It is assumed that all players have an equal chance of making a shot. The probability of the shot succeeding depends on the skill and experience of the player. A professional basketball player is more likely to make a shot because that player would be more skilled. So, the chances are going to be greater that the professional will succeed in getting the ball in the basket. The probability of the player's success would be based on previous statistics. Someone who plays very little basketball is more likely to miss the basket than someone who plays every day.

313. B

According to the study Jill recently found, 60% of dog owners report that their dogs help them stay in shape. This statement supports Jill's position that they should purchase a dog.

314. D

Subjective judgment is based on someone's feelings or emotions. When decisions are based on subjective judgments, they are rooted in a particular feeling someone has about an event occurring.

Anton believes that if he kills a spider, it will rain. Since he does not want it to rain, he made the decision to avoid killing the spider based on subjective judgment.

EXERCISE #2—EVALUATING OUTCOMES USING PROBABILITY

Use the following information to answer the next question.

A car company conducts a survey of their customers that have been in non-life threatening car accidents in the past five years. They want to determine what saved the lives of their customers in the accident. Their results were as follows:

Accessory	Percentage of customers who believe it saved their lives
Front airbags	72
Side airbags	56
Seatbelt	88
Brake	44

315. If this company wants to make their cars safer, which accessory should they spend the **most** money on when they redesign their cars?
    A. Front airbags   B. Side airbags
    C. Seatbelts   D. Brakes

Use the following information to answer the next question.

Steven and Joel are studying together for the final exam in Grade 9 Math. Steven noticed that the math teacher used questions from the class notes 45% of the time, questions from the textbook 30% of the time, and questions from an unknown source 25% of the time on previous exams. Steven's plan is to only study the class notes.

316. Which of the following statements is **not** an argument Joel could use to oppose Steven's plan?
    A. By studying the textbook and the class notes, they will most likely cover 75% of the material.
    B. The teacher may choose to use questions from another source for the final exam.
    C. The largest proportion of test questions will come from the class notes.
    D. The class notes cover less than half of the material.

Exercise #2   534   Castle Rock Research

Use the following information to answer the next question.

Brent wants to go fishing and has a choice of going to one of four lakes. After some research, he discovers the given table, which shows statistics of the success that one professional fisherman has had at the four lakes. Brent wants to take his friend Kevin with him to Chinook Lake, but Kevin refuses to fish there because he believes it is haunted and that ghosts will scare away the fish.

Lake	Probability of Catching a Fish
Chinook Lake	0.43
Lake Willow	0.15
Marigold Lake	0.32
Lake Soho	0.04

317. Kevin's decision not to fish at Chinook Lake is based on
   A. rational thinking
   B. subjective judgment
   C. theoretical probability
   D. experimental probability

EXERCISE #2—EVALUATING OUTCOMES USING PROBABILITY ANSWERS AND SOLUTIONS

| 315. D | 316. C | 317. B |

315. D

To make the cars safer the car company should redesign the accessory that has the least percentage in saving lives.

Identify the accessory that has the minimum percentage of safety. From the table, the brakes have the minimum percentage in saving lives. Therefore, the company should put the most money into redesigning their brakes to make their cars safer.

316. C

Statistically, the class notes are the largest source for test questions at 45%, whereas only 30% of test questions typically come from the textbook, and 25% of test questions typically come from an unknown source. This statement supports Steven's plan.

317. B

Subjective judgment is based on someone's feelings or emotions. When decisions are based on subjective judgments, they are based on a particular feeling someone has about an event occurring. In this case, there is no scientific evidence to prove that Chinook Lake is haunted or that there is a low probability of catching a fish. This claim is based on something Kevin believes or may have heard someone say. Based on this belief, he concludes that the probability of catching a fish there is low. Kevin's decision not to fish at Chinook Lake is based on a subjective judgment.

NOTES

NOTES

NOTES

NOTES

SOLARO Study Guides
Ordering Information

Every SOLARO Study Guide unpacks the curriculum standards and provides an overview of all curriculum concepts, practice questions with full solutions, and assignment questions for students to fully test their knowledge.

Visit www.solaro.com/orders to buy books and learn how SOLARO can offer you an even more complete studying solution.

SOLARO Study Guides

SOLARO Study Guide—$29.95 each plus applicable sales tax

SOLARO Common Core State Standard Titles	
Mathematics 3	Algebra I
Mathematics 4	Algebra II
Mathematics 5	Geometry
Mathematics 6	English Language Arts 3
Mathematics 7	English Language Arts 4
Accelerated Mathematics 7 (Int.)	English Language Arts 5
Accelerated Mathematics 7 (Trad.)	English Language Arts 6
Mathematics 8	English Language Arts 7
Accelerated Mathematics I	English Language Arts 8
Mathematics I	English Language Arts 9
Mathematics II	English Language Arts 10
Mathematics III	English Language Arts 11
Accelerated Algebra I	English Language Arts 12

To order books, please visit
www.solaro.com/orders

Volume pricing is available. Contact us at orderbooks@solaro.com